How to
Master Skills for the

TOEFL® iBT

LISTENING

Advanced

Second Edition

How to
Master Skills for the

TOEFL® iBT

LISTENING Advanced

Second Edition

Publisher Kyudo Chung
Editor Sangik Cho
Authors Gerald de la Salle, Jasmine C. Swaney, Monika N. Kushwaha, E2K
Proofreaders Michael A. Putlack, Will Link
Designers Minji Kim, Yeji Kim

First Published in March 2007 By Darakwon, Inc.
Second edition first published in Novemver 2024 by Darakwon, Inc.
Darakwon Bldg., 211, Munbal-ro, Paju-si, Gyeonggi-do 10881
Republic of Korea
Tel: 02-736-2031 (Ext. 250)
Fax: 02-732-2037

ISBN 978-89-277-8094-6 14740
978-89-277-8084-7 14740 (set)

www.darakwon.co.kr

Photo Credits
Shutterstock.com

Components Main Book / Answer Key / Free MP3 Downloads
7 6 5 4 3 2 1 24 25 26 27 28

Table of Contents

INTRODUCTION

1 Information on the TOEFL® iBT

A The Format of the TOEFL® iBT

Section	Number of Questions or Tasks	Timing	Score
Reading	**20 Questions** • 2 reading passages – with 10 questions per passage – approximately 700 words long each	35 Minutes	30 Points
Listening	**28 Questions** • 2 conversations – 5 questions per conversation – 3 minutes each • 3 lectures – 6 questions per lecture – 3-5 minutes each	36 Minutes	30 Points
Speaking	**4 Tasks** • 1 independent speaking task – 1 personal choice/opinion/experience – preparation: 15 sec. / response: 45 sec. • 2 integrated speaking tasks: Read-Listen-Speak – 1 campus situation topic reading: 75-100 words (45 sec.) conversation: 150-180 words (60-80 sec.) – 1 academic course topic reading: 75-100 words (50 sec.) lecture: 150-220 words (60-120 sec.) – preparation: 30 sec. / response: 60 sec. • 1 integrated speaking task: Listen-Speak – 1 academic course topic lecture: 230-280 words (90-120 sec.) – preparation: 20 sec. / response: 60 sec.	17 Minutes	30 Points
Writing	**2 Tasks** • 1 integrated writing task: Read-Listen-Write – reading: 230-300 words (3 min.) – lecture: 230-300 words (2 min.) – a summary of 150-225 words (20 min.) • 1 academic discussion task – a minimum 100-word essay (10 min.)	30 Minutes	30 Points

B What Is New about the TOEFL® iBT?

- The TOEFL® iBT is delivered through the Internet in secure test centers around the world at the same time.
- It tests all four language skills and is taken in the order of Reading, Listening, Speaking, and Writing.
- The test is about 2 hours long, and all of the four test sections will be completed in one day.
- Note taking is allowed throughout the entire test, including the Reading section. At the end of the test, all notes are collected and destroyed at the test center.
- In the Listening section, one lecture may be spoken with a British or Australian accent.
- There are integrated tasks requiring test takers to combine more than one language skill in the Speaking and Writing sections.
- In the Speaking section, test takers wear headphones and speak into a microphone when they respond. The responses are recorded and transmitted to ETS's Online Scoring Network.
- In the Writing section, test takers must type their responses. Handwriting is not possible.
- Test scores will be reported online. Test takers can see their scores online 4-8 business days after the test and can also receive a copy of their score report by mail.

2 Information on the Listening Section

The Listening section of the TOEFL® iBT measures test takers' ability to understand spoken English in English-speaking colleges and universities. This section has 2 conversations that are 12-25 exchanges (about 3 minutes) long and 3 lectures that are 500-800 words (3-5 minutes) long. Each conversation is followed by 5 questions and each lecture by 6 questions. Therefore, test takers have to answer 28 questions in total. The time allotted to the Listening section is 36 minutes, including the time spent listening to the conversations and lectures and answering the questions.

A Types of Listening Conversations and Lectures

- Conversations
  - Between a student and a professor or a teaching assistant during office hours
  - Between a student with a person related to school services such as a librarian, a housing director, or a bookstore employee

- Lectures
  - Monologue lectures delivered by a professor unilaterally
  - Interactive lectures with one or two students asking questions or making comments
    cf. One lecture may be spoken with a British or Australian accent.

B Types of Listening Questions

- Basic Comprehension Questions
  - Listening for Main Ideas Question: This type of question asks you to identify the overall topic or main

idea of a lecture or conversation.

– Listening for Main Purpose Question: This type of question asks you why the speakers are having a conversation or why a lecture is given.

– Listening for Major Details Question: This type of question asks you to understand specific details or facts from a conversation or lecture.

- Pragmatic Understanding Questions
  – Understanding the Function of What Is Said Question: This type of question asks you why a speaker mentions some point in the conversation or lecture. It may involve replaying part of the listening passage.
  – Understanding the Speaker's Attitude Question: This type of question asks you what a speaker's feelings, opinions, or degree of certainty is about some issue, idea, or person. It may involve replaying part of the listening passage.

- Connecting Information Questions
  – Understanding Organization Question: This type of question asks you how the listening passage is organized or how two portions of the listening passage are related to each other.
  – Connecting Content Question: This type of question asks you to classify or sequence information in a different way from the way it was presented in the listening passage.
  – Making Inferences Question: This type of question asks you to draw a conclusion based on information given in the listening passage.

C Question Formats

- There are four question formats in the Listening section: traditional multiple-choice questions with four answer choices and one correct answer, multiple-choice questions with more than one answer, questions that ask test takers to make the order of events or steps in a process, and questions that ask test takers to match objects or text to categories in a chart.

HOW TO USE THIS BOOK

How to Master Skills for the TOEFL® iBT Listening Advanced is designed to be used either as a textbook for a TOEFL® iBT listening preparation course or as a tool for individual learners who are preparing for the TOEFL® test on their own. With a total of eight units, this book is organized to prepare you for the test with a comprehensive understanding of the test and thorough analysis of every question type. Each unit consists of seven parts and provides a step-by-step program that provides question-solving strategies and the development of test-taking abilities. At the back of the book are two actual tests of the Listening section of the TOEFL® iBT.

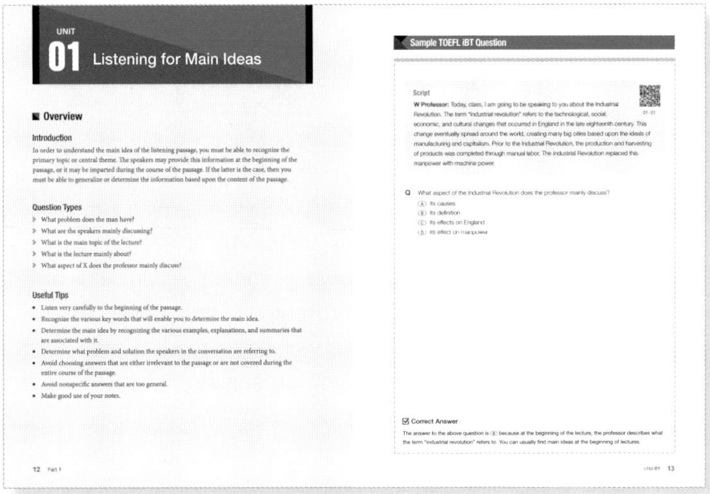

❶ Overview

This part is designed to prepare you for the type of question the unit covers. You will be given a full description of the question type and its application in the passage. You will also be given some useful tips as well as an illustrated introduction and a sample.

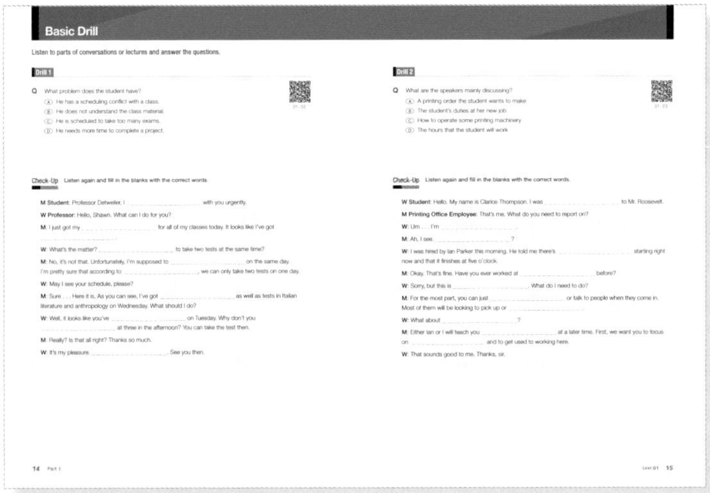

❷ Basic Drill

The purpose of this section is to ensure that you understand the new types of questions that were described in the overview. You will be given a chance to confirm your understanding in brief scripts before starting on the practice exercises. You will listen to some simple conversations or lectures and answer questions of a particular type. This part will help you learn how to deal with each type of question on the Listening section of the TOEFL® iBT.

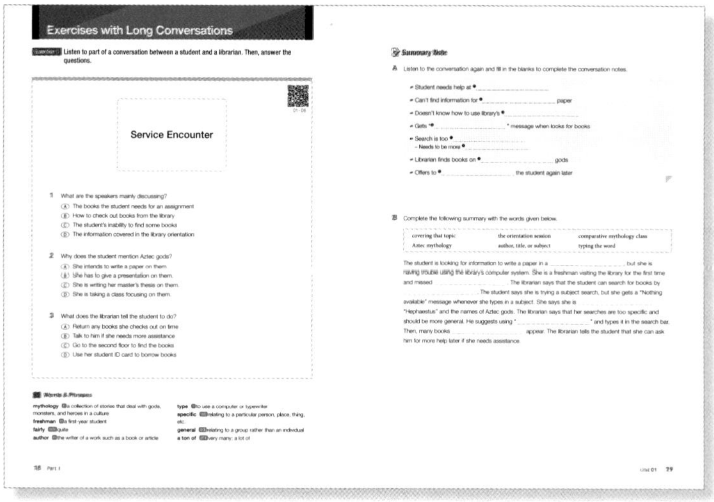

❸ Exercises with Long Conversations

This part is one of the two practical exercise sections where you can actually practice and improve your ability to solve questions. With a total of four conversations, you will be able to confirm your understanding of the question types and master skills presented in each unit. Glossed vocabulary and well-organized notes will be given to help you understand the material and answer the questions.

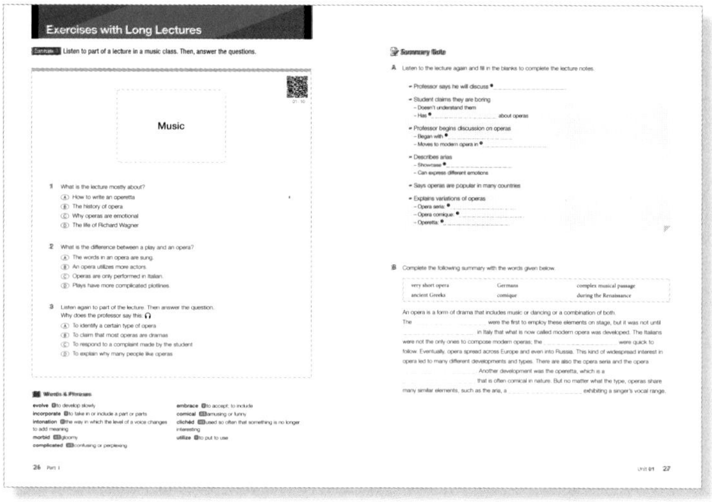

❹ Exercises with Long Lectures

This part is the other practical exercise section where you can actually practice and improve your ability to solve questions. With a total of four lectures, you will be able to confirm your understanding of the question types and master skills presented in each unit. Glossed vocabulary and well-organized notes will be given to help you understand the material and answer the questions.

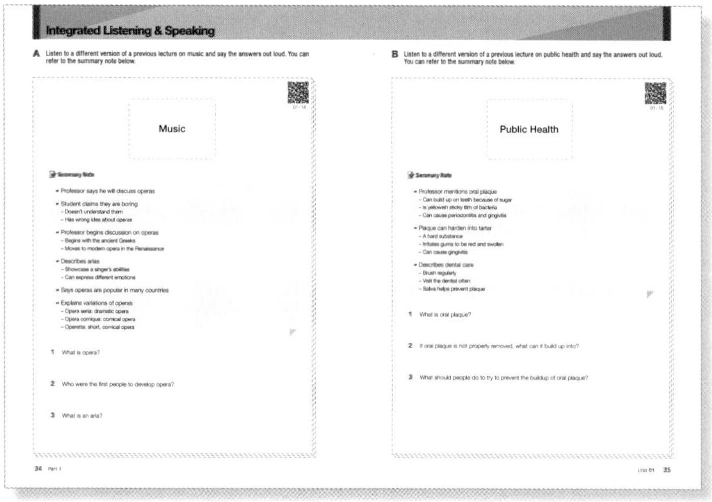

❺ Integrated Listening & Speaking

The TOEFL® iBT is different from previous tests in that it is more integrated than ever. So in this part, you are given the chance to experience the iBT style study by linking your listening skills with your speaking skills. Listen to the different versions of the previous lectures and answer the questions. But remember that this time, you have to say the answers. There is no writing.

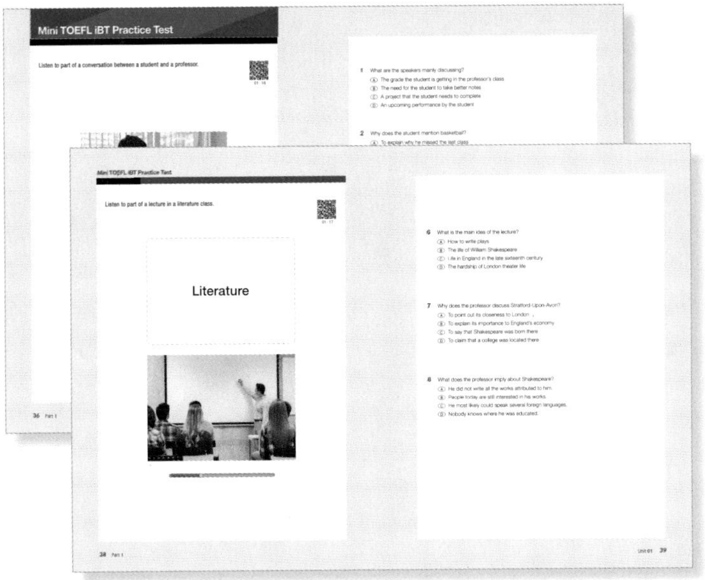

❻ Mini TOEFL iBT Practice Test

This part will give you a chance to experience an actual TOEFL® iBT test. You will be given a conversation with five questions and a lecture with six questions. The topics are similar to those on the actual test, as are the questions.

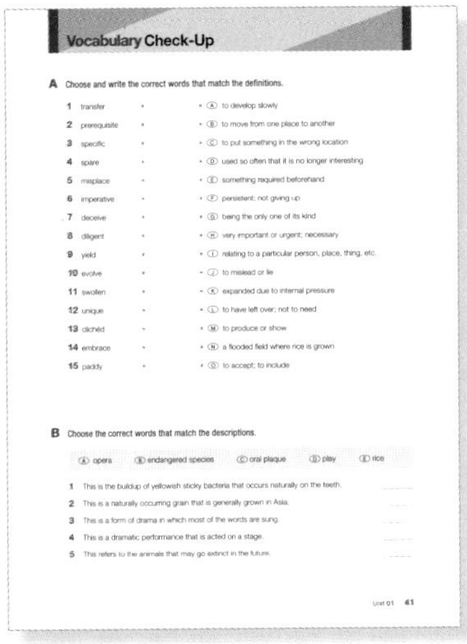

❼ Vocabulary Check-Up

This part offers you a chance to review some of the words you need to remember after finishing each unit. Vocabulary words for each unit are also provided at the back of the book to help you prepare for each unit.

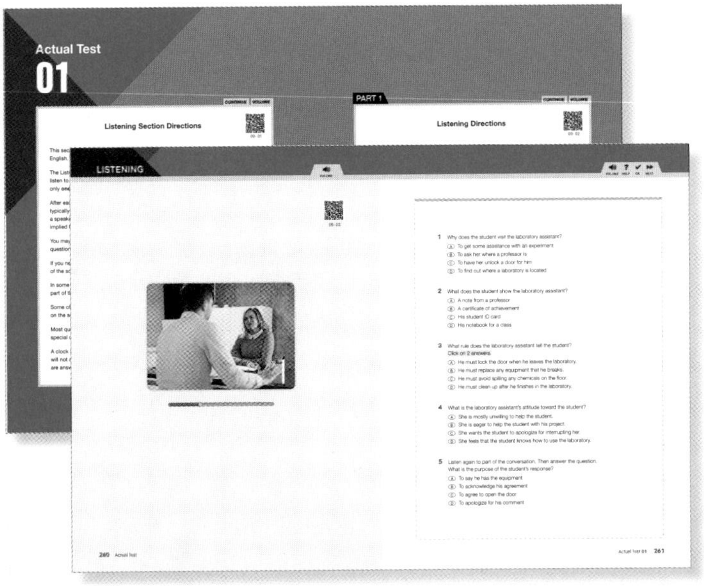

❽ Actual Test

This part offers two full practice tests that are modeled on the Listening section of the TOEFL® iBT. This will familiarize you with the actual test format of the TOEFL® iBT.

PART I

Basic Comprehension

Basic comprehension of the listening passage is tested in three ways: listening for the main ideas, listening for the main purpose, and listening for the major details. Listening for the main idea is to identify the overall topic of the contents. Listening for the main purpose is to search for the reason behind the contents. For questions about the major details, you must understand and remember explicit details and facts from a lecture or conversation.

UNIT

01 Listening for Main Ideas

Overview

Introduction

In order to understand the main idea of the listening passage, you must be able to recognize the primary topic or central theme. The speakers may provide this information at the beginning of the passage, or it may be imparted during the course of the passage. If the latter is the case, then you must be able to generalize or determine the information based upon the content of the passage.

Question Types

- What problem does the man have?
- What are the speakers mainly discussing?
- What is the main topic of the lecture?
- What is the lecture mainly about?
- What aspect of X does the professor mainly discuss?

Useful Tips

- Listen very carefully to the beginning of the passage.
- Recognize the various key words that will enable you to determine the main idea.
- Determine the main idea by recognizing the various examples, explanations, and summaries that are associated with it.
- Determine what problem and solution the speakers in the conversation are referring to.
- Avoid choosing answers that are either irrelevant to the passage or are not covered during the entire course of the passage.
- Avoid nonspecific answers that are too general.
- Make good use of your notes.

Sample TOEFL iBT Question

Script

01 - 01

W Professor: Today, class, I am going to be speaking to you about the Industrial Revolution. The term "industrial revolution" refers to the technological, social, economic, and cultural changes that occurred in England in the late eighteenth century. This change eventually spread around the world, creating many big cities based upon the ideals of manufacturing and capitalism. Prior to the Industrial Revolution, the production and harvesting of products was completed through manual labor. The Industrial Revolution replaced this manpower with machine power.

Q What aspect of the Industrial Revolution does the professor mainly discuss?

(A) Its causes
(B) Its definition
(C) Its effects on England
(D) Its effect on manpower

☑ Correct Answer

The answer to the above question is (B) because at the beginning of the lecture, the professor describes what the term "industrial revolution" refers to. You can usually find main ideas at the beginning of lectures.

Basic Drill

Listen to parts of conversations or lectures and answer the questions.

Drill 1

01 - 02

Q What problem does the student have?

(A) He has a scheduling conflict with a class.
(B) He does not understand the class material.
(C) He is scheduled to take too many exams.
(D) He needs more time to complete a project.

Check-Up Listen again and fill in the blanks with the correct words.

M Student: Professor Detweiler, I ______________ with you urgently.

W Professor: Hello, Shawn. What can I do for you?

M: I just got my ______________ for all of my classes today. It looks like I've got ______________.

W: What's the matter? ______________ to take two tests at the same time?

M: No, it's not that. Unfortunately, I'm supposed to ______________ on the same day. I'm pretty sure that according to ______________, we can only take two tests on one day.

W: May I see your schedule, please?

M: Sure . . . Here it is. As you can see, I've got ______________ as well as tests in Italian literature and anthropology on Wednesday. What should I do?

W: Well, it looks like you've ______________ on Tuesday. Why don't you ______________ at three in the afternoon? You can take the test then.

M: Really? Is that all right? Thanks so much.

W: It's my pleasure. ______________. See you then.

Drill 2

Q What are the speakers mainly discussing?

Ⓐ A printing order the student wants to make
Ⓑ The student's duties at her new job
Ⓒ How to operate some printing machinery
Ⓓ The hours that the student will work

01-03

Check-Up Listen again and fill in the blanks with the correct words.

W Student: Hello. My name is Clarice Thompson. I was .... to Mr. Roosevelt.

M Printing Office Employee: That's me. What do you need to report on?

W: Um . . . I'm ....

M: Ah, I see. .... ?

W: I was hired by Ian Parker this morning. He told me there's .... starting right now and that it finishes at five o'clock.

M: Okay. That's fine. Have you ever worked at .... before?

W: Sorry, but this is .... What do I need to do?

M: For the most part, you can just .... or talk to people when they come in. Most of them will be looking to pick up or ....

W: What about .... ?

M: Either Ian or I will teach you .... at a later time. First, we want you to focus on .... and to get used to working here.

W: That sounds good to me. Thanks, sir.

Drill 3

01 - 04

Q What is the lecture mainly about?
Click on 2 answers.

Ⓐ Baroque architecture
Ⓑ Baroque composers
Ⓒ Baroque music characteristics
Ⓓ Baroque musical instruments

Check-Up

Listen again and fill in the blanks with the correct words.

M Professor: I'm sure that all of you .... Baroque architecture as there are some very famous examples of it throughout .... However, fewer people know about .... even though they have surely heard it numerous times. Baroque music was popular from around 1600 to 1750. It became popular in countries throughout Europe, but it was .... in England, Germany, France, and Italy. Two of .... in history lived and produced work during this period. I'm talking, of course, about Johann Sebastian Bach and George Frideric Handel. We're going to listen to some music by both of .... in just a moment. But I need to finish .... of the period first. Oh, I shouldn't forget Antonio Vivaldi, who was yet another .... Baroque composer.

Now, uh, what were .... of the period? First, ... became popular during it. You see, uh, prior to the Baroque Period, a lot of music was .... Baroque music also .... thanks to the use of the pianoforte. The pianoforte was a .... that many composers utilized in place of the harpsichord. It allowed composers to create music that was .... Much Baroque music has .... to it as well since composers embellished their works in various ways.

Drill 4

Q What is the main topic of the lecture?

Ⓐ Irrigation methods in ancient times
Ⓑ Agriculture in the Roman Empire
Ⓒ Egyptian farming methods
Ⓓ The discovery of farming in Mesopotamia

01-05

Check-Up Listen again and fill in the blanks with the correct words.

W Professor: Nowadays, if you ______________, watering your plants is a simple process. You take a hose to the garden, turn it on, and ______________ with water. You might also ______________ in the garden and let it run for a few minutes. In the past, people didn't have hoses and sprinklers though. But they did have crops they ______________. So . . . how did they get water to their crops? That's what I would like to discuss with you right now.

______________ that you need to know is irrigation. This refers to the using of ______________ in order to water land to make plants grow. Well, in ancient times, people in some cultures ______________ in containers from a river or lake or other source of water to their fields. But this was a long, arduous process that was ______________ with small plots of land. ______________, large-scale irrigation projects were necessary. Several thousand years ago, humans in Egypt and Mesopotamia learned how to build ______________ which could transport water to fields. The Egyptians did this by the Nile. Ah, they also ______________ that could capture floodwaters from the Nile which they could use later. And the Mesopotamians did this near the Tigris and Euphrates rivers. Other cultures ______________. The Romans, for instance, built enormous aqueducts and used ______________ to move water to fields.

Exercises with Long Conversations

Exercise 1 Listen to part of a conversation between a student and a librarian. Then, answer the questions.

01 - 06

Service Encounter

1 What are the speakers mainly discussing?

Ⓐ The books the student needs for an assignment
Ⓑ How to check out books from the library
Ⓒ The student's inability to find some books
Ⓓ The information covered in the library orientation

2 Why does the student mention Aztec gods?

Ⓐ She intends to write a paper on them.
Ⓑ She has to give a presentation on them.
Ⓒ She is writing her master's thesis on them.
Ⓓ She is taking a class focusing on them.

3 What does the librarian tell the student to do?

Ⓐ Return any books she checks out on time
Ⓑ Talk to him if she needs more assistance
Ⓒ Go to the second floor to find the books
Ⓓ Use her student ID card to borrow books

Words & Phrases

mythology n a collection of stories that deal with gods, monsters, and heroes in a culture
freshman n a first-year student
fairly adv quite
author n the writer of a work such as a book or article
type v to use a computer or typewriter
specific adj relating to a particular person, place, thing, etc.
general adj relating to a group rather than an individual
a ton of phr very many; a lot of

Summary Note

A Listen to the conversation again and fill in the blanks to complete the conversation notes.

- Student needs help at ❶ ______________
- Can't find information for ❷ ______________ paper
- Doesn't know how to use library's ❸ ______________
- Gets "❹ ______________" message when looks for books
- Search is too ❺ ______________
  - Needs to be more ❻ ______________
- Librarian finds books on ❼ ______________ gods
- Offers to ❽ ______________ the student again later

B Complete the following summary with the words given below.

covering that topic	the orientation session	comparative mythology class
Aztec mythology	author, title, or subject	typing the word

The student is looking for information to write a paper in a ______________, but she is having trouble using the library's computer system. She is a freshman visiting the library for the first time and missed ______________. The librarian says that the student can search for books by ______________. The student says she is trying a subject search, but she gets a "Nothing available" message whenever she types in a subject. She says she is ______________ "Hephaestus" and the names of Aztec gods. The librarian says that her searches are too specific and should be more general. He suggests using "______________" and types it in the search bar. Then, many books ______________ appear. The librarian tells the student that she can ask him for more help later if she needs assistance.

Exercise 2 Listen to part of a conversation between a student and a professor. Then, answer the questions.

01-07

Office Hours

1 What problem does the student have?

Ⓐ He does not know which classes to take.
Ⓑ He has not studied for the midterm exam yet.
Ⓒ He could not understand the day's lecture.
Ⓓ He does not know how to do an assignment.

2 What is the professor's attitude toward the student?

Ⓐ She expresses confidence in his writing abilities.
Ⓑ She is sympathetic regarding his problem.
Ⓒ She believes he is asking improper questions.
Ⓓ She is hesitant to give him too much information.

3 What can be inferred about the student?

Ⓐ He is majoring in archaeology.
Ⓑ He visits the professor's office regularly.
Ⓒ He enjoys doing research on various topics.
Ⓓ He appreciates the professor's explanation.

Words & Phrases

spare v to have left over; not to need
recall v to remember
process n a method; a way of doing something
lost adj confused
artifact n an object from a time in the past
precisely adv exactly
sum up phr to describe briefly
get the hang of phr to understand; to know how to do something

Summary Note

A Listen to the conversation again and fill in the blanks to complete the conversation notes.

- Student meets ❶ ______________ about problem
- Needs to talk about ❷ ______________
  - Isn't sure what to do
- Professor suggests writing on ❸ ______________
- Student asks ❹ ______________ research paper
  - Never wrote ❺ ______________ in high school
  - Doesn't know ❻ ______________ to use
- Professor says to make ❼ ______________
- Must have introduction, ❽ ______________, and conclusion

B Complete the following summary with the words given below.

facts and data	classes to take	will sum up
how to write	a thesis statement	he is lost

The student asks the professor if she can talk for a moment. The professor wonders if the student needs help choosing which ______________ next semester, but the student says he is there about something else. He says he does not know ______________ the research paper. The professor suggests writing about archaeological methods. The student then states that he has never written a research paper before, so ______________ and does not know what to do. The professor tells him that he needs to come up with ______________, which is one sentence explaining what he will be discussing. Then, he should divide his paper into three parts. The introduction should explain what he will discuss. The body will contain ______________ defending the argument. And the conclusion ______________ the paper.

Exercise 3 Listen to part of a conversation between a student and a bookstore employee. Then, answer the questions.

01-08

Service Encounter

1 What problem does the student have?

Ⓐ She cannot find some material she needs.
Ⓑ She believes a book's price is too high.
Ⓒ She forgot to bring her credit card with her.
Ⓓ She is unable to sign up for a class she needs.

2 What type of class is the student taking?

Ⓐ An accounting class
Ⓑ A literature class
Ⓒ An international relations class
Ⓓ A psychology class

3 What will the student probably do next?

Ⓐ Go to another section
Ⓑ Look for something else
Ⓒ Ask another question
Ⓓ Make a purchase

Words & Phrases

organize v to arrange; to put in the correct order
mistake n an error
odd adj strange
roughly adv around; about; approximately
identical adv same
misplace v to put something in the wrong location
transfer v to move from one place to another

Summary Note

A Listen to the conversation again and fill in the blanks to complete the conversation notes.

- Student can't ❶ ____________
- Man says books aren't organized ❷ ____________
  - Are organized according to ❸ ____________
  - Finds the ❹ ____________ section
- Book student needs is not in the ❺ ____________
  - ❻ ____________ for class are there
  - Man says book must have been ❼ ____________
- Finds book in different location
- Gives book to student to take to ❽ ____________

B Complete the following summary with the words given below.

requests assistance	this is odd	transfer the books
name of the author	for French 134	the wrong place

The student ____________ from the man because she cannot find a book. However, she is looking in ____________ because the books are not organized alphabetically. They are organized according to which class they are for. The student says she needs a book ____________. The man shows her to the French section and asks for the ____________. However, the book the student needs is missing whereas the other six books for that class are on the shelf. The man says that ____________, so he guesses the book must have been misplaced. He looks for it and finds it in the French 234 section. He gives the student the book and says he has to ____________ to the correct location.

Exercise 4 Listen to part of a conversation between a student and a professor. Then, answer the questions.

01-09

Office Hours

1 What are the speakers mainly discussing?

(A) How to become a good journalist
(B) Registering for courses
(C) Securing a job at a university
(D) How to take proper notes during a lecture

2 What class does the professor tell the student to take next semester?

(A) Biology
(B) Journalism
(C) Mass communication
(D) History

3 What does the student imply about the geology class?

(A) Many students are trying to take it.
(B) There is not much work required for it.
(C) It will be difficult to get an A in.
(D) She wants to study with the professor.

Words & Phrases

requirement n something demanded or obligatory
register v to enter or record on an official list
prerequisite n something required beforehand
appointment n a scheduled meeting
consideration n a careful thought
definitely adv for certain
suspect v to believe to be true; to imagine
afford v to manage

Summary Note

A Listen to the conversation again and fill in the blanks to complete the conversation notes.

- Student visits professor for ❶ ______________
- Wants to ❷ ______________ next semester's classes
- Professor asks about hours
  - Wants to know ❸ ______________
  - Student wants to finish in ❹ ______________
  - Student wants to take ❺ ______________
- Both discuss classes
  - Student has not taken a prerequisite mass communication class
  - Student needs to ❻ ______________

B Complete the following summary with the words given below.

cannot afford	interest in geology	major she was choosing
graduate on time	scheduling classes	prerequisite

The student visits her professor to go over her choices for next semester's classes. The student wants to make sure that she is taking the right classes for her journalism major. The professor agrees that a very important part of succeeding in college is ______________ correctly, and she looks at the student's records. The professor asks the student if she wants to ______________ in the usual four years. The student says she wants to graduate on time as she ______________ to stay longer. The professor tells the student that, considering the ______________, she should think about taking the mass communication class since it is a ______________ for other classes that she will need. The professor also inquires if there are any other science classes the student is interested in taking. The student indicates that she has an ______________.

Exercises with Long Lectures

Exercise 1 Listen to part of a lecture in a music class. Then, answer the questions.

01 - 10

Music

1 What is the lecture mostly about?

Ⓐ How to write an operetta
Ⓑ The history of opera
Ⓒ Why operas are emotional
Ⓓ The life of Richard Wagner

2 What is the difference between a play and an opera?

Ⓐ The words in an opera are sung.
Ⓑ An opera utilizes more actors.
Ⓒ Operas are only performed in Italian.
Ⓓ Plays have more complicated plotlines.

3 Listen again to part of the lecture. Then answer the question.
Why does the professor say this: 🎧

Ⓐ To identify a certain type of opera
Ⓑ To claim that most operas are dramas
Ⓒ To respond to a complaint made by the student
Ⓓ To explain why many people like operas

Words & Phrases

evolve v to develop slowly
incorporate v to take in or include a part or parts
intonation n the way in which the level of a voice changes to add meaning
morbid adj gloomy
complicated adj confusing or perplexing
embrace v to accept; to include
comical adj amusing or funny
clichéd adj used so often that something is no longer interesting
utilize v to put to use

Summary Note

A Listen to the lecture again and fill in the blanks to complete the lecture notes.

- Professor says he will discuss ❶ ______________________
- Student claims they are boring
  - Doesn't understand them
  - Has ❷ ______________________ about operas
- Professor begins discussion on operas
  - Began with ❸ ______________________
  - Moves to modern opera in ❹ ______________________
- Describes arias
  - Showcase ❺ ______________________
  - Can express different emotions
- Says operas are popular in many countries
- Explains variations of operas
  - Opera seria: ❻ ______________________
  - Opera comique: ❼ ______________________
  - Operetta: ❽ ______________________

B Complete the following summary with the words given below.

very short opera	Germans	complex musical passage
ancient Greeks	comique	during the Renaissance

An opera is a form of drama that includes music or dancing or a combination of both. The ______________________ were the first to employ these elements on stage, but it was not until ______________________ in Italy that what is now called modern opera was developed. The Italians were not the only ones to compose modern operas; the ______________________ were quick to follow. Eventually, opera spread across Europe and even into Russia. This kind of widespread interest in opera led to many different developments and types. There are also the opera seria and the opera ______________________. Another development was the operetta, which is a ______________________ that is often comical in nature. But no matter what the type, operas share many similar elements, such as the aria, a ______________________ exhibiting a singer's vocal range.

Exercise 2 Listen to part of a lecture in a history class. Then, answer the questions.

01 - 11

History

1 What is the lecture mainly about?

- (A) How to harvest rice
- (B) The uses for domestic rice
- (C) The origins of wild and domestic rice
- (D) How China became a major producer of rice

2 What is the main difference between wild and domestic rice?

- (A) Wild rice has more flavor than domestic rice.
- (B) Domestic rice is planted according to desired traits.
- (C) Wild rice is only found in Australia.
- (D) Domestic rice has more flavor.

3 What does the professor imply about domestic rice?

- (A) It is the most nutritious grain.
- (B) The Chinese make the best rice.
- (C) Wild rice is better than domestic rice.
- (D) It is hard to identify its exact date of origin.

Words & Phrases

cultivate v to prepare and work on land in order to raise crops
yield v to produce or show
distribution n an arrangement
origin n the point at which something is born
precise adj exact
microscopic adj too small to be seen by the naked eye
paddy n a flooded field where rice is grown
generation n offspring that is at the same stage from a common ancestor
sow v to scatter seeds for growing

Summary Note

A Listen to the lecture again and fill in the blanks to complete the lecture notes.

- Professor discusses ❶ ______________________
- Describes wild rice
  - Occurs ❷ ______________________
  - Existed 16,000 years ago
  - Probably originated ❸ ______________________
- Describes domestic rice
  - Goes back to ❹ ______________________
  - Carries certain desired ❺ ______________________
- Discusses a ❻ ______________________ about rice
  - *The Gift of the Sky Flood*

B Complete the following summary with the words given below.

China	rice paddies	ancestors were harvesting
to yield desired traits	occurs naturally	nearly impossible

The origin of rice is a complicated question because it can potentially contain three parts: the origins of wild rice and domestic rice or the mythological stories surrounding rice. The exact origin of wild rice is ______________________ to pinpoint, but evidence suggests that early human ______________________ it as early as 16,000 years ago. The evidence also suggests that wild rice spread over four continents: Australia, Asia, Africa, and North America. Domestic rice originated in ______________________ in Hunan Province; evidence of ancient ______________________ has been discovered there. The difference between wild rice and domestic rice is that wild rice ______________________ while domestic rice seeds are selectively planted according to the potential ______________________. Finally, another way that the origin of rice is explained is through the use of ancient myths. One such myth about the origin of rice is the story of Shuhwa, a girl who planted a seed she found in a dog's fur during a flood and which later produced rice.

Exercise 3 Listen to part of a lecture in a public health class. Then, answer the questions.

01-12

Public Health

1 What is the lecture mainly about?

(A) How to diagnose a case of gingivitis
(B) A good technique to brush one's teeth
(C) Oral plaque and how to prevent it
(D) How to schedule visits to the dentist

2 What is one way that oral plaque can affect teeth?

(A) It hardens and becomes tartar.
(B) It makes teeth healthy.
(C) It can cause teeth to fall out.
(D) It can cause oral cancer.

3 How does the professor organize the lecture?

(A) By having an informal question-and-answer session
(B) By speaking chronologically about the history of dentistry
(C) By reading from the textbook and then explaining the passage
(D) By providing examples and then discussing them

Words & Phrases

imperative adj very important or urgent; necessary
diligent adj persistent; not giving up
incorporate v to take in or include as part or parts
rigorous adj very exact
ingest v to take food into the body via the mouth
failure n a lack of success
defense n a method of protecting something
swollen adj expanded due to internal pressure
neutralize v to counterbalance
penetrate v to enter something

Summary Note

A Listen to the lecture again and fill in the blanks to complete the lecture notes.

- Professor mentions ❶ ____________
  - Can build up on teeth because of ❷ ____________
  - Is yellowish sticky film of ❸ ____________
  - Can cause periodontitis and ❹ ____________
- Plaque can harden into tartar
  - A hard ❺ ____________
  - Irritates gums so that they are red and ❻ ____________
  - Can cause gingivitis
- Describes dental care
  - Brush ❼ ____________
  - Visit the dentist often
  - ❽ ____________ helps prevent plaque

B Complete the following summary with the words given below.

hard substance	remove	natural defense
gingivitis	actively neutralizing	yellowish sticky film

Oral plaque is a ____________ of bacteria that forms naturally on the teeth. However, if not properly removed, oral plaque can form into a ____________ known as tartar. In turn, if tartar is not properly treated, it can lead to much more serious diseases like ____________ and periodontitis. The body does its best to combat the buildup of oral plaque into tartar; it even has its own ____________: saliva. Saliva helps break down the bacteria by ____________ the acidic environment. The best way to prevent plaque from building up in the mouth is to incorporate a rigorous daily routine of brushing and flossing with regular visits to the dentist to ____________ all the plaque from the teeth and gums.

Exercise 4 Listen to part of a lecture in a zoology class. Then, answer the questions.

01 - 13

Zoology

1 What is the lecture mainly about?

Ⓐ How to hunt large cats
Ⓑ How to identify various tigers
Ⓒ The characteristics of tigers
Ⓓ Where to find large cats in Asia

2 According to the professor, how have humans affected tigers?

Ⓐ They have made it illegal to kill tigers.
Ⓑ They have moved many to animal sanctuaries.
Ⓒ They have reduced the sizes of tigers' habitats.
Ⓓ They have hunted large numbers of tigers.

3 What can be inferred about tigers?

Ⓐ They are worth saving from extinction.
Ⓑ People are permitted to hunt them in some places.
Ⓒ There are more tigers in zoos than in the wild.
Ⓓ Albino tigers are superior to other tigers.

Words & Phrases

deficiency n the state of not having enough
deceive v to mislead or lie
poacher n a person who kills an animal illegally
mention v to refer to something
unique adj being the only one of its kind
hereditary adj transmitted from parent to offspring
illusion n a wrong perception of reality

Summary Note

A Listen to the lecture again and fill in the blanks to complete the lecture notes.

- Professor describes ❶ ______________
  - A mammal
  - Has ❷ ______________ striped fur
  - Has ❸ ______________ in some places
- Describes the albino tiger
  - Has a deficiency of ❹ ______________
  - Has no ❺ ______________
- Gives physical characteristics of tigers
  - Is the largest cat
    → Up to ❻ ______________ feet long
    → Weighs 200–700 pounds
- Are ❼ ______________ subspecies of tigers
- Describes current situation of tigers
  - About 2,500–5,000 tigers alive
  - Some species are ❽ ______________
  - Others species are endangered
  - Live only in Asia

B Complete the following summary with the words given below.

Javan tigers	largest	eight different subspecies
Siberian tiger	endangered species	poached

A tiger is a mammal that generally has orange fur and black stripes with white markings on its face, chest, and underside. Tigers are also the ______________ of all the cats. The largest is the ______________. Tigers can range in length from four to thirteen feet and can weigh anywhere between 200 and 700 pounds. They are broken down into ______________, three of which are extinct. The extinct subspecies are the Bali, Caspian, and ______________. The fact that there are extinct subspecies of tigers is also a reason why tigers are listed as ______________. While tigers once roamed anywhere between eastern Turkey and Asia, what tigers remain are now only found in certain parts of Asia. Tigers are becoming extinct because they are being ______________ for their skins and because they sometimes kill cattle and other livestock.

Integrated Listening & Speaking

A Listen to a different version of a previous lecture on music and say the answers out loud. You can refer to the summary note below.

01-14

Music

Summary Note

- Professor says he will discuss operas
- Student claims they are boring
  - Doesn't understand them
  - Has wrong idea about operas
- Professor begins discussion on operas
  - Begins with the ancient Greeks
  - Moves to modern opera in the Renaissance
- Describes arias
  - Showcase a singer's abilities
  - Can express different emotions
- Says operas are popular in many countries
- Explains variations of operas
  - Opera seria: dramatic opera
  - Opera comique: comical opera
  - Operetta: short, comical opera

1 What is opera?

2 Who were the first people to develop opera?

3 What is an aria?

B Listen to a different version of a previous lecture on public health and say the answers out loud. You can refer to the summary note below.

01 - 15

Public Health

Summary Note

- Professor mentions oral plaque
  - Can build up on teeth because of sugar
  - Is yellowish sticky film of bacteria
  - Can cause periodontitis and gingivitis
- Plaque can harden into tartar
  - A hard substance
  - Irritates gums to be red and swollen
  - Can cause gingivitis
- Describes dental care
  - Brush regularly
  - Visit the dentist often
  - Saliva helps prevent plaque

1 What is oral plaque?

2 If oral plaque is not properly removed, what can it build up into?

3 What should people do to try to prevent the buildup of oral plaque?

Mini TOEFL iBT Practice Test

Listen to part of a conversation between a student and a professor.

01-16

1 What are the speakers mainly discussing?

(A) The grade the student is getting in the professor's class
(B) The need for the student to take better notes
(C) A project that the student needs to complete
(D) An upcoming performance by the student

2 Why does the student mention basketball?

(A) To explain why he missed the last class
(B) To note that he enjoys playing it with friends
(C) To ask for permission to attend practice
(D) To say he is on the school's basketball team

3 What can be inferred about the student?

(A) He usually turns in schoolwork late.
(B) He does not attend class very often.
(C) He has a part-time job on weekends.
(D) He is majoring in physical education.

4 What is the professor's attitude toward the student?

(A) She praises him for his diligence.
(B) She becomes upset about his poor attitude.
(C) She is surprised by his knowledge.
(D) She is unhappy with his responses.

5 Which topic does the student express interest in?

(A) Tunnels
(B) Suspension bridges
(C) Deep-water ports
(D) Skyscrapers

Listen to part of a lecture in a literature class.

01-17

Literature

6 What is the main idea of the lecture?

(A) How to write plays
(B) The life of William Shakespeare
(C) Life in England in the late sixteenth century
(D) The hardship of London theater life

7 Why does the professor discuss Stratford-Upon-Avon?

(A) To point out its closeness to London
(B) To explain its importance to England's economy
(C) To say that Shakespeare was born there
(D) To claim that a college was located there

8 What does the professor imply about Shakespeare?

(A) He did not write all the works attributed to him.
(B) People today are still interested in his works.
(C) He most likely could speak several foreign languages.
(D) Nobody knows where he was educated.

9 According to the professor, how did the bubonic plague affect England?

Ⓐ It killed large numbers of people there.

Ⓑ It resulted in theaters being closed down.

Ⓒ It made plays more popular than ever.

Ⓓ It caused people to move away from cities.

10 Based on the information in the lecture, when did Shakespeare write the following plays? Click on the correct box for each statement.

	1589-1594	1599-1608
1 *The Comedy of Errors*		
2 *Othello*		
3 *King Lear*		
4 *Titus Andronicus*		

11 Listen again to part of the lecture. Then answer the question.
What does the professor mean when he says this: 🎧

Ⓐ There are many mysterious things regarding Shakespeare.

Ⓑ Very little is known about the works of Shakespeare.

Ⓒ Shakespeare's works can be difficult to understand.

Ⓓ There are some works of Shakespeare that are lost.

Vocabulary Check-Up

A Choose and write the correct words that match the definitions.

1 transfer	•	• Ⓐ	to develop slowly
2 prerequisite	•	• Ⓑ	to move from one place to another
3 specific	•	• Ⓒ	to put something in the wrong location
4 spare	•	• Ⓓ	used so often that it is no longer interesting
5 misplace	•	• Ⓔ	something required beforehand
6 imperative	•	• Ⓕ	persistent; not giving up
7 deceive	•	• Ⓖ	being the only one of its kind
8 diligent	•	• Ⓗ	very important or urgent; necessary
9 yield	•	• Ⓘ	relating to a particular person, place, thing, etc.
10 evolve	•	• Ⓙ	to mislead or lie
11 swollen	•	• Ⓚ	expanded due to internal pressure
12 unique	•	• Ⓛ	to have left over; not to need
13 clichéd	•	• Ⓜ	to produce or show
14 embrace	•	• Ⓝ	a flooded field where rice is grown
15 paddy	•	• Ⓞ	to accept; to include

B Choose the correct words that match the descriptions.

Ⓐ opera Ⓑ endangered species Ⓒ oral plaque Ⓓ play Ⓔ rice

1 This is the buildup of yellowish sticky bacteria that occurs naturally on the teeth.

2 This is a naturally occurring grain that is generally grown in Asia.

3 This is a form of drama in which most of the words are sung.

4 This is a dramatic performance that is acted on a stage.

5 This refers to the animals that may go extinct in the future.

UNIT

02 Listening for Main Purpose

Overview

Introduction

In order to understand the purpose of the listening passage, you must be able to recognize the reason why various topics are discussed or mentioned. This type of question occurs more frequently in conversations rather than in lectures. Just like main idea questions, the speakers may provide this information at the beginning of the passage, or it may be imparted during the course of the passage. If the latter is the case, then you must be able to generalize or determine the information based upon the content of the passage.

Question Types

- Why does the student visit the professor?
- Why does the student visit the Registrar's office?
- Why did the professor ask to see the student?
- Why does the professor explain X?

Useful Tips

- Understand the reason for having the lecture or conversation.
- Listen very carefully to the ends of conversations.
- Determine the purpose by recognizing the solution to the problem.
- Avoid choosing answers that are either irrelevant to the passage or are not covered during the entire course of the passage.
- Avoid nonspecific answers that are too general.
- Make good use of your notes.

Sample TOEFL iBT Question

Script

02-01

M Student: Professor Drexler, may I speak with you for a moment, please? You're not too busy right now, are you?

W Professor: No, not at all, Adrian. Come into my office, and have a seat . . . So tell me . . . What's on your mind right now?

M: Well, you may or may not know this, but I'm applying to several graduate schools, so I was hoping that you would be able to write a few letters of recommendation that I could send out along with my applications.

W: I'm honored that you've asked me, Adrian, and I'm more than happy to help you out, but don't you think you ought to ask Professor Smith instead? After all, he is your advisor, and he's the professor that you've worked with the most in all of your years here. I would think that he would be able to write the best, most comprehensive letter of recommendation for you.

M: Yes, ma'am. You're absolutely right. The only problem is that I can't get in touch with Professor Smith at this moment. Apparently, he is still at that conference somewhere in Europe, and I don't know when he's coming back. I left him a couple of voice messages, and I've e-mailed him several times, but he hasn't responded to any of them.

Q Why does the student visit the professor?

Ⓐ To inquire as to Professor Smith's whereabouts
Ⓑ To ask about some different graduate schools
Ⓒ To request a favor from the professor
Ⓓ To submit a letter of recommendation to the professor

☑ Correct Answer

The answer to the above question is Ⓒ. The reason the student visits the professor is that he wants the professor to write some letters of recommendation for him, so he is asking the professor for a favor.

Basic Drill

Listen to parts of conversations or lectures and answer the questions.

Drill 1

02-02

Q Why does the student visit the gym?

Ⓐ To lift weights

Ⓑ To speak with a coach

Ⓒ To go swimming

Ⓓ To get a membership

Check-Up **Listen again and fill in the blanks with the correct words.**

W Student: Hello. I'm here to use ________________. But, uh, I don't know where it is.

M Gym Employee: The pool is located ________________. To get there, you can go down the stairs in the back.

W: Great. Thanks.

M: Hold on a moment. You ________________ right now. The swim team is ________________.

W: Oh . . . Well, they aren't using ________________, are they?

M: Actually, they are. The swim team expanded ________________ this year, so the entire pool ________________ to everyone else each day between four and six PM.

W: Okay. That's fine. But I can use it ________________, right? And do I need to pay to use it?

M: If you're a ________________ here, you don't need to pay anything at all. And yes, you can use the pool ________________.

W: That's wonderful. Oh, one last question . . . Is the pool open ________________?

M: Yes, but the hours are ________________. If you go to the pool, you'll see the hours ________________ for each day.

Drill 2

Q Why did the professor ask to see the student?

Ⓐ To give him a new assignment
Ⓑ To ask him about a homework project
Ⓒ To discuss a story that he wrote
Ⓓ To talk about how to improve his grade

02-03

Check-Up Listen again and fill in the blanks with the correct words.

W Professor: Hello, Theo. Thanks for ______________.

M Student: No problem, Professor Evergreen. You know, uh, I was going to ______________ even if you hadn't asked me to. I think you forgot to ______________ the short story I wrote today. ______________ received their story.

W: I didn't hand it back to you ______________, Theo. And ______________ I asked you to come to my office.

M: Oh . . . I guess ______________ my story. That's too bad.

W: ______________, I loved it.

M: Huh?

W: I found it to be a very intriguing and well-written ______________. Where did you ______________ for it?

M: Uh . . . I don't know really. I just read a lot of fantasy works and wrote something ______________.

W: You didn't copy it from ______________, did you?

M: Not at all. I would ______________. I just had an idea and went with it.

W: Well, it's ______________, and you got an A+ on the assignment. If you don't mind, I'm going to ______________ to the class the next time we meet.

Drill 3

Q Why does the professor explain the effects of gravity on dwarf planets?

Ⓐ To claim that it is making their orbits irregular

Ⓑ To point out how powerful the sun's gravity is

Ⓒ To state that their masses are less than Neptune's

Ⓓ To argue why Planet X probably exists

02-04

Check-Up

Listen again and fill in the blanks with the correct words.

W Professor: ____________________ that there are eight planets in the solar system. In addition, there are ____________________. Pluto is the best-known of them, but there are several others, ____________________ in the Kuiper Belt. This is an area which is way beyond the orbit of Neptune, ____________________ from the sun. However, there are ____________________ who believe there is yet another planet—a ninth planet—that is orbiting the sun much farther away than Neptune and Pluto. Despite not having been discovered, ____________________ has been given the name Planet X.

Astronomers who ____________________ that Planet X exists but hasn't been located yet believe the planet is around the same size as Neptune. It likely has a mass which is ____________________ that of Earth, and it probably takes between 10,000 and 20,000 years to complete ____________________ around the sun. You're ____________________ why astronomers believe Planet X is real. Well, the main reason ____________________ gravity. You see, astronomers have noticed ____________________ in the dwarf planets and the other objects located in the Kuiper Belt. ____________________ they have is that a large planet—uh, you know, Planet X—is having an effect on them due to the strength of its gravity. Here, um, let me show you how some of these dwarf planets are behaving, and then ____________________.

Drill 4

Q Why does the professor explain the Mohs Hardness Scale?

Ⓐ To tell the students about the person who created it
Ⓑ To focus on a characteristic of various minerals
Ⓒ To answer a question asked by a student in class
Ⓓ To let the students know why diamond cannot be scratched

02-05

Check-Up **Listen again and fill in the blanks with the correct words.**

M Professor: In our geology class, one of the most important things you need to ________________ is the Mohs Hardness Scale. It's something I'm going to mention ________________ I lecture, particularly when I introduce a new kind of rock or mineral. What is the Mohs Hardness Scale? Well, it's a scale that measures, ________________, the hardness of various minerals. And just so you know, in this case, hardness refers to the ability of a mineral ________________.

At the bottom of the scale is talc, which has ________________. Number two is gypsum while number three is calcite. So just to make sure you understand, talc ________________ either gypsum or calcite because it is too soft. However, both gypsum and calcite can scratch talc while calcite can also scratch gypsum since it has a ________________. Let me continue . . . Fluorite is four, apatite is five, and orthoclase is six. Now, we're getting to ________________. Quartz is seven while topaz is eight. Corundum is nine, and diamond ________________ at ten. This means that diamond is ________________ known to us. It is ________________ anything else on this list.

Exercises with Long Conversations

Exercise 1 Listen to part of a conversation between a student and a professor. Then, answer the questions.

02-06

Office Hours

1 Why does the student visit the professor?

Ⓐ She is upset with her grade in history class.
Ⓑ She wants more information about the final examination.
Ⓒ She is thinking about withdrawing from his course.
Ⓓ She would like to rewrite her paper.

2 How do HIT tutors help students?
Click on 2 answers.

Ⓐ They summarize the textbooks.
Ⓑ They provide assistance with assignments.
Ⓒ They do projects for students.
Ⓓ They lead study groups of students.

3 What can be inferred about the student?

Ⓐ She will drop the course.
Ⓑ She will quit her part-time job.
Ⓒ She will stay enrolled in the class.
Ⓓ She will become an HIT tutor.

Words & Phrases

cumulative adj total
consult v to ask someone for advice
drop v to quit something
entire adj all of
session n a lesson or meeting
tutoring n informal teaching
undergraduate n a university student who has not earned a degree yet
withdraw v to quit

Summary Note

A Listen to the conversation again and fill in the blanks to complete the conversation notes.

- Student meets professor
- Claims the book is ❶ ______________ so must drop the class
- Professor says it is ❷ ______________ to drop
- Professor says student's grades are ❸ ______________
- Student claims she needs a high grade for ❹ ______________
- Professor recommends ❺ ______________
  - Is called HIT
  - Graduate students tutor students
  - Is a ❻ ______________
- Student decides to look into the program

B Complete the following summary with the words given below.

she is not worried	becomes excited	withdrawing
summarizing the textbook	it will be too difficult	too much material

The student tells the professor that she is thinking of ______________ from his history course because she has a part-time job, she does not have enough time to study, and the textbook contains ______________ to read. The professor tells her that it would be a shame if she dropped out of the course because she has already completed five weeks and has done well on the assignments. He also tells her not to worry about failing the course. The student replies that ______________ about failing but that her concern is ______________ to attain a high grade. The professor then mentions the history tutoring program. He says that the tutors are graduate students who can probably do a good job of ______________. Upon hearing this news, the student ______________ and tells the professor that she will check out the History Department's website as soon as she gets back to her computer.

Exercise 2 **Listen to part of a conversation between a student and a cafeteria manager. Then, answer the questions.**

02-07

Service Encounter

1 Why does the student visit the cafeteria manager?

(A) To complain about the food in the cafeteria
(B) To apply for a job in the cafeteria
(C) To request that the snack bar extend its hours
(D) To get permission to study in the cafeteria late at night

2 According to the conversation, why does the student want to extend the snack bar's hours? Click on 2 answers.

(A) Students like to hang out late at the snack bar.
(B) Students enjoy eating the food at the snack bar.
(C) It is inconvenient to go out for a snack late at night.
(D) Students want to eat more during exam week.

3 What can be inferred from the conversation?

(A) The snack bar is a popular place.
(B) The unionized employees are too powerful.
(C) The snack bar has very cheap food.
(D) The cafeteria manager does not like the student.

Words & Phrases

appreciate (v) to be thankful for
complaint (n) a negative comment
custodian (n) someone that is paid to clean a building
extend (v) to make longer
hang out (phr) to spend time together
petition (n) a formal written request made to an authority
snack (n) a short, small meal
steady (adj) not changing suddenly; consistent

Summary Note

A Listen to the conversation again and fill in the blanks to complete the conversation notes.

- Student visits cafeteria manager
- Student wants snack bar to ❶ ______________
  - Says students like to hang out there late and study
  - Is too far to walk to ❷ ______________
- Manager understands student's argument
  - Has to close early for ❸ ______________
  - Students cannot clean
  - Only ❹ ______________ can clean
- Students suggests selling ❺ ______________ from 10:00 to 12:00
- Manager agrees to do that during ❻ ______________

B Complete the following summary with the words given below.

allow the custodians	cafeteria manager	disappointed
packaged goods	the manager agrees	are not allowed

The student visits the ______________ to talk about the hours of the snack bar in the cafeteria. The student says that many students enjoy hanging out and working there at night. He notes that the students are ______________ that the snack bar closes at 10:00 every day. He indicates it would be better if the snack bar stayed open until midnight. The manager replies that it is necessary to close the snack bar by 10:00 to ______________, who stop working at 10:30, time to clean up. He says that student employees ______________ to clean the snack bar. The student then suggests that they keep the snack bar open during midterm exam week and only permit the sale of ______________ after 10:00. The student also shows the manager a petition. Upon hearing the student's suggestion and seeing the petition, ______________ to extend the snack bar's hours during the midterm exam week and possibly during final exam week, too.

Exercise 3 Listen to part of a conversation between a student and a student activities office employee. Then, answer the questions.

02-08

Service Encounter

1 Why did the man ask to see the student?

Ⓐ To provide her with funding
Ⓑ To complement her for her work
Ⓒ To provide her with some advice
Ⓓ To discuss a problem with her

2 What kind of club does the student belong to?

Ⓐ A hiking club
Ⓑ A birdwatching club
Ⓒ A movie club
Ⓓ A photography club

3 What can be inferred about the student?

Ⓐ She is not interested in being president of the club.
Ⓑ She intends to meet her club members tonight.
Ⓒ She has already recruited some new club members.
Ⓓ She is unfamiliar with the rules regarding clubs.

Words & Phrases

respond v to answer
remain v to stay
dictate v to state
recognize v to acknowledge officially
disband v to break up, as in a group or organization
fund v to provide money for someone or something
signature n a person's name in written form
precisely adv exactly

Summary Note

A Listen to the conversation again and fill in the blanks to complete the conversation notes.

- Student says she got the man's ❶ ______________
- ❷ ______________ for not coming in sooner
  - Finished last class ten minutes ago
  - Man says he ❸ ______________ student for one or two days
- Student is president of ❹ ______________
- Club doesn't have enough members
  - Has seven members
  - Needs ❺ ______________ to be recognized by school
- Will be hard to ❻ ______________
- Cannot get funding
- Man tells student to get ❼ ______________ of students to be members
- Will talk to student later about how ❽ ______________ can help her

B Complete the following summary with the words given below.

school rules dictate	get funding	sign up as members
his text message	not be recognized	did not expect

The student visits the man in his office and says that she got ______________. She apologizes for not coming sooner, but she just finished her last class of the day ten minutes ago. The man says that he ______________ her to come until the next day or two. The student says she is the president of the birdwatching club at the school and that they are having a great time. The man says that ______________ that clubs have at least twelve members, but her club only has seven. He says that if the club does not get more members soon, then the club will ______________ by the school. That means it will be hard to reserve a room for meetings and the club cannot ______________ from the school. The student has no idea that funding is available. The man tells the student to get some students to ______________. Then, he will talk to the student about what his office can do for her club.

Exercise 4 Listen to part of a conversation between a student and a professor. Then, answer the questions.

02-09

Office Hours

1 Why does the student visit the professor?

(A) To ask about how to find a nursing job
(B) To respond to her inquiry about volunteer work
(C) To request her help in organizing a conference
(D) To tell the professor about her work experience

2 Why does the student want the professor's help?

(A) She does not have much experience.
(B) Most of her contacts are limited.
(C) The professor has plenty of spare time.
(D) The professor is eager to help the student.

3 What can be inferred from the conversation?

(A) The student wants the professor's full participation.
(B) The professor is eager to help the student.
(C) The professor is very busy nowadays.
(D) The student has lots of experience overseas.

Words & Phrases

accomplish v to reach a goal or objective
association n a formal club, group, league, or organization
exclusively adv only
huge adj very big
logistics n the way something is organized or arranged
numerous adj many
respond v to answer

Summary Note

A Listen to the conversation again and fill in the blanks to complete the conversation notes.

- Student wants to speak with a professor
  - – Had ❶ ________________ many times
  - – Professor never ❷ ________________
- Professor said had been ❸ ________________
- Student wants to set up employment conferences
- Professor suggests using ❹ ________________
- Student doesn't want to do that
  - – Thinks the center's contacts are ❺ ________________
  - – Can't find good jobs through it
- Student offers to do the work
  - – Has many contacts
  - – Professor has to do ❻ ________________ work
- Professor agrees to help

B Complete the following summary with the words given below.

good idea	set up an employment conference	insufficient experience
pleasantly surprised	unsuccessful	do much work

A nursing student goes to speak to her professor. She asks the professor to help ________________. The professor does not think the conference is a ________________. She says she is too busy. She says this type of event should be conducted through the student employment center. She also indicates that the Nursing Department held employment conferences in the past and that all of these conferences were ________________. She says the students did not ________________ and had ________________ in organizing conferences. The student then advises the professor not to worry about the above factors because she used to work for the American Nursing Association and helped organize numerous nursing conferences. The professor is ________________ to hear this and then agrees to make a few phone calls to help arrange the conference.

Exercises with Long Lectures

Exercise 1 Listen to part of a lecture in a zoology class. Then, answer the questions.

02-10

Zoology

1 Why does the professor explain the harshness of the Arctic environment?

(A) To discourage the students from visiting it
(B) To emphasize how impressive polar bears are
(C) To explain why many animals there are dying
(D) To let the students know how cold the Arctic is

2 What comparison does the professor make between polar bears and brown bears?

(A) The amount of fish that each can eat
(B) The type of diet that each one has
(C) The relative size of each bear
(D) The swimming ability of each bear

3 What does the professor imply about polar bears?

(A) They need long summers for maximum energy.
(B) They are a serious threat to humans in the Arctic.
(C) They are reproducing at a rapid rate.
(D) They have changed their diets in recent years.

Words & Phrases

amazingly adv surprisingly
camouflage v to disguise one's appearance
endangered adj being in a dangerous situation
extremely adv very
frequently adv often
harsh adj severe
insulate v to provide a warm layer
roam v to walk all over the place with no specific destination in mind

Summary Note

A Listen to the lecture again and fill in the blanks to complete the lecture notes.

- Professor discusses ❶ ____________
  - Live in Arctic in ❷ ____________
  - Few species can survive there
  - Roam the land and ice hunting; eat seals, fish, and other food
  - Have no ❸ ____________
- Shows pictures of polar bears
  - Are ❹ ____________ than brown and black bears
  - Can weigh up to 1,600 pounds
  - Have ❺ ____________ fur
  - Are strong swimmers
- Are becoming ❻ ____________
  - ❼ ____________ decreases the amount of ice
  - Bears have less time to hunt

B Complete the following summary with the words given below.

front paws	looking for seals	harsh environment
the ice	endangered species	favorite food

Polar bears live in the Arctic, which has an extremely ____________. It's one of the coldest places on the Earth. The temperature in the Arctic frequently drops below minus forty degrees centigrade. The polar bear, however, thrives in this kind of environment. The polar bear roams on land, swims in freezing sea water, and floats on sheets of ice while ____________, which is its ____________. Polar bears are very large. They have a very thick coat of fur and large ____________ that allow them to swim far from land. Unfortunately, polar bears are an ____________ because the Arctic is becoming too warm for them. ____________ is disappearing, and so are the seals.

Exercise 2 Listen to part of a lecture in a geology class. Then, answer the questions.

02-11

Geology

1 Why does the professor explain seismic waves?

(A) To illustrate how scientists managed to learn about them
(B) To explain the most common causes of earthquakes
(C) To explain why they are so dangerous during earthquakes
(D) To illustrate the differences between various types of them

2 According to the professor, which of the following describes surface waves?
Click on 2 answers.

(A) They are the fastest kind of seismic wave.
(B) They travel at half the speed of P waves.
(C) They are the most destructive seismic waves.
(D) They move at or near the Earth's surface.

3 What can be inferred about earthquakes?

(A) There are hundreds of them each day.
(B) Not all of them are dangerous.
(C) Those with body waves are the most dangerous.
(D) They can be caused by sound waves.

Words & Phrases

amplitude (n) the height of a wave
catastrophic (adj) having a very harmful impact
destructive (adj) causing damage
duration (n) a period of time
frequency (n) the regularity that something happens
material (n) content; an ingredient
ripple (n) a small wave
tremor (n) small shaking

Summary Note

A Listen to the lecture again and fill in the blanks to complete the lecture notes.

- Professor discusses ❶ ____________
  - Some cannot be felt on the Earth
  - Some are violent with ❷ ____________
- People feel seismic waves
  - Are similar to ❸ ____________ waves
  - Can reflect and ❹ ____________
  - Can change speed
- Two major kinds of seismic waves
  - ❺ ____________
    - → P wave or primary wave
    - → S wave or secondary wave
  - ❻ ____________
    - → Move at the Earth's surface
    - → Are very destructive
    - → Love wave and Rayleigh wave

B Complete the following summary with the words given below.

feel or hear them	during an earthquake	lower frequency
moving up and down	major explosions	deep inside

Seismic waves are caused by earthquakes and ____________. Sometimes it is possible to feel seismic waves ____________. If one feels shaking during an earthquake, what is felt are seismic waves. Seismic waves have similar properties to sound waves and light waves. The first kinds of waves that one can feel are body waves. These might not be very powerful because they move ____________ the Earth's surface. But because some of them travel very fast, they are the waves that a person feels first. Perhaps a person will not ____________. If they are felt, they are usually minor tremors. Some body waves travel slower and might cause more damage at the Earth's surface. Surface waves travel at or near the Earth's surface. They are usually more destructive than body waves because of their ____________, larger amplitude, and longer duration. One type of body wave, when it reaches the Earth's surface, might appear as a wave ____________, sometimes making it appear as though cars are moving up and down.

Exercise 3 Listen to part of a lecture in an astronomy class. Then, answer the questions.

02-12

Astronomy

1 Why does the professor explain the Jovian planets?

(A) To detail the manner in which they were formed
(B) To point out their similarities to Earth
(C) To explain why there are so big
(D) To describe their characteristics

2 According to the professor, which of the following describes Jupiter?
Click on 2 answers.

(A) It is very cold.
(B) It has the Great Dark Spot.
(C) It is much bigger than the other planets.
(D) It is very hot.

3 Listen again to part of the lecture. Then answer the question.
Why does the professor say this: 🎧

(A) To distinguish between Jovian planets and gas giants
(B) To avoid confusing the students
(C) To get the students to look in their textbooks
(D) To compare Jovian planets with rocky planets

Words & Phrases

bombard (v) quickly to hit, shoot, or target something many times
blend (v) to mix together; to combine with
core (n) the center of an object
diameter (n) the distance across a circle
fixture (n) something that is permanent
halo (n) a circle of light
massive (adv) very large in size; enormous
radiate (v) to deflect
reiterate (v) to repeat

Summary Note

A Listen to the lecture again and fill in the blanks to complete the lecture notes.

- Professor discusses ❶ ____________
  - Neptune, Uranus, Saturn, and Jupiter
  - Are different from Earth and Mars
  - Are mostly composed of ❷ ____________
- Jovian planets do not have solid surfaces
  - Are ❸ ____________
  - Can't land spacecraft on them
- Gives more facts about them
  - Have many ❹ ____________
  - Are very large
- Weather patterns are very different
  - Have violent ❺ ____________
  - Have many ❻ ____________
- Is probably no life on Jovian planets

B Complete the following summary with the words given below.

exterior	number of rings	a layer of clouds
twice as massive	landing on	rocky core

There are two types of planets. One type is those with a ____________ such as Earth and Mars. The other type is the gaseous planets, which are Neptune, Uranus, Saturn, and Jupiter. The biggest of these is Jupiter. The rocky planets and the gaseous planets are very different. For example, the ____________ of a gaseous planet does not have a solid surface. Therefore, a spacecraft would be incapable of ____________ such a planet. The Jovian planets have a ____________ and moons. Jupiter has ninety-five moons. It is also the biggest planet in the solar system. In fact, it is ____________ as all of the other planets combined. Jupiter has the Great Red Spot, a storm which is at least 350 years old. Wind speeds on Jupiter often reach up to 600 kilometers per hour. Jupiter's innermost ring is 22,000 kilometers wide. And Jupiter is always covered by ____________.

Exercise 4 Listen to part of a lecture in a climatology class. Then, answer the questions.

02-13

Climatology

1 What aspect of monsoons does the professor mainly discuss?

- (A) The damage caused by them
- (B) How they are caused by global warming
- (C) The monsoon season in Asia
- (D) Their benefits to people

2 Why does the professor explain the effect of monsoons on India?

- (A) To illustrate how heavy the rainfall is
- (B) To inform the students that India has too much water
- (C) To indicate that they can be beneficial
- (D) To illustrate why other countries do not receive much rainfall

3 According to the professor, which of the following describes monsoons?
Click on 2 answers.

- (A) They are more common in the Northern Hemisphere.
- (B) India is almost completely reliant on monsoon rains.
- (C) All monsoons have roughly the same duration.
- (D) Monsoons are very common in the United States.

Words & Phrases

annual adj occurring every year
ample adj plenty; a lot
derive from phr to come from
drenched adj extremely wet
famine n starvation
moist adj wet
porous adj having many holes
reliant on adj dependent on
urge v to encourage, recommend, or suggest
shabby adj old; broken-down

Summary Note

A Listen to the lecture again and fill in the blanks to complete the lecture notes.

- Professor discusses ❶ ____________________
  - Are annual weather phenomena
  - Are heavy rains
  - Occur in ❷ ____________________ places
- Can be beneficial
  - Supply ❸ ____________________ of India's water
  - Essential for ❹ ____________________
- Can be harmful
  - Can cause ❺ ____________________
  - Inconvenience people in cities
- Are hard to ❻ ____________________

B Complete the following summary with the words given below.

these rains	primarily in Asia	over the ocean
causing flooding	large landmasses	impossible to predict

Monsoons are annual weather phenomena that occur ____________________. More specifically, they are very heavy rains which originate from moist air masses that move inland from the ocean. Typically, cool air ____________________ reaches warm dry air above India, causing it to rain throughout South Asia. Monsoons can be destructive, ____________________ and subsequent famines. But unlike most natural weather phenomena, they also have a beneficial impact. For example, monsoon rains supply about ninety percent of India's total water supply. They are essential for crops. Poor subsistence farmers are totally reliant on ____________________ for their livelihoods. Too little rain may result in famine. The precise dates and durations of monsoons are ____________________. Monsoons are more common in the Northern Hemisphere, where there are more ____________________, than in the Southern Hemisphere, which is mostly comprised of sea water.

Integrated Listening & Speaking

A Listen to a different version of a previous lecture on zoology and say the answers out loud. You can refer to the summary note below.

02-14

Zoology

Summary Note

- Professor discusses polar bears
  - Live in Arctic in freezing temperature
  - Few species can survive there
  - Roam the land and ice hunting; eat seals, fish, and other food
  - Have no natural enemies
- Shows pictures of polar bear
  - Are bigger than brown and black bears
  - Can weigh up to 740 kilograms
  - Have thick white fur
  - Are strong swimmers
- Are becoming endangered
  - Global warming decreases the amount of ice
  - Bears have less time to hunt

1 What do polar bears look like?

2 What do polar bears like to eat?

3 Why are polar bears an endangered species?

B Listen to a different version of a previous lecture on climatology and say the answers out loud. You can refer to the summary note below.

02-15

Climatology

Summary Note

- Professor discusses monsoons
  - Are annual weather phenomena
  - Are heavy rains
  - Occur in various places
- Can be beneficial
  - Supply ninety percent of India's water
  - Essential for crops
- Can be harmful
  - Can cause flooding
  - Inconvenience people in cities
- Are hard to predict

1 What causes monsoons to occur in India?

2 How do monsoons benefit farmers?

3 Why are most monsoons in the Northern Hemisphere?

Listen to part of a conversation between a student and a student services center employee.

02-16

1 Why does the student visit the student center?

Ⓐ To schedule an interview for a job
Ⓑ To find out some job requirements
Ⓒ To receive the results of an application
Ⓓ To ask questions about Bestviews

2 According to the woman, what does a media assistant do?

Ⓐ Makes pickups and deliveries
Ⓑ Works on a computer in an office
Ⓒ Helps make movies
Ⓓ Assists actors while they are working

3 Why does the woman mention a driver's license?

Ⓐ The student needs to get one at once.
Ⓑ She thinks the student cannot do the job.
Ⓒ She believes the student is wrong for the job.
Ⓓ The job requires a lot of driving.

4 What will the student probably do next?

Ⓐ Send an email to Emily
Ⓑ Contact his supervisor
Ⓒ Start working at his job
Ⓓ Look for another job

5 Listen again to part of the conversation. Then answer the question.
What does the woman imply when she says this: 🎧

Ⓐ Bestviews has good experiences with students from the university.
Ⓑ Many students working at Bestviews have careers in media.
Ⓒ The job that the student will do might be a bit dangerous at times.
Ⓓ The student will be working primarily on educational films.

Listen to part of a lecture in a history class.

02-17

6 What aspect of calendars does the professor mainly discuss?

(A) The similarities between the Chinese and Egyptian calendars

(B) The uses of the different calendars kept by the Egyptians

(C) The manner in which the Egyptians calculated days and months

(D) The development of the Egyptian lunar calendar

7 What does the professor imply about ancient cultures?

(A) They were primitive compared to modern times.

(B) They were capable of doing difficult mathematics.

(C) They were surprisingly advanced in some ways.

(D) They were very different from modern ones.

8 What is the professor's opinion of the Egyptian calendar based on star movements?

(A) He considers it to be practical.

(B) He thinks it had too many mistakes.

(C) He believes it was overly complicated.

(D) He calls it unnecessary for most Egyptians.

9 According to the professor, how did the Egyptians use their calendars?
Click on 2 answers.

Ⓐ For confirming the seasons
Ⓑ For religious events
Ⓒ For remembering kings' birthdates
Ⓓ For farming purposes

10 What is a Sothic cycle?

Ⓐ The amount of time from one rainy season to the next
Ⓑ The time it took for two calendars to be in sync
Ⓒ A period of time lasting for the life of an Egyptian king
Ⓓ A complete year in the Egyptian lunar calendar

11 Listen again to part of the lecture. Then answer the question.
Why does the student say this: 🎧

Ⓐ To claim that the professor cannot be right
Ⓑ To express her thoughts on the topic
Ⓒ To ask the professor to repeat himself
Ⓓ To request confirmation from the professor

Vocabulary Check-Up

A Choose and write the correct words that match the definitions.

1 camouflage	•	• (A) to disguise something
2 drenched	•	• (B) not changing suddenly; consistent
3 blend	•	• (C) old; broken down
4 shabby	•	• (D) someone that is paid to clean a building
5 respond	•	• (E) to answer
6 accomplish	•	• (F) very wet
7 custodian	•	• (G) able to do something
8 capable	•	• (H) to reach a goal or objective
9 insulate	•	• (I) to make longer
10 extend	•	• (J) a formal written request made to an authority
11 ripple	•	• (K) to break up, as in a group or organization
12 porous	•	• (L) having many holes
13 petition	•	• (M) to provide a warm layer
14 steady	•	• (N) to mix together; to combine with
15 disband	•	• (O) a small wave

B Choose the correct words that match the descriptions.

(A) polar bears (B) monsoon (C) seismic waves (D) Jupiter (E) Jovian planets

1 This weather phenomenon is a heavy rain that occurs when cool, moist air over the ocean reaches dry, warm air above the Asian continent. ....

2 Neptune, Uranus, Saturn, and Jupiter are examples of these planets. Their exteriors are gaseous. ....

3 These waves move through the Earth whenever there is an earthquake or a major explosion. ....

4 These large creatures are very comfortable living in the harsh Arctic environment. ....

5 This is the largest planet in the solar system. ....

UNIT

03 Listening for Major Details

Overview

Introduction

In order to answer detail questions correctly, you must both understand and remember various details and facts given in the listening passage. The details asked about are often related to the main idea. They may be examples or may expand upon the main topic in the form of supporting statements. The majority of questions asked about details are concerned with major, not minor, details.

Question Types

- According to the professor, what is one way that X can affect Y?
- What are X?
- What resulted from the invention of the X?
- According to the professor, what is the main problem with the X theory?

Useful Tips

- Be sure to take excellent notes with regards to details. Make good use of your notes on details.
- Listen very carefully to the major details, not the minor details, which are given in the passage.
- Answers to detail questions are often paraphrased sentences, not the exact words as they appear in the passage.
- When you are not positive about the correct answer, look at the answer choices and determine which of them most closely resembles the main idea of the passage.

Sample TOEFL iBT Question

Script

03-01

W Professor: For the most part, the most important method of auditioning an actor is through the use of the monologue. A monologue is a, um, speech made by one person speaking his or her thoughts aloud or directly addressing a reader, audience, or character. It is a common feature in drama. Monologues are also a feature of, um, opera when an aria, a recitative, or another sung section may carry out a function similar to that of spoken monologues in the theater. In addition, comic monologues have become a standard element of entertainment routines on stage and television. Has everyone got this? Good!

In addition, there's much more to this than just doing a monologue. Some auditions involve cold reading or performing from a script that the actor is not familiar with. Sight-reading is a much-needed requirement in drama as it is often used in conjunction with improvisations to gauge a performer's ability to perform new works. It is particularly useful during auditions. A good drama sight reader is able to communicate with fluency and clarity and is able to project speech rhythms and rhymes well. He or she should also be able to bring out the intent, the mood, and the characterization of a piece through appropriate articulation and body language.

Q According to the professor, what is a common practice in auditions?

Ⓐ Interviews
Ⓑ Cold readings
Ⓒ Impromtu speeches
Ⓓ Movement exercises

☑ Correct Answer

The correct response to the above question is Ⓑ. The professor says, "In addition, there's much more to this than just doing a monologue. Some auditions involve cold reading or performing from a script that the actor is not familiar with."

Basic Drill

Listen to parts of conversations or lectures and answer the questions.

Drill 1

03-02

Q What does the professor recommend the student do after graduation?

Ⓐ Find a job
Ⓑ Travel abroad
Ⓒ Take some time off
Ⓓ Attend graduate school

Check-Up Listen again and fill in the blanks with the correct words.

M Student: Before I ________________, may I discuss one more thing with you, please?

W Professor: Sure. But we ________________. Several other students are waiting to talk to me, and ________________ in fifteen minutes.

M: Sure. Well, uh, I'm trying to ________________.

W: What are you considering doing?

M: I'm not really sure. Part of me wants to ________________, but another part would prefer to ________________.

W: I think you'd be ________________ for more studying.

M: Why do you think so?

W: Your grades are good, you enjoy studying, and you're ________________ at research. You're exactly the kind of person that grad schools ________________ as students.

M: Thanks for saying that. Do you have any idea which schools I should apply to?

W: Let's have this conversation ________________. I can talk to you ________________ after tomorrow's class ends. How does that sound?

M: Perfect. Thanks so much.

Drill 2

03-03

Q What does the man tell the student to do?

(A) Stop playing loud music
(B) Be nicer to her roommate
(C) Study more for her exams
(D) Choose a new dorm to live in

Check-Up **Listen again and fill in the blanks with the correct words.**

M Residential Assistant: Rebecca, I need to talk to you about ______________ for a moment.

W Student: Sure, Reggie. What's going on?

M: There have been ______________ about you by other students in this dorm.

W: Complaints? About what?

M: ______________. Apparently, you play your music ______________, so you are disturbing a lot of people's sleep.

W: But . . . I don't think it's too loud.

M: Well, the other students do. I need for you to stop playing loud music ______________. If you keep doing it and more students complain, you're going to ______________.

W: Oh, that wouldn't be good.

M: No, it wouldn't. If you get fined, you not only have to pay money, but you have a harder time ______________ in the future.

W: I wasn't ______________. I'm really sorry, Reggie. ______________ my music isn't loud from now on.

M: Thanks a lot, Rebecca.

Drill 3

Q Which of the plays of Aristophanes does the professor like the most?

Ⓐ *The Knights*
Ⓑ *The Wasps*
Ⓒ *Lysistrata*
Ⓓ *The Birds*

03-04

Check-Up Listen again and fill in the blanks with the correct words.

W Professor: The three biggest names in ______________ are Aeschylus, Euripides, and Sophocles. They were primarily responsible for popularizing ______________ in ancient times. Arguably the ______________ playwright in ancient Greece was Aristophanes. He lived from 446 to around 386 B.C. He is called the Father of Comedy, and he was quite a ______________. Let me tell you a bit more about him.

Aristophanes is known to have written ______________. Of those plays, eleven survive ______________ or are almost in their entirety. There are also around 1,000 fragments of his other works ______________. In most cases, they are merely a line or two, so those remaining plays ______________ forever. Aristophanes wrote in the genre known as Old Comedy and was a master both of ______________.

Among his surviving plays, *The Birds*, *The Wasps*, and *Lysistrata* are surely the best known and ______________. Personally, I'm a big fan of *The Knights*, which is a satire on ______________ life in Athens in the fifth century B.C. We're going to read it in class, so please be sure to ______________. Aristophanes often ______________ of Athens, and he was despised by men like Cleon, whom he wrote of disparagingly in *The Knights*.

Drill 4

Q According to the professor, how does the walking stick insect use camouflage?

Ⓐ To try to catch various insects
Ⓑ To ambush animals that come near it
Ⓒ To avoid being hunted
Ⓓ To protect itself from bats

03-05

Check-Up Listen again and fill in the blanks with the correct words.

M Professor: Everyone, please ______________ this picture up on the screen . . . Can anyone tell me what you see?

W Student: Um . . . It's just a picture of ______________. It looks like an oak tree. Is that what we're studying today?

M: I'm impressed you can ______________, Leslie, but look a bit more closely. ______________ is a walking stick insect. You can see it in the upper lefthand corner of the picture . . . uh, right there . . .

The walking stick insect is a ______________ of camouflage. This insect basically, as you can see, resembles ______________ on a tree. It may even sway ______________ when the wind blows to make it look more realistic.

There are around 3,000 species of walking stick insects around the world, and this creature can be found on ______________ except for Antarctica. It prefers ______________ areas though, so you're more likely to find it in places with warm or hot weather. Interestingly, the walking stick is an herbivore, so its camouflage is used for ______________. Despite the fact that ______________, the walking stick insect's camouflage is very effective. Unfortunately, it ______________ due to their reliance on echolocation, so bats are among the ______________ of this insect.

Exercises with Long Conversations

Exercise 1 Listen to part of a conversation between a student and a student housing office employee. Then, answer the questions.

03-06

Service Encounter

1 What does the student complain about?

Ⓐ He dislikes how dirty his roommate is.
Ⓑ He disagrees with his roommate's opinions.
Ⓒ His roommate wakes up too early in the morning.
Ⓓ He and his roommate keep different hours.

2 What does the woman tell the student to do?

Ⓐ Speak with her manager later in the day
Ⓑ Get signed confirmation from other students
Ⓒ Wait to make a change until the next semester
Ⓓ Move into a single room in another dormitory

3 What can be inferred about the student?

Ⓐ He will look for off-campus housing.
Ⓑ He will work things out with his roommate.
Ⓒ He will ask the school administration for help.
Ⓓ He will have a new roommate soon.

Words & Phrases

upheaval n a strong change
exception n a decision that is against the general rule
signature n a person's signed name on a document
invite v to ask a person to attend an event
compromise v to give up some demands in order to reach an agreement
proof n evidence that shows something is true
interruption n something that causes a break in the middle of something

Summary Note

A Listen to the conversation again and fill in the blanks to complete the conversation notes.

- Student speaks with student housing office employee
  - Has problem with ❶ ____________
    - → Has different hours than roommate
    - → Doesn't like roommate's ❷ ____________
  - Wants to change roommates
- Woman says is ❸ ____________ to change
- Student has already found ❹ ____________
- Woman refuses
  - Student complains that grades are low and ❺ ____________
  - Woman suggests studying in ❻ ____________
- Woman agrees to allow the roommate switch

B Complete the following summary with the words given below.

halfway through the semester	sleep poorly	the same schedule
plays loud music	living situation	signatures

The student is unhappy with his ____________. The student wants to change roommates because his current one keeps a different schedule. The student complains that his roommate stays up late and ____________ when he is trying to sleep. This causes him to ____________, so when he gets up in the morning to study, he is too tired. The student says his studies are suffering and asks to switch roommates. The woman says she is sorry, but the college does not allow students to switch roommates ____________. The student responds that he has found the perfect roommate: a student who keeps ____________. The woman says she will allow the student to change roommates if he gets ____________ from his friend and from the other roommates agreeing to this. The woman concludes by pointing out that difficult living situations can teach the student a lot about compromising.

Exercise 2 Listen to part of a conversation between a student and a professor. Then, answer the questions.

03-07

Office Hours

1 Which of the professor's classes does the student want to take?

Ⓐ Modern Theater
Ⓑ Shakespeare
Ⓒ Theater History
Ⓓ Dance in Theater

2 Why does the professor advise the student to take the class next semester?
Click on 2 answers.

Ⓐ She is already taking enough classes.
Ⓑ The class is already full.
Ⓒ He wants her to participate in class.
Ⓓ The class has a heavy workload.

3 Why does the student mention auditing the class?

Ⓐ To suggest a way to take the class for free
Ⓑ To enable her to learn the class material
Ⓒ To ask the professor if he allows students to do that
Ⓓ To avoid having to do any homework

Words & Phrases

currently adv at the present time
secure v to get hold of something
audit v to attend a class but not receive credit or a grade
regarding prep in relation with something else
audience n a group of people at an event
participate v to take part in something

Summary Note

A Listen to the conversation again and fill in the blanks to complete the conversation notes.

- Student goes to speak with professor
- Wants to take his ❶ ______________________ class
- Professor suggests she wait until ❷ ______________________
- Student wants to ❸ ______________________ class
  - Can attend class
  - But does not get ❹ ______________________
- Professor believes it is not a good idea
  - Cannot participate in ❺ ______________________
  - Should get credit for ❻ ______________________
- Student agrees to take class later

B Complete the following summary with the words given below.

following semester	will not be able	theater history class
theater history major	eighteen credits	until next semester

A student goes to her professor's office because she wishes to take the professor's ______________________ this semester even though she is already taking ______________________. The professor tells the student that eighteen credits is a lot of work and asks the student to wait ______________________ to take the class. The student says she wants to be a ______________________ and worries that she should take the class now. The student asks the professor if she can audit this semester's theater history class for no credit. The professor says that she can although he wonders if the student will be okay with the fact that she ______________________ to participate in the discussions during class. The professor also points out that the school recommends that students take all of their major classes for credit. The student says she did not consider this and decides to take the theater history class for credit the ______________________.

Exercise 3 Listen to part of a conversation between a student and a Registrar's office employee. Then, answer the questions.

03-08

Service Encounter

1 According to the woman, why is the student unable to register for classes?

Ⓐ The student has an unpaid library fine.
Ⓑ The student failed too many classes previously.
Ⓒ The student has not paid his tuition yet.
Ⓓ The student does not have permission from his advisor.

2 According to the woman, what will happen tonight?

Ⓐ A fine will be sent to the student.
Ⓑ The computer system will be upgraded.
Ⓒ Unregistered students will be removed from school.
Ⓓ Online class registration will end.

3 Listen again to part of the conversation. Then answer the question.
What is the purpose of the student's response?

Ⓐ To confirm that he used the library
Ⓑ To indicate that he did not make a mistake
Ⓒ To argue that the woman is incorrect
Ⓓ To say that he should be able to register

Words & Phrases

specify v to mention in detail
distinctly adv unmistakably
reminisce v to remember past experiences
receipt n a written acknowledgment of having paid for something
fine n something paid as a penalty
update v to make something current

Summary Note

A Listen to the conversation again and fill in the blanks to complete the conversation notes.

- Student has trouble registering for class
  - Cannot use ❶ ______________
  - Wants to know the problem
- Employee says student has unpaid ❷ ______________
- Student claims to have paid
  - Employee says ❸ ______________ record is not in the system
  - Student realizes that librarian did not ❹ ______________ it
- Must register for classes today
- Student decides to go to library and ❺ ______________
- Will register later from ❻ ______________

B Complete the following summary with the words given below.

stands out in his mind	has not paid a library fine	ends at 4:00 PM
register online	get a receipt	complete his registration

The student approaches the Registrar's office employee because he is having trouble registering online. Whenever he tries to ______________, he receives a notice that he must see an employee to proceed. The woman checks her computer and finds that the reason the student cannot register is that he ______________. The student tells the woman that he paid the fine and that the incident ______________ because the librarian he paid was someone he knows. The woman tells the student that the only way to resolve the issue is to ______________ from the library, but he must hurry because in-person registration ______________, and online registration ends at 10:00 PM. To give himself more time, the student decides he will get the library receipt after dinner and then ______________.

Exercise 4 Listen to part of a conversation between a student and a professor. Then, answer the questions.

03-09

Office Hours

1 According to the student, why is she doing poorly in her physics class? Click on 2 answers.

Ⓐ Her study group is not very helpful.
Ⓑ She cannot understand some concepts.
Ⓒ She forgot to turn in her homework.
Ⓓ She is having problems with her lab partners.

2 What solution does the professor offer the student?

Ⓐ To do an extra-credit project
Ⓑ To study with a tutor
Ⓒ To redo a lab assignment
Ⓓ To have an extra study session with him

3 What can be inferred about the student?

Ⓐ She does not appreciate the professor's response.
Ⓑ She intends to drop the professor's class.
Ⓒ She has little time to study because of her job.
Ⓓ She believes she can improve her grade.

Words & Phrases

remedy v to mend or fix
salvage v to save or rescue
concept n an idea
extend v to lengthen
curious adj eager to learn or know
suffer v to endure pain or grief
familiar adj easy to recognize because of prior experience

Summary Note

A Listen to the conversation again and fill in the blanks to complete the conversation notes.

- Student meets professor
- Student has problems in ❶ ______________ class
  - Professor suggests getting ❷ ______________
- Student has problem with ❸ ______________
- Professor suggests ❹ ______________
- Student apologizes for not asking for help sooner

B Complete the following summary with the words given below.

part-time tutor	upcoming physics project	lab partners
learning new concepts	become upset	concerned about her grades

The professor scheduled the meeting with the student because he is ______________. He asks her if she can list any reasons why she might be having so much trouble in his class. The student admits she is having trouble ______________, and even though she stayed up late to study, she still did poorly on the test. The professor says he just hired a ______________ who can help her. The student then says that she is also having trouble with her ______________. They are leaving her to do parts of the lab that she does not understand and then ______________ with her efforts. The professor promises to switch her to a different lab group and also allows her to hand in her ______________ at a later date so she will have a chance to catch up on the material.

Exercises with Long Lectures

Exercise 1 Listen to part of a lecture in a drama class. Then, answer the questions.

03-10

Drama

1 How were amphitheaters built to let the audience hear more clearly?
Click on 2 answers.

- (A) They were built to be round in shape.
- (B) They were built with large stages.
- (C) They were built with sloped seating.
- (D) They were built on parts of hills.

2 According to the professor, what happened to the original Globe Theater?

- (A) It was torn down.
- (B) It burned in a fire.
- (C) It was renovated 100 years ago.
- (D) It was moved to a new location.

3 How does the professor organize the information about theaters?

- (A) By comparing theaters in Greece and London
- (B) By talking about the audience's effect on theaters
- (C) By focusing primarily on theaters in England
- (D) By discussing the information in chronological order

Words & Phrases

balcony n a raised gallery in a theater
spectator n a person who watches
resonate v to cause to sound again
harness v to gain control of
octagonal adj eight-sided
erect v to raise
drawback n a disadvantage
replica n a copy

Summary Note

A Listen to the lecture again and fill in the blanks to complete the lecture notes.

- Professor discusses ❶ ________________
- Originated in ❷ ________________
- First theaters were ❸ ________________
  - Built into ❹ ________________
  - Were round
  - ❺ ________________ and Theater of Dionysus
  - Couldn't be used in ❻ ________________
- William Shakespeare's Globe Theater was famous
  - Was much improved over ❼ ________________
  - ❽ ________________ but was later rebuilt

B Complete the following summary with the words given below.

trapdoors	octagonal	ancient Greeks
very few props	open air	amphitheaters

Theater architecture and Western drama were first developed by the ________________. The Greeks constructed what were known as ________________. These were round in shape with high wooden seats built into hillsides so that an audience could better see and hear a performance. Two of the earliest and most famous Greek theaters were the theater at Delphi, known as the Attic Theater, and the Theater of Dionysus in Athens. The Greeks used ________________ for their dramas, and plays were always performed in the ________________. By Elizabethan times, however, theater architecture had evolved. Shakespeare's Globe Theater, for instance, was ________________ in shape with three-story-high walls and an elevated stage. The pit was for standing room only. Some of the developments featured such things as ________________ on the stage floor and rigging in the wings. In 1613, a fire destroyed the Globe Theater, but during the mid-1990s, an exact replica was made in the city of London.

Exercise 2 Listen to part of a lecture in a literature class. Then, answer the questions.

03-11

Literature

1 According to the professor, where did Pearl S. Buck spend the better part of the first forty years of her life?

Ⓐ In Nanking
Ⓑ In China
Ⓒ In Pennsylvania
Ⓓ At Cornell University

2 What novel by Pearl S. Buck was made into a motion picture?

Ⓐ *The Patriot*
Ⓑ *The Child Who Never Grew*
Ⓒ *Chinese Culture*
Ⓓ *The Good Earth*

3 Listen again to part of the lecture. Then answer the question.
What can be inferred about Pearl S. Buck when she said this:

Ⓐ She was not religious.
Ⓑ She did not trust her fellow human beings.
Ⓒ She thought that humans were naturally greedy.
Ⓓ She experienced many bad relationships in her life.

Words & Phrases

interpreter n a person who translates languages
hysterectomy n surgery to remove a woman's uterus
impoverished adj very poor
humanitarian adj having concern for other people
span v to extend over or across
tutor n a person who instructs another privately
seek v to go in search of something or someone
candor n sincerity; honesty

Summary Note

A Listen to the lecture again and fill in the blanks to complete the lecture notes.

- Professor discusses ❶ ______________________
  - Born in West Virginia but moved to ❷ ____________________
  - Spent almost forty years in China
  - Went to college, got married, and had different jobs
- Had an eventful private life
- Published ❸ ______________________
  - Sold two million copies in its first years
  - Describes life of Wang Lung
- Won the ❹ ______________________ for literature
- Published over eighty works

B Complete the following summary with the words given below.

publisher	China	Presbyterian missionaries
worked as a teacher	Pulitzer Prize	was adopted

Pearl S. Buck was a great American literary figure born in West Virginia to two ______________________. Soon afterward, Pearl's family moved to ______________________. Pearl grew up speaking both English and Chinese, and in 1910, she enrolled at Randolph-Macon Women's College in Virginia. In 1917, Pearl married John Lossing Buck, and the two settled in Anhwei Province in China, where Pearl ______________________ and interpreter. Pearl had two children. Carol, their first child, was born with considerable birth defects, and their second daughter, Janice, ______________________ since Pearl underwent a hysterectomy after the birth of Carol. Pearl and John's marriage did not last, and in 1935, she divorced her husband and married her ______________________, Richard Walsh. They moved back to the United States. In 1931, she wrote her most famous novel, *The Good Earth*, which sold nearly two million copies and earned her the ______________________. Pearl continued writing until her death in 1973. During her life, she wrote over eighty works of literature and won the Nobel Prize.

Exercise 3 Listen to part of a lecture in a hieroglyphics class. Then, answer the questions.

03-12

Hieroglyphics

1 According to the professor, what did Thomas Young do?

Ⓐ He learned how to pronounce some hieroglyphs.
Ⓑ He translated the inscription on the Rosetta Stone.
Ⓒ He created the first dictionary of hieroglyphics.
Ⓓ He discovered the tomb of an ancient Egyptian pharaoh.

2 What can be inferred about the professor?

Ⓐ She has visited Egypt several times in the past.
Ⓑ She intends to give the students a test soon.
Ⓒ She is meeting the students for the first time.
Ⓓ She rarely asks her students any questions.

3 What will the professor probably do next?

Ⓐ Ask the students some questions
Ⓑ Take a short break
Ⓒ Let the students go for the day
Ⓓ Begin studying with the students

Words & Phrases

reign n the time when a king or queen rules
pharaoh n a king in ancient Egypt
prominent adj leading; widely known
outlaw v to make illegal
gargantuan adj very large; huge
component n an important part or ingredient of something
decree n an official announcement, often from a king
ascertain v to determine

Summary Note

A Listen to the lecture again and fill in the blanks to complete the lecture notes.

- Professor says hieroglyphics used in ❶ ______________
  - Christianity became more prominent
  - ❷ ______________ stopped being used
  - Forgot how to read it
- People interested in ❸ ______________
- Had to learn hieroglyphics
- Thought was just ❹ ______________
  - Thought was no ❺ ______________
- Found Rosetta Stone in 1799
  - Decree written in ❻ ______________
  - Could use stone to translate hieroglyphics
- Thomas Young learned to ❼ ______________ several hieroglyphs
- Jean-Francois Champollion translated hieroglyphics in 1822
  - Used knowledge of Coptic
  - Learned ❽ ______________ words

B Complete the following summary with the words given below.

in Egyptology	how to pronounce	knowledge of Coptic
in ancient Egypt	the Rosetta Stone	picture writing

The professor welcomes the students to the class and says she needs to talk about hieroglyphics. It was a type of writing used ______________ for thousands of years. Once Christianity became more prominent, people stopped using hieroglyphics, and they forgot how to read it. Later, when people were interested ______________, they needed to learn how to read hieroglyphics. Most people thought it was just ______________ and had no phonetic component. In 1799, ______________ was discovered. It was the key to letting people translate hieroglyphics. First, Thomas Young learned ______________ several hieroglyphs properly. Then, Jean-Francois Champollion managed to translate hieroglyphics in 1822. He used his ______________ to figure out how to pronounce the words.

Exercise 4 Listen to part of a lecture in an entomology class. Then, answer the questions.

03-13

Entomology

1 What is another name for swarmer white ants?

(A) Workers
(B) Alates
(C) Termites
(D) Nymphs

2 Why must worker white ants feed the other white ants?

(A) Worker ants have the largest appetites.
(B) Soldier white ants do not have time to find food.
(C) Worker white ants have special bacteria in their stomachs.
(D) The king and queen white ants do not know how to find food.

3 What can be inferred about white ants?

(A) They are dangerous to other species of insects.
(B) They are deadlier than carpenter ants.
(C) They often fight white ants in other colonies.
(D) They are highly organized and very destructive.

Words & Phrases

subterranean adj below ground
nymph n the young of an insect
regurgitate v to expel undigested food
pheromone n a chemical that attracts the opposite sex
exterminator n a person that eliminates insects
refrain v to stop
considerable adj worthy of attention
gather v to bring together in one group
groom v to clean or otherwise tend to something
invade v to enter forcefully

Summary Note

A Listen to the lecture again and fill in the blanks to complete the lecture notes.

- Professor discusses ❶ ____________________
  - Is another name for ❷ ____________________
  - Resembles ant but is closer to ❸ ____________________
- Live in ❹ ____________________
  - Different kinds of termites
  - Have different duties
    - → Workers feed others and care for the nest
    - → Queen ❺ ____________________
    - → Soldiers ❻ ____________________ the nest
    - → Alates become kings and queens in future colonies
- Are difficult to ❼ ____________________
- Can cause much damage to ❽ ____________________

B Complete the following summary with the words given below.

digestive bacteria	cellulose	considerable damage
reproduction of young	in damp timber	grooming and feeding

White ants are termites mainly found in Australia and feed on ____________________, which causes them to live underground or ____________________. They live in highly organized colonies with each type of white ant serving a particular function within the nest. The king and queen white ants are responsible for the ____________________, or nymphs. Soldier white ants protect the colony from intruders. Worker white ants have many tasks from building and maintaining the colony to ____________________ the other termites. Worker white ants feed the others because they are the only white ants to have special ____________________ in their stomachs. Finally, swarmers, or alates, are future kings and queens of other colonies as they have reproductive capabilities. White ants cause ____________________ to buildings and homes in Australia. The best way to deal with white ants is to steer clear of them in the wild and to call an exterminator if they are in a home or office.

Integrated Listening & Speaking

A Listen to a different version of a previous lecture on drama and say the answers out loud. You can refer to the summary note below.

03-14

Drama

Summary Note

- Professor discusses development of theater
- Originated in ancient Greece
- First theaters were amphitheaters
  - Built into hillside
  - Were round
  - Attic Theater and Theater of Dionysus
  - Couldn't be used in bad weather
- William Shakespeare's Globe Theater was famous
  - Was much improved over amphitheaters
  - Burned down but was later rebuilt

1 What is an advantage of having round and octagonal-shaped theaters?

2 Where is the Globe Theater located?

3 In ancient Greece, where did the audience sit when they were watching a performance?

B Listen to a different version of a previous lecture on entomology and say the answers out loud. You can refer to the summary note below.

03-15

Entomology

Summary Note

- Professor discusses white ants
  - Is another name for termite
  - Resembles ant but is closer to cockroach
- Live in colonies
  - Different kinds of termites
  - Have different duties
    - → Workers feed others and care for the nest
    - → Queen lays eggs
    - → Soldiers protect the nest
    - → Alates become kings and queens in future colonies
- Are difficult to exterminate
- Can cause much damage to structures

1 Why do white ants cause so much destruction to homes and buildings?

2 How would you describe the physical characteristics of a white ant?

3 What is a responsibility of soldier white ants?

Mini TOEFL iBT Practice Test

Listen to part of a conversation between a student and a professor.

03-16

1 What problem does the student have?

Ⓐ She does not like the topic of her paper.
Ⓑ She is not a very good writer.
Ⓒ She needs more sources for her report.
Ⓓ She needs an extension on her essay.

2 What kind of play is *A Midsummer Night's Dream*?

Ⓐ A history
Ⓑ A comedy
Ⓒ A tragedy
Ⓓ A romance

3 According to the professor, what is one way to examine the wedding scene in the play *A Midsummer Night's Dream?*

Ⓐ By looking at another play with a wedding in it
Ⓑ By comparing it to factual information about marriage traditions
Ⓒ By contrasting the play with another one written by William Shakespeare
Ⓓ By imagining that there is no wedding scene in the play

4 What is the professor's attitude toward the student?

Ⓐ He is very encouraging.
Ⓑ He is not too helpful.
Ⓒ He is a bit critical.
Ⓓ He is concerned about the student.

5 Listen again to part of the lecture. Then answer the question.
What does the professor mean when he says this: 🎧

Ⓐ The student needs to reread the play several times.
Ⓑ The student ought to compare different versions of the play.
Ⓒ The student had better write about a different play.
Ⓓ The student should watch a film version of the movie.

Listen to part of a lecture in an American history class.

03-17

American History

6 What aspect of the Erie Canal does the professor mainly discuss?

(A) Its construction
(B) Its importance
(C) Its locks
(D) Its appearance

7 Why does the professor discuss Lake Erie?

(A) To call it the biggest Great Lake
(B) To stress its importance to the American economy
(C) To point out the destination of the canal
(D) To explain where the canal got its name from

8 According to the professor, what does a lock in a canal do?

(A) Enable one ship to pass another one
(B) Allow ships to go uphill or downhill
(C) Let ships dock in a certain place
(D) Help large ships get through the canal

9 Why does the professor explain the Erie Canal's locks' dimensions?

Ⓐ To show how impressive the canal's construction was

Ⓑ To explain why some ships cannot use the canal

Ⓒ To prove that two ships can pass side by side in the canal

Ⓓ To point out the drawbacks of nineteenth-century technology

10 What can be inferred about the Erie Canal?

Ⓐ It was the first canal built in North America.

Ⓑ It is not used today as much as it was in the past.

Ⓒ It is the longest canal in the United States.

Ⓓ It remains an important aspect of American shipping.

11 What is the professor's opinion of the Erie Canal?

Ⓐ She thinks that it should have never been built.

Ⓑ She believes it needs to be enlarged as soon as possible.

Ⓒ She wants more ships to use the canal these days.

Ⓓ She considers it an important part of American history.

Vocabulary Check-Up

A Choose and write the correct words that match the definitions.

1 salvage	Ⓐ the young of an insect
2 decree	Ⓑ a person who translates languages
3 impoverished	Ⓒ to make illegal
4 hysterectomy	Ⓓ an official announcement, often from a king
5 resonate	Ⓔ to bring together in a group
6 harness	Ⓕ a disadvantage
7 nymph	Ⓖ to gain control of
8 interpreter	Ⓗ surgery to remove a woman's uterus
9 gargantuan	Ⓘ a person who instructs another privately
10 regurgitate	Ⓙ very large; huge
11 outlaw	Ⓚ to cause to sound again
12 drawback	Ⓛ very poor
13 invade	Ⓜ to enter forcefully
14 tutor	Ⓝ to expel undigested food
15 gather	Ⓞ to save or rescue

B Choose the correct words that match the descriptions.

Ⓐ Globe Theater Ⓑ subterranean Ⓒ hieroglyphics Ⓓ Pearl S. Buck Ⓔ amphitheater

1 This was a form of writing that was used thousands of years ago in ancient Egypt. ....

2 This was built in an octagonal shape with three stories. It was first built in London. ....

3 This term means living underground and is a characteristic of the white ant. ....

4 This was a structure first created by the ancient Greeks. ....

5 This woman won the Pulitzer Prize for her work in literature. ....

PART Ⅱ

Pragmatic Understanding

Pragmatic Understanding questions test understanding of certain features that go beyond basic comprehension. Generally, two question types test pragmatic understanding: Function of What Is Said and Speaker's Attitude. Function of What Is Said questions test whether you can understand the underlying intentions of what is said. Speaker's Attitude questions test whether you can understand a speaker's attitude or opinion that has not been directly expressed. Pragmatic Understanding questions typically involve a replay of a small portion of the listening passage.

UNIT

04 Understanding the Function of What Is Said

Overview

Introduction

These questions determine whether or not you understand the speaker's intentions. You must often determine the speaker's intentions by understanding the context of the passage surrounding the sentence in question. By analyzing the passage as a whole, you can determine the speaker's intentions. These questions typically replay a part of the listening passage.

Question Types

- What does the professor imply when he says this: (replay)
- What can be inferred from the professor's response to the student? (replay)
- What is the purpose of the woman's response? (replay)
- Why does the student say this: (replay)

Useful Tips

- Practice recognizing the unspoken meanings of words.
- Make notes on the context of the passage.
- Recognize what tone of voice the speakers are using in the passage.

Sample TOEFL iBT Question

Script

W Professor: Hmm . . . You also worked at an orphanage for two summers?

04-01

M Student: Well, ah . . . actually, that, ah . . . that was a volunteer job. My mother works there, and she made me do that.

W: **Well, thank God for your mother.** When you go home tonight, give her a big hug. And then tomorrow tell the interviewers you worked at an orphanage. What did you do there?

M: I helped them take the children on field trips and special outings. I also helped organize special events at the orphanage. For example, I organized baseball games, soccer games, and birthday parties. Some of the children were disabled, so I taught them to play wheelchair basketball. Sometimes I took blind children for a walk.

Q Listen again to part of the conversation. Then answer the question.
What can be inferred from the professor's response to the student?

(A) She is happy the student's mother made him work at the orphanage.
(B) She is pleased to have met the student's mother at the orphanage.
(C) She does not want the student to disappoint his mother again.
(D) She believes the student should work at the orphanage some more.

☑ Correct Answer

The answer to the above question is (A). The professor is happy the student's mother made him work at the orphanage because he now has some valuable work experience.

Basic Drill

Listen to parts of conversations or lectures and answer the questions.

Drill 1

Q Listen again to part of the conversation. Then answer the question.
What is the purpose of the professor's response?

04-02

- (A) To reject the student's suggestion
- (B) To encourage the student to think harder
- (C) To remind the student to write a good paper
- (D) To approve the student's request

Check-Up Listen again and fill in the blanks with the correct words.

M Student: Professor Garber, may I have ______________ with you about today's lecture, please?

W Professor: Of course, Nate. ______________ are you interested in discussing?

M: The part about ______________. I have a question about it.

W: Go ahead.

M: My home has ______________ with a lot of trees. We try to keep the yard looking nice, but I've noticed that weeds ______________ right around the trees.

W: Go on.

M: Well, I was wondering . . . Is this an example of ______________? I mean, uh, are birds sitting on the tree branches and ______________ from various plants? Is that ______________ all of those weeds to grow in the grass?

W: I'd say that you're ______________.

M: Thanks. Would it be all right with you if I wrote ______________ about this? I think it would be ______________.

W: I ______________ to that.

Drill 2

Q Listen again to part of the conversation. Then answer the question.
What does the librarian imply when he says this: 🎧

04-03

Ⓐ The student should put her books elsewhere.
Ⓑ He will return the student's books for her.
Ⓒ The student cannot renew the books she has.
Ⓓ He is not allowed to check out the student's books.

Check-Up

Listen again and fill in the blanks with the correct words

M Librarian: That's a big ____________ you have there. Are you planning to check all of them out?

W Student: Actually, I ____________ these three books. Can I do that here?

M: You're supposed to put them in ____________ over there. But I'll ____________ in your case since you have so many books here.

W: Great. Thanks so much. Here you are . . .

M: You're welcome. And ____________ to check those books out now?

W: Yes, please. I've got a report to write for ____________, so I really need all of these books.

M: ____________ with that. May I see your student ID card, please?

W: Oh . . . no. I must ____________ in my dorm room. ____________ to check these books out, right?

M: I'm afraid so. But I can hold these books here at ____________ for you if you want to go to your dorm and come back with your card.

W: That would be wonderful. Thanks so much. I'll be back in ____________.

M: Great. I'll see you then.

Drill 3

Q Listen again to part of the lecture. Then answer the question.
What does the professor imply when he says this?

04-04

- (A) He grows plants to help the environment.
- (B) He grows lilacs in her backyard.
- (C) He is not very good at gardening.
- (D) He has a variety of flowers in her garden.

Check-Up

Listen again and fill in the blanks with the correct words.

M Professor: If any of you ______________ at your home, you have almost surely come across some plant diseases. There are many different kinds of them, and ______________ can range from merely making the leaves of plants change colors to ______________. I'd like to spend the rest of the lecture on talking to you about a few plant diseases that you're ______________ in your home garden.

You know, uh, I have ______________ myself and grow a lot of flowers there. Lilacs are some of my favorite flowers, but, unfortunately, mine have a tendency to ______________ a disease called powdery mildew. If you've ever seen, hmm . . . it's basically a ______________ that can be on the stems, the leaves, and even the flowers of plants . . . then you've almost surely encountered powdery mildew. In addition to lilacs, daisies and roses are some flowers it affects while ______________ grapevines and apple trees plus cucumbers and peas. Fortunately, ______________ by various fungicides. Or if you're like me and prefer to ______________, you can simply mix ______________ and spray it on the affected areas. You'll find that the problem goes away fairly quickly. However, you also need to make sure that you remove leaves that have mildew on them so that ______________.

Drill 4

Q Listen again to part of the lecture. Then answer the question.
What is the purpose of the professor's response?

04-05

Ⓐ To tell the students to contribute more in class
Ⓑ To point out that Borlaug helped many people
Ⓒ To indicate that the student is correct
Ⓓ To chastise the student for not speaking earlier

Check-Up

Listen again and fill in the blanks with the correct words.

W Professor: Have any of you ever heard the name Norman Borlaug . . . ? No . . . ? Hmm . . . I must say I find that ______________. After all, Borlaug was one of the ______________ who lived during the twentieth century. He was a man who contributed ______________ to the Green Revolution. And it was thanks primarily to him that millions of people around the world were ______________.

Borlaug was an American who was born in 1914. He had an ______________ while growing up. In the 1940s, he found himself in Mexico, where he observed farmers struggling to ______________. You see, uh, there were two major problems. Yes?

M Student: The farmers had issues with productivity and their corn crops ______________, right?

W: Ah, it seems that someone ______________ Borlaug before. Yes, those were the two major problems which farmers there faced. Borlaug basically created various ______________ that were able to resist disease and that could also grow well in the climate in Mexico. ______________ for Mexican farmers, which resulted in people getting more to eat. His methods would ______________ by people around the world. The result was the Green Revolution, which, as I said a minute ago, saved ______________. Let's continue looking into Borlaug and his work, which ______________.

Exercises with Long Conversations

Exercise 1 Listen to part of a conversation between a student and a professor. Then, answer the questions.

04-06

Office Hours

1 Listen again to part of the conversation. Then answer the question.
What can be inferred from the student's response to the professor?

Ⓐ He believes he lacks the skill to make a business card.
Ⓑ He thinks making business cards requires no skill.
Ⓒ He already made a business card in another class.
Ⓓ He likes the assignment the professor gave the class.

2 Listen again to part of the conversation. Then answer the question.
What is the purpose of the student's response?

Ⓐ To disagree with the professor's comment
Ⓑ To show his dislike of the assignment
Ⓒ To ask the professor to reconsider her opinion
Ⓓ To admit the professor made a good point

3 Why did the professor ask to see the student?

Ⓐ To give him a grade on some work he submitted
Ⓑ To check his progress on an assignment
Ⓒ To ask him to work together with a partner
Ⓓ To assign him an extra-credit project

Words & Phrases

beneficial adj helpful
conduct v to do
design v to create or draw something
elaborate adj having lots of details or information
essential adj required; needed
purchaser n a buyer
simultaneously adv at the same time

Summary Note

A Listen to the conversation again and fill in the blanks to complete the conversation notes.

- Professor wants to see student's ❶ ____________
- Student did ❷ ____________ instead
- Professor says student did ❸ ____________
- Student thinks business cards are ❹ ____________
- Professor disagrees
  - Cards are good for ❺ ____________
  - Are basic but ❻ ____________
- Student agrees to do the business card assignment

B Complete the following summary with the words given below.

designing business cards	networking	another project
a project of his choice	an important marketing tool	a car magazine

The professor asks the student to show her his business card. But the student is working on ____________. He is designing a cover for ____________. The professor tells the student that the assignment is to design a basic business card. The student suggests that ____________ is a waste of time and says that he wants to work on something more elaborate. He says that business cards are not ____________. The professor replies that business cards are a valuable marketing tool and are also very important for establishing contacts and for ____________. The professor insists that the student work on a business card and tells the student there will be plenty of opportunities later on to work on ____________. The student agrees to do so.

Exercise 2 Listen to part of a conversation between a student and a student services center employee. Then, answer the questions.

04-07

Service Encounter

1 Listen again to part of the conversation. Then answer the question.
What can be inferred from the man's response to the student?

Ⓐ He expects the student to attend orientation.
Ⓑ He believes the student has no money.
Ⓒ He thinks the student will get good grades.
Ⓓ He considers the student a freshman.

2 Listen again to part of the conversation. Then answer the question.
Why does the student say this: 🎧

Ⓐ To explain that she is not inexperienced
Ⓑ To indicate to the man that she needs help
Ⓒ To tell the man about her old school
Ⓓ To ask how to transfer credits from another school

3 What does the man suggest doing for the student?

Ⓐ Arranging extensions on some work
Ⓑ Introducing her to some professors
Ⓒ Checking out some library books
Ⓓ Purchasing her textbooks for her

Words & Phrases

adjust v to get used to; to become accustomed to
arrange v to organize something in a certain way
coupon book n a book with many coupons in it
freshman n a first-year student
itinerary n a schedule
orientation program n a program for new members
perhaps adv maybe; possibly
syllabus n an outline for a course
transfer student n a student who has changed schools

Summary Note

A Listen to the conversation again and fill in the blanks to complete the conversation notes.

- Student visits man
  - Asks for ❶ ______________ and ❷ ______________
  - Man gives her big package
- Student says won't be around for ❸ ______________
  - Man describes events
  - But student has trip planned
- Student says is ❹ ______________ with campus already
- Man offers to provide extra help

B Complete the following summary with the words given below.

around campus	booked a vacation	including a name tag
agrees to gather	orientation	upcoming semester

The man gives a student a package containing various items, ______________ for the orientation program and an orientation itinerary. Upon hearing about the ______________, the student informs the man that she will not be going to the program. The man is very surprised to hear this because, in his view, the program is very valuable. The student explains to the man that she has already ______________ during orientation week and that it will be impossible for her to attend. She also advises the man that her brother, who graduated from the same university, can show her ______________ if necessary. Because the student cannot attend the orientation, the man ______________ whatever helpful information he can get to help the student prepare for the ______________.

Exercise 3 Listen to part of a conversation between a student and a professor. Then, answer the questions.

04-08

Office Hours

1 Listen again to part of the conversation. Then answer the question.
Why does the student say this: 🎧

Ⓐ She believes the professor thinks her major is psychology.
Ⓑ She is considering changing her major to commerce.
Ⓒ She plans to take classes on psychology and commerce.
Ⓓ She has not yet declared a major.

2 Why does the student visit the professor?

Ⓐ To talk about his time in France
Ⓑ To ask about how to learn French
Ⓒ To get help finding a job in France
Ⓓ To describe her love for France

3 Why does the professor apologize to the student?

Ⓐ He did not remember her name.
Ⓑ He was impolite to her in class.
Ⓒ He gave her a difficult assignment.
Ⓓ He made a mistake grading her test.

Words & Phrases

complain v to indicate unhappiness or displeasure
contact v to speak with or write to
hook up with phr to connect with; to meet
major n an area of specialized study
mention v to speak about something or someone
recognize v to remember having seen someone or something
suggestion n a recommendation

Summary Note

A Listen to the conversation again and fill in the blanks to complete the conversation notes.

- Student visits professor's office
- Says is looking for job in ❶ ____________
  - Knows professor lived in France
  - Wants help from professor
  - Wants to work at ❷ ____________
- Professor doesn't know ❸ ____________
- Professor knows ❹ ____________ who worked in France
  - Thinks friend may help
  - Offers to give an introduction

B Complete the following summary with the words given below.

look for a job	banking jobs	he lived in France
can find a job	a commerce major	to contact him

The student tells the professor that she is planning to ____________ in France. The professor remarks that ____________ as a teenager. He asks her what kind of job she is looking for. She replies that she wants a banking job. He tells her that ____________ are difficult work. But the student is ____________, is studying European banking, and can speak French. However, she needs advice on where she can stay in Paris and how she ____________ there. The professor says that he cannot answer those two questions but says he will contact his friend, a businessman in France, and arrange for the student ____________.

Exercise 4 Listen to part of a conversation between a student and a security guard. Then, answer the questions.

04-09

Service Encounter

1 Listen again to part of the conversation. Then answer the question.
What can be inferred from the student's response to the man?

Ⓐ She does not have enough money.
Ⓑ This is her first parking offense.
Ⓒ She will have to pay with her credit card.
Ⓓ Her friend owes her some money.

2 What problem does the student have?

Ⓐ Her car has a flat tire.
Ⓑ Her car has been damaged.
Ⓒ She did not have the right sticker.
Ⓓ She cannot find her vehicle.

3 What will the student probably do next?

Ⓐ Visit the impound lot
Ⓑ Return to her dormitory
Ⓒ Contact the police
Ⓓ Purchase a parking sticker

Words & Phrases

sedan n a car with two or four doors that can carry four or more people
on duty phr working
tow truck n a truck that can carry another vehicle by using a winch
absolutely adv completely; totally
overnight adv during the night; for the entire night
overlook v to miss; not to see
offense n a violation of a rule, regulation, or law
impound lot n a place where cars that have been towed are brought

Summary Note

A Listen to the conversation again and fill in the blanks to complete the conversation notes.

- Student's car is ❶ ______________ from lot
- Security guard did not see any red cars driving
- Student shows where car was ❷ ______________
- Security guard saw it ❸ ______________
  - No ❹ ______________ allowed in lot
- Needs to visit ❺ ______________ to get car back
- Must pay fine of ❻ ______________

B Complete the following summary with the words given below.

a tow truck take it	of fifty dollars	no red vehicles
a parking sticker	car is missing	overnight parking

The student tells the security guard that she needs help. Her problem is that her ______________. It is a red sedan, but the security guard says that he saw ______________ driving in or out the lot this morning. The student shows the man where she was parked, and then he remembers that he saw ______________ and two other cars away early in the morning. The student asks why it got towed and mentions that she has ______________ that allows her to park anywhere on campus. The man states that ______________ is not permitted in the lot. He then tells the student how to get her car back. She has to pay a fine ______________. He gives her directions to the impound lot and advises her not to park in the lot overnight again.

Exercises with Long Lectures

Exercise 1 Listen to part of a lecture in an agricultural technology class. Then, answer the questions.

04-10

Agricultural Technology

1 Listen again to part of the lecture. Then answer the question.
Why does the professor say this:

Ⓐ To point out how the student's response can be improved
Ⓑ To praise the student for her response
Ⓒ To indicate that the student's answer is not complete
Ⓓ To disregard the student's answer to his question

2 What aspect of crop rotation does the professor mainly discuss?

Ⓐ Its historical practice
Ⓑ Its benefits and drawbacks
Ⓒ Its use in some countries
Ⓓ Its requirements

3 Why does the professor discuss labor-intensive crops?

Ⓐ To claim that they are often very profitable
Ⓑ To show how much time they take to grow
Ⓒ To point out their disadvantages to farmers
Ⓓ To explain why farmers like to grow them

Words & Phrases

replenish v to renew; to provide with more of something
exhausted adj used up; empty
acclimate v to get used to
topsoil n the fertile earth at the top of the ground
labor n work
mend v to fix; to repair
sizable adj very large
endeavor n an effort; an activity

Summary Note

A Listen to the lecture again and fill in the blanks to complete the lecture notes.

- ❶ ________________ has been used for long time
  - ❷ ________________ used three-field crop rotation
- ❸ ________________ nutrients in soil
- Other benefits
  - Fewer pests, weeds, and diseases
  - Retains water well
  - Prevents ❹ ________________
  - Non-labor-intensive crops give farmers ❺ ________________
- Some disadvantages
  - Labor-intensive crops make farmers ❻ ________________
  - Some crops need ❼ ________________, which costs money
  - Not all crops worth the same amount of money
  - Some crops require ❽ ________________

B Complete the following summary with the words given below.

costs money	replenish nutrients	three-field crop rotation
farmers exhausted	labor intensive	pests, weeds, and diseases

The professor mentions that crop rotation has been practiced for a long time and that one of the most famous examples of it is the ________________ practiced during the Middle Ages. He notes that people used it to ________________ in the soil and to keep it from becoming exhausted. He then mentions that there are other benefits to crop rotation. It can keep the numbers of ________________ down, the soil retains water well, and it helps prevent soil erosion. When farmers grow crops that are not ________________, they have more time for other activities, too. As for disadvantages, labor-intensive crops can make ________________. Some crops require the use of machinery, which ________________. All crops are not worth the same amount of money, and some crops can be knowledge-intensive endeavors.

Exercise 2 Listen to part of a lecture in a geography class. Then, answer the questions.

04-11

Geography

1 Listen again to part of the lecture. Then answer the question.
What does the professor imply when he says this:

- (A) He does not enjoy the hot weather of the Nile.
- (B) He is planning another trip to the Amazon soon.
- (C) He enjoys spending time outside his office.
- (D) He would like to take his students on a trip to the Nile.

2 Listen again to part of the lecture. Then answer the question.
Why does the professor say this:

- (A) To claim that the Amazon is more accessible than the Nile
- (B) To point out why the Nile is not interesting to him
- (C) To state that the Amazon is much less expensive to visit
- (D) To note that Nile is the longest river in the world

3 Why does the professor mention the harpy eagle?

- (A) To compare it with the macaw parrot
- (B) To explain where it mostly lives
- (C) To describe an interesting fact about it
- (D) To talk about its grooming habits

Words & Phrases

basin (n) the entire area of a river, including nearby land and streams
canopy (n) a covering
chilling (adj) scary
consider (v) to think about
creature (n) a type of life form
ecosystem (n) an entire community of living organisms in a certain area
electrifying (adj) very exciting
immense (adj) very many or very much
species (n) a type of plant, animal, or insect
varied (adj) having different types

Summary Note

A Listen to the lecture again and fill in the blanks to complete the lecture notes.

- Professor compares ❶ ______________ rivers
  - Has done work in both places
  - ❷ ______________ students to visit the Amazon
- Describes the Amazon
  - Has a ❸ ______________
  - Has much diversity of life
  - Has a varied ❹ ______________
- Describes animals there
  - ❺ ______________: large, powerful cat
  - Giant otter: over six-feet long
  - Piranhas, dolphins, and anacondas
- Has thick ❻ ______________
  - Many kinds of trees
  - Some are very tall

B Complete the following summary with the words given below.

the treetop canopy	may contain	creatures
dry desert	immense vegetation	tropical rainforest

The Amazon River is the second longest river in the world, but the Amazon basin and its ______________ are the largest on the planet. It is an interesting place to visit and contains more life than any other place on the Earth. This can be contrasted with the Nile River. Although the Nile is longer, it has less wildlife and less plant life. It is surrounded mainly by ______________. The Amazon is home to 500 species of mammals, one-third of the world's bird population, hundreds of reptiles, 175 different kinds of lizards, up to 300 million types of insects, and ______________. The trees are so dense that their treetops form a canopy. The Amazon is home to ______________ such as the jaguar, the most powerful cat in the Western Hemisphere, twenty species of piranhas, 300-pound dolphins, and the anaconda. ______________ is nine times bigger than Texas and home to millions of undiscovered species. Some scientists believe this canopy alone ______________ half of the world's animal species.

Exercise 3 Listen to part of a lecture in a sociology class. Then, answer the questions.

04-12

Sociology

1 Listen again to part of the lecture. Then answer the question.
Why does the professor say this:

Ⓐ To encourage the student to continue speaking
Ⓑ To tell the student his answer is incorrect
Ⓒ To ask the student to reconsider his comments
Ⓓ To indicate that the student has explained enough

2 How does the professor organize the information about cultural diffusion that she presents to the class?

Ⓐ By discussing them in chronological order
Ⓑ By talking about them according to their importance
Ⓒ By explaining each type individually
Ⓓ By covering them alphabetically

3 According to the professor, what was Queen Victoria's wedding dress an example of?

Ⓐ Stimulus diffusion
Ⓑ Hierarchical diffusion
Ⓒ Expansion diffusion
Ⓓ Contagious diffusion

Words & Phrases

innovation n something new, such as an idea or invention
ethnic adj relating to a certain foreign group
global adj relating to the entire world
conquer v to defeat, often in battle
diminish v to make lesser or smaller
fad n something that becomes popular quickly and often loses popularity quickly
authority n people in command, often in government

Summary Note

A Listen to the lecture again and fill in the blanks to complete the lecture notes.

- Professor describes ❶ ______________
  - Way ❷ ______________, language, aspects of culture, and innovation spread
  - ❸ ______________ is example
- ❹ ______________ spreads to other cultures but stays strong in original place
  - English language and ❺ ______________
- Contagious diffusion spreads quickly, like ❻ ______________
- Hierarchical diffusion spreads from ❼ ______________
  - Queen Victoria's ❽ ______________
- Stimulus diffusion results in ❾ ______________ in something as it spreads
- ❿ ______________ is different around the world

B Complete the following summary with the words given below.

expansion diffusion	aspects of culture	white wedding dress
such as fads	in some ways	ethnic food

The professor remarks that cultural diffusion is the way in which knowledge, language, ______________, and innovation spread from one place to another. A student says that he believes ______________ is an example of cultural diffusion, and the professor says that he is right. The professor says there are four main types of cultural diffusion. ______________ happens when something spreads to another culture while remaining strong in its own culture. The English language and Hellenism are examples of that. Contagious diffusion is for things ______________ that spread very quickly. Hierarchical diffusion happens when powerful people or those in positions of authority influence others. Queen Victoria's ______________ is an example of that. Stimulus diffusion happens when something spreads to another culture but changes ______________. Pizza is the example that the professor uses.

Exercise 4 Listen to part of a lecture in a botany class. Then, answer the questions.

04-13

Botany

1 Listen again to part of the lecture. Then answer the question.
What does the professor imply when she says this: 🎧

(A) Deer prefer chestnuts to other types of nuts.
(B) Most forest animals eat chestnuts before hibernating.
(C) It is possible to find chestnut trees in many forests.
(D) Chestnut trees were important to their ecosystems.

2 Listen again to part of the lecture. Then answer the question.
Why does the professor say this: 🎧

(A) To encourage the students to help the foundation
(B) To indicate that the foundation will reach its goal soon
(C) To say that many people support the foundation
(D) To point out the mission of the foundation

3 Why does the professor discuss the American Chestnut Foundation?

(A) To claim that it can cure trees with chestnut blight
(B) To explain how it is trying to save chestnut trees
(C) To say that it is the only foundation dedicated to trees
(D) To compare its work with that of other foundations

Words & Phrases

extinct adj no longer existing
breed v to create
gene n something inherited with DNA and RNA
progeny n the offspring of plants and animals
resistant adj immune to
susceptible adj vulnerable; likely to suffer hardship
thwart v to slow down or stop something
twig n a small branch

Summary Note

A Listen to the lecture again and fill in the blanks to complete the lecture notes.

- Professor discusses ❶ ______________
  - Spread through ❷ ______________ and southern Canada
  - Belongs to beech and oak family
  - Has many uses
- Almost became ❸ ______________ by 1940s
- Chestnut blight kills many trees
- ❹ ______________ tries to save trees
  - Are creating ❺ ______________
  - Hoping to make ❻ ______________ trees

B Complete the following summary with the words given below.

the process is repeated	a wonderful supply	swept across
fully resistant	American chestnut trees	a breeding program

Until about 100 years ago, there were millions of American chestnut trees throughout eastern North America. Some of these trees reached up to 150 feet tall and were a valuable source of timber. They also provided ______________ of chestnuts. But in the early 1900s, a disease known as chestnut blight ______________ the forests of eastern North America, wiping out ______________. Only a few trees still exist today. However, the tree is not totally extinct, and the American Chestnut Foundation has started ______________ to revive these trees. It accomplishes this by breeding Chinese trees resistant to the disease with susceptible American trees. Then, it breeds the hybrids with more American trees, which pass on two resistant genes to the progeny. ______________ until eventually the percentage of American genes in the hybrids is very high and one of the progeny receives four resistance genes, making it ______________ to the blight fungus.

Integrated Listening & Speaking

A Listen to a different version of a previous lecture on agricultural technology and say the answers out loud. You can refer to the summary note below.

04-14

Agricultural Technology

Summary Note

- Crop rotation has been used for long time
  - Middle Ages used three-field crop rotation
- Replenish nutrients in soil
- Other benefits
  - Fewer pests, weeds, and diseases
  - Retains water well
  - Prevents soil erosion
  - Non-labor-intensive crops give farmers more time
- Some disadvantages
  - Labor-intensive crops make farmers exhausted
  - Some crops need machinery, which costs money
  - Not all crops worth the same amount of money
  - Some crops require lots of knowledge

1 What is a well-known example of crop rotation?

2 How do most people use crop rotation?

3 What is a disadvantage of crop rotation?

B **Listen to a different version of a previous lecture on geography and say the answers out loud. You can refer to the summary note below.**

04-15

Geography

Summary Note

- Professor compares Nile and Amazon rivers
  - – Has done work in both places
  - – Encourages students to visit the Amazon
- Describes the Amazon
  - – Has a rainforest
  - – Has much diversity of life
  - – Has a varied ecosystem
- Describes animals there
  - – Jaguar: large, powerful cat
  - – Giant otter: over six-feet long
  - – Piranhas, dolphins, and anacondas
- Has thick vegetation
  - – Many kinds of trees
  - – Some are very tall

1 How would you describe the Amazon River basin?

2 Where do most of the Amazon's species live?

3 Which percentage of the Earth's species live in the Amazon Rainforest?

Mini TOEFL iBT Practice Test

Listen to part of a conversation between a student and a professor.

04-16

1 Why does the student visit the professor?

Ⓐ To talk about possible graduate schools
Ⓑ To request a letter of recommendation
Ⓒ To discuss his career after graduation
Ⓓ To ask about his upcoming interview

2 Why is the student not considering graduate school?

Ⓐ His grades are not high enough.
Ⓑ He thinks it is too expensive.
Ⓒ He does not need it for his career.
Ⓓ He cannot decide what to study.

3 What can be inferred about the professor?

Ⓐ She has a high opinion of the student.
Ⓑ She has taught the student in several classes.
Ⓒ She is not willing to assist the student.
Ⓓ She has to attend a class in the next few minutes.

4 What is the professor's attitude toward the student?

Ⓐ She is a bit impatient due to a lack of time.
Ⓑ She is considerate of his opinion.
Ⓒ She is upset about the choice he is making.
Ⓓ She is very complimentary toward him.

5 Listen again to part of the conversation. Then answer the question.
What is the purpose of the student's response?

Ⓐ To reject the information that the professor tells him
Ⓑ To acknowledge the professor has made a good point
Ⓒ To admit that he is interested in going to graduate school
Ⓓ To ask the professor to give him some more information

Listen to part of a lecture in a civil engineering class.

04-17

Civil Engineering

6 What aspect of the Hoover Dam does the professor mainly discuss?

Ⓐ Its design

Ⓑ Its construction

Ⓒ Its completion

Ⓓ Its surrounding infrastructure

7 Why does the professor mention third-world nations?

Ⓐ To give a description of the United States in a previous time

Ⓑ To say that the dam could not have been built in one

Ⓒ To state how they were harmed by the completion of the dam

Ⓓ To note that the dam's design has been copied by them

8 According to the professor, what did Gordon Kaufman do?

Ⓐ He made the original design of the Hoover Dam.

Ⓑ He simplified the original design of the Hoover Dam.

Ⓒ He designed the town near the Hoover Dam.

Ⓓ He added an overhanging balcony.

9 Which of the following are features of the Hoover Dam?
Click on 2 answers.

Ⓐ Art Deco sculptures on the outer towers
Ⓑ Towers with simple appearances
Ⓒ Tunnels leading to the towers
Ⓓ An ornamental concrete panel

10 What will the professor probably do next?

Ⓐ Show the students a video
Ⓑ Have the students look at pictures
Ⓒ Talk about the Golden Gate Bridge
Ⓓ Ask the students some questions

11 Listen again to part of the lecture. Then answer the question.
What does the professor imply when he says this: 🎧

Ⓐ There will be at least two more lectures next week.
Ⓑ There will be an exam during the next class.
Ⓒ He will not speak about the Empire State Building today.
Ⓓ The Golden Gate Bridge took a long time to design.

Vocabulary Check-Up

A Choose and write the correct word that matches each definition.

1 acclimate	Ⓐ necessary; required
2 purchaser	Ⓑ to defeat, often in battle
3 simultaneously	Ⓒ to stop or slow something down
4 basin	Ⓓ the entire area of a river, including nearby land and streams
5 essential	Ⓔ maybe
6 thwart	Ⓕ at the same time
7 beneficial	Ⓖ helpful
8 ethnic	Ⓗ to tell someone that something is not satisfactory
9 conquer	Ⓘ an effort; an activity
10 replenish	Ⓙ a buyer
11 perhaps	Ⓚ relating to a certain foreign group
12 endeavor	Ⓛ to get used to
13 mention	Ⓜ to say something to someone
14 complain	Ⓝ to provide with more of something; to renew
15 exchange	Ⓞ to trade one thing for another

B Choose the correct words that match the descriptions.

Ⓐ crop rotation Ⓑ teaching assistant Ⓒ fad Ⓓ the Amazon River Ⓔ chestnut blight

1 This is a graduate student who may also teach some classes. ....

2 This is the second longest river in the world and home to the world's largest tropical rainforest. ....

3 This is the practice of planting different crops in a field each growing season. ....

4 In the early 1900s, this disease spread throughout the forests of eastern North American and killed almost all of the American chestnut trees. ....

5 This refers to something that becomes popular quickly but also loses popularity very fast. ....

UNIT

05 Understanding the Speaker's Attitude

Overview

Introduction

These questions determine whether or not you understand the attitude or opinion of the speaker. These questions ask about the speaker's feelings, the speaker's likes and dislikes, and the reasons for the emotions the speaker displays. These questions often ask about the speaker's degree of certainty. These questions typically replay a part of the listening passage.

Question Types

- What can be inferred about the student?
- What is the professor's attitude toward X?
- What is the professor's opinion of X?
- What can be inferred about the student when she says this: (replay)
- What does the woman mean when she says this: (replay)

Useful Tips

- Recognize the tone of voice, the intonation, and the sentence stress that the speakers use throughout the passage.
- Distinguish between referencing and giving personal opinions.
- Avoid choosing answers that are not connected with the passage's general tone.
- Take notes on the context of the passage.
- Take note of adjectives and verbs of feeling.

Sample TOEFL iBT Question

Script

05-01

W Student: Hi, Professor Smith. Do you have a minute?

M Professor: Of course, Sally. What can I help you with?

W: I want to talk to you about my grade in your calculus class.

M: Okay. Give me a second to find your information on this spreadsheet. Here it is. **It looks like you're lagging behind on your homework assignments.** Hmm . . . You've also missed quite a number of classes so far this semester. Is everything okay?

W: Well, I've been having a hard time this semester because I broke up with my boyfriend. We've been seeing each other for a bit, but he recently moved away from here. It's been hard trying to keep focused on school.

M: I'm sorry to hear that. It's certainly hard when someone important in our lives moves away. Coping with the end of a relationship can be difficult for anyone.

Q Listen again to part of the conversation. Then answer the question.
What does the professor mean when he says this:

- (A) The student has not been turning in her homework lately.
- (B) The student has been copying someone else's homework.
- (C) The student should get some assistance with her homework.
- (D) The student is not doing very well on her homework.

☑ Correct Answer

The correct answer to the above question is (D). When the professor says that the student is lagging on her homework, it means that she is not doing well on her assignments and is therefore getting lower grades on them.

Basic Drill

Listen to parts of conversations or lectures and answer the questions.

Drill 1

05-02

Q Listen again to part of the conversation. Then answer the question.
What does the professor mean when she says this?

- (A) She will be in her office for the rest of the day.
- (B) She has some time to help the student later on.
- (C) She does not approve of the student's suggestion.
- (D) She has a couple more classes before the day ends.

Check-Up

Listen again and fill in the blanks with the correct words.

M Student: Professor Schmidt, here is the ______________ I'm planning to write for your class.

W Professor: Thank you, Dave. Hold on a minute and ______________, please.

M: Sure thing.

W: Hmm . . . I'm sorry, Dave, but it looks like you didn't ______________.

M: What do you mean? This is a description of what I intend to write about on ______________.

W: I ______________ to do that. I asked all the students to ______________ for their paper. This is ______________ that describes your topic.

M: How is an outline different?

W: Well, it would be ______________. In addition, it would ______________ what you're going to write about, the arguments you're going to make, and the examples you're going to give. You ______________ this.

M: Okay. Can I give it to you when our class ______________ this Friday?

W: I'd like it by ______________ today.

Drill 2

05-03

Q Listen again to part of the conversation. Then answer the question.
What can be inferred about the man when he says this?

(A) He believes a classical music show would be fine.
(B) He frequently listens to classical music.
(C) He is not interested in hearing classical music.
(D) He thinks a classical music show would fail.

Check-Up Listen again and fill in the blanks with the correct words.

W Student: Hello. My name is Andrea Garvey. I ________________ on the air here, but my application ________________. I wonder if you could tell me ________________.

M Radio Station Employee: Andrea Garvey? Ah, yes. I remember your application.

W: And?

M: Well, you wanted to ________________ about politics. However, we've tried that in the past, and ________________ were very low. In addition, almost nobody called in to the station ________________.

W: I see. Well, I'd really like to have ________________. What would you recommend that I do?

M: Why don't you apply again and suggest a ________________ this time?

W: What kind of show are you looking for?

M: Most students who listen to the ________________ just want to hear music with the DJ talking about the musicians a bit in between songs.

W: Oh, okay. How do you think a show ________________ would go over?

M: ________________. Why don't you try it?

Drill 3

Q What is the professor's opinion of coral reefs?

Ⓐ There should be laws that protect them from harm.
Ⓑ They are places that are important to the Earth.
Ⓒ They are the best places for fish to lay their eggs.
Ⓓ They are some of the planet's most beautiful areas.

05-04

Check-Up Listen again and fill in the blanks with the correct words.

W Professor: Take a look at these pictures up here on the screen, please . . . Here's one . . . and another . . . and another one . . . Can anyone tell me what ______________________?

M Student: It's ______________________. I'm not sure where it is, but it's almost surely in some kind of ______________________.

W: That's correct, Brian. The pictures of the coral reef ______________________ were taken in the South Pacific by the way. And those waters are definitely tropical. You see, uh, with ______________________, coral reefs can only exist in tropical waters. The water ______________________. It can't be too hot or too cold, or the coral will die.

And that's a big problem nowadays. Coral reefs are some of the ______________________ on the planet, yet they are disappearing in some places. And, uh, sure, ______________________ in other places, but the rate of expansion is less than the rate of destruction. What makes coral reefs so important? Well, for one, an enormous variety of ocean life ______________________. I'm not just referring to fish. I'm also talking about ______________________, including mammals and reptiles.

Many animals use coral reefs as ______________________ since the reefs provide many places for them to hide and to ______________________ so that they aren't vulnerable to predators. Coral reefs also tend to have ______________________ of food.

Drill 4

05-05

Q What can be inferred about the student?

(A) She comes from a place that gets red rain.
(B) She has seen red rain in person before.
(C) She does not know much about red rain.
(D) She dislikes the idea of seeing red rain.

Check-Up

Listen again and fill in the blanks with the correct words.

M Professor: Did any of you read ______________? There was an article in the paper about red rain falling . . . Huh, okay. I guess nobody read it. Well, red rain is a ______________. It's also called blood rain for ______________.

W Student: Is it . . . blood falling from the sky? That ______________.

M: No, it's not blood. But in the past, people thought ______________. Red rain ______________ as falling in places around the world for thousands of years. People typically thought it was an ______________ to come. I mean, uh, it makes sense, doesn't it? ______________ if you saw red rain falling to the ground?

W: I would be expecting ______________.

M: That's exactly what people thought . . . and still think today. So, uh, red rain ______________ as falling in many places. But nobody is really sure why. Apparently, lots of incidents ______________ have happened soon after meteor showers. So there could be ______________ involved. Other times, ______________ have been followed by red rain, so it could be volcanic ash causing the problem. Some people attribute it to ______________ that mix with raindrops and even lichens that get in the atmosphere. Basically, we just don't know.

Exercises with Long Conversations

Exercise 1 Listen to part of a conversation between a student and a student housing office employee. Then, answer the questions.

05-06

Service Encounter

1 Listen again to part of the conversation. Then answer the question.
What can be inferred about the student when she says this: 🎧

- (A) She is sad because she is being fined.
- (B) She is angry that she is being fined.
- (C) She is sorry for having a halogen lamp.
- (D) She is worried about paying a fine.

2 What is the man's attitude toward the student?

- (A) He acts in a reasonable manner toward her.
- (B) He is upset about her actions in the dorm.
- (C) He is intolerant of her attitude.
- (D) He finds her careless and unconcerned about others.

3 What will the student probably do next?

- (A) Speak with the man's boss
- (B) Ask the man a question
- (C) File a protest
- (D) Visit a store

Words & Phrases

disregard v to pay no attention to
clause n a provision in a contract
cautious adj showing hesitation or carefulness
hazard n a danger or risk
minor adj not serious or important
responsible adj having the duty of taking care of something; accountable for something

Summary Note

A Listen to the conversation again and fill in the blanks to complete the conversation notes.

- Student asks secretary about ❶ ______________
  - Doesn't understand why she was fined
  - Is quiet and ❷ ______________
- Secretary explains fine is for ❸ ______________
- Student doesn't understand
- Secretary says halogen lamps are ❹ ______________
  - A halogen lamp once ❺ ______________ at school
  - Must follow the rules
- Student won't have to pay fine if buys ❻ ______________

B Complete the following summary with the words given below.

pose a fire danger	stands by the school rules	halogen lamp
inquires about a fine	buy a new lamp	brings the man

The student goes to the housing office and ______________ she has received. The man checks his computer and finds that the student has been fined for keeping a ______________ in her dorm room. The student is shocked by the news. She does not understand how having a lamp could result in a fine. She tells the man that she is a very responsible student. The man explains that although the student may be cautious, halogen lamps ______________ because the bulbs heat up to such a high degree. The man suggests that the student ______________ as soon as possible. The student asks if she can keep the lamp if she is very careful where she places it, but the man ______________. The student then complains that the fine is too high, so the man offers to waive the fine if the student goes out and buys a new lamp immediately and then ______________ the receipt.

Exercise 2 Listen to part of a conversation between a student and a professor. Then, answer the questions.

05-07

Office Hours

1 What is the professor's attitude toward the student?

Ⓐ He is confident in the student's abilities.
Ⓑ He is hesitant to tell the student more.
Ⓒ He is positive the student already knows everything.
Ⓓ He is unsure the student can do the job.

2 What can be inferred about the student?

Ⓐ He plays soccer as a hobby.
Ⓑ He enjoys public speaking.
Ⓒ He is a chemistry major.
Ⓓ He performs as an actor.

3 According to the professor, what is an optional activity for visiting students?

Ⓐ Visiting the recreation center
Ⓑ Sitting in on a lecture
Ⓒ Watching a football game
Ⓓ Doing a class assignment

Words & Phrases

inquire v to ask
entail v to cover
prospective adj potential; likely
mandatory adj necessary; required
drama n a play
orientation n an introduction to show people new surroundings
logistics n the planning and coordination of an event

Summary Note

A Listen to the conversation again and fill in the blanks to complete the conversation notes.

- Student talks to professor about ❶ ....
  - Will host ❷ ....
  - Professor is pleased
- Professor explains student's duties
  - Show prospective students ❸ ....
  - Answer any questions
  - Be ❹ .... and ❺ ....
- Student says is not good with big crowds
- Professor says will only have to escort ❻ ....
- Student may have to help prospective students sit in on various classes

B Complete the following summary with the words given below.

not obligatory	on a tour	have the option
accept the job	mandatory orientations	host visiting students

The student wants to volunteer to help .... at his college, so he visits the professor to see how he can do that. The professor tells the student that he would be responsible for leading a small group of students .... around campus. The professor also says that the students .... of sitting in on a class of their choice, but this is .... The student says he will ...., so the professor gives him the final details, which are to have each of his students attend at least one of two ...., either on Monday afternoon or on Thursday at night.

Exercise 3 Listen to part of a conversation between a student and a post office employee. Then, answer the questions.

05-08

Service Encounter

1 Listen again to part of the conversation. Then answer the question.
What can be inferred about the student?

Ⓐ She is frustrated with the post office.
Ⓑ She is indecisive about what to do with her mail.
Ⓒ She is happy to speak with the post office employee.
Ⓓ She feels angry that the post office will not hold her mail.

2 Listen again to part of the conversation. Then answer the question.
Why does the student say this: 🎧

Ⓐ She wants to get good advice from the employee.
Ⓑ She wants to know what the employee thinks of her idea.
Ⓒ She wants the employee to imagine what studying in Spain is like.
Ⓓ She wants to know if there are any other options.

3 Why does the man mention the student newspaper?

Ⓐ To state that he reads it regularly
Ⓑ To advise the student to subscribe to it
Ⓒ To tell the student to read an article in it
Ⓓ To say that the post office cannot hold it

Words & Phrases

indefinitely adv for a period of time with no fixed limit
urgent adj requiring immediate action
cancel v to stop something
storage n a space for keeping things
handle v to manage something
subscription n the regular reception of published material

Summary Note

A Listen to the conversation again and fill in the blanks to complete the conversation notes.

- Student visits ❶ ______
  - Is going to Spain for ❷ ______
  - Is worried about ❸ ______
- Employee explains choices
  - Can have mail forwarded
  - Or can hold mail for ❹ ______
- Employee recommends ❺ ______ if she won't receive anything urgent
- Student agrees with employee
  - Fills out form
  - Must cancel ❻ ______

B Complete the following summary with the words given below.

school newspaper	concerned about	up to three months
forwarded to Spain	cancel her subscription	leaving the country

The student goes to the school post office because she is ______ for three months and is ______ what will happen to her mail during that time. The student asks the post office employee about her options. The man tells her that she either has the option of having her mail ______ or having the post office hold her mail. The only provisions are that if the she chooses to have her mail held, the post office can only hold it for ______, and it cannot hold the ______ as it would take up too much space. The student tells the man that because she does not have anything urgent coming to her in the mail, she would like to have her mail held. She tells the man that she currently receives the school newspaper but will ______ since she does not read it regularly.

Exercise 4 Listen to part of a conversation between a student and a professor. Then, answer the questions.

05-09

Office Hours

1 Listen again to part of the conversation. Then answer the question.
What does the student mean when he says this:

Ⓐ He believes the professor made a mistake.
Ⓑ He has not received his final grade yet.
Ⓒ He would like to see his final exam paper.
Ⓓ He needs the professor to explain an idea.

2 What is the professor's attitude toward classroom attendance?

Ⓐ It is not an important part of the grading process.
Ⓑ It is an important part of the student's grade.
Ⓒ It is impossible to have high test scores with poor attendance.
Ⓓ It is offensive for a student to miss too many classes.

3 According to the professor, what did the student miss?

Ⓐ Some minor quizzes
Ⓑ A presentation
Ⓒ Some discussions
Ⓓ A guest lecturer

Words & Phrases

baffled adj confused
apparent adj obvious
conduct v to lead or guide
analogy n a similarity between two like features of two separate things
comparable adj similar to something else
anticipate v to expect something beforehand
apply v to put to use
amoeba n a one-celled organism

Summary Note

A Listen to the conversation again and fill in the blanks to complete the conversation notes.

- Student visits professor to talk about ❶ ______________
  - Got ❷ ______________ and doesn't know why
  - Says did well on tests
- Professor consults grades
  - Agrees that test scores were ❸ ______________
  - Says attendance was ❹ ______________
- Student questions ❺ ______________
- Professor says it is ❻ ______________
  - Can ❼ ______________ class discussions
  - Can learn things not in the book
  - Can get ❽ ______________ in labs
- Student realizes importance of going to class

B Complete the following summary with the words given below.

a third of her classes	confused	learning all of the material
very good test scores	problem	lively discussions

The student makes an appointment with his professor because he is ______________ by his final score in her class. The student points out that he received ______________ on the last few tests, so he cannot understand why his final grade was so low, especially when he enjoyed learning about so many of the concepts. The professor checks her records to find that the student did receive good test scores but failed to attend ______________. The student does not see how this is a ______________. He believes that if his test scores are good, it proves he is ______________. The professor points out that what the student is missing when he does not attend classes are ______________, evidence of new and cutting-edge research, and important hands-on experience in labs, which can be applied to the ideas and research of the current time.

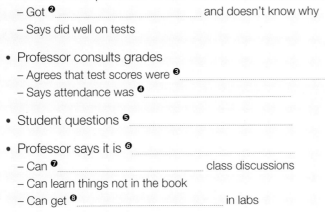

Exercises with Long Lectures

Exercise 1 Listen to part of a lecture in an environmental science class. Then, answer the questions.

05-10

Environmental Science

1 Listen again to part of the lecture. Then answer the question.
What does the professor mean when he says this:

(A) The student's guess is not close to correct.
(B) The student appears to be studying a lot.
(C) The student's thoughts are well organized.
(D) The student should reconsider her answer.

2 What is the lecture mainly about?

(A) How the carbon cycle works
(B) Different forms of carbon
(C) Carbon in the Earth's oceans
(D) Carbon dioxide

3 According to the professor, what is an elemental form of carbon?
Click on 2 answers.

(A) Carbon dioxide
(B) Fullerene
(C) Graphite
(D) Carbonate

Words & Phrases

abundant adj plentiful; available in large amounts
transparent adj able to be seen through
opaque adj blocking the passage of light through something
miniscule adj tiny; very small
emit v to give off
absorb v to take in
consume v to eat; to devour
convert v to change

Summary Note

A Listen to the lecture again and fill in the blanks to complete the lecture notes.

- Professor will discuss ❶ ______________________
- Important since humans are ❷ ______________________
- Carbon has many forms
  - Graphite, diamond, and fullerene as elemental forms
  - Carbonates when combines with ❸ ______________________
  - ❹ ______________________ as gas
- Plants take in carbon dioxide when ❺ ______________________
- Animals eat plants
- Plants and animals die
  - Some carbon released as gas
  - Other carbon becomes ❻ ______________________
- People burn fossil fuels, so carbon enters ❼ ______________________ again
- ❽ ______________________ absorb carbon as well

B Complete the following summary with the words given below.

photosynthesis	carbon-based	plants and animals
carbon dioxide	periodic chart	becomes fossil fuels

The professor says that he will cover the carbon cycle. Since humans are ______________________ lifeforms, it is of great importance. Carbon has an atomic number of six, and its symbol on the ______________________ is C. It can be found in elemental forms as graphite, diamond, and fullerene, it can be carbonates when it combines with elements, and its gaseous form is often ______________________. The carbon cycle begins when plants take in carbon dioxide when they undergo ______________________. Then, plants are eaten by animals, so both ______________________ have carbon. When the plants and animals die, some carbon is released as a gas. Other carbon remains in the ground and ______________________. When the fossil fuels are used by humans, the carbon returns to the atmosphere as a gas. The ocean can also absorb lots of carbon, which is used by shellfish to create their hard shells.

Exercise 2 Listen to part of a lecture in a climatology class. Then, answer the questions.

05-11

Climatology

1 What is the professor's opinion of dust devils?

(A) They are entertaining to see.
(B) They should be avoided by people.
(C) They are like desert tornadoes.
(D) They are mostly harmless.

2 Why does the student mention Australia?

(A) To ask if dust devils happen there
(B) To answer a question that the professor asks
(C) To claim that he saw a dust devil there
(D) To point out that it never gets dust devils

3 According to the professor, what are Martian dust devils like?

(A) They are much larger than those on the Earth.
(B) They tend to be highly destructive.
(C) They can last for hours at a time.
(D) They are short lived and fairly small.

Words & Phrases

phenomenon n something that is impressive or extraordinary
prevalent adj widespread
momentum n the speed of movement
sustain v to support
terrestrial adj pertaining to land
crucial adj extremely important
threat n a declaration of intent to harm someone or something
swirl v to move around in a whirling motion
harmless adj without the power to cause injury; safe

Summary Note

A Listen to the lecture again and fill in the blanks to complete the lecture notes.

- Professor discusses ❶ ______________________
  - Are a weather phenomenon
  - Are similar to ❷ ______________________
  - Form an updraft when hot air rises quickly into ❸ ______________________
  - Are common in ❹ ______________________
- Professor describes creation in detail
  - Hot air quickly rises and passes through ❺ ______________________
  - The air rotates and makes a ❻ ______________________
  - Looks like a ❼ ______________________
- Mars has large dust devils
- Scientists learned about them from ❽ ______________________

B Complete the following summary with the words given below.

ten times higher	air speed and friction	very hot air
cleaned the solar panels	creates a swirling motion	forms an updraft

Dust devils are formed when ______________________ near the ground ______________________ into cooler, low pressure air. The quickly rising hot air ______________________ that forms into a funnel-shaped column of air capable of moving along the ground due to ______________________. Dust devils on the Earth are relatively small and harmless while Martian dust devils, as evidenced by pictures from space probes, can be up to fifty times wider and ______________________ than their earthbound cousins. Some concern arose regarding the safety of terrestrial space equipment on Mars should a dust devil form and destroy the equipment due to its size and power. However, there was an instance when a Martian dust devil actually ______________________ on a robot.

Exercise 3 Listen to part of a lecture in a sociology class. Then, answer the questions.

05-12

Sociology

1 What is the professor's opinion of the Industrial Revolution?

(A) It was harmful to the environment in many places.
(B) It led to the rise of communist thought in England.
(C) It allowed goods to be produced faster than before.
(D) It made Manchester and London important cities.

2 According to the professor, what resulted from the invention of the cotton mill?

(A) Most people could afford to buy new pants.
(B) Artisans had a difficult time finding new jobs.
(C) Cotton production became a mechanized industry.
(D) England became the world's most powerful country.

3 Why does the professor mention Cottonopolis?

(A) To discuss a large cotton farm
(B) To explain the importance of cotton
(C) To express her dislike of cotton
(D) To give a nickname for a city

Words & Phrases

capitalism n an economic system in which investment, ownership, and profit are in the private sector
culminate v to reach the highest point
utilize v to put to use
proliferation n a rapid increase
lament v to express grief
prior adj earlier in time; previous
harsh adj physically uncomfortable
model n an example used for comparison
slightly adv a little

Summary Note

A Listen to the lecture again and fill in the blanks to complete the lecture notes.

- Professor discusses ❶ ______
  - Began in England in ❷ ______
  - Spread around the world
  - Based on ❸ ______ and capitalism
  - Replaced manpower with ❹ ______
- Mentions steam engine
  - Helped make ❺ ______ faster
  - Made faster manufacturing machines
  - Thomas Savery and Richard Trevithick worked on ❻ ______
- Britain changed greatly
  - Manchester became manufacturing city
  - Roller spinning machine created
  - Richard Arkwright made ❼ ______
- Modern cities created
  - New laws made to ❽ ______
  - Communist writings became popular

B Complete the following summary with the words given below.

protect the working class	man or horsepower	steam engine locomotive
socioeconomic	allowing machinery	Industrial Revolution

The Industrial Revolution refers to the technological, ______, and cultural changes that took place in Britain in the late eighteenth century. Prior to this period, goods and services were provided through ______. The development of the steam engine revolutionized manufacturing forever by ______ to do the jobs of men and at much faster rates. Factories sprang up and grew into what we now know as modern cities as people left their rural homes and flocked to the cities for work. Trade unions sprang up to ______ from harsh laws and intolerable conditions. Transportation was also changed forever with the invention of the ______. As a result, people and goods could be transported across the country at a much faster rate. Many British historians and philosophers at the time wrote manifestos concerning the state of the working class in England and how the ______ would change their lives forever.

Exercise 4 Listen to part of a lecture in a biology class. Then, answer the questions.

05-13

Biology

1 What is the professor's attitude toward crocodiles?

Ⓐ He is concerned about the parasites in their bodies.
Ⓑ He is sad about the way they kill many other animals.
Ⓒ He is amazed they do not eat the Egyptian plover.
Ⓓ He is upset about the number of people killing them.

2 What is the professor's opinion of the student's question?

Ⓐ He is surprised by it.
Ⓑ He believes it is unnecessary.
Ⓒ He is impressed by it.
Ⓓ He finds it juvenile.

3 According to the professor, how does the oxpecker have relationships with certain African animals?
Click on 2 answers.

Ⓐ As a parasite
Ⓑ As a symbiont
Ⓒ As a host
Ⓓ As a predator

Words & Phrases

intimate adj very personal or close
merge v to join together; to combine
lethal adj deadly
predator n an organism that exists by eating other organisms
parasite n an organism that lives off of another organism
unlikely adj not liable to happen
scenario n an outline of what might happen

Summary Note

A Listen to the lecture again and fill in the blanks to complete the lecture notes.

- Professor defines ❶ ______________
  - Two ❷ ______________ interact intimately or merge into one
  - Larger one is host
  - Smaller is ❸ ______________
- Discusses mutualism
  - Relationship where ❹ ______________ profit
    - → Egyptian plover and ❺ ______________
    - → Goby fish and shrimp
- Sometimes mutualism is not always ❻ ______________ to one party
  - Oxpecker and some large animals

B Complete the following summary with the words given below.

potentially fatal parasites	eats the parasites benefit	form of symbiosis
will draw blood	merge into parasitism	African land mammals

Mutualism is defined as a ______________ in which two differing organisms benefit from a close relationship. An example of mutualism is the relationship between the Egyptian plover and the crocodile, in which the Egyptian plover ______________ off of the crocodile's body. The Egyptian plover benefits from the relationship by getting an easy meal, and the crocodile benefits from the relationship by having ______________ removed from its body. Mutualism can sometimes ______________, however, if one of the organisms begins harming the other. For example, a different kind of bird, the oxpecker, normally enjoys a relationship of mutualism with certain ______________. However, once in a while, the oxpecker ______________ from the mammals to drink so therefore benefits when the mammal does not.

Integrated Listening & Speaking

A Listen to a different version of a previous lecture on environmental science and say the answers out loud. You can refer to the summary note below.

05-14

Environmental Science

Summary Note

- Professor will discuss carbon cycle
- Important since humans are carbon-based lifeforms
- Carbon has many forms
  - Graphite, diamond, and fullerene as elemental forms
  - Carbonates when combines with other elements
  - Carbon dioxide as gas
- Plants take in carbon dioxide when undergo photosynthesis
- Animals eat plants
- Plants and animals die
  - Some carbon released as gas
  - Other carbon becomes fossil fuels
- People burn fossil fuels, so carbon enters atmosphere again
- Oceans absorb carbon as well

1 What kind of lifeforms are humans?

2 What are three elemental forms of carbon?

3 What is the first step in the carbon cycle?

B Listen to a different version of a previous lecture on biology and say the answers out loud. You can refer to the summary note.

05-15

Biology

Summary Note

- Professor defines symbiosis
  - Two dissimilar organisms interact intimately or merge into one
  - Larger one is host
  - Smaller is symbiont
- Discusses mutualism
  - Relationship where both partners profit
    - → Egyptian plover and crocodile
    - → Goby fish and shrimp
- Sometimes mutualism is not always beneficial to one party
  - Oxpecker and some large animals

1 If you come down with a cold, is your relationship with the virus considered mutualism or parasitism, and why?

2 In the case of the Egyptian plover and the crocodile, how does the Egyptian plover benefit from the relationship?

3 When is the relationship between the oxpecker bird and a buffalo not an example of mutualism but one of parasitism?

Mini TOEFL iBT Practice Test

Listen to part of a conversation between a student and a professor.

05-16

1 Why does the student visit the professor?

(A) To receive a letter of recommendation from him
(B) To inquire about her academic future
(C) To seek information on what jobs are available
(D) To get his opinion on life in a large city like London

2 According to the student, which job is she considering?
Click on 2 answers.

(A) Psychologist
(B) Counselor
(C) Elementary school teacher
(D) College professor

3 Why does the professor mention London?

(A) To note where he attended graduate school
(B) To say that many good jobs are there
(C) To state that he is going there during vacation
(D) To suggest that the student study there

4 What is the professor's opinion of the student?

(A) He thinks she needs to study much harder.
(B) He considers her to be very hard working.
(C) He believes she is an excellent student.
(D) He thinks she should work instead of study.

5 What will the student probably do next?

(A) Give the professor an application form
(B) Attend her next seminar
(C) Visit the library
(D) Leave the professor's office

Listen to part of a lecture in a life science class.

05-17

Life Science

6 What is the lecture mainly about?

(A) How plants move from place to place

(B) Why plants can be invasive species

(C) People and their efforts to import plants

(D) The effects of plants on new environments

7 How is the discussion organized?

(A) The professor provides examples of the effects of naturalized plants.

(B) The professor gives definitions of both naturalized and endemic plants.

(C) The professor describes various naturalized plants in North America.

(D) The professor discusses the reasons why people introduce nonnative species.

8 Why does the professor discuss the Norway maple?

(A) To complain about how it has spread through North America

(B) To explain why Scandinavians brought it with them

(C) To give an example of a harmless naturalized plant

(D) To state that it has harmed several native species

9 According to the professor, how can the purple loosestrife affect other plant species? Click on 2 answers.

- Ⓐ By spreading too quickly
- Ⓑ By preventing other plants from growing
- Ⓒ By overconsuming water resources
- Ⓓ By removing nutrients from the soil

10 What does the professor imply about national parks?

- Ⓐ They can be quickly overcome by nonnative plants.
- Ⓑ They need nonnative plants to feed their animal populations.
- Ⓒ They can be testing grounds for the introduction of nonnative plants.
- Ⓓ They have helped keep various plants from becoming extinct.

11 What is the professor's attitude toward the extinction of plants?

- Ⓐ It is something that happens over time.
- Ⓑ It should be prevented as much as possible.
- Ⓒ It is something governments should prevent.
- Ⓓ It is not always negative when it happens.

Vocabulary Check-Up

A Choose and write the correct words that match the definitions.

1 clause	Ⓐ to reach the highest point
2 merge	Ⓑ to express grief
3 momentum	Ⓒ a rapid increase
4 terrestrial	Ⓓ an example used for a comparison
5 miniscule	Ⓔ plentiful; available in large amounts
6 proliferation	Ⓕ tiny; very small
7 abundant	Ⓖ pertaining to land or ground
8 culminate	Ⓗ to put to use
9 urgent	Ⓘ having the duty of taking care of something; accountable for something
10 lament	Ⓙ requiring immediate action
11 apply	Ⓚ not serious or important
12 minor	Ⓛ a provision in a contract
13 responsible	Ⓜ without the power to cause injury
14 harmless	Ⓝ to join together; to combine
15 model	Ⓞ the speed of movement

B Choose the correct words that match the descriptions.

Ⓐ dust devil   Ⓑ exotic species   Ⓒ mutualism   Ⓓ trade union   Ⓔ carbon dioxide

1 This is a form of symbiosis in which two organisms both benefit from a close relationship. ....

2 This is the term used for a plant that is being introduced into a new habitat. ....

3 This is a gaseous form of the element carbon. ....

4 This is created when very hot air spirals upward from the ground and forms a swirling column. ....

5 This was something created during the Industrial Revolution to protect men, women, and children working in factories. ....

PART Ⅲ

Connecting Information

Connecting Information questions test your ability to integrate information from different parts of the listening passage to make inferences, to draw conclusions, to form generalizations, and to make predictions. To choose the right answer, these question types require you to make connections between or among pieces of information in the text and to identify the relationships between the ideas and the details.

UNIT

06 Understanding Organization

Overview

Introduction

In order to answer these questions correctly, you must either recognize how the entire listening passage is organized or recognize how different portions of the passage are related to one another. These questions ask you to recognize the importance of information like topic changes, exemplifying, digressing, and inducing introductory and concluding remarks. These questions test whether you understand how a part of the passage is related to the passage as a whole. These questions often occur in lectures rather than conversations, and they sometimes ask for more than one answer.

Question Types

- How does the professor organize the information about X that he presents to the class?
- How is the discussion organized?
- Why does the professor discuss X?
- Why does the professor mention X?

Useful Tips

- The questions often include the following patterns:
  - giving examples
  - contrasting
  - comparing
  - classifying or categorizing
  - describing causes and effects
  - explaining in chronological order
- Listen very carefully to recognize when there is a transition in the sequence.
- Take note of the transitional words and the relationships between the contents.

Sample TOEFL iBT Question

Script

06-01

W Professor: Now, you're probably aware that the Arctic is an extremely harsh environment and one of the coldest places on the Earth. But let me remind you of what it's really like in the Arctic, especially in late December or early January. The temperature frequently drops below minus forty degrees centigrade and sometimes gets even colder. Combine that with strong winds, little or no sunlight, and very little vegetation, and what you get is an environment in which very few species are capable of surviving. The polar bear, however, thrives in this kind of environment. The polar bear spends his time roaming throughout the Arctic, walking on land and ice, swimming in freezing sea water, and floating on sheets of ice while looking for seals, fish, and other food. Its favorite food is seals, which its finds along the edges of the ice, in holes in the ice, and under cracks in the ice. It has no natural enemies in this environment, which is perfectly suited for it.

Q Why does the professor mention the harsh Arctic environment?

Ⓐ To explain why polar bears have no natural enemies anywhere
Ⓑ To show how strong the polar bear is to be able to survive there
Ⓒ To prove that the Arctic is one of the coldest places on the Earth
Ⓓ To describe the kinds of animals that can survive in the Arctic

☑ Correct Answer

The correct answer to the above question is Ⓑ. The professor describes the harshness of the environment to show the strength of the polar bear in being able to survive there.

Basic Drill

Listen to parts of conversations or lectures and answer the questions.

Drill 1

06-02

Q Why does the student mention English literature?

(A) To ask about a course in that department
(B) To find out how he can major in it
(C) To inquire about a professor who teaches it
(D) To say that he is getting a minor in it

Check-Up Listen again and fill in the blanks with the correct words.

M Student: Professor Wallace, ______________ for a quick chat?

W Professor: Sure, Edward. What can I do for you?

M: I saw that you're going to be ______________ next semester. Would it be possible for me to ______________?

W: Hmm . . . Are you going to be a ______________ next semester?

M: I'll be a senior. Is that important?

W: Yes, it is. Attendance for seminars is restricted ______________. It's usually eighteen or twenty. So seniors are ______________ to sign up for seminars first.

M: I had no idea. But, um . . . I'm not an English literature major. I'm just ______________ in it.

W: That's quite all right. You can still ______________ from me to sign up for the class. Would you like that?

M: Definitely. I'm really ______________ nineteenth-century novels.

W: I'm glad that you're so interested in the class. I'll ______________ on the list.

Drill 2

Q Why does the man mention the deadline for dropping classes?

Ⓐ To state that the school is thinking of changing it
Ⓑ To explain why the student gets a partial refund
Ⓒ To point out that it happens one week after classes start
Ⓓ To say that it is going to happen two days from now

06-03

Check-Up Listen again and fill in the blanks with the correct words.

M Bursar's Office Employee: Good afternoon. How may I ______________ today?

W Student: Hello. I'd like to ______________ on my classes.

M: Could you be ______________, please?

W: Sure. I was signed up for two classes during ______________. But I had to drop both of them because I got a ______________ for the summer.

M: I see. May I have ______________, please? I need to call your name up on the screen.

W: Of course. Here you are . . .

M: Let me see . . . Doris Mercer . . . According to the computer, you ______________ 1,000 dollars.

W: Huh? I thought it should be ______________. After all, I paid 2,000 dollars for the classes.

M: Yes, but you dropped the classes on July 10. ______________ for dropping classes to get a full refund was July 8. You missed it ______________.

W: Okay. I didn't realize that. I guess ______________.

Drill 3

Q How does the professor organize the information about Sandro Botticelli that she presents to the class?

06-04

Ⓐ By discussing his life in chronological order

Ⓑ By showing some of his paintings and discussing them

Ⓒ By asking questions about him and answering them herself

Ⓓ By focusing on the painting methods that he preferred

Check-Up Listen again and fill in the blanks with the correct words.

W Professor: One of the ______________ in history was Sandro Botticelli. He was an Italian who lived during the Renaissance. He was born in 1445 and died in 1510. Let me show you a couple of ______________ right now so that you can ______________. Here is one . . . Here is another . . . And another . . . Impressive, aren't they?

Botticelli lived during the Early Renaissance, and he was ______________. This means he didn't focus so much on ______________ like artists did during the Middle Ages. Botticelli instead focused on ______________. He was strongly affected by the introduction of Greek and Roman ideas ______________. ______________ that he didn't paint religious topics. He did. Here is his painting called *The Adoration of the Magi*. Take a close look . . . It's one of my favorites. However, his paintings focusing on ______________ are much better known. Here is *The Birth of Venus*. Venus was the ______________ in Greek mythology. She is depicted sailing to shore on ______________. This painting is entitled *Venus and Mars*. Mars was the Greek god of war and ______________ Venus. You've probably seen this one, too. It's called *Primavera*. It ______________ from mythology. It's one of my personal favorites.

Drill 4

Q Why does the professor mention specialized equipment?

06-05

Ⓐ To say that archaeologists have it in their laboratories
Ⓑ To point out an expense of doing underwater archaeology
Ⓒ To claim that it is used to unearth artifacts under the water
Ⓓ To argue that it costs too much for most archaeologists

Check-Up **Listen again and fill in the blanks with the correct words.**

M Professor: ______________ take place on land. Archaeologists dig in the ground to unearth ______________ buried in the past. There's also something called ______________. This can be done for various reasons. Many times, archaeologists ______________ in order to study ships and to recover their contents. In some places, ______________ have covered entire civilizations, so archaeologists must go down into the water to ______________.

This is one of the ______________ of archaeology to practice for obvious reasons. Let me tell you some of the difficulties. First, the conditions ______________ can be very harsh, especially in ocean and river environments. Currents can make it hard for archaeologists simply to go ______________, and visibility can be low at times. Second, people who practice underwater archaeology require ______________. They have to know ______________. Even experienced divers have problems when they are deep in the ocean, and accidents, some of which ______________, happen from time to time. Specialized equipment, which can cost ______________, is required. And divers not only have to focus on doing proper dives but then also have to examine artifacts or ______________. Underwater archaeology is really extremely difficult and dangerous, and few people are ______________ enough to do it.

Exercises with Long Conversations

Exercise 1 Listen to part of a conversation between a student and a professor. Then, answer the questions.

06-06

Office Hours

1 Why does the student mention her midterm exam grade?

(A) To express her confusion about the professor's comment
(B) To claim that she has the top grade in the class
(C) To agree that she requires assistance with the course material
(D) To argue that her grade on the test should have been higher

2 Why did the professor ask to see the student?

(A) To encourage her to meet one of his friends
(B) To ask her about her upcoming presentation
(C) To find out why she has been absent a lot lately
(D) To discuss her performance in his class

3 What is the professor's attitude toward the student?

(A) He is pleased with the effort she is making.
(B) He is concerned about her wellbeing.
(C) He is disturbed by the comments she makes.
(D) He is upset with her actions in class.

Words & Phrases

hand back phr to give back, such as a homework assignment
vital adj important
chime in phr to speak up; to add to a conversation
stutter n the act of speaking while repeating words or sounds
contribute v to give; to supply
phobia n a fear, often irrational, of something
mad adj upset; angry

Summary Note

A Listen to the conversation again and fill in the blanks to complete the conversation notes.

- Student visits professor in his office
- Professor is concerned about ❶ ____________________
- Student says homework and ❷ ____________________ were good
- Professor says ❸ ____________________ is twenty percent of grade
- Student ❹ ____________________ in class
- Student gets nervous doing ❺ ____________________
- Professor offers to introduce student to ❻ ____________________

B Complete the following summary with the words given below.

gets nervous	class participation	concerned about
getting mad at	homework and exam	with a specialist

The student visits the professor because he wants to speak with her. He states that he is ____________________ the student's class performance, and the student is surprised. She states that her ____________________ grades were high, so she feels she is doing well in the class. The professor remarks that ____________________ is twenty percent of her grade, but she has never said anything during class discussions. The student says she ____________________ when speaking in front of others. The professor asks if she would like to speak ____________________ at the school. The student agrees, so the professor volunteers to introduce her to one of the specialists. The student expresses her thanks that the professor is helping her rather than ____________________ her.

Exercise 2 Listen to part of a conversation between a student and the dean of students. Then, answer the questions.

06-07

Service Encounter

1 Why does the student discuss Professor Lombard?

(A) To describe her problem with the professor
(B) To praise the professor for her teaching
(C) To complain about the professor's grading
(D) To talk about why she likes the professor's class

2 What does the man promise to do?

(A) Help the student with her classes
(B) Have a talk with a professor
(C) Arrange for a tutor for the student
(D) Meet the student later in the day

3 What will the student probably do next?

(A) Study for an anthropology class
(B) Go to her next class
(C) Give the man her email address
(D) Speak with the man's secretary

Words & Phrases

adjust v to change in order to get used to something
raise v to lift
annoying adj bothersome
ignore v not to pay attention to someone or something
pause n a brief rest or halt

Summary Note

A Listen to the conversation again and fill in the blanks to complete the conversation notes.

- Student has problem with ❶ ____________________
- May be ❷ ____________________
- Student wants to ❸ ____________________ in class
  - Professor ❹ ____________________ her
  - Would not talk to student after class
- Dean of students will talk to professor
- Will ❺ ____________________ with professor and student
- Student will tell secretary ❻ ____________________

B Complete the following summary with the words given below.

raises her hand	dean of students	professor ignores
something cultural	what time	says nothing

The student arranged to meet the ____________________ because she has a problem. She thinks it might be ____________________ because she is from a foreign land. She says that she has a problem with one of her professors. When the student ____________________ to ask a question in class, the ____________________ her. She calls on other students but ignores the student. The student tries speaking up in class and has waited for the professor after class, but the professor ____________________ to her. The man says that he will talk to the professor and then arrange for the two of them to meet in his office on Friday. He tells the student to let his secretary know ____________________ is good for her on Friday.

Exercise 3 Listen to part of a conversation between a student and a professor. Then, answer the questions.

06-08

Office Hours

1 Why does the student mention his exam and quiz grades?

Ⓐ To ask how he can improve his scores
Ⓑ To respond to the professor's question
Ⓒ To confirm he is paying attention in class
Ⓓ To explain why there must be a mistake

2 What can be inferred about the professor?

Ⓐ She has a class in a few minutes.
Ⓑ She can admit when she is wrong.
Ⓒ She will give an exam the next day.
Ⓓ She is bothered by the student's questions.

3 What will the professor probably do next?

Ⓐ Go over the other grades in her class
Ⓑ Prepare for her next class
Ⓒ Leave her office for the day
Ⓓ Help the student with his research

Words & Phrases

error n a mistake
grade n a score
hesitate v to pause
inconvenience n an annoyance; a bother
nonsense n silliness
quantum n an amount of energy in nuclear physics

Summary Note

A Listen to the conversation again and fill in the blanks to complete the conversation notes.

- Student asks to speak with professor
  - Says made mistake on ❶ ....
  - Professor doesn't believe him
- Student shows ❷ ....
- Professor can't find student on ❸ ....
  - Was looking at ❹ ....
- Professor agrees grade was ❺ ....
  - ❻ .... for error

B Complete the following summary with the words given below.

are correct	made a mistake	be higher
late at night	calculating grades	the professor's spreadsheet

The student goes to the professor's office to tell her that he suspects that the professor .... when she calculated the student's quantum physics grade. The student says that according to ...., his grade is only a seventy-two, but his midterm score was an eighty-five, and his quiz score was a ninety. Therefore, he feels that his grade should .... than a seventy-two. The professor tells him that she sometimes makes mistakes .... She asks for the student's ID number but cannot find the student on the class list. Eventually, the professor realizes that she is looking at the wrong list. Then, she finds the right list and confirms that student's statements .... She informs the student that .... is an eighty-six. She apologizes for the mistake and tells the student that she did the grades ....

Exercise 4 Listen to part of a conversation between a student and a librarian. Then, answer the questions.

06-09

Service Encounter

1 Why does the librarian mention the returned books section?

(A) She is certain that the book the student wants is there.
(B) She wants the student to put all of his overdue books there.
(C) She believes the book the student is looking for may be there.
(D) She is going to go there and look for a book for the student.

2 Why does the student visit the library?

(A) To renew some books he checked out
(B) To pay a fine on overdue books
(C) To ask about a book's availability
(D) To request a book's call number

3 What is the librarian's attitude toward the student?

(A) She is not particularly interested in talking to him.
(B) She likes joking about everything.
(C) She is eager to be of assistance.
(D) She is pleased he has renewed his books.

Words & Phrases

due adj expected; scheduled
relief n comfort; ease
crucial adj vital; important
fascinating adj captivating; gripping

Summary Note

A Listen to the conversation again and fill in the blanks to complete the conversation notes.

- Student visits ❶ ____________
  - Asks to ❷ ____________
  - Hopes he does not have to ❸ ____________
- Librarian renews his books
- Student asks about another book
  - Needs it for ❹ ____________
  - Is expensive so does not want to ❺ ____________
- Librarian finds that book is available
  - Gives man ❻ ____________
  - Tells him what to do if book is not there

B Complete the following summary with the words given below.

to renew	his ID card	his research project
currently checked out	checks its availability	on the shelves

The student goes to the library ____________ some of his books. He asks the librarian if he needs to bring the books with him, but she tells him that is not necessary. He gives her ____________, and she calls his name up on the computer. She then renews the student's books for him. The student proceeds to ask a question about a book that he needs to complete ____________. He says that the book is ____________, and because it is so expensive, he does not want to purchase it. The librarian ____________ and notices that the book was returned that day. She gives the man the book's call number and then tells him that if the book is not ____________, he should tell her, and she will find the book in the returned books section.

Exercises with Long Lectures

Exercise 1 Listen to part of a lecture in an economics class. Then, answer the questions.

06-10

Economics

1 How does the professor organize the lecture?

(A) By comparing domestic trade with foreign trade
(B) By comparing two types of trade throughout history
(C) By comparing the characteristics of two types of trading policies
(D) By discussing one type of trade commonly used nowadays

2 Why does the professor mention India?

(A) To compare its trading policies with those of China
(B) To claim that it has many garment manufacturers
(C) To note that it has engaged in free trade in recent times
(D) To point out an advantage of employing workers there

3 What is the likely outcome of a country adopting protectionist policies?

(A) Consumers will pay lower prices for foreign goods.
(B) The country will lose jobs to foreign competition.
(C) The prices of most goods in that country will rise.
(D) Trade will increase between various countries.

Words & Phrases

dump (v) to throw away
import (n) something brought in from another country
manufacture (v) to make
nation (n) a country
outsource (v) to delegate work outside a company
prevent (v) to stop something before it happens
quota (n) a numerical limit
regulation (n) a rule
subsidy (n) economic funding or assistance

Summary Note

A Listen to the lecture again and fill in the blanks to complete the lecture notes.

- Professor discusses ❶ ______________
  - Is free flow of ❷ ______________
  - Lets people buy and sell anything
  - Will create ❸ ______________ for both partners
- Free trade has ❹ ______________ to people
- Describes protectionism
  - Prevents people from ❺ ______________
  - Can include ❻ ______________
- Describes advantages of free trade
  - ❼ ______________ manufacturing
  - Outsource jobs
  - Improves economies of ❽ ______________

B Complete the following summary with the words given below.

protective policies	absence of tariffs	many domestic businesses
at the same time	goods and services	free flow of business

Free trade is the free flow of goods and services between nations. Some of the characteristics of free trade are the ______________, quotas, subsidies, and various other regulations that limit the ______________. Free trade agreements usually involve some ______________. Protectionism is government restraint on trade between two nations. It is one nation's efforts to prevent its own people from trading. Such protective measures include tariffs, restrictive quotas, government regulations, anti-dumping laws, and subsidies. One major advantage of free trade is that it keeps prices down, but ______________, a big disadvantage is that it might cause ______________ to suffer economically, domestic jobs to disappear, and domestic wages to decrease. Foreign businesses, especially in poorer countries, can provide the same ______________ at cheaper prices because of lower labor costs.

Exercise 2 Listen to part of a lecture in an art history class. Then, answer the questions.

06-11

Art History

1 How does the professor organize the lecture?

- (A) By discussing technical details of cameras in order
- (B) By focusing on the most important events in the 1800s
- (C) By providing biographies of important people in the history of cameras
- (D) By providing information in chronological order

2 Who was the first person to make multiple copies of the same image?

- (A) Joseph Nicéphore Niépce
- (B) Louis Daguerre
- (C) William Henry Talbot
- (D) Frederick Scott Archer

3 What does the professor imply about the ancient Greeks?

- (A) They created the world's first camera.
- (B) They understood optics better than the Chinese.
- (C) They lacked the technology to make a camera.
- (D) They knew what white light is formed of.

Words & Phrases

accomplish v to achieve
capture v to catch
be composed of phr to be made of
expose v to uncover, reveal, or show
jeopardize v to put in danger
immerse v to be put completely into
instant adj immediate
practical adj useful
resemble v to look the same as; to look like
snowball v to grow quickly in size; to spread

Summary Note

A Listen to the lecture again and fill in the blanks to complete the lecture notes.

- Professor gives ❶ ____________
  - ❷ ____________ philosophers described its principles
  - Isaac Newton discovered light is made of ❸ ____________
  - Johann Heinrich Schulze learned light can ❹ ____________ silver nitrate
  - Joseph Nicéphore Niépce created first ❺ ____________
- Louis Daguerre experimented with photography
  - Captured an image that ❻ ____________
  - Developed photographic plates
- William Henry Talbot developed ❼ ____________ process
- Frederick Scott Archer invented Collodion process
- Cameras first ❽ ____________ in 1900s
- More inventions later

B Complete the following summary with the words given below.

at least eight hours	in salt	photographic plates
required a few seconds	familiar with	exposure to light

The history of photography is a long one. In the fourth and fifth centuries B.C., Greek and Chinese philosophers were already ____________ the basic principles of cameras. In 1727, Johann Heinrich Schulze discovered that ____________ would darken silver nitrate. Finally, in 1814, a Frenchman, Joseph Nicéphore Niépce, created a photographic image, but it was not very practical because it needed to be exposed to light for ____________ and the image quickly faded. In 1833, his business partner, Louis Daguerre, became the first to capture a permanent image. He accomplished this by immersing the image ____________. He also developed ____________, which significantly reduced the required exposure time to thirty minutes. In 1841, William Henry Talbot invented a process that only ____________ to have multiple copies of the same image. Finally, in 1851, Frederick Scott Archer invented the Collodion process, in which images made it possible of light exposure.

Exercise 3 Listen to part of a lecture in an archaeology class. Then, answer the questions.

06-12

Archaeology

1 How does the professor organize the lecture?

Ⓐ By comparing American and European excavations
Ⓑ By comparing two types of excavations
Ⓒ By discussing the history of excavations
Ⓓ By discussing the different types of rescues

2 Why does the professor mention Mexico?

Ⓐ To say it has more digs than the United States
Ⓑ To compare digs there with those in Peru
Ⓒ To state that research excavations are rare there
Ⓓ To discuss rescue archaeology operations there

3 According to the professor, what is one way that land development can affect archaeological sites?

Ⓐ It can help uncover valuable artifacts.
Ⓑ It can destroy valuable archaeological sites.
Ⓒ It is an inexpensive way to practice archaeology.
Ⓓ It can unearth sites that have been hidden for years.

Words & Phrases

artifact n a relic
erosion n a process by which something is broken down
inevitable adj unable to be avoided; bound to happen
imminent adj looming
reconstruct v to put together again
remains n remnants
peril n serious danger
source n an origin
urgent adj needing to be done soon

Summary Note

A Listen to the lecture again and fill in the blanks to complete the lecture notes.

- Professor describes ❶ ______________________
  - Study of ❷ ____________________ and human activities
  - Examine ❸ ____________________
  - Must dig for them
- Describes rescue archaeology
  - Survey ❹ ____________________
  - Must excavate quickly
  - Is common in ❺ ____________________
- Thousands of digs throughout world
  - Many in ❻ ____________________
  - Mentions Pompeii

B Complete the following summary with the words given below.

with no deadlines	ancient remains	digging or excavating
examination of sites	a lot of erosion	chief source of knowledge

Ancient cultures left little or no written history, but archaeologists can learn a lot about these cultures by examining ______________________ such as buildings, tools, graves, and artifacts. These remains are the ______________________ of prehistoric and ancient cultures. Archaeologists get their information by ______________________. One kind of archaeology is rescue archaeology, which is the ______________________ threatened by land development. Usually, development is imminent, so archaeologists must urgently excavate before the bulldozers move in. Many sites also suffer ______________________, which adds to the peril of the situation. In such a case, excavation becomes an exercise in damage control. Sometimes excavation can be done at a relaxed pace ______________________. This is called research excavation. During this type of excavation, archaeologists have more resources and can excavate more fully. Right now, there are thousands of digs taking place all over the world. The countries where ancient civilizations were located tend to have the most archaeological sites.

Exercise 4 Listen to part of a lecture in an art class. Then, answer the questions.

06-13

Art

1 How does the professor organize the information about ceramics that he presents to the class?

Ⓐ By providing a chronological history of ceramics
Ⓑ By focusing on how it is made and its uses
Ⓒ By talking about how it was first created
Ⓓ By stressing the places where it is made

2 According to the professor, where is most kitchenware produced?

Ⓐ In ceramics studios
Ⓑ In people's homes
Ⓒ In factories
Ⓓ In art classes

3 What can be inferred about pottery?

Ⓐ It was first invented thousands of years ago.
Ⓑ It is too expensive for many people to afford.
Ⓒ Its manufacturing process has changed since ancient times.
Ⓓ It was highly decorated in most prehistoric civilizations.

Words & Phrases

decorative adj used for decoration or adornment
devote v to dedicate time or attention
durability n strength
glaze v to paint or coat something and to give it a shiny appearance
modify v to change
nonporous adj having no holes or gaps
practical adj useful
refined adj polished
utilitarian adj useful

Summary Note

A Listen to the lecture again and fill in the blanks to complete the lecture notes.

- Professor describes ❶ ____________________
  - Are objects made from ❷ ____________________
  - Often called ❸ ____________________
  - Are used as ❹ ____________________
  - Oldest form of art
- Describes manufacturing process
  - Create pot with ❺ ____________________ and hands
  - Heat clay in kiln
  - Hardens
  - Glazed before ❻ ____________________

B Complete the following summary with the words given below.

various minerals	combination	always glazed
oldest form of art	shapes it with his hands	mass-produced in factories

Generally, ceramic arts, which are sometimes referred to as pottery, are pieces made from a ____________________ of inorganic nonmetallic materials and heat. The most common ingredient is clay, but it is usually mixed with ____________________. Typically, pottery is something people have used their entire lives: kitchenware. It usually has utilitarian purposes, but sometimes it is designed purely for decorative reasons. It is very durable, and it is the ____________________. Many pieces date back to the age of prehistoric man. Much of the kitchenware seen in the stores is ____________________. However, many pots are made in old-fashioned, modest studios. They are also made by hand. The potter starts with a hunk of clay, ____________________, and then heats it up in a kiln. This hardens the clay. Pots and other ceramic arts are usually heated at extremely high temperatures, but they are ____________________ before the final firing, which gives them a refined look and makes them nonporous. Artists may add a final touch to them as well.

Integrated Listening & Speaking

A Listen to a different version of a previous lecture on economics and say the answers out loud. You can refer to the summary note below.

06-14

Economics

Summary Note

- Professor discusses free trade
  - Is free flow of goods and services
  - Lets people buy and sell anything
  - Will create wealth for both partners
- Free trade has different meanings to people
- Describes protectionism
  - Prevents people from trading
  - Can include tariffs
- Describes advantages of free trade
  - Cheap manufacturing
  - Outsource jobs
  - Improve economies of developing nations

1 What is free trade?

2 Which type of trade is more likely to result in higher domestic prices?

3 What are some advantages of protectionism?

B **Listen to a different version of a previous lecture on art and say the answers out loud. You can refer to the summary note below.**

06-15

Art

Summary Note

- Professor describes ceramics
  - Objects made from clay
  - Often called pottery
  - Used as kitchenware
  - Oldest form of art
- Describes manufacturing process
  - Create pot with potter's wheel and hands
  - Heat clay in kiln
  - Hardens
  - Glazed before firing again

1 What do people often use pottery for?

2 What are the steps to making a pot?

3 What does glazing do?

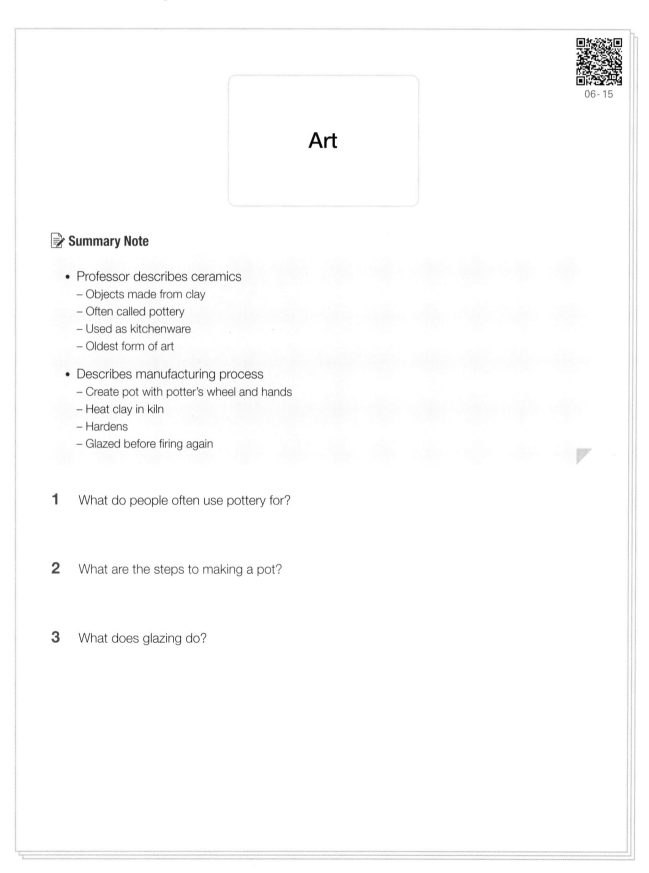

Mini TOEFL iBT Practice Test

Listen to part of a conversation between a student and a professor.

06-16

1 What are the speakers mainly discussing?

Ⓐ A homework assignment that the student must do
Ⓑ A field trip that the student went on last semester
Ⓒ A part-time position that the student wants to have
Ⓓ A favor that the professor asks the student for

2 According to the professor, what will one of the exhibits feature?

Ⓐ Works by Renaissance artists
Ⓑ Works by Impressionists
Ⓒ Works by Realist artists
Ⓓ Works by medieval artists

3 What is the professor's opinion of the student?

Ⓐ She believes he is a very skilled artist.
Ⓑ She appreciates the comments he makes in class.
Ⓒ She thinks very highly of his knowledge.
Ⓓ She considers him her most outstanding student.

4 Why does the professor mention Granderson Hall?

Ⓐ To say that is where she is going next
Ⓑ To tell the student where he should go
Ⓒ To state that she teaches a class there
Ⓓ To have the student go there right now

5 Listen again to part of the conversation. Then answer the question.
What does the student imply when he says this: 🎧

Ⓐ He is willing to agree to the professor's request.
Ⓑ He does not have much time to meet the professor.
Ⓒ He hopes that he does not have to leave too early.
Ⓓ He has some time to meet later on in the morning.

Listen to part of a lecture in a biology class.

06-17

Biology

6 What is the lecture mainly about?

(A) Why bears are not true hibernators
(B) Characteristics of certain hibernators
(C) The details of predictive dormancy
(D) Various kinds of deep hibernators

7 How does the professor organize the lecture?

(A) By responding to questions that the students ask
(B) By explaining how hibernation affects the body
(C) By providing various information about bears
(D) By talking about different types of hibernators

8 What is true hibernation?

(A) A state of complete inactivity for a long period of time
(B) A condition of sensing winter approaching and acting accordingly
(C) A state of unconsciousness that lasts for a short period of time
(D) A condition in which an animal can rouse itself from dormancy

9 According to the professor, how do some hibernators practice predictive dormancy?

Ⓐ They hibernate as the days grow longer.
Ⓑ They hibernate all year round.
Ⓒ They hibernate as the days decrease in length.
Ⓓ They only hibernate when they do not have enough food.

10 Based on the information in the lecture, are the following animals torpor hibernators or deep hibernators?
Click in the correct box for each statement.

	Torpor Hibernators	Deep Hibernators
1 Raccoons		
2 Toads		
3 Skunks		
4 Woodchucks		

11 Listen again to part of the lecture. Then answer the question.
What does the professor imply when he says this:

Ⓐ Most animals around the world are non-hibernating ones.
Ⓑ People can expect to see gray squirrels in winter.
Ⓒ Red foxes sleep longer than bears during winter.
Ⓓ It is hard to tell which animals hibernate and which do not.

Vocabulary Check-Up

A Choose and write the correct words that match the definitions.

1	chime in	•	• (A)	economic funding or assistance
2	subsidy	•	• (B)	a process by which something is broken down
3	jeopardize	•	• (C)	to put back together
4	resemble	•	• (D)	not to pay attention to someone or something
5	reconstruct	•	• (E)	to speak up; to add to a conversation
6	inevitable	•	• (F)	to put in danger
7	ignore	•	• (G)	to change in order to get used to something
8	stutter	•	• (H)	to look the same as
9	erosion	•	• (I)	able to exist for a long time; long-lasting
10	durable	•	• (J)	the act of speaking while repeating words or sounds
11	phobia	•	• (K)	unable to be avoided; bound to happen
12	adjust	•	• (L)	a fear, often irrational, of something
13	accomplish	•	• (M)	an amount of energy in nuclear physics
14	snowball	•	• (N)	to glow quickly in size; to spread
15	quantum	•	• (O)	to achieve

B Choose the correct words that match the descriptions.

 (A) archeology (B) excavation (C) pottery (D) photography (E) free trade

1 This is the digging of a big hole to expose ancient remains and other findings to learn more about ancient cultures.

2 This is a government policy that allows people to trade whatever they want with whomever they want without any government interference.

3 This art is made from clay and other materials. Usually, it requires a very hot kiln.

4 This technology slowly developed over several hundred years but finally started to capture images in the nineteenth century.

5 This is the study of ancient cultures by examining ancient remains.

UNIT

07 Connecting Content

Overview

Introduction

In order to answer these questions correctly, you must identify the relationships between various ideas in the listening passage. Sometimes these ideas are stated openly; other times, they must be inferred. These questions sometimes ask you to classify items into categories, identify a sequence of events or the steps involved in a process, or specify the relationship between various ideas in a manner that was not presented in the passage. Other questions may ask you to make inferences about information in the passage and then make a prediction, come to a conclusion, or extrapolate some other information.

Question Types

- What is the likely outcome of doing procedure X before procedure Y?
- What can be inferred about X?
- What does the professor imply about X?
- What comparison does the professor make between X and Y?

Useful Tips

- Pay attention to the way that you take your notes.
- Take note of the category words, their characteristics, and examples.

Sample TOEFL iBT Question

Script

07-01

M Student: Professor Bates, do you think that I can sign up for math 33 next semester?

W Professor: Hmm . . . You haven't completed math 21 yet, have you? That's a prerequisite for the course I'll be teaching.

M: No, ma'am, I haven't taken that class yet. Do you think that I need to take it first?

W: Student learn lots of new concepts in math 21. Those concepts are all applied in math 33. If you don't know them, you'll have a difficult time learning the material well. I suggest that you take math 21 first, Kyle.

Q What is the likely outcome of the student taking math 33 before math 21?

Ⓐ He will get a higher grade.
Ⓑ He will learn many new concepts.
Ⓒ He will not do well in the class.
Ⓓ He will have to take the course again.

☑ Correct Answer

The right answer to the above question is Ⓒ. The professor says that math 21 is a prerequisite for math 33 and that there are many new concepts taught in math 21. So if the student takes math 33 before math 21, the likely outcome is that he will not do well in the class.

Basic Drill

Listen to parts of conversations or lectures and answer the questions.

Drill 1

Q What comparison does the professor make between history and chemistry?

Ⓐ The amount of work involved in each subject
Ⓑ The difficulty of the material in each subject
Ⓒ The job prospects for majoring in each subject
Ⓓ The number of classes needed to take in each subject

07-02

Check-Up Listen again and fill in the blanks with the correct words.

W Student: Good afternoon. I have something ______________, Professor Daniels, so I'd like to speak with you, please.

M Professor: Can you ______________? I've got a seminar to teach in five minutes.

W: Sure. This ______________.

M: Great. What's up?

W: I've been thinking of doing ______________, but I'm not sure which subject to choose. My major is art history, but I have enough time to ______________.

M: What are you considering?

W: I'm thinking about either doing ______________. What do you think?

M: Well, both of them are ______________. You'll have to do a lot of work ______________ because of the labs. You won't be quite so busy in history. But history might be ______________.

W: Why is that?

M: You'll be able to understand ______________ in which many artists worked. As you know, ______________ by their times, so I would go with history if I were you.

Drill 2

Q What can be inferred about the woman?

- Ⓐ She is not supposed to keep the museum open late.
- Ⓑ She has a personal collection of Chinese pottery.
- Ⓒ She will allow the student to come back tomorrow.
- Ⓓ She is friends with the student's professor.

07-03

Check-Up Listen again and fill in the blanks with the correct words.

W Museum Curator: I'm very sorry, young man, but we're about to ______________.

M Student: Really? That's too bad. I was hoping to see ______________ of Chinese pottery.

W: It's ______________. Are you planning to view it because of a class you're taking?

M: Yes, that's right. My professor suggested that ______________ look at it. Professor Westin spoke ______________ in class.

W: Ah, so Candice sent you.

M: Candice?

W: That's Professor Westin's first name. We ______________ a long time ago.

M: Ah, I see. Well, I guess that I'll come back tomorrow.

W: That's quite all right. Since you're here for her class, I can ______________ for around twenty minutes. Will that be enough time?

M: ______________. Thank you so much, ma'am.

Drill 3

Q Based on the information in the lecture, do the following statements refer to reptiles or amphibians?
Click on the correct box for each statement.

07-04

	Reptiles	Amphibians
1 Have skin that is capable of helping with breathing		
2 Have both dry and scaly skin		
3 May be brightly colored when they are toxic		
4 Can suffer damage from the sun and the wind		

Check-Up

Listen again and fill in the blanks with the correct words.

W Professor: We all know that __________ are different kinds of animals. Nevertheless, people often __________ with each other. Just remember that __________, lizards, turtles, snakes, alligators, and crocodiles are reptiles. __________, they include toads, frogs, salamanders, and newts.

Of course, uh, both reptiles and amphibians are vertebrates, meaning that __________. However, their skin is different. Amphibians have moist skin whereas the skin of reptiles is __________. Reptiles' skin helps protect them __________. As for amphibians, their skin is permeable both to __________ as they sometimes breathe __________. Amphibians also live parts of their lives in water and __________. While some reptiles live in the water, __________ into it. For instance, crocodiles, alligators, and some species of snakes spend __________ in the water. Ah, yes, turtles as well. However, various reptiles and snakes don't __________ at all.

Something else you often see is that __________ are brightly colored. This __________ to stay away from them. This is __________ for certain species of frogs. Oh, I nearly forgot. Because of __________, they need unique living conditions. If they get too much sun, their skin cells __________. And if the wind blows too much, their skin __________, which dehydrates them.

Drill 4

Q Based on the information in the lecture, do the following statements refer to Sir Francis Drake or Horatio Nelson?
Click on the correct box for each statement.

07-05

	Sir Francis Drake	Horatio Nelson
1 Was shot and killed during a battle		
2 Utilized fireships to win a battle		
3 Was a privateer who attacked Spanish shipping		
4 Engaged in fights against the Spanish and the French		

Check-Up

Listen again and fill in the blanks with the correct words.

M Professor: ______________, Great Britain has always depended upon its navy for protection. As such, it has produced countless ______________. Two of the greatest were Sir Francis Drake and Horatio Nelson. Interestingly, the two men ______________ in different ways.

Drake lived in the 1500s, which was when Great Britain was ______________ ships across the Atlantic Ocean to the Americas. He was a privateer, which is basically ______________ pirate. He ______________ against the Spanish, so he mostly attacked Spanish ships. He plundered their cargo and ______________, becoming a rich man in the process. In 1588, the Spanish sent an enormous fleet—now called the Spanish Armada—to invade Britain. The queen made Drake an admiral, and he led ______________. Thanks to Drake's use of fireships and ______________, Drake managed to defeat the Spanish Armada.

Horatio Nelson lived from 1758 to 1805. He served ______________, where he fought both the French and the Spanish during the Napoleonic Wars. He fought in ______________, and he lost an eye and ______________ in two of them. In 1798, he won the Battle of the Nile ______________. In 1805, he led the British fleet at the Battle of Trafalgar. Prior to battle, he made the famous quote "England expects that every man ______________." Nelson was ______________, but Britain won the battle.

Exercises with Long Conversations

Exercise 1 Listen to part of a conversation between a student and a professor. Then, answer the questions.

07-06

Office Hours

1 What does the professor imply about ascending too quickly?

Ⓐ It is only dangerous to babies and handicapped people.
Ⓑ It can affect people who are in good physical condition.
Ⓒ It can have long-term consequences lasting for years.
Ⓓ It affects animals more than humans in most cases.

2 According to the professor, how can acclimatization affect people?

Ⓐ It can cause heart attacks.
Ⓑ It can deprive people of fluids.
Ⓒ It can make people pass out.
Ⓓ It can cause altitude sickness.

3 Listen again to part of the conversation. Then answer the question.
What does the professor imply when she says this: 🎧

Ⓐ She is proud of the student's actions.
Ⓑ She is always happy to answer students' questions.
Ⓒ She wants the student to return for more help later.
Ⓓ She expects the student to do well on the test.

Words & Phrases

ascend v to climb or go upward
strenuous adj vigorous
hydrate v to take in water
replenish v to make full or complete again
nausea n sickness of the stomach; queasiness
reduce v to make less or smaller
accompany v to go along with someone

Summary Note

A Listen to the conversation again and fill in the blanks to complete the conversation notes.

- Student wants to speak to professor
  - Had problem understanding lecture
  - Professor offers to ❶ ______________
- Discusses ❷ ______________
  - Occurs in people ❸ ______________
  - Caused by lack of ❹ ______________
  - Can cause feelings of lightheadedness or ❺ ______________
- Some are acclimatized to it
- ❻ ______________ helps prevent it

B Complete the following summary with the words given below.

ways to acclimatize	understand a concept	forty percent fewer
oxygen molecules	ascend into the atmosphere	strenuous activity

The student asks the professor to help him ______________ from an earlier lecture. The lecture was about high-altitude sickness. The professor starts by defining high-altitude sickness as an illness that occurs when people ______________ too quickly. People tend to feel ill because they are not breathing as many ______________ as they normally do. If a person were on a plane that was flying at 12,000 feet, he would be taking in ______________ oxygen molecules with each breath. This depletion of oxygen intake can cause the person to feel dizzy or nauseous. The professor then tells the student about some of the ______________ in high altitudes. The person could start to ascend from no more than 10,000 feet and ascend slowly. The professor also points out the benefits of drinking plenty of fluids and of refraining from ______________ for the first twenty-four hours after flying.

Exercise 2 Listen to part of a conversation between a student and a student housing office employee.

07-07

Service Encounter

1 What comparison does the man make between the student and an incoming foreign student?

- (A) Making friends with various foreigners
- (B) Studying at a school in a different country
- (C) Learning how to speak another language
- (D) Attempting to find housing in another country

2 According to the student, why does she have to remain for one more semester?

- (A) She has to do student-teaching.
- (B) She does not have enough class credits.
- (C) She does not have any other place to go.
- (D) She loves her dorm very much.

3 What does the man imply about foreign students?

- (A) They should be made to feel as welcome as possible.
- (B) They should have to fend for themselves on campus.
- (C) They make up a large percentage of the student body.
- (D) They are the most important students on campus.

Words & Phrases

allocate v to set apart for a particular purpose
upgrade n an improvement or increase
desperate adj having an urgent need
initially adv at the beginning
extend v to make longer
mistake n an error

Summary Note

A Listen to the conversation again and fill in the blanks to complete the conversation notes.

- Student visits ❶ ________________
  - Wants to ❷ ________________ longer
  - Gives personal information
- Employee says can't stay there because of ❸ ________________
- Student becomes ❹ ________________
- Employee refuses to kick ❺ ________________ out
- Student ❻ ________________ situation

B Complete the following summary with the words given below.

she is a senior	an extra semester	help them get comfortable
needs a roommate	complete her student-teaching	a foreign student

The student stops by the student housing office to let the man know that she needs to remain in her dorm room for ________________ because she forgot she had to ________________. The man checks the computer and finds that her room has already been allocated to ________________ for next semester, so the student must find new housing arrangements. This angers the student since she feels she should be able to remain in her room since ________________. The man kindly informs her that the reason the university puts foreign students in dorm rooms is to ________________ in a new country and on a new campus. The man suggests that she find an off-campus house with one of her friends. The student understands the man's point of view and mentions a friend she knows that ________________.

Exercise 3 Listen to part of a conversation between a student and a music hall employee. Then, answer the questions.

07-08

Service Encounter

1 What is the likely outcome of the student accepting the man's offer?

(A) She can borrow an instrument from the man.
(B) She can continue using the practice room.
(C) She can practice with no interruptions.
(D) She can rehearse together with another student.

2 Why does the student visit the man?

(A) To offer a compromise
(B) To ask about a concert
(C) To book a practice room
(D) To complain about noise

3 What instrument does the student play?

(A) The flute
(B) The piano
(C) The cello
(D) The violin

Words & Phrases

inconvenience n something that causes discomfort or trouble
guarantee n a promise or assurance
prior adj earlier in time or order; beforehand
utilize v to make use of
mobile adj able to move
pushy adj trying too hard to persuade someone to do something; self-assertive
polish v to make exact or better
convenient adj suitable or agreeable
crew n a group of people working together for one purpose

Summary Note

A Listen to the conversation again and fill in the blanks to complete the conversation notes.

- Student complains about noise
  - ❶ ______________ causes noise
  - Can't concentrate on ❷ ______________
- Employee says workers can't stop construction
- Student needs to ❸ ______________
- Employee offers to let student use different piano for ❹ ______________
- Student agrees

B Complete the following summary with the words given below.

practicing the piano	one week	complains to the employee
making too much noise	before the big concert	written permission

The student visits Lincoln Hall and complains to the employee on duty that she cannot hear herself ______________ because there are construction workers in the building ______________. The man apologizes but tells her that the upgrades on Lincoln Hall are necessary ______________ and that the construction workers are only booked for ______________. The student says that she requires a full ______________ of practice on her Bach piece and simply cannot have that much noise. The man offers her a compromise. He will give her ______________ to use the piano in the theater building for one week while the construction workers finish their job. The student agrees to this compromise and thanks the man.

Exercise 4 Listen to part of a conversation between a student and a student services center employee. Then, answer the questions.

07-09

Service Encounter

1 What is the likely outcome of the student waiting at the bus stop?

(A) He will get to go on the field trip.
(B) The bus will arrive on schedule.
(C) He will have to stand on the bus.
(D) The bus can carry his bags for him.

2 Why was the student's application rejected?

(A) He applied to go on the trip too late.
(B) He did not cancel his booking last semester.
(C) He did not pay the registration fee in advance.
(D) He was not approved to go by his professor.

3 Why does the student need to go on the field trip?

(A) To be able to graduate
(B) To get points in a class
(C) To get extra credit
(D) To satisfy his professor

Words & Phrases

forfeit v to lose something as a result of a fault
crucial adj extremely important
consolation n the act of offering comfort
vacancy n an unoccupied place
preferential adj given special consideration
delete v to erase
attend v to be present; to go to
basis n the base upon which something rests

Summary Note

A Listen to the conversation again and fill in the blanks to complete the conversation notes.

- Student visits office worker
  - – Needs to ❶ ____________
  - – But application was ❷ ____________
- Worker says student ❸ ____________ last time
- Student never called to cancel
  - – Trip is ❹ ____________
  - – If didn't cancel last time, cannot go on trip
- Student needs trip to ❺ ____________
- Can show up early in case another student doesn't ❻ ____________

B Complete the following summary with the words given below.

forfeited his chance	did not show up	in order to graduate
he had the flu	has been denied	fill a vacancy

The student goes to the science office because he does not understand why his application to attend the Inglewood Forest field trip ____________. The woman informs him that the reason he was denied was that he submitted an application for the same field trip last term but ____________ on that day. The student explains that he did not attend the trip because ____________. The clerk tells him that because he did not bother to call in and inform the science office, he ____________ to go on the trip. The student tells the woman that he needs to attend the field trip ____________ and that there must be a way he can go. The woman says that she is sorry, but the only way he has a chance at going is to wait at the bus stop on the day of the trip and hope to ____________ left by another student.

Exercises with Long Lectures

Exercise 1 Listen to part of a lecture in a psychology class. Then, answer the questions.

07-10

Psychology

1 Based on the information in the lecture, do the following statements refer to the causes or effects of stress?
Click on the correct box for each statement.

	Cause	Effect
1 May produce skin problems for some people		
2 May give people headaches or upset stomachs		
3 May result in a person gaining or losing weight		
4 May result from an upcoming marriage		

2 What does the professor indicate about stress?

- (A) It affects people in the same way.
- (B) It can last for a short or long time.
- (C) It frequently results in people dying.
- (D) It can be cured by taking medicine.

3 What will the professor probably do next?

- (A) Answer some questions
- (B) Let the students take a short break
- (C) Ask the students to submit their homework
- (D) Give the students a short quiz

Words & Phrases

overly adv too much; exceedingly
workload n the amount of work a person has or does
impending adj happening or coming soon
divorce n the act of legally ending a marriage
chronic adj continuing again and again; happening for a long time
concentrate v to focus on something
irritable adj easily angered
mitigate v to reduce; to make less harmful or painful

Summary Note

A Listen to the lecture again and fill in the blanks to complete the lecture notes.

- Professor describes ❶ ________________
- Can ❷ ________________ by many things
- Includes ❸ ________________, school, and personal issues
  - Work issues include ❹ ________________ and heavy workloads
  - School issues include ❺ ________________, homework, and assignments
  - Personal issues include ❻ ________________, death, and money
- Short-term effects can be ❼ ________________, upset stomachs, a lack of sleep, and being irritable
- Long-term effects including weight gain or loss, skin problems, and ❽ ________________

B Complete the following summary with the words given below.

personal issues	bigger problems	cause stress
worry or tension	impending deadline	upset stomachs

The professor defines stress as a state of ________________ in the mind caused by something unpleasant or difficult. He then notes that many things can cause stress and that what causes stress for some people may not ________________ for others. He then states that there are some things that tend to cause stress in most people. Among them are work, school, and ________________. A demanding boss, a heavy workload, and an ________________ can cause stress at work. Tests, homework, and assignments can cause stress at school. Divorce, death, money problems, and illnesses can cause stress in private lives. The effects of stress include headaches, ________________, a lack of sleep, and being irritable. Long-term stress can lead to ________________, including weight gain or loss, skin problems, and even heart attacks.

Exercise 2 Listen to part of a lecture in a zoology class. Then, answer the questions.

07-11

Zoology

1 Based on the information in the lecture, are the following whales toothed or baleen whales? Click on the correct box for each statement.

	Toothed Whale	Baleen Whale
1 Blue whale		
2 Humpback whale		
3 Bottlenose whale		
4 Sperm whale		

2 According to the professor, why do whales migrate to warmer waters?

(A) To escape from cold water
(B) To visit their feeding grounds
(C) To breed and to give birth
(D) To avoid predators

3 What can be inferred about a whale's intelligence?

(A) Whales panic in stressful situations and generally are killed.
(B) A whale uses its intelligence to adapt to stressful situations.
(C) Whales are able to communicate with other marine creatures.
(D) Whales are not particularly intelligent due to their small brains.

Words & Phrases

migration n the movement of large numbers of animals from one place to another
distinct adj different in nature
distinguish v to recognize as different
formation n a particular arrangement of different parts
gorge v to stuff with food
sieve n a container used to separate large parts from smaller parts
activity n a specific action
typical adj showing a particular characteristic

Summary Note

A Listen to the lecture again and fill in the blanks to complete the lecture notes.

- Professor discusses ❶ ________
  - Humpback whale
  - Blue whale
- Mentions baleen
  - Filters water from ❷ ________
  - Made of keratin
- Toothed whales
  - Sperm whale
  - Bottlenose whale
  - ❸ ________
- Whale migration
  - For food
  - For ❹ ________
- Whale intelligence
  - Have very large ❺ ________
  - Are social
  - Communicate through ❻ ________

B Complete the following summary with the words given below.

to breed and give birth	those with baleen	blue whale
sperm whale	to feed	work together in groups

The mammals known as whales can be divided into two main groups: ________ and those with teeth. Baleen is a sieve-like structure made of keratin that filters out plankton for baleen whales to eat. Two types of baleen whales are the ________ and the humpback whale. Toothed whales, such as the ________ and the killer whale, prey on larger animals such as fish or squid. Whales also migrate. They migrate to warmer waters ________, and then they migrate into colder waters ________. One would think that the energy spent for these mass migrations would not be worth it; however, once whales are in their feeding waters, they are able to gorge to their hearts' content. Whales are very intelligent and often ________ to try to avoid danger.

Exercise 3 Listen to part of a lecture in an American history class. Then, answer the questions.

07-12

American History

1 Based on the information in the lecture, do the following sentences refer to Mount Rushmore or the Statue of Liberty?
Click on the correct box for each statement.

	Mount Rushmore	The Statue of Liberty
1 Was constructed in France		
2 Required fourteen years to make		
3 Was shipped across the ocean when completed		
4 Was made for a cost of almost one billion dollars		

2 What can be inferred about the Statue of Liberty?

(A) It is considered the most important symbol in the United States.
(B) It is no longer open for people to visit.
(C) It is considered an important site by American citizens.
(D) Most Americans visit the statue once in their lifetime.

3 How does the professor organize the discussion?

(A) By talking separately about two monuments
(B) By covering the events in chronological order
(C) By discussing the more famous monument first
(D) By focusing on how each monument was constructed

Words & Phrases

origin n a beginning
conceive v to think; to create
visage n a face
persuade v to convince
precarious adj uncertain; unstable
frigate n a fast military and cargo ship
dedicate v to set apart for some purpose
icon n a representation of something well known
tourist n a person traveling for pleasure
construct v to build or make
immigrant n a person who goes to live in a different country

Summary Note

A Listen to the lecture again and fill in the blanks to complete the lecture notes.

- Professor mentions ❶ ____________
  - In South Dakota
  - ❷ ____________ of four U.S. presidents
  - Made to increase ❸ ____________
  - Took fourteen years to finish
- Professor discusses ❹ ____________
  - Woman in robe wearing ❺ ____________
  - Given to U.S. by ❻ ____________
  - In New York Harbor
  - Has many ❼ ____________
  - ❽ ____________ American icon

B Complete the following summary with the words given below.

gesture of friendship	pure copper	a large sculpture
granite hillside	bring more tourists	holding a stone tablet

Two famous monuments in the United States are Mount Rushmore and the Statue of Liberty. Mount Rushmore is located in South Dakota and is ____________ of four United States presidents etched into the ____________ of the tallest peak in the Black Hills. The four presidents represented are George Washington, Thomas Jefferson, Theodore Roosevelt, and Abraham Lincoln. The monument was conceived by Doane Robinson, who was trying to think of a way to ____________ to the Black Hills region. A sculptor by the name of Gutzon Borglum and four hundred workers completed Mount Rushmore in 1941. The Statue of Liberty is a monument of a woman wearing a robe and crown while ____________ and a flaming torch. She was given to the Americans by the French in 1884 as a ____________ and goodwill. One of its designers was Alexandre Gustave Eiffel, the same man who designed the Eiffel Tower in Paris, France. The Statue of Liberty is made of ____________ and stands on an island in the middle of New York Harbor.

Exercise 4 Listen to part of a lecture in a history class. Then, answer the questions.

07-13

History

1 What can be inferred about early Greek tyrants?

Ⓐ They were not supported by the poor.
Ⓑ They were supported by the elite they opposed.
Ⓒ They were opposed by the elite.
Ⓓ They ruled without any problems.

2 What is the lecture mainly about?

Ⓐ The history of Greek democracy
Ⓑ Tyrants in ancient Greece
Ⓒ Greek monarchies
Ⓓ The history of populists

3 According to the professor, what type of government was originally used in Greek cities?

Ⓐ Tyrannical governments
Ⓑ Monarchical governments
Ⓒ Democratic governments
Ⓓ Constitutional governments

Words & Phrases

brutal adj savage or cruel
aristocrat n a person born of nobility
conjure v to make something appear by magic; to produce
negative adj unfavorable
lofty adj elevated in style or tone
aspiration n a strong desire
appealing adj attracting interest or desire
rural adj of the country; not of the city
connotation n the associated meaning of a word

Summary Note

A Listen to the lecture again and fill in the blanks to complete the lecture notes.

- Professor describes ❶ ______________ in ancient Greece
  - Past definition is different from current one
  - Aristocrats secured power by ❷ ______________
  - Was during ❸ ______________
- Describes ancient Greece
  - Democracy was starting
  - Mostly ❹ ______________
  - Aristocrats ❺ ______________ them
- Mentions ❻ ______________
  - Type of tyrant
  - Tried to stand up for ❼ ______________
  - Wanted ❽ ______________

B Complete the following summary with the words given below.

known as populists	unjust exercising	mistreated
poor people	was to bribe them	absolute ruler

The term tyranny is defined as the ______________ of power by one ______________ over a group of people. Although the current term has negative connotations, the first tyrants were not harsh rulers but were in fact a group of aristocrats ______________ who wished to represent the ______________ who were being undervalued and ______________ by the elite. Some of these populists gained control and became known as tyrants because their method of amassing support from the poor or slaves ______________ with money or promises of freedom.

Integrated Listening & Speaking

A Listen to a different version of a previous lecture on American history and say the answers out loud. You can refer to the summary note below.

07-14

American History

Summary Note

- Professor mentions Mount Rushmore
  - – In South Dakota
  - – Sculptures of four U.S. presidents
  - – Made to increase tourism
  - – Took fourteen years to finish
- Professor discusses Statue of Liberty
  - – Woman in robe wearing crown
  - – Given to U.S. by France
  - – In New York Harbor
  - – Has many symbols
  - – Very recognizable American icon

1 In what U.S. state is Mount Rushmore located?

2 What does Mount Rushmore represent?

3 The Statue of Liberty is a statue of a woman. What two things is she holding?

B **Listen to a different version of a previous lecture on history and say the answers out loud. You can refer to the summary note below.**

07-15

History

Summary Note

- Professor describes tyranny in ancient Greece
  - Past definition is different from current one
  - Aristocrats secured power by helping poor
  - Was during archaic period
- Describes ancient Greece
  - Democracy was starting
  - Mostly monarchies
  - Aristocrats overthrew them
- Mentions populists
  - Type of tyrant
  - Tried to stand up for poor people
  - Wanted equal representation

1 How did tyrants gain the support of the poor or slaves?

2 In what way did tyrants evolve so that today's definition of them is no longer seen as positive?

3 Where did tyranny originate?

Mini TOEFL iBT Practice Test

Listen to part of a conversation between a student and a professor.

07-16

1 Why does the student visit the professor?

- (A) To ask about a trip to Egypt
- (B) To talk about a recent class
- (C) To request that he be her advisor
- (D) To discuss her term paper

2 What is the professor's attitude toward the student?

- (A) He is very complimentary toward her.
- (B) He is hesitant to accept her opinion.
- (C) He is a bit impatient with her.
- (D) He is generous to her.

3 What does the professor imply about majoring in archaeology?

- (A) It can be an expensive hobby to have.
- (B) It limits the jobs some people can get.
- (C) It lets people travel abroad very often.
- (D) It requires people to study languages.

4 What can be inferred about the student?

- (A) She has studied several ancient languages.
- (B) She is having trouble learning hieroglyphics.
- (C) She has visited a foreign country in the past.
- (D) She believes she can get permission to go to Egypt.

5 What will the student do the next time she visits the professor?
Click on 2 answers.

- (A) Give him a form to sign
- (B) Submit her most recent assignment
- (C) Let him know about the summer project
- (D) Show him a paper to review

Listen to part of a lecture in an education class.

07-17

Education

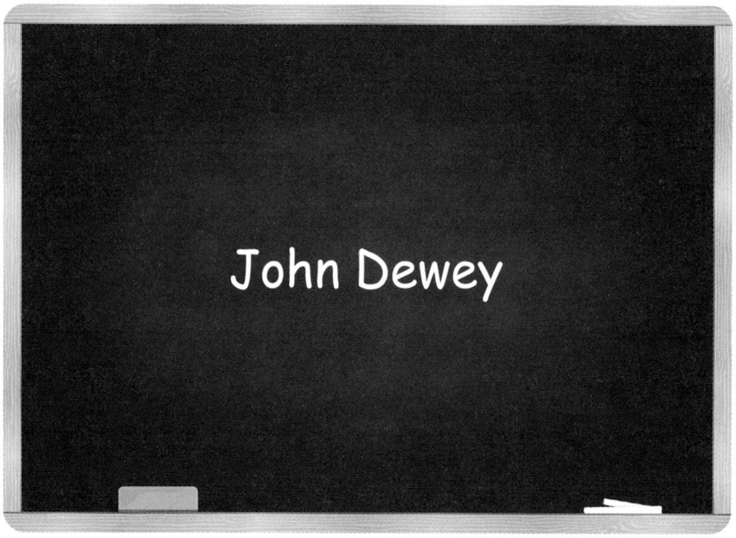

6 What aspect of John Dewey does the professor mainly discuss?

Ⓐ His personal life

Ⓑ His teaching philosophy

Ⓒ His connections with educational progressives

Ⓓ His five-step approach to learning

7 What does the professor imply about John Dewey's philosophy of progressive education?

Ⓐ It is better than the rote learning teaching philosophy.

Ⓑ It is not a good teaching philosophy and is best forgotten.

Ⓒ It is an outdated philosophy of education.

Ⓓ The history of his philosophy is not important.

8 According to the professor, what is one way that humans can learn better?

Ⓐ By participating in real-life activities

Ⓑ By memorizing information

Ⓒ By using different tools to help them learn

Ⓓ By doing both memorization and various activities

9 Why does the professor explain educational progressivism?

Ⓐ To describe Dewey's five-step process for learning

Ⓑ To explain Dewey's thoughts on how people learn best

Ⓒ To summarize Dewey's philosophy of education

Ⓓ To connect it with Dewey's personal biography

10 According to John Dewey's philosophy, what would be the best way to learn how to make a pancake?

Ⓐ Listen to a teacher recite the ingredients and recipe

Ⓑ Gather the ingredients and recipe and try to make a pancake

Ⓒ Listen to a lecture about pancakes given by an actual chef

Ⓓ Buy quality ingredients in order to try to make pancakes

11 Listen again to part of the lecture. Then answer the question.
What does the student imply when she says this: 🎧

Ⓐ Dewey copied the laboratory processes for his learning approaches.

Ⓑ She does not need to learn this since she studied it in the laboratory.

Ⓒ She was not aware she has already been using Dewey's methods.

Ⓓ The laboratory process is much simpler than the methods Dewey used.

Vocabulary Check-Up

A Choose and write the correct words that match the definitions.

1 mitigate	•	• Ⓐ	to convince
2 toxic	•	• Ⓑ	trying too hard to persuade someone to do something; self-assertive
3 impending	•	• Ⓒ	something that causes discomfort or trouble
4 persuade	•	• Ⓓ	to stuff with food
5 inconvenience	•	• Ⓔ	very interesting
6 upgrade	•	• Ⓕ	to recognize as different
7 workload	•	• Ⓖ	a person traveling for pleasure
8 conjure	•	• Ⓗ	to reduce; to make less harmful or painful
9 visage	•	• Ⓘ	an improvement or increase
10 distinguish	•	• Ⓙ	happening or coming soon
11 tourist	•	• Ⓚ	poisonous
12 connotation	•	• Ⓛ	the associated meaning of a word
13 gorge	•	• Ⓜ	the face
14 fascinating	•	• Ⓝ	to make something appear by magic; to produce
15 pushy	•	• Ⓞ	the amount of work a person has or does

B Choose the correct words that match the descriptions.

Ⓐ Mount Rushmore Ⓑ progressive education Ⓒ excavation Ⓓ inhibition Ⓔ tyrant

1 This is a philosophy of teaching and learning that emphasizes a hands-on approach and integration into society.

2 This is a monument in South Dakota that features the sculpted faces of four American presidents.

3 This concept defines what happens when the brain stops the body from reacting instinctively.

4 This was a type of ruler that gained support from the poor by promising them money.

5 This is a dig that archaeologists do to try to unearth ancient artifacts.

UNIT

08 Making Inferences

Overview

Introduction

In order to answer these questions correctly, you must come to conclusions based upon facts given in the listening passage. You must take the information given and determine a future outcome. These questions may ask about various things like a simple process, a cause and effect, or a comparison and contrast.

Question Types

- What does the professor imply about X?
- What will the student probably do next?
- What can be inferred about X?
- What does the professor imply when he says this: (replay)

Useful Tips

- Try to come to a conclusion about the details you hear while you are taking notes.
- Try to generalize about the information you hear.
- Think about what is implied by the speakers.
- Concentrate on answer choices that use words which do not appear in the passage.

Sample TOEFL iBT Question

Script

08-01

M Student: Professor Yeltsin, here's my term paper for your psychology 304 class.

W Professor: Thank you, Reggie, but you know it's three days late. It was due on Monday, and today is Thursday. You're going to lose points for that.

M: I'm really sorry, ma'am, but I just got out of the hospital. I was admitted on Saturday morning and was released only a couple of hours ago. I had no way to get you the paper until now.

W: Oh, that's terrible. Are you okay now?

M: Yes, ma'am. I'm much better. Here's a note from my doctor explaining the problem.

W: Hmm . . . Okay. Thanks for letting me have this. It's all right that you didn't turn it in on time. Don't worry about it.

Q What can be inferred about the student?

Ⓐ He missed taking a test in the professor's class.
Ⓑ He will not lose any points for being late.
Ⓒ He has to return to the hospital soon.
Ⓓ He cannot attend class for the rest of the semester.

☑ Correct Answer

The correct answer is Ⓑ. The professor tells the student he will lose points for turning in the paper late. After he shows her the note from the doctor, she says that it is all right that he did not turn the paper in on time and that he should not worry about it. So it can be inferred that the student will not lose any points for being late.

Basic Drill

Listen to parts of conversations or lectures and answer the questions.

Drill 1

08-02

Q What will the student probably do next?

Ⓐ Rewrite her paper for the professor
Ⓑ Return to her dormitory room
Ⓒ Print some research documents
Ⓓ Find some books for her term paper

Check-Up

Listen again and fill in the blanks with the correct words.

M Professor: Janet, I need you to rewrite ______________ you submitted on Tuesday.

W Student: Rewrite it? What did I do wrong?

M: You failed to ______________ in your paper.

W: Really? I ______________ writing one.

M: Apparently, you remember incorrectly. You had ______________, and the body of your paper was quite good, but then it just ended. There was no paragraph ______________.

W: Hmm . . . Would you mind if I looked at the paper for a minute, please?

M: Not at all . . . Here you are.

W: Oh . . . Oh, no. I see what happened. I ______________ the last page of the paper. I can go back to my dorm, print it, and ______________. Is that all right?

M: Sure. That's fine. ______________ from time to time.

W: Thanks so much, sir. I'll be back in around thirty or forty minutes.

Drill 2

Q What does the woman imply about the student?

Ⓐ He needs to improve his grades this semester.
Ⓑ He did not bring all of the necessary information.
Ⓒ He should consider majoring in a different subject.
Ⓓ He will probably receive some financial aid.

08-03

Check-Up Listen again and fill in the blanks with the correct words.

M Student: Hello. My name is Brad Welker. I ______________ with you for 3:30.

W Financial Aid Office Employee: It's a pleasure to meet you, Mr. Welker. Please come in and ______________.

M: Thank you very much. I appreciate it.

W: So . . . what kind of ______________ are you looking for?

M: Well, as you know, ______________ is going up next semester. ______________, and it's hard for my family to support me. I have three younger sisters, so my parents are trying to ______________.

W: I see. About ______________ financial aid are you looking for?

M: Around two thousand dollars would be great. I brought along all of my family's ______________ so that you can look at it. ______________ are good, too. I have a 3.74 GPA.

W: That's a very impressive GPA. You must ______________.

M: I do my best. I want to be successful so that I can ______________ all the money they've spent on me.

W: I like your attitude. Let me look at ______________ you've provided. I'm pretty sure that we will be able to help you out ______________ you mentioned. I'll call you back in ______________.

M: That sounds perfect. Thank you very much.

Drill 3

Q What can be inferred about the professor?

Ⓐ She is showing students actual meteorological devices.
Ⓑ She has never used some of the tools before.
Ⓒ She is meeting the students for the first time.
Ⓓ She expects the students to take good notes in class.

08-04

Check-Up **Listen again and fill in the blanks with the correct words.**

W Professor: Good morning, everyone. My name is Professor Powell. This semester, I'll be teaching you ______________. I hope we can all learn a lot in this class.

Now, uh, meteorologists have ______________ that we use to measure the weather. I'd like you to ______________ as I explain them to you. I'm going to talk about them in every class, so you must ______________. Please take a look up here at the screen as I'll show you some pictures of ______________ in our endeavors.

The first is something I'm sure ______________: the thermometer. This simple device ______________. That is, it tells us how ______________ the conditions are in a place. Next is this device, which is a barometer. It ______________, which is quite useful for telling when it's going to rain or snow or if ______________ is coming. An anemometer is a device that measures ______________. You can see it here . . . And a weather vane, which I'm sure everyone has seen on the tops of barns, tells us the direction that ______________. Here's one you may not know . . . It's a hygrometer. This device measures ______________ in the air. And a rain gauge tells us ______________ has fallen. Those are ______________. Let me show you some ______________ now.

Drill 4

Q What does the professor imply about ancient Egyptian art?

Ⓐ It was well made to have survived thousands of years.
Ⓑ It included pottery and sculptures.
Ⓒ It had less variety than Western art.
Ⓓ It depicted people realistically.

08-05

Check-Up Listen again and fill in the blanks with the correct words.

M Professor: Some of ______________ other than cave paintings comes from Egypt. I'm referring, of course, to the Egyptian art which can be seen in the ruins of old buildings as well as ______________. Some of the oldest art ever found in Egypt ______________ around 5,000 years ago.

There are ______________ about ancient Egyptian art that I'm sure most of you have seen but may not ______________ much attention to. Take a look at this picture here . . . and this one . . . and this one . . . You all saw that the paintings were ______________, right? Now . . . how were they similar? First, each character in the pictures was ______________. That means you can only ______________. The pose each character was making ______________, too, wasn't it? And you only saw one eye. Finally, each picture was ______________. The Egyptians never learned how to give the appearance of ______________ in their paintings. Or, uh, if they did learn it, they ______________.

Interestingly, this style of art ______________ for thousands of years. Think about all of the ______________ that have taken place in the Western world. Hmm . . . Wait. ______________ the different styles there were in the 1900s. There were Cubism . . . Dadaism . . . Impressionism, Art Deco, Pop Art, and numerous others. But for thousands of years, Egyptian art simply ______________.

Exercises with Long Conversations

Exercise 1 Listen to part of a conversation between a student and a bookstore employee. Then, answer the questions.

08-06

Service Encounter

1 What will the student probably do next?

- (A) Look for a used bookstore
- (B) Accept money from the woman
- (C) Buy some books online
- (D) Search for a book that he wants

2 Why does the student visit the bookstore?

- (A) To purchase some new textbooks
- (B) To return some textbooks he bought
- (C) To look for a new novel to read
- (D) To sell back some of his textbooks

3 According to the woman, why does the bookstore avoid buying some textbooks?
Click on 2 answers.

- (A) The books are in poor condition.
- (B) A newer edition is coming out.
- (C) It already has too many books.
- (D) Students rarely buy the books.

Words & Phrases

warning (n) an advisory about something bad
desire (v) to want
inventory (n) the goods that a business has in stock
in luck (phr) lucky; fortunate
refuse (v) not to agree to do something; to reject
pile (n) a stack; several things on top of one another
rather (adv) somewhat; quite

Summary Note

A Listen to the conversation again and fill in the blanks to complete the conversation notes.

- Student goes to ❶ ________________
  - Wants to sell ❷ ________________
  - Doesn't need them anymore
- Woman says bookstore might ❸ ________________ them
  - Will not buy ❹ ________________
  - Will not buy if too many books in ❺ ________________
- Woman checks books
  - Will pay ❻ ________________ for some books
  - Cannot take other books
- Student agrees to offer

B Complete the following summary with the words given below.

a publishing company	sixty dollars	buy back books
the old edition	a huge stack	half price

The student visits the bookstore with ________________ of books. They are textbooks that he does not need anymore, so he wants to sell them. The woman says that the bookstore sometimes does not ________________, and when it does buy them, the prices are not high. The student asks why the bookstore does not buy books at times. The student responds that if ________________ is making a new edition, the bookstore will not buy ________________. In addition, if it has too many of a certain textbook in stock, it will not buy more of them. The woman checks one book and says the bookstore will give the student ________________ for that. She thinks it is a good offer. Then, she scans all of the books and offers him ________________ for some. She cannot buy the others. The student agrees to her offer.

Exercise 2 Listen to part of a conversation between a student and a residential assistant. Then, answer the questions.

08-07

Service Encounter

1 Listen again to part of the conversation. Then answer the question.
What does the student imply when he says this:

(A) He has not yet received any grades.
(B) He does not have to declare a major yet.
(C) He has never experienced a quiet period.
(D) He is living in the freshman dormitory.

2 What does the student imply about his roommate?

(A) He studies hard most of the time.
(B) He is going to graduate this year.
(C) He usually visits the library to study.
(D) He likes to play music in his room.

3 Why does the student mention Eddie and Lewis?

(A) To say that he is good friends with both of them
(B) To claim that they make the most noise of everyone
(C) To indicate that they will not enjoy the quiet period
(D) To point out their location to the woman

Words & Phrases

flyer n a poster, usually advertising or announcing something
disturb v to bother; to annoy
chat n an informal talk
precisely adv exactly
emphasize v to stress
beneficial adj helpful
uninterrupted adj unbroken

Summary Note

A Listen to the conversation again and fill in the blanks to complete the conversation notes.

- Student asks about ❶ ______________ for quiet period
- Happens during ❷ ______________ period
- Students must be ❸ ______________
  - Cannot ❹ ______________ others
  - No making loud noises
- Loud period from seven to eight PM
- Loud students get fined or talk to ❺ ______________
- Student is ❻ ______________ so should be fine

B Complete the following summary with the words given below.

midterm exam	student's roommate	he is quiet
get fined	a flyer	avoid disturbing

The student asks the residential assistant about ______________ he saw. It provided information about a quiet period that is going to happen during the ______________ period. Because he is a freshman, he does not know about it. The woman says that it starts two days before midterm exams and finishes when the last exam ends. All students must be quiet to ______________ other students. There should be no yelling, shouting, singing, listening to music, or playing musical instruments. The woman will talk to the ______________ since he is a musician. From seven to eight PM every day, students can make as much noise as they want. Students who make noise during the quiet period will ______________ and may have to talk to the dean of students. The woman says that the student should be fine since ______________, but other students may have difficulty during this time.

Exercise 3 Listen to part of a conversation between a student and a professor. Then, answer the questions.

08-08

Office Hours

1 What can be inferred about the professor?

Ⓐ She is familiar enough with the student to know his family finances.
Ⓑ She is fluent in several different European languages.
Ⓒ She encourages international relations majors to study abroad.
Ⓓ She wants to meet the student again later in the week.

2 What is the professor's opinion of the student's schedule for next semester?

Ⓐ She thinks he needs another class in his major.
Ⓑ She believes his classes are too easy.
Ⓒ She says his schedule is very difficult.
Ⓓ She approves of the classes he chose.

3 Where does the professor think the student should go?

Ⓐ To China
Ⓑ To Germany
Ⓒ To France
Ⓓ To England

Words & Phrases

elective n a class not necessary for a student's major
abroad adv to a foreign country
afford v to have enough money to buy something
firsthand adv through direct observation or personal experience
fluent adj competent in another language

Summary Note

A Listen to the conversation again and fill in the blanks to complete the conversation notes.

- Professor compliments student on choice of classes for ❶ ________________
- Student ❷ ________________ taking classes
- Professor asks student about studying abroad ❸ ________________
- Thinks ❹ ________________ major should go abroad
- Student good at ❺ ________________ and Italian
- Professor suggests going to Germany or Italy
  – Can ❻ ________________ in foreign language
- Student will talk to parents

B Complete the following summary with the words given below.

German and Italian	choice of classes	to his parents
become fluent	studying abroad	international relations

The professor compliments the student on his ________________ to take next semester. The student says that he is looking forward to taking all of the classes. The professor then asks the student if he has considered ________________ during his junior year. The student says he has not thought about it. The professor thinks that since the student is an ________________ major, he should go abroad. She asks what languages he knows, and he says that he is pretty good at ________________. She recommends that he go to Germany or Italy since he will ________________ in either German or Italian when he is there. The student says that he needs to talk ________________ but that he will come back later to talk to the professor.

Exercise 4 Listen to part of a conversation between a student and a professor. Then, answer the questions.

08-09

Office Hours

1 What can be inferred about the student?

(A) She will write a paper to get some extra credit.
(B) She will work hard to improve her grade.
(C) She will complain to the dean about the professor.
(D) She will drop out of the professor's class.

2 Why does the student visit the professor?

(A) To request that she take a test a second time
(B) To inquire about why her grade was bad
(C) To find out when an exam will take place
(D) To ask for some help studying for a test

3 What did the student do on her test?

(A) She got some names wrong on her essay.
(B) She forgot to write some of the answers.
(C) She got confused about some chemical formulas.
(D) She put the correct answers in the wrong blanks.

Words & Phrases

chief adj main; primary
mess up phr to make a mistake; to do something badly
repeat v to do or say again
improve v to do or make better

Summary Note

A Listen to the conversation again and fill in the blanks to complete the conversation notes.

- Student wants to talk about ❶ ______________ on test
- Has never gotten ❷ ______________ before
- Looks at test
  - Wrote correct answers in ❸ ______________
  - Got some ❹ ______________ wrong
- Professor tells her to learn from ❺ ______________
- Still has three tests and ❻ ______________
- Can get an A if does well

B Complete the following summary with the words given below.

wrong blanks	a lot of dates	remaining exams
is upset	low grade	multiple-choice

The student wants to talk about the ______________ she got on an exam. The professor says that he was surprised the grade was so low, so he checked it again. The student wants to see the test because she ______________ about getting a D. She checks the ______________ part and realizes that she had the correct answers but put them in the ______________. Then, on the other part of the test, she got ______________ wrong. She says that she just messed up on the test. The professor tells her to learn from her mistakes and to do well on the three ______________ and paper. He thinks she can get an A in the class if she does well.

Exercises with Long Lectures

Exercise 1 Listen to part of a lecture in an art class. Then, answer the questions.

08-10

Art

1 What can be inferred about the term Eskimo?

(A) Inuit people do not like its usage.
(B) Inuit people came up with the name.
(C) Few people are aware of its meaning.
(D) It was created from an old Inuit word.

2 What will the professor probably do next?

(A) Dismiss the class for the day
(B) Answer a student's question
(C) Talk about Inuit carvings
(D) Go over the midterm exam

3 According to the professor, what material is used to make Inuit carvings?
Click on 2 answers.

(A) Wood
(B) Soapstone
(C) Shells
(D) Serpentine

Words & Phrases

authentic adj real; not artificial
carving n a sculpture
derogatory adj expressing criticism; insulting
flourish v to grow fast and healthily
humorous adj funny
incorporate v to include as part of
miniature adj very small
nomadic adj always moving
perception n a belief as to what is true
primitive adj very old style; simple

Summary Note

A Listen to the lecture again and fill in the blanks to complete the lecture notes.

- Professor discusses ❶ ____________________
  - Live in ❷ ____________________
  - Mostly associated with ❸ ____________________
  - Have many kinds of artwork
- Inuit ❹ ____________________
  - Are becoming commercialized
  - Are miniature carvings
  - Are polished and ❺ ____________________
  - Animal and human subjects
  - Made of many raw materials but not ❻ ____________________

B Complete the following summary with the words given below.

green to black	hold in one's fist	realistic
available from the land	never made of wood	permanent settlements

The Inuit are northern people who live in the Arctic areas of Canada, Alaska, Russia, and Greenland. Inuit art includes sculptures, paintings, and prints. Prior to the 1950s, Inuit carvings were small enough to ____________________. Today, the carvings have become bigger because the Inuit have settled into ____________________ and are trying to satisfy market demand. So there are now miniatures and larger sculptures. In addition, since the 1980s, Inuit carvings have become more polished and ____________________. The subjects of these carvings are usually animals and humans. The animals are bears, seals, whales, walruses, and sometimes birds. Some themes are humorous while others are more serious. A unique characteristic of Inuit carvings is that they are ____________________. The artists use whatever raw materials are ____________________ and sea. The most common substance is a stone called serpentine. It's available in a range of colors from ____________________. Other stones used include marble, quartz, and dolomite.

Exercise 2 Listen to part of a lecture in a meteorology class. Then, answer the questions.

08-11

Meteorology

1 What can be inferred from the lecture?

(A) La Nina seems to be getting worse every year it occurs.
(B) Scientists must learn more about El Nino and La Nina.
(C) The Pacific Ocean has more weather problems than the other oceans.
(D) Peru and Bolivia receive bad weather all year round.

2 Why does the professor mention the Southern Hemisphere?

(A) To respond to a student's inquiry
(B) To say El Nino does not have its origins there
(C) To point out the area that La Nina affects
(D) To note how few landforms it has

3 According to the professor, what is a characteristic of La Nina?

(A) It brings warm water to the coast of South America.
(B) It originates in the Northern Hemisphere.
(C) In winter, it tends to accentuate weather patterns.
(D) It essentially has the same impact as El Nino.

Words & Phrases

accentuate v to emphasize
desert n very dry land
drastically adv severely; seriously
drought n an extended period of dry weather without rain
forecast n a prediction
obliterate v to destroy something completely
originate v to start
meteorologist n a person who studies climate
uncharacteristic adj unusual

Summary Note

A Listen to the lecture again and fill in the blanks to complete the lecture notes.

- Discusses ❶ ....
- Mentions EL Nino
  - Brings ❷ .... to South America
  - Occurs every 5–8 years
  - Reduces ❸ .... in area
  - Can change weather worldwide
- Mentions La Nina
  - Brings ❹ .... to South America
  - Happens ❺ .... as often as El Nino
- Gives ❻ .... effects of El Nino

B Complete the following summary with the words given below.

Pacific Ocean	South America	unusual weather phenomena
water at the surface	the amount of plant life	hurricane development

El Nino and La Nina are weather phenomena that both originate in the Southern Hemisphere and occur in the .... Both cause major temperature changes in the surface waters of the Pacific Ocean and eventually trigger .... worldwide. El Nino brings warm water to the west coast of ...., and La Nina brings cold water to the west coast of South America. The warm water El Nino brings to the coastal waters of Peru rises, replaces the cool nutrient-rich ...., and drastically reduces .... and fish in the area. El Nino causes unusual weather in many different areas, including droughts and severe rainstorms. La Nina contributes to .... and in winter accentuates the climate in certain areas. For example, in winter, it may cause Florida to be warmer and drier than usual.

Exercise 3 Listen to part of a lecture in a writing class. Then, answer the questions.

08-12

Writing

1 What does the professor imply about memoirs?

(A) Anyone can write them.
(B) They are similar to biographies.
(C) They focus on people's entire lives.
(D) It is fun to read them.

2 What will the students probably do next?

(A) Start giving their class presentations
(B) Begin writing their assignment in class
(C) Watch a short video with the professor
(D) Ask the professor some questions

3 Why does the professor mention *Angela's Ashes?*

(A) To describe her impression of it
(B) To claim it is a bestselling memoir
(C) To name a memoir by a regular person
(D) To talk about the events covered in it

Words & Phrases

chronological adj organized according to time
conflict n a fight, disagreement, argument, or war
emotion n a feeling such as happiness, sadness, and anger
essentially adv mainly
hardship n a difficult time; a difficult experience
interview v to ask questions to get information
flashback n a quick memory from the past
foreshadow n a hint as to what might happen in the future
in retrospect phr looking back in time
significant adj important

Summary Note

A Listen to the lecture again and fill in the blanks to complete the lecture notes.

- Professor gives assignment to ❶ ____________
- Explains ❷ ____________
  - Account of another person's life
  - Autobiography describes ❸ ____________
- Describes memoir
  - Does not need much research like ❹ ____________
  - Has narrow focus
  - About important part of one's life
  - Usually written by ❺ ____________
  - Is in ❻ ____________ form

B Complete the following summary with the words given below.

a lot of research	an autobiography	a public figure
a part of someone's life	a detailed story	military leaders

A biography is an account of another person's life rather than one's own. An autobiography is ____________ of one's own life, usually from childhood to old age. It is a chronological, detailed, personal history that requires ____________ and interviews. A memoir, however, is a type of autobiography which focuses on only ____________. The writer merely needs to recall some events that occurred in his or her life. No research is required. It is usually shorter than ____________. It focuses on events that are significant to the writer. If the person is ____________, then that person writes his or her recollections and emotions regarding some of the important public events of his or her life. Historically, they were written by world leaders, politicians, ____________, and other famous people, but that is changing nowadays.

Exercise 4 Listen to part of a lecture in a geology class. Then, answer the questions.

08-13

Geology

1 What can be inferred about the lithosphere?

- (A) It is found deep within the Earth.
- (B) It is the largest part of the Earth.
- (C) It changes appearance rapidly.
- (D) It includes both land and water.

2 Why does the professor mention puzzle globes?

- (A) To make a comparison using them
- (B) To suggest that the students buy them
- (C) To show how the Earth's plates move
- (D) To point out a problem with plate tectonics

3 According to the professor, what will happen to the core in the future?

- (A) It will grow much larger in size.
- (B) It will stop being so hot.
- (C) It will make tectonic plates move more.
- (D) It will begin to cause more earthquakes.

Words & Phrases

churn (v) to move violently
core (n) the center part of object
fluid (n) a liquid
generate (v) to create movement of action
glide (n) a smooth, sliding motion
stabilize (v) to stop moving; to stop changing

Summary Note

A Listen to the lecture again and fill in the blanks to complete the lecture notes.

- Describes ❶ ______________
  - Earth's exterior: ❷ ______________
  - Includes continents, rocks, and ❸ ______________
  - Like a giant puzzle
- Describes asthenosphere
  - Is semi-plastic ❹ ______________
  - Is fluid
  - Causes ❺ ______________ to move
- Describes plate tectonics
  - Causes ❻ ______________
  - Makes mountains
  - 7 major and 12 minor plates

B Complete the following summary with the words given below.

Earth's exterior	slide along	seven major plates
the upper part	a few inches	the extremely hot interior

The lithosphere is the ______________. It is the crust, which includes the continents, the rocks, and the ocean floor. It also includes ______________ of the asthenosphere, which is located just below the crust. On the continents, the crust is about eighty kilometers deep, but below the ocean, it is about five kilometers thick. The exterior of the Earth is like many pieces broken into giant plates that fit together like a jigsaw puzzle. These pieces are called tectonic plates. The continents rest on these plates. They ______________ the upper part of the asthenosphere, which consists of a semi-plastic molten rock material. It is more fluid and moves as it responds to the churning motions of ______________ of the Earth below. These movements in the asthenosphere cause the tectonic plates to move as they glide or float on the moving asthenosphere. There are ______________ and twelve minor plates. Because the plates only move ______________ a year, it takes millions of years for the continents to move. But at one time, the continents were mostly connected.

Integrated Listening & Speaking

A Listen to a different version of a previous lecture on art and say the answers out loud. You can refer to the summary note below.

08-14

Art

Summary Note

- Professor discusses Inuit art
  - – Live in Arctic areas
  - – Mostly associated with Canada
  - – Have many kinds of artwork
- Inuit sculptures
  - – Becoming commercialized
  - – Are miniature carvings
  - – Are polished and realistic
  - – Animal and human subjects
  - – Made of many raw materials but not wood

1 What are traditional Inuit sculptures like?

2 Where do most Inuit live?

3 What are Inuit carvings made of?

B Listen to a different version of a previous lecture on writing and say the answers out loud. You can refer to the summary note below.

08-15

Writing

Summary Note

- Professor gives assignment to write memoir
- Explains biography
  - – Account of another person's life
  - – Autobiography describes writer's own life
- Describes memoir
  - – Does not need much research like autobiography
  - – Has narrow focus
  - – About important part of one's life
  - – Usually written by important people
  - – Is in narrative form

1 What is the main difference between autobiographies and memoirs?

2 How much research is required to write a memoir?

3 Historically, what kinds of people wrote memoirs?

Mini TOEFL iBT Practice Test

Listen to part of a conversation between a student and a gym employee.

08-16

1 Why does the student visit the gym?

(A) To pay his membership fee
(B) To lift some weights
(C) To ask about the swimming pool
(D) To inquire about its usage

2 According to the student, what happened at his previous school?

(A) He had to pay several hundred dollars to join the gym.
(B) He was allowed to use all the facilities for free.
(C) He could use the basketball court when the team was not there.
(D) He was robbed once while he was exercising.

3 What is the woman's attitude toward the student?

(A) She is disinterested in his questions.
(B) She is somewhat aggressive.
(C) She is very patient with him.
(D) She is concerned about his welfare.

4 What can be inferred about the man?

(A) He will visit the gym again.
(B) He will pay for a gym membership.
(C) He wants to continue speaking with the woman.
(D) He enjoys working out every day.

5 Listen again to part of the conversation. Then answer the question.
Why does the woman say this: 🎧

(A) To invite the student to try out for a sports team
(B) To ask the student about his status at the university
(C) To indicate that the student does not get his own locker
(D) To tell the student that he needs to pay a small fee

Listen to part of a lecture in a zoology class.

08-17

Zoology

6 What is the main topic of the lecture?

Ⓐ The types of foods spiders consume
Ⓑ The habitats of various spiders
Ⓒ Some characteristics of spiders
Ⓓ Various species of spiders

7 What can be inferred about spiders?

Ⓐ Most of them try to avoid humans as much as possible.
Ⓑ There are more spiders on the Earth than there are humans.
Ⓒ Scientists have learned little about spiders in recent times.
Ⓓ The vast majority have probably not been discovered yet.

8 According to the professor, where do spiders' webs come from?

Ⓐ They come from their feet and hands.
Ⓑ They come from their tongues.
Ⓒ They come from their spinnerets.
Ⓓ They come from their heads.

9 How does the professor organize the information about spider's silk that she presents to the class?

Ⓐ By explaining the process by which it is formed

Ⓑ By making note of its numerous uses

Ⓒ By listing the species that make use of it

Ⓓ By refuting incorrect information students believe about it

10 According to the professor, which of the following is a use of spider's silk?
Click on 2 answers.

Ⓐ Poisoning their prey

Ⓑ Raising their young

Ⓒ Assisting in molting

Ⓓ Climbing structures

11 Listen again to part of the lecture. Then answer the question.
What does the professor imply when she says this: 🎧

Ⓐ The black widow spider lives in many habitats.

Ⓑ The black widow spider is dangerous to people.

Ⓒ The black widow spider has a powerful bite.

Ⓓ The black widow spider is a large type of spider.

Vocabulary Check-Up

A Choose and write the correct words that match the definitions.

1 fluid	•	• Ⓐ a liquid
2 glide	•	• Ⓑ the central part of an object
3 nomadic	•	• Ⓒ relating to people with no permanent homes
4 chat	•	• Ⓓ a class not necessary for a student's major
5 flourish	•	• Ⓔ to hint about what will happen in the future
6 derogatory	•	• Ⓕ to slide smoothly
7 inventory	•	• Ⓖ expressing criticism; insulting
8 obliterate	•	• Ⓗ to destroy something completely
9 foreshadow	•	• Ⓘ an informal talk
10 authentic	•	• Ⓙ real and genuine
11 elective	•	• Ⓚ to grow well
12 mess up	•	• Ⓛ a person who studies the climate
13 core	•	• Ⓜ through direct observation or personal experience
14 meteorologist	•	• Ⓝ to make a mistake; to do something badly
15 firsthand	•	• Ⓞ the goods that a business has in stock

B Choose the correct words that match the descriptions.

Ⓐ lithosphere　Ⓑ Inuit　Ⓒ spiders　Ⓓ memoir　Ⓔ El Nino

1 This is a type of autobiography which describes only a part of a person's life. ....

2 These people live in the Arctic. They produce various forms of art including many carvings. ....

3 This weather phenomenon brings warm water to the west coast of South America and causes strange weather all over the world. ....

4 This is the seventh most diverse species in the world and uses silk to capture and kill prey. ....

5 This part of the Earth includes the crust, the continents, the ocean floor, the tectonic plates, and the upper part of the asthenosphere. ....

Actual
Test

Actual Test 01

CONTINUE VOLUME

Listening Section Directions

09-01

This section measures your ability to understand conversations and lectures in English.

The Listening section is divided into separately timed parts. In each part, you will listen to 1 conversation and 1 or 2 lectures. You will hear each conversation or lecture only **one** time.

After each conversation and lecture, you will answer questions about it. The questions typically ask about the main idea and supporting details. Some questions ask about a speaker's purpose or attitude. Answer the questions based on what is stated or implied by the speakers.

You may take notes while you listen. You may use your notes to help you answer the questions. Your notes will not be scored.

If you need to change the volume while you listen, click on the **Volume** icon at the top of the screen.

In some questions, you will see this icon: 🎧 This means that you will hear, but not see, part of the question.

Some of the questions have special directions. These directions appear in a gray box on the screen.

Most questions are worth 1 point. If a question is worth more than 1 point, it will have special directions that indicate how many points you can receive.

A clock at the top of the screen will show you how much time is remaining. The clock will not count down while you are listening. The clock will count down only while you are answering the questions.

PART 1

CONTINUE VOLUME

Listening Directions

09-02

In this part, you will listen to 1 conversation and 1 lecture.

You must answer each question. After you answer click on **Next**. Then click on **OK** to confirm your answer and go on to the next question. After you click on **OK**, you cannot return to previous questions.

You may now begin this part of the Listening section. You will have **7 minutes** to answer the questions.

Click on **Continue** to go on.

VOLUME

09-03

1 Why does the student visit the laboratory assistant?

(A) To get some assistance with an experiment
(B) To ask her where a professor is
(C) To have her unlock a door for him
(D) To find out where a laboratory is located

2 What does the student show the laboratory assistant?

(A) A note from a professor
(B) A certificate of achievement
(C) His student ID card
(D) His notebook for a class

3 What rule does the laboratory assistant tell the student?
Click on 2 answers.

(A) He must lock the door when he leaves the laboratory.
(B) He must replace any equipment that he breaks.
(C) He must avoid spilling any chemicals on the floor.
(D) He must clean up after he finishes in the laboratory.

4 What is the laboratory assistant's attitude toward the student?

(A) She is mostly unwilling to help the student.
(B) She is eager to help the student with his project.
(C) She wants the student to apologize for interrupting her.
(D) She feels that the student knows how to use the laboratory.

5 Listen again to part of the conversation. Then answer the question.
What is the purpose of the student's response?

(A) To say he has the equipment
(B) To acknowledge his agreement
(C) To agree to open the door
(D) To apologize for his comment

VOLUME

09-04

Psychology

6 What is the main topic of the lecture?

(A) Adolescent and adult lives
(B) The basis of attachment theory
(C) The work of John Bowlby
(D) The Harlow experiments

7 In the lecture, the professor describes a number of facts about affectional bonds. Indicate whether each of the following is a fact about affectional bonds.
Click in the correct box for each sentence.

	Fact	Not a Fact
1 It involves a relationship that is emotionally insignificant.		
2 The individual who formed the bond wants to remain physically close to the person with whom he has bonded.		
3 It is persistent rather than transitory.		
4 The individual will become happy when separated from the person with whom the bond was formed.		

8 Why does the professor explain Bowlby's scientific work?

(A) To explain its importance in establishing attachment theory
(B) To say that Bolby was a famous scientist
(C) To mention that Bolby was the first to work on rhesus monkeys
(D) To show that deep-seeded attachments are important to understand

9 What is the professor's opinion of the Harlow experiments?

Ⓐ They were not as significant as the work conducted by John Bowlby.
Ⓑ They were unethical because they mistreated rhesus monkeys.
Ⓒ They were important because they involved monkeys.
Ⓓ They were important because they could not be done on humans.

10 What can be inferred about rhesus monkeys?

Ⓐ They are kind creatures in general.
Ⓑ They will act normally if raised apart from their mothers.
Ⓒ They do not like being used in scientific experiments.
Ⓓ They have some similarities to humans.

11 What will the professor probably do next?

Ⓐ Confirm that the students understand the information
Ⓑ Continue talking about a similar topic
Ⓒ Ask the students to conduct a small experiment
Ⓓ Give the students a quiz to test their knowledge

PART 2

CONTINUE VOLUME

Listening Directions

09-05

In this part, you will listen to 1 conversation and 2 lectures.

You must answer each question. After you answer click on **Next**. Then click on **OK** to confirm your answer and go on to the next question. After you click on **OK**, you cannot return to previous questions.

You may now begin this part of the Listening section. You will have **10 minutes** to answer the questions.

Click on **Continue** to go on.

VOLUME

09-06

1 Why did the professor ask to see the student?

- (A) To ask her about her progress in his class
- (B) To give her a new topic to write about
- (C) To go over a story that she wrote line by line
- (D) To provide some feedback on an assignment

2 What is the professor's attitude toward the student?

- (A) He is pleased with her pleasant attitude.
- (B) He finds her to be a bit abrupt in her behavior.
- (C) He is complimentary of her punctuality.
- (D) He approves of her disinterest in idle chitchat.

3 What does the professor say about the student's story?
Click on 2 answers.

- (A) It has a large number of grammar mistakes.
- (B) It has sentences that are well written.
- (C) It was double the length he requested.
- (D) It was a very creative work.

4 What does the student imply about her story?

- (A) It contains almost all exposition.
- (B) It involves some aspects of the supernatural.
- (C) It is based in a fantasy world.
- (D) It could use better dialogue between characters.

5 What will the student probably do next?

- (A) Conduct a science experiment
- (B) Do a freewriting project
- (C) Continue talking to the professor
- (D) Give a presentation in her literature class

VOLUME

09-07

Environmental Science

6 What is the main topic of the lecture?

(A) Different forms of pollution
(B) Different forms of water pollution
(C) Different forms of water diseases
(D) Different forms of air pollution

7 What does the professor imply about nature?

(A) It takes thousands of years to eliminate pollution.
(B) It has been entirely overwhelmed by manmade pollution.
(C) It can heal damage caused by natural disasters.
(D) It will never improve due to the actions of humans.

8 How does the professor describe the worldwide pollution situation?

(A) It is slowly but surely improving.
(B) It is not as bad as it was ten years ago.
(C) It is the leading cause of death.
(D) It does not receive enough press.

9 Why does the professor discuss pollution's effect on fish?

(A) To show how it can deplete an important food source

(B) To show how it can attack weaker species

(C) To show how it affects every step of the food chain

(D) To show how fish have built up immunity against it

10 What will the professor probably do next?

(A) Assign the students a group project

(B) Show the students a short video

(C) Talk to the students about their exam

(D) Answer any questions the students have

11 Listen again to part of the lecture. Then answer the question.
What does the professor mean when he says this: 🎧

(A) The student understands correctly.

(B) The student should think again.

(C) The student needs to consider all options.

(D) The student made a wrong assumption.

VOLUME

09-08

Archaeology

12 What is the main topic of the lecture?

(A) The ancient Egyptians
(B) Archaeological evidence
(C) Radiocarbon dating
(D) Willard Libby

13 What can be inferred about the professor?

(A) He is not confident in his lecture notes.
(B) He is worried the lecture might be too difficult.
(C) He is excited about the students' expertise.
(D) He wishes he had chosen a different topic.

14 What is a half-life?

(A) The time expected for carbon to be depleted from a sample
(B) The time it takes for half of the carbon to disappear from a sample
(C) The time it takes for carbon to multiply in a given sample
(D) The time it takes for carbon to thrive in a given sample

15 According to the professor, why is carbon so helpful in the dating process?

- (A) It is a universal element of the life cycle.
- (B) Its atoms are easily identifiable.
- (C) It is found in dinosaurs.
- (D) Its half-life is more easily measurable than nitrogen.

16 What resulted from Willard Libby's discovery?

- (A) It became easier to date specimens older than 70,000 years.
- (B) It created a lot of controversy among his colleagues.
- (C) It showed that Egyptian culture was much older than originally thought.
- (D) It allowed scientists to be more accurate in determining the ages of objects.

17 How does the professor organize the information about Willard Libby that he presents to the class?

- (A) By covering all of the information in chronological order
- (B) By focusing on the multiple discoveries Willard Libby made
- (C) By stressing the methods used in Willard Libby's experiments
- (D) By asking questions and then answering the questions himself

Actual Test

02

CONTINUE VOLUME

Listening Section Directions

09-09

This section measures your ability to understand conversations and lectures in English.

The Listening section is divided into separately timed parts. In each part, you will listen to 1 conversation and 1 or 2 lectures. You will hear each conversation or lecture only **one** time.

After each conversation and lecture, you will answer questions about it. The questions typically ask about the main idea and supporting details. Some questions ask about a speaker's purpose or attitude. Answer the questions based on what is stated or implied by the speakers.

You may take notes while you listen. You may use your notes to help you answer the questions. Your notes will not be scored.

If you need to change the volume while you listen, click on the **Volume** icon at the top of the screen.

In some questions, you will see this icon: 🎧 This means that you will hear, but not see, part of the question.

Some of the questions have special directions. These directions appear in a gray box on the screen.

Most questions are worth 1 point. If a question is worth more than 1 point, it will have special directions that indicate how many points you can receive.

A clock at the top of the screen will show you how much time is remaining. The clock will not count down while you are listening. The clock will count down only while you are answering the questions.

CONTINUE VOLUME

09-10

Listening Directions

In this part, you will listen to 1 conversation and 1 lecture.

You must answer each question. After you answer click on **Next**. Then click on **OK** to confirm your answer and go on to the next question. After you click on **OK**, you cannot return to previous questions.

You may now begin this part of the Listening section. You will have **7 minutes** to answer the questions.

Click on **Continue** to go on.

VOLUME

09-11

1 Why does the student visit the woman?

Ⓐ To submit a job application
Ⓑ To confirm his hours of employment
Ⓒ To inquire about employment
Ⓓ To complete some paperwork

2 What can be inferred about Mr. Carrington?

Ⓐ He is the owner of a business establishment.
Ⓑ He is good friends with the woman.
Ⓒ He is willing to hire the student.
Ⓓ He is a long-time employee at the school.

3 What kind of experience does the student have?

Ⓐ He worked at a bakery.
Ⓑ He worked at a fast-food restaurant.
Ⓒ He worked at a coffee shop.
Ⓓ He worked at a convenience store.

4 What will the student probably do next?

Ⓐ Respond to the woman's question
Ⓑ Complete some paperwork
Ⓒ Go to speak to Mr. Carrington
Ⓓ Change his course schedule

5 Listen again to part of the conversation. Then answer the question.
What does the woman mean when she says this:

Ⓐ She is willing to give the student the hours he wants.
Ⓑ She hopes that the student will not have any problems.
Ⓒ She thinks that the café sometimes has problems.
Ⓓ She does not agree with the student's proposal.

VOLUME

09-12

Drama

6 What aspect of theater does the professor mainly discuss?

Ⓐ Opposition to theater in the American colonies
Ⓑ The history of American theater
Ⓒ The rise of Broadway in New York
Ⓓ Burlesque shows in the United States

7 How is the discussion organized?

Ⓐ Important people and their lives are covered.
Ⓑ The information is discussed chronologically.
Ⓒ Europe's influence is heavily stressed.
Ⓓ Some plays and their content are described.

8 Why does the professor mention Massachusetts?

Ⓐ To call it one of the first American colonies
Ⓑ To say that plays were banned there in the 1700s
Ⓒ To credit it for the origins of minstrel shows
Ⓓ To claim that many playwrights were educated there

9 Where is the oldest continuously operating theater in the United States?

(A) In Philadelphia
(B) In New York City
(C) In Boston
(D) In New Orleans

10 According to the professor, what influenced modern theater in the United States?
Click on 2 answers.

(A) Burlesque shows
(B) Broadway
(C) Vaudeville
(D) Minstrel shows

11 Listen again to part of the lecture. Then answer the question.
Why does the student say this: 🎧

(A) To agree with the professor's remark
(B) To express his surprise at the professor's comment
(C) To ask the professor to provide more information
(D) To show that he doubts the statement the professor made

PART 2

CONTINUE VOLUME

Listening Directions

09-13

In this part, you will listen to 1 conversation and 2 lectures.

You must answer each question. After you answer click on **Next**. Then click on **OK** to confirm your answer and go on to the next question. After you click on **OK**, you cannot return to previous questions.

You may now begin this part of the Listening section. You will have **10 minutes** to answer the questions.

Click on **Continue** to go on.

VOLUME

09- 14

1 Why does the student visit the professor?

(A) To ask him to let her change groups
(B) To get help choosing a leader for her group
(C) To complain about the topic that she was assigned
(D) To get some advice concerning a project

2 What problem does the student have?

(A) Her group has not made any progress.
(B) She believes she will get a poor grade.
(C) Her understanding of the material is low.
(D) She believes the class is too hard for her.

3 According to the professor, how can the student benefit by taking his advice?
Click on 2 answers.

(A) She will develop more confidence.
(B) She will learn managerial skills.
(C) She will get a higher grade.
(D) She will learn more about the topic.

4 What will the student probably do next?

(A) Begin preparing for the exam
(B) Ask the professor more questions
(C) Speak to the other group members
(D) Select a topic for her group

5 Listen again to part of the conversation. Then answer the question.
What does the professor imply when he says this:

(A) The student needs to speak more in class.
(B) He wants the student to solve her own problem.
(C) There is not much he can do for the student.
(D) The solution to the problem is obvious.

09-15

Zoology

6 What is the lecture mainly about?

Ⓐ The life cycle of badgers
Ⓑ Habitats of badgers
Ⓒ Hunting practices of badgers
Ⓓ Characteristics of badgers

7 How does the professor organize the information about badgers that she presents to the class?

Ⓐ She only discusses general facts about badgers.
Ⓑ She starts by telling a story about hunter and a badger.
Ⓒ She starts discussing general facts and moves to details about coloring.
Ⓓ She only discusses specific facts about badger coloration.

8 Why does the professor mention the students' textbook?

Ⓐ To tell them to look at a picture in it
Ⓑ To remind them to do the reading
Ⓒ To say that they should bring it to class
Ⓓ To note that the information in it is important

9 In the lecture, the professor describes a number of facts about badgers. Indicate whether each of the following is a fact about badgers.
Click in the correct box for each sentence.

	Fact	Not a Fact
1 They live in underground dwellings.		
2 They are mostly active during the day.		
3 They bear young around the same time of the year.		
4 They prefer to consume various types of vegetation.		

10 Why does the professor explain melanin pigmentation in badgers?

(A) To say that that badgers completely lack melanin
(B) To indicate how badgers build their homes
(C) To state that it can cause harm to many badgers
(D) To show what determines badgers' coloring

11 According to the professor, what will happen next week?

(A) The students will go on a field trip for class.
(B) The professor will give the students a test.
(C) The semester will come to an end.
(D) The students will give their presentations.

VOLUME

09-16

Biology

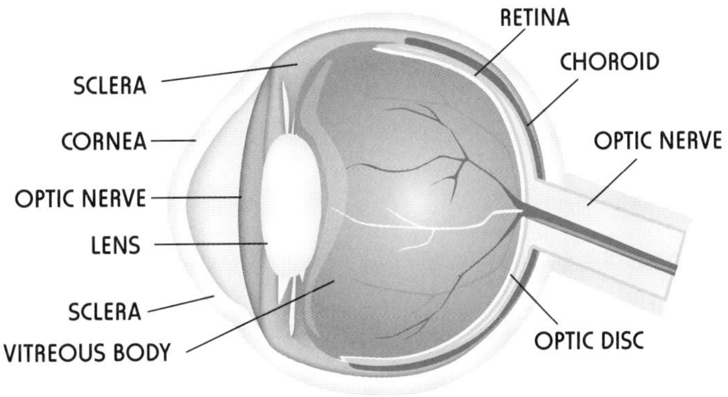

12 What aspect of the eye does the professor mainly discuss?

Ⓐ The lens
Ⓑ The choroid
Ⓒ The hyaloids artery
Ⓓ The zonules of Zinn

13 How is the lecture organized?

Ⓐ The professor shows a chart and then uses it as he lectures.
Ⓑ The professor covers the information in alphabetical order.
Ⓒ The professor describes individual parts of the lens in detail.
Ⓓ The professor responds to questions asked by the students.

14 According to the professor, how does the index gradient affect the optical power of the lens?

Ⓐ By causing damage to it
Ⓑ By decreasing its ability
Ⓒ By causing it to suffer more strain
Ⓓ By enhancing its performance

15 According to the professor, which of the following is the crystalline lens composed of?
Click on 2 answers.

(A) The cortex
(B) The ciliary muscle
(C) The zonules of Zinn
(D) The nucleus

16 Why does the professor explain the process of accommodation?

(A) To say it is important to understand the way the lens ages
(B) To describe it as the most important part of the eye
(C) To mention that the zonules of Zinn are controlled by this process
(D) To state that the lens has too many organelles

17 What can be inferred about the professor?

(A) He understands the difficulty of the material he covered.
(B) He prefers that students email him rather than visit him.
(C) He has performed several eye operations on patients before.
(D) He needs to continue the lecture before the class ends.

Appendix

Mastering Word List

This part provides lists of important vocabulary words in each unit. They are essential words for understanding any academic scripts. Many of the words are listed with their derivative forms so that students can expand their vocabulary in an effective way. These lists can be used as homework assignments.

UNIT 01 Listening for Main Ideas

Step A

- ☐ acidity
- ☐ advise
- ☐ albino
- ☐ anthropology
- ☐ aria
- ☐ bubonic
- ☐ buckwheat
- ☐ cavity
- ☐ clichéd
- ☐ deficiency
- ☐ discrepancy
- ☐ domestication
- ☐ extinct
- ☐ gingivitis
- ☐ habitat
- ☐ hereditary
- ☐ overview
- ☐ registration
- ☐ saliva
- ☐ scavenge
- ☐ soldiering
- ☐ specific
- ☐ speculate
- ☐ subspecies
- ☐ suspension
- ☐ trait
- ☐ trinity

Step B

- ☐ *n.* alphabet
- ☐ *v.* alphabetize
- ☐ *adv.* alphabetically

- ☐ *n.* assistance
- ☐ *v.* assist
- ☐ *adj.* assistive

- ☐ *n.* composer
- ☐ *v.* compose
- ☐ *adj.* composed

- ☐ *n.* consideration
- ☐ *v.* consider
- ☐ *adj.* considerate
- ☐ *adv.* considerately

- ☐ *n.* cultivation
- ☐ *v.* cultivate
- ☐ *adj.* cultivatable

- ☐ *n.* deceiver
- ☐ *v.* deceive
- ☐ *adj.* deceivable
- ☐ *adv.* deceivingly

- ☐ *n.* distribution
- ☐ *v.* distribute
- ☐ *adj.* distributive
- ☐ *adv.* distributively

- ☐ *n.* emphasis
- ☐ *v.* emphasize
- ☐ *adj.* emphatic

- ☐ *n.* individual
- ☐ *adj.* individual
- ☐ *adv.* individually

- ☐ *n.* intonation
- ☐ *v.* intonate
- ☐ *adj.* intonational
- ☐ *adv.* intonationally

- ☐ *n.* poacher
- ☐ *v.* poach
- ☐ *adj.* poachable

- ☐ *n.* rigorousness
- ☐ *adj.* rigorous
- ☐ *adv.* rigorously

- ☐ *n.* recommendation
- ☐ *v.* recommend
- ☐ *adj.* recommendable

- ☐ *n.* registration
- ☐ *v.* register

- ☐ *n.* regular
- ☐ *v.* regulate
- ☐ *adj.* regular
- ☐ *adv.* regularly

- ☐ *n.* requirement
- ☐ *v.* require

UNIT 02 Listening for Main Purpose

Step A

- ☐ amplitude
- ☐ bizarre
- ☐ breathtaking
- ☐ camouflage
- ☐ centigrade
- ☐ climatology
- ☐ cumulative
- ☐ custodian
- ☐ diameter
- ☐ disband
- ☐ equatorial
- ☐ exterior
- ☐ fixture
- ☐ gaseous
- ☐ hydrogen
- ☐ intriguing
- ☐ magnificent
- ☐ porous
- ☐ predict
- ☐ scratch
- ☐ seismic
- ☐ signature
- ☐ Sothic
- ☐ spectacular
- ☐ sophisticated
- ☐ undue
- ☐ Uranus
- ☐ urban

Step B

- ☐ *n.* amplitude
- ☐ *v.* amplify

- ☐ *n.* catastrophe
- ☐ *adj.* catastrophic
- ☐ *adv.* catastrophically

- ☐ *n.* derivative
- ☐ *v.* derive
- ☐ *adj.* derivative
- ☐ *adv.* derivatively

- ☐ *n.* dwarf
- ☐ *v.* dwarf
- ☐ *adj.* dwarfish
- ☐ *adv.* dwarfishly

- ☐ *n.* entirety
- ☐ *adj.* entire
- ☐ *adv.* entirely

- ☐ *n.* expansion
- ☐ *v.* expand
- ☐ *adj.* expansive
- ☐ *adv.* expansively

- ☐ *n.* extension
- ☐ *v.* extend
- ☐ *adj.* extended
- ☐ *adv.* extendedly

- ☐ *n.* fixture
- ☐ *v.* fixate
- ☐ *adj.* fixated

- ☐ *n.* initiation
- ☐ *v.* initiate
- ☐ *adj.* initial
- ☐ *adv.* initially

- ☐ *n.* insulation
- ☐ *v.* insulate

- ☐ *n.* minimum
- ☐ *v.* minimize
- ☐ *adj.* minimal
- ☐ *adv.* minimally

- ☐ *n.* regulation
- ☐ *v.* regulate
- ☐ *adj.* regulated

- ☐ *n.* reiteration
- ☐ *v.* reiterate
- ☐ *adj.* reiterative
- ☐ *adv.* reiteratively

- ☐ *n.* response
- ☐ *v.* respond
- ☐ *adj.* responsive
- ☐ *adv.* responsively

- ☐ *n.* withdrawal
- ☐ *v.* withdraw

UNIT 03 Listening for Major Details

Step A

- ☐ amphitheater
- ☐ aqueduct
- ☐ candor
- ☐ cellulose
- ☐ considerate
- ☐ complaint
- ☐ drawback
- ☐ exterminator
- ☐ familiarize
- ☐ frustrate
- ☐ genetic
- ☐ handicapped
- ☐ hysterectomy
- ☐ impoverish
- ☐ invade
- ☐ keen
- ☐ moisture
- ☐ overdue
- ☐ pheromone
- ☐ Presbyterian
- ☐ rectangular
- ☐ regurgitate
- ☐ ridicule
- ☐ salvage
- ☐ sacred
- ☐ talented
- ☐ termite
- ☐ translate

Step B

- ☐ *n.* complaint
- ☐ *v.* complain
- ☐ *adv.* complainingly

- ☐ *n.* concept
- ☐ *v.* conceive
- ☐ *adj.* conceivable
- ☐ *adv.* conceivably

- ☐ *n.* distinction
- ☐ *v.* distinguish
- ☐ *adj.* distinct
- ☐ *adv.* distinctly

- ☐ *n.* exception
- ☐ *v.* except
- ☐ *adj.* exceptional
- ☐ *adv.* exceptionally

- ☐ *n.* exterminator
- ☐ *v.* exterminate
- ☐ *adj.* exterminable

- ☐ *n.* inscription
- ☐ *v.* inscribe
- ☐ *adj.* inscriptional

- ☐ *n.* interpreter
- ☐ *v.* interpret
- ☐ *adj.* interpretative
- ☐ *adv.* interpretatively

- ☐ *n.* invasion
- ☐ *v.* invade
- ☐ *adj.* invasive
- ☐ *adv.* invasively

- ☐ *n.* moisture
- ☐ *v.* moisten
- ☐ *adj.* moist
- ☐ *adv.* moistly

- ☐ *n.* octagon
- ☐ *adj.* octagonal
- ☐ *adv.* octagonally

- ☐ *n.* popularity
- ☐ *v.* popularize
- ☐ *adj.* popular
- ☐ *adv.* popularly

- ☐ *n.* regurgitation
- ☐ *v.* regurgitate
- ☐ *adj.* regurgitative

- ☐ *n.* reproduction
- ☐ *v.* reproduce
- ☐ *adj.* reproductive
- ☐ *adv.* reproductively

- ☐ *n.* resonation
- ☐ *v.* resonate
- ☐ *adj.* resonant
- ☐ *adv.* resonantly

UNIT 04 Understanding the Function of What Is Said

Step A

- ☐ aesthetically
- ☐ afford
- ☐ airline
- ☐ allude
- ☐ anaconda
- ☐ backyard
- ☐ beech
- ☐ blight
- ☐ canopy
- ☐ diameter
- ☐ elaborate
- ☐ exception
- ☐ façade
- ☐ fad
- ☐ fallow
- ☐ fungicide
- ☐ fungus
- ☐ hybrid
- ☐ irrigation
- ☐ itinerary
- ☐ legume
- ☐ majestic
- ☐ mildew
- ☐ otter
- ☐ powdery
- ☐ progeny
- ☐ reminiscent
- ☐ sedan
- ☐ sprout
- ☐ startle
- ☐ tendency
- ☐ thwart
- ☐ weed

Step B

- ☐ *n.* benefit
- ☐ *v.* benefit
- ☐ *adj.* beneficial
- ☐ *adv.* beneficially

- ☐ *n.* chill
- ☐ *v.* chill
- ☐ *adj.* chilling
- ☐ *adv.* chillingly

- ☐ *n.* circulation
- ☐ *v.* circulate
- ☐ *adj.* circulatory

- ☐ *n.* complication
- ☐ *v.* complicate
- ☐ *adj.* complicated
- ☐ *adv.* complicatedly

- ☐ *n.* consideration
- ☐ *v.* consider
- ☐ *adj.* considerable
- ☐ *adv.* considerably

- ☐ *n.* contribution
- ☐ *v.* contribute

- ☐ *n.* dispersal
- ☐ *v.* disperse
- ☐ *adj.* dispersible
- ☐ *adv.* dispersedly

- ☐ *n.* electricity
- ☐ *v.* electrify
- ☐ *adj.* electrifying

- ☐ *n.* impression
- ☐ *v.* impress
- ☐ *adj.* impressive
- ☐ *adv.* impressively

- ☐ *n.* objection
- ☐ *v.* object
- ☐ *adj.* object

- ☐ *n.* orientation
- ☐ *v.* orient
- ☐ *adj.* oriented

- ☐ *n.* network
- ☐ *v.* network

- ☐ *n.* resistance
- ☐ *v.* resist
- ☐ *adj.* resistant

- ☐ *n.* retention
- ☐ *v.* retain
- ☐ *adj.* retentive
- ☐ *adv.* retentively

- ☐ *n.* rotate
- ☐ *adj.* rotation
- ☐ *adj.* rotatable

- ☐ *n.* struggle
- ☐ *v.* struggle

- ☐ *n.* typicality
- ☐ *v.* typify
- ☐ *adj.* typical
- ☐ *adv.* typically

- ☐ *n.* variety
- ☐ *v.* vary
- ☐ *adj.* various
- ☐ *adv.* variously

UNIT 05 Understanding the Speaker's Attitude

Step A

- ☐ aesthetic
- ☐ amoeba
- ☐ argument
- ☐ artisan
- ☐ bachelor
- ☐ baffle
- ☐ breed
- ☐ celestial
- ☐ choke
- ☐ cohabitate
- ☐ culminate
- ☐ definitely
- ☐ drape
- ☐ eliminate
- ☐ enthusiasm
- ☐ exotic
- ☐ fabric
- ☐ foster
- ☐ funnel
- ☐ garlic
- ☐ hazard
- ☐ merge
- ☐ mutualism
- ☐ parasite
- ☐ perennial
- ☐ photosynthesis
- ☐ pluck
- ☐ politics
- ☐ redo
- ☐ reject
- ☐ transparent
- ☐ tropical

Step B

- ☐ *n.* atom
- ☐ *v.* atomize
- ☐ *adj.* atomic

- ☐ *n.* comparison
- ☐ *v.* compare
- ☐ *adj.* comparable
- ☐ *adv.* comparably

- ☐ *n.* consumption
- ☐ *v.* consume
- ☐ *adj.* consumable

- ☐ *n.* culmination
- ☐ *v.* culminate
- ☐ *adj.* culminating

- ☐ *n.* description
- ☐ *v.* describe
- ☐ *adj.* describable

- ☐ *n.* disregard
- ☐ *v.* disregard

- ☐ *n.* document
- ☐ *v.* document
- ☐ *adj.* documentable

- ☐ *n.* fascination
- ☐ *v.* fascinate
- ☐ *adj.* fascinating

- ☐ *n.* indefiniteness
- ☐ *adj.* indefinite
- ☐ *adv.* indefinitely

- ☐ *n.* intimacy
- ☐ *adj.* intimate
- ☐ *adv.* intimately

- ☐ *n.* phenomenon
- ☐ *adj.* phenomenal
- ☐ *adv.* phenomenally

- ☐ *n.* predator
- ☐ *v.* predate
- ☐ *adj.* predatory

- ☐ *n.* prevalent
- ☐ *v.* prevail
- ☐ *adj.* prevalent
- ☐ *adv.* prevalently

- ☐ *n.* proliferation
- ☐ *v.* proliferate
- ☐ *adj.* proliferative

- ☐ *adj.* prospective
- ☐ *adv.* prospectively

- ☐ *n.* rotation
- ☐ *v.* rotate
- ☐ *adj.* rotational
- ☐ *adv.* rotationally

UNIT 06 Understanding Organization

Step A

- ☐ adjust
- ☐ ancient
- ☐ arousal
- ☐ aspect
- ☐ depict
- ☐ dormancy
- ☐ drop
- ☐ durability
- ☐ entitled
- ☐ excavate
- ☐ feat
- ☐ garment
- ☐ hibernate
- ☐ humanist
- ☐ imminent
- ☐ impede
- ☐ metabolism
- ☐ nitrate
- ☐ peril
- ☐ reptile
- ☐ restrictive
- ☐ sculpture
- ☐ seminar
- ☐ shipwreck
- ☐ specialized
- ☐ stutter
- ☐ verdict
- ☐ vital

Step B

- ☐ *n.* brilliance
- ☐ *adj.* brilliant
- ☐ *adv.* brilliantly

- ☐ *n.* decoration
- ☐ *v.* decorate
- ☐ *adj.* decorative
- ☐ *adv.* decoratively

- ☐ *n.* devotion
- ☐ *v.* devote
- ☐ *adj.* devoted
- ☐ *adv.* devotedly

- ☐ *n.* erosion
- ☐ *v.* erode
- ☐ *adj.* erosive
- ☐ *adv.* erosively

- ☐ *n.* exposition
- ☐ *v.* expose
- ☐ *adj.* exposed

- ☐ *n.* focus
- ☐ *v.* focus
- ☐ *adj.* focused

- ☐ *n.* inevitability
- ☐ *adj.* inevitable
- ☐ *adv.* inevitably

- ☐ *n.* instant
- ☐ *adj.* instantaneous
- ☐ *adv.* instantaneously

- ☐ *n.* jeopardy
- ☐ *v.* jeopardize
- ☐ *adj.* jeopardized

- ☐ *n.* observation
- ☐ *v.* observe
- ☐ *adv.* observably

- ☐ *n.* modification
- ☐ *v.* modify
- ☐ *adj.* modified

- ☐ *n.* pause
- ☐ *v.* pause

- ☐ *n.* permission
- ☐ *v.* permit
- ☐ *adj.* permittable

- ☐ *n.* practicality
- ☐ *v.* practice
- ☐ *adj.* practical
- ☐ *adv.* practically

- ☐ *n.* refund
- ☐ *v.* refund
- ☐ *adj.* refundable

- ☐ *n.* urgency
- ☐ *v.* urge
- ☐ *adj.* urgent
- ☐ *adv.* urgently

- ☐ *n.* visibility
- ☐ *adj.* visible
- ☐ *adv.* visibly

UNIT 07 Connecting Content

Step A

- ☐ acclimatize
- ☐ altitude
- ☐ archaic
- ☐ chronic
- ☐ commonplace
- ☐ communal
- ☐ condition
- ☐ connotation
- ☐ corruption
- ☐ defeat
- ☐ exhibit
- ☐ frigate
- ☐ hump
- ☐ infancy
- ☐ influence
- ☐ inhale
- ☐ molecule
- ☐ monument
- ☐ nauseous
- ☐ pottery
- ☐ privateer
- ☐ regurgitate
- ☐ replenish
- ☐ robe
- ☐ squid
- ☐ tablet
- ☐ venture
- ☐ visage

Step B

- ☐ *n.* ascension
- ☐ *v.* ascend
- ☐ *adj.* ascendable

- ☐ *n.* aspiration
- ☐ *v.* aspire
- ☐ *adj.* aspirational

- ☐ *adj.* brutal
- ☐ *adv.* brutally

- ☐ *n.* consolation
- ☐ *v.* console
- ☐ *adj.* consolable
- ☐ *adv.* consolingly

- ☐ *adj.* crucial
- ☐ *adv.* crucially

- ☐ *n.* dehydration
- ☐ *v.* dehydrate
- ☐ *adj.* dehydrated

- ☐ *n.* desperateness
- ☐ *v.* desperate
- ☐ *adj.* desperate
- ☐ *adv.* desperately

- ☐ *n.* distinction
- ☐ *v.* distinguish
- ☐ *adj.* distinct
- ☐ *adv.* distinctly

- ☐ *n.* forfeit
- ☐ *v.* forfeit
- ☐ *adj.* forfeit

- ☐ *n.* migration
- ☐ *v.* migrate
- ☐ *adj.* migratory

- ☐ *n.* moisture
- ☐ *v.* moisten
- ☐ *adj.* moist

- ☐ *n.* persuasion
- ☐ *v.* persuade
- ☐ *adj.* persuadable
- ☐ *adv.* persuadably

- ☐ *n.* strenuousness
- ☐ *adj.* strenuous
- ☐ *adv.* strenuously

- ☐ *n.* tyranny
- ☐ *v.* tyrannize
- ☐ *adj.* tyrannical
- ☐ *adv.* tyrannically

- ☐ *n.* utilization
- ☐ *v.* utilize
- ☐ *adj.* utilizable

UNIT 08 Making Inferences

Step A

- ☐ abdomen
- ☐ accentuate
- ☐ appendage
- ☐ ash
- ☐ athletic
- ☐ beneficial
- ☐ churn
- ☐ collide
- ☐ contribution
- ☐ crust
- ☐ derogatory
- ☐ dolomite
- ☐ dimension
- ☐ foreshadow
- ☐ indigenous
- ☐ infirm
- ☐ intimate
- ☐ literally
- ☐ meteorologist
- ☐ miniature
- ☐ molten
- ☐ nomadic
- ☐ obliterate
- ☐ paragraph
- ☐ precipitation
- ☐ primitive
- ☐ repeat
- ☐ retrospect
- ☐ susceptible
- ☐ tectonic
- ☐ tomb

☐ tuition

Step B

☐ *n.* admission
☐ *v.* admit
☐ *adj.* admissible
☐ *adv.* admissibly

☐ *n.* apology
☐ *v.* apologize
☐ *adj.* apologetic
☐ *adv.* apologetically

☐ *n.* authenticity
☐ *v.* authenticate
☐ *adj.* authentic
☐ *adv.* authentically

☐ *n.* consideration
☐ *v.* consider
☐ *adj.* considerate
☐ *adv.* considerably

☐ *n.* desire
☐ *v.* desire
☐ *adj.* desirable

☐ *n.* finance
☐ *v.* finance
☐ *adj.* financial

☐ *n.* forecast
☐ *v.* forecast
☐ *adj.* forecasted

☐ *n.* frequency
☐ *v.* frequent
☐ *adj.* frequent
☐ *adv.* frequently

☐ *n.* gauge
☐ *v.* gauge

☐ *n.* generation
☐ *v.* generate
☐ *adj.* generational

☐ *n.* glider
☐ *v.* glide

☐ *n.* humor
☐ *v.* humor
☐ *adj.* humorous
☐ *adv.* humorously

☐ *n.* measurement
☐ *v.* measure
☐ *adj.* measurable

☐ *n.* perception
☐ *v.* perceive
☐ *adj.* perceived
☐ *adv.* perceptively

☐ *n.* scan
☐ *v.* scan
☐ *adj.* scannable

☐ *n.* significance
☐ *v.* signify
☐ *adj.* significant
☐ *adv.* significantly

☐ *n.* stability
☐ *v.* stabilize
☐ *adj.* stable
☐ *adv.* stably

☐ *n.* support
☐ *v.* support
☐ *adj.* supportive

MEMO

MEMO

MEMO

Second Edition

How to Master Skills for the TOEFL® iBT

LISTENING

Answers, Scripts, and Translations

Advanced

DARAKWON

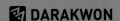

How to
Master Skills for the

Second Edition

TOEFL® iBT

LISTENING Advanced

Answers, Scripts, and Translations

DARAKWON

PART I Basic Comprehension

UNIT 01 Listening for Main Ideas

Basic Drill p.14

Drill 1 Ⓒ

Script 01-02

M Student: Professor Detweiler, I need to speak with you urgently.

W Professor: Hello, Shawn. What can I do for you?

M: I just got my final exam schedule for all of my classes today. It looks like I've got a big problem.

W: What's the matter? Are you scheduled to take two tests at the same time?

M: No, it's not that. Unfortunately, I'm supposed to take three tests on the same day. I'm pretty sure that according to school regulations, we can only take two tests on one day.

W: May I see your schedule, please?

M: Sure . . . Here it is. As you can see, I've got your economics test as well as tests in Italian literature and anthropology on Wednesday. What should I do?

W: Well, it looks like you've only got one test on Tuesday. Why don't you come to my office at three in the afternoon? You can take the test then.

M: Really? Is that all right? Thanks so much.

W: It's my pleasure. Study hard. See you then.

해석

M Student: Detweiler 교수님, 급하게 교수님께 드릴 말씀이 있어요.

W Professor: 안녕하세요, Shawn. 어떻게 도와 드릴까요?

M: 오늘 저의 전체 수업에 대한 기말고사 시간표를 받았어요. 제게 큰 문제가 생긴 것 같아요.

W: 무슨 문제인가요? 두 개의 시험을 동시에 보게 되나요?

M: 아니요, 그건 아니에요. 불행히도, 같은 날에 세 개의 시험을 보도록 되어 있어요. 학교 규정에 따르면, 시험은 하루에 두 개만 볼 수 있는 것으로 알고 있거든요.

W: 제가 시간표를 볼 수 있을까요?

M: 그럼요… 여기 있어요. 보시다시피, 교수님의 경제학 시험과 이탈리아 문학 및 인류학 시험이 수요일에 잡혀 있죠. 제가 어떻게 해야 할까요?

W: 음, 화요일에는 시험이 하나만 있는 것으로 보이는군요. 오후 3시에 제 사무실로 오는 것이 어때요? 그때 시험을 봐도 좋아요.

M: 정말인가요? 그래도 될까요? 정말 고맙습니다.

W: 천만에요. 열심히 공부하세요. 그때 보죠.

Drill 2 Ⓑ

Script 01-03

W Student: Hello. My name is Clarice Thompson. I was advised to report to Mr. Roosevelt.

M Printing Office Employee: That's me. What do you need to report on?

W: Um . . . I'm your new employee.

M: Ah, I see. Who hired you?

W: I was hired by Ian Parker this morning. He told me there's an open shift starting right now and that it finishes at five o'clock.

M: Okay. That's fine. Have you ever worked at a printing office before?

W: Sorry, but this is my first time. What do I need to do?

M: For the most part, you can just answer the phone or talk to people when they come in. Most of them will be looking to pick up or make orders.

W: What about using the machines?

M: Either Ian or I will teach you how to use them at a later time. First, we want you to focus on doing simple stuff and to get used to working here.

W: That sounds good to me. Thanks, sir.

해석

W Student: 안녕하세요. 제 이름은 Clarice Thompson이에요. Roosevelt 선생님께 보고를 하라는 이야기를 들었어요.

M Printing Office Employee: 바로 저예요. 무엇에 대한 보고를 하셔야 하나요?

W: 음… 저는 신입 직원이에요.

M: 아, 그렇군요. 누가 고용을 했나요?

W: 오늘 아침에 Ian Parker 선생님께서 고용하셨죠. 지금 바로 시작해서 5시에 끝나는 근무 시간이 비어 있다고 말씀해 주시더군요.

M: 그래요. 좋아요. 전에 프린터실에서 일해 본 적이 있나요?

W: 유감이지만 이번이 처음이에요. 제가 무엇을 하면 되나요?

M: 주로 전화를 받거나 사람들이 들어올 때 말을 주고받으면 돼요. 대부분의 사람들은 주문한 것을 찾거나 주문을 하려고 하죠.

W: 기기 사용에 관해서는요?

M: Ian과 저 중 한 명이 나중에 사용법을 가르쳐 드릴 거예요. 우선은 단순한 업무를 처리하는 것에 집중하면서 이곳 일에 익숙해지면 좋겠어요.

W: 좋아요. 감사합니다, 선생님.

Drill 3 Ⓑ, Ⓒ

Script 01-04

M Professor: I'm sure that all of you are familiar with Baroque architecture as there are some very famous examples of it throughout cities in Europe. However, fewer people know about Baroque music even though they have surely heard it numerous times. Baroque music was popular from around 1600 to 1750. It became popular in countries throughout Europe, but it was especially beloved in England, Germany, France, and Italy. Two of the greatest composers in history lived and produced work during this period. I'm talking, of course, about Johann Sebastian Bach and George Frideric Handel. We're going to listen to some music by both of those geniuses in just a moment. But I need to finish this brief overview of the period first. Oh, I shouldn't forget Antonio Vivaldi, who was yet another highly talented and famous Baroque composer.

Now, uh, what were the primary characteristics of the period? First, instrumental music became popular during it. You see, uh, prior to the Baroque Period, a lot of music was vocal in nature. Baroque music also emphasized dynamics thanks to the use of the pianoforte. The pianoforte was a keyboard instrument that many composers utilized in place of the harpsichord. It allowed composers to create music that was soft and loud. Much Baroque music has a certain flair to it as well since composers embellished their works in various ways.

해석

M Professor: 유럽의 많은 도시에 매우 유명한 바로크 건축물들이 있기 때문에 여러분 모두 바로크 건축을 익히 알고 있을 것으로 생각해요. 하지만 바로크 음악에 대해서는, 비록 분명 그에 대해 여러 번 들어 보았음에도 불구하고, 아는 사람이 적습니다. 바로크 음악은 약 1600년부터 1750년까지 인기를 끌었던 음악이었어요. 유럽의 여러 나라에서 인기를 얻었지만, 특히 영국, 독일, 프랑스, 그리고 이탈리아에서 사랑을 받았죠. 역사상 가장 위대했던 작곡가 두 명이 이 시기에 살면서 작곡을 했습니다. 물론, 요한 세바스찬 바흐와 조지 프레드릭 헨델을 말씀드리는 거예요. 잠시 후에 이 두 명의 천재들의 음악을 몇 곡 들어보도록 하죠. 하지만 먼저 이 시대에 대한 간략한 소개를 마치도록 하겠습니다. 오, 안토니오 비발디를 잊었는데, 그 역시 재능이 매우 뛰어나고 유명했던 바로크 시대의 작곡가였어요.

자, 어, 이 시대의 주요한 특징은 무엇이었을까요? 우선, 이 당시에 기악곡이 인기를 얻었습니다. 아시다시피, 어, 바로크 시대 이전에는 많은 음악들이 본질적으로 성악곡이었죠. 또한 바로크 음악은 강약을 강조했는데, 이는 피아노포르테의 사용 덕분이었어요. 피아노포르테는 많은 작곡가들이 하프시코드 대신 사용했던 건반 악기였죠. 이로써 작곡가들은 부드럽고 소리가 큰 음악을 작곡할 수 있었습니다. 또한 작곡가들이 다양한 방법으로 자신들의 작품을 장식했기 때문에 많은 바로크 음악들이 특정한 세련미를 나타냅니다.

Drill 4 Ⓐ

Script 01-05

W Professor: Nowadays, if you have a garden, watering your plants is a simple process. You take a hose to the garden, turn it on, and spray your plants with water. You might also put a sprinkler in the garden and let it run for a few minutes. In the past, people didn't have hoses and sprinklers though. But they did have crops they grew and watered. So . . . how did they get water to their crops? That's what I would like to discuss with you right now.

The key word that you need to know is irrigation. This refers to the using of various artificial means in order to water land to make plants grow. Well, in ancient times, people in some cultures simply transported water in containers from a river or lake or other source of water to their fields. But this was a long, arduous process that was only effective with small plots of land. For enormous fields, large-scale irrigation projects were necessary. Several thousand years ago, humans in Egypt and Mesopotamia learned how to build ditches or canals which could transport water to fields. The Egyptians did this by the Nile. Ah, they also dug out pools that could capture floodwaters from the Nile which they could use later. And the Mesopotamians did this near the Tigris and Euphrates rivers. Other cultures developed different methods. The Romans, for instance, built enormous aqueducts and used cement pipes to move water to fields.

해석

W Professor: 오늘날 정원이 있는 경우에는 식물에게 물을 주는 일이 간단한 편이에요. 정원으로 호스를 가지고 가서 물을 틀고 식물에게 물을 주면 되죠. 정원에 스프링클러를 설치하고 몇 분 동안 작동을 시킬 수도 있고요. 하지만 과거에는 사람들에게 호스와 스프링클러가 없었습니다. 하지만 기르고 물을 주어야 할 식물은 있었죠. 그러면… 그들이 어떻게 작물에게 물을 주었을까요? 바로 이러한 점에 대해 지금 여러분들과 논의하고자 합니다.

여러분들이 알아야 할 키워드는 관개입니다. 땅에 물을 공급해 작물들이 자라도록 다양한 인공적인 수단을 이용하는 것을 가리키죠. 음, 고대에는 몇몇 문화권의 사람들이 강이나 호수, 또는 기타 수원의 물을 통에 담아서 밭으로 가져갔어요. 하지만 이는 시간이 많이 걸리고 고된 일로, 땅 크기가 작은 경우에만 효과적이었죠. 거대한 농장에는 대규모의 관개 시설이 필요했어요. 수천 년 전 이집트와 메소포타미아 사람들은 도랑이나 운하를 파서 물을 밭으로 옮기는 방법을 알게 되었습니다. 이집트 사람들이 나일강 주변에서 그렇게 했죠. 아, 또한 웅덩이를 파서 나일강에서 넘친 물을 가두고 이를 나중에 사용할 수도 있었습니다. 그리고 메소포타미아 사람들은 티그리스강과 유프라테스강 근처에서 그렇게 했어요. 기타 문화권에서도 다양한 방법들이 개발되었습니다. 예를 들어 로마인들은 거대한 수로를 건설하고 시멘트 파이프를 이용해 농장에 물을 댔죠.

Exercises with Long Conversations

Exercise 1 1 Ⓒ 2 Ⓐ 3 Ⓑ p.18

Script 01-06

W Student: Excuse me. I wonder if you can give me some assistance, please.

M Librarian: Of course. What do you require help with?

W: I'm trying to get some information for a paper I'm writing on a comparative mythology class I'm taking, but I'm having problems using the computer system.

M: Okay. Have you ever used it before?

W: I'm a freshman, and this is my first visit to the library. I missed the orientation session, so I didn't get a chance to take the library tour.

M: Don't worry about that. It's fairly simple to use the system.

W: Okay.

M: You can see the search bar right here on the screen . . . If you know the author of the work you're looking for, type the author's name there. You can also type the title of the book you're looking for.

W: I don't know either of those.

M: In that case, you can type the subject.

W: See, uh, that's the problem. I have been typing the subject, but no matter what I type, the computer doesn't show me any books. I simply get "Nothing available" on the screen. This is really driving me crazy because I'm sure the library has plenty of books on my topic.

M: That's odd. What have you been typing in as the subject?

W: First, I typed in the name Hephaestus. He's a Greek god. Then, I typed the names of a couple of ancient Aztec gods. But the computer says you don't have any books about them.

M: Ah, I see what you're doing wrong. Your search is way too specific. There are probably no books in our collection with the name Hephaestus or the names of any Aztec gods in their titles. So you're not going to get any positive results. Instead, you need to type in a more general subject. I'm sure we have a large number of books on both Greek and Aztec mythology in our collection. In fact, I can tell you exactly where in the library you can find them.

W: Really? So, uh, what should I type to do a subject search then?

M: You said you're looking for some information on Aztec gods. In that case, why don't you type "Aztec mythology" into the search bar? Here, uh, I'll do it for you . . . There you go.

W: Wow. The library has a ton of books about this topic. So, uh, should I type "Greek mythology" as well to get information about Hephaestus?

M: Yes, exactly. You should be able to find out all the information you need by checking out some of the books we have. Good luck. If you need anything else, my desk is right over there. You can feel free to ask me for more assistance.

해석

W Student: 실례합니다. 제게 도움을 주실 수 있는지 궁금해서요.

M Librarian: 그럼요. 어떤 도움이 필요하신가요?

W: 수강 중인 비교 신화학 수업의 보고서에 필요한 정보를 찾고 있는데, 컴퓨터 시스템 사용에 문제를 겪고 있어요.

M: 그렇군요. 전에 사용해 본 적이 있으신가요?

W: 저는 신입생이고 오늘 처음 도서관에 방문했어요. 오리엔테이션에 참가를 하지 못했기 때문에 도서관 견학의 기회를 놓쳤죠.

M: 그 점에 대해서는 걱정하지 마세요. 컴퓨터 시스템을 사용하는 법은 꽤 쉬우니까요.

W: 알겠어요.

M: 화면 여기에서 검색창을 보실 수 있는데··· 찾고 있는 책의 저자를 알고 있는 경우, 그곳에 저자의 이름을 입력하세요. 또한 찾고 있는 책의 제목을 입력하셔도 되고요.

W: 둘 다 모르겠어요.

M: 그런 경우에는 주제를 입력하면 되어요.

W: 그게, 어, 그것이 문제예요. 주제를 입력하고 있었는데, 제가 입력하는 것과 상관없이 컴퓨터 화면에 어떤 책도 나타나지가 않아요. 화면에 "결과 없음"이라고만 나오고요. 제 주제에 대한 책들이 분명 도서관에 많이 있다고 알고 있기 때문에 정말로 미치겠어요.

M: 이상하군요. 주제로서 어떤 것을 입력하고 있었나요?

W: 우선 헤파이스토스라는 이름을 입력했어요. 그리스의 신이죠. 그리고는 고대 아즈텍 신들의 이름을 두어 개 입력했어요. 하지만 컴퓨터에는 그에 관한 책이 없다고 나오더군요.

M: 아, 어떤 점이 잘못되었는지 알겠어요. 학생의 검색이 너무 특정되어 있어요. 아마도 책 제목에 헤파이스토스라는 이름이나 아즈텍 신들의 이름이 들어 있는 책은 도서관에 없을 거예요. 그래서는 긍정적인 결과를 얻을 수 없을 거예요. 대신 보다 일반적인 주제를 입력해야 해요. 도서관에 그리스 신화나 아즈텍 신화와 관련된 책은 분명 상당히 많이 있을 거예요. 사실 학생이 그 책들을 정확히 도서관 어디에서 찾을 수 있는지 제가 말씀을 드릴 수도 있죠.

W: 정말인가요? 그러면, 어, 주제 검색을 하려면 어떻게 입력해야 하나요?

M: 아즈텍 신들에 관한 정보를 찾고 있다고 말했잖아요. 그런 경우에는 검색창에 "아즈텍 신화"라고 입력해 보는 것이 어떨까요? 여기, 어, 제가 해 드리면··· 나왔어요.

W: 와. 이 주제에 관한 책들이 도서관에 정말 많이 있군요. 그러면, 어, 헤파이스토스에 대한 정보를 얻기 위해서는 마찬가지로 "그리스 신화"를 입력해야 할까요?

M: 네, 맞아요. 저희가 소장하고 있는 책들을 확인하면 학생에게 필요한 모든 정보를 찾을 수 있을 거예요. 행운을 빌어요. 기타 필요한 것이 있으면 제 책상이 바로 저쪽에 있어요. 편하게 도움을 요청하셔도 좋아요.

Summary Note

A

❶ the library
❷ comparative mythology
❸ computer system
❹ Nothing available
❺ the library
❻ general
❼ Aztec
❽ help

B

The student is looking for information to write a paper in a comparative mythology class, but she is having trouble using the library's computer system. She is a freshman visiting the library for the first time and missed the orientation session. The librarian says that the student can search for books by author, title, or subject. The student says she is trying a subject search, but she gets a "Nothing available" message whenever she types in a subject. She says she is typing the word "Hephaestus" and the names of Aztec gods. The librarian says that her searches are too specific and should be more general. He suggests using "Aztec mythology" and types it in the search bar. Then, many books covering that topic appear. The librarian tells the student that she can ask him for more help later if she needs assistance.

Exercise 2 1 Ⓓ 2 Ⓑ 3 Ⓓ p.20

Script 01-07

M Student: Professor McClanahan, I would like to have a word with you if you could spare a couple of minutes. Would that be all right?

W Professor: Certainly, Trent. What do you need to talk about today? Is this about the upcoming course registration for next semester? Do you need some assistance choosing which classes to take?

M: Uh, no, ma'am. I already know which classes I'm planning to take. I'll be signing up for your class on Chinese archaeology if there's space available by the time I get to register.

W: Ah, that's a really fun class. I'm glad you intend to take it.

M: Yes, I'm expecting to learn a lot in it.

W: So . . . if that's not what you're here for, what do you need to talk to me about?

M: It's about the research paper you assigned in class today. I guess, uh . . . I guess I'm just not sure what to do.

W: You need a topic? Well, I recall the essay you wrote about archaeological methods on the midterm exam was quite well done. Why don't you choose that?

M: Er . . . Okay. But I mean . . . um . . . How do I write a research paper?

W: Ah . . . Do you mean the entire process?

M: Yes, that's right. I'm sorry, but I never had to write a long paper in high school. I think the longest paper I have ever written is three pages. And I know the style I used for that paper is not what I'm supposed to do for your class. So I guess I'm just a bit lost. I hate to admit it, but it's true.

W: There's absolutely no need to feel embarrassed about that. It's not your fault that nobody ever taught you what to do.

M: Thanks for saying that.

W: Okay . . . So how do you write a research paper? First of all, you need to come up with a thesis statement. That's basically one sentence explaining what you will be discussing. This should be something like, hmm . . . The methods some archaeologists use in recovering artifacts are problematic and damage ancient sites.

M: Oh, I like that. So in other words, I need to state an opinion or an argument. Is that correct?

W: Precisely. Then, you need to divide your paper into three parts. There should be an introduction, a body, and a conclusion. The introduction is one paragraph which explains what you're going to discuss and what your major arguments are. The body includes those arguments and the facts and various data you use to defend the points you make. Lastly, the conclusion basically sums up the paper.

M: You make it sound so easy.

W: It really is once you get the hang of it. If you have any problems while writing your paper, you know my email address.

해석

M Student: McClanahan 교수님, 잠깐 시간이 되시면 교수님과 이야기를 나누고 싶은데. 괜찮으신가요?

W Professor: 그럼요, Trent. 무엇에 대해 이야기를 하면 되나요? 곧 있을 다음 학기 수강 신청에 관한 것인가요? 어떤 수업을 들어야 하는지에 대해 도움이 필요한가요?

M: 어, 아니에요, 교수님. 제가 듣게 될 수업들은 이미 알고 있어요. 수강 신청할 때 빈 자리가 있는 경우에는 교수님의 중국 고고학 수업에도 등록할 거예요.

W: 아, 정말로 재미있는 수업이죠. 학생이 듣고자 한다니 기쁘군요.

M: 네, 그 수업에서 많은 것을 배우게 될 것으로 기대하고 있어요.

W: 그러면⋯ 여기에 온 이유가 그게 아니라면 무엇에 대해 저와 이야기를 해야 하나요?

M: 오늘 수업에서 내 주신 연구 보고서에 대해서요. 제가, 어⋯ 제가 무엇을 해

야 하는지 잘 모르겠어요.

W: 주제가 필요한가요? 음, 중간고사 때 학생이 고고학적 방법에 대해 썼던 에세이가 매우 훌륭했던 것으로 기억해요. 그걸 선택하는 것은 어때요?

M: 어… 좋아요. 하지만 제 말은… 음… 연구 보고서를 어떻게 써야 하나요?

W: 아… 전체 과정을 말하는 건가요?

M: 네, 맞아요. 죄송하지만, 제가 고등학교 때 장문의 보고서를 써야 했던 적이 없어서요. 제가 지금까지 써 본 가장 긴 보고서는 3페이지 보고서였던 것 같아요. 그리고 그러한 보고서에 제가 사용했던 방식이 교수님 수업에서는 적합하지 않은 걸로 알고 있어요. 그래서 어떻게 해야 할지 잘 모르겠어요. 인정하기는 싫지만, 사실이에요.

W: 그에 대해서 전혀 당황해 할 필요가 없어요. 학생이 어떻게 해야 하는지 알려 준 사람이 없었다는 것은 학생 잘못이 아니죠.

M: 그렇게 말씀해 주시다니 감사합니다.

W: 좋아요… 그러면 연구 보고서를 어떻게 쓰면 될까요? 먼저, 주제문을 생각해 내야 해요. 기본적으로 학생이 논의하려는 바를 설명하는 한 개의 문장이죠. 다음과 같은 것이 될 수 있는데, 흠… 일부 고고학자들이 사용하는 유물 발굴 방법에 문제가 있으며 이로 인해 고대 유적지가 손상되고 있다.

M: 오, 마음에 들어요. 그러면 다시 말해서 제가 한 가지 의견이나 주장을 제시해야 하는군요. 맞나요?

W: 맞아요. 그런 다음 보고서를 세 개의 부분으로 나누어야 해요. 서론, 본론, 그리고 결론이 있어야 하죠. 서론은 학생이 무엇에 대해 논의할 것인지, 그리고 주된 논점들이 무엇인지 설명하는 한 개의 단락이에요. 본론에는 그러한 논점 및 학생이 제시하는 요점을 뒷받침하기 위해 사용되는 사실과 다양한 자료들이 포함되고요. 마지막으로 결론은 기본적으로 보고서를 요약해 주죠.

M: 말씀만으로는 쉽게 들리네요.

W: 요령만 알면 정말 쉬워요. 보고서를 작성하면서 문제가 생기는 경우, 제 이메일 주소를 알고 있을 거예요.

Summary Note

A

❶ professor
❷ research paper
❸ archaeological methods
❹ how to write
❺ long paper
❻ what style
❼ thesis statement
❽ body

B

The student asks the professor if she can talk for a moment. The professor wonders if the student needs help choosing which classes to take next semester, but the student says he is there about something else. He says he does not know how to write the research paper. The professor suggests writing about archaeological methods. The student then states that he has never written a research paper before, so he is lost and does not know what to do. The professor tells him that he needs to come up with a thesis statement, which is one sentence explaining what he will be discussing. Then, he should divide his paper into three parts. The introduction should explain what he will discuss. The body will contain facts and data defending the argument. And the conclusion will sum up the paper.

Exercise 3 1 Ⓐ 2 Ⓑ 3 Ⓓ p.22

Script 01-08

W Student: Good morning. I wonder if you could possibly give me some assistance.

M Bookstore Employee: Sure thing. Are you having trouble locating a book?

W: Yes, that's right. The author's last name is Bradley, so I'm over here in this section where the B's should be, but I can't find it. In fact, the books appear to be completely out of order.

M: Actually . . . the books are not organized alphabetically. Instead, we organize books according to which class they are for. As you can see here, you're in the psychology section. So unless the book you want is for a psychology class, you're not going to find it.

W: Oh . . . I get it. My mistake.

M: What class is the book for?

W: It's for French 134. It's a French literature class.

M: Ah, the books for French classes are right over here . . . Follow me, please . . .

W: Oh, it's over in another aisle. I would have been here all day.

M: Here we are. What did you say that the author's name is? I don't recall.

W: It's Bradley. Emil Bradley.

M: And French 134, right?

W: That's correct.

M: I'm sorry, but it appears that we don't have any more copies of that book. It looks like there are seven books required for that class. We have six of them on the shelf, but the Bradley book just isn't there.

W: Is that something that often happens? I mean, uh, it seems a bit odd that all of the books for the class except for one are here on the shelf.

M: You're right. It really is strange. In fact, in most cases, students buy one of each book. As you can see, there appear to be a roughly identical number of each of the six other books here. So what that tells me is that the book you want has almost surely been misplaced. In other words, we have the book somewhere, but it's just not in the right location. Hold on a moment while I look . . . No, not here . . . Not here . . . Aha!

W: You found it! That's so wonderful. It looks like

someone put it on the shelf for French 234. I guess that kind of mistake could happen to anyone.

M: Yeah, these things happen sometimes when you have so many books to stock. Anyway, here's your book. Why don't you take it to the cash register to pay for it? I need to transfer the rest of the Bradley books to the right place so that the other students in your class can find it more easily than you did.

해석

W Student: 안녕하세요. 혹시 저를 도와 주실 수 있는지 궁금하군요.

M Bookstore Employee: 그럼요. 책을 찾는데 문제가 있나요?

W: 네, 맞아요. 작가의 성이 브래들리라서 B로 시작하는 사람의 책이 있어야 하는 이곳 섹션으로 왔는데 찾을 수가 없어요. 실제로 책들이 완전히 뒤섞여 있는 것처럼 보이는군요.

M: 사실… 책들이 알파벳 순으로 정리되어 있는 것은 아니에요. 대신 저희가 관련 수업에 따라 책을 정리해 두죠. 여기에서 알 수 있는 것처럼, 학생은 심리학 섹션에 있어요. 그러니 원하는 책이 심리학 수업과 관련된 것이 아니라면 찾을 수 없을 거예요.

W: 오… 알겠어요. 제가 잘못했군요.

M: 어떤 수업에 관한 책인가요?

W: 프랑스어 134 수업에 관한 것이에요. 프랑스 문학 수업이죠.

M: 아, 프랑스어 수업과 관련된 책들은 바로 이쪽에 있어요… 저를 따라 오세요…

W: 오, 다른 코너에 있군요. 하루 종일 여기에 있을 뻔 했네요.

M: 여기 있어요. 작가의 이름이 뭐라고 했죠? 기억이 안 나서요.

W: 브래들리예요. 에밀 브래들리.

M: 그리고 프랑스어 134 수업이죠, 그렇죠?

W: 맞아요.

M: 죄송하지만 그 책은 더 이상 없는 것 같군요. 그 수업에서 필요한 책은 7개인 것 같아요. 그중 6개는 선반에 있는데, 브래들리의 책은 없네요.

W: 이런 일이 자주 일어나나요? 제 말은, 어, 하나만 빼고 수업에 필요한 모든 책들이 이곳 책장에 있다는 것이 좀 이상하게 보여서요.

M: 학생 말이 맞아요. 정말 이상하네요. 사실, 대부분의 경우, 학생들이 각각의 책들을 한 권씩 구입하죠. 보시다시피, 여기 다른 6개의 책들은 수량이 대충 동일한 것으로 보여요. 그러면 학생이 원하는 책은 거의 틀림없이 다른 자리에 있는 것 같군요. 즉 어딘가에 책이 있는데, 제 자리에 있지는 않은 것이죠. 제가 살펴볼 테니 잠시 기다리시면… 여기에는 없고… 여기에도 없는데… 아하!

W: 찾으셨군요! 정말 놀랍네요. 누군가가 프랑스 234 수업을 위한 책장에 둔 것 같군요. 이런 실수는 누구나 흔히 겪을 수 있는 것이라고 생각해요.

M: 그래요, 두어야 할 책들이 너무 많은 경우에 때때로 그런 일들이 일어나죠. 어쨌든, 여기 학생의 책이요. 계산대로 가지고 가서 계산을 하는 것이 어떨까요? 저는 같은 수업을 듣는 다른 학생들이 학생보다 더 쉽게 책을 찾을 수 있도록 나머지 브래들리의 책들을 제자리로 옮겨 놓아야 할 것 같아요.

Summary Note

A

❶ find book
❷ alphabetically
❸ class
❹ French
❺ correct place
❻ Other books
❼ misplaced
❽ cash register

B

The student requests assistance from the man because she cannot find a book. However, she is looking in the wrong place because the books are not organized alphabetically. They are organized according to which class they are for. The student says she needs a book for French 134. The man shows her to the French section and asks for the name of the author. However, the book the student needs is missing whereas the other six books for that class are on the shelf. The man says that this is odd, so he guesses the book must have been misplaced. He looks for it and finds it in the French 234 section. He gives the student the book and says he has to transfer the books to the correct location.

Exercise 4 1 Ⓑ 2 Ⓒ 3 Ⓓ p.24

Script 01-09

W1 Student: Hi, Professor Samuels. I am here for my 9:00 appointment.

W2 Professor: Good morning. So you're here to register for next semester's classes?

W1: Yes, that's right. I want to make sure that I am signing up for the courses that I need for my journalism major.

W2: Let me get out the journalism requirements checklist so we can make sure that you're taking the classes you need. Here we go. Okay, now, how many course hours do you want to take next semester?

W1: As few as possible. I really don't want to get burned out.

W2: Well, I can understand that. I was a student once, too. But remember that you need 126 credit hours to graduate, and I suspect you want to graduate in the usual four years.

W1: Oh, yes, I really can't afford to stay longer than four years.

W2: Okay, so keeping that in consideration, I would

recommend that you take at least fifteen to eighteen hours each semester.

W1: Well, okay. I took fifteen credit hours each for the last two semesters. And I'm signed up for six credit hours of summer school. Fifteen hours hasn't been so bad, so maybe I'll continue with that. But can we try to schedule my classes so that I get to sleep in a little bit in the mornings?

W2: Sure, absolutely. And the fact that you took so many credits last semester means you've gotten off to a good start. Have you taken all the required courses for first-year journalism students?

W1: Yes, I have. Oh, wait a minute! I actually took a biology class instead of a mass communication class. Is that a problem?

W2: No, it's not a problem. Actually, you need to take two science classes before you graduate, so now you have filled one of those two requirements. But you definitely need to take the mass communication class next semester because it is a prerequisite for other classes that you need.

W1: Oh, that's good to know. Well, I'll write down that course to take next semester. Should I take my other science class in the fall semester as well?

W2: It would be a good idea to take that class in one of the next two semesters so that you can focus on the classes in your major. Is there a science class offered next semester that interests you?

W1: There is a geology class that looks interesting, and I've heard good things about the professor. It's offered at three different times, so I should be able to work that in around my other classes.

W2: Great. So I will sign this for you now. Do you have any other questions while you're here?

W1: Not that I can think of at the moment. Thank you very much for helping me, Professor.

W2: No problem. That's what I'm here for. Good luck next semester.

해석

W1 Student: 안녕하세요, Samuels 교수님. 9시 약속 때문에 왔어요.

W2 Professor: 좋은 아침이군요. 다음 학기 수업에 등록을 하려고 온 거죠?

W1: 네, 맞아요. 언론학 전공을 위해 들어야 하는 수업을 제가 수강하게 될 것인지 확인하고 싶어서요.

W2: 언론학 전공 필수 과목 리스트를 꺼내서 학생이 들어야 하는 수업을 듣게 될 것인지 확인해 보죠. 여기 있군요. 좋아요, 자, 다음 학기에는 몇 학점을 듣고자 하나요?

W1: 가능한 적게요. 정말로 녹초가 되고 싶지는 않거든요.

W2: 음, 무슨 말인지 알겠어요. 저도 학생이었던 때가 있었죠. 하지만 학생이 졸업을 하기 위해서는 126학점이 필요하다는 점을 기억해야 하는데, 학생은 보통의 경우처럼 4년 안에 졸업을 하고 싶어하는 것 같군요.

W1: 오, 네. 4년 이상 대학을 다닐 형편은 되지 않아서요.

W2: 좋아요, 그러한 점을 염두에 두면, 학생에게 매 학기마다 최소 15학점에서 18학점씩 듣는 것을 추천할게요.

W1: 음, 좋아요. 저는 지난 두 학기 동안 각각 15학점씩 들었어요. 그리고 여름 학기에 6학점을 신청할 예정이에요. 15학점은 그다지 빡빡하지 않았으니, 계속 그렇게 할 거예요. 하지만 아침에 잠을 좀 잘 수 있도록 수업 시간표를 조정할 수 있을까요?

W2: 물론 가능하죠. 그리고 지난 학기에 그렇게 많은 학점을 얻었다는 사실은 출발이 좋았다는 점을 뜻하죠. 언론학과 1학년의 필수 과목들은 다 들었나요?

W1: 네, 들었어요. 오, 잠깐만요! 사실 매스컴 수업 대신 생물학 수업을 들었어요. 그게 문제가 될까요?

W2: 아뇨, 문제가 되지는 않아요. 사실 졸업하기 전에 과학 수업을 두 개 들어야 하는데, 이러한 두 개의 필수 과목 중 하나를 들은 셈이네요. 하지만 매스컴 수업은 학생에게 필요한 또 다른 수업의 선수 과목이기 때문에 반드시 다음 학기에는 들어야 해요.

W1: 오, 알게 되어 다행이군요. 음, 다음 학기에 들을 수 있도록 그 수업을 적어 놓을게요.

W2: 전공 수업에 집중할 수 있도록 다음 두 학기 중 한 학기 때 그 수업을 듣는 것이 좋을 거예요. 다음 학기에 개설되는 과학 수업 중에서 흥미가 가는 것이 있나요?

W1: 지질학 수업이 흥미롭게 보이는데, 그 교수님에 관한 좋은 이야기들을 들었어요. 서로 다른 세 개의 시간대에 개설이 되기 때문에 다른 수업들과 병행할 수 있을 것 같아요.

W2: 잘 됐군요. 그러면 이제 서명을 해 드리죠. 온 김에 혹시 다른 질문이 있나요?

W1: 지금은 생각나는 것이 없어요. 도와주셔서 정말 감사합니다, 교수님.

W2: 천만에요. 할 일을 한 것뿐이죠. 다음 학기에 행운이 있기를 빌게요.

Summary Note

A

❶ her appointment
❷ sign up for
❸ when student would like to graduate
❹ four years
❺ fifteen credit hours
❻ take science class

B

The student visits her professor to go over her choices for next semester's classes. The student wants to make sure that she is taking the right classes for her journalism major. The professor agrees that a very important part of succeeding in college is scheduling classes correctly, and she looks at the student's records. The professor asks the student if she wants to graduate on time in the usual four years. The student says she wants to graduate on time as she cannot afford to stay longer. The professor tells the student that, considering the major she is choosing, she should think about taking the mass communication class since it is a prerequisite for other classes that she will need. The professor also inquires if there are any other science classes the student is interested in taking. The student indicates that she has an interest in geology.

Exercises with Long Lectures

Exercise 1 1 Ⓑ 2 Ⓐ 3 Ⓒ p.26

Script 01-10

M Professor: Today, we are going to be talking about opera.

W Student: Opera? Oh, no. Operas are so boring.

M: **Boring? Not at all.** Operas are dramas that employ the use of music.

W: They are dramas? I thought an opera is when performers dress up in costumes and then sing in foreign languages on stage.

M: Well, I am sure an opera appears that way if you don't know what is happening. Why don't we look at the history of opera to find out exactly what an opera is and how this form of drama evolved? We have the ancient Greeks to thank for inspiring this form of expression. The ancient Greeks performed dramas that incorporated music and singing and sometimes even dancing.

W: The ancient Greeks? But when I think of opera, I think of a large woman wearing a horned helmet, and she is singing in . . . I don't know . . . German? Italian?

M: Either one is correct as both the Germans and the Italians embraced operatic performances. Modern opera began in Italy during the Renaissance. One of the very first modern operas was composed during the late sixteenth century by Jacopo Peri. It was called *Dafne* and was an opera based on a Greek myth.

W: It is hard enough to follow a play. Why must they add such complicated songs? Sometimes it sounds like the singers are screaming.

M: Those "complicated songs," as you refer to them, are known as arias. An aria is a complex musical passage created to showcase a singer's vocal range. But can you think of another reason why a wide range in vocal sound might be important?

W: To show . . . when someone is angry?

M: Close. An aria allows a performer to express a varied range of emotions through the tone of his or her singing. It can be compared to how babies cry using differing intonations depending on their need, say, hunger or tiredness.

W: Are Italy and Germany the only places where operas are performed?

M: Not at all. The art form of opera is very popular all over the world but are especially popular in Europe. Venice, Italy, was where the first opera house was created, but there are opera houses in England, France, Portugal, Spain, and Russia. Still, because opera is thought of as an Italian art form, composers from other countries, such as Germany's Handel and Austria's Mozart, wrote their works in Italian. It wasn't until later that composers felt confident enough to write operas in their own language.

W: It seems that everyone ends up dying in an opera. Are all operas so?

M: Again, you are thinking of opera in its clichéd form. Just as a play can be a comedy or a tragedy, so too can operas. The most popular is the one you mentioned, the opera seria, which has a dramatic plot that may involve death, but there is also the opera comique, which is a comical opera. Operettas are shorter versions of operas that often have comical plots.

W: Can you recommend an opera to us? They don't appear so boring after all.

M: Certainly. There are, of course, Puccini's *Madame Butterfly*, Mozart's The *Marriage of Figaro*, George Bizet's *Carmen*, and Wagner's *Der Ring des Nibelungen*. They are all examples of dramas that utilize music, singing, and dancing.

해석

M Professor: 오늘은 오페라에 대해 논의해 보죠.

W Student: 오페라요? 오, 이런. 오페라는 너무 지루해요.

M: 지루해요? 전혀 그렇지 않습니다. 오페라는 음악을 사용하는 드라마예요.

W: 드라마라고요? 저는 배우들이 의상을 갖춰 입고 무대에서 외국어로 노래를 하는 것이라고 생각했는데요.

M: 음, 무슨 얘긴지 모르는 경우에는 분명 오페라가 그렇게 보일 거예요. 오페라의 역사를 살펴보고 오페라가 정확히 무엇인지, 그리고 이러한 형태의 드라마가 어떻게 발전했는지 알아보는 것이 어떨까요? 이러한 표현 방식이 등장한 것은 고대 그리스인 덕분이었어요. 고대 그리스인들이 음악과 노래, 그리고 때로는 무용이 합쳐진 드라마를 공연했죠.

W: 고대 그리스인들이요? 하지만 오페라를 떠올리면 장식이 달린 모자를 쓴 덩치 큰 여자가 생각나는데, 노래를… 잘 모르겠지만… 독일어인가요? 아니면 이탈리아어로 하나요?

M: 독일인과 이탈리아인 모두 오페라 공연을 받아들였으니 어느 쪽이든 맞아요. 현대의 오페라는 르네상스 시대의 이탈리아에서 시작되었습니다. 최초의 현대 오페라 중 하나는 16세기 후반에 야코포 페리가 작곡한 것이었어요. *다프네*라는 오페라로, 이는 그리스 신화에 기초를 둔 오페라였습니다.

W: 극을 이해하기가 어려워요. 왜 그렇게 복잡한 노래를 덧붙여야 하는 건가요? 때로는 가수가 비명을 지르는 것처럼 들리기도 해요.

M: 학생이 지칭한 그 "복잡한 노래"들은 아리아로 알려져 있죠. 아리아는 가수의 음역을 보여 주기 위해 만들어진 복잡한 악곡이에요. 하지만 넓은 음역의 발성이 중요한 또 다른 이유를 생각해 볼 수 있나요?

W: 보여 주기 위해서··· 누군가 화가 나 있다는 점을 나타내기 위해서요?

M: 정답에 가까워요. 아리아는 노래의 톤을 통해 배우가 다양한 감정을 표현하도록 만듭니다. 이는 아기가 필요에 따라, 가령 배고프거나 피곤한 경우 서로 다른 억양을 이용해 우는 법과 비교될 수 있죠.

W: 이탈리아와 독일에서만 오페라가 공연되나요?

M: 전혀 그렇지 않아요. 오페라라는 예술 형태는 전 세계적으로 매우 인기가 있는데, 특히 유럽에서 인기가 많죠. 이탈리아의 베니스에서 최초의 오페라 극장이 만들어졌지만, 영국, 프랑스, 포르투갈, 스페인, 그리고 러시아에도 오페라 극장이 존재합니다. 하지만 오페라가 이탈리아의 예술로 생각되기 때문에 독일의 헨델이나 오스트리아의 모차르트 같은 다른 나라의 작곡가들도 이탈리아어로 작품을 썼어요. 작곡가들이 자부심을 가지고 자국 언어로 오페라를 쓴 것은 그 이후의 일이었습니다.

W: 오페라에서는 결국 모두가 죽는 것처럼 보여요. 모든 오페라가 그처럼 무시무시한가요?

M: 또 다시 진부한 형태의 오페라를 생각하고 있군요. 극이 희극일 수도 있고 비극일 수도 있듯이 오페라도 마찬가지입니다. 가장 인기 있는 오페라는 학생이 언급한 오페라인 정가극으로, 이는 죽음과 관련이 있을 수 있는 극적인 줄거리를 가지고 있지만, 희극적인 오페라인 희가극도 존재해요. 오페레타는 보다 짧은 형식의 오페라로 종종 희극적인 줄거리를 가지고 있죠.

W: 저희에게 오페라를 추천해 주실 수 있으신가요? 들어보니 그렇게 지루한 것 같지는 않네요.

M: 당연하죠. 물론 푸치니의 *나비 부인*, 모차르트의 *피가로의 결혼*, 조르주 비제의 *카르멘*, 그리고 바그너의 *니벨룽겐의 반지*가 있어요. 이들 모두 음악, 노래, 그리고 무용을 이용한 극에 해당됩니다.

Summary Note

A

❶ operas
❷ wrong ideas
❸ the ancient Greeks
❹ the Renaissance
❺ a singer's abilities
❻ dramatic opera
❼ comical opera
❽ short, comical opera

B

An opera is a form of drama that includes music or dancing or a combination of both. The ancient Greeks were the first to employ these elements on stage, but it was not until during the Renaissance in Italy that what is now called modern opera was developed. The Italians were not the only ones to compose modern operas; the Germans were quick to follow. Eventually, opera spread across Europe and even into Russia. This kind of widespread interest in opera led to many different developments and types. There are also the opera seria and the opera comique. Another development was the operetta, which is a very short opera that is often comical in nature. But no matter what the type, operas share many similar elements, such as the aria, a complex musical passage exhibiting a singer's vocal range.

Exercise 2 1 Ⓒ 2 Ⓑ 3 Ⓓ p.28

Script 01-11

W Student: We've been talking a lot about how rice is prepared, but what is the actual origin of rice?

M Professor: An excellent question, but one that is complicated.

W: Complicated?

M: Yes, because it all depends on which way you approach the question. Do you mean the origin of wild rice or domestic rice? Are you interested in the scientific origin of rice, or are you interested in the mythological stories surrounding it?

Let's assume you are interested in all the possibilities and begin with wild rice. Now, because wild rice grows in many places, it is very hard to pin down a precise date in history when it first developed. What is known, however, is that the earliest evidence of rice dates back more than 16,000 years ago, when the last ice age was coming to an end. Early humans, who were once mainly hunters, cultivated the land and gathered, among other things, wild rice. Scientists know this because microscopic rice cells have been discovered near the sites of these ancient civilizations. What is also known, through a process called electrophoresis, is that cultivated rice from areas as widespread as Australia, Asia, Africa, and North America all stem from one common type of rice that existed when the continents were connected. Despite the widespread distribution of rice—there are twenty wild species spread across four continents—experts believe the likely location of its origin is Asia due to a finding of rice imprints from the Yang-shao site in northern China that dates back to between 3200 and 2500 B.C. in the 1920s.

W: That is wild rice, but what about the rice that we eat today?

M: Domestic rice originates back to the early days of Chinese culture. Various archaeological sites revealed deep rice paddies in Hunan Province. The oldest paddy sites date from nearly 12,000 years ago in an area just south of the Three Gorges Dam in the middle of Yangtze River.

W: But what do you mean by domestic? Does domestic just mean that it is collected by people?

M: No. People can harvest wild rice, but that doesn't make it domestic. Domestication happens when people plant seeds to form a new generation of rice that carries certain desired traits. For example, early humans would have tried to grow heartier crops and crops that yielded more volume, so they would have sown only seeds from crops that exhibited those positive traits.

W: That is the science behind the origin of rice, but I want to hear the myths.

M: Well, I am certain there's more than one myth behind the origin of rice, but I will briefly summarize one such legend, called *The Gift of the Sky Flood*. The Chinese story states that a long time ago, a girl named Shuhwa lived with her family cultivating buckwheat along the banks of the Yangtze River. One year, however, powerful rains flooded the area, so Shuhwa and her family were driven to higher ground. During the flood, Shuhwa spied a wild dog clinging to a floating log. Shuhwa saved the dog, and, later, as she was running her fingers through the dog's fur, Shuhwa found a small seedling. The very next day, Shuhwa planted the seedling on the higher, yet still marshy ground, and year after year, the plant thrived, yielding grains which were later to be known as rice. So you see, there are three different ways to look at the origin of rice.

해석

W Student: 쌀을 만드는 과정에 대해서는 논의를 많이 했는데, 실제로 쌀의 기원은 무엇인가요?

M Professor: 훌륭한 질문이지만 복잡한 질문이기도 하군요.

W: 복잡하다고요?

M: 네, 그 문제에 어떻게 접근하느냐에 따라 답이 완전히 달라져요. 야생벼의 기원을 말하는 건가요, 아니면 재배벼의 기원을 말하는 건가요? 쌀의 과학적인 기원에 관심이 있나요, 아니면 쌀을 둘러싼 신화에 관심이 있나요?

모든 것에 관심이 있다고 가정을 하고 야생벼로부터 시작해 보죠. 자, 야생벼는 여러 지역에서 자라기 때문에 역사상 쌀이 처음 등장한 정확한 시기를 꼬집어 말하기란 매우 어렵습니다. 하지만 알려진 바에 따르면, 쌀에 대한 최초의 증거는 마지막 빙하기가 끝나고 있던 16,000년 전의 것이에요. 한때 주로 사냥을 했던 초기 인류가 땅을 경작하고 채집 생활을 하면서, 특히 야생벼를 채집했어요. 과학자들이 이러한 점을 알게 된 것은 그러한 고대 문명지 인근에서 미세한 쌀 세포가 발견되었기 때문이었습니다. 또한 전기 영동이라는 과정을 통해 알려진 점은 호주, 아시아, 아프리카, 그리고 북아메리카와 같은 넓은 지역에서 경작된 쌀들이, 이 대륙들이 모두 연결되었을 당시 존재했던 하나의 공통된 쌀 종류에서 비롯되었다는 것이에요. 네 개의 대륙 전역에 20개의 야생벼가 분포되어 있을 정도로 쌀은 넓은 지역에 퍼져 있었는데, 1920년대에 기원전 3200년에서 2500년 사이에 만들어진 쌀 흔적이 중국 북부의 양샤오 지역에서 발견됨으로써 전문가들은 쌀의 기원지가 아시아라고 믿고 있습니다.

W: 그건 야생벼 이야기지만, 오늘날 우리가 먹는 쌀은 어떤가요?

M: 재배벼의 기원은 중국 문화의 초기로 거슬러 올라갑니다. 후난성의 여러 고고학 유적지에서 깊이가 깊은 논이 발견되었어요. 가장 오래된 논은 양쯔강 중류의 삼협댐 바로 남쪽 지역에 있는데, 약 12,000년 전의 것입니다.

W: 그런데 재배벼는 무엇을 말하는 건가요? 사람에 의해 수확이 된다는 의미인가요?

M: 아니에요. 야생벼도 수확을 할 수 있지만 이를 재배벼라고 하지는 않죠. 재배는 바람직한 특정 형질을 가진 새로운 세대의 쌀을 생산하기 위해 씨를 심는 경우와 관련이 있어요. 예를 들어 초기 인류는 알이 더 굵고 더 많은 양을 수확할 수 있는 작물을 기르기 위해 노력했기 때문에 그러한 긍정적인 형질을 나타냈던 작물의 씨만을 심었을 거예요.

W: 그것이 바로 쌀의 기원에 숨어 있는 과학일 텐데, 저는 신화도 듣고 싶어요.

M: 음, 쌀의 기원과 관련된 신화는 분명 한 가지 이상 존재할 것이지만, *홍수의 선물*이라고 불리는 하나의 전설에 대해 짧게 이야기하겠습니다. 이 중국 전설에 따르면 옛날에 슈화라는 이름의 소녀가 양쯔강 둑에서 메밀을 경작하며 가족과 함께 살고 있었어요. 하지만 어느 해에 폭우로 그 지역이 범람을 해서 슈화와 그녀의 가족은 보다 높은 곳으로 가야만 했죠. 홍수가 일어났을 때 슈화는 한 마리의 들개가 물위에 떠 있는 통나무에 매달려 있는 것을 보았습니다. 슈화는 개를 구해 주었고, 이후 손가락으로 개의 털을 훑다가 작은 묘목을 발견했어요. 바로 그 다음날 슈화는 보다 높은 곳에 있는, 하지만 여전히 축축한 상태였던 땅에 묘목을 심었는데, 이 식물이 잘 자라서 나중에 쌀이라고 알려진 낟알을 생산했습니다. 이제 쌀의 기원을 바라보는 서로 다른 세 가지 방식이 존재한다는 점을 아셨을 거예요.

Summary Note

A

❶ origins of rice
❷ naturally
❸ in China
❹ Chinese culture
❺ traits
❻ myth

B

The origin of rice is a complicated question because it can potentially contain three parts: the origins of wild rice and domestic rice or the mythological stories surrounding rice. The exact origin of wild rice is nearly impossible to pinpoint, but evidence suggests that early human ancestors were harvesting it as early as 16,000 years ago. The evidence also suggests that wild rice spread over four continents: Australia, Asia, Africa, and North America. Domestic rice originated in China in Hunan Province; evidence of ancient rice paddies has been discovered there. The difference between wild rice and domestic rice is that wild rice occurs naturally while domestic rice seeds are selectively planted according to the potential to yield desired traits. Finally, another way that the origin of rice is explained is through the use of ancient myths. One such myth about the origin of rice is the story of Shuhwa, a girl who planted a seed she found in a dog's fur during a flood and which later produced rice.

Exercise 3 1 Ⓒ 2 Ⓐ 3 Ⓐ p.30

Script 01-12

M1 Professor: Yesterday, we ended our lecture with a discussion of cavities. Today, we will be discussing oral plaque. Does anyone know the definition of oral plaque?

W Student: Is oral plaque a buildup of sugar on your teeth?

M1: That is a good guess. Plaque can build up on your

teeth due to the ingestion of too much sugar, but oral plaque is actually a yellowish sticky film of bacteria. It is not so much the presence of this particular bacteria that is bad for your teeth. After all, it occurs naturally within our mouths. It is the failure properly to clean the plaque from our teeth on a day-to-day basis that leads to what we discussed yesterday: dental cavities or even more serious diseases such as periodontitis and gingivitis.

M2 Student: But if the bacteria that makes up plaque occurs naturally, then it must be good for us. And if it is good for us, why would it lead to cavities or diseases?

M1: Good question. The reason is that if the plaque is not removed regularly, it hardens into what is known as tartar. Tartar is a very hard substance that irritates our gums, causing them to grow red and swollen. And once tartar starts collecting near the gum line, it becomes very difficult to clean your teeth properly. Your gums may even start to bleed, leading to one of the diseases I named earlier, gingivitis.

M2: Eww! That sounds disgusting.

M1: It is very disgusting and a serious problem if people fail to take proper care of their teeth. The good news is that the body has a natural defense against plaque, so with regular brushing and regular visits to the dentist, you can help protect your teeth from the buildup of plaque.

W: Would diligent brushing be good enough? I just hate going to the dentist.

M1: I wish I could say yes, but it is imperative that you see a dentist at least twice a year so that he or she can clean plaque not only from your teeth but also from below the gum line. Once the dentist has cleaned your teeth thoroughly, it takes three to four months for the plaque to return. In the meantime, your own saliva is doing its utmost to help you keep plaque at bay by actively neutralizing the acidic environment caused by the bacteria. Eventually, however, the plaque builds up to such a level that your saliva is no longer able to penetrate and neutralize the acidity. When that happens, the microorganisms in the plaque release their acids, which attack your tooth enamel and cause it to break down.

W: I guess I never considered the serious consequences of not brushing my teeth regularly.

M1: Well, don't worry too much. The practice of good oral hygiene—daily brushing and flossing—is the best way to prevent the buildup of plaque. This, combined with regular visits to the dentist, should keep you in good oral health.

해석

M1 Professor: 어제는 충치에 대한 논의로 강의가 끝났죠. 오늘은 치태에 대해 논의할 예정입니다. 치태의 정의를 아는 사람이 있나요?

W Student: 치태는 치아에 당이 쌓이는 건가요?

M1: 괜찮은 대답이군요. 치태는 당을 너무 많이 섭취해서 치아에 쌓일 수도 있지만, 치태는 사실 노란색의 끈적끈적한 박테리아 막입니다. 이 특정 박테리아가 있다는 사실 자체가 치아에 나쁜 것은 아니에요. 어쨌거나 입안에서 자연적으로 생기니까요. 어제 논의했던 충치 또는 치주염 및 치은염과 같은 보다 심각한 질환을 일으키는 것은 매일 치아에서 치태를 적절하게 제거해 내지 못하기 때문이죠.

M2 Student: 하지만 치태를 만드는 박테리아가 자연적으로 생기는 것이라면, 틀림없이 우리에게 좋은 것일 텐데요. 그리고 우리에게 좋은 것이라면, 왜 그로 인해 충치나 질병이 발생하나요?

M1: 좋은 질문이군요. 그 이유는 치태가 규칙적으로 제거되지 않는 경우 단단해져서 치석이라는 것이 되기 때문이죠. 치석은 잇몸에 염증을 일으키고 잇몸을 빨갛고 붓게 만드는 매우 딱딱한 물질입니다. 일단 잇몸에 치석이 쌓이기 시작하면 제대로 양치질을 하는 일이 매우 힘들어져요. 잇몸에서 피가 날 수도 있고, 이로 인해 제가 앞서 언급했던 질병 중 하나인 치은염이 발생할 수도 있죠.

M2: 웩! 끔찍하게 들리는군요.

M1: 치은염은 매우 끔찍한 것으로 치아를 적절하게 관리하지 못하는 경우 심각한 문제가 됩니다. 좋은 소식은 신체에 치태에 대한 자연적인 방어 시스템이 있기 때문에 규칙적으로 양치질을 하고 정기적으로 치과를 방문하면 치아에 치태가 쌓이는 것을 막을 수 있다는 점이에요.

W: 양치질만 부지런히 해도 충분할까요? 치과에 가는 건 정말 싫거든요.

M1: 저도 그렇다고 대답할 수 있으면 좋겠지만, 치아뿐만 아니라 잇몸선 아래쪽의 치태까지 제거하기 위해서는 최소한 1년에 한 번은 치과에 가야 합니다. 치과 의사가 치아를 깨끗하게 만들면 다시 치태가 생기기까지 3개월에서 4개월이 걸리죠. 이 시기에는 여러분의 침이 박테리아 때문에 생기는 산성 환경을 적극적으로 중화시키기 때문에 치태가 끼지 못합니다. 하지만 결국에는 침이 산성을 뚫고 이를 중화시킬 수 없는 수준으로 치태가 쌓이게 되죠. 이런 일이 발생하면 치태 안의 미생물들이 산성 물질을 분비해서 치아 법랑을 공격해 이를 부서지게 만듭니다.

W: 규칙적으로 양치질을 하지 않는 경우의 심각한 결과에 대해서는 한 번도 생각해 보지 않았던 것 같아요.

M1: 음, 너무 걱정할 필요는 없어요. 건강에 좋은 구강 위생 습관, 즉 매일 양치질을 하고 치실을 사용하는 것이 치태가 쌓이는 것을 막는 최선의 방법이죠. 그렇게 하면서 정기적으로 치과를 방문한다면 건강한 구강 상태를 유지할 수 있어요.

Summary Note

A

❶ oral plaque
❷ sugar
❸ bacteria
❹ gingivitis
❺ substance
❻ swollen
❼ regularly
❽ Saliva

B

Oral plaque is a yellowish sticky film of bacteria that forms naturally on the teeth. However, if not properly removed, oral plaque can form into a hard substance known as tartar. In turn, if tartar is not properly treated, it can lead to much more serious diseases like gingivitis and periodontitis. The body does its best to combat the buildup of oral plaque into tartar; it even has its own natural defense: saliva. Saliva helps break down the bacteria by actively neutralizing the acidic environment. The best way to prevent plaque from building up in the mouth is to incorporate a rigorous daily routine of brushing and flossing with regular visits to the dentist to remove all the plaque from the teeth and gums.

Exercise 4 1 Ⓒ 2 Ⓓ 3 Ⓐ p.32

Script 01-13

M1 Professor: Today, we are going to be discussing a beautiful yet intimidating animal, the tiger. First of all, I assume everyone knows what animal I'm talking about when I mention the word tiger. Is that right?

M2 Student: A tiger is a mammal with orange and black striped fur. It also has white markings on its face, chest, and underside.

M1: Good. And did you also know that no two tigers share the same stripe pattern?

M2: So their stripes are like our fingerprints. Each has its own unique print.

M1: Yes, an excellent analogy.

M2: Professor, one time I was at a zoo, and I saw an all-white tiger. Was it sick?

M1: Oh, no. It wasn't sick. What you saw was something very rare: an albino tiger.

M2: An albino tiger? What is that?

M1: An albino tiger is a tiger with a marked deficiency in skin pigmentation—for example, white fur, pinkish eyes, and no stripes—due to a hereditary defect.

M2: The tiger I saw was enormous. When you see tigers on television or in a magazine or book, they never appear that big.

M1: A tiger's size can be very deceiving. Did you know that it is the largest of all the cats?

M2: No way. Lions are the largest cat.

M1: One would think so. But a lion's mane can actually add to the illusion that it is bigger than a tiger. It is, however, the tiger that can grow up to thirteen feet in length and weigh as much as 700 pounds or as little as 200 pounds. Nevertheless, some tigers are as small as four feet.

M2: That's a pretty big discrepancy in the range of tigers' length and weight. There must be a lot of different types of tigers.

M1: Good observation. Most people may think that all tigers are the same. Besides the size differences that occur between males and females, there are also eight subspecies of tigers that scientists have identified. The biggest is the Siberian tiger.

M2: With eight different subspecies, you'd think we would see lots of tigers, but aren't tigers on the endangered species list?

M1: Unfortunately, yes. About 100 years ago, there were an estimated 100,000 tigers in the wild. Today, estimates are anywhere from 2,500 to 5,000, both in the wild and in wildlife preserves and zoos. And not all of the subspecies of tigers are still in existence. The Bali tiger, for example, became extinct in the 1940s. The Caspian and Javan tigers are also extinct. Of the remaining subspecies, all are endangered. These include the Siberian, Bengal, Indochinese, Sumatran, and South China tigers.

M2: Where are all of these tigers? Are they in North America? Australia?

M1: In the past, tigers ranged anywhere between eastern Turkey and Asia. Now, sadly, most tigers are found only in parts of Asia.

M2: But why are tigers endangered species? They seem too beautiful and majestic to kill.

M1: It is for this precise reason that tigers are becoming extinct. Poachers hunt them for their skins mainly. And many hunters consider them valuable as big game trophies. In addition, as humans move into tiger habitats, people increasingly see the tigers as a threat to humans and their livestock and crops.

해석

M1 Professor: 오늘은 아름답지만 무서운 동물인 호랑이에 대해서 살펴보도록 하죠. 먼저, 제가 호랑이라는 단어를 언급할 때 제가 어떤 동물을 말하는지는 모두 알고 있으리라 생각합니다.

M2 Student: 호랑이는 주황색과 검정색의 줄무늬가 있는 털을 가진 포유 동물이죠. 또한 얼굴, 가슴, 그리고 배 아래쪽에 하얀 무늬가 있어요.

M1: 잘 대답했어요. 그런데 두 마리의 호랑이가 똑같은 줄무늬를 갖는 경우는 없다는 점도 알고 있나요?

M2: 그러면 줄무늬가 우리의 지문과 같은 것이겠군요. 각각 고유한 무늬를 갖고 있으니까요.

M1: 네, 비유가 훌륭하군요.

M2: 교수님, 저는 예전에 동물원에 갔다가 하얀색 호랑이를 봤어요. 병에 걸린 것이었을까요?

M1: 오, 아니에요. 학생이 본 것은 매우 드문 것으로, 백호였어요.

M2: 백호요? 그것이 무엇인가요?

M1: 백호는 유전적인 결함으로 인해, 예컨대 하얀색 털과 분홍색 눈을 가지고 있지만 줄무늬는 가지고 있지 않은 경우처럼, 피부 색소가 심각하게 결핍되어 있는 호랑이에요.

M2: 제가 본 호랑이는 엄청나게 컸어요. 텔레비전이나 잡지 혹은 책에서 보는 경우에는 그렇게 커 보이지 않지만요.

M1: 호랑이의 크기에 속기가 매우 쉬워요. 고양이과 동물 중에서 호랑이가 가

장 크다는 것을 알고 있었나요?

M2: 아니에요. 사자가 가장 큽니다.

M1: 그렇게 생각할 수도 있죠. 하지만 사자의 갈기 때문에 사자가 호랑이보다 더 크다는 착각을 할 수 있어요. 하지만 호랑이는 13피트의 길이까지 자랄 수 있고, 많게는 700파운드, 적게는 200파운드의 몸무게가 나갑니다. 그럼에도 불구하고 4피트 정도의 작은 호랑이들도 있죠.

M2: 호랑이의 몸길이와 몸무게의 범위가 매우 크군요. 틀림없이 종류도 여러가지일 것 같아요.

M1: 관찰력이 좋군요. 대부분의 사람들은 호랑이가 모두 똑같다고 생각할 수도 있어요. 암컷과 수컷 간에 존재하는 크기 차이 외에도, 과학자들은 여덟 개의 아종이 존재한다는 점을 알아냈습니다. 가장 큰 것은 시베리아호랑이에요.

M2: 여덟 개의 아종이 있으면 호랑이를 많이 볼 수 있을 것으로 생각되는데, 호랑이는 멸종 위기종이 아닌가요?

M1: 안타깝게도 그렇습니다. 약 100년 전에는 야생 상태의 호랑이가 10만 마리 정도 있었던 것으로 생각되었어요. 오늘날에는 야생 및 야생 동물 보호 구역과 동물원을 합쳐 2,500에서 5,000마리 정도가 존재한다고 생각됩니다. 호랑이의 모든 아종이 현존하는 것은 아니에요. 예를 들어 발리호랑이는 1940년대에 멸종했습니다. 카스피아호랑이와 자바호랑이 역시 멸종했고요. 남아 있는 아종 모두 멸종 위기에 처해 있습니다. 여기에는 시베리아호랑이, 벵갈호랑이, 인도차이나호랑이, 수마트라호랑이, 그리고 남중국호랑이가 포함되죠.

M2: 그 호랑이들은 전부 어디에 있나요? 북아메리카에 있나요? 호주인가요?

M1: 과거에는 터키 동부와 아시아 사이의 어디에서나 호랑이가 돌아다녔습니다. 지금은 안타깝게도 대부분의 호랑이들이 아시아의 일부 지역에서만 관찰되고 있죠.

M2: 그런데 왜 호랑이가 멸종 위기종인가요? 죽이기에는 너무 아름답고 근엄하게 보이잖아요.

M1: 호랑이가 멸종되고 있는 이유는 바로 다음과 같은 이유 때문이에요. 밀렵꾼들이 주로 호랑이 가죽을 얻기 위해 호랑이를 사냥합니다. 그리고 많은 사냥꾼들이 호랑이 가죽을 커다란 사냥물의 전리품으로서 귀하게 생각하죠. 게다가 사람들이 호랑이 서식지 안으로 들어가면서 점점 더 호랑이를 인간 및 인간의 가축과 농작물을 위협하는 존재로 여기고 있어요.

Summary Note

A

❶ the tiger
❷ orange and black
❸ white markings
❹ skin pigmentation
❺ stripes
❻ 13
❼ eight
❽ extinct

B

A tiger is a mammal that generally has orange fur and black stripes with white markings on its face, chest, and underside. Tigers are also the largest of all the cats. The largest is the Siberian tiger. Tigers can range in length from four to thirteen feet and can weigh anywhere between 200 and 700 pounds. They are broken down into eight different subspecies, three of which are extinct. The extinct subspecies are the Bali, Caspian, and Javan tigers. The fact that there are extinct subspecies of tigers is also a reason why tigers are listed as endangered species. While tigers once roamed anywhere between eastern Turkey and Asia, what tigers remain are now only found in certain parts of Asia. Tigers are becoming extinct because they are being poached for their skins and because they sometimes kill cattle and other livestock.

Integrated Listening & Speaking p.34

A

Script 01-14

M Professor: Last week, we defined an opera as a form of drama that incorporates music or dancing or both. Modern opera developed in Italy during the Renaissance, but the origin of operas goes further back to the days of the ancient Greeks. The operatic movement quickly spread throughout Europe and into Russia during and after the Renaissance. Such widespread interest in the composition and production of operas naturally led to the art form acquiring many different elements. One such development was the operetta, a short opera often comical in nature. Opera seria is a dramatic opera, often involving death, and opera comique is an opera comical in nature. However, one of the most famous elements of opera is the aria, a complex musical passage that exhibits a singer's amazing vocal range.

1 An opera is a drama that incorporates music or dancing or a combination of both.

2 The Italians were the first to develop modern opera, but the ancient Greeks first developed the art form.

3 It is a complex musical passage exhibiting a singer's vocal range.

B

Script 01-15

M Professor: Oral plaque is a yellowish sticky film of bacteria that forms naturally on the teeth. However, if it is not properly removed, oral plaque can form into a hard substance that is known as tartar. It can irritate the gums to make them red and swollen and also cause gingivitis. In turn, if tartar is not properly treated, it can lead to much more serious diseases, such as gingivitis and periodontitis. The body does its best to combat the buildup of oral plaque into tartar; it even has its own natural defense, which is saliva. Saliva helps break down the bacteria by actively neutralizing the acidic environment. The best way to prevent plaque from building up in the mouth is to incorporate a rigorous daily routine of brushing and flossing with regular visits to the dentist to remove all the plaque from the teeth and gums.

1 Oral plaque is yellowish sticky bacteria that occur naturally in the mouth and form on the teeth.

2 If not properly removed, plaque can build up into tartar.

3 They should brush and floss daily and make regular visits to the dentist.

Mini TOEFL iBT Practice Test p.36

1 Ⓒ 2 Ⓓ 3 Ⓑ 4 Ⓓ 5 Ⓑ

6 Ⓑ 7 Ⓒ 8 Ⓓ 9 Ⓑ 10 1589-1594: [1], [4] 1599-1608: [2], [3] 11 Ⓐ

[1-5]

Script 01-16

M Student: Professor Willis, I just received your email a few minutes ago. I was on my way to the gym to attend basketball practice, but the tone of your email was a bit urgent, so I thought I'd be sure to come here first.

W Professor: That's very admirable of you, Adrian. Thank you. I didn't know that you play on the school's basketball team.

M: Ah, yes, ma'am. I'm just a bench player this year, but I get to play a few minutes each game. I hope to become a starter next year if I can keep improving.

W: Well, good luck to you. I hope you can do it.

M: Thanks a lot. So, um . . . your email didn't mention why you want to talk to me.

W: That's right. I would rather speak with you about this matter in person.

M: Okay.

W: You haven't turned in the topic of your project assignment to me yet. It was due last week, and everyone else in the class turned theirs in. You're the only one left. So . . . what's the topic of your individual project going to be?

M: Individual project?

W: Seriously?

M: Um . . . I'm sorry, but I'm not sure what you're talking about.

W: Adrian, I've talked about the project almost every class during the first six weeks of the semester. How could you possibly not know about it?

M: Um . . .

W: Have you been attending classes?

M: I go to most of them . . . Well, I guess I have been to about half of the classes.

W: You know, you might want to focus on class a bit more and less on basketball. If you don't do well in your classes, your grades won't be high enough, and you won't be able to come back to be on the team next semester. You realize that we have a midterm exam coming up next week, right?

M: Er, yes. I'm well aware of the test. I haven't started studying for it yet, but I will probably start doing that on the weekend. So . . . the project?

W: You need to do an individual project based on something we have studied in class up to this point. All of the other students chose their own topics, but I think it would be best if you simply chose from this list that I have right here. There are five topics on it. Why don't you read through them and see which one you like?

M: Okay. I can do that . . . Hmm . . . Suspension bridges and how they work . . . The construction process of a skyscraper . . . Erecting a tower . . . How to build a tunnel through a mountain . . . And the way to construct a deep-water port . . . Those are some interesting topics. I think I'd like to go with the first one. I'll do my project on suspension bridges.

W: That's great. Now remember you not only need to write a report, but you also have to construct a model suspension bridge. As this is an engineering class, I expect your bridge to look good and to be able to stay up.

M: Yes, ma'am. I'll do my best.

해석

M Student: Willis 교수님, 조금 전에 교수님의 이메일을 받았어요. 농구 연습을 하러 체육관에 가던 길이었는데, 이메일의 어조를 보니 약간 급한 일 같아서 먼저 이곳으로 와야겠다고 생각했죠.

W Professor: 칭찬할 만하군요, Adrian. 고마워요. 학생이 교내 농구팀에 소속되어 있다는 점은 제가 모르고 있었네요.

M: 아, 네, 교수님. 올해는 후보 선수일 뿐이지만 경기마다 잠깐씩 경기에 참가하고 있죠. 실력을 향상시켜서 내년에 선발 선수가 되기를 바라고 있어요.

W: 음, 행운을 빌어요. 그렇게 되기를 바랄게요.

M: 정말 고맙습니다. 그러면, 음… 교수님 이메일에 저와 왜 이야기를 나누셔야 하는지는 나와 있지 않더군요.

W: 맞아요. 이번 문제에 대해 학생과 직접 이야기를 하는 것이 좋을 것 같아서요.

M: 그렇군요.

W: 학생은 아직 프로젝트 과제의 주제를 제출하지 않았어요. 마감이 지난 주였

는데, 수업을 듣는 다른 모든 학생들은 제출을 했죠. 학생 혼자만 남았어요. 그래서… 개별 프로젝트의 주제가 무엇인가요?

M: 개별 프로젝트요?

W: 진심인가요?

M: 음… 죄송하지만 무슨 말씀이신지 잘 모르겠어요.

W: Adrian, 학기 첫 6주 동안 거의 모든 수업에서 제가 프로젝트에 대해 이야기했어요. 어떻게 그에 대해 모를 수가 있는 거죠?

M: 음…

W: 수업에 참석하고 있었나요?

M: 대부분 수업에 참석을… 음, 수업의 절반 정도에 참석했던 것 같아요.

W: 알겠지만, 수업에 조금 더 집중하고 농구에는 조금 덜 집중하는 것이 좋을 것 같아요. 수업 성적이 좋지 않으면 학점이 충분히 높지 않을 것이고, 그러면 다음 학기에 팀으로 돌아갈 수 없을 거예요. 다음 주에 중간고사가 있다는 건 알고 있죠, 그렇죠?

M: 어, 네. 중간고사에 대해서는 잘 알고 있어요. 아직 시험 공부를 시작하지는 않았지만, 아마도 주말에는 시작하게 될 거예요. 그러면… 프로젝트는요?

W: 지금까지 수업에서 우리가 공부했던 것을 바탕으로 개별 프로젝트를 수행해야 해요. 다른 학생들은 모두 자신의 주제를 선택했지만, 학생의 경우에는 여기 제가 가지고 있는 이 리스트에서 그냥 하나를 고르는 것이 최선일 것 같군요. 여기에 5개의 주제가 있어요. 읽어보고 마음에 드는 것을 확인해 볼래요?

M: 좋아요. 그럴게요… 흠… 현수교와 현수교의 원리… 고층 건물의 건설 과정… 타워 건설… 산을 관통하는 터널 공사 방식… 그리고 심해항 건설법… 흥미로운 주제들이군요. 첫 번째 것이 마음에 드는 것 같아요. 현수교에 관한 프로젝트를 하도록 할게요.

W: 잘 되었군요. 이제 보고서를 써야 할 뿐만 아니라 현수교 모형도 제작해야 한다는 점을 기억해 주세요. 이번 수업은 공학 수업이기 때문에 학생의 다리가 멋지게 보이고 잘 서 있을 수 있기를 기대할게요.

M: 네, 교수님. 최선을 다하겠습니다.

[6-11]

Script 01-17

W Student: I really loved reading *Hamlet, Prince of Denmark*. Who was William Shakespeare that he could write such an amazing play?

M Professor: **Ah, Shakespeare was truly an amazing man and such an enigma.**

W: An enigma? But why?

M: Well, there are many conflicting historical reports of the great English bard. For instance, no one knows exactly on which date Shakespeare was born. All that is known is that he was most likely born at one of his father's two houses on Henley Street in Stratford-Upon-Avon, England. The earliest record of Shakespeare was recorded on April 26, 1564, in Holy Trinity Church in Stratford but only because it was custom to baptize a child three days after his birth. So Shakespeare's birthday is recognized as April 23, which, coincidentally enough, was the same day as his burial fifty-two years later.

W: Wow! That is a coincidence. But did he learn to write plays when he was at school? How did he become such a great writer?

M: Actually, there is no record of Shakespeare having gone to school. Things were not recorded as meticulously as they are today. What is known is that William Shakespeare married Anne Hathaway in 1582, when Shakespeare was just eighteen years old and Anne Hathaway was twenty-six years old. Soon after, they had three children. From 1585 through 1592, there is no official record as to what William Shakespeare was up to. It is speculated, based on the range of knowledge revealed in his plays, that Shakespeare could have been doing as many things as money lending, gardening, sailing, scavenging, soldiering, printing, and even working as a school master during those "lost" years. Whatever the case, Shakespeare moved to London in 1592, and that is when Shakespeare's name first started showing up in records, most of them surrounding the realm of theater.

From 1589 to 1594, Shakespeare was working hard writing the plays, *Henry VI*, *Titus Andronicus*, and *The Comedy of Errors*. It was also during that time that the dreaded bubonic plague hit England, closing down the London theaters, so Shakespeare spent most of his time writing poetry. For the next two years, he would be busy writing both plays and poetry, and in 1597, he purchased New Place, the second largest house in Stratford-Upon-Avon, where his wife and his children lived, making frequent trips between there and London as he balanced his work and family life. In 1599, he became one of the prime shareholders in the popular playhouse The Globe in London, and he had a hand in all aspects of play production.

The following nine years would prove to be Shakespeare's most productive. During that time, he wrote the great plays *Twelfth Night*, *Troilus and Cressida*, *Hamlet*, *Othello*, *Measure for Measure*, *King Lear*, *Macbeth*, and more. He continued writing plays until 1613, and he moved permanently out of London around the year 1611 to live out the rest of his days in Stratford. On April 23, 1616, the great English bard, William Shakespeare, breathed his last and died.

해석

W Student: 저는 *햄릿, 덴마크의 왕자*를 정말 재미있게 읽었어요. 그처럼 놀라운 희곡을 쓴 윌리엄 셰익스피어는 도대체 어떤 사람이었나요?

M Professor: 아, 셰익스피어는 정말 대단한 사람이자 불가사의한 인물이었어요.

W: 불가사의하다고요? 왜죠?

M: 음, 이 위대한 영국의 극작가에 대한 많은 역사적인 기록들이 모순적이기 때문이에요. 예를 들어 셰익스피어가 태어난 정확한 날짜는 아무도 모릅니다. 알려진 것이라고는 그가 영국 스트랫퍼드-어폰-에이번의 헨리가에 있는 그의 아버

지 소유의 두 채의 집 중 한 곳에서 태어났을 것이라는 점이에요. 셰익스피어에 관한 최초의 기록은 1564년 4월 26일 스트랫퍼드의 홀리 트리니티 교회에서 작성되었는데, 아이의 출생 후 3일 뒤에 아이에게 세례를 주는 것이 관습이었기 때문이었죠. 그래서 셰익스피어가 태어난 날이 4월 23일로 생각되는데, 공교롭게도 그는 52년 후 정확히 같은 날에 사망을 했습니다.

W: 와! 정말 우연의 일치군요. 그런데 셰익스피어는 학교에서 희곡을 쓰는 법을 배웠나요? 어떻게 그처럼 위대한 작가가 되었나요?

M: 사실 셰익스피어가 학교에 다녔다는 기록은 존재하지 않아요. 오늘날처럼 자세하게 기록되는 경우가 없었죠. 알려진 바에 따르면 윌리엄 셰익스피어는 1582년에 앤 해서웨이와 결혼을 했는데, 이때 셰익스피어의 나이는 18세였고 앤 해서웨이는 26세였어요. 이후 그들은 세 명의 아이를 낳았습니다. 1585년부터 1592년 사이에 윌리엄 셰익스피어가 한 일에 대해서는 공식적인 기록이 없어요. 그의 희곡에 드러나 있는 내용에 기초해 볼 때 셰익스피어는 "사라진" 해 동안 대부, 원예, 항해, 청소, 군생활과 관련 일, 그리고 심지어는 학교 수업도 했을 것으로 추측되고 있죠. 사실이 무엇이든 셰익스피어는 1592년에 런던으로 이사했는데, 이때 셰익스피어라는 이름이 처음으로 기록에 나타났고, 이 중 대부분은 연극과 관련된 것들이었습니다.

1589년과 1594년까지 셰익스피어는 열심히 *헨리 6세*, *타이투스 안드로니카스*, 그리고 *실수 연발*과 같은 희곡 작품을 썼습니다. 또한 끔찍한 선페스트가 유럽을 강타해 런던의 극장들이 문을 닫은 것도 이때였는데, 그러자 셰익스피어는 대부분의 시간을 씨를 쓰면서 보냈어요. 그 뒤로 2년 간 그는 희곡과 시 모두를 쓰느라 바쁘게 지냈을 것이며, 1597년에는 스트랫퍼드-어폰-에이번에서 두 번째로 큰 저택인 뉴 플레이스를 구입하고, 이곳에서 아내와 자식들과 함께 살면서 이곳과 런던을 자주 오가며 일과 가정 생활 간의 균형을 맞추었습니다. 1599년 그는 런던의 인기 극장이었던 더 글로브의 최대 주주 중 한 명이 되었고, 모든 측면에서 연극 제작에 관여했어요.

그 이후의 9년은 셰익스피어에게 가장 생산적인 시기였습니다. 이때 *십이야*, *트로일로스와 크레시다*, *햄릿*, *오델로*, *자에는 자로*, *리어왕*, *맥베드* 등의 위대한 희곡을 썼죠. 그는 1613년까지 계속해서 희곡 작품을 썼고, 1611년 즈음에는 런던에서 완전히 빠져 나와 스트랫퍼드에서 여생을 보냈어요. 1616년 4월 23일, 영국의 위대한 음유 시인이었던 윌리엄 셰익스피어는 마지막 숨을 거두었습니다.

Vocabulary Check-Up

p.41

A

1 Ⓑ	2 Ⓔ	3 Ⓘ	4 Ⓛ	5 Ⓒ
6 Ⓗ	7 Ⓙ	8 Ⓕ	9 Ⓜ	10 Ⓐ
11 Ⓚ	12 Ⓖ	13 Ⓓ	14 Ⓞ	15 Ⓝ

B

1 Ⓒ	2 Ⓔ	3 Ⓐ	4 Ⓓ	5 Ⓑ

UNIT 02 Listening for Main Purpose

Basic Drill

p.44

Drill 1 Ⓒ

Script 02-02

W Student: Hello. I'm here to use the swimming pool. But, uh, I don't know where it is.

M Gym Employee: The pool is located in the basement. To get there, you can go down the stairs in the back.

W: Great. Thanks.

M: Hold on a moment. You can't go swimming right now. The swim team is having practice.

W: Oh . . . Well, they aren't using the entire pool, are they?

M: Actually, they are. The swim team expanded by several members this year, so the entire pool is off limits to everyone else each day between four and six PM.

W: Okay. That's fine. But I can use it any other time, right? And do I need to pay to use it?

M: If you're a full-time student here, you don't need to pay anything at all. And yes, you can use the pool whenever it's open.

W: That's wonderful. Oh, one last question . . . Is the pool open on the weekend?

M: Yes, but the hours are different from weekdays. If you go to the pool, you'll see the hours posted on the door for each day.

해석

W Student: 안녕하세요. 수영장을 이용하려고 왔는데요. 하지만, 어, 어디에 있는지 모르겠어요.

M Gym Employee: 수영장은 지하에 있어요. 그곳에 가려면 뒤쪽 계단으로 내려가시면 돼요.

W: 잘 되었군요. 고맙습니다.

M: 잠시만요. 지금은 수영을 하실 수 없어요. 수영부가 연습 중이라서요.

W: 오… 음, 그들이 수영장 전체를 사용하는 것은 아니죠, 그런가요?

M: 실은 전체를 사용하고 있어요. 수영부 인원이 올해 몇 명 늘어나서 매일 오후 6시에서 6시까지는 다른 사람들이 수영장 출입을 할 수가 없어요.

W: 그렇군요. 괜찮아요. 하지만 다른 시간에는 이용할 수 있죠, 그렇죠? 그리고 이용하려면 얼마를 내야 하나요?

M: 이곳 정규 학생이라면 전혀 비용을 낼 필요가 없어요. 그리고, 그래요, 개방된 때에는 언제라도 수영장을 이용할 수 있어요.

W: 잘 되었군요. 오, 마지막으로 질문을 드리면… 주말에도 수영장이 개방되나요?

M: 네, 하지만 주중과 개방 시간이 달라요. 수영장에 오면 문앞에서 각 날짜에 해당되는 이용 시간표를 보시게 될 거예요.

Drill 2 ⓒ

Script 02-03

W Professor: Hello, Theo. Thanks for dropping by my office.

M Student: No problem, Professor Evergreen. You know, uh, I was going to come by here even if you hadn't asked me to. I think you forgot to hand me back the short story I wrote today. Everyone but me received their story.

W: I didn't hand it back to you on purpose, Theo. And that's the reason I asked you to come to my office.

M: Oh . . . I guess you didn't like my story. That's too bad.

W: On the contrary, I loved it.

M: Huh?

W: I found it to be a very intriguing and well-written work of fantasy. Where did you get the idea for it?

M: Uh . . . I don't know really. I just read a lot of fantasy works and wrote something in a similar vein.

W: You didn't copy it from anyone else's writing, did you?

M: Not at all. I would never do that. I just had an idea and went with it.

W: Well, it's a fabulous work, and you got an A+ on the assignment. If you don't mind, I'm going to read it out loud to the class the next time we meet.

해석

W Professor: 안녕하세요, Theo. 제 사무실에 와 줘서 고마워요.

M Student: 천만에요, Evergreen 교수님. 아시다시피, 어, 제게 요청을 하지 않으셨어도 여기에 올 생각이었어요. 제가 오늘 작성했던 단편 소설을 교수님께서 잊으시고 돌려 주지 않으신 것 같아서요. 저만 빼고 모두들 소설을 받았으니까요.

W: 저는 의도적으로 돌려 주지 않은 것이었어요, Theo. 그리고 제 사무실로 오라고 요청한 것도 그 때문이고요.

M: 오… 제 소설이 마음에 들지 않으신 것 같군요. 유감이네요.

W: 그와 반대로, 정말 마음에 들었어요.

M: 네?

W: 매우 흥미롭고 잘 쓰여진 판타지 작품이라고 생각했어요. 어디에서 그에 대한 아이디어를 얻었나요?

M: 어… 사실 잘 모르겠어요. 저는 판타지 작품을 많이 읽었는데, 비슷한 방식으로 글을 쓴 것 같아요.

W: 다른 사람의 글을 따라 쓴 것이 아니었군요, 그런가요?

M: 전혀 그렇지 않았어요. 저는 결코 그런 일을 하지 않아요. 아이디어가 떠올라서 썼을 뿐이에요.

W: 음, 훌륭한 작품이기 때문에 학생은 과제에서 A+를 받았어요. 괜찮다면 다음 수업 시간에 제가 큰 소리로 학생들에게 읽어 줄게요.

Drill 3 ⓓ

Script 02-04

W Professor: It's well known that there are eight planets in the solar system. In addition, there are various dwarf planets. Pluto is the best-known of them, but there are several others, including a few in the Kuiper Belt. This is an area which is way beyond the orbit of Neptune, the farthest planet from the sun. However, there are many astronomers who believe there is yet another planet—a ninth planet—that is orbiting the sun much farther away than Neptune and Pluto. Despite not having been discovered, this theoretical planet has been given the name Planet X.

Astronomers who subscribe to the notion that Planet X exists but hasn't been located yet believe the planet is around the same size as Neptune. It likely has a mass which is ten times that of Earth, and it probably takes between 10,000 and 20,000 years to complete a single orbit around the sun. You're surely wondering why astronomers believe Planet X is real. Well, the main reason has to do with gravity. You see, astronomers have noticed some strange behavior in the dwarf planets and the other objects located in the Kuiper Belt. The best explanation they have is that a large planet—uh, you know, Planet X—is having an effect on them due to the strength of its gravity. Here, um, let me show you how some of these dwarf planets are behaving, and then you'll understand better.

해석

W Professor: 태양계에 8개의 행성이 있다는 점은 잘 알려져 있습니다. 게다가 다양한 왜행성들도 존재하죠. 그중에서 가장 유명한 것은 명왕성이지만, 카이퍼 벨트에 있는 몇 개를 포함하여 다른 외행성들도 존재합니다. 카이퍼 벨트는 태양에서 가장 멀리 떨어져 있는 행성인 해왕성의 궤도 밖에 있는 지역이에요. 하지만 해왕성과 명왕성보다 훨씬 더 멀리 떨어진 곳에서 태양 주위를 돌고 있는 또 다른 행성, 즉 아홉 번째 행성이 존재한다고 믿는 천문학자들이 다수 있습니다. 발견된 것은 아니지만, 이러한 이론상의 행성에게 행성 X라는 이름이 붙어졌어요.

행성 X가 존재하지만 아직 그 위치가 밝혀지지 않았다는 주장을 지지하는 천문학자들은 이 행성의 크기가 해왕성과 비슷하다고 믿습니다. 질량은 지구의 10배에 이를 것으로 생각되며, 태양 주위를 한 바퀴 도는데 아마 10,000년에서 20,000년이 걸릴 거예요. 왜 천문학자들이 행성 X가 실제로 존재한다고 믿는지 분명 궁금하실 것입니다. 아시다시피, 천문학자들은 왜행성 및 카이퍼 벨트에 위치한 기타 천체들의 이상한 궤도에 주목해 왔어요. 그들이 제시하는 최선의 설명은 커다란 행성이, 어, 아시다시피 행성 X가 강력한 중력으로 이들에게 영향을 미치고 있다는 것이죠. 이제, 음, 이러한 일부 왜행성들의 궤도를 보여 드릴 텐데, 그 후에는 보다 이해하기가 쉬울 거예요.

Drill 4 Ⓑ

Script 02-05

M Professor: In our geology class, one of the most important things you need to be familiar with is the Mohs Hardness Scale. It's something I'm going to mention virtually every time I lecture, particularly when I introduce a new kind of rock or mineral. What is the Mohs Hardness Scale? Well, it's a scale that measures, from one to ten, the hardness of various minerals. And just so you know, in this case, hardness refers to the ability of a mineral to be scratched.

At the bottom of the scale is talc, which has a hardness of one. Number two is gypsum while number three is calcite. So just to make sure you understand, talc cannot scratch either gypsum or calcite because it is too soft. However, both gypsum and calcite can scratch talc while calcite can also scratch gypsum since it has a higher hardness number. Let me continue . . . Fluorite is four, apatite is five, and orthoclase is six. Now, we're getting to the harder minerals. Quartz is seven while topaz is eight. Corundum is nine, and diamond tops the scale at ten. This means that diamond is the hardest mineral known to us. It is capable of scratching anything else on this list.

해석

M Professor: 이번 지질학 수업에서 여러분들이 잘 알고 있어야 할 가장 중요한 것 중의 하나가 모스 경도계입니다. 실제로 제가 강의를 할 때마다, 특히 새로운 종류의 암석이나 광물질을 소개할 때, 언급하게 될 것이에요. 모스 경도계란 무엇일까요? 음, 이는 다양한 광물질의 단단한 정도를 1에서 10까지로 측정한 등급입니다. 그리고 아시다시피 이 경우 단단함이란 광물이 긁힘에 대항할 수 있는 능력을 가리키죠.

모스 경도계의 가장 아래에는 활석이 있으며, 활석의 경도는 1입니다. 두 번째가 석고이고, 세 번째는 방해석이죠. 이해를 돕기 위해 말씀을 드리면, 활석은 무르기 때문에 석고나 방해석에 흠집을 낼 수 없습니다. 하지만 석고와 방해석 모두 활석에 흠집을 낼 수 있고, 또한 방해석은 보다 높은 경도를 갖고 있기 때문에 석고에 흠집을 낼 수가 있어요. 계속해 보면… 형석이 4, 인회석은 5, 그리고 정장석이 6입니다. 자, 보다 단단한 광물질로 넘어가고 있군요. 석영이 7이고 토파즈는 8이에요. 강옥이 9이고, 경도의 가장 위쪽에는 10인 다이아몬드가 있습니다. 이는 다이아몬드가 우리에 알려진 가장 단단한 광물질이라는 점을 의미하죠. 이 리스트에 있는 그 밖의 모든 것에 흠집을 낼 수가 있습니다.

Exercises with Long Conversations

Exercise 1 1 Ⓒ 2 Ⓐ, Ⓑ 3 Ⓒ p.48

Script 02-06

M Professor: It's great to see you. Please have a seat.

W Student: Thank you.

M: How can I help you?

W: Well, in the last lecture, you mentioned that the final exam would be a cumulative test and that it would cover the entire textbook and at least one other history book. I think the textbook is too big. It has over 800 pages. So I'm thinking of withdrawing from your history course.

M: Oh, that's a shame.

W: I really don't want to drop the course, so I thought I'd consult you in case you had any helpful advice.

M: Well, first of all, it's unusual for students to withdraw this far into the semester. We've already completed five weeks of the course.

W: Yes, I know, but the deadline for withdrawal isn't until next week. I enjoy your class, and I love history, but there's too much information to study. I also have a part-time job here on campus, so I don't have much time to study.

M: Let me take a quick look at your record . . . Hmm . . . I see . . . Uh-huh! It looks good. You're doing fine. I don't think there is any danger of you failing the course.

W: No, there isn't.

M: It appears to me that you're working quite hard. Uh, so far, you have done well on the quiz and on the book report. Your participation is good, too. So I think it would be a real shame to see you withdraw after having done so much work.

W: Yeah, I know. To be honest, I'm not worried about passing the course. The problem is that I need high grades so that I can get into law school or graduate school. I don't want to risk getting a low grade, and there's too little time to study the entire textbook. What do you think I should do?

M: Well, are you familiar with HIT? It's our history tutoring program.

W: No, I'm not. I've heard about math tutors and ESL tutors, but I've never heard anything about tutors for history classes.

M: Let me tell you about it. It's not a well-known program because we just started it this semester. Graduate students can provide you with free tutoring three times a week. Some of the HIT tutors reported to me that they spend a lot of time summarizing the textbook and providing advice for exams and assignments.

W: Yes, but unfortunately, most of these university services are offered only in the daytime, and that's when I have to work. I usually work until the early evening.

M: Oh, no problem. The tutoring sessions usually don't start until after 8:00 PM. This service is also available free of charge for all undergraduate students. For more information, visit the department's homepage. Click on the HIT icon, and you should be well on your way.

W: Okay, now I'm excited. I'm going to check this out as soon as I get back to my computer.

해석

M Professor: 만나서 반가워요. 자리에 앉으세요.

W Student: 감사합니다.

M: 어떻게 도와 드리면 될까요?

W: 음, 지난 번 강의에서 교수님께서 말씀하시기를 기말고사 범위는 누적될 것이고 시험 범위에 교재 전체와 적어도 한 권 이상의 다른 역사 서적이 포함될 것이라고 하셨잖아요. 제 생각에는 교재의 양이 너무 많아요. 800페이지가 넘죠. 그래서 교수님의 역사 수업은 수강을 취소할까 생각 중이에요.

M: 오, 안타깝군요.

W: 저도 정말로 취소하고 싶지는 않아서, 교수님께서 도움이 될 만한 충고를 해 주실 수도 있으니 교수님과 상담을 해야겠다고 생각했어요.

M: 음, 우선, 학기 중 이렇게 늦은 시기에 학생들이 수업을 취소하는 건 특이한 경우예요. 이미 수업을 5주나 했잖아요.

W: 네, 저도 알지만, 수강 취소의 마감일은 다음 주에 있어요. 교수님 수업이 마음에 들고 역사도 좋아하는데, 공부해야 할 내용이 너무 많아요. 게다가 저는 교내 아르바이트도 하고 있어서 공부를 할 시간이 그렇게 많지는 않거든요.

M: 잠깐 학생의 성적을 확인해 보면… 흠… 그래요… 어허! 성적이 좋네요. 잘 하고 있어요. 이번 수업에서 학생이 낙제할 위험성은 전혀 없어 보이는군요.

W: 네, 그래요.

M: 제게는 학생이 매우 열심히 공부하는 것처럼 보여요. 어, 지금까지 퀴즈와 독후감에서의 성적이 좋아요. 수업 참여도 역시 좋고요. 그래서 이렇게 잘 하는 학생이 수강을 취소하는 모습을 보게 된다면 정말로 안타까울 것 같군요.

W: 예, 저도 알아요. 솔직히 말씀을 드리면, 수업을 통과하는 것에 대해서는 걱정을 하지 않아요. 문제는 제가 로스쿨이나 대학원에 가기 위해서는 좋은 성적을 받아야 한다는 점이죠. 낮은 점수를 받을 위험을 감수하고 싶지는 않고, 교재 전체를 공부할 시간은 너무 부족해요. 제가 어떻게 해야 한다고 생각하시나요?

M: 음, HIT를 알고 있나요? 역사 개인 교습 프로그램이죠.

W: 아니요, 몰라요. 수학 개인 교사와 ESL 개인 교사에 대해서는 들어본 적이 있는데, 역사 수업을 위한 개인 교사에 대해서는 들어본 적이 없어요.

M: 제가 설명해 드리죠. 이번 학기에는 얼마 전에 시작을 해서 잘 알려져 있지가 않아요. 대학원생들이 일주일에 세 번 무료로 개인 지도를 해 줄 수 있어요. 몇몇 HIT 개인 교사들은 제게 자신들이 교재를 요약해 주고 시험 및 과제에 대한 조언을 하는데 많은 시간을 할애하고 있다고 알려 주더군요.

W: 네, 하지만 안타깝게도 대부분의 그러한 대학 서비스들은 주간에만 제공되는데, 저는 그때 일을 해야 해요. 보통 초저녁까지 일을 하죠.

M: 오, 전혀 문제될 것이 없어요. 개인 교습은 보통 저녁 8시 이후에 시작되니까요. 또한 모든 학부생들에게 무료로 제공되고 있어요. 더 많은 정보가 필요한 경우에는 학과 홈페이지를 방문해 보세요. HIT 아이콘을 클릭하면 잘 알 수 있을 거예요.

W: 좋아요, 기대가 되는군요. 제 컴퓨터 자리에 돌아가는 대로 확인해 볼게요.

Summary Note

A

❶ too long
❷ very late
❸ fine
❹ law or graduate school
❺ tutoring program
❻ free service

B

The student tells the professor that she is thinking of withdrawing from his history course because she has a part-time job, she does not have enough time to study, and the textbook contains too much material to read. The professor tells her that it would be a shame if she dropped out of the course because she has already completed five weeks and has done well on the assignments. He also tells her not to worry about failing the course. The student replies that she is not worried about failing but that her concern is it will be too difficult to attain a high grade. The professor then mentions the history tutoring program. He says that the tutors are graduate students who can probably do a good job of summarizing the textbook. Upon hearing this news, the student becomes excited and tells the professor that she will check out the History Department's website as soon as she gets back to her computer.

Exercise 2 1 Ⓒ 2 Ⓐ, Ⓒ 3 Ⓐ p.50

Script 02-07

M Student: Are you the cafeteria manager?

W Cafeteria Manager: Yes.

M: You're just the person I want to see.

W: Yes, I heard you want to talk to me about the snack bar.

M: That's right. I live in the dormitory next door, and for the past month, some of my friends and I have tried to buy things from your snack bar late in the evening, but it usually closes at 10:00. We want it to stay open until later.

W: We've already extended the snack bar hours to 10:00 PM. Last year, we closed at 9:00.

M: I know, and I appreciate the extended hours. But many students, especially those in the dormitory, like to hang out in the cafeteria in the evening to relax, do homework, work on group projects, or study. There's usually a steady flow of traffic there until late in the evening, especially during exam week. It would be convenient if you stayed open until midnight. Late at night, students don't always feel like walking ten minutes to the nearest convenience store. And during exam week, we're too busy to go for a walk late at night.

W: I understand your situation. But we need to close by ten o'clock so that the janitorial staff can clean the snack bar and the surrounding area. Our custodians finish work at 10:30, and there's nobody to clean the snack bar after then.

M: Why don't you ask the snack bar staff to clean up?

W: I'd like to, but we usually only employ them to serve in the snack bar rather than to do cleaning work. The custodians are also unionized, and there's a clause in the collective bargaining agreement that prevents other people from doing their work.

M: Then why don't you just extend the hours until 12:00 but not allow any cooking after 10:00? Just sell packaged goods after 10:00.

W: Well . . . I don't know. Hmm . . . I don't really know what to say.

M: I started a petition. Let me show it to you . . . Here it is . . . I've already got over 100 signatures from students. Many of them live in the dormitory, and I think I can get more.

W: My goodness! Well, in that case, I don't think we need to have a big debate over this. When are the midterm exams?

M: They start on October 22.

W: All right. I'll ask the snack bar staff to keep it open until 12:00 from October 22 to 27.

M: That would be good, but we'd appreciate if you could start doing it on Sunday, October 21, the evening before the exams begin.

W: Okay, we'll keep it open until midnight for a full week. If everything goes well, or, uh, if there are no complaints, we can do it again during final exam week.

M: We would appreciate that.

해석

M Student: 구내 식당 관리자신가요?

W Cafeteria Manager: 네.

M: 제가 만나고 싶은 분이셨군요.

W: 네, 학생이 저와 스낵바에 대해 이야기하고 싶어한다는 말을 들었어요.

M: 맞아요. 저는 바로 옆 기숙사에 사는데, 지난 달에 친구 몇 명과 함께 저녁 늦은 시간에 스낵바에서 무언가 사려고 했지만, 보통 10시면 그곳 문이 닫히더군요. 저희는 더 늦게까지 문이 열려 있으면 좋겠어요.

W: 이미 스낵바 영업 시간을 10시로 연장한 것이에요. 작년에는 9시에 문을 닫았죠.

M: 그건 저도 아는데, 영업 시간이 연장된 것에 대해서는 감사해요. 하지만 많은 학생들이, 특히 기숙사에 사는 학생들은 저녁에 구내 식당에 모여 휴식을 취하거나, 과제를 하거나, 그룹 프로젝트를 하거나, 혹은 공부하는 것을 좋아해요. 저녁 늦은 시간까지, 특히 시험 기간에는, 꾸준하게 이곳으로 모여들죠. 그래서 자정까지 문을 열면 편리할 것 같아요. 밤늦은 시간에 가장 가까운 편의점까지 가기 위해서는 10분 동안 걸어야 한다는 점을 학생들이 항상 불편해 하거든요. 그리고 시험 기간에는 너무 바빠서 밤늦게 걸어갈 수도 없고요.

W: 사정은 이해해요. 하지만 청소 직원들이 스낵바와 그 주변을 청소하기 위해서는 우리가 10시에 문을 닫아야 해요. 미화원들은 10시 30분에 일이 끝나는데, 그 후에는 스낵바를 청소할 사람이 아무도 없죠.

M: 스낵바 직원들에게 청소를 하라고 하는 건 어떤가요?

W: 저도 그렇게 하고 싶지만, 저희는 보통 스낵바에서 서빙을 할 사람을 뽑는 것이지 청소를 할 사람을 뽑는 것은 아니에요. 또한 미화원들은 조합을 결성하고 있는데, 단체 교섭 협정에는 다른 사람들이 그들의 업무를 하지 못하도록 만드는 조항이 있어요.

M: 그러면 영업 시간을 12시까지로 연장하되 10시 이후에는 조리를 금지시키는 것이 어떨까요? 10시 이후에는 포장이 된 제품만 판매하고요.

W: 음… 잘 모르겠네요… 흠… 정말 어떻게 말을 해야 할지 모르겠어요.

M: 저는 청원을 신청했어요. 보여 드리면… 여기 있어요… 이미 100명의 학생들로부터 서명을 받았죠. 그중 다수는 기숙사에서 살고 있는데, 저는 더 많은 서명을 받을 수 있을 것이라고 생각해요.

W: 맙소사! 음, 그런 경우라면 그에 대해 토론을 벌일 필요가 없을 것 같군요. 중간고사가 언제인가요?

M: 10월 22일에 시작해요.

W: 좋아요. 스낵바 직원들에게 10월 22일부터 27일까지는 12시까지 문을 열어 두라고 요청할게요.

M: 그러면 좋을 것 같은데, 시험 시작 전날인 10월 21일 일요일 저녁부터 시행해 주시면 감사하겠어요.

W: 좋아요. 일주일 내내 자정까지 문을 열어 두도록 하죠. 모든 일이 잘 풀리는 경우나, 어, 아무런 불만이 접수되지 않는 경우에는 기말시험 주간에 또 다시 그렇게 할 수도 있어요.

M: 그렇게 해 주시면 고맙겠네요.

Summary Note

A

❶ extend hours
❷ convenience store
❸ cleaning
❹ union members
❺ only packaged goods
❻ exam week

B

The student visits the cafeteria manager to talk about the hours of the snack bar in the cafeteria. The student says that many students enjoy hanging out and working there at night. He notes that the students are disappointed that the snack bar closes at 10:00 every day. He indicates it would be better if the snack bar stayed open until midnight. The manager replies that it is necessary to close the snack bar by 10:00 to allow the custodians, who stop working at 10:30, time to clean up. He says that student employees are not allowed to clean the snack bar. The student then suggests that they keep the snack bar open during midterm exam week and only permit the sale of packaged goods after 10:00. The student also shows the manager a petition. Upon hearing the student's suggestion and seeing the petition, the manager agrees to extend the snack bar's hours during the midterm exam week and possibly during final exam week, too.

Exercise 3 1 Ⓓ 2 Ⓑ 3 Ⓓ p.52

Script 02-08

W Student: Excuse me. Are you Mr. Glenn?

M Student Activities Office Employee: Yes, that's me. May I ask your name, please?

W: Yes. I'm Wilma Jinks. I received your text message this morning. I'm sorry I couldn't come any earlier, but Wednesday is my busiest day of the week. I just finished my last class of the day ten minutes ago. I've been so busy today that I didn't even have time for lunch.

M: That's quite all right, Wilma. I understand that students are busy. Honestly, I wasn't expecting you to come until tomorrow or maybe even Friday, so I'm rather pleased that you responded so quickly.

W: Ah, I see.

M: So . . . you probably want to know what's going on, don't you?

W: Yes, sir.

M: You are the president of the birdwatching club, aren't you?

W: Yes, that's right. We're a brand-new club on campus. We've only been in existence since the start of last semester, but we're having a great time.

M: I'm pleased to hear that. Now, uh . . . I would like for your club to remain in existence, so I need to tell you something important.

W: Yes?

M: School rules dictate that a club must have at least twelve members to be considered an official club. According to the numbers your club turned in last week, you only have seven members. Is that correct?

W: Unfortunately, it is. We had a few members that didn't come back this semester for various reasons. Most of them are studying abroad this spring.

M: Okay, well, I need you to get some new members soon, or the school is not going to recognize your club.

W: What does that mean? We'll be forced to disband?

M: Hmm . . . Not exactly. You will, of course, still have the right to meet. The school can't prevent you from doing that. However, the school will not recognize you as an official club. This means that your club won't have access to any of the benefits it provides other clubs. For instance, it will be more difficult for you to reserve a room on campus to have meetings in. And you won't be able to apply for funding for various activities. For example, if you want to go birdwatching at a national park, we won't be able to fund a rental van to take you there.

W: We can get funding from the school? Um . . . I had no idea.

M: Oh . . . I guess nobody told you that. Okay, I think you and I need to have a long talk, but first, you need to get some more people signed up. It doesn't matter if they don't attend meetings. Just get some students' signatures down on this form and bring it back to me by Friday. Then, we'll talk about what my office can do for you. Can you do that?

W: Definitely. I know precisely who to ask.

해석

W Student: 실례합니다. Glenn 선생님이신가요?

M Student Activities Office Employee: 네, 저예요. 이름을 물어봐도 될까요?

W: 네. 저는 Wilma Jinks예요. 오늘 아침에 선생님의 문자 메시지를 받았죠. 더 일찍 오지 못해서 죄송하지만, 수요일은 일주일 중에서 제가 가장 바쁜 날이거든요. 10분 전에 마지막 수업이 끝났어요. 오늘 너무 바빠서 점심을 먹을 시간조차 없었죠.

M: 괜찮아요, Wilma. 학생들이 바쁘다는 점은 이해해요. 솔직히 말해서 저는 학생이 내일이나 혹은 금요일까지도 오지 못할 것으로 예상했기 때문에 상당히 빨리 응답해 준 것에 대해 기쁘게 생각해요.

W: 아, 그렇군요.

M: 그러면… 무슨 일인지 알고 싶겠군요, 그렇지 않나요?

W: 네, 선생님.

M: 학생은 조류 관찰 동아리의 회장이죠, 그렇지 않나요?

W: 네, 맞아요. 저희는 새로 생긴 교내 동아리예요. 지난 학기가 시작한 이후에 활동하고 있지만, 멋진 시간을 보내고 있죠.

M: 그런 말을 들으니 기쁘군요. 자, 어… 저는 학생의 동아리가 계속 남아 있기를 바라기 때문에 학생에게 중요한 점을 알려 드려야 해요.

W: 네?

M: 교내 규정에 따르면 공식적인 동아리로 간주되기 위해서는 동아리에 최소한 12명의 회원들이 가입되어 있어야 해요. 지난 주 학생의 동아리가 제출한 인원 수에 따르면 회원이 7명뿐이더군요. 맞나요?

W: 안타깝지만 그래요. 다양한 이유들로 이번 학기에 돌아오지 못한 회원들이 몇 명 있었죠. 그들 대부분은 이번 봄에 유학을 떠날 거예요.

M: 그래요, 음, 곧 새로운 회원들을 모집해야 하는데, 그렇지 않으면 학교측은 학생 동아리를 인정하지 않을 거예요.

W: 그게 무슨 말씀이신가요? 저희가 강제로 해산을 당하게 된다는 건가요?

M: 흠… 꼭 그런 것은 아니에요. 학생에게, 물론, 모임을 가질 수 있는 권리는 있을 거예요. 학생이 그렇게 하는 것을 학교측이 막을 수는 없죠. 하지만 학교측은

학생들을 공식적인 동아리로 인정하지 않을 거예요. 이는 다른 동아리에 제공되는 혜택 중 어떤 것도 학생 동아리는 받을 수 없을 것이라는 의미에요. 예를 들어 학생이 교내에서 모임을 가질 장소를 예약하는 일이 더 어려워질 거예요. 그리고 다양한 활동을 위한 지원금도 신청하지 못하게 될 것이고요. 예를 들면 국립 공원에서 조류를 관찰하고자 하는 경우, 그곳까지 타고 갈 승합차를 렌트하는데 필요한 지원금을 받을 수 없을 거예요.

W: 학교로부터 지원금을 받을 수 있다고요? 음… 저는 몰랐어요.

M: 오… 아무도 학생에게 이야기를 해 주지 않은 것 같군요. 좋아요, 학생과 제가 긴 대화를 나누어야 할 것 같은데, 하지만 우선 더 많은 사람들을 등록시켜야 해요. 모임에 참석하는지는 상관 없어요. 이 양식에 학생들의 서명을 받은 후 금요일까지 제게 다시 가져다 주세요. 그 후 저희 사무실에서 학생을 위해 무엇을 할 수 있는지에 대해 이야기하게 될 거예요. 그렇게 할 수 있나요?

W: 물론이죠. 누구에게 요청해야 할지 정확히 알고 있어요.

Summary Note

A

❶ text message
❷ Apologizes
❸ didn't expect
❹ birdwatching club
❺ twelve members
❻ reserve room
❼ signatures
❽ his office

B

The student visits the man in his office and says that she got his text message. She apologizes for not coming sooner, but she just finished her last class of the day ten minutes ago. The man says that he did not expect her to come until the next day or two. The student says she is the president of the birdwatching club at the school and that they are having a great time. The man says that school rules dictate that clubs have at least twelve members, but her club only has seven. He says that if the club does not get more members soon, then the club will not be recognized by the school. That means it will be hard to reserve a room for meetings and the club cannot get funding from the school. The student has no idea that funding is available. The man tells the student to get some students to sign up as members. Then, he will talk to the student about what his office can do for her club.

Exercise 4 1 Ⓒ 2 Ⓑ 3 Ⓒ p.54

Script 02-09

W Student: Professor Smith, can I speak with you for a minute?

M Professor: Sure.

W: I tried to call you three times this week, and I sent you three emails in the last few days, but you never responded.

M: Jennifer, I'm very sorry. I have been out of town for the last few days. I didn't have time to open all of my emails yet. In fact, yesterday, I didn't get home until well past midnight. And I couldn't receive any phone calls while I was out of town.

W: That's okay. I understand.

M: What can I do for you?

W: I want to know if you can help us set up an employment conference for November 20 and 21.

M: Conferences are a lot of work, and I already have a lot on my plate. Conferences can be better accomplished through the student employment center. That's what the center is there for.

W: The student employment center indicated that it won't set up an employment conference exclusively for nursing majors.

M: Well, maybe you don't need an employment conference because the center has a lot of connections, so it can introduce you to a number of employers. Isn't that enough?

W: No, not at all. The center isn't necessarily the best way to find a nursing job. Most of its contacts are outdated.

M: That's too bad. But I'm already overworked. More importantly, we tried this a few times before, and the conferences were a huge failure. The students were unwilling to do any work. They expected the faculty to do everything, so very little was accomplished. Part of the problem is that the students had no experience arranging conferences. Meanwhile, the faculty didn't have enough time to make it a success.

W: Don't worry about that. I have lots of experience arranging conferences. I used to work for the American Nursing Association and helped organize numerous nursing conferences. So I already have a lot of names and key contacts, and I know a lot of people in the industry.

M: Good for you. I didn't know that about you.

W: But most of my contacts are regional. You've worked abroad and in other states, so you have a lot of contacts in areas where I don't. All we need you to do is make a few phone calls to see who is interested in participating and who's looking for nurses next year. I think that with your contacts and mine, that should be enough. Other than making phone calls, your participation will be very limited. The students will take care of the logistics and do most of the work.

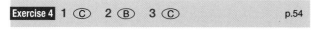

M: It sounds like you've really thought this out and know what you're doing. I wish you were here the last time we had a conference. It was quite embarrassing. I'd love to help you, so go ahead and start organizing.

W: Thanks.

M: But don't expect me to do all the work.

W: I won't.

해석

W Student: Smith 교수님, 잠깐 말씀을 나눌 수 있을까요?

M Professor: 그럼요.

W: 제가 이번 주에 교수님께 세 차례 전화를 드렸고, 지난 며칠 동안 세 통의 이메일을 보냈는데도 답을 받지 못해서요.

M: Jennifer, 정말 미안해요. 제가 지난 며칠 동안 이곳에 없었어요. 이메일을 열어 볼 수 있는 시간이 없었죠. 사실 어제 자정이 지나서야 집에 도착했어요. 그리고 이곳에 없는 동안 전화를 받을 수도 없었고요.

W: 괜찮습니다. 이해해요.

M: 무슨 일인가요?

W: 11월 20일과 21일 동안 취업 컨퍼런스를 개최하는데 교수님께서 도움을 주실 수 있는지 궁금해서요.

M: 컨퍼런스에는 많은 노력이 필요한데, 제게는 이미 해야 할 일들이 많이 있어요. 컨퍼런스 일이라면 학생 취업 센터를 통해 진행하는 것이 더 나을 거예요. 그것이 그곳 센터가 존재하는 이유이니까요.

W: 학생 취업 센터에서 간호학 전공자만을 위한 취업 컨퍼런스는 개최할 수 없다고 알려 주었어요.

M: 음, 센터와 연결되어 있는 곳이 많아서 아마 취업 컨퍼런스가 필요 없을 수도 있고, 그곳에서 학생에게 여러 군데의 직장을 소개시켜 줄 수도 있을 거예요. 그것으로 충분하지 않나요?

W: 전혀 그렇지 않아요. 센터가 반드시 간호 관련 일자리를 찾아 주는 가장 좋은 곳은 아니에요. 대부분의 연락처도 오래된 것들이고요.

M: 정말 안됐군요. 하지만 저는 이미 과도한 업무에 시달리고 있어요. 더 중요한 것은 전에도 몇 번 그러한 일을 시도해 봤는데, 컨퍼런스들이 큰 실패로 끝났어요. 학생들이 어떤 일도 하려고 하지 않았죠. 교직원들이 모든 것을 다 해 줄 것이라고 기대했기 때문에 성과가 거의 없었어요. 그러한 문제는 부분적으로 학생들이 컨퍼런스를 준비해 본 경험이 없기 때문이었죠. 동시에 교직원들의 경우, 컨퍼런스를 성공적으로 만들기 위한 시간이 부족했고요.

W: 그 점에 대해서는 걱정하지 마세요. 저는 컨퍼런스를 준비해 본 경험이 많으니까요. 미 간호 협회의 일을 하면서 다수의 간호 컨퍼런스를 준비해 본 적이 있어요. 그래서 많은 사람들의 이름과 주요 연락처도 이미 알고 있고, 업계의 사람들도 많이 알고 있죠.

M: 잘 되었군요. 학생의 그런 점은 제가 모르고 있었네요.

W: 하지만 제 연락처들은 대부분 이 지역에 한정된 것들이에요. 교수님은 해외나 다른 주에서도 일을 하셨으니 제게 없는 지역의 연락처도 많이 가지고 계실 거예요. 저희가 교수님께 바라는 일은 단지 전화를 몇 통 하셔서 어느 곳이 참여에 관심이 있는지, 그리고 어느 곳에서 내년에 간호사를 채용할 것인지를 알아봐 주시는 거예요. 교수님 연락처와 제 연락처가 있으면 충분할 것으로 생각해요. 전화 통화를 제외하고 교수님께서 관여하시게 될 일은 매우 한정적일 거예요. 학생들이 모든 계획을 세우고 대부분의 일을 처리할 거예요.

M: 정말 이번 일을 잘 계획하고 무엇을 하게 될 것인지 잘 알고 있는 것처럼 들리는군요. 지난 번 컨퍼런스를 열었을 때 학생이 있었으면 좋았을 것 같아요. 상당히 힘들었거든요. 기꺼이 도와 줄 테니 가서 준비를 하도록 해요.

W: 감사합니다.

M: 하지만 제가 모든 걸 다 해 줄 것으로 바라지는 말아요.

W: 그러지 않을게요.

Summary Note

A

❶ called and emailed
❷ responded
❸ out of town
❹ student employment center
❺ outdated
❻ minimal

B

A nursing student goes to speak to her professor. She asks the professor to help set up an employment conference. The professor does not think the conference is a good idea. She says she is too busy. She says this type of event should be conducted through the student employment center. She also indicates that the Nursing Department held employment conferences in the past and that all of these conferences were unsuccessful. She says the students did not do much work and had insufficient experience in organizing conferences. The student then advises the professor not to worry about the above factors because she used to work for the American Nursing Association and helped organize numerous nursing conferences. The professor is pleasantly surprised to hear this and then agrees to make a few phone calls to help arrange the conference.

Exercises with Long Lectures

Exercise 1 1 Ⓑ 2 Ⓒ 3 Ⓐ p.56

Script 02-10

M Professor: The next kind of bear I'd like to discuss with you today is the polar bear. As I already mentioned on Tuesday, polar bears only live in the Arctic, primarily in northern Canada, northern Russia, and Alaska. If, for example, you are in southern Canada, you won't see any of these bears.

Now, you're probably aware that the Arctic is an extremely harsh environment and one of the coldest places on the Earth. But let me remind you of what it's really like in the Arctic, especially in late December or early January. The temperature frequently drops below minus forty degrees centigrade and sometimes gets even colder. Combine that with strong winds, little or no sunlight, and very little vegetation, and what you get is an environment in which very few species are capable of surviving. The polar bear, however, thrives in this kind of environment. The polar bear spends its time roaming throughout the Arctic, walking on land and ice, swimming in freezing sea water and floating on sheets of ice while looking for seals, fish, and other food. Its favorite food is seals, which it finds along the edges of the ice, in holes in the ice, and under cracks in the ice. It has no natural enemies in this environment, which is perfectly suited for it.

Now, what you see on the screen behind me is a photo of a polar bear. As you can see, it's very beautiful. But what's not apparent in this and other similar photos is the bear's actual size. Polar bears are much bigger than the brown and black bears we discussed earlier. In fact, they're huge. They weigh up to 1,600 pounds, which is about 720 kilograms. And they're designed to survive in their environment. They have very thick white fur, which camouflages them from the snow and ice and insulates them from the extreme cold. It's much thicker than the fur of the bears that we discussed earlier. Polar bears are also strong swimmers. They have large front paws that amazingly allow them to swim a few hundred kilometers from land.

Despite their impressiveness, polar bears, unlike black bears, are an endangered species. This is a result of global warming, which will be a topic of our next film. The Arctic is becoming too warm for the bears. That ice I just mentioned to you is now disappearing. It breaks up much earlier in the spring, and now it's a lot further from land. Ice thickness in the Arctic has decreased by forty percent in the last thirty years, and some scientists predict that the Arctic basin might not have any ice in another fifty years. For polar bears, this is terrible. Ice is essential to their existence. Less ice means fewer seals and less food.

Polar bears do their hunting in winter, but because winter is getting shorter and the ice is disappearing earlier, they have less time to restore their fat. In summer, they're forced to remain on land for longer periods of time, and during that time, they live off the fat stored in their bodies. Thirty years ago, they spent just over three months on land. Now it's almost four months. The shorter the winter and the earlier the ice breaks up, the less time they have to restore their fat. This reduces their strength and energy. With less ice, polar bears must swim farther to reach it. This further reduces their strength and energy.

해석

M Professor: 오늘 여러분과 공부하고자 하는 다음 종류의 곰은 북극곰입니다. 이미 화요일에 언급했던 것처럼, 북극곰은 북극에서만, 주로 캐나다 북부, 러시아 북부, 그리고 알래스카에서 서식합니다. 예컨대 캐나다 남부에서는 전혀 북극곰을 볼 수가 없을 거예요.

자, 여러분들은 아마 북극의 환경이 극도로 혹독하며 그곳이 지구에서 가장 추운 곳 중 하나라는 점을 아실 것입니다. 하지만 북극이, 특히 12월 말이나 1월 초에, 실제로 어떤지를 상기시켜 드리죠. 기온이 종종 영하 40℃ 아래로 떨어지며, 때로는 훨씬 더 추운 경우도 있습니다. 강한 바람이 불고, 햇빛이 거의 비치지 않거나 전혀 비치지 않으며, 식물도 거의 없는 환경에서는 살아남을 수 있는 종이 거의 없어요. 하지만 북극곰은 이러한 환경에서 잘 살고 있습니다. 북극곰은 북극을 돌아다니고, 육지 및 얼음 위를 걸어 다니고, 차가운 바닷물에서 수영을 하고, 물개, 물고기, 그리고 기타 먹이를 찾아 얼음 덩어리를 타고 다니면서 대부분의 시간을 보내죠. 가장 좋아하는 먹이는 물개로, 북극곰은 얼음의 가장 자리, 얼음의 구멍, 그리고 얼음에 있는 틈 아래에서 물개를 찾습니다. 천적이 존재하지 않는 이러한 환경은 북극곰에게 완벽한 곳이에요.

자, 제 뒤 화면에 북극곰의 사진이 있습니다. 보시다시피 매우 아름답죠. 하지만 이 사진 및 기타 이와 비슷한 사진들에서 볼 수 없는 것은 북극곰의 실제 크기입니다. 북극곰은 앞서 논의했던 불곰이나 흑곰보다 훨씬 더 덩치가 커요. 실제로 거대합니다. 몸무게가 최대 1,600파운드, 즉 720kg까지 나가죠. 그리고 이들은 자신의 환경에서 생존할 수 있도록 디자인되어 있습니다. 매우 두꺼운 흰색 털을 가지고 있어서 눈 및 얼음 속에서 위장을 할 수 있고 추위로부터 열을 빼앗기지 않아요. 북극곰의 털은 앞서 이야기했던 곰들의 털보다 훨씬 더 두껍습니다. 또한 북극곰은 헤엄을 잘 쳐요. 커다란 앞발을 가지고 있기 때문에 놀랍게도 육지에서 수백 킬로미터나 떨어진 곳까지 헤엄을 칠 수가 있죠.

인상적이긴 하지만 북극곰은 흑곰과 달리 멸종 위기종입니다. 이는 지구 온난화의 한 가지 결과이기도 한데, 지구 온난화는 다음 영상의 주제가 될 거예요. 북극곰이 살기에 북극이 너무 더워지고 있습니다. 제가 여러분께 조금 전 언급했던 얼음이 현재 사라지고 있어요. 훨씬 이른 봄부터 갈라지기 시작해서 육지로부터 훨씬 멀리 떨어져 있습니다. 북극의 얼음 두께는 지난 30년간 40퍼센트가 줄어들었고, 일부 과학자들은 50년 후에는 북극 분지에서 얼음이 사라질 것으로 예상하고 있어요. 북극곰에게는 끔찍한 일이죠. 얼음은 이들의 생존에 필수적인 것입니다. 얼음이 줄어든다는 것은 곧 물개와 먹이가 줄어든다는 것을 의미하니까요.

북극곰은 겨울에 사냥을 하지만 겨울이 짧아지고 얼음이 보다 일찍 사라지고 있는 탓에 북극곰이 지방을 비축할 시간이 점점 줄어들고 있어요. 여름에는 보다 오랫동안 육지에 남아있어야 하는데, 이 기간에는 몸속에 저장된 지방으로 살아갑니다. 30년 전에는 3개월 정도만 육지에서 지냈어요. 지금은 거의 4개월 정도고요. 겨울이 짧아질수록 얼음이 더 빨리 갈라지기 때문에 이들이 지방을 저장할 수 있는 시간은 점점 더 줄어들고 있습니다. 이로써 이들의 힘과 에너지가 감소하게 되죠. 얼음이 줄어들면 북극곰은 보다 먼 거리를 헤엄쳐야 해요. 이로 인해 힘과 에너지가 더욱 감소하게 됩니다.

Summary Note

A

❶ polar bears
❷ freezing temperature
❸ natural enemies
❹ bigger
❺ thick white
❻ endangered
❼ Global warming

B

Polar bears live in the Arctic, which has an extremely harsh environment. It's one of the coldest places on the Earth. The temperature in the Arctic frequently drops below minus forty degrees centigrade. The polar bear, however, thrives in this kind of environment. The polar bear roams on land, swims in freezing sea water, and floats on sheets of ice while looking for seals, which is its favorite food. Polar bears are very large. They have a very thick coat of fur and large front paws that allow them to swim far from land. Unfortunately, polar bears are an endangered species because the Arctic is becoming too warm for them. The ice is disappearing, and so are the seals.

Exercise 2 1 Ⓓ 2 Ⓒ, Ⓓ 3 Ⓑ p.58

Script 02-11

W Professor: Uhhh . . . okay now, um . . . I don't have anything further to say about volcanoes. Unless there are any more questions. Uh, are there any questions? Uh, okay, good. I shall continue our discussion on waves, but this time, I'd like to focus more on earthquakes. As you know, some earthquakes are not powerful enough to be felt on the Earth's surface while during others, people can indeed feel the earth shaking. And, of course, there might be violent movement, often with catastrophic results. What we feel during an earthquake or huge explosion are a series of waves called seismic waves. These waves are similar to sound waves and light waves. For example, they reflect and refract. And they change speeds and directions as they travel through different densities of rocks.

In an earthquake, you might initially feel some minor trembling, then perhaps violent shaking, and then some more tremors. The reason why you feel these different types of movement is that there are different kinds of seismic waves. Some of them may easily be felt at the Earth's surface while others are not. The reason for this is that not all waves travel at the Earth's surface or with equal amplitude.

There are two major types of seismic waves: body waves and surface waves. The waves that you feel first are body waves. These mainly travel deep through the Earth's interior rather than at the surface. Some of them travel very fast, and that's why you feel them first. But because they travel deep inside the Earth, they're felt only as tremors. There are two types of body waves. The first type of body wave is the P wave, or primary wave. It's the fastest kind of seismic wave. P waves can move through any type of material, including rock and fluids. Because of this and because of their speed, these waves are the first to reach the Earth's surface. You likely won't even hear or feel these waves, but animals may hear them. They're not strong enough to cause significant damage. The other type of body wave is the S wave, or secondary wave. Because S waves travel at half the speed of P waves, you don't feel them in the beginning. These kinds of waves move rocks from side to side or up and down. Their amplitude is several times higher than P waves, and they are more destructive than P waves.

The second major category of wave is the surface wave. Unlike body waves, surface waves move at or near the Earth's surface. These waves are similar to ripples on water. They are usually the most destructive type of seismic wave because of their lower frequency, larger amplitude, and longer duration. There are two types of surface waves. The first kind of surface wave is called a love wave. It's the fastest surface wave. These waves make the ground move from side to side. The other kind of surface wave is the Rayleigh wave. It rolls along the ground just like a wave rolls across a lake or an ocean. As a result, it moves the ground up and down and side to side in the same direction that the wave is moving. Most of the shaking felt from an earthquake is due to Rayleigh waves, which can be much larger than the other waves. They are slower than body waves, and sometimes cars might appear to be moving up and down with these waves.

해석

W Professor: 어… 좋아요, 이제, 음… 화산에 대해서는 더 이상 이야기할 것이 없네요. 질문이 더 없다면요. 어, 질문이 있나요? 어, 그래요, 좋습니다. 계속해서 파동에 대한 논의를 해야하는데, 이번 시간에는 지진에 대해 보다 초점을 맞추고자 해요. 여러분도 아시다시피, 너무 약해서 지표면에서 느껴지지 않는 지진들도 있지만, 땅이 흔들리는 것을 느낄 수 있는 지진들도 있습니다. 그리고 물론 종종 엄청난 피해를 수반하는 격렬한 지진도 일어날 수 있죠. 지진이나 큰 폭발이 일어났을 때 우리가 느끼는 것은 지진파라고 불리는 파동이에요. 이러한 파동은 음파 및 광파와 비슷합니다. 예를 들어 반사되기도 하고 굴절되기도 하죠. 그리고 서로 다른 밀도를 가진 암석을 통과하는 경우에는 속도 및 방향이 바뀌게 됩니다.

지진이 발생하면 처음에는 약한 진동이 느껴지고, 그 후에는 격렬한 흔들림이, 그리고 그 다음에는 미동이 느껴질 수 있어요. 이처럼 다양한 형태의 움직임을 느끼게 되는 이유는 다양한 종류의 지진파가 존재하기 때문입니다. 어떤 지진파는 지표면에서 쉽게 느껴질 수 있는 반면 그렇지 않는 지진파들도 있어요. 그러한 이유는 모든 지진파들이 지표면에서 이동하거나 동일한 진폭을 가지는 것은 아니기 때문이죠.

지진파의 두 가지 유형은 실체파와 표면파입니다. 여러분이 처음 느끼는 파동은 실체파예요. 이는 주로 지표면보다 지구 내부의 깊은 곳을 통과하면서 이동을 합니다. 일부 실체파는 이동 속도가 매우 빠르기 때문에 이들을 제일 먼저 느끼게 돼요. 하지만 지구 내부의 깊은 곳에서 이동을 하기 때문에 미동으로만 느껴집니다. 실체파에는 두 가지가 있어요. 첫번째는 P파, 또는 일차파예요. 지진파 가운데 가장 빠른 파동이죠. P파는 암석 및 유체를 포함하여 어떠한 물질도 관통할 수 있습니다. 이러한 점 및 이들의 속도 때문에 P파가 가장 먼저 지표면에 도달합니다. 여러분은 아마 이 파동을 듣거나 느낄 수 없을 테지만, 동물들은 들을 수도 있어요. 이들은 심각한 피해를 가져다 줄 만큼 강력하지는 않습니다. 또 다른 종류의 실체파는 S파 또는 이차파예요. S파는 P파 속도의 반밖에 되지 않는 속도로 이동하기 때문에 처음에는 느껴지지가 않습니다. 이러한 파동은 암석들을 좌우 또는 상하로 이동시켜요. 진폭이 P파에 비해 몇 배나 크며, P파보다 파괴력이 큽니다.

두 번째 유형의 파장은 표면파예요. 표면파는 실체파와 달리 지표면이나 지표면 가까이에서 이동합니다. 이 파동은 수면 위에 생기는 물결과 비슷해요. 주파수가 낮고, 진폭이 크며, 그리고 지속 시간이 길기 때문에 일반적으로 지진파 중에서 가장 파괴력이 크죠. 표면파에는 두 종류가 있습니다. 하나는 러브파라고 불리는 파동이에요. 속도가 가장 빠른 파동이죠. 이 파동은 땅을 좌우로 흔들리게 만듭니다. 또 다른 종류의 표면파는 레일리파예요. 이는 호수나 바다에서 출렁이는 파도처럼 지면에서 출렁거립니다. 그 결과, 이 파동이 움직이는 방향과 동일한 방향으로 땅이 상하 및 좌우로 움직이게 되죠. 지진에서 느껴지는 대부분의 흔들림은 레일리파 때문인데, 이는 다른 파동들보다 훨씬 더 클 수 있어요. 이들은 실체파보다 속도가 느리며, 때로는 이 파동 때문에 자동차가 상하로 움직이는 것처럼 보일 수도 있습니다.

Summary Note

A

❶ earthquakes
❷ catastrophic results
❸ sound and light
❹ refract
❺ Body waves
❻ Surface waves

B

Seismic waves are caused by earthquakes and major explosions. Sometimes it is possible to feel seismic waves during an earthquake. If one feels shaking during an earthquake, what is felt are seismic waves. Seismic waves have similar properties to sound waves and light waves. The first kinds of waves that one can feel are body waves. These might not be very powerful because they move deep inside the Earth's surface. But because some of them travel very fast, they are the waves that a person feels first. Perhaps a person will not feel or hear them. If they are felt, they are usually minor tremors. Some body waves travel slower and might cause more damage at the Earth's surface. Surface waves travel at or near the Earth's surface. They are usually more destructive than body waves because of their lower frequency, larger amplitude, and longer duration. One type of body wave, when it reaches the Earth's surface, might appear as a wave moving up and down, sometimes making it appear as though cars are moving up and down.

Exercise 3 1 Ⓓ 2 Ⓒ, Ⓓ 3 Ⓑ p.60

Script 02-12

M Professor: Your textbook uses the terms Jovian planets and gas giants interchangeably. **And I'm going to do the same.** There are four of these planets in our solar system: Neptune, Uranus, Saturn, and Jupiter. The biggest of these is Jupiter, and that's the planet I'll be focusing on. Jupiter and the Jovian planets are very different than Earth, Mars, and even our moon. These gas giants have rocky or solid cores, but they're composed mostly of gases such as hydrogen, helium, methane, and various others. They're also composed of liquids.

One huge difference between the Jovian planets and the rocky planets is that the Jovian planets do not have solid surfaces. Their exteriors are gaseous, and these gases blend with their atmospheres. Therefore, you wouldn't be able to land a spacecraft on Jupiter nor on any of the other gaseous planets, nor would you be able to walk on them. You could possibly float through them, but if you tried that on Jupiter, you would eventually burn up because Jupiter is extremely hot.

Now here are some more facts about the Jovian planets. These planets have a number of rings and moons. Saturn has the most spectacular rings and has 146 moons, the most in the solar system. Neptune has some faint rings and fourteen moons. Uranus has thirteen faint rings and twenty-seven moons while Jupiter has ninety-five moons. Jovian planets are also the largest planets; they are much larger than the rocky planets. Jupiter is the biggest planet in the solar system, and it's huge. It's several times bigger than any of the other planets in the solar system. In fact, it's twice as massive as all of the other planets combined. By comparison, it's about 318 times more massive than Earth, with a diameter eleven times greater than Earth. Now, believe it or not, despite its magnificent size, Jupiter is not the largest planet in the universe. Larger planets have recently been discovered outside the solar system, and I'm sure more will be discovered in the future.

Weather patterns on the Jovian planets are much different than the rocky planets. For example, they don't have any oceans or landmasses, which greatly influence weather conditions on Earth. Jupiter has the Great Red Spot, a storm which is at least 350 years old and seems to be a permanent fixture on the planet. The storm is bigger than Earth. Wind speeds on Jupiter often reach up to 600 kilometers per hour. Neptune has a similar phenomenon, called the Great Dark Spot, a cyclonic storm about the same size as Europe and Asia combined. This type of phenomenon does not exist on the rocky planets. Again, I reiterate, the Jovian planets are much different than Earth.

The rings that surround Jupiter are composed of smoke-like particles that are sprayed about when its moons are bombarded by energetic meteor impacts. The halo, which is the innermost ring, is 22,000 kilometers wide. And Jupiter is always covered by a layer of clouds. The rings surrounding the other Jovian planets are composed of similar particles.

Spacecraft have taken numerous closeup photos of the Jovian planets. Some of these photos appear in your textbook. The word closeup has to be taken with a grain of salt. The photo I'm showing you now, uh, just a minute . . . Would someone turn off the light, please . . . ? Okay, there it is. This breathtaking view was obtained by *Voyager 1* when the spacecraft was 9.2 million kilometers from Jupiter . . . Oh, and here's another. This is Neptune. I think it's the most beautiful planet. I love the blue color. It looks like one gigantic ocean, but it's not ocean.

Is there life on the Jovian planets? Is that possible? Well, scientists seem to agree that there probably wouldn't be any Earthlike life on these planets because there's little water in their atmospheres, and any possible solid surface deep inside these planets, for example, in Jupiter, would be under too much pressure.

해석

M Professor: 여러분 교재에서는 목성형 행성과 거대 가스형 행성이라는 용어가 섞여서 사용되고 있어요. 그리고 저 역시 그렇게 하겠습니다. 우리의 태양계에서 이러한 행성들은 4개가 존재하는데, 해왕성, 천왕성, 토성, 그리고 목성이 여기에 해당됩니다. 이들 중 가장 큰 행성은 목성으로, 이에 대해 초점을 맞추어 보죠. 목성 및 목성형 행성들은 지구, 화성, 그리고 심지어 우리의 달과도 크게 다릅니다. 이 거대 가스형 행성들의 핵은 암석이나 고체로 되어 있지만, 대부분은 수소, 헬륨, 메탄, 그리고 기타 기체들로 이루어져 있어요.

목성형 행성과 암석형 행성 사이의 커다란 차이점 중 하나는 목성형 행성들의 표면이 고체가 아니라는 점이에요. 이들의 바깥층은 기체로 이루어져 있고, 이 기체는 대기와 섞여 있습니다. 그래서 목성이나 다른 기체형 행성에서는 우주선을 착륙시킬 수도 없고, 그 위를 걸어 다닐 수도 없죠. 아마 그 속에서 둥둥 떠다닐 수는 있겠지만, 목성에서 그렇게 하려고 했다가는 목성의 뜨거운 열기 때문에 결국 몸이 타버릴 것입니다.

이제 목성형 행성에 관한 사실을 몇 개 더 알려 드릴게요. 이 행성들은 많은 고리와 위성을 지니고 있습니다. 토성에는 가장 멋진 고리와 146개의 위성이 존재하는데, 이는 태양계에서 가장 큰 수치입니다. 해왕성에는 몇 개의 희미한 고리들과 14개의 위성이 존재해요. 천왕성에는 13개의 희미한 고리와 27개의 위성이 존재하고, 목성에는 95개의 위성이 존재하죠. 또한 목성형 행성은 크기가 가장 큰 행성들로, 암석형 행성 보다 크기가 훨씬 더 큽니다. 목성은 태양계에서 가장 큰 행성으로, 그 크기가 거대합니다. 태양계의 다른 어떤 행성들보다도 몇 배 이상 크기가 커요. 실제로 다른 모든 행성들을 합친 크기보다 두 배 더 큽니다. 비교를 해 보면, 목성은 지구보다 약 318배 더 무겁고, 직경은 지구 직경의 11배에 이르죠. 자, 믿거나 말거나이지만, 엄청난 크기에도 불구하고, 목성이 우주에서 가장 큰 행성은 아닙니다. 최근에 태양계 밖에서 보다 큰 행성들이 발견되었는데, 저는 미래에 더 많이 발견될 것으로 확신합니다.

목성형 행성의 날씨 패턴은 암석형 행성과 크게 다릅니다. 예를 들어 목성형 행성에는 지구의 날씨 상황에 큰 영향을 미치는 바다나 육지가 없어요. 목성에는 대적반이 존재하는데, 이는 적어도 350년 전에 발생해서 이 행성에서 사라지지 않을 것으로 보이는 폭풍입니다. 이 폭풍이 지구보다도 커요. 목성에서의 풍속은 종종 시속 600킬로미터에 이르기도 합니다. 해왕성도 비슷한 현상인 대암반이 존재하는데, 이는 유럽과 아시아를 합한 것과 크기가 동일한 격렬한 폭풍이에요. 이러한 현상은 암석형 행성에서는 존재하지 않습니다. 다시 한 번 말씀을 드리면, 목성형 행성은 지구와 크게 다릅니다.

목성을 둘러싸고 있는 고리는 그곳 위성들이 강력한 유성 충격을 받을 때 뿌려지는, 연기와 같은 입자들로 이루어져 있어요. 가장 안쪽에 있는 고리인 헤일로의 폭은 22,000킬로미터예요. 그리고 목성은 항상 구름층으로 덮여 있습니다. 다른 목성형 행성들을 둘러싸고 있는 고리들도 비슷한 입자로 이루어져 있어요.

우주선들이 목성형 행성들을 여러 차례 근접 촬영했습니다. 그러한 사진 중 몇 개를 여러분 교재에서 보실 수 있어요. 근접 촬영이라는 말은 좀 감안해서 들어야 합니다. 제가 지금 여러분들께 보여 드릴 사진은, 어, 잠깐만요… 누가 불 좀 꺼 줄래요…? 좋아요, 여기 있군요. 이 놀라운 광경은 *보이저 1호*가 목성으로부터 920만 킬로미터 떨어진 곳에서 촬영한 것입니다. 오, 그리고 여기에 한 장 더 있군요. 해왕성입니다. 제 생각에는 해왕성이 가장 아름다운 행성인 것 같아요. 푸른빛이 정말 마음에 듭니다. 거대한 바다같이 보이지만, 바다는 아니에요.

목성형 행성에 생명체가 존재할까요? 그것이 가능한 일일까요? 음, 과학자들은 그곳 대기에 수분이 거의 없고, 이러한 행성들, 예컨대 목성 내부의 깊은 곳에 있을지도 모르는 고체 표면에는 너무 큰 압력이 존재할 것이기 때문에, 이러한 행성들에는 지구의 생명체와 같은 생명체가 존재하지 않을 것이라는 의견에 동의하는 것 같습니다.

Summary Note

A

❶ Jovian planets
❷ gases and liquids
❸ gaseous
❹ rings and moons
❺ storms
❻ clouds

B

There are two types of planets. One type is those with a rocky core such as Earth and Mars. The other type is the gaseous planets, which are Neptune, Uranus, Saturn, and Jupiter. The biggest of these is Jupiter. The rocky planets and the gaseous planets are very different. For example, the exterior of a gaseous planet does not have a solid surface. Therefore, a spacecraft would be incapable of landing on such a planet. The Jovian planets have a number of rings and moons. Jupiter has ninety-five moons. It is also the biggest planet in the solar system. In fact, it is twice as massive as all of the other planets combined. Jupiter has the Great Red Spot, a storm which is at least 350 years old. Wind speeds on Jupiter often reach up to 600 kilometers per hour. Jupiter's innermost ring is 22,000 kilometers wide. And Jupiter is always covered by a layer of clouds.

Exercise 4 1 Ⓓ 2 Ⓒ 3 Ⓐ, Ⓑ p.62

Script 02-13

W Professor: The last thing I want to discuss with you today are monsoons. Because we don't have much time remaining in today's lecture and because the next class will be our physical geography midterm examination, I'm not going to go into a lot of detail. Your textbook provides you with more than ample information on this topic, so please refer to it before next Monday's examination.

Needless to say, I can guarantee there will be at least a few examination questions on this topic.

Very briefly, I'd like to tell you that monsoons are an annual weather phenomenon. In fact, the word monsoon derives from an old Arabic word which means "season" because these rainstorms occur every year. More specifically, monsoons are very heavy rains which originate from moist air masses that move inland from the ocean. What actually happens is that air masses move from cool air to warm air or from a high-pressure system above the Indian Ocean to a low-pressure system over the continent, causing it to rain in South Asia. And as your textbook indicates, most monsoons happen in continental Asia. Smaller ones occur in northern Australia, equatorial Africa, and, to a much lesser extent, right here in the southwestern U.S.

Now, unlike earthquakes, volcanoes, flash floods, ice storms, droughts, and most of the other natural phenomenon that we discussed during the last few weeks, monsoons, surprisingly, have a very beneficial impact. Although the heavy rains might be unwanted in some places, monsoon rains supply about ninety percent of India's total water supply. So right there, you have more than a billion people benefiting from and relying on this rain. This rain is essential for crops. Imagine the hardship a billion people would endure if there were no monsoons. In fact, Asia, where most monsoons occur, contains half of the world's population. In other words, three billion people live in areas affected by monsoons. Many of these people are poor subsistence farmers who are totally reliant on monsoons for their livelihoods. Too little rain would result in famine.

By the same token, these same people can suffer undue hardship if there's too much rain, which can result in disastrous floods. Flooding leads to severe damage and famine. Monsoons are also less appreciated in the urban areas, where many people, both poor and wealthy, are greatly inconvenienced by too much rain. Again, imagine the millions of poor people in third-world cities, living in porous, shabby homes, drenched by extensive leakage.

I mentioned that monsoons occur annually. But the precise date, duration, and quantity are impossible to predict. In addition, monsoons are more common in the Northern Hemisphere, where there are more large landmasses than in the Southern Hemisphere, which is mostly comprised of sea water.

So to reiterate, monsoons have positive and negative impacts. I'd like to continue this discussion on monsoons, but, unfortunately, we've run out of time today, and our examination will be during the next class. So I urge you to read more about this in your textbook.

해석

W Professor: 오늘 마지막으로 논의하고자 하는 것은 몬순입니다. 오늘 수업 시간이 얼마 남지 않았고 다음 수업 시간에 자연 지리학 중간고사를 볼 예정이기 때문에 깊이 들어가지는 않을 거예요. 이 주제와 관련된 내용들은 교재에 충분할 정도로 나와 있으니 다음 월요일 시험 전까지 그 부분을 참고해 주세요. 말할 필요도 없겠지만, 이번 주제와 관련된 문제들이 최소한 몇 개는 나온다고 장담할 수 있어요.

간단하게 이야기하면, 몬순은 매년 일어나는 기상 현상이라고 말씀을 드리고 싶군요. 사실 몬순이라는 단어는 "계절"을 뜻하는 오래된 아랍어 단어에서 유래된 것으로, 그 이유는 이러한 폭풍우가 매년 일어나기 때문입니다. 보다 자세하게 말씀을 드리면, 몬순은 바다에서 내륙으로 이동하는 습윤 기단에서 발생하는 강력한 폭우예요. 실제로 기단들이 차가운 공기에서 따뜻한 공기 쪽으로, 혹은 인도양의 고기압에서 아시아 대륙의 저기압 쪽으로 이동함으로써 아시아 남부에 비가 내리는 것이죠. 그리고 교재에도 나와 있듯이, 대부분의 몬순은 아시아 대륙에서 발생합니다. 작은 규모의 몬순은 호주 북부와 적도 부근의 아프리카에서도 발생을 하고, 훨씬 적기는 하지만, 이곳 미국 남서부에서도 발생을 하죠.

자, 지난 몇 주 동안 우리가 논의했던 지진, 화산, 돌발 홍수, 얼음 폭풍, 가뭄 그리고 기타 대부분의 자연 현상들과 달리, 몬순은 놀랍게도 매우 긍정적인 영향을 가져다 줍니다. 일부 지역에서는 폭우가 반갑지 않을 수도 있지만, 몬순으로 인한 강수는 인도의 전체 급수량의 약 90퍼센트를 차지해요. 그래서 그곳에서는 10억명의 사람들이 이러한 강수의 혜택을 받으면서 강수에 의지해서 살아갑니다. 이러한 강수는 농작물에 필수적이에요. 몬순이 없는 경우 10억명의 사람들이 겪게 될 고통을 생각해 보세요. 실제로 대부분의 몬순이 발생하는 아시아에서 전 세계 인구의 절반이 살고 있습니다. 다시 말해서 30억명의 사람들이 몬순의 영향을 받는 지역에서 살고 있는 것이죠. 이러한 사람들 중 다수가 가난한 자급자족 농부로, 이들은 생계를 전적으로 몬순에 의존하고 있습니다. 비가 너무 적게 내린다면 그 결과로 기아를 겪게 될 거예요.

같은 이유로 비가 너무 많이 내려서 엄청난 홍수가 발생하는 경우에도 똑같은 사람들이 고통을 겪을 수 있습니다. 홍수는 심각한 피해와 기아로 이어지죠. 또한 몬순은 가난하든 부유하든 많은 사람들이 폭우로 인해 엄청난 불편을 겪는 도시 지역에서도 덜 반가운 존재예요. 또 다시, 구멍이 많이 나 있는 초라한 주택에서 심각한 누수로 물에 젖은 채 살아가는 제3세계 도시의 빈민들을 떠올려 보세요.

제가 몬순이 매년 일어난다고 언급을 했죠. 하지만 정확한 날짜, 기간, 그리고 강수량은 예측이 불가능합니다. 또한 몬순은 북반구에서 보다 일반적인데, 대부분 바닷물로 이루어진 남반부보다 북반부에 육지가 더 많이 발생해요.

그래서 다시 한 번 말씀을 드리면, 몬순은 긍정적인 효과와 부정적인 효과를 모두 가지고 있어요. 몬순에 대한 논의를 계속하고 싶지만 안타깝게도 오늘은 시간이 다 지났는데, 다음 수업 시간에는 시험이 예정되어 있습니다. 그러니 이와 관련된 내용을 교재에서 꼭 찾아서 읽어보세요.

Summary Note

A

❶ monsoons
❷ various
❸ ninety percent
❹ crops
❺ flooding
❻ predict

B

Monsoons are annual weather phenomena that occur primarily in Asia. More specifically, they are very heavy rains which originate from moist air masses that move inland from the ocean. Typically, cool air over the ocean reaches warm dry air above India, causing it to rain throughout South Asia. Monsoons can be destructive, causing flooding and subsequent famines. But unlike most natural weather phenomena, they also have a beneficial impact. For example, monsoon rains supply about ninety percent of India's total water supply. They are essential for crops. Poor subsistence farmers are totally reliant on these rains for their livelihoods. Too little rain may result in famine. The precise dates and durations of monsoons are impossible to predict. Monsoons are more common in the Northern Hemisphere, where there are more large landmasses, than in the Southern Hemisphere, which is mostly comprised of sea water.

Integrated Listening & Speaking

p.64

A

Script 02-14

M Professor: Last week we talked about polar bears. I told you they lived in the Arctic, a very harsh environment. In late December and early January, the temperature falls below minus forty degrees, and there is little or no sunlight. Very few species can survive in this environment. But as I mentioned to you, this environment is perfect for polar bears. They cannot live without it. They are huge, white animals, weighing up to 740 kilograms. They have thick white fur and are camouflaged from the environment. They have large front paws, allowing them to swim a few hundred kilometers from land. These meat eaters spend most of their waking hours hunting seals under or near the ice. Unfortunately, these beautiful animals are now an endangered species. The reason is that the Arctic is becoming too warm for the bears. There is less ice, so there are fewer seals to feed on. They have to swim farther to reach the ice, and this reduces their condition.

1 They are huge white bears covered by thick white fur, and they have large front paws.

2 They eat meat, especially seals.

3 The Arctic climate is perfectly suited for polar bears, but now it is getting too warm for them. There is less ice, so there are fewer seals.

B

Script 02-15

W Professor: Now, just as a brief review, monsoons are an annual weather phenomenon that usually occur in Asia. Typically, what happens is that cool, moist air above the ocean collides with dry, warm air above India. When this happens, it turns into heavy rain. The rainfall can impact all areas of Asia, especially India. Unlike other natural phenomenon, monsoons can be extremely beneficial. For example, they supply India with ninety percent of its water supply and water for subsistence farmers throughout Asia, who use it for their crops. Unfortunately, too much rain can result in disaster, such as flooding and famine. The precise dates and durations of monsoons are impossible to predict. Monsoons are more common in the Northern Hemisphere, where there are more large landmasses, than in the Southern Hemisphere, which is mostly comprised of sea water.

1 Cool, moist air above the ocean collides with dry, warm air above India.

2 Monsoons provide farmers with water for their crops.

3 The Northern Hemisphere is where most of the large landmasses are located.

Mini TOEFL iBT Practice Test

p.66

1 Ⓒ 2 Ⓐ 3 Ⓓ 4 Ⓑ 5 Ⓐ
6 Ⓑ 7 Ⓓ 8 Ⓐ 9 Ⓑ, Ⓓ
10 Ⓑ 11 Ⓓ

[1-5]

Script 02-16

M Student: Excuse me. I was here last week for a few interviews. I'm just checking if you've heard from any of the employers yet?

W Student Services Center Employee: Yes, we've started to hear from a few. I have a list here . . .

M: Oh! That's me . . . right there . . . What job is that?

W: This is the media assistant position. It's a three-month contract, and it starts soon.

M: Media assistant? I didn't even have an interview for that job. How did I get it?

W: Well, I guess the company received your application and then hired you based on your experience and qualifications. Or perhaps someone at the company contacted your references.

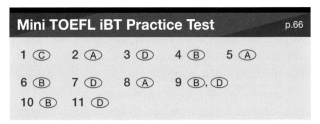

M: That's great! I mean, I hope it's a good job . . . I don't know anything about it. Do you know exactly what it's about? Is it a good job?

W: Well, first of all, the job is with Bestviews. It's a local company that produces a lot of educational films, documentaries, news clips, and sometimes special events. In addition, many of the professors from this university work on those films. But to answer your question, I think it is a good job. It's not dirty or dangerous or anything like that. **A lot of students here have had that job, and they liked it.** It's very interesting, and it's a lot better than most of the work students end up getting.

M: Well, what exactly does a media assistant do?

W: A number of things. It's not really an office job or a sedentary job. You have to travel a lot.

M: Really? That's good. I don't mind traveling. Which cities would I have to travel to?

W: Well, I didn't mean road trips, but you have to travel a lot around the city or near the city. You have to pick up and deliver any movies, videos, and films that are being edited. So perhaps the filming might take place at an event just outside of the city. You'd take the film back to the Bestviews Media Center, which is located just across the street from campus, and then return any edited films to other destinations throughout the city. You have a driver's license, right?

M: Yes, sure. I used to have a part-time job as a taxi driver. I drove full time last summer.

W: I see. Well, maybe that's why you got hired. This job is going to require a lot of driving, and you'll be driving vans. Bestviews has nice vans.

M: Okay. When does the job start?

W: You'll have to get all of the details directly from the employer. But most of these jobs are supposed to begin early next month. Here's the phone number. Just call this person. Her name is Emily. I've met her a few times. She's very nice. She should be able to answer all of your questions. I think she might be your supervisor.

M: I'll do that. Thanks a lot.

W: No problem. I hope it all works out for you.

해석

M Student: 실례합니다. 지난 주 이곳에서 면접을 몇 번 보았어요. 혹시 연락 온 곳이 있었는지 확인하려고요.

W Student Services Center Employee: 네, 몇 군데에서 연락이 오기 시작했어요. 여기에 목록이 있는데…

M: 오! 저예요… 바로 거기요… 어떤 일인가요?

W: 미디어 어시스턴트 자리예요. 3개월 계약직이고, 곧 일이 시작돼요.

M: 미디어 어스스턴트요? 그에 대한 면접은 보지도 않았는데요. 제가 어떻게 구한 거죠?

W: 음, 제 생각에는 그곳 회사가 학생의 지원서를 받고 학생의 경력과 자격 조건에 근거해서 학생을 채용한 것 같아요. 아니면 그곳 회사의 누군가가 학생의 추천인에게 연락을 했을 수도 있고요.

M: 잘 됐군요! 제 말은, 좋은 일자리이면 좋겠다는 뜻인데… 그에 대해서는 전혀 아는 바가 없네요. 그 자리가 정확히 어떤 것인지 아시나요? 좋은 자리인가요?

W: 음, 우선, Bestviews에서 하게 되는 일이에요. 많은 교육 프로그램, 다큐멘터리, 뉴스, 그리고 때로는 특별 영상물을 제작하는 지역 회사죠. 또한 이곳 대학 출신의 많은 교수님들께서 그러한 영상물 제작에 참여하고 계세요. 하지만 학생의 질문에 답하자면 저는 좋은 자리라고 생각해요. 지저분하거나 위험한 일 등은 아니에요. 이곳의 많은 학생들이 그 일자리를 얻고는 마음에 들어 했어요. 일이 매우 재미있어서, 학생들이 구하게 되는 대부분의 일자리보다 훨씬 낫죠.

M: 음, 미디어 어시스턴트가 정확히 무슨 일을 하나요?

W: 많은 일들을 해요. 사실 사무실 업무나 비서 업무를 하지는 않죠. 많이 돌아다녀야 해요.

M: 정말인가요? 잘 됐군요. 돌아다니는 것은 상관없어요. 어떤 도시로 가게 될까요?

W: 음, 장거리 이동이 아니라 시내 또는 시 외곽 지역을 많이 돌아다녀야 한다는 뜻이었어요. 편집 중인 영화, 영상, 혹은 필름을 수거해서 전달해야 해요. 아마 시 외곽에서 진행되는 행사에서 촬영이 이루어질 수도 있겠죠. 학생은 그 필름을 학교 길 건너편에 있는 Bestviews 미디어 센터로 다시 가지고 와야 하고, 그 후에는 편집된 필름을 시내 곳곳의 목적지로 다시 가져다 주어야 할 거예요. 운전면허증은 가지고 있죠, 그렇죠?

M: 네, 물론이죠. 아르바이트로 택시 운전도 해 봤어요. 지난 여름에 풀타임으로 운전을 했죠.

W: 그렇군요. 음, 학생을 고용한 이유가 그것 때문일 수도 있겠네요. 이 일을 하면 운전을 많이 하게 될 것인데, 아마도 그 회사의 승합차를 운전하게 될 거예요. Bestviews에는 좋은 승합차들이 많거든요.

M: 좋아요. 일은 언제부터 시작하나요?

W: 자세한 이야기는 모두 그쪽 회사로부터 들어야 해요. 하지만 이 일자리들은 대부분 다음 달 초에 시작될 예정이죠. 여기 전화번호가 있어요. 이 사람에게 전화해 보세요. 이름이 Emily에요. 저도 몇 번 만난 적이 있어요. 매우 친절한 사람이에요. 학생의 모든 질문에 대답해 줄 수 있을 거예요. 어쩌면 학생의 상사가 될 수도 있겠네요.

M: 그럴게요. 정말 감사합니다.

W: 천만에요. 모든 일이 잘 풀리기를 바랄게요.

[6-11]

Script 02-17

M Professor: Are there any more questions about the Chinese calendar . . . ? No . . . ? Okay, then let me continue . . .The ancient Chinese were not the only ones who had a calendar. Other ancient cultures, including the Romans, the Assyrians, and the Babylonians, all had calendars, and, of course, so did the Egyptians. Many of the ancient calendars were relatively useless. In Egypt, for instance, there were different kinds of calendars.

W Student: What do you mean different kinds of calendars?

M: Well, for example, the Egyptians had a civil calendar for the government and another one for agriculture.

W: Wait . . . Do you mean that they had two calendars at the same time?

M: Yes. In fact, for 2,000 years, they had three. They used three concurrent calendars.

W: That sounds so confusing. Why did they have so many different calendars? I mean, uh, I just don't get the point of doing that.

M: Well, different calendars developed for different reasons or different purposes. And, yes, it probably was confusing because these calendars varied in length. One was a little shorter than the others, so they had to wait a long time before the calendars got in sync again.

W: That sounds so bizarre.

M: Well, let's not forget that these were ancient times and that people then did things differently from how we do them today. They might think that our methods are strange if they could come to the future to see us.

W: Were these calendars any good?

M: Yes, in fact, the first usable calendar started in Egypt, a very long time ago . . . in 4236 B.C. This was originally a lunar calendar, but over time, the Egyptians started to use the stars rather than the moon to make more accurate predictions. It was a useful calendar because it predicted precisely when the Nile would flood. At that time, farmers depended heavily on the Nile and its flooding to supply water for their crops. The floods also deposited rich soil throughout the plains. Because of this rich soil, the Egyptians were able to develop a sophisticated agricultural system which helped sustain a large population. So the calendar was useful and important for planting and harvesting crops.

The year was divided into three seasons, each of which had four months. There were thirty days in a month. They added five days at the end of the year to make it 365 days. The civil calendar regulated the government and its administrators.

One problem was the discrepancy between these two calendars. Months in the lunar calendar occurred at the same time every year. But this was not the case for the civil calendar. It was a few hours shorter than the lunar year, and, therefore, its months occurred at different times every year. In fact, it took 1,460 years for the two calendars to agree or be in sync with one another. This 1,460-year period is referred to as, uh . . . a Sothic cycle. Therefore, a second lunar calendar was created based upon the civil year. Its purpose was to regulate religious affairs, and it was designed to agree with the civil calendar. However, the original lunar calendar was never abandoned and was continued to be used because of its usefulness for agricultural purposes. Thus, three different calendars coexisted, each with a different purpose. The years were counted according to the duration of the reign of a king. For example, there might be "the eighth year of King A" and "the second year of King B." Additionally, of note, the Egyptians started their day at sunrise rather than at sundown, so a month would begin at sunrise as well.

해석

M Professor: 중국력에 대해서 질문이 더 있나요…? 없나요…? 좋아요, 그럼 계속하겠습니다… 고대 중국인들만 달력을 가지고 있던 것은 아니었어요. 다른 고대 문화권에서도, 예컨대 로마, 아시리아, 그리고 바빌로니아에도 모두 달력이 존재했으며, 당연하게도, 이집트에도 달력이 존재했어요. 고대의 달력 중 다수는 비교적 쓸모 없는 것이었습니다. 예를 들어 이집트에는 각기 다른 종류의 달력이 존재했어요.

W Student: 각기 다른 종류의 달력이라는 것이 어떤 의미인가요?

M: 음, 예를 들어 이집트에는 정부에서 사용하는 민간력과 농사에서 사용되는 역법이 있었어요.

W: 잠깐만요… 그러니까 두 개의 달력이 동시에 존재했다는 말씀이신가요?

M: 네. 실제로 2천 년 동안 세 개가 존재했어요. 세 개의 달력이 병행해서 사용되었죠.

W: 그러면 굉장히 혼란스러울 것 같아요. 왜 그렇게 많은 달력이 있었나요? 제 말은, 어, 저는 그렇게 했던 이유를 모르겠어요.

M: 음, 서로 다른 이유 때문에, 혹은 서로 다른 목적을 위해 다양한 달력들이 만들어졌습니다. 그리고, 네, 이러한 달력들은 길이가 서로 달랐기 때문에 아마도 혼란을 가져다 주었을 거예요. 한 달력이 나머지 달력보다 약간 짧았기 때문에, 오랜 시간을 기다린 후에야 달력들의 시간이 다시 맞춰졌어요.

W: 정말 이상하게 들리는군요.

M: 음, 이때는 고대였고, 당시 사람들은 오늘날 우리가 하는 것과 다른 방식으로 일을 처리했다는 점을 잊지 맙시다. 그들이 미래로 와서 우리를 본다면 우리의 방식들을 이상하게 생각할 수도 있어요.

W: 그러한 달력들이 유용하기는 했나요?

M: 네, 사실 처음으로 유용했던 달력은 오래 전 이집트에서… 기원전 4236년에 등장했어요. 본래 음력 달력이었지만 시간이 흐르면서 이집트인들은 보다 정확한 예상을 하기 위해 달보다는 별을 이용하기 시작했죠. 이러한 달력은 나일강의 범람 시기를 정확히 예측해 주었기 때문에 유용했어요. 그 당시 농부들은 농작물에 물을 대기 위해 나일강과 나일강의 범람에 크게 의존하고 있었습니다. 홍수는 또한 평야 전체에 비옥한 토양을 가져다 주기도 했어요. 이러한 비옥한 토양 덕분에 이집트인들은 많은 인구를 부양할 수 있는 정교한 농법을 개발해 낼 수 있었죠. 따라서 달력이 농작물을 심고 수확하는데 유용하고 중요했습니다.

한 해는 세 개의 계절로 나뉘었고, 각 계절은 4개월로 이루어졌어요. 한 달은 30일이었고요. 한 해의 마지막에 5일을 더함으로써 365일이 만들어졌죠. 민간력은 정부와 정부 관리들이 사용했습니다.

한 가지 문제는 이 두 달력 사이에 존재하는 차이였어요. 음력의 달들은 매년 같은 시기에 찾아왔습니다. 하지만 민간력의 경우에는 그렇지가 않았죠. 이는 음력보다 몇 시간 짧았으며, 그 때문에 달들이 매년 다른 시기에 찾아왔어요. 실제로 두 달력이 일치하거나 서로 맞아 떨어지기 위해서는 1,460년이 걸렸습니다. 이 1,460년의 기간을, 어… 천랑성 주기라고 부릅니다. 따라서 역년에 기반한 두 번째 음력이 만들어졌어요. 이 달력의 목적은 종교 행사를 조정하는 것이었고, 이는 민간력과 일치시키기 위해 고안되었습니다. 하지만 원래의 음력은 농사에 유용했기 때문에 폐기된 적이 없었으며 계속해서 사용되었어요. 그래서 각기 다른 목적을 가진 세 가지 달력이 공존했던 것이죠. 연도는 왕의 통치 기간에 따라

정해졌어요. 예를 들어 "A왕 8년"과 "B왕 2년"과 같은 식이 될 수 있었죠. 게다가 흥미롭게도, 이집트인들은 일몰보다는 일출과 함께 하루를 시작했기 때문에, 한 달 역시 일출로 시작되었습니다.

Vocabulary Check-Up p.71

A 1 Ⓐ 2 Ⓕ 3 Ⓝ 4 Ⓒ 5 Ⓔ 6 Ⓗ 7 Ⓓ 8 Ⓖ 9 Ⓜ 10 Ⓘ 11 Ⓞ 12 Ⓛ 13 Ⓙ 14 Ⓑ 15 Ⓚ

B 1 Ⓑ 2 Ⓔ 3 Ⓒ 4 Ⓐ 5 Ⓓ

UNIT 03 Listening for Major Details

Basic Drill p.74

Drill 1 Ⓓ

Script 03-02

M Student: Before I leave your office, may I discuss one more thing with you, please?

W Professor: Sure. But we need to be quick. Several other students are waiting to talk to me, and I have class in fifteen minutes.

M: Sure. Well, uh, I'm trying to think about my future.

W: What are you considering doing?

M: I'm not really sure. Part of me wants to get a job, but another part would prefer to attend graduate school.

W: I think you'd be a good candidate for more studying.

M: Why do you think so?

W: Your grades are good, you enjoy studying, and you're pretty talented at research. You're exactly the kind of person that grad schools love to have as students.

M: Thanks for saying that. Do you have any idea which schools I should apply to?

W: Let's have this conversation another time. I can talk to you in more detail after tomorrow's class ends. How does that sound?

M: Perfect. Thanks so much.

해석

M Student: 사무실을 나가기 전에 한 가지 더 말씀을 드려도 될까요?

W Professor: 그럼요. 하지만 빨리 말해야 할 거예요. 다른 학생들도 저와 이야기하기 위해 기다리고 있고, 15분 후에는 제가 수업에 들어가야 해요.

M: 그럴게요. 음, 어, 저는 제 장래에 대해 생각해 보고 있어요.

W: 어떤 일을 할 생각인가요?

M: 정말로 잘 모르겠어요. 한편으로는 취직을 하고 싶기도 하고, 다른 한편으로는 대학원에 다니는 것이 좋을 것 같기도 해요.

W: 제 생각에는 공부를 더 하는 편이 좋을 것 같아요.

M: 왜 그렇게 생각하시나요?

W: 학생의 학점이 좋고, 학생은 공부하는 것도 좋아하고, 그리고 연구에 꽤 소질이 있으니까요. 대학원들은 정확히 학생 같은 사람을 학생으로 삼고자 하죠.

M: 그렇게 말씀해 주셔서 감사합니다. 제가 어떤 학교에 지원해야 한다고 생각하시나요?

W: 이번 대화는 다음에 다시 하기로 해요. 내일 수업이 끝난 후에 보다 자세한 이야기를 나눌 수 있을 거예요. 어떻게 들리나요?

M: 좋아요. 정말 고맙습니다.

Drill 2 Ⓐ

Script 03-03

M Residential Assistant: Rebecca, I need to talk to you about something important for a moment.

W Student: Sure, Reggie. What's going on?

M: There have been some complaints about you by other students in this dorm.

W: Complaints? About what?

M: About your music. Apparently, you play your music too loudly at night, so you are disturbing a lot of people's sleep.

W: But . . . I don't think it's too loud.

M: Well, the other students do. I need for you to stop playing loud music after nine at night. If you keep doing it and more students complain, you're going to get fined.

W: Oh, that wouldn't be good.

M: No, it wouldn't. If you get fined, you not only have to pay money, but you have a harder time getting into certain dorms in the future.

W: I wasn't aware of that. I'm really sorry, Reggie. I'll make sure my music isn't loud from now on.

M: Thanks a lot, Rebecca.

해석

M Residential Assistant: Rebecca, 잠시 학생과 중요한 이야기를 해야 할 것 같아요.

W Student: 그래요, Reggie. 무슨 일인가요?

M: 이곳 기숙사의 다른 학생들로부터 학생에 관한 불만 사항이 몇 건 제기되었

어요.

W: 불만 사항이요? 어떤 점 때문인가요?

M: 음악 때문이에요. 듣자 하니 학생이 밤에 음악을 너무 크게 틀어서 여러 사람들의 수면을 방해한다고 하더군요.

W: 하지만… 제가 그렇게 크게 틀지는 않는 것 같은데요.

M: 음, 다른 학생들은 크게 튼다고 생각해요. 더 이상 저녁 9시 이후에는 음악을 크게 틀지 않도록 해요. 계속 음악을 크게 틀어서 더 많은 학생들이 불만을 제기하면 학생에게 벌금이 부과될 거예요.

W: 오. 그럼 좋지 않겠군요.

M: 그래요, 좋지 않을 거예요. 학생에게 벌금이 부과되면 학생은 벌금을 내야 할 뿐만 아니라 추후에 특정 기숙사에 들어가는 일이 더 어려워질 거예요.

W: 그 점은 제가 몰랐군요. 정말 미안해요, Reggie. 지금부터는 확실히 음악을 크게 틀지 않도록 할게요.

M: 정말 고마워요, Rebecca.

Drill 3 Ⓐ

Script 03-04

W Professor: The three biggest names in ancient Greek drama are Aeschylus, Euripides, and Sophocles. They were primarily responsible for popularizing various styles of drama in ancient times. Arguably the next most important playwright in ancient Greece was Aristophanes. He lived from 446 to around 386 B.C. He is called the Father of Comedy, and he was quite a brilliant writer. Let me tell you a bit more about him.

Aristophanes is known to have written at least forty plays. Of those plays, eleven survive in complete form or are almost in their entirety. There are also around 1,000 fragments of his other works that exist elsewhere. In most cases, they are merely a line or two, so those remaining plays are likely lost forever. Aristophanes wrote in the genre known as Old Comedy and was a master both of ridicule and satire.

Among his surviving plays, *The Birds*, *The Wasps*, and *Lysistrata* are surely the best known and most studied. Personally, I'm a big fan of *The Knights*, which is a satire on social and political life in Athens in the fifth century B.C. We're going to read it in class, so please be sure to pay close attention. Aristophanes often ridiculed leading citizens of Athens, and he was despised by men like Cleon, whom he wrote of disparagingly in *The Knights*.

해석

W Professor: 고대 그리스 드라마에서 가장 중요한 세 개의 이름은 아이스킬로스, 에우리피데스, 그리고 소포클레스입니다. 주로 이들 덕분에 다양한 스타일의 드라마들이 고대에 유행을 할 수 있었죠. 고대 그리스에서 그 다음으로 중요한 희곡 작가는 아마도 아리스토파네스일 거예요. 그는 약 기원전 446년부터 기원전 386년까지 살았어요. 그는 희극의 아버지라고 불리는데, 상당히 뛰어난 작가였어요. 그에 대해서 약간 더 이야기를 해 보죠.

아리스토파네스는 최소 40편의 희곡을 썼던 것으로 알려져 있어요. 이들 희곡 중에서 11개가 완전한 형태로, 혹은 거의 온전한 형태로 현재까지 전해지고 있습니다. 또한 기타 작품들 중 일부에 해당되는 1,000여편의 글들도 존재해요. 대부분의 경우, 이들은 한 줄이나 두 줄로 되어 있기 때문에, 이렇게 남아 있는 희곡들은 영원히 묻혀 있을 가능성이 큽니다. 아리스토파네스는 구희극이라고 알려진 장르의 작품을 썼으며, 조소와 풍자의 대가였어요.

현재 남아 있는 그의 희곡 중에서 *새*, *벌*, 그리고 *여자의 평화*가 분명 가장 유명하고 가장 많이 연구되고 있습니다. 개인적으로 저는 *기사*의 열렬한 팬인데, 이 작품은 기원전 5세기 아테네의 사회적 및 정치적 삶에 대한 풍자극이에요. 수업에서 이를 읽어볼 것이기 때문에 반드시 많은 주의를 기울여 주시기 바랍니다. 아리스토파네스는 종종 아테네의 유력한 시민들을 조롱했으며, *기사*에서 모욕적으로 묘사된 클레온과 같은 사람들로부터 경멸을 받았습니다.

Drill 4 Ⓒ

Script 03-05

M Professor: Everyone, please take a look at this picture up on the screen . . . Can anyone tell me what you see?

W Student: Um . . . It's just a picture of a tree branch. It looks like an oak tree. Is that what we're studying today?

M: I'm impressed you can identify an oak tree, Leslie, but look a bit more closely. Hiding in plain sight is a walking stick insect. You can see it in the upper lefthand corner of the picture . . . uh, right there . . .

The walking stick insect is a highly effective user of camouflage. This insect basically, as you can see, resembles a stick or twig on a tree. It may even sway back and forth when the wind blows to make it look more realistic.

There are around 3,000 species of walking stick insects around the world, and this creature can be found on every continent except for Antarctica. It prefers tropical and temperate areas though, so you're more likely to find it in places with warm or hot weather. Interestingly, the walking stick is an herbivore, so its camouflage is used for defensive purposes. Despite the fact that many animals hunt it, the walking stick insect's camouflage is very effective. Unfortunately, it doesn't trick bats due to their reliance on echolocation, so bats are among the most successful hunters of this insect.

해석

M Professor: 모두들 화면에 있는 이 사진을 봐 주세요… 무엇이 보이는지 말해볼 사람이 있나요?

W Student: 음… 나뭇가지 사진이군요. 떡갈나무처럼 보여요. 이것이 오늘 우리가 공부할 내용인가요?

M: 떡갈나무를 알아보다니 인상적이지만, Leslie, 조금 더 자세히 보세요. 뻔히 잘 보이는 곳에 대벌레가 있습니다. 사진의 왼쪽 구석 위에서 보실 수 있는데… 어, 여기에 있죠…

대벌레는 매우 효과적으로 위장을 하는 곤충이에요. 이 곤충은 기본적으로, 보시다시피, 막대기 혹은 나뭇가지처럼 생겼습니다. 심지어 바람이 불면 몸이 앞

뒤로 흔들리기 때문에 더욱 진짜처럼 보입니다.

전 세계에 약 3,000종의 대벌레가 존재하며, 이 생물은 남극을 제외한 모든 대륙에서 찾아볼 수 있습니다. 하지만 열대 및 온대 지역을 선호하기 때문에 날씨가 따뜻하거나 더운 곳에서 찾아보기가 더 쉬워요. 흥미롭게도, 대벌레는 초식동물이어서 방어 목적으로 위장을 사용합니다. 많은 동물들이 이를 사냥한다는 사실에도 불구하고, 대벌레의 위장은 매우 효과적이에요. 안타깝게도, 반향 위치 측정을 이용하는 박쥐들은 속이지 못하기 때문에, 박쥐는 이 곤충을 가장 잘 사냥하는 동물들 중 하나입니다.

Exercises with Long Conversations

Exercise 1 1 Ⓓ 2 Ⓑ 3 Ⓓ p.78

Script 03-06

M Student: Hi, Ms. Jones. Could I speak with you, please?

W Student Housing Office Employee: Certainly, Rudy. What's the problem?

M: I am having some trouble with my roommate. We have completely different schedules. I go to bed early and get up in the morning to do my studying. My roommate stays up late and then sleeps through the morning. This wouldn't be too much of a problem if he were quiet when I am trying to sleep, but at night he likes to play loud music and talk on the telephone. He's not considerate either. One night, I invited a few classmates over to work on a project. My roommate got upset when they wouldn't leave by 10 PM, but the very next night, he invited a friend over, and they stayed up until 2 AM.

W: That certainly does sound like a problem, Rudy, but I'm afraid I cannot allow you to switch roommates as it's the middle of a semester.

M: But I already found another roommate. His name is Frederick, and he has the same problem as me. He and his roommate have totally different hours. All four of us would be much happier if we switched roommates.

W: Yes, I understand that you would like to change roommates, Rudy, but the rules state that students cannot switch roommates in the middle of a semester.

M: But my studies are suffering because my sleep keeps getting interrupted, and then I am too tired to study in the morning. There would be fewer interruptions of my studies if you allowed us to switch roommates.

W: Have you tried talking to your roommate first? How about studying in the library instead of in your room?

M: I did try talking to my roommate, but he said that the only way he can study is if he stays up late and plays music. And I would go study at the library, but it's all the way across campus. It's more than an hour's walk.

W: Okay, I am going to make an exception as I don't want to see your studies suffer. However, I want to have signed proof from your friend Frederick attesting that he agrees to change roommates mid-semester. I also want to have signed proof that both of your roommates are willing to do this. If you return with the signatures, then I will allow you to switch. Is that understood?

M: Yes! Thank you, Ms. Jones. I will bring the signatures to you as soon as possible. Now we all will be able to study without being so distracted. Again, thank you!

W: You're welcome, Rudy. And remember that although I am allowing you to switch roommates, sometimes having the experience of living with a difficult person teaches us valuable lessons about how to compromise. It sounds like in this case you did all that you could.

M: I certainly did, Ms. Jones. I tried my best.

해석

M Student: 안녕하세요, Jones 선생님. 이야기를 나눌 수 있을까요?

W Student Housing Office Employee: 그럼요, Rudy. 무슨 일인가요?

M: 룸메이트와 문제를 겪고 있어서요. 우리는 스케줄이 완전히 달라요. 저는 일찍 자고 아침에 일어나서 공부를 해요. 제 룸메이트는 늦게까지 깨어 있다가 오전 내내 잠을 자고요. 제가 자려고 할 때 그가 조용히 있으면 큰 문제가 안 되겠지만, 그는 밤에 음악을 크게 틀고 전화로 이야기하는 것을 좋아해요. 그는 또한 배려심도 없어요. 어느 날 밤, 저는 친구들을 몇 명 초대해서 프로젝트를 하고 있었어요. 친구들이 저녁 10시까지 머무르자 룸메이트가 화를 냈는데, 바로 그 다음 날 밤에 그는 한 친구를 초대해서 새벽 2시까지 같이 있더군요.

W: 분명 심각한 문제로 들리지만, Rudy, 안타깝게도 학기 중이라서 룸메이트를 바꾸는 것은 허락할 수 없어요.

M: 하지만 저는 이미 다른 룸메이트를 구했어요. 그의 이름은 Frederick인데, 저와 똑같은 문제를 겪고 있죠. 그와 그의 룸메이트의 활동 시간대도 완전히 달라요. 룸메이트를 바꾸면 저희 네 사람 모두 훨씬 더 행복해질 거예요.

W: 네, 룸메이트를 바꾸고 싶어하는 점은 이해가 가지만, Rudy, 규정에 따르면 학기 중에는 학생들이 룸메이트를 바꿀 수가 없어요.

M: 하지만 계속 수면에 방해를 받아서 오전에 공부하기가 너무 힘들기 때문에 제 학업에 차질이 생기고 있는걸요. 룸메이트를 바꾸는 것을 허락해 주신다면 제 학업이 방해를 덜 받게 될 거예요.

W: 먼저 룸메이트와 이야기를 해 봤나요? 방에서 공부하는 대신 도서관에서 공부를 하는 것은 어때요?

M: 룸메이트와도 이야기를 나누었지만, 그는 밤늦은 시간에 음악을 틀고 있는 경우에만 공부가 된다고 하더군요. 그리고 저도 도서관에서 공부를 하려고 했는데, 도서관은 캠퍼스 반대편에 있어요. 걸어서 한 시간 이상 가야 하죠.

W: 좋아요, 학생의 학업에 지장이 생기는 것은 원하지 않으니 예외를 두도록 하죠. 하지만 학기 도중 룸메이트를 바꾸는데 동의한다는, 학생의 친구 Frederick의 서명이 들어 있는 증거 서류가 있어야 해요. 또한 두 명의 룸메이트 모두 이에 동의한다는 서명이 들어 있는 증거 서류도 있어야 하고요. 서명을 받아서 다시 여기로 오면 제가 룸메이트 바꾸는 것을 허락할게요. 이해했나요?

M: 네! 감사합니다, Jones 선생님. 최대한 빨리 서명을 받아 올게요. 이제 우리 모두 방해 받지 않고 공부하게 되겠군요. 다시 한 번 고맙습니다!

W: 천만에요, Rudy. 그리고 제가 룸메이트 바꾸는 것을 허락하기는 했지만, 때

로는 까다로운 사람과 함께 지냈던 경험이 타협하는 법에 관한 소중한 교훈을 알려 준다는 점을 기억하세요. 이번 경우에는 학생이 할 수 있는 최선을 다했던 것으로 들리지만요.

M: 정말 그랬어요, Jones 선생님. 저는 최선을 다했어요.

Summary Note

A

❶ roommate
❷ loud music
❸ impossible
❹ new roommate
❺ can't study
❻ library

B

The student is unhappy with his living situation. The student wants to change roommates because his current one keeps a different schedule. The student complains that his roommate stays up late and plays loud music when he is trying to sleep. This causes him to sleep poorly, so when he gets up in the morning to study, he is too tired. The student says his studies are suffering and asks to switch roommates. The woman says she is sorry, but the college does not allow students to switch roommates halfway through the semester. The student responds that he has found the perfect roommate: a student who keeps the same schedule. The woman says she will allow the student to change roommates if he gets signatures from his friend and from the other roommates agreeing to this. The woman concludes by pointing out that difficult living situations can teach the student a lot about compromising.

Exercise 2 1 Ⓒ 2 Ⓐ, Ⓒ 3 Ⓑ p.80

Script 03-07

W Student: Hi, Professor Williams. I just have a quick question.

M Professor: Hello, Julie. Yes, what is it?

W: I am currently taking eighteen credits, which is a full load, but I would really like to take your theater history class as well.

M: I would love to have you in class, Julie, but it sounds as though you are taking enough classes as it is. Why don't you take my class next semester?

W: I would, but I am going to be majoring in theater history, and I feel as though I should take it right now since I'll need to take other classes in the future.

M: I am sorry, Julie, but I don't see how it would be possible. If you were to take my class on top of another eighteen credits, you would be studying all the time and would have no time for anything else.

W: I have considered this, which is why I've come up with an idea. What if I were to audit your class? That way, I would listen to the lectures and learn the material, but I wouldn't get credit for taking the class.

M: That is certainly an idea, Julie. You could audit the class for no credit, according to the policy at this school, but then you would not be able to participate in any class discussions. What if you have a question concerning a lecture I am giving? Are you going to feel okay about not participating?

W: Wow, I never considered that. I would have to say that I would be frustrated if I weren't able to ask questions in class or add my own comments to a discussion.

M: You should also consider how not having a theater history credit is going to affect your theater major. Ideally, we would like you to have credit for all of your major classes. And if you decide to do something in the theater world later on, then it would also be a good idea to get credit for those classes. Don't worry, Julie. You are a great student, and putting off my class for one semester is not going to set you back. Take your eighteen credits this semester, and I will get you into my theater history class next semester. Okay?

W: Okay. I guess I just got worried that I would not have time to fit in all of my theater history classes. But it is more important to me that I receive full credit for my major courses and that I participate in the discussions. I look forward to taking your class next semester though. Thanks very much for talking to me.

M: No problem, Julie. It's always a pleasure to talk to you, and I will pencil you in for next semester's class right now. Have a good afternoon.

해석

W Student: 안녕하세요, Williams 교수님. 간단히 여쭤볼 것이 있어서요.

M Professor: 안녕하세요, Julie. 그래요, 어떤 것인가요?

W: 저는 현재 들을 수 있는 최대 학점인 18학점을 듣고 있는데, 교수님의 연극사 수업이 정말로 듣고 싶어요.

M: 학생이 제 수업을 들으면 좋겠지만, Julie, 학생은 현재로도 충분히 많은 수업을 듣고 있는 것처럼 보이는군요. 다음 학기에 제 수업을 듣는 것이 어떨까요?

W: 그럴 수도 있지만, 저는 연극사를 전공할 생각인데, 나중에 다른 과목들을 들어야 해서 지금 당장은 그 수업을 들어야만 할 것 같아요.

M: 유감이지만, Julie, 그런 일은 가능할 것 같지가 않네요. 만약 학생이 18학점 외에 제 수업까지 듣는다면 내내 공부만 하게 될 것이고 그 밖의 일들을 할 시간은 없을 거예요.

W: 저도 그러한 점은 생각해 보았는데, 그래서 한 가지 아이디어가 떠올랐어요. 제가 교수님 수업을 청강하는 것은 어떨까요? 그렇게 하면 강의를 듣고 수업 내용을 익힐 수 있지만, 과목 이수에 대한 학점은 인정받지 못하게 되죠.

M: 확실히 아이디어이기는 하네요, Julie. 이곳 학교 규정에 따르면 학점을 인정

받지 않고 수업을 청강할 수는 있지만, 수업 토론에는 참여할 수 없을 거예요. 제 강의 내용과 관련된 질문이 있다면 어떻게 할 건가요? 참여를 하지 않아도 괜찮나요?

W: 와, 그 점은 결코 생각해 보지 못했어요. 수업 시간에 질문을 할 수 없고 토론에서도 의견을 낼 수 없다면 당황스러울 것 같아요.

M: 또한 연극사 수업에서 학점을 얻지 못하면 연극 전공에 어떤 영향이 미칠 것인지도 생각해 봐야 해요. 이상적으로는 모든 전공 수업에서 학점을 얻는 것이 좋아요. 그리고 나중에 연극계에서 일을 하기로 결심한다면, 이들 수업에서 학점을 얻는 것 또한 좋은 아이디어가 될 거예요. 걱정하지 말아요, Julie. 학생은 우수한 학생이고, 제 수업을 한 학기 미룬다고 해서 학생이 뒤쳐지는 것도 아니에요. 이번 학기에 18학점을 들으면 다음 학기에는 제 연극사 수업을 들을 수 있게 해 줄게요. 알겠죠?

W: 알겠어요. 연극사 수업을 들을 수 있는 시간이 없을 것 같아서 걱정을 했던 것 같아요. 하지만 전공에 필요한 학점을 다 채우고 수업 토론에 참여하는 것이 더 중요해 보이네요. 하지만 다음 학기에 교수님 수업을 들을 수 있기를 고대하고 있을게요. 말씀을 나눠 주셔서 정말 고맙습니다.

M: 천만에요, Julie. 학생과 이야기하는 것은 제게도 항상 즐거운 일이고, 지금 내년 학기 수강생 명단에 학생 이름을 적어 두도록 하죠. 즐거운 오후 보내세요.

Summary Note

A

❶ theater history
❷ next semester
❸ audit
❹ credit
❺ discussion
❻ major classes

B

A student goes to her professor's office because she wishes to take the professor's theater history class this semester even though she is already taking eighteen credits. The professor tells the student that eighteen credits is a lot of work and asks the student to wait until next semester to take the class. The student says she wants to be a theater history major and worries that she should take the class now. The student asks the professor if she can audit this semester's theater history class for no credit. The professor says that she can although he wonders if the student will be okay with the fact that she will not be able to participate in the discussions during class. The professor also points out that the school recommends that students take all of their major classes for credit. The student says she did not consider this and decides to take the theater history class for credit the following semester.

Exercise 3 1 Ⓐ 2 Ⓓ 3 Ⓑ p.82

Script 03-08

W Registrar's Office Employee: Good afternoon. How can I help you?

M Student: Good afternoon. I seem to be having trouble registering for classes.

W: Can you specify what kind of trouble?

M: I am having trouble when I try to register for next semester's classes online. Whenever I press the "Complete Registration" button, I get a notice that reads, "Sorry. We cannot complete this registration. Please see an employee for details." I am not sure what the problem is. I am a good student and always make sure I choose classes to complete my major.

W: Let me take a look on my computer here. Ah! It seems that your problem has nothing to do with your classes. My computer screen shows that you have an overdue fee at the library. It says you owe the library ten dollars for a book entitled *Psychology and the Universe*. Do you remember checking this book out?

M: What? I paid that fee just last week! I remember that book because I checked it out for a psychology paper. I did forget to return the book on time, but I received a notice last week and went to the library and paid the fine.

W: Hmm . . . It's possible that the librarian forgot to log the information into the main computer. In that case, my computer wouldn't be updated. You paid the fine, right? You're certain you didn't pay a fine for a different book?

M: **I haven't checked out any other books at the library in a long time.** In fact, I distinctly remember paying the fine because when I was in the library, the librarian who took my money was someone I knew, so we talked for forty-five minutes. Hey! Perhaps she got sidetracked and forgot to update the computer.

W: I'm sure it has happened before, and that could very well be the situation again. However, the only way to resolve this is to get a receipt from the library. But hurry as today is the last day you can register for classes.

M: Today is the last day I can register? I thought registration ended next week.

W: I'm afraid it's today. If you hurry, you can go to the library and come back before we close at 4:00. Otherwise, online registration will continue until 10:00 PM.

M: I doubt I can get to the library and then back here by 4:00. I will just go to the library after dinner and then make sure I go home directly afterward and register online.

W: Wonderful. Just make sure the library enters the receipt into the system. That way, your name will be cleared, and you can register. However, please bring me the receipt tomorrow so that we have a paper trail in case there is a problem.

M: I will make sure to let them know. Thank you very much for your help.

해석

W Registrar's Office Employee: 안녕하세요. 어떻게 도와 드릴까요?

M Student: 안녕하세요. 수강 신청을 하는데 문제가 있는 것 같아요.

W: 어떤 문제인지 구체적으로 알려 주실 수 있나요?

M: 다음 학기 수업을 온라인으로 신청하려는 중인데 문제가 있어요. "신청 완료" 버튼을 누를 때마다 "죄송합니다. 신청을 완료할 수 없습니다. 자세한 내용은 직원에게 문의하십시오."라는 안내만 나와요. 문제가 무엇인지 잘 모르겠어요. 저는 성적도 좋고, 항상 전공 이수에 필요한 수업들을 선택하고 있죠.

W: 여기 제 컴퓨터로 한 번 볼게요. 아! 학생의 문제는 수업과 아무런 관련이 없는 것 같군요. 제 컴퓨터 화면에는 학생에게 도서관 연체료가 있다고 나오네요. *심리학과 우주*라는 제목의 책에 대해서 10달러의 연체료를 내야한다고 나와요. 이 책을 대출했던 것이 기억나시나요?

M: 뭐라고요? 저는 지난 주에 연체료를 냈어요! 심리학 수업의 보고서를 작성하기 위해 대출했던 책이라 기억을 해요. 제때 반납하는 것을 잊었지만, 지난 주에 연락을 받고 도서관에 가서 연체료를 납부했어요.

W: 흠… 사서가 깜빡 잊고 해당 정보를 메인 컴퓨터에 입력하지 않았을 수도 있겠군요. 그런 경우라면 제 컴퓨터에 정보가 업데이트되지 않았을 거예요. 연체료를 납부하셨죠, 그렇죠? 다른 책에 대한 연체료를 지불한 것은 분명 아니죠?

M: 다른 책들은 한동안 도서관에서 대출한 적이 없었어요. 사실 제가 도서관에 갔을 때 제 연체료를 받은 사람이 제가 알던 사람이라 45분 동안 이야기를 나누었기 때문에 제가 연체료를 냈다는 건 분명 기억하고 있어요. 그래요! 어쩌면 그 직원이 정신이 팔려서 컴퓨터에 정보를 입력하는 것을 잊었을 수도 있어요.

W: 전에도 그런 일이 있었기 때문에 이번에도 같은 상황일 것으로 생각되네요. 하지만 이 문제를 해결할 수 있는 유일한 방법은 도서관에서 영수증을 받아오는 것이에요. 그런데 오늘이 수강 신청 마지막 날이니 서두르세요.

M: 오늘이 수강 신청 마감일이라고요? 수강 신청 마감이 다음 주인 줄 알았는데요.

W: 안타깝지만 오늘이에요. 서두르면 도서관에 갔다가 사무실이 문을 닫는 4시까지 여기에 다시 올 수 있을 거예요. 하지만 온라인 수강 신청은 오후 10시까지 가능해요.

M: 도서관에 갔다가 4시까지 여기로 돌아올 수는 없을 것 같아요. 저녁 식사 후 도서관에 들린 다음 곧바로 집으로 가서 온라인으로 수강 신청을 할게요.

W: 그래요. 도서관에서 시스템에 영수증을 입력하는지 확인하세요. 그러면 학생 이름이 삭제 될 테고 온라인 수강 신청이 가능해질 거예요. 하지만 혹시 문제가 생기는 경우를 대비해서 저희가 문서상 기록을 가지고 있을 수 있도록 내일 제게 영수증을 가져다 주세요.

M: 꼭 그들에게 알려 줄게요. 도움을 주셔서 정말 고맙습니다.

Summary Note

A

❶ online registration
❷ library fine
❸ payment
❹ record
❺ pay the fine
❻ home

B

The student approaches the Registrar's office employee because he is having trouble registering online. Whenever he tries to complete his registration, he receives a notice that he must see an employee to proceed. The woman checks her computer and finds that the reason the student cannot register is that he has not paid a library fine. The student tells the woman that he paid the fine and that the incident stands out in his mind because the librarian he paid was someone he knows. The woman tells the student that the only way to resolve the issue is to get a receipt from the library, but he must hurry because in-person registration ends at 4:00 PM, and online registration ends at 10:00 PM. To give himself more time, the student decides he will get the library receipt after dinner and then register online.

Exercise 4 1 Ⓑ, Ⓓ 2 Ⓑ 3 Ⓓ p.84

Script 03-09

M Professor: Hello, Sarah. Thank you for answering my email and coming here. You're probably wondering why I want to see you.

W Student: Is it about the upcoming physics project?

M: Well, yes and no. You see, I'm very worried about your grade. You've failed the last two tests, and you've not been handing in your homework. Is there something going on outside class that is making your work suffer? I checked and found out that you did fine in your entry-level physics class.

W: I guess I have done pretty poorly lately, haven't I? It's a combination of things. First off, I'm finding the new things we're covering in class very challenging. Before the last test, I stayed up and studied most of the night, but I still had trouble understanding the concepts.

M: I can help remedy this particular problem. In fact, I just hired a part-time tutor. Perhaps you would be interested in meeting him for a few sessions until you get caught up with the material.

W: That would be very helpful.

M: Is there anything else affecting your performance?

W: I'm experiencing some trouble with my lab partners. We can never agree on a time to do our lab because of our schedules, so we often do parts of it on our own. This is causing problems for me, especially when I have to do the harder parts or equations I'm not familiar with. When we get together to exchange information, they get angry at me for not doing the work right and then complete it themselves without sharing the correct answers or showing me how to do it. I know you put the lab groups together, but do you think I could change groups?

M: Certainly, Sarah. I would be happy to move you to a different group. In fact, if you give me a copy of your schedule, I can match it with some other students who have similar schedules so that you can all do the lab work together. Do you think meeting with a tutor and switching lab groups will help you get back on track again?

W: I think so. Thank you for being so understanding, Professor Miller.

M: You're welcome, Sarah. I just wish you'd come to me sooner so that we could have sorted this out. You need to work really hard now to salvage your grade this semester.

W: I know. I guess I was so embarrassed by how badly I was doing that I didn't want to say anything.

M: That is nonsense. You are always welcome in my office. I want you to do the best you can. In fact, I am going to extend the deadline for the upcoming project I assigned today in class just to give you enough time to catch up with the tutor.

W: Thank you, Professor Miller. I really appreciate it.

해석

M Professor: 안녕하세요, Sarah. 내가 보낸 이메일에 답장도 해 주고 찾아와 줘서 고마워요. 아마도 제가 왜 학생을 보자고 했는지 궁금해할 것 같군요.

W Student: 곧 있을 물리학 프로젝트 때문인가요?

M: 음, 그렇기도 하고 아니기도 해요. 저는 학생의 성적이 매우 걱정스러워요. 학생은 지난 두 번의 시험에서 낙제 점수를 받았고 과제물도 제출하지 않았죠. 수업 외적으로 학업에 지장을 주는 일이라도 있나요? 확인해 봤더니 초급 물리학 수업에서는 성적이 좋았더군요.

W: 최근에 제 성적이 꽤 부진했죠, 그렇죠? 복합적인 이유가 있어요. 우선 수업에서 다루고 있는 새로운 내용들이 제게 너무 어려워요. 지난 번 시험을 보기 전에 늦게까지 잠도 안자고 거의 밤을 새다시피 공부를 했는데도 개념을 이해하기가 어려웠어요.

M: 그와 같은 특정한 문제는 제가 해결해 드릴 수 있어요. 사실 조금 전에 아르바이트 과외 교사를 고용했죠. 아마도 수업을 따라올 수 있을 때까지 그와 만나서 몇 차례 지도를 받는 것에 관심이 있을 것 같군요.

W: 그러면 많은 도움이 될 것 같아요.

M: 성적에 영향을 미치는 또 다른 문제가 있나요?

W: 실험 조원들과도 문제를 겪고 있어요. 시간표 때문에 실험 일정을 정할 수가 없어서 각자가 실험 일부를 혼자서 진행하고 있죠. 이러한 점은 제게 문제가 되는데, 특히 제가 어려운 부분이나 익숙하지 않은 방정식을 다루어야 할 때 문제가 돼요. 서로 모여서 내용을 공유하는 경우, 조원들은 제게 실험을 제대로 안했다고 화를 내고, 정답이나 하는 방법을 알려 주지도 않은 채 그들 스스로 실험을 마무리하죠. 교수님께서 조 배정을 하신 걸로 알고 있는데, 제가 다른 조에 들어갈 수 있을까요?

M: 물론이죠, Sarah. 기꺼이 다른 조로 바꿔 줄게요. 실제로 학생의 시간표를 알려 주면 비슷한 시간표를 가진 학생들과 조를 이루도록 해서 모두가 함께 실험을 할 수 있도록 할게요. 과외 교사를 만나고 실험 조를 바꾸면 다시 예전처럼 잘 할 수 있을 것으로 생각하나요?

W: 그럴 것 같아요. 이해해 주셔서 감사합니다, Miller 교수님.

M: 천만에요, Sarah. 더 빨리 저를 찾아와서 이 문제를 해결했으면 좋았을 것 같군요. 이번 학기에 성적을 회복하려면 정말로 열심히 해야 해요.

W: 저도 알아요. 성적이 너무 엉망이라 당황해서 아무런 말도 하고 싶지 않았던 것 같아요.

M: 말도 안 돼요. 제 사무실에서 학생은 언제라도 환영이에요. 학생이 최선을 다했으면 좋겠어요. 실제로 학생이 과외 수업으로 수업 내용을 따라잡을 수 있는 충분한 시간을 가질 수 있도록 오늘 수업 시간에 내 준 프로젝트의 마감일은 연장하려고 해요.

W: 감사합니다, Miller 교수님. 정말 고맙습니다.

Summary Note

A

❶ physics
❷ a tutor
❸ lab partners
❹ changing lab partners

B

The professor scheduled the meeting with the student because he is concerned about her grade. He asks her if she can list any reasons why she might be having so much trouble in his class. The student admits she is having trouble learning new concepts, and even though she stayed up late to study, she still did poorly on the test. The professor says he just hired a part-time tutor who can help her. The student then says that she is also having trouble with her lab partners. They are leaving her to do parts of the lab that she does not understand and then become upset with her efforts. The professor promises to switch her to a different lab group and also allows her to hand in her upcoming physics project at a later date so she will have a chance to catch up on the material.

Exercises with Long Lectures

Exercise 1 1 Ⓐ, Ⓓ 2 Ⓑ 3 Ⓓ p.86

Script 03-10

W Student: We have been talking a lot about different kinds of plays, but when did the idea of having theater develop?

M Professor: That is a very excellent question. We can find the first theaters in the same place that Western drama was first developed: ancient Greece.

W: So the ancient Greeks had theaters like we have today . . . with a big curtain and comfortable seats and sometimes balconies?

M: Well, not exactly. You see, the first theaters were called amphitheaters. The word amphitheater comes from the Greek work *theatron*, which referred to the large wooden stands that the Greeks erected on hillsides so that an audience could watch the unfolding drama.

By having spectators sit on the hillsides with the action taking place downslope from themselves in a hollowed-out part of a hill, sounds such as actors' voices and music resonated better throughout the space, so the audience was able to hear clearly. Another key feature of amphitheaters was that they were round in shape so as to harness sounds better. The orchestra was situated on a raised platform near the actors that was also round in shape. Two of the earliest theaters were the theater at Delphi, also known as the Attic Theater, and the Theater of Dionysus in Athens.

W: Did the ancient Greeks have any props or a set?

M: Most of the early plays were done in the open air during the daytime with few or no props. Later, however, scene buildings were used, not only for the purpose of a set but also as changing rooms for actors and sounding boards. Initially, the buildings were only temporary. They were put up and taken down each time a play was completed. Eventually, however, the buildings were left standing and served as stages for plays, like what we have today.

W: But we don't watch plays in amphitheaters now. Why did things change?

M: Well, just like other things in life, theaters evolved over time and through technology. For example, one of the drawbacks to performing plays in amphitheaters was that a play could not be performed in bad weather. Now, however, we can see a play any time of the year regardless of the weather. What was not lost during the changes was that the most important thing about putting on a play is that you must make sure your audience can hear the performance. It's not like going to watch a movie, where the sound can be turned up to accommodate the crowd. A play is a living thing, not a recording. Actors are speaking, and musicians are playing live.

One of the most famous theaters in the world is William Shakespeare's Globe Theater. The Globe was built in London sometime around the year 1598. Just like the Greek amphitheaters, it is open aired yet octagonal in shape. It is three stories high with enough seating for 3,000 people and a pit, or floor, for people to stand in. The stage itself is rectangular and has such features as trapdoors and other riggings for special effects.

W: Does the Globe Theater still exist?

M: Sadly, the original Globe Theater burned down in a fire in 1613; however, a new one was built—an exact replica of the original—in the mid-1990s.

해석

W Student: 다양한 종류의 희곡에 대해 많은 논의를 했는데, 극장을 만들어야겠다는 생각은 언제 시작되었나요?

M Professor: 매우 훌륭한 질문이군요. 서양 드라마가 처음 등장했던 곳과 같은 곳에서 최초의 극장을 찾아볼 수 있죠. 바로 고대 그리스입니다.

W: 그럼 고대 그리스에 오늘날과 같은 극장들이… 커다란 커튼과 편안한 좌석, 그리고 때로는 2층의 특별석이 갖춰져 있는 극장들이 있었나요?

M: 음, 그렇지는 않았어요. 아시다시피 최초의 극장은 원형 극장이라고 불렸습니다. 원형 극장이라는 말은 그리스어 단어인 *theatron*에서 비롯되었는데, 이는 관객들이 진행되는 연극을 관람할 수 있도록 그리스인들이 언덕에 세웠던 거대한 목재 관람석을 가리켰어요. 관객들은 언덕에 앉아 있었고 공연은 언덕 아래쪽의 움푹한 곳에서 이루어졌기 때문에 배우들의 목소리 및 음악과 같은 소리가 그곳 공간에 더 잘 울려 퍼졌고, 이로 인해 관객들은 소리를 선명하게 들을 수 있었습니다. 원형 극장의 또 다른 중요한 특징은 소리가 더 잘 울려 퍼질 수 있도록 이들의 형태가 원형이었다는 점이었어요. 오케스트라는 배우들 근처에 있는 높은 단상에 위치했는데, 이 단상 역시 원형이었고요. 최초의 극장 중 두 개는 애틱 시어터라고도 알려진 델파이에 있는 극장과 아테네에 있는 디오니소스 극장이었습니다.

W: 고대 그리스인들에게도 소도구나 세트가 있었나요?

M: 대부분의 초창기 연극은 낮 시간에 노천에서 이루어졌고, 소도구는 거의 사용되지 않거나 전혀 사용되지 않았어요. 하지만 이후 세트 목적으로, 아울러 배우들의 의상실 및 공명판으로 사용하기 위해 무대 건물이 사용되었습니다. 처음에 이러한 건물들은 일시적인 것이었어요. 연극이 공연될 때마다 세워지고 허물어졌죠. 하지만 결국 건물들을 계속 세워둠으로써 오늘날과 같은 연극 무대가 마련되었습니다.

W: 하지만 지금은 원형 극장에서 연극을 관람하지는 않잖아요. 왜 바뀐 거죠?

M: 음, 인생의 다른 것들과 마찬가지로 극장도 시간이 흐르고 기술이 발전하면서 진화했습니다. 예를 들어 원형 극장에서 이루어지는 공연의 한 가지 단점은 악천후인 경우 공연이 불가능하다는 점이었어요. 하지만 지금은 날씨에 상관없이 일 년 내내 공연을 볼 수가 있죠. 이러한 변화를 겪으면서도 바뀌지 않은 것은 연극 공연에서 가장 중요한 것이 관객으로 하여금 공연 내용을 들을 수 있도록 만들어야 한다는 점이에요. 이는 영화를 보러 가는 것과 다른 점인데, 영화관에서는 관중을 수용하기 위해 소리를 키울 수가 있죠. 연극은 살아 있는 것으로, 녹음된 것이 아닙니다. 배우들이 말을 하고 연주자들은 라이브로 음악을 연주하죠.

세계에서 가장 유명한 극장 중 하나는 윌리엄 셰익스피어의 글로브 극장입니다. 글로브 극장은 1598년 무렵 런던에 세워졌어요. 그리스의 원형 극장과 마찬가지로 노천 극장이고 8각형의 형태를 띠고 있어요. 3층으로 되어 있으며, 3,000명의 관객을 수용할 수 있는 좌석이 있고, 맨 아랫부분, 즉 플로어에서는 사람들이 서서 관람을 할 수가 있죠. 무대는 직사각형 형태이고, 트랩도어 및 특수 효과를 위한 기타 장치들이 있는 것이 특징이에요.

W: 글로브 극장이 아직도 존재하나요?

M: 안타깝게도 원래의 글로브 극장은 1613년에 화재로 소실되었습니다. 하지만 1990년대 중반에 원형대로 복원한 건물이 새로 지어졌죠.

Summary Note

A

❶ development of theater
❷ ancient Greece
❸ amphitheaters
❹ hillside
❺ Attic Theater
❻ bad weather
❼ amphitheaters
❽ Burned down

B

Theater architecture and Western drama were first developed by the ancient Greeks. The Greeks constructed what were known as amphitheaters. These were round in shape with high wooden seats built into hillsides so that an audience could better see and hear a performance. Two of the earliest and most famous Greek theaters were the theater at Delphi, known as the Attic Theater, and the Theater of Dionysus in Athens. The Greeks used very few props for their dramas, and plays were always performed in the open air. By Elizabethan times, however, theater architecture had evolved. Shakespeare's Globe Theater, for instance, was octagonal in shape with three-story-high walls and an elevated stage. The pit was for standing room only. Some of the developments featured such things as trapdoors on the stage floor and rigging in the wings. In 1613, a fire destroyed the Globe Theater, but during the mid-1990s, an exact replica was made in the city of London.

Exercise 2 1 Ⓑ 2 Ⓓ 3 Ⓐ p.88

Script 03-11

W Professor: Today, we are going to be discussing the life and work of the American literary figure Pearl S. Buck. Pearl was born in West Virginia in the year 1892 to Absalom and Caroline Sydenstricker. Pearls' parents were Presbyterian missionaries, and when Pearl was only three months old, they moved to China, where Pearl spent the better part of the first forty years of her life. From early childhood, Pearl was able to speak both English and Chinese, being taught by both her mother and a Chinese tutor, Mr. Kung. In 1910, Pearl enrolled in Randolph-Macon Women's College in Virginia. After graduation in 1914, Pearl returned to China for a short time as her mother was seriously ill. The following year, Pearl met an agricultural biologist, John Lossing Buck, and the two married in 1917 and settled in the rural Chinese province Anhwei. Pearl worked as a teacher and also as an interpreter for her husband, whose job required that he travel around China. In the early 1920s, Pearl and her husband moved to Nanking, China, where Pearl took up a position teaching English and American literature at a university.

It was during these years in Nanking that Pearl gave birth to a daughter, Carol, who had a rare genetic disorder that left her mentally handicapped. During delivery, it was also discovered that Pearl had a tumor, so she underwent a hysterectomy. In 1925, Pearl and her husband adopted a second daughter, Janice, but that did little to ease the strain of the stressful marriage between them. In 1926, Pearl returned to the United States with her first daughter, Carol, to seek medical attention for her condition, and it was during this time also that Pearl studied for and achieved a master's degree in literature from Cornell University. The Bucks returned to China in the year 1927 only to be evacuated to Japan during the Chinese Civil War. Pearl was never to return to China again. In 1935, she divorced her husband and married her publisher, Richard Walsh, with whom she moved to Pennsylvania, and it was there that Pearl penned her most famous novel, namely *The Good Earth*, which was published in 1931.

The Good Earth follows the life of Wang Lung, an impoverished man who eventually becomes a rich landowner. *The Good Earth* gained a worldwide audience, sold nearly two million copies in its first year of publication, earned her the Pulitzer Prize, and was eventually made into a motion picture. Many books were to follow, for example, *The Patriot* in 1939 and *The Child Who Never Grew* in 1950 with many stories and essays in between. In 1936, she was made a member of the National Institute of Arts and Letters, and in the year 1938, she won the Nobel Prize for literature.

After the death of her second husband, Richard Walsh, she began a relationship with a young dance instructor, Ted Harris, who was forty years younger than her. She died at the age of eighty in Vermont on March 6, 1973. She is remembered for her work in literature but also for her humanitarian work, for her candor, and for her faith in her fellow peers. **In 1939, she said, "I feel no need for any other faith than my faith in human beings."** Pearl's work spanned forty years, during which she published over eighty works of literature.

해석

W Professor: 오늘은 미국 문학 작가인 펄 S. 벅의 삶과 작품에 대해 논의해 보겠습니다. 펄은 1892년 웨스트버지니아에서 압살롬 사이든스트리커와 캐롤린 사이든스트리커의 딸로 태어났어요. 펄의 부모는 장로교 선교사들로 펄이 겨우 3달 되던 때 중국으로 건너갔는데, 펄은 이곳에서 거의 40년 동안 지냈습니다. 펄은 어려서부터 어머니와 중국어 가정 교사였던 쿵 씨로부터 영어와 중국어를 배웠기 때문에 두 가지 언어를 모두 구사했어요 1910년 펄은 버지니아에 있는 랜돌프-메이콘 여대에 입학했습니다. 1914년에 졸업을 한 후 펄은 잠시 중국으로 돌아왔는데, 어머니의 병이 위중했기 때문이었죠. 이듬해 펄은 농생물학자인 존 로싱 벅을 만났고, 두 사람은 1917년에 결혼을 해서 중국 안후이성의 시골에 정착했어요. 펄은 교사로 일하면서 남편의 통역가 역할을 하기도 했는데, 남편은 직업상 중국 전역을 여행해야 했죠. 1920년대 초반, 펄과 그녀의 남편은 중국의 난징으로 이사를 했고, 펄은 한 대학에서 영국 문학과 미국 문학을 가르치는 일자리를 얻었습니다.

난징에서의 이 기간 동안 펄은 딸 캐롤을 낳았는데, 캐롤은 희귀한 유전 질환에 가지고 있어서 정신 장애를 앓았습니다. 출산 도중 펄에게 종양이 있다는 점이 발견되었기 때문에 그녀는 자궁 절제술을 받았어요. 1925년 펄과 그녀의 남편은 둘째 딸 재니스를 입양했지만, 이것이 결혼 생활에서 오는 긴장감을 완화시켜 주지는 못했습니다. 1926년 펄은 장녀인 캐롤을 데리고 미국으로 돌아와 장애에 대한 치료를 받게끔 했고, 또한 바로 이 시기에 코넬 대학에서 공부를 해서 문학 석사 학위를 땄어요. 벅 가족은 1927년에 다시 중국으로 돌아갔지만 중국의 내전 기간 동안에는 일본으로 피난을 가야만 했죠. 펄은 결코 중국으로 돌아가지 못했어요. 1935년 그녀는 남편과 이혼하고 출판업자였던 리처드 월쉬와 재혼해서 그와 함께 펜실베이니아로 갔으며, 그곳에서 자신의 가장 유명한 소설인 *대지*를 썼는데, 이 책은 1931년 출판되었습니다.

*대지*는 결국 부유한 지주가 된 왕룽이라는 가난한 남자의 일생을 다루고 있어요. *대지*는 전 세계에서 독자층을 확보했고, 출간 첫해에 2백만 부가 팔렸으며, 퓰리처상을 수상했고, 결국에는 영화로도 만들어졌죠. 이후 많은 책들이, 예컨대 1939년에는 *애국자*, 1950년에는 *자라지 않는 아이*가 발표되었고, 그 사이에도 많은 소설과 에세이가 발표되었습니다. 1936년에 그녀는 미국 문예 아카데미의 회원이 되었으며, 1938년에는 노벨 문학상을 수상했어요.

두 번째 남편인 리처드 월쉬가 사망한 후 그녀는 젊은 댄스 강사인 테드 해리스와 교제하기 시작했는데, 그는 그녀보다 마흔 살이나 젊었습니다. 그녀는 1973년 3월 6일 버몬트에서 80세의 나이로 사망했어요. 그녀는 문학 분야에서의 업적으로 기억되고 있지만, 인도주의적인 작품, 솔직함, 그리고 주변 사람들에 대한 믿음으로도 기억되고 있어요. 1939년에는 "인간에 대한 믿음 외에는 어떠한 믿음도 필요하지 않다고 생각합니다."라는 말을 하기도 했죠. 펄은 40년에 걸쳐 80편이 넘는 문학 작품들을 발표했습니다.

Summary Note

A

❶ Pearl S. Buck
❷ China
❸ *The Good Earth*
❹ Nobel Prize

B

Pearl S. Buck was a great American literary figure born in West Virginia to two Presbyterian missionaries. Soon afterward, Pearl's family moved to China. Pearl grew up speaking both English and Chinese, and in 1910, she enrolled at Randolph-Macon Women's College in Virginia. In 1917, Pearl married John Lossing Buck, and the two settled in Anhwei Province in China, where Pearl worked as a teacher and interpreter. Pearl had two children. Carol, their first child, was born with considerable birth defects, and their second daughter, Janice, was adopted since Pearl underwent a hysterectomy after the birth of Carol. Pearl and John's marriage did not last, and in 1935, she divorced her husband and married her publisher, Richard Walsh. They moved back to the United States. In 1931, she wrote her most famous novel, *The Good Earth*, which sold nearly two million copies and earned her the Pulitzer Prize. Pearl continued writing until her death in 1973. During her life, she wrote over eighty works of literature and won the Nobel Prize.

Exercise 3 1 Ⓐ 2 Ⓒ 3 Ⓓ p.90

Script 03-12

W Professor: Welcome to Hieroglyphics 101. My name is Professor Watson, and we're going to spend this semester learning to read ancient Egyptian hieroglyphics. Now before we begin, I need to inform you about a few things regarding this language.

First, hieroglyphics was used as a type of writing for thousands of years during the reigns of the pharaohs in ancient Egypt. Hieroglyphs, which is what we call the individual characters, can be found inscribed on temples, tombs, and other buildings from ancient Egypt.

After the pharaohs were no more and Christianity became more prominent, the use of hieroglyphics came to an end. In fact, its usage was outlawed at one time. Thus, over time, the knowledge of how to read this language was lost to people. Many centuries later, when people began to be interested in learning about ancient Egypt, they were faced with the gargantuan task of trying to translate hieroglyphics. Most people who looked at the hieroglyphs believed that it was merely simple picture writing. They didn't believe there was a phonetic component at all, so they tried translating the hieroglyphs according to what each picture showed.

Then, in 1799, an enormous discovery was made that changed everything. In a way, I suppose, we Egyptologists owe a debt of gratitude to Napoleon Bonaparte. Does anyone know what I'm talking about? Yes?

M Student: It was some French soldiers who discovered the Rosetta Stone when Napoleon was invading Egypt. The Rosetta Stone was the key to people being able to translate hieroglyphics.

W: Exactly. I'm sure you've all heard of the Rosetta Stone, but let me give you the details to make sure because without it, none of you would be sitting here listening to me. The Rosetta Stone had writing on three sides. One contained hieroglyphics, another was written in demotic, and the third was written in ancient Greek. Well, the French didn't have their hands on the Rosetta Stone for too long. It was handed over to the British in 1802 and taken to the British Museum in London.

Soon afterward, the ancient Greek section was translated. It was a decree issued by Ptolemy V in 196 B.C. The translators realized the importance of their discovery when one of the lines in Greek read that the proclamation would be made in three languages: Greek, document writing, and sacred writing. Document writing referred to demotic while sacred writing was hieroglyphics. People realized that since they knew ancient Greek and demotic, they should then be able to translate the hieroglyphics on the stone.

In 1814, Thomas Young made an important discovery. You see, even though people might be able to learn how to read hieroglyphics, they still had no idea how to pronounce the words. Young managed to ascertain the correct pronunciations of several hieroglyphs, yet he soon gave up his work. Then, in 1822, Jean-Francois

Champollion solved the puzzle. He used his knowledge of Coptic, an ancient dead language, to understand hieroglyphics. He realized it was a phonetic language and not merely picture writing. Champollion managed to translate various inscriptions in temples in Egypt. He learned how to pronounce a large number of hieroglyphs in the correct manner. He also took extensive notes on his discoveries, which was a fortunate thing since he died a mere three years later. It was then that other Egyptologists used his work to make more discoveries. Today, much of the language is understood, and people around the world study hieroglyphics, just like all of you are doing.

I think that's enough for now. I'll talk more about the history of hieroglyphics as we study the language. But why don't we dive right in to the material now and get started? Please turn your books to the first page of chapter 1.

해석

W Professor: 상형 문자학 101 수업에 오신 걸 환영해요. 저는 Watson 교수이고, 우리는 이번 학기 동안 고대 이집트의 상형 문자 읽는 법을 배우게 될 거예요. 시작하기에 앞서, 이 언어에 대한 몇 가지 사항들을 알려 드릴게요.

먼저, 상형 문자 표기법은 고대 이집트에서 파라오가 통치를 했던 수천 년 동안 사용되었어요. 상형 문자는, 각각의 문자를 이렇게 부르는데, 사원, 무덤, 그리고 고대 이집트에서 만들어진 기타 건물에서 새겨져 있는 형태로 찾아볼 수 있습니다.

파라오가 사라지고 기독교가 보다 널리 퍼진 후에는 상형 문자가 더 이상 사용되지 않았어요. 실제로 사용이 금지된 적도 있었죠. 그래서 시간이 지남에 따라 이 언어를 읽는 방법은 사람들에게 잊혀졌어요. 수 세기 후 사람들이 고대 이집트를 공부하는데 흥미를 갖기 시작하자, 사람들은 상형 문자를 해독해야 하는 엄청난 과제에 직면하게 되었습니다. 상형 문자를 본 대부분의 사람들이 이것이 단순한 그림 문자라고 생각했어요. 음성과 관련된 부분은 전혀 없다고 생각했기 때문에 각 그림이 나타내는 바에 따라 상형 문자를 해석하려고 했죠.

그러다가 1799년에 중요한 발견이 이루어지면서 모든 것이 바뀌었어요. 어떤 면에서는, 제 생각에, 우리 이집트학자들이 보나파르트 나폴레옹에게 큰 마음의 빚을 지고 있다고 생각해요. 제가 무슨 말을 하는지 아는 사람이 있나요? 네?

M Student: 나폴레옹이 이집트를 침략했을 때 프랑스 군인들이 로제타석을 발견했습니다. 로제타석은 사람들이 상형 문자를 해독하는데 열쇠가 되었고요.

W: 정확하군요. 여러분 모두 로제타석에 대해 분명 들어보셨을 텐데, 그것이 없었다면 여러분 중 누구도 이 자리에 앉아 제 말을 듣고 있지 않으실 테니 제가 몇 가지 세부적인 내용들을 확인해 드릴게요. 로제타석의 세 면에는 글자가 쓰여 있었습니다. 한 면에는 상형 문자가, 다른 면에는 이집트 민중 문자가, 그리고 세 번째 면에는 고대 그리스어가 적혀 있었죠. 음, 프랑스인들이 오랫동안 로제타석을 가지고 있지는 못했습니다. 1802년 영국인들에게 넘겨져 런던의 대영 박물관으로 가게 되었죠.

이후 얼마 되지 않아 고대 그리스어로 된 부분이 해석되었습니다. 기원전 196년에 프톨레마이오스 5세가 발표한 법령이었죠. 그리스어로 쓰여진 줄 하나가 이 법령은 세 가지 언어, 즉 그리스어, 기록 문자, 그리고 신성 문자로 쓰여졌다고 읽혀지자 번역가들은 자신들이 발견한 것의 중요성을 깨달았어요. 기록 문자는 민중 문자를 가리켰고 종교 문자는 상형 문자였죠. 사람들은 고대 그리스어와 민중 문자를 알고 있었기 때문에 돌에 새겨진 상형 문자를 해독할 수 있다는 점을 깨달았어요.

1814년 토마스 영이 중요한 발견을 했습니다. 아시다시피, 상형 문자의 뜻을 이해할 수는 있어도 사람들은 단어를 어떻게 발음하는지 여전히 알지 못했어요. 영은 몇몇 상형 문자에 대한 올바른 발음은 알아낼 수 있었지만, 곧 자신의 연구를 포기했죠. 이후 1822년에 장프랑스아 샹폴리옹이 퍼즐을 풀었습니다. 그는 고대 사어인 콥트어에 대한 지식을 이용하여 상형 문자를 이해했어요. 그는 그것이 단순한 그림 문자가 아니라 음성 언어였다는 점을 깨달았죠. 샹폴리옹은 이집트 사원에 있던 다양한 비문을 해석할 수 있었어요. 그리고 다수의 상형 문자들을 올바르게 발음하는 법도 알게 되었죠. 또한 자신이 발견한 것에 대해 광범위한 기록을 남겼는데, 그후 불과 3년 만에 그가 사망했기 때문에 이는 매우 다행한 일이었어요. 이때 다른 이집트학자들도 자신의 연구를 이용하여 더 많은 것을 발견했습니다. 오늘날 이 언어의 상당 부분이 이해되고 있고, 전 세계 사람들이, 여러분 모두와 마찬가지로, 상형 문제를 배우고 있죠.

지금으로서는 이 정도면 충분한 것 같군요. 이 언어에 대해 공부하면서 상형 문자의 역사에 대해 더 이야기하도록 할게요. 하지만 이제 본격적으로 학습을 시작해 보는 것이 어떨까요? 여러분 교재 1장의 첫 페이지를 펴 주세요.

Summary Note

A

❶ ancient Egypt
❷ Hieroglyphics
❸ Egyptology
❹ picture writing
❺ phonetic component
❻ three languages
❼ pronounce
❽ how to pronounce words

B

The professor welcomes the students to the class and says she needs to talk about hieroglyphics. It was a type of writing used in ancient Egypt for thousands of years. Once Christianity became more prominent, people stopped using hieroglyphics, and they forgot how to read it. Later, when people were interested in Egyptology, they needed to learn how to read hieroglyphics. Most people thought it was just picture writing and had no phonetic component. In 1799, the Rosetta Stone was discovered. It was the key to letting people translate hieroglyphics. First, Thomas Young learned how to pronounce several hieroglyphs properly. Then, Jean-Francois Champollion managed to translate hieroglyphics in 1822. He used his knowledge of Coptic to figure out how to pronounce the words.

Exercise 4 1 Ⓑ 2 Ⓒ 3 Ⓓ p.92

Script 03-13

M Professor: Today, we'll be discussing the insect known as the white ant. Actually, it isn't an ant at all but a termite, and in our case, we will be focusing specifically on the subterranean form. These termites are called white ants because, for the most part, they resemble ants even though they are more closely related to cockroaches.

Now, before we look at their genetic makeup, let's talk about the living systems of these termites. White ants live in colonies and work in highly organized units. Within each colony there are a king and a queen termite, soldiers, swarmers or alates, nymphs, and thousands of worker termites. White ants are mainly found in parts of Australia and can cause considerable damage to timber, homes, and commercial buildings because they feed on cellulose, which is a form of a plant tissue. These little creatures require contact with soil and with moisture, so they tend to make their nests in the ground, which stand out as visible mounds, and they sometimes build their nests in damp and rotting trees. They have soft bodies and are relatively small, roughly half the size of a matchstick.

It is only worker white ants that can digest cellulose due to certain bacteria in their guts. Therefore, the workers are also responsible for feeding the other white ants by partly digesting the cellulose and then regurgitating it for the other ants. Imagine having to regurgitate your food to feed your brothers and sisters. It is also the responsibility of worker ants to maintain the nest, to make subterranean tunnels from the nest to nearby food sources, to gather and distribute food, to groom themselves and the other white ants, and to care for young nymphs until they are adults. Now, compared to worker white ants, the queen has a much lazier lifestyle. Her sole responsibility is to lay eggs. She can live for more than twenty-five years and lay up to 2,000 eggs every day. These eggs are then tended to by the worker ants.

There are also soldier white ants, which look slightly different from their worker counterparts. They have orange-colored heads and pinchers to crush their enemies. Some solider white ants even have pointed noses, which emit a sticky substance that helps hold their prey. Soldier termites protect the nest and the other termites from invading insects. The final type of white ant is the swarmers or alates. They have wings and become future king and queen termites of different colonies as they are equipped with reproductive organs. Once a colony is well established, swarmers fly off in groups of thousands, land, shed their wings, and attract mates by emitting chemical pheromones. It is the sight of these swarmers flying in large groups that signals that a white ant colony is well established. If homeowners see this, they should call an exterminator as soon as possible.

White ants cause considerable damage to homeowners and business owners in Australia. Millions of dollars are spent each year trying to keep these little timber eaters from causing too much damage, especially structural damage. Professionals instruct people that if they find a white ant nest, they should refrain from disturbing it. White ants have very keen survival instincts and if their colony is disturbed, they are likely to move on and cause further damage to a different part of the tree or building. If a white ant nest is found in a rural or nonresidential area, the best thing to do is to stay away from it. If the colony is found in a residential or business area, a professional exterminator should be contacted.

해석

M Professor: 오늘은 흰개미로 알려져 있는 곤충에 대해 논의할 거예요. 사실 이들은 개미가 아니라 흰개미인데, 이번 수업에서는 특별히 땅속에 사는 종에 초점을 맞출 것입니다. 이 흰개미들은 주로 개미와 닮았기 때문에 흰개미라고 불리지만 바퀴벌레에 보다 가까운 편이죠.

자, 이들의 유전적인 구조를 살펴보기 전에 흰개미들이 생활하는 방식에 대해 논의해 봅시다. 흰개미들은 군락을 이루고 살며 매우 조직적인 형태로 일을 해요. 각 군락에는 왕개미, 여왕개미, 병정개미, 스워머 혹은 유시충, 유충, 그리고 수천 마리의 일개미가 존재합니다. 흰개미는 주로 호주에서 찾아볼 수 있으며, 이들이 식물 조직의 일종인 섬유소를 먹고 살기 때문에 목재, 주택, 그리고 상업용 건물에 상당한 피해를 입힐 수 있어요. 이 작은 생물들은 흙 및 수분과 접촉해야 해서 눈에 띄는 둔덕 형태의 개미집을 땅에 만드는 경향이 있는데, 때로는 축축한 썩은 나무에 보금자리를 만들기도 하죠. 몸은 부드럽고 비교적 작은 편으로, 크기가 성냥개비의 약 절반 정도입니다.

일개미만이 소화관에 있는 특정 박테리아 때문에 섬유소를 소화시킬 수 있어요. 따라서 일개미들은 부분적으로 섬유소를 소화시켰다가 이를 게워내 다른 개미들에게 줌으로써 다른 흰개미들에게 먹이를 공급하는 역할도 합니다. 여러분이 먹었던 음식을 게워내서 형제와 자매들에게 주어야 한다고 상상해 보세요. 또한 개미집을 보수하고, 개미집에서 먹이가 있는 곳까지 땅굴을 파고, 먹이를 모아서 나누고, 자신과 다른 흰개미들을 위해 그루밍을 하고, 그리고 유충이 다 자랄 때까지 유충을 돌보는 것도 일개미의 책무입니다. 자, 일개미와 비교해 볼 때 여왕개미는 훨씬 더 게으른 생활을 해요. 여왕개미의 유일한 역할은 알을 낳는 것이죠. 25년 이상 살면서 매일 최대 2천 개의 알을 낳을 수가 있습니다. 이후 이러한 알들은 일개미들이 보살펴 주죠.

또한 병정개미도 있는데, 이들은 일개미와 약간 다르게 생겼어요. 머리는 오랜지색을 띠며 적을 무찌르기 위한 한 쌍의 집게가 달려 있죠. 일부 병정개미들은 뾰족한 코를 가지고 있으며, 코에서는 먹이를 붙잡는데 도움을 주는 끈적한 물질이 분비됩니다. 병정개미는 곤충들의 공격으로부터 개미집과 다른 흰개미들을 보호해 줍니다. 마지막 종류의 흰개미는 스워머 혹은 유시충이에요. 이들은 날개를 가지고 있으며, 그리고 생식 기관을 가지고 있기 때문에 추후 서로 다른 군락의 왕개미와 여왕개미가 됩니다. 일단 군락이 잘 만들어지면 스워머들이 수천 마리씩 떼를 지어 날아 오르고, 땅에 내려앉아 날개를 떨어뜨리고, 그리고 화학 물질인 페로몬을 분비해 짝을 유인합니다. 흰개미 군락이 잘 형성되었다는 점은 이 스워머들이 거대한 무리를 지어 날아다니는 광경을 보면 알 수가 있어요. 만약 집주인들이 이러한 광경을 본다면 최대한 빨리 해충 구제업자에게 연락을 해야 할 거예요.

흰개미는 호주의 주택 소유자들과 사업가들에게 상당한 피해를 입히고 있습니다. 목재를 먹어 치우는 이 작은 동물들이 과도한 피해를, 특히 건물에 대한 피해를 입히지 못하도록 매년 수백만 달러가 쓰이고 있죠. 전문가들은 만약 흰개미의 개미집을 발견하는 경우 이를 건드리지 말라고 사람들에게 충고합니다. 흰개미의 생존 본능은 매우 강하며, 만약 이들의 군락이 피해를 받는 경우, 다른 곳으로 이동을 해서 나무나 건물의 다른 부분에 보다 큰 피해를 입힐 가능성이 높아요. 시골이나 비주거 지역에서 흰개미가 목격되는 경우, 최선의 방법은 그곳을 떠나는 것입니다. 주거 지역이나 상업 지역에서 군락이 발견되는 경우에는 전문적인 해충 구제업체에 연락을 해야 하죠.

Summary Note

A

❶ white ant
❷ termite
❸ cockroach
❹ colonies
❺ lays eggs
❻ protect
❼ exterminate
❽ structures

B

White ants are termites mainly found in Australia and feed on cellulose, which causes them to live underground or in damp timber. They live in highly organized colonies with each type of white ant serving a particular function within the nest. The king and queen white ants are responsible for the reproduction of young, or nymphs. Soldier white ants protect the colony from intruders. Worker white ants have many tasks from building and maintaining the colony to grooming and feeding the other termites. Worker white ants feed the others because they are the only white ants to have special digestive bacteria in their stomachs. Finally, swarmers, or alates, are future kings and queens of other colonies as they have reproductive capabilities. White ants cause considerable damage to buildings and homes in Australia. The best way to deal with white ants is to steer clear of them in the wild and to call an exterminator if they are in a home or office.

Integrated Listening & Speaking p.94

A

Script 03-14

M Professor: The other day, I gave a lecture concerning the history of theater architecture. Initially, we identified ancient Greece as the origin of drama and then went on to discuss the architecture of Greek amphitheaters. I listed the qualities of amphitheater design. For example, an amphitheater is round in shape and open aired. There was a round platform for the orchestra, and the audience was seated on high wooden stands that were built into the hillside. The seating arrangement allowed for better sound and sight quality during the performance. We then skipped ahead in time and saw that theater architecture had evolved. The modern theater we used as an example was Shakespeare's Globe Theater in London, England. The Globe Theater was octagonal in shape with wooden seating three stories high and a pit in front of the stage in the middle that was standing room only. On stage, there were various trapdoors and riggings to aid with props and special effects during the performance.

1 The round shape of theaters helps with the sound so that the audience members can hear the performers better.

2 London, England

3 The audience was seated on high wooden seats on the hillside.

B

Script 03-15

M Professor: Last week, we looked at the insect known as the white ant, otherwise known as a termite. White ants are mainly found in Australia. Each year, these little creatures cause considerable damage to homes and commercial buildings due to their appetite for wood. White ants are small insects with soft off-white bodies. They live in colonies either in old, damp trees or in mounded earth, and different white ants perform different duties. King and queen white ants are solely responsible for reproduction while soldier ants protect the nest. Swarmer white ants, otherwise known as alates, are future king and queen white ants of other colonies as they are born with reproductive organs. Finally, worker white ants are responsible for a number of tasks within the colony, such as building and maintaining the nest, finding food, feeding others, grooming, and caring for young.

1 They are termites, so white ants eat away at the structural timber in homes and buildings.

2 White ants are small insects with soft off-white bodies.

3 Soldier white ants are responsible for protecting nests from enemies.

Mini TOEFL iBT Practice Test p.96

1 Ⓒ 2 Ⓑ 3 Ⓑ 4 Ⓐ 5 Ⓓ
6 Ⓑ 7 Ⓒ 8 Ⓑ 9 Ⓑ 10 Ⓑ
11 Ⓓ

[1-5]

Script 03-16

W Student: Hello, Professor Adams. I was wondering if you could help me for a minute.

M Professor: Certainly, Heather. Come on in. What can I

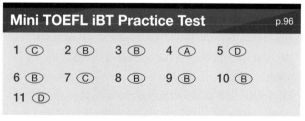

help you with?

W: I have chosen to write about Shakespeare's play *A Midsummer Night's Dream* for the literature project you assigned, but I am having a little trouble finding sources for my essay.

M: Ah! *A Midsummer Night's Dream*, my favorite Shakespearean comedy! I am glad you have chosen that play. Before we talk about sources, why don't you tell me what aspect of the work you are going to write about? That may help us in our search for source material.

W: Well, I especially like *A Midsummer Night's Dream* as it is a wedding play. I also like many of the characters in the play, particularly the weaver, Bottom, and how he convinces his friends to put on their own play in the enchanted woods. I guess I just don't know how to combine these elements into one idea.

M: **One idea would be not only to read the play, as you have done, but also to look at it through another medium.** I suggest you go to see a production of the play and also see it on film. There was a film version of *A Midsummer Night's Dream* done in 1999 by director Michael Hoffman. I would suggest you familiarize yourself with both the written and visual material of the play before you begin. Now, after you have done that, you can decide how you wish to narrow your focus. You mentioned the aspect of marriage in the play.

W: Yes, I was thinking that maybe I could write about the treatment of women during those times in relationship to the marriages in the play. Marriages were decided by the father, and if the daughter did not obey and marry her father's choice of husband, then she could be put to death or sent to a nunnery under Athenian law.

M: That sounds like an excellent avenue to follow in terms of an essay. One book that I would highly recommend is called *A Midsummer Night's Dream Manual and Study Guide*. This book is full of information not only about the play but also about Shakespeare. It has a timeline and many cross-references. What it also contains, which would be of considerable help to you, is a bibliography, which lists even more sources regarding the play.

W: That sounds like the perfect reference book for my essay.

M: Another thing I would suggest is to look online and in an encyclopedia regarding the issue of marriage and the treatment of women during Elizabethan times. This way, you will have some factual information about marriage tradition to compare to the themes of marriage and the treatment of women in the play.

W: Thank you so much, Professor Adams. Now I not only have the play to take information from, but I also have a film to watch, a new book to order, and ideas on how to look up more information online and in the encyclopedia.

M: You are very welcome, Heather. And good luck on your essay. I look forward to reading it.

해석

W Student: 안녕하세요, Adams 교수님. 잠깐 저를 도와 주실 수 있는지 궁금해서요.

M Professor: 물론이에요, Heather. 들어오세요. 어떻게 도와 드리면 될까요?

W: 교수님께서 내 주신 문학 과제로 셰익스피어의 희곡인 *한여름 밤의 꿈*에 관한 글을 쓰기로 했는데, 에세이에 필요한 자료를 찾기가 약간 힘들어서요.

M: 아! 제가 가장 좋아하는 셰익스피어의 희극인 *한여름 밤의 꿈*이군요! 학생이 그 희곡을 선택했다니 기쁘네요. 자료에 대한 이야기를 하기 전에, 그 작품의 어떤 면에 대한 글을 쓸 것인지 이야기해 보는 것이 어떨까요? 그러면 자료를 찾는 데 도움이 될 수 있을 거예요.

W: 음, 저는 *한여름 밤의 꿈*이 결혼과 관련된 희곡이라서 특히 마음에 들어요. 게다가 희곡의 여러 등장 인물들, 특히 직공인 보텀이 마음에 들고, 그가 친구들을 설득시켜 마법의 숲에서 자신의 연극을 공연하는 과정도 마음에 들어요. 그런데 이러한 요소들을 어떻게 하나의 아이디어로 통합해야 할지 잘 모르겠어요.

M: 한 가지 방법은 학생이 한 것처럼 희곡을 읽기만 하지 말고 또 다른 매체를 통해 희곡을 바라보는 것이에요. 연극 공연도 보고 영화로도 보는 것을 추천할게요. 1999년 마이클 호프만 감독에 의해 *한여름 밤의 꿈*이 영화로 만들어졌죠. 시작하기에 앞서 글로 쓰여진 형태와 영상으로 된 형태 모두에 익숙해지기를 추천할게요. 자, 그렇게 한 뒤에는 초점 범위를 어떻게 좁힐 것인지 결정할 수 있을 거예요. 학생이 희곡에서 결혼에 관한 측면을 언급했잖아요.

W: 네, 저는 희곡 속의 결혼과 관련된 당시 여성의 처우에 관한 글을 쓸 수도 있겠다고 생각했어요. 결혼이 아버지에 의해 결정되었고, 딸이 명령에 따르지 않고 아버지가 선택한 남편과 결혼하지 않았다면 그녀는 아테네의 법에 따라 사형을 당하거나 수녀원에 보내졌을 거예요.

M: 에세이 작성 시 따라야 할 훌륭한 지침처럼 들리는군요. 제가 강력하게 추천하고자 하는 것은 *한여름 밤의 꿈 매뉴얼 및 스터디 가이드*라는 책이에요. 이 책은 그 작품뿐만 아니라 셰익스피어에 관한 정보들로 가득하죠. 연대표와 많은 상호 참조표들이 들어 있어요. 게다가 학생에게 큰 도움이 될 수 있는 참고 문헌이 포함되어 있는데, 여기에서 그 희곡과 관련된 자료들의 목록을 훨씬 더 많이 볼 수 있어요.

W: 에세이 작성에 필요한 완벽한 참고 도서가 될 것 같군요.

M: 한 가지 더 제안하고 싶은 것은 엘리자베스 시대의 결혼 문제 및 여성 처우와 관련된 내용을 온라인과 백과 사전에서 찾아보는 것이에요. 그러면 희곡 속의 결혼 및 여성 처우와 비교할 수 있는 결혼 전통에 관한 사실들을 알게 될 거예요.

W: 정말 감사합니다, Adams 교수님. 이제 정보를 가져와야 할 희곡뿐만 아니라 봐야 할 영화와 주문해야 할 책도 생겼고, 온라인과 백과 사전에서 더 많은 정보를 찾는 법에 관한 아이디어도 얻게 되었군요.

M: 천만에요, Heather. 그리고 에세이를 잘 쓰길 바라요. 읽기를 고대하고 있을게요.

[6-11]

Script 03-17

W Professor: Now, class, we have been discussing the Great Lakes in North America, and no lecture on this subject would be complete without mentioning the Erie

Canal. Has anyone here heard of the Erie Canal or know where it is located?

M Student: The Erie Canal is a system of waterways, right? Doesn't it run through the state of New York?

W: Yes, that is correct. There are four main waterways that run through New York—the Erie, the Champlain, the Oswego, and the Cayuga-Seneca—which are connected by a five-hundred-and-twenty-four-mile system of canals. What is most important about the Erie Canal, however, is that it allows boats to pass from the Hudson River into Lake Erie, one of the five Great Lakes.

M: When was the canal built and why?

W: Let me take your second question first. Can anyone tell me why it would be advantageous to have the Hudson River connect to the Great Lakes?

M: Well, I suppose it would be important for shipping because the Hudson River empties into the Atlantic Ocean, so it would mean that imports and exports could be transported through the waterways all the way from the east coast of America to the Midwest.

W: Excellent. When you think about it, you see that you can answer your own question. That is one of the main reasons that the canal was built. Another reason was that it was another method of transportation for the migration of American settlers westward. To address your first question, the Erie Canal was proposed by the governor of New York, Dewitt Clinton, around 1818. The idea was dismissed at first and dubbed "Clinton's Folly" because the project seemed impossible. What Clinton was proposing was to build a canal that would cut through three hundred and sixty-three miles of wilderness. When finished some seven years later in 1825, the Erie Canal had eighteen aqueducts and eighty-three locks.

M: What exactly is a lock?

W: A lock is a piece of engineering in a canal system that allows for a boat to go either uphill or downhill. There are so many locks in the Erie Canal system because Lake Erie sits five hundred and sixty-eight feet higher in elevation than the Hudson River.

M: Five hundred and sixty-eight feet higher? You mean a big ship can go that far uphill or downhill?

W: There are some length and height restrictions. A vessel up to three hundred feet long and forty feet wide can pass through the canal system; however, there are bridge clearance restrictions of fifteen and a half to twenty feet in height. Still, this allows for just about any boat or barge to go through the canal.

M: Is the system still used for imports and exports?

W: Well, transportation has come a long way in the last one hundred and fifty-some years. We can now transport goods by truck, train, and plane. Today, the Erie Canal is mainly used for pleasure and recreation. It is a tourist hotspot with many neat sites along the way. There are quaint inns and waterway restaurants along the way as well as beautiful scenery and canal museums to take in as you travel through the canal system. If any of you ever have the opportunity to go there and check it out, I highly recommend that you do so. You will definitely not be disappointed. It's a great piece of American history that you should try to get a firsthand look at.

해석

W Professor: 자, 여러분, 우리는 북아메리카에 있는 오대호에 대해 공부했는데, 이리 운하를 이야기하지 않는다면 이 주제에 관한 강의는 불완전할 수 밖에 없을 거예요. 이리 운하에 관해 들어본 적이 있거나, 이리 운하가 어디에 있는지 아는 사람이 있나요?

M Student: 이리 운하는 수로입니다, 그렇죠? 뉴욕주를 관통하지 않나요?

W: 네, 맞아요. 뉴욕주를 관통하는 수로는 네 개, 즉 이리, 샴플레인, 오스위고, 그리고 카유가-세네카 운하로, 이들은 524마일에 이르는 운하로 연결되어 있죠. 하지만 이리 운하와 관련된 가장 중요한 점은 이리 운하를 통해 허드슨강에서 오대호의 하나인 이리호까지 배로 갈 수 있다는 점입니다.

M: 이리 운하는 언제, 그리고 왜 건설되었나요?

W: 두 번째 질문에 먼저 답을 할게요. 허드슨강과 오대호를 연결하면 어떤 이점이 있는지 누가 말해 볼까요?

M: 음, 허드슨강이 대서양으로 흘러 들어가기 때문에 운송에서 중요했을 것 같은데, 그렇게 되면 미국의 동부 해안에서 중서부까지 수로로 곧장 수출입품들을 운송할 수 있었을 거예요.

W: 훌륭하군요. 생각해 보면 자신의 질문에 스스로 답을 할 수 있을 거예요. 그것이 이리 운하를 건설한 주된 이유 중 하나이죠. 다른 이유로는 이리 운하가 미식민지 정착민들을 서부로 이동시키는 또 다른 주요 교통 수단이 되었다는 점이었어요. 학생의 첫 번째 질문에 답을 하면, 이리 운하는 1818년경 뉴욕의 주지사였던 드윗 클린턴에 의해 제안되었습니다. 이러한 아이디어는 처음에 무시를 당했고, 공사가 불가능해 보였기 때문에 "클린턴의 바보짓"이라는 별명을 얻었어요. 클린턴이 제안한 것은 363마일의 황무지를 관통하는 운하 건설이었죠. 7년 후인 1825년에 완공되었을 당시, 이리 운하에는 18개의 수로와 83개의 갑문이 존재했습니다.

M: 갑문이 정확히 무엇인가요?

W: 갑문은 배를 위 또는 아래쪽으로 이동시키는 운하의 기계 장치예요. 이리호에는 다수의 갑문이 존재하는데, 그 이유는 이리호가 허드슨강보다 568피트 높은 곳에 있기 때문이죠.

M: 568피트 높은 곳이요? 그러니까 거대한 선박이 그 정도까지 위아래로 이동할 수 있다는 말씀이신가요?

W: 길이 및 높이 제한은 있어요. 길이가 300피트, 폭이 40피트 이하의 선박만이 운하를 통과할 수 있죠. 하지만 15.5피트에서 20피트의 교각 통과 높이 제한이 있어요. 그래도 거의 모든 선박이나 바지선은 이리 운하를 통과할 수 있죠.

M: 그러한 시스템이 아직도 수출입에 사용되나요?

W: 음, 지난 150년 동안 운송 수단은 크게 발전했어요. 지금은 트럭, 기차, 그리고 비행기로 물품을 운송하죠. 오늘날 이리 운하는 주로 관광 및 레저용으로 이용되고 있어요. 운하를 따라 멋진 곳들이 많이 있는 관광 명소이죠. 운하를 따라 예스러운 숙박 시설과 수상 식당들이 있을 뿐만 아니라 멋진 풍경 및 운하를 여행하면서 들어가볼 수 있는 운하 박물관들도 있습니다. 여러분들이 그곳에 가서 둘러볼 기회가 있는 경우, 그렇게 하는 것을 강력히 추천할게요. 결코 실망하지 않을 거예요. 미국 역사의 위대한 한 부분을 직접 눈으로 보게 될 거예요.

Vocabulary Check-Up
p.101

A

1 Ⓞ	2 Ⓓ	3 Ⓛ	4 Ⓗ	5 Ⓚ
6 Ⓖ	7 Ⓐ	8 Ⓑ	9 Ⓙ	10 Ⓝ
11 Ⓒ	12 Ⓕ	13 Ⓜ	14 Ⓘ	15 Ⓔ

B

1 Ⓒ	2 Ⓐ	3 Ⓑ	4 Ⓔ	5 Ⓓ

PART II Pragmatic Understanding

UNIT 04 Understanding the Function of What Is Said

Basic Drill
p.106

Drill 1 Ⓓ

Script 04-02

M Student: Professor Garber, may I have a quick word with you about today's lecture, please?

W Professor: Of course, Nate. What aspect of it are you interested in discussing?

M: The part about seed dispersal. I have a question about it.

W: Go ahead.

M: My home has a big yard with a lot of trees. We try to keep the yard looking nice, but I've noticed that weeds tend to grow up right around the trees.

W: Go on.

M: Well, I was wondering . . . Is this an example of seed dispersal? I mean, uh, are birds sitting on the tree branches and defecating seeds from various plants? Is that what's causing all of those weeds to grow in the grass?

W: I'd say that you're almost surely correct.

M: Thanks. Would it be all right with you if I wrote my final paper about this? I think it would be an interesting topic.

W: **I have no objections to that.**

해석

M Student: Garber 교수님, 오늘 강의와 관련해서 잠깐 이야기를 나눌 수 있으신가요?

W Professor: 물론이에요, Nate. 어떤 점에 대해 이야기하고 싶나요?

M: 종자 분산에 관한 부분이요. 그에 대한 질문이 있어서요.

W: 얘기해 보세요.

M: 저희 집의 큰 마당에 나무들이 많이 있어요. 마당을 보기 좋게 가꾸려고 노력 중인데, 나무 주변에서 잡초가 자라는 경향이 있다는 것을 알게 되었죠.

W: 계속해 보세요.

M: 음, 제가 궁금했던 것은… 이것이 종자 분사의 예인가요? 제 말은, 어, 새들이 나뭇가지에 앉아서 다양한 식물로부터 얻은 씨앗을 배설물로 내보내는 것인가요? 그래서 잔디밭에 그러한 잡초들이 모두 자라는 것인가요?

W: 거의 정답에 가깝다고 얘기하고 싶군요.

M: 감사합니다. 제가 그에 대해 기말 보고서를 작성해도 괜찮으신가요? 흥미로운 주제가 될 것 같아서요.

W: 반대하지 않을게요.

Drill 2 Ⓑ

Script 04-03

M Librarian: That's a big stack of books you have there. Are you planning to check all of them out?

W Student: Actually, I need to return these three books. Can I do that here?

M: You're supposed to put them in the drop-off box over there. **But I'll make an exception in your case since you have so many books here.**

W: Great. Thanks so much. Here you are . . .

M: You're welcome. And do you need to check those books out now?

W: Yes, please. I've got a report to write for my art history class, so I really need all of these books.

M: Good luck with that. May I see your student ID card, please?

W: Oh . . . no. I must have left it back in my dorm room. I need it to check these books out, right?

M: I'm afraid so. But I can hold these books here at the circulation desk for you if you want to go to your dorm and come back with your card.

W: That would be wonderful. Thanks so much. I'll be back in around fifteen minutes.

M: Great. I'll see you then.

해석

M Librarian: 책이 한 무더기군요. 전부 대출할 생각인가요?

W Student: 사실 이 책 세 권은 반납해야 해요. 여기에서 할 수 있나요?

M: 저쪽에 있는 반납함에 넣으셔야 해요. 하지만 가지고 있는 책이 너무 많으니 학생의 경우에는 제가 예외를 두도록 할게요.

W: 잘 되었군요. 정말 고맙습니다. 여기 있어요…

M: 천만에요. 그리고 이 책들은 대출을 해야 하나요?

W: 네, 그렇게 해 주세요. 미술사 수업의 보고서를 작성해야 해서 이 책들 전부가 꼭 필요하거든요.

M: 행운이 있기를 바랄게요. 학생증을 보여 주시겠어요?

W: 오… 이런. 틀림없이 제 기숙사에 놔두고 온 것 같아요. 이 책들을 대출하려면 필요하죠, 그렇죠?

M: 유감이지만 그래요. 하지만 학생이 기숙사로 가서 카드를 가지고 다시 오고자 한다면 제가 이 책들을 이곳 대출대에 보관하고 있을게요.

W: 그렇게 해 주시면 좋겠어요. 정말 고맙습니다. 약 15분 후에 다시 올게요.

M: 좋아요. 그때 뵙죠.

Drill 3 Ⓑ

Script 04-04

M Professor: If any of you have a garden at your home, you have almost surely come across some plant diseases. There are many different kinds of them, and their effects on plants can range from merely making the leaves of plants change colors to killing plants entirely. I'd like to spend the rest of the lecture on talking to you about a few plant diseases that you're likely to encounter in your home garden.

You know, uh, I have a backyard garden myself and grow a lot of flowers there. **Lilacs are some of my favorite flowers, but, unfortunately, mine have a tendency to fall prey to a disease called powdery mildew.** If you've ever seen, hmm . . . it's basically a white dusty coating that can be on the stems, the leaves, and even the flowers of plants . . . then you've almost surely encountered powdery mildew. In addition to lilacs, daisies and roses are some flowers it affects while it can also harm grapevines and apple trees plus cucumbers and peas. Fortunately, it can be killed by various fungicides. Or if you're like me and prefer to avoid chemicals, you can simply mix baking soda and water and spray it on the affected areas. You'll find that the problem goes away fairly quickly. However, you also need to make sure that you remove leaves that have mildew on them so that it can't spread.

해석

M Professor: 여러분 집에 정원이 있는 경우, 여러분들은 분명 식물병을 접해 본 적이 있을 것입니다. 다양한 종류의 식물병이 존재하며, 식물병이 식물에 미치는 영향은 단순히 잎의 색깔이 변하는 것에서 식물이 완전히 죽는 경우까지 다양할 수 있습니다. 남은 강의 시간은 여러분 가정의 정원에서 목격하기 쉬운 몇 가지 식물병에 대한 이야기로 보내고자 합니다.

아시다시피, 어, 저희 집에도 뒷마당이 있어서 저는 그곳에서 여러 가지 꽃을 키웁니다. 라일락은 제가 가장 좋아하는 꽃 중 하나이지만, 안타깝게도 제 라일락은 흰가루병이라는 질병에 희생되는 경향이 있어요. 보신 적이 있으시면, 흠… 기본적으로 줄기, 잎, 그리고 식물의 꽃에도 하얀색 가루가 붙게 되는데… 그러면 거의 흰가루병을 보신 것이죠. 라일락 외에도 데이지와 장미도 이 병에 걸리며, 또한 포도 덩굴과 사과 나무, 그리고 오이와 완두콩도 피해를 입을 수 있습니다. 다행히도 이는 다양한 살진균제로 제거할 수 있어요. 혹은 여러분도 저와 같이 화학 물질 사용을 기피하는 경우, 베이킹 소다와 물을 섞어서 피해 지역에 뿌려도 됩니다. 문제가 상당히 빨리 해결되는 것을 보시게 될 거예요. 하지만 확산을 막기 위해서는 반드시 흰가루가 붙어 있는 잎들을 제거해야 합니다.

Drill 4 ⓒ

Script 04-05

W Professor: Have any of you ever heard the name Norman Borlaug . . . ? No . . . ? Hmm . . . I must say I find that a bit surprising. After all, Borlaug was one of the most important people who lived during the twentieth century. He was a man who contributed a great deal to the Green Revolution. And it was thanks primarily to him that millions of people around the world were saved from starvation.

Borlaug was an American who was born in 1914. He had an interest in biology while growing up. In the 1940s, he found himself in Mexico, where he observed farmers struggling to raise their crops. You see, uh, there were two major problems. Yes?

M Student: The farmers had issues with productivity and their corn crops suffering from disease, right?

W: **Ah, it seems that someone has heard of Borlaug before.** Yes, those were the two major problems which farmers there faced. Borlaug basically created various strains of corn that were able to resist disease and that could also grow well in the climate in Mexico. This increased yields for Mexican farmers, which resulted in people getting more to eat. His methods would later be reproduced by people around the world. The result was the Green Revolution, which, as I said a minute ago, saved millions of lives. Let's continue looking into Borlaug and his work, which I find fascinating.

해석

W Professor: 노먼 볼로그라는 이름을 들어 보신 분이 있나요…? 없나요…? 흠… 약간 놀랐다고 말씀을 드려야겠네요. 어쨌거나, 볼로그는 20세기에 살았던 가장 중요한 인물 중 한 명이었습니다. 그는 녹색 혁명에 막대한 기여를 한 사람이었어요. 그리고 전 세계 수백만 명의 사람들이 기아에서 해방된 것도 부분적으로 이 사람 덕분이었습니다.

볼로그는 미국인으로 1914년에 태어났습니다. 그는 자라면서 생물학에 흥미를 갖게 되었어요. 1940년대에 그는 멕시코에서 농부들이 작물을 기르느라 애쓰고 있는 모습을 목격하게 되었습니다. 아시다시피, 어, 두 가지 커다란 문제가 있었죠. 네?

M Student: 농부들이 생산량과 관련된 문제를 겪고 있었고 그들의 옥수수는 병에 걸려 있었죠, 맞나요?

W: 아, 볼로그에 대해 들어본 사람이 있는 것 같군요. 네, 그곳 농부들이 직면했던 두 가지 커다란 문제가 바로 그것이었죠. 주로 볼로그는 질병에 대한 저항력을 나타내고 또한 멕시코의 기후에서도 잘 자랄 수 있는 다양한 옥수수 품종을 개발했습니다. 이로써 멕시코 농부들의 생산량이 증가했는데, 그 결과 사람들이 더 많은 식량을 얻게 되었죠. 그의 방법은 이후 전 세계 사람들에 의해 사용되었습니다. 그 결과 제가 조금 전에 말씀드린 녹색 혁명이 일어났고, 이로써 수백만 명의 사람들이 목숨을 건질 수 있었어요. 볼로그와, 제가 대단하다고 생각하는, 그의 업적에 대해 계속해서 살펴보죠.

Exercises with Long Conversations

Exercise 1 1 Ⓑ 2 Ⓓ 3 Ⓑ p.110

Script 04-06

W Professor: Pardeep, how is your design going? May I see it?

M Student: Oh, sure . . . Here you are.

W: What's this . . . ? I don't understand . . . What are these photographs for? I just want to see the business card you designed. That's what this assignment is all about.

M: Oh, uh . . . sorry . . . I changed my mind and decided to do something more elaborate. I want to design a cover page for a car magazine. So that's why I . . . I have all these photos of classic cars. But . . . I'm just not sure which ones to choose.

W: Pardeep, I think you misunderstood what this assignment is all about. And it looks like you're already doing too much work. All you have to do is design a simple, basic business card.

M: Yes, I know, but I decided to do something different and more beneficial even if that means doing extra work.

W: Well, save that for another assignment. You'll get plenty of opportunity to do that later in the semester. You're getting too far ahead of yourself.

M: **But anyone can make a business card, and they all look the same.** A business card also isn't much of a marketing tool.

W: Oh, I disagree. They're very valuable marketing tools . . . and . . . uh, businesspeople need them for networking and establishing contacts. You might have a customer that insists on a specific design, and it would be embarrassing if you couldn't design a card according to the purchaser's requirements. Business cards are basic, but they're also important, so that's why we're doing this for our first assignment.

M: **Oh, I didn't think about that.** I had the impression they aren't particularly important.

W: You're not looking at the whole picture. Business cards are not just for marketing. They're essential for conducting business. You might be busy during a meeting or conference, perhaps simultaneously talking to several people, many of whom are potential customers, and you'll want to maintain contact with them. There might not be enough time to exchange names and phone numbers, but if you have some business cards, you'll at least be able to maintain your contacts and develop further business relationships. The cards also need a variety of designs so that when people collect several cards, yours will be easy to identify. That's why it's important for you to develop a unique design.

M: I see . . . So after we design a business card, may I work on a magazine cover?

W: No, not yet. Our second assignment will be another business card assignment. For now, I just want you to think of ways to design basic business cards. But next month, I'll give everyone an opportunity to design their own product, and, of course, for your final project, you can do whatever you want.

M: Okay. So you just want me to design a basic business card. Is that it?

W: Yes, and next time, we'll do a more elaborate design.

해석

W Professor: Pardeep, 디자인은 어떻게 되고 있나요? 제가 봐도 될까요?

M Student: 오, 물론이죠… 여기 있습니다.

W: 이건 뭐죠…? 이해가 안 가는데… 이 사진들은 뭔가요? 저는 학생이 디자인한 명함을 보고 싶어요. 이번 과제가 바로 그것이잖아요.

M: 오, 어… 죄송해요… 생각이 바뀌어서 보다 노력이 필요한 것을 하기로 결심했어요. 저는 자동차 잡지의 표지를 디자인하고 싶어요. 그런 이유에서… 이 클래식 자동차들의 사진이 있는 것이죠. 하지만… 어떤 사진들을 택해야 할지 잘 모르겠어요.

W: Pardeep, 학생이 과제에 대해 잘못 생각했던 것 같군요. 그리고 이미 상당히 많은 작업을 한 것처럼 보이네요. 학생이 해야 할 일은 단순하고 기본적인 명함을 만드는 것이에요.

M: 네, 저도 알지만, 추가적인 작업이 필요하더라도 색다르고 보다 유익한 것을 하기로 결심했어요.

W: 음, 그건 아껴 두었다가 다른 과제에서 쓰세요. 학기 후반에 그럴 수 있는 기회가 많이 있을 거예요. 너무 앞서 나가고 있어요.

M: 하지만 명함은 누구라도 만들 수 있고 다 똑같이 보이잖아요. 또한 명함을 마케팅 수단으로 이용하기도 힘들고요.

W: 오, 저는 그렇게 생각하지 않아요. 명함은 매우 훌륭한 마케팅 수단이고… 그리고… 어, 사업을 하는 사람들이 네트워크를 형성하고 연락을 취하기 위해서는 명함이 필요해요. 특별한 디자인을 요구하는 고객이 있을 수도 있는데, 만약 구매자의 요구 조건에 따라 명함을 디자인하지 못한다면 당황스러울 거예요. 명함은 기본적인 것이지만 중요한 것이기도 해서, 우리의 첫 번째 과제로 그러한 일을 하고 있는 것이죠.

M: 오, 그러한 점은 생각해 보지 못했어요. 전 명함이 그다지 중요하지 않다는 느낌을 받았거든요.

W: 학생은 전체적인 그림을 보지 못하고 있어요. 명함은 마케팅을 위한 것만이 아니에요. 사업을 하는데 필수적인 것이죠. 회의나 컨퍼런스로 바쁜 상황에서 몇몇 사람들과 이야기를 나누게 될 수도 있는데, 그들 중 다수가 잠재적 고객이어서 그들과 계속 연락을 취하고 싶을 수도 있을 거예요. 이름과 전화번호를 교환할 수 있는 시간은 충분하지 않을 수도 있지만, 명함이 있는 경우에는 최소한 연락을 유지하고 사업 관계를 발전시켜 나갈 수 있을 거예요. 또한 사람들이 여러 장의 명함을 가지고 있는 경우, 자신의 명함이 쉽게 눈에 띌 수 있도록 명함에 다양한 디자인이 필요하죠. 독특한 디자인을 만드는 것이 중요한 이유가 바로 그러한 점 때문이에요.

M: 그렇군요… 그러면 명함을 디자인한 후에 잡지 표지 작업을 해도 될까요?

W: 아니요, 아직은 안 돼요. 두 번째 과제 역시 명함과 관련된 과제가 될 거예요. 지금으로서는 기본적인 명함을 디자인하는 방법에 대해 생각했으면 좋겠어요. 하지만 다음 달에는 자기 자신의 제품을 디자인할 수 있는 기회를 모두에게 줄 예정인데, 물론, 학생의 기말 프로젝트로 원하는 것은 무엇이든 해도 좋아요.

M: 알겠습니다. 그러니까 제가 기본적인 명함을 디자인하는 것을 원하시는군요. 그렇죠?

W: 네, 그리고 다음 번에 보다 노력이 필요한 디자인 작업을 하게 될 거예요.

Summary Note

A

❶ business card design
❷ car magazine cover
❸ wrong assignment
❹ useless
❺ networking
❻ important

B

The professor asks the student to show her his business card. But the student is working on another project. He is designing a cover for a car magazine. The professor tells the student that the assignment is to design a basic business card. The student suggests that designing business cards is a waste of time and says that he wants to work on something more elaborate. He says that business cards are not an important marketing tool. The professor replies that business cards are a valuable marketing tool and are also very important for establishing contacts and for networking. The professor insists that the student work on a business card and tells the student there will be plenty of opportunities later on to work on a project of his choice. The student agrees to do so.

Exercise 2 1 Ⓐ 2 Ⓐ 3 Ⓑ p.112

Script 04-07

W Student: Hi. I'm just checking to see if my schedule and course outlines are available.

M Student Services Center Employee: Your name, please?

W: Yes, I'm Nancy Carter.

M: Oh! Nancy, I have a package for you. This package has everything you need: your schedule, your psychology syllabus, a campus map, a coupon book, your name tag for the orientation program, your orientation itinerary, and . . .

W: Oh, I won't be here for the orientation.

M: **Sure, you will.** Orientation day is the most enjoyable day on campus. You'll meet a lot of people, get a tour of the campus, meet some of your professors, and receive valuable information about life here at the university. By the way, there are a variety of festivities . . . a free dinner followed by the orientation night party.

W: I know. But I won't be going.

M: Why not? You don't have to worry about the costs. They're already included in your student activity fees.

W: Yes, but the orientation festivities are during the final week of summer vacation. I worked all summer, so orientation week is my only chance to go on vacation. I've already paid for my airline ticket. I'm going to Quebec City and Niagara Falls.

M: Aw . . . that's too bad. The program has a lot to offer. It's great that you get to go to Canada, but I'm worried that perhaps you'll have some difficulty adjusting to life on campus.

W: I think I'll be okay. My older brother graduated from this university, so I'm already familiar with the campus. When I return from my trip, my brother can show me around if necessary. And another thing . . . I'm a transfer student. **I've already completed two years of university, so I don't need the orientation as much as freshmen do.**

M: Well, you should take this package just in case. I think some of it will be of use.

W: Thanks.

M: I really hope you have a good trip. I envy you. I've never been to Canada . . . Anyway, since you won't be attending orientation, is there anything I can do for you?

W: Yes, this package only has my psychology syllabus. Could you find out what textbooks I'll need and who my professors are?

M: Okay. I'll try to gather whatever information I can. When are you leaving for vacation?

W: Two weeks from today.

M: Okay. Maybe I can even arrange for you to meet some of your professors before you leave for Canada.

W: That would be great.

M: You also have to get a library card. That's usually done on orientation day. If you'd like, I'll arrange for you to come and get your photo before you leave, and then you won't have to do it when you return from Canada.

W: Okay, I think I'll be back here next week. So I'll talk to you then.

해석

W Student: 안녕하세요. 제 시간표와 수업 요강을 받을 수 있는지 확인하려고 하는데요.

M Student Services Center Employee: 이름을 알려 주시겠어요?

W: 네, 저는 Nancy Carter예요.

M: 오! Nancy, 이 봉투를 드릴게요. 이 봉투 안에 학생에게 필요한 모든 것이 다 들어 있어요. 시간표, 심리학 강의 계획서, 캠퍼스 지도, 쿠폰북, 오리엔테이션에 필요한 이름표, 그리고 오리엔테이션 일정⋯

W: 오, 저는 오리엔테이션에 참가하지 못할 거예요.

M: 꼭 오셔야 해요. 오리엔테이션 날이 학교에서 가장 재미있는 날이죠. 많은 사람들도 만나고, 캠퍼스도 둘러보고, 교수님들도 몇 분 뵙고, 그리고 이곳 대학 생활과 관련된 소중한 정보도 얻게 될 거예요. 그건 그렇고, 다양한 행사들이 있는데⋯ 무료로 저녁 식사가 제공된 후에는 오리엔테이션 나이트 파티도 있을 거예요.

W: 저도 알아요. 하지만 가지 못할 거예요.

M: 왜요? 비용은 걱정하지 않으셔도 돼요. 이미 학생활동비에 포함되어 있죠.

W: 그렇기는 하지만 오리엔테이션 행사는 여름 방학 마지막 주에 진행되잖아요. 저는 여름 내내 일을 했기 때문에 오리엔테이션 주간이 휴가를 갈 수 있는 유일한 때예요. 이미 비행기표를 구입했어요. 저는 퀘벡시와 나이아가라 폭포에 갈 거예요.

M: 어⋯ 정말 안 되었군요. 프로그램에서 많은 것이 제공될 거예요. 캐나다에 가는 건 멋진 일이지만, 학생이 대학 생활에 적응하는데 어려움을 겪게 될 것 같아 걱정이 되는군요.

W: 괜찮을 거예요. 우리 오빠가 여기 대학을 졸업했기 때문에 이미 캠퍼스에 익숙해요. 여행에서 돌아오면, 필요한 경우, 오빠가 제게 대학을 구경시켜 줄 수도 있고요. 그리고 한 가지 더⋯ 저는 편입생이에요. 이미 2년 동안 대학 생활을 했으니 신입생들만큼 오리엔테이션이 필요하지는 않을 거예요.

M: 음, 만약을 위해 이 봉투는 가지고 가세요. 그중 일부는 유용할 것으로 생각해요.

W: 감사합니다.

M: 재미있는 여행이 되기를 진심으로 바랄게요. 부럽군요. 저는 캐나다에 가본 적이 없어서요⋯ 어쨌든, 오리엔테이션에 참석하지 못한다니, 제가 도와 드릴 일이 있을까요?

W: 네, 이 봉투에는 심리학 수업의 강의 계획서만 있네요. 어떤 교재가 필요하고 교수님이 누구신지 알아봐 주실 수 있나요?

M: 좋아요. 찾을 수 있는 정보는 다 구해 놓을게요. 언제 휴가를 떠날 예정이죠?

W: 오늘부터 2주 후에요.

M: 좋아요. 어쩌면 캐나다로 떠나기 전에 몇 분의 교수님들을 만나도록 자리를 마련해 드릴 수도 있을 거예요.

W: 그러면 정말 좋을 것 같군요.

M: 도서관 카드도 받으셔야 해요. 보통 오리엔테이션이 진행되는 날에 발급되죠. 원하시면 떠나기 전에 오셔서 사진을 찍을 수 있도록 준비해 놓을 수도 있는데, 그러면 캐나다에서 돌아와서 또 그러실 필요가 없을 거예요.

W: 좋아요, 다음 주에 여기로 다시 올 수 있을 거예요. 그때 다시 말씀을 드릴게요.

Summary Note

A

❶ schedule
❷ course outline
❸ orientation
❹ familiar

B

The man gives a student a package containing various items, including a name tag for the orientation program and an orientation itinerary. Upon hearing about the orientation, the student informs the man that she will not be going to the program. The man is very surprised to hear this because, in his view, the program is very valuable. The student explains to the man that she has already booked a vacation during orientation week and that it will be impossible for her to attend. She also advises the man that her brother, who graduated from the same university, can show her around campus if necessary. Because the student cannot attend the orientation, the man agrees to gather whatever helpful information he can get to help the student prepare for the upcoming semester.

Exercise 3 1 Ⓐ 2 Ⓒ 3 Ⓐ p.114

Script 04-08

W Student: Hello. Can . . . can I come in?

M Professor: Most certainly! Come on in . . . I wasn't expecting anyone this early . . . Just a minute, and I'll clear my sofa so you can sit down . . . Okay, there you are. Please have a seat. Now, I recognize your face, and I know you're in my Psych 420 class, but I don't remember your name.

W: I'm Michelle.

M: Yes! I'm sorry, Michelle. How are your classes going?

W: Everything is fine. I just thought I'd let you know that I'm looking for a job in France.

M: France? That's wonderful! I spent two years there when I was in high school.

W: Yes, you've said that a few times in class, so that's why I am mentioning it to you.

M: Can you speak French?

W: Yes. In fact, I've already been to France. I loved it. I fell in love with every element of French society. I'm hoping to work at a bank there.

M: A bank . . . Are you sure you want to do that? Banking is a very complicated business, especially in Europe. The last time I was there, I met a few people who complained about the complexities. Have you studied banking?

W: Yes. In fact, psychology is not my major. **My major is commerce.** Prior to this semester, I hadn't taken any banking courses, but I'm currently taking a course in European banking.

M: That's good. Unfortunately, I don't know anyone in the industry there. Most of the people I know in Europe are in the social sciences.

W: Oh, I understand. But I'm wondering . . . I've never lived in France. I'm thinking of maybe moving there and then looking for a job. Do you have any suggestions as to where I could stay? I also wonder if you have any advice on getting a banking job there.

M: Hmm . . . I haven't lived in France for twenty-five years. When I lived there, I was still a teen and didn't have to worry about finding a place . . . Oh, hold on! I have a friend. I actually met him when I lived there, and his major was the same as yours, and now he's a businessman. He still has family living in France, and he spends most of his time there. His daughter is your age, and she lives there. He also does a lot of business there. I think he would be glad to help you out. I'm sure if you talk to him, he can give you some good ideas and hook you up with some people. Maybe you can meet his daughter.

W: Oh, that would be great.

M: Here's his business card. His name is Frank. But don't call him. I'll talk to him, and the next time we meet, I'll let you know the best way for you to contact him.

W: Okay. I'll get back to you next week. Thank you so much.

해석

W Student: 안녕하세요. 제가… 들어가도 되나요?

M Professor: 물론이죠! 들어와요… 이렇게 일찍 누가 올 줄은 몰랐네요… 잠시 기다리면 앉을 수 있게 소파를 치울게요… 됐어요, 앉으세요. 자, 학생의 얼굴도 알겠고, 학생이 제 심리학 420 수업을 듣는다는 것도 알겠는데, 학생의 이름은 기억이 나지 않는군요.

W: 저는 Michelle이에요.

M: 그래요! 미안해요, Michelle. 수업은 어떤가요?

W: 모든 것이 좋아요. 저는 제가 프랑스에서 일자리를 찾고 있다는 말씀을 교수님께 드리고 싶었어요.

M: 프랑스요? 멋지군요! 저도 고등학생 때 그곳에서 2년 동안 살았어요.

W: 네, 수업 중에 몇 번 말씀하신 적이 있어서, 그래서 말씀을 드리는 거예요.

M: 불어는 할 줄 알아요?

W: 네. 사실 저는 프랑스에 가본 적이 있어요. 너무 마음에 들었죠. 프랑스 사회의 모든 것에 푹 빠졌어요. 저는 그곳 은행에서 일을 하기를 바라고 있어요.

M: 은행이라… 그 일을 하고 싶은 것이 확실한가요? 금융 업무는 매우 복잡한데, 특히 유럽에서 복잡하죠. 제가 지난 번 프랑스에 갔을 때 만났던 몇몇 사람들도 복잡하다고 불평을 했어요. 금융 업무에 대해 공부해 본 적이 있나요?

W: 네. 사실 제 전공은 심리학이 아니에요. 제 전공은 무역이죠. 이전 학기에는 금융 수업을 듣지 않았지만, 지금은 유럽 금융에 관한 수업을 듣고 있어요.

M: 잘 되었군요. 안타깝게도 금융 분야에 제가 아는 사람은 없어요. 유럽에서 제가 아는 사람들은 사회 과학 분야의 사람들이죠.

W: 오, 그러시군요. 하지만 궁금한 점이 있는데… 저는 프랑스에서 살아본 적이 없어요. 그곳으로 이사를 가서 일자리를 구할까 생각 중이죠. 제가 지낼 만한 곳과 관련해서 추천하실 곳이 있을까요? 그리고 그곳 은행에 취직하는 것에 대해서 충고해 주실 말씀이 있는지도 궁금해요.

M: 흠… 저는 25년간이나 프랑스를 떠나 있었어요. 거기에 살았을 때에도 저는 십대였기 때문에 집을 구할 걱정을 할 필요가 없었죠… 오, 잠깐만요! 제게 친구가 한 명 있어요. 사실 제가 그곳에서 살 때 만났던 친구인데, 그의 전공이 학생과 같았고, 지금은 사업을 하죠. 그의 가족들이 아직 프랑스에서 살고 있고, 그도 대부분의 시간을 그곳에서 보내요. 그의 딸이 학생 나이인데, 그녀도 그곳에서 살죠. 또한 그 친구가 그곳에서 여러 가지 사업을 하고 있어요. 제 생각에는 그가 기꺼이 학생에게 도움을 줄 수 있을 것 같아요. 그 친구에게 이야기를 하면 분명 그

가 몇 가지 좋은 아이디어도 얘기해 주고 사람들도 소개시켜 줄 거예요. 어쩌면 그 친구 딸을 만날 수도 있겠군요.

W: 오, 그렇게 된다면 정말 좋겠어요.

M: 여기 그의 명함이 있어요. 이름이 Frank죠. 하지만 그에게 전화를 하지는 마세요. 제가 그와 이야기를 할 테니, 우리가 다음 번에 만나면 제가 그와 연락할 수 있는 가장 좋은 방법을 학생에게 알려 줄게요.

W: 알겠습니다. 다음 주에 다시 찾아뵐게요. 정말 고맙습니다.

Summary Note

A

❶ France
❷ bank
❸ any bankers
❹ businessman

B

The student tells the professor that she is planning to look for a job in France. The professor remarks that he lived in France as a teenager. He asks her what kind of job she is looking for. She replies that she wants a banking job. He tells her that banking jobs are difficult work. But the student is a commerce major, is studying European banking, and can speak French. However, she needs advice on where she can stay in Paris and how she can find a job there. The professor says that he cannot answer those two questions but says he will contact his friend, a businessman in France, and arrange for the student to contact him.

Exercise 4 1 Ⓑ 2 Ⓓ 3 Ⓐ p.116

Script 04-09

W Student: Good morning. I have a huge problem, and I really hope that you can help me out in solving it.

M Security Guard: I'll do my best, miss. Are you in any danger right now?

W: No, I'm all right. But . . . my car is missing. Did you see anyone drive out of here in a red sedan? The license plate number is K54-283.

M: Hmm . . . I can't say that I noticed any red cars leaving this lot. There aren't too many of them, you know. I've been on duty in this parking lot since seven in the morning as well, so I've seen everyone entering and leaving the lot.

W: Well, I parked the car right over there in front of that big pine tree. Do you remember seeing it?

M: Oh, yeah. Now I remember. A tow truck came here and took it away pretty early this morning. I think it was right around when I got here that it happened.

W: What?

M: Yeah, it was one of . . . hmm . . . three cars, I think, that got towed this morning.

W: Why on earth did it get towed? The car has a parking sticker on it. I'm allowed to park anywhere on campus.

M: On the contrary, your car was parked here overnight, and there is absolutely no overnight parking permitted in this lot. Didn't you see the signs?

W: I guess I must have overlooked them.

M: Well, I'm sorry that it happened, but the rules are the rules.

W: So . . . how am I supposed to get my car back? Where did it get towed to?

M: Hold on a moment . . . Here you are . . . This is a business card for the towing company that the school has a contract with. You're kind of in luck since it's located fairly close to the school, so you won't need to take a taxi there. You just need to go down to the company, show your driver's license, and pay the fine. Then, you'll be able to get your car back.

W: How much is the fine?

M: It's fifty dollars for a first offense, and then it increases to one hundred dollars for a second offense. How much are you going to have to pay?

W: **Fifty dollars.** I guess it could be worse.

M: That's true. Some students just keep parking here overnight. It's like they never learn. Some of them wind up paying several hundred dollars in fines each semester. Anyway, just go down that street and turn left at the light. You'll see the impound lot as soon as you turn. I'm really sorry that this happened to you. You seem like a nice person. Just try to remember that you can't park here overnight. So don't do that again. Okay?

해석

W Student: 안녕하세요. 제게 심각한 문제가 있는데, 선생님께서 문제를 해결하는데 도움을 주셨으면 좋겠어요.

M Security Guard: 최선을 다할게요. 지금 위험에 처해 있나요?

W: 아니요, 저는 괜찮아요. 하지만… 제 차가 없어졌어요. 빨간색 세단을 몰고 여기에서 나간 사람을 보셨나요? 자동차 번호가 K54-283이에요.

M: 흠… 이곳 주차장에서 빨간색 차가 나가는 것은 보지 못한 것 같아요. 아시다시피 그런 차가 아주 많지는 않으니까요. 또한 제가 이곳 주차장에서 오전 7시부터 근무를 하고 있었기 때문에 주차장에서 들어오고 나가는 사람들은 모두 보았어요.

W: 음, 저는 저기 커다란 소나무 앞쪽에 차를 주차했어요. 보신 기억이 있나요?

M: 오, 그래요. 이제 기억나는군요. 오늘 아침 꽤 이른 시간에 이곳으로 견인차가 와서 끌고 갔어요. 제가 이곳에 왔을 무렵에 그런 일이 있었던 것 같아요.

W: 뭐라고요?

M: 그래요, 그 차가 그중 하나였는데… 흠… 제 생각으로는 세 대의 차량이 오늘 아침에 견인되었어요.

W: 도대체 왜 견인이 되었나요? 차에는 주차 스티커가 붙어 있어요. 저는 캠퍼스 내 어디에서나 주차를 할 수 있는걸요.

M: 그와 반대로, 학생의 차는 밤새 여기에 주차되어 있었는데, 이곳 주차장에는 밤새 주차를 하는 것이 절대로 허용되지 않아요. 안내판을 보지 못했나요?

W: 제가 분명 못보고 넘어갔던 것 같군요.

M: 음, 그런 일이 발생해서 유감이지만, 규정은 규정이니까요.

W: 그러면… 제가 어떻게 해야 차를 다시 가져올 수 있나요? 어디로 견인이 되었나요?

M: 잠시만요… 여기 있군요… 학교와 계약을 맺은 견인업체의 명함이에요. 학교에서 상당히 가까운 곳에 위치하고 있기 때문에 학생은 운이 좋은 편인데, 그곳까지 택시를 타고 갈 필요는 없어요. 견인업체에 가서 운전면허증을 보여 주고 과태료를 납부하기만 하면 되죠. 그러면 다시 차를 가지고 올 수 있을 거예요.

W: 과태료가 얼마인가요?

M: 첫 번째 위반시에는 50달러이고 두 번째 위반시에는 100달러로 올라가요. 얼마를 납부해야 하나요?

W: 50달러요. 그만하면 다행이군요.

M: 맞아요. 일부 학생들은 계속 이곳에서 밤새 차를 세워 둬요. 결코 모르는 것 같더라고요. 그중 일부는 매 학기마다 결국 수백 달러의 과태료를 내게 되죠. 어쨌거나, 저기 거리를 따라 가다가 신호등에서 좌회전을 하세요. 좌회전을 하자마자 견인 보관소가 보일 거예요. 학생에게 이런 일이 일어나서 정말 유감이에요. 학생은 좋은 사람 같네요. 이곳에서는 밤새 주차를 할 수가 없다는 점을 기억하세요. 그리고 다시는 그러지 마시고요. 아시겠죠?

Summary Note

A

❶ missing
❷ parked
❸ get towed
❹ overnight parking
❺ towing company
❻ fifty dollars

B

The student tells the security guard that she needs help. Her problem is that her car is missing. It is a red sedan, but the security guard says that he saw no red vehicles driving in or out the lot this morning. The student shows the man where she was parked, and then he remembers that he saw a tow truck take it and two other cars away early in the morning. The student asks why it got towed and mentions that she has a parking sticker that allows her to park anywhere on campus. The man states that overnight parking is not permitted in the lot. He then tells the student how to get her car back. She has to pay a fine of fifty dollars. He gives her directions to the impound lot and advises her not to park in the lot overnight again.

Exercises with Long Lectures

Exercise 1 1 Ⓑ 2 Ⓑ 3 Ⓒ p.118

Script 04-10

M Professor: Everyone here knows what crop rotation is, right? Patricia, would you give me a quick explanation of it, please?

W Student: Crop rotation is the act of growing different crops in the same field—or leaving it fallow at times—to prevent the soil from losing all of its nutrients.

M: **I couldn't have said it any better myself.** By the way, the word fallow that Patricia used means to grow nothing in a field during a growing season. Crop rotation has been practiced for a long, long time. Arguably the most famous instances of it took place in Europe in the Middle Ages. Then, many people began practicing three-field crop rotation. One field would be a grain such as wheat or barley, another field would be a legume such as peas, and the third field would lie fallow. People in medieval times found that an effective method of crop rotation.

Now, uh, what most people learn about crop rotation is that it is used to replenish nutrients in the soil and to keep the soil from becoming exhausted. That's true. But there are also other benefits to crop rotation, and I am going to tell you about them now.

One of the most overlooked—yet most important—features is that it keeps the numbers of pests, weeds, and diseases down. You see, uh, when the plants keep changing, pests are not able to acclimate. That's especially true since most pests prefer specific types of plants. As for weeds and diseases, without regular hosts, they too cannot prosper, so they disappear. Another advantage is that crop rotation helps prevent soil erosion. When the soil is ideal for growing crops, it retains water very well, which makes the soil healthier and also prevents the wind from blowing topsoil away. Something else that people do not consider is that not all crops require the same amount of work by farmers. Some are fairly easy to grow whereas others are much more labor intensive. Well, when crops that don't require much work are grown, then farmers have more time to dedicate to other pursuits. These may include mending equipment, building new facilities, taking care of animals, and simply getting some much-needed rest.

W: What about disadvantages? Are there any drawbacks to using crop rotation?

M: Yes, there are a few. Let me think . . . Well, I just talked about some crops being labor intensive while others aren't. One disadvantage of growing labor-intensive crops is that there is less time to do other activities. Farmers may find themselves exhausted from growing certain crops. In addition, some crops require the use of machinery to grow or harvest, so farmers may have to invest more money in them. Yet another disadvantage is that not all crops have the same value. Perhaps a farmer cannot grow corn in his field one year because he is practicing crop rotation. Instead, he has to grow peas in it. Well, it's entirely possible that the price of corn is higher than that of peas, so the farmer may be losing a sizable amount of money.

Oh, uh, there's another disadvantage that you should be aware of. Farming isn't just putting seeds in the ground, watering them, and watching them grow into plants which can be harvested. There's a considerable amount of knowledge required to be a farmer. The more crops that farmers grow, the more they need to learn. So practicing crop rotation can be a knowledge-intensive endeavor for farmers, which can take up a lot of their time.

해석

M Professor: 여기 계신 모든 분들은 윤작이 무엇인지 아실 거예요, 그렇죠? Patricia, 간단하게 설명해 볼래요?

W Student: 윤작은 동일한 경작지에서 서로 다른 작물을 재배하거나 때때로 휴한을 하는 행위로, 토양에서 모든 영양분이 빠져나가는 것을 막기 위한 것입니다.

M: 제 자신도 그보다 설명을 잘 할 수는 없을 것 같군요. 그건 그렇고, Patricia가 사용한 휴한이라는 단어는 성장 시기 동안 경작지에 아무것도 재배하지 않는 것을 의미합니다. 윤작은 아주 오랫동안 실행되어 왔어요. 거의 틀림없이, 윤작의 가장 유명한 예는 중세 시대의 유럽에서 이루어진 윤작일 거예요. 당시 많은 사람들이 삼모작을 하기 시작했습니다. 한 경작지에는 밀이나 보리 같은 곡물이 있었고, 또 다른 경작지에는 완두콩과 같은 콩들이 있었고, 그리고 세 번째 경작지는 휴한 상태에 있었습니다. 중세 시대의 사람들은 그것이 효과적인 윤작법이라는 점을 알아냈죠.

자, 어, 윤작에 대해 대부분의 사람들이 알고 있는 것은 윤작이 토양에 영양분을 다시 채워 넣기 위해 사용된다는 점과 토양의 영양분이 고갈되는 것을 막기 위해 사용된다는 점입니다. 그건 사실이죠. 하지만 윤작에는 또 다른 이점들이 존재하는데, 이제 그에 대해서 말씀을 드리겠습니다.

가장 많이 간과되는, 하지만 가장 중요한 점 중 하나는 윤작으로 해충, 잡초, 그리고 병해가 감소한다는 것입니다. 아시다시피, 어, 식물이 바뀌면 해충이 적응을 하지 못해요. 특히 대부분의 해충들이 특정 식물을 좋아하기 때문에 그런 것이죠. 잡초 및 병해에 대해 말씀을 드리면, 통상적인 숙주가 존재하지 않는 경우, 이들 역시 확산을 하지 못해서 사라지게 됩니다. 또 다른 이점은 윤작으로 토양의 침식이 예방된다는 점이에요. 토양이 곡식 재배에 이상적인 경우, 토양에는 많은 물이 포함되어 있는데, 이로써 토양이 보다 건강해지고 표토가 바람에 날려가지 않습니다. 사람들이 생각하지 못하는 그 밖의 이점은 모든 작물에 농부들의 동일한 노동이 필요한 것은 아니라는 점이에요. 일부는 재배하기가 쉬운 반면 훨씬 더 노동 집약적인 것들도 있습니다. 음, 그다지 많은 노동을 필요로 하지 않는 작물이 재배되는 경우, 농부들이 다른 일에 할애할 수 있는 시간이 더 많아집니다. 그러한 일에는 장비 수선, 새로운 시설 구축, 동물 관리, 그리고 충분한 휴식이 포함되죠.

W: 단점은 어떤가요? 윤작을 하는 경우 문제점이 있나요?

M: 네, 몇 가지 있어요. 생각해 보면… 음, 일부 작물들은 노동 집약적인 반면 그렇지 않은 작물들도 있다고 방금 말씀을 드렸습니다. 노동 집약적인 작물을 재배하는 경우의 한 가지 단점은 다른 활동을 할 수 있는 시간이 줄어든다는 것이에요. 농부들은 특정 작물을 재배하느라 지친 자신의 모습을 볼 수도 있습니다. 게다가 일부 작물들을 재배하거나 수확하기 위해서는 기계를 사용해야 하기 때문에 농부들은 기계에 더 많은 돈을 투자해야 할 수도 있습니다. 또 다른 단점은 모든 작물이 동일한 가치를 지니는 것은 아니라는 점에 있어요. 한 농부가 윤작을 하기 때문에 어느 해에는 자신의 경작지에서 옥수수를 재배할 수 없다고 해 보죠. 대신 그는 완두콩을 심어야만 합니다. 음, 옥수수 가격이 콩보다 높을 가능성이 크기 때문에 농부는 금전적으로 상당한 손실을 보게 될 수도 있습니다.

오, 어, 여러분들이 알아야 하는 또 다른 단점이 있습니다. 농사는 단지 땅에 씨를 뿌리고, 물을 주고, 그리고 수확이 가능한 식물로 자라기까지 이들을 지켜보는 것이 아니에요. 농부가 되기 위해서는 상당한 지식이 필요합니다. 농부들은 더 많은 작물을 재배할수록 더 많이 배워야 해요. 그래서 윤작은 농부들에게, 시간을 많이 잡아먹을 수도 있는, 지식 집약적인 일이 될 수도 있습니다.

Summary Note

A

❶ Crop rotation
❷ Middle Ages
❸ Replenish
❹ soil erosion
❺ more time
❻ exhausted
❼ machinery
❽ lots of knowledge

B

The professor mentions that crop rotation has been practiced for a long time and that one of the most famous examples of it is the three-field crop rotation practiced during the Middle Ages. He notes that people used it to replenish nutrients in the soil and to keep it from becoming exhausted. He then mentions that there are other benefits to crop rotation. It can keep the numbers of pests, weeds, and diseases down, the soil retains water well, and it helps prevent soil erosion. When farmers grow crops that are not labor intensive, they have more time for other activities, too. As for disadvantages, labor-intensive crops can make farmers exhausted. Some crops require the use of machinery, which costs money. All crops are not worth the same amount of money, and some crops can be knowledge-intensive endeavors.

Exercise 2 1 Ⓒ 2 Ⓑ 3 Ⓒ p.120

Script 04-11

M Professor: You probably learned in middle school that the Nile River is the longest river in the world and is the cradle of civilization. But even more impressive is the Amazon River, the second longest river in the world. **As**

you know, I have spent a lot of time working along both of these rivers, doing research, filming, and sometimes just relaxing. If you ever get a chance to visit one of these rivers, go for it. However, if you have to choose between visiting the Amazon or the Nile, then you should definitely visit the Amazon. In my opinion, it's way more interesting than the Nile. In fact, it's the most interesting place I've been to, and I've been everywhere, including all seven continents. To me, it's more interesting than regular tourist destinations such as the Swiss Alps and the Himalayas.

The main reason why I like it so much is that the Amazon delta is the largest tropical rainforest in the world. And where there's a rainforest, there's life. Plenty of it. **The Nile flows mostly through dry desert, where there's little wildlife or plant life.** Meanwhile, there's more life in the Amazon than in any other place in the world. For example, there are 500 species of mammals, one-third of the world's bird population, hundreds of reptiles, 175 different kinds of lizards, up to 300 million types of insects, and immense vegetation. The trees are so dense that they form a canopy. The basin contains the Earth's richest and most varied ecosystem. It will startle your senses . . . your sight, your hearing, and your sense of smell.

Let me briefly describe for you some of the impressive creatures you'll see on the video next week. The first is the jaguar. It is the largest and most powerful cat in the Western Hemisphere. It measures up to six feet in length and weighs up to 350 pounds. Its powerful jaws can crush a turtle shell. I heard three of them roar one night as I was paddling in a stream a few hundred meters away. The sound was electrifying, though chilling. As you'll learn, they prefer to do their hunting near the river and its streams at night. In the river, there are giant otters over six feet long, twenty species of piranha, and 300-pound dolphins. And not far away is the world's largest snake, the anaconda.

As I alluded to a moment ago, the Amazon basin is thick with vegetation, including a very dense forest of tall trees. By far the most amazing thing in the basin is the treetop world. The canopy, as scientists call it, is nine times bigger than Texas and home to millions of undiscovered species. It consists of trees, shrubs, vines, and other plants and covers much of the forest. Eighty percent of the forest's food is found in the canopy. Most of the animals live on the trees' branches. Many of the trees are 150 feet tall with canopies exceeding eighty feet. The trees have narrow trunks and can therefore be described as top heavy. Some scientists believe the canopy alone may contain half of the world's species.

Among these species is the harpy eagle, which has a six or seven-foot wingspan and is perhaps the most powerful bird in the world. It's big enough to carry a full-grown monkey and then eat it. There is the macaw parrot, considered by many to be the largest and most beautiful of its species. The video will illustrate what I'm talking about.

해석

M Professor: 여러분들은 아마도 중학교 때 나일강은 세계에서 가장 긴 강이며 문명의 발상지라고 배웠을 것입니다. 하지만 훨씬 더 인상적인 강은 세계에서 두 번째로 긴 강인 아마존강이에요. 아시다시피, 저는 이들 두 강 근처에서 일하면서, 예컨대 조사를 하고, 영상을 제작하고, 그리고 그냥 휴식을 취하면서 많은 시간을 보냈습니다. 만약에 이들 강 중 한 곳에 갈 기회가 생긴다면 가 보세요. 하지만 아마존강과 나일강 중에서 선택을 해야 하는 경우, 반드시 아마존강으로 가도록 하세요. 제 생각에, 그곳이 나일강보다 훨씬 더 흥미롭습니다. 실제로 제가 가 본 곳 중에서 가장 흥미로운 곳인데, 저는 7개의 대륙을 모두 포함해서 안 가 본 곳이 없어요. 이곳은 제게 스위스의 알프스나 히말라야산맥과 같은 일반적인 관광 명소보다도 더 흥미로운 곳입니다.

제가 그곳을 그처럼 좋아하는 주된 이유는 아마존 삼각지가 세계에서 가장 큰 열대 우림이기 때문이에요. 그리고 열대 우림이 있는 곳에는 생명이 존재합니다. 그것도 아주 많이요. 나일강은 주로 야생 동물이나 식물이 거의 존재하지 않는 건조한 사막 지대를 관통합니다. 반면에 아마존에는 전 세계 어떤 곳보다 많은 생명체가 살고 있어요. 예를 들어 500종의 포유류, 전 세계 조류의 3분의 1, 수백 종의 파충류, 175종류의 각기 다른 도마뱀, 최대 3억 종류에 이르는 곤충, 그리고 엄청난 식물들이 존재하죠. 나무들은 너무 울창해서 캐노피가 형성되어 있어요. 아마존 분지에는 지구에서 가장 풍요롭고 가장 다양한 생태계가 존재합니다. 여러분의 감각을… 시각, 청각, 그리고 후각을 깜짝 놀라게 만들 것입니다.

다음 주에 동영상으로 보게 될 인상적인 몇몇 생물들을 간단히 소개해 드리죠. 첫 번째는 재규어입니다. 서반구에서 가장 크고 힘이 센 고양이과 동물이죠. 길이는 최고 1.8미터, 그리고 체중은 최대 350파운드까지 나갈 수 있어요. 강력한 턱은 거북이의 등껍질도 부술 수가 있습니다. 저는 어느 날 밤 강에서 노를 젓다가 수백 미터 떨어진 곳에서 재규어 세 마리가 울부짖는 것을 들은 적이 있습니다. 서늘하긴 했지만 짜릿했죠. 여러분도 알게 되겠지만, 이들은 야간에 강과 개울가에서 사냥하는 것을 선호합니다. 강에는 길이가 6피터 이상인 대형 수달, 20종의 피라냐, 무게가 300파운드에 이르는 돌고래들이 있어요. 그리고 세상에서 가장 큰 뱀인 아나콘다도 그 근처에 있죠.

조금 전에 제가 언급했던 것처럼 아마존 분지는, 키 큰 나무들로 이루어진 울창한 숲을 포함해서, 많은 식물들로 가득합니다. 이곳 분지에서 가장 놀라운 점은 나무 꼭대기 부분이에요. 과학자들은 이를 캐노피라고 부르는데, 이는 텍사스보다 9배나 크고 알려지지 않은 수백 만 종의 생물들의 터전이기도 합니다. 이는 나무, 관목, 넝쿨, 그리고 기타 식물들로 이루어져 있으며 우림의 많은 부분을 덮고 있어요. 우림에 있는 먹이의 80%를 캐노피에서 찾아볼 수 있습니다. 대부분의 동물들이 나뭇가지에서 살고 있어요. 많은 나무들의 높이가 150피트에 이르며 캐노피의 높이는 80피트 이상입니다. 나무 몸통들이 얇기 때문에 윗부분이 무겁다고 말할 수도 있을 거예요. 일부 과학자들은 캐노피에만 전 세계 생물 종의 절반이 존재할 수도 있다고 생각합니다.

이러한 종들 사이에는 날개폭이 6피트에서 7피트에 이르는, 아마도 지구에 존재하는 조류 중 가장 힘이 센 남미수리가 있습니다. 이 새는 매우 크기 때문에 다 자란 원숭이를 낚아채서 잡아먹기도 하죠. 또한 많은 사람들에게 가장 크고 가장 아름답다고 생각되는 마코앵무새도 있습니다. 동영상에 제가 말씀드리는 것들이 나올 거예요.

Summary Note

A

❶ Nile and Amazon
❷ Encourages
❸ rainforest
❹ ecosystem
❺ Jaguar
❻ vegetation

B

The Amazon River is the second longest river in the world, but the Amazon basin and its tropical rainforest are the largest on the planet. It is an interesting place to visit and contains more life than any other place on the Earth. This can be contrasted with the Nile River. Although the Nile is longer, it has less wildlife and less plant life. It is surrounded mainly by dry desert. The Amazon is home to 500 species of mammals, one-third of the world's bird population, hundreds of reptiles, 175 different kinds of lizards, up to 300 million types of insects, and immense vegetation. The trees are so dense that their treetops form a canopy. The Amazon is home to creatures such as the jaguar, the most powerful cat in the Western Hemisphere, twenty species of piranhas, 300-pound dolphins, and the anaconda. The treetop canopy is nine times bigger than Texas and home to millions of undiscovered species. Some scientists believe this canopy alone may contain half of the world's animal species.

Exercise 3 1 Ⓐ 2 Ⓒ 3 Ⓑ p.122

Script 04-12

W Professor: I'd like to speak with you a bit about cultural diffusion right now. This refers to the way in which knowledge, language, aspects of culture, and even innovation spread from one place to another. It has been happening all throughout history. Any time people in one culture interact with another, there is the possibility of cultural diffusion taking place. Can anyone provide me with an example of cultural diffusion? Todd, your hand is up. What do you think?

M Student: Would an example be ethnic food?

W: **Possibly, but you need to expand on your idea.**

M: I guess I mean that when people from one culture move to another one, they often bring their food with them. When people in the new country learn about that food, eat it, like it, and start making it themselves, that would be an example of cultural diffusion. Uh, or at least I think it is.

W: Well done, Todd. Yes, that's a good example of cultural diffusion. Many people here in our country have started eating ethnic food, and that's definitely one way that foreign cultures have affected ours. Food, uh, as well as music and clothing, can often be cited as an example of cultural diffusion. There are four main types of cultural diffusion. They are contagious, hierarchical, stimulus, and expansion diffusion. I'll tell you about each of them one by one now.

Let's start with expansion diffusion, which is the process through which something spreads to another culture or a different place while it still remains practiced in its place of origin. I think we can use the English language as an example of this kind of diffusion. English, of course, started in England, but as England became a global power, the usage of the English language spread everywhere around the world. Today, people in countries everywhere learn English. Hellenism, which refers to Greek culture, is another example of this kind of cultural diffusion. When Alexander the Great conquered large parts of the world, Hellenism spread with his armies. At the same time, it was not diminished at all in Greece, where it originated.

What about contagious diffusion? It happens when something spreads through a population incredibly quickly. It's basically like a disease, uh, except it doesn't harm people. I'm referring to how rapidly the concept spreads. In the modern world, this has become much more prominent than it was in the past. Can anyone tell me why?

M: I would guess it has to do with the Internet. It's pretty easy for fads to spread around the world over the Internet.

W: You are correct. Fads can spread this way. Music, uh, especially pop music, can spread throughout contagious diffusion in a way that simply wouldn't have been possible even forty years ago.

Let's move on to hierarchical diffusion. This happens when powerful individuals or those in positions of authority spread ideas or customs to others. Easily the best-known example of this happened in the 1800s. When Queen Victoria of England got married, she wore a white wedding dress. Almost immediately afterward, there was a global trend of brides wearing white on their wedding day. You can also see this nowadays when people we call influencers attempt to get other individuals to use certain products. These individuals are essentially using their status to get other people to do something.

The fourth one is stimulus diffusion, which happens when some aspect of one culture is adopted by a new culture after the second culture has been exposed to it. However, the new culture gives this idea or concept or whatever a new form. Do you know what a great example of it is? It's pizza. Even here in the United States, there are different types of pizza in different states. Go abroad, and you will find even more numerous varieties. The sauce, the toppings, and the crust are all different in different places.

해석

W Professor: 이제 문화 전파에 대해서 잠시 이야기를 드리고 싶군요. 이는 지식, 언어, 문화의 측면들, 그리고 심지어는 기술 혁신이 한 곳에서 다른 곳으로 전파되는 과정을 가리킵니다. 문화 전파는 역사를 통틀어 이루어져 왔어요. 한 문화권의 사람들이 다른 사람들과 상호 작용을 하는 경우에 언제라도 문화 전파가 일어날 수 있습니다. 문화 전파의 예를 들어볼 사람이 있나요? Todd, 손을 들었군요. 어떻게 생각하나요?

M Student: 전통 음식도 한 가지 예가 될까요?

W: 가능할 것 같은데, 아이디어를 확대시켜 보세요.

M: 한 문화권에서 다른 문화권으로 사람들이 이주하는 경우에 종종 음식을 가져가는 것 같아요. 새로운 나라의 사람들이 그 음식을 알게 되고, 먹고, 좋아하고, 그리고 스스로 만들기 시작하면, 그것이 문화 전파가 예가 될 수 있을 거예요. 음, 적어도 저는 그렇게 생각해요.

W: 잘 했어요, Todd. 네, 그것이 문화 전파의 한 가지 적절한 사례입니다. 우리나라의 많은 사람들이 외국의 전통 음식을 먹기 시작했는데, 이는 분명 다른 문화가 우리에게 영향을 끼치고 있는 한 가지 방식이죠. 음식은, 어, 음악과 옷과 마찬가지로, 종종 문화 전파의 예로 언급될 수 있습니다. 문화 전파에는 네 가지 주요 유형이 존재해요. 전염 전파, 위계적 전파, 자극 전파, 그리고 확대 전파가 그것이죠. 이들 각각에 대해 하나씩 말씀을 드리겠습니다.

확대 전파로 시작해 볼 텐데, 이는 어떤 것이 원래의 장소에서 계속 존재하면서 다른 문화 혹은 다른 장소로 확산되는 과정이에요. 저는 이러한 전파의 한 가지 예가 영어라고 생각합니다. 영어는 물론 영국에서 시작되었지만, 영국이 전 세계적인 강대국이 되면서 영어 사용이 전 세계 모든 곳으로 확대되었습니다. 오늘날 모든 국가의 사람들이 영어를 배우고 있죠. 그리스 문화를 가리키는 헬레니즘도 이러한 문화 전파의 한 가지 사례입니다. 알렉산더 대왕이 전 세계 넓은 지역을 정복하자 그의 군대와 함께 헬레니즘이 확산되었죠. 동시에 헬레니즘은, 헬레니즘이 탄생했던 그리스에서 결코 사라지지 않았어요.

전염 전파는 어떨까요? 이는 무언가가 매우 빠르게 사람들 사이에서 확산되는 경우에 일어납니다. 기본적으로, 어, 해를 끼치지 않는다는 점을 제외하고는, 마치 질병과 같죠. 그러한 개념이 얼마다 빨리 확산되는지 말씀드리는 거예요. 현대에는 이러한 일이 과거보다 훨씬 더 두드러지게 나타나고 있습니다. 그 이유가 무엇인지 누가 말해 볼까요?

M: 인터넷과 관련이 있을 것 같아요. 유행이 인터넷을 타고 전 세계로 확산되기가 꽤 쉬우니까요.

W: 맞아요. 유행이 그러한 방식으로 확산될 수 있습니다. 음악, 어, 특히 대중 음악이 전염 전파로 확산될 수 있는데, 이러한 방식은 불과 40년 전만 해도 가능하지 않았던 것이에요.

위계적 확산으로 넘어가 보죠. 이는 영향력을 가진 개인이나 권위자들이 아이디어나 관습을 다른 이들에게 확산시키는 경우에 일어납니다. 아마도 이에 대한 가장 잘 알려진 예는 1800년대에 일어날 것일 거예요. 영국의 빅토리아 여왕이 결혼을 할 때 하얀색 웨딩 드레스를 입었습니다. 그 후 즉각적으로, 신부들이 결혼식 날에 하얀색 옷을 입는 것이 전 세계적인 유행이 되었어요. 이는 오늘날에도 인플루언서라고 불리는 사람들이 다른 사람들에게 영향을 미쳐 특정 제품을 사용하도록 만드는 경우에서도 찾아볼 수 있습니다. 이러한 개인들은 기본적으로 자신들의 지위를 이용해서 다른 사람에게 특정한 행동을 하도록 영향을 미칩니다.

네 번째는 자극 전파로, 이는 한 문화의 일정 측면이, 두 번째 문화가 그것에 노출된 후, 새로운 문화에 의해 채택되는 경우에 일어납니다. 하지만 새로운 문화가 여기에 아이디어나 개념, 혹은 새로운 형식을 부여하게 되죠. 그에 대한 유명한 예가 무엇인지 아시나요? 피자입니다. 심지어 이곳 미국에서도 다양한 주에 다양한 종류의 피자가 존재하죠. 해외에 나가면 훨씬 더 다양한 것들을 찾아 볼 수 있어요. 지역마다 소스, 토핑, 그리고 크러스트가 모두 다릅니다.

Summary Note

A

❶ cultural diffusion
❷ knowledge
❸ Ethnic food
❹ Expansion diffusion
❺ Hellenism
❻ fads
❼ powerful people
❽ white wedding dress
❾ change
❿ Pizza

B

The professor remarks that cultural diffusion is the way in which knowledge, language, aspects of culture, and innovation spread from one place to another. A student says that he believes ethnic food is an example of cultural diffusion, and the professor says that he is right. The professor says there are four main types of cultural diffusion. Expansion diffusion happens when something spreads to another culture while remaining strong in its own culture. The English language and Hellenism are examples of that. Contagious diffusion is for things such as fads that spread very quickly. Hierarchical diffusion happens when powerful people or those in positions of authority influence others. Queen Victoria's white wedding dress is an example of that. Stimulus diffusion happens when something spreads to another culture but changes in some ways. Pizza is the example that the professor uses.

Exercise 4 1 Ⓓ 2 Ⓓ 3 Ⓑ p.124

Script 04-13

W Professor: Until about 100 years ago, the American chestnut tree was an important tree spread throughout the forests of the eastern United States and southern Canada. It was a majestic hardwood, belonging to the beech and oak tree family. Some of these chestnut trees reached up to 150 feet tall and were around ten feet in diameter. They were a valuable source of timber. **They were also a wonderful supply of nuts, which fell to the ground in the fall, helping feed deer, bears, and other animals.** At one time, these trees numbered in the hundreds of millions.

But by the 1940s, these trees were virtually extinct. This was the result of a disease that had accidentally been imported to North America between 1900 and 1908. After that, it quickly spread through the forests, wiping out the American chestnut trees . . . By the way, when people sell roasted chestnuts in the United States, those chestnuts are not from the U.S. They're imported.

Anyway, getting back to the disease . . . It is called chestnut blight. It's a fungal disease that affects the bark of the chestnut trees. Sometimes it's called chestnut bark disease. Normally, the fungus enters a wound in the tree and then gets under the bark and grows. Gradually, it goes around the trunk, a branch, or a twig and kills the cambium. Now, cambium is the tissue that divides the bark from the wood. It also forms those rings you're all familiar with. I mean the annual rings that go around a tree's wood, making it possible for you determine the age of a tree. The fungal infection causes the tree trunk to split. If the cambium is cut, the tree will die. However, the tree's root system is quite resistant to the blight. Sprouts will develop at the base of the tree, and, therefore, several small American chestnut trees still exist. But they are only shoots from existing bases. The reason is that before they can reproduce, the disease will eventually attack and infect the tree again. It dies, and then the process starts again. Are there any questions?

No questions? Okay. Then, I'll continue. Although the American chestnut tree is all but extinct, it's not totally extinct. Efforts are now being made not only to thwart its extinction but also to revive the tree. One is a breeding plan conducted by the American Chestnut Foundation. It is known that Japanese chestnut trees and some Chinese chestnut trees are resistant to the fungus. Even when they're infected, they rarely die. You see, uh, they have two genes that are resistant to chestnut blight. The foundation made simple hybrids of susceptible American trees with Asian trees. The results showed that the hybrids carried at least two genes resistant to chestnut blight. Then they started back-crossing, where the partially resistant hybrid trees were then crossed with the susceptible American trees. One-fourth of the progeny inherited both of the resistant genes and was therefore resistant. These are then crossed with the American trees. This back-crossing process will be repeated over and over so that the percentage of American genes in the hybrids increases and insures passage of the resistance genes. Eventually, a final cross will be made between a pair of trees carrying two resistant genes. One out of sixteen of these trees will have four resistance genes, making it fully resistant to the blight fungus. In short, the foundation is breeding the trees for resistance to blight. **Its goal is to reintroduce blight-resistant American chestnut trees to the forests of eastern North America within the next few decades.**

해석

W Professor: 약 100년 전까지만 해도 미국 밤나무는 미국 동부와 캐나다 남부의 산림 지대 전역에 분포되어 있던 중요한 수목이었어요. 이들은 너도밤나무 및 참나무과에 속하는 거대한 견목이었습니다. 이들 밤나무 중 일부는 높이가 최고 150피트에 이르렀고 지름은 10피터 정도였어요. 이들은 귀중한 목재였습니다. 또한 엄청나게 많은 견과를 제공해 주었는데, 견과는 가을이면 땅에 떨어져 사슴, 곰, 그리고 기타 동물들의 먹이가 되었죠. 한때는 이 나무들의 수가 수억 그루에 이르기도 했어요.

하지만 1940년경 이 나무는 사실상 멸종했습니다. 1900년과 1908년 사이에 우연히 북아메리카로 들어온 질병 때문이었어요. 그 후 질병이 산림 지대 전역으로 급속히 퍼지면서 미국 밤나무들은 멸종을 했는데… 그건 그렇고, 미국에서 구운 밤을 판매하는 경우, 이 밤들은 미국산이 아닙니다. 수입산이에요.

어쨌든, 질병으로 다시 돌아가면… 이 질병은 밤나무줄기마름병이라고 불립니다. 밤나무 껍질에 영향을 미치는 진균성 질병이죠. 때로는 밤나무껍질병이라고도 불리고요. 주로 균류가 나무의 상처를 통해 나무 껍질 아래로 들어가서 자라게 되죠. 서서히 몸통, 가지, 혹은 잔가지로 퍼져서 형성층을 죽게 만듭니다. 자, 형성층이란 나무껍질과 목질부를 나누는 조직이에요. 또한 여러분 모두가 잘 알고 있는 테를 만듭니다. 나무의 나이를 알 수 있게 해 주는, 목질부 주변에 생기는 나이테를 말씀드리는 거예요. 진균 감염으로 인해 나무의 몸통이 갈라집니다. 형성층이 떨어져 나가면 나무는 죽게 될 것입니다. 하지만 나무의 뿌리는 밤나무줄기마름병에 상당히 잘 견뎌요. 나무의 아랫부분에서 싹이 자라날 것이기 때문에 소수의 작은 미국 밤나무들은 여전히 존재합니다. 하지만 남아 있는 나무 밑동에 싹이 나 있을 뿐이에요. 그러한 이유는 이들이 번식을 하기 전에 결국 또 다시 질병이 공격을 해서 나무를 감염시킬 것이기 때문이죠. 나무가 죽은 다음에는 그러한 과정이 다시 시작되고요. 질문이 있나요?

질문이 없나요? 좋아요. 그럼 계속하겠습니다. 미국 밤나무가 거의 멸종하기는 했지만 완전히 멸종한 것은 아니에요. 멸종을 막으려는 노력뿐만 아니라 이 나무들을 소생시키려는 노력이 이루어지고 있습니다. 하나는 미국 밤나무 협회에서 이루어지고 있는 번식 계획이에요. 일본 밤나무와 일부 중국 밤나무들은 이 균류에 내성을 가지고 있는 것으로 알려져 있어요. 이들은 감염이 되어도 거의 죽는 경우가 없죠. 아시다시피, 어, 이들이 밤나무줄기마름병에 내성을 나타내는 두 개의 유전자를 갖고 있기 때문입니다. 이 협회는 감염에 취약한 미국 나무와 아시아 나무들을 단순히 교배시켰어요. 그 결과 교배종은 밤나무줄기마름병에 내성을 나타내는 최소 두 개의 유전자를 갖게 되었죠. 이후 이들은 여교배되어 부분적으로 내성을 지닌 이들 교배종과 병에 취약한 미국 나무들이 다시 교배되었습니다. 이들 자손의 4분의 1은 두 내성 유전자 모두를 물려받아서 내성을 나타냈어요. 이들은 다시 미국의 나무들과 교배가 되었습니다. 이러한 여교배 과정을 계속 반복하면 교배종 내의 미국 유전자의 비중이 증가하고 내성 유전자들의 전달이 보장될 거예요. 결국에는 두 개의 내성 유전자를 지닌 한 쌍의 나무들 사이에서 최종 교배종이 만들어질 것입니다. 이러한 16그루의 나무 중 하나가 네 개의 내성 유전자를 갖게 되면 균류에 대한 완전한 내성을 나타낼 거예요. 간단히 말해서, 이 협회는 줄기마름병에 내성을 지닌 나무 품종을 만들고 있는 것입니다. 이들의 목표는 향후 수십 년 내에 북아메리카 동부의 산림 지대에서 줄기마름병에 내성을 나타내는 미국 밤나무들이 다시 자라도록 만드는 것이에요

Summary Note

A

❶ chestnut tree
❷ eastern U.S.
❸ extinct
❹ American Chestnut Foundation

❺ hybrid trees
❻ disease-resistant

B

Until about 100 years ago, there were millions of American chestnut trees throughout eastern North America. Some of these trees reached up to 150 feet tall and were a valuable source of timber. They also provided a wonderful supply of chestnuts. But in the early 1900s, a disease known as chestnut blight swept across the forests of eastern North America, wiping out American chestnut trees. Only a few trees still exist today. However, the tree is not totally extinct, and the American Chestnut Foundation has started a breeding program to revive these trees. It accomplishes this by breeding Chinese trees resistant to the disease with susceptible American trees. Then, it breeds the hybrids with more American trees, which pass on two resistant genes to the progeny. The process is repeated until eventually the percentage of American genes in the hybrids is very high and one of the progeny receives four resistance genes, making it fully resistant to the blight fungus.

Integrated Listening & Speaking p.126

A

Script 04-14

M Professor: Let's review the information about crop rotation. It has been practiced for a long time, and one of the most famous examples of it is the three-field crop rotation practiced during the Middle Ages. Most people used it to replenish nutrients in the soil and to keep it from becoming exhausted. But there are other benefits to crop rotation. For example, it can keep the numbers of pests, weeds, and diseases down, the soil retains water well, and it helps prevent soil erosion. In addition, when farmers grow crops that are not labor intensive, they have more time for other activities, too. There are some disadvantages though. One is that labor-intensive crops can make farmers exhausted. Some crops require the use of machinery, which costs money. All crops are not worth the same amount of money, and some crops can be knowledge-intensive endeavors.

1 In the Middle Ages, people used the three-field crop rotation system.

2 They use it to replenish nutrients in the soil.

3 One disadvantage is that labor-intensive crops can make farmers exhausted.

B

Script 04-15

M Professor: Last week, we talked about the Amazon River. I indicated to you that although it isn't the largest river in the world, its basin is the largest, and it's also home to the world's largest tropical rainforest. It's rich with life as well and contains more life than any other place on the Earth. The Amazon is home to 500 species of mammals, one-third of the world's bird population, hundreds of reptiles, 175 different kinds of lizards, up to 300 million types of insects, and immense vegetation. The trees are so dense that their tops form a canopy. The Amazon is home to such creatures as the jaguar, the most powerful cat in the Western Hemisphere, twenty species of piranhas, 300-pound dolphins, and the anaconda. The treetop canopy is nine times bigger than Texas and home to millions of undiscovered species. Some scientists believe this canopy alone may contain half of the world's species.

1 The Amazon River is the second longest river in the world. It has the largest river basin in the world and is home to the largest tropical rainforest in the world. It's rich with life.

2 In the canopy (the treetops)

3 About fifty percent

Mini TOEFL iBT Practice Test p.128

1 Ⓓ 2 Ⓑ 3 Ⓐ 4 Ⓓ 5 Ⓑ
6 Ⓐ 7 Ⓐ 8 Ⓑ 9 Ⓑ, Ⓓ
10 Ⓑ 11 Ⓒ

[1-5]

Script 04-16

M Student: Professor Chambliss, I'd like to talk to you for a few minutes.

W Professor: Of course, Harold. Please have a seat and tell me what's going on.

M: I wonder if you can give me some advice. You see, uh, tomorrow, I've got a job interview.

W: A job interview? Congratulations. What kind of job are you applying for?

M: It's a teaching position at a local school. You know, uh, I'm not really sure if teaching is for me, but I need to do something after I graduate. After all, I've got to earn money.

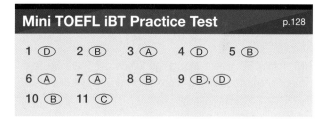

W: Hmm . . . Haven't you considered attending graduate school?

M: Graduate school? Why would I want to do that?

W: Well, there are a couple of reasons. First, most schools want their teachers to have at least a master's degree. So if you become a teacher, at some point, you're almost surely going to have to attend graduate school. If you do that while you are working, that means night school. And you'll be really busy when you're attending classes and working.

M: Huh. You know, I hadn't ever considered that.

W: It's definitely something you should think about.

M: But . . . graduate school is pretty expensive. There's no way that I can afford to pay for it, and I'm not interested in taking out any loans. I prefer to have a debt-free life. And my parents can't afford to help me out as I have two younger brothers and a younger sister, so they need to help pay for my siblings' college educations as well.

W: Okay. But you probably don't need to worry about paying for graduate school.

M: Er . . . why not?

W: Well, if you get accepted to a grad school and are offered a position as a teaching assistant, then your tuition will be paid for by the university. You'll even get paid for the teaching work you do.

M: Seriously? You're not joking?

W: I wouldn't joke about something like that. A university education is expensive nowadays, and graduate school can cost even more. But by becoming a TA or a research assistant, you'd be able to go to school for free. Interested?

M: Totally. But where should I go to school? There are so many grad schools, and I don't know anything about them.

W: Well, let me tell you something . . . If you were to apply to grad school here, I'd make sure you are accepted into this department. I could also use a teaching assistant for one of my classes. Now, uh, you'd have to work really hard because grad school isn't easy, but you'd be able to get your master's degree in two years. Then, you'd have no problem getting a job as a teacher at a school, and your starting salary would be higher than what you would get with just a bachelor's degree.

M: Wow. That's a lot for me to take in right now. I'm inclined to say yes. But I'd still like to think about it.

W: Well, you'd better think quickly because the deadline for applying to this school is in two weeks.

M: Okay. I'll let you know by tomorrow. Now, uh, back to the original reason why I came here . . . My interview. Do you think you could give me a few tips on what I need to do?

W: Of course, I can.

해석

M Student: Chambliss 교수님, 잠시 이야기를 나누고 싶은데요.

W Professor: 그래요, Harold. 앉아서 무슨 일인지 얘기해 보세요.

M: 제게 조언을 좀 해 주실 수 있는지 궁금해서요. 아시다시피, 어, 내일 면접이 있거든요.

W: 면접이요? 축하해요. 어떤 일자리에 지원했나요?

M: 인근 학교의 교사직이에요. 아시겠지만, 어, 저는 교사 업무가 제게 맞는 것인지 정말로 잘 모르겠는데, 졸업을 한 후에는 무언가를 해야 하죠. 어쨌거나 돈을 벌어야 하니까요.

W: 흠… 대학원에 다니는 것은 생각해 본 적이 없나요?

M: 대학원이요? 제가 왜 대학원에 가야 하나요?

W: 음, 두 가지 이유가 있어요. 첫째, 대부분의 학교들은 교사가 최소한 석사 학위를 가지고 있기를 바라요. 그래서 학생이 교사가 되는 경우, 어느 시점에 이르면 거의 확실하게 대학원에 다녀야 할 거예요. 일을 하면서 다닐 수도 있지만, 그렇게 하려면 야간 대학에 다녀야 하죠. 그리고 수업을 들으면서 일을 하면 정말로 바쁠 거예요.

M: 이런. 아시겠지만 그에 대해서는 생각해 본 적이 없었어요.

W: 반드시 생각해 봐야 할 문제예요.

M: 하지만… 대학원은 학비가 상당히 비싸잖아요. 제게 학비를 감당할 수 있는 방법이 없는데다가, 저는 대출을 받는 것도 내키지가 않아요. 빚이 없는 삶을 선호하거든요. 그리고 저한테는 남동생 두 명과 여동생 한 명이 있어서 부모님들이 제 형제자매의 대학 등록금 납부에도 도움을 주셔야 하기 때문에 부모님들도 저를 도울 수 있는 여유가 없으세요.

W: 그렇군요. 하지만 대학원 학비는 걱정할 필요가 없을 수도 있어요.

M: 어… 왜 그렇죠?

W: 음, 대학원에 입학을 해서 수업 조교 업무를 제안받는 경우, 학교측이 학비를 납부해 줄 거예요. 학생이 하는 수업 업무에 대해 급여도 지급받게 될 것이고요.

M: 정말인가요? 농담 아니시죠?

W: 전 그런 농담은 하지 않아요. 요즘 대학 학비가 비싼 편인데, 대학원을 다니면 훨씬 더 많은 비용이 들 수 있죠. 하지만 수업 조교나 연구 조교가 됨으로써 무료로 대학원에 다닐 수도 있어요. 관심이 있나요?

M: 많이요. 하지만 어디에 다녀야 하나요? 대학원들은 많은데, 그에 대해서는 전혀 아는 바가 없거든요.

W: 음, 한 마디만 하자면… 학생이 이곳 대학원에 지원을 하는 경우, 제가 분명 우리 학과에 입학할 수 있도록 할게요. 또한 제 수업 중 하나에서 학생을 수업 조교로 고용할 수도 있죠. 자, 어, 대학원은 쉽지가 않기 때문에 학생이 정말로 열심히 해야 할 텐데, 하지만 2년 후에는 석사 학위를 받을 수 있을 거예요. 그런 다음에는 교사 일자리를 얻는 것에 아무런 문제가 없을 것이고, 학사 학위만 가지고 있을 때보다 초봉도 높아질 거예요.

M: 와. 당장 받아들이기에는 내용이 많군요. '네'라고 말씀을 드리고 싶어요. 하지만 그에 대해 계속 생각해 보고 싶어요.

W: 음, 이곳 학교의 지원 마감일이 2주 후에 있기 때문에 빨리 생각해 보는 편이 좋을 거예요.

M: 알겠습니다. 내일까지 알려 드릴게요. 이제, 어, 제가 이곳에 온 원래의 이유로 돌아가서… 면접이요. 제가 어떻게 해야 하는지에 대해서 몇 가지 팁을 주실 수 있으신가요?

W: 물론이죠.

[6-11]

Script 04-17

M Professor: During the 1930s, America was in the middle of the Great Depression. If one of us were to take a time machine back to the United Sates of the 1930s, it would have looked like a third-world nation compared to what it is today. Despite the harshness of the era, it was also a time of gigantic architectural and engineering accomplishments. The Empire State Building, the Hoover Dam, and the Golden Gate Bridge were all erected during this period. These achievements were impressive, even by today's standards. **We don't have much time left today, so I'll begin by talking about one of these, the Hoover Dam, and then next week, we can discuss some of the other architectural accomplishments of the 1930s.**

What I'm showing you on the screen now is a series of photos of the Hoover Dam. Some were taken before the dam was completed, and some others were shot after its completion . . . The creators of the Hoover Dam wanted to build a modern façade, and they wanted to make the entire thing aesthetically pleasing. The dam's original design was very functional, but it was unbalanced with massive eagles. It had been designed by engineers, so it therefore wasn't modern or good looking. To acquire a more modern and pleasant look, Gordon Kaufman, an architect from Los Angeles, was hired, and most of his suggestions were subsequently implemented. He simplified the design, giving it the modern and pleasing appearance that had been sought. He replaced the four unequal towers and the overhanging balcony with a series of observation niches and towers that were very balanced. You can see them in this photo I'm showing to you now, rising from the wall as they continue upward with no interference.

Now, if you look to where I'm pointing, you can see that the new design emphasized a series of small vertical shadows and larger shadows from the elevator and utility towers. Kaufman treated this as part of the dam's face. In addition, the four large towers, which you see, uh . . . up here, are reminiscent of a building we just looked at last week, the Los Angeles Times Building, with its cutback corners. But in this case, the corners and the towers have a simpler look. They are more modern. The two inner towers were public entrances to the dam, and the outer ones were for utilities and public washrooms.

By the way, the two inner towers contained an ornament . . . Here it is . . . This was the only ornament on the dam. It's a large, concrete panel depicting various subjects, including irrigation, flood control, and some of the history of the area. The sculpture was a semi-classical cubist work. As you might have already guessed, this is an Art Deco sculpture, the modern style of art and architecture popular throughout the 1920s and 1930s. Putting small ornaments on buildings was typical of the Art Deco style.

Now, as I think I mentioned earlier, the Hoover Dam was no minor undertaking. First, in 1930 or 1931, the workers had to install a town of houses and the infrastructure to support the four or five thousand workers who would be needed to work on the dam. A railway was set up nearby to supply the town and the project. And a year or two before they started to pour any cement, tunnels had to be carved through the walls of the canyon so that water could be diverted away from the project. This took time. The employees worked different shifts so that the project could continue twenty-four hours a day. The first bucket of cement was not poured until 1933. This continued for two years until the last bucket was poured in May of 1936. It was finally completed a year later. And like the Empire State Building, it was completed ahead of time. It was finished two years ahead of schedule. Now, let's take a look at some more pictures of the dam. I think you'll like them.

해석

M Professor: 1930년대 미국은 대공황의 시기를 겪고 있었어요. 만약 우리 중 한 명이 타임머신을 타고 1930년대의 미국으로 돌아간다면 미국은, 오늘날과 비교해 볼 때, 제3세계 국가처럼 보일 것입니다. 힘든 시대였음에도 불구하고, 이때는 대규모 건축 및 공학적 성과들이 이루어진 때이기도 했어요. 엠파이어스테이트 빌딩, 후버 댐, 그리고 금문교 모두 이 시기에 건설되었죠. 이러한 성과들은 오늘날의 기준으로 볼 때에도 인상적인 것이었습니다. 오늘은 남은 시간이 얼마 없으니 이들 중 하나인 후버 댐에 대한 이야기로 시작을 하고, 다음 주에 1930년대의 기타 건축물들을 살펴보도록 하겠습니다.

이제 스크린에서 후버 댐 사진들을 보여 드릴게요. 일부는 댐이 완공되기 전에 촬영된 것이고 일부는 완공 후에 촬영된 것인데… 후버 댐을 생각해 낸 사람들은 외관이 현대적이기를 바랐고 댐 전체가 미적인 아름다움을 나타내기를 바랐어요. 댐의 원래 디자인은 매우 기능적인 것이었지만, 거대한 독수리 형상들로 균형이 맞지 않았습니다. 공학자들이 설계를 했기 때문에 댐은 현대적이지도 않았고 외적으로도 멋있게 보이지 않았어요. 보다 현대적이고 멋진 외관을 나타낼 수 있도록 로스앤젤레스 출신의 건축가 고든 카우프만이 고용되었는데, 그가 한 제안들은 이후 대부분 받아들여졌어요. 그는 설계를 단순화해서 댐에 요구되었던 현대적이고 멋진 외관을 댐이 가질 수 있도록 만들었습니다. 그는 네 개의 각기 다르게 생긴 타워와 돌출된 발코니를 없애고 전망대와 매우 균형이 잡힌 타워를 설치했어요. 지금 여러분께 보여 드리는 사진에서 아무런 방해도 받지 않고 벽에서부터 위로 뻗어나 있는 이들의 모습을 보실 수 있습니다.

자, 제가 가리키는 곳을 보시면, 새로운 설계에서는 수직 형태의 작은 그림자들과 엘리베이터 및 시설 관리실로부터 나오는 보다 큰 그림자들이 강조되어 있다는 점을 아실 수 있을 거예요. 카우프만은 이것을 댐의 얼굴로 간주했어요. 또한 네 개의 커다란 타워가 여기 위쪽에 보이는데, 어… 우리가 지난 주에 보았던 모서리가 잘려나간 로스앤젤레스 타임즈 빌딩을 연상시키죠. 하지만 이 경우에는 모서리와 타워의 외관이 보다 단순하게 보입니다. 이들이 보다 현대적이죠. 안쪽에 있는 두 개의 타워는 일반 대중들이 댐 안으로 들어가는 입구이고, 바깥쪽 타워는 시설 관리실 및 공용 화장실입니다.

그건 그렇고, 안쪽 두 개의 타워에는 장식이 있는데… 여기에 있습니다… 이것이 댐에 있는 유일한 장식이에요. 관개, 홍수 조절, 그리고 이 지역의 일부 역사를 포함하여 다양한 주제들을 묘사하고 있는 거대한 콘크리트 판넬이죠. 조각은 반고전적인 입체파 작품입니다. 이미 짐작하셨겠지만, 이것은 1920년대와 1930년대에 인기를 끌었던 현대 미술 및 건축 양식인 아르데코 양식의 조각이에요. 건물에 작은 장식을 입히는 것은 전형적인 아르데코 양식이었습니다.

자, 제가 앞서 언급했듯이 후버 댐 건설은 결코 만만한 작업이 아니었어요. 우선 1930년 혹은 1931년에 댐 건설에 필요한 4천명 또는 5천 명의 인부를 수용할 수 있는 주택 및 기반 시설을 갖춘 마을을 건설해야 했습니다. 마을과 공사 현상에 물자를 공급하기 위해 인근에 철도가 건설되었어요. 그리고 처음 시멘트를 붓기 1년이나 2년 전에, 공사 현장으로부터 물을 빼낼 수 있도록, 협곡의 벽에 터널을 뚫어야만 했습니다. 이 작업에 상당한 시간이 걸렸어요. 공사가 하루 24시간 동안 계속 진행될 수 있도록 인부들은 교대로 작업을 했습니다. 1933년이 되어서야 첫 시멘트가 부어졌어요. 공사는 2년 동안 계속되었고, 1936년 5월에 마지막 시멘트 작업이 이루어졌습니다. 그 후 1년이 지나서 마침내 댐이 완공되었죠. 엠파이어스테이트 빌딩과 마찬가지로 일정보다 2년 빨리 완공이 되었어요. 자, 댐의 사진을 몇 장 더 보도록 하겠습니다. 마음에 드실 거예요.

Vocabulary Check-Up p.133

A

1 Ⓛ	2 Ⓙ	3 Ⓕ	4 Ⓓ	5 Ⓐ
6 Ⓒ	7 Ⓖ	8 Ⓚ	9 Ⓑ	10 Ⓝ
11 Ⓔ	12 Ⓘ	13 Ⓜ	14 Ⓗ	15 Ⓞ

B

1 Ⓑ	2 Ⓓ	3 Ⓐ	4 Ⓔ	5 Ⓒ

UNIT 05 Understanding the Speaker's Attitude

Basic Drill p.136

Drill 1 Ⓒ

Script 05-02

M Student: Professor Schmidt, here is the description of the paper I'm planning to write for your class.

W Professor: Thank you, Dave. Hold on a minute and let me review it, please.

M: Sure thing.

W: Hmm . . . I'm sorry, Dave, but it looks like you didn't follow my instructions.

M: What do you mean? This is a description of what I intend to write about on the term paper.

W: I didn't ask you to do that. I asked all the students to submit an outline for their paper. This is just one paragraph that describes your topic.

M: How is an outline different?

W: Well, it would be much more specific. In addition, it would show me precisely what you're going to write about, the arguments you're going to make, and the examples you're going to give. You need to redo this.

M: Okay. Can I give it to you when our class meets again this Friday?

W: **I'd like it by the end of the day today.**

해석

M Student: Schmidt 교수님, 교수님 수업에서 제가 작성할 보고서를 설명한 것이에요.

W Professor: 고마워요, Dave. 잠시 기다리시면 제가 살펴볼게요.

M: 알겠습니다.

W: 흠… 유감이지만, Dave, 제 지시를 따르지 않은 것 같군요.

M: 무슨 말씀이신가요? 이것은 제 기말 보고서에서 제가 쓰려고 하는 것을 설명한 것인데요.

W: 제가 그렇게 하라고 요청하지는 않았어요. 저는 모든 학생들에게 자신의 보고서에 대한 개요를 제출하라고 했죠. 이건 학생의 주제를 설명하는 하나의 단락일 뿐이에요.

M: 개요는 어떻게 다른가요?

W: 음, 훨씬 더 구체적이죠. 게다가 정확히 학생이 무엇에 대해 쓰고자 하는지, 학생이 하게 될 주장, 그리고 학생이 제시할 사례를 제게 보여 주어야 해요. 다시 하도록 하세요.

M: 그럴게요. 다음 수업이 있는 이번 주 금요일에 드려도 될까요?

W: 오늘 중으로 받았으면 좋겠군요.

Drill 2 Ⓐ

Script 05-03

W Student: Hello. My name is Andrea Garvey. I applied for a position on the air here, but my application was rejected. I wonder if you could tell me the reason why.

M Radio Station Employee: Andrea Garvey? Ah, yes. I remember your application.

W: And?

M: Well, you wanted to do a talk show about politics. However, we've tried that in the past, and the ratings for it were very low. In addition, almost nobody called in to the station during that time.

W: I see. Well, I'd really like to have my own show. What would you recommend that I do?

M: Why don't you apply again and suggest a different kind of show this time?

W: What kind of show are you looking for?

M: Most students who listen to the university's radio station just want to hear music with the DJ talking about the musicians a bit in between songs.

W: Oh, okay. How do you think a show featuring classical music would go over?

M: **Not too badly.** Why don't you try it?

해석

W Student: 안녕하세요. 제 이름은 Andrea Garvey입니다. 생방송 프로그램 일자리에 지원을 했는데, 제 지원서가 거부되었어요. 그 이유를 알려 주실 수 있는지 궁금합니다.

M Radio Station Employee: Andrea Garvey라고요? 아, 그래요. 학생의 지원서가 기억나는군요.

W: 그래서요?

M: 음, 학생은 정치와 관련된 토크쇼를 하고 싶다고 했죠. 하지만 그건 예전에 시도해 본 적이 있는데, 그에 대한 청취율이 매우 낮았어요. 게다가 그 기간 동안 방송국으로 전화를 걸어온 사람도 거의 없었죠.

W: 알겠어요. 음, 저는 정말로 저만의 쇼를 진행해 보고 싶어요. 제게 추천해 주실 만한 것이 있나요?

M: 다시 지원을 해서 이번에는 다른 종류의 쇼를 제안해 보는 것이 어떨까요?

W: 어떤 종류의 쇼를 찾고 계신가요?

M: 대학교의 라디오 방송을 듣는 대부분의 학생들은 음악을 듣고 싶어하는데, 노래 사이에는 어느 정도 음악가에 대한 DJ의 이야기도 듣고 싶어하죠.

W: 오, 알겠어요. 클래식 음악을 다루는 쇼는 받아들여질 것 같나요?

M: 그다지 나쁘게 들리지는 않는군요. 한번 시도해 볼래요?

Drill 3 Ⓑ

Script 05-04

W Professor: Take a look at these pictures up here on the screen, please . . . Here's one . . . and another . . . and another one . . . Can anyone tell me what we're looking at?

M Student: It's a coral reef. I'm not sure where it is, but it's almost surely in some kind of tropical location.

W: That's correct, Brian. The pictures of the coral reef you're looking at were taken in the South Pacific by the way. And those waters are definitely tropical. You see, uh, with very few exceptions, coral reefs can only exist in tropical waters. The water needs to be warm. It can't be too hot or too cold, or the coral will die.

And that's a big problem nowadays. Coral reefs are some of the most vital ecosystems on the planet, yet they are disappearing in some places. And, uh, sure, they are expanding in other places, but the rate of expansion is less than the rate of destruction. What makes coral reefs so important? Well, for one, an enormous variety of ocean life resides in them. I'm not just referring to fish. I'm also talking about other marine creatures, including mammals and reptiles.

Many animals use coral reefs as their breeding grounds since the reefs provide many places for them to hide and to lay their eggs so that they aren't vulnerable to predators. Coral reefs also tend to have abundant amounts of food.

해석

W Professor: 여기 화면 위에 있는 이 사진들을 봐 주세요… 여기에 하나가 있고… 여기에 하나가… 그리고 여기에도 하나가 있습니다… 무엇을 보고 있는지 말해 볼 사람이 있나요?

M Student: 산호초입니다. 어디에 있는지는 잘 모르겠지만, 분명 열대 지방과 같은 곳에 있을 거예요.

W: 맞아요, Brian. 그건 그렇고, 여러분이 보고 계신 것은 남태평양에서 찍은 산호의 사진입니다. 그리고 이곳 바다는 분명 열대 지역이죠. 아시다시피, 어, 극소수의 예외가 있기는 하지만 산호초는 열대 수역에서만 존재할 수 있어요. 바닷물이 따뜻해야 합니다. 너무 뜨겁거나 차가워도 안 되며, 그렇지 않은 경우에는 산호초가 죽게 되죠.

그리고 그러한 점이 현재 큰 문제가 되고 있어요. 산호초는 지구에서 가장 중요한 생태계 중 하나이지만 일부 지역에서 산호초가 사라지고 있습니다. 그리고, 어, 물론, 다른 곳에서는 확대되고 있지만, 확대되는 속도가 파괴되는 속도보다 느립니다. 어떤 점에서 산호초가 중요할까요? 음, 우선, 그곳에 매우 다양한 바다 생물들이 살고 있습니다. 어류만을 말씀드리는 것이 아니에요. 포유류와 파충류를 포함한 기타 해양 생물들도 말씀을 드리는 것입니다.

많은 동물들이 산호초를 번식지로 이용하는데, 그 이유는 산호초가 이들에게 몸을 숨기고 알을 낳을 수 있는 많은 장소를 제공해 주기 때문에 이들이 포식자들을 피할 수 있기 때문이에요. 또한 산호초에는 풍부한 먹이가 존재하는 경우가 많습니다.

Drill 4 Ⓓ

Script 05-05

M Professor: Did any of you read yesterday's newspaper? There was an article in the paper about red rain falling . . . Huh, okay. I guess nobody read it. Well, red rain is a real phenomenon. It's also called blood rain for obvious reasons.

W Student: Is it . . . blood falling from the sky? That would be gross.

M: No, it's not blood. But in the past, people thought it was blood. Red rain has been recorded as falling in places around the world for thousands of years. People typically thought it was an omen of bad things to come. I mean, uh, it makes sense, doesn't it? How would you feel if you saw red rain falling to the ground?

W: I would be expecting the end of the world.

M: That's exactly what people thought . . . and still think today. So, uh, red rain has been documented as falling in many places. But nobody is really sure why. Apparently, lots of incidents involving red rain have happened soon after meteor showers. So there could be a celestial element involved. Other times, volcanic eruptions have been followed by red rain, so it could be volcanic ash causing the problem. Some people attribute it to dust particles that mix with raindrops and even lichens that get in the atmosphere. Basically, we just don't know.

해석

M Professor: 어제 날짜의 신문을 보신 분이 있나요? 신문에서 붉은 비가 내린다는 기사가 실렸는데⋯ 허, 그래요. 읽은 사람이 없는 것 같군요. 음, 붉은 비는 실제로 존재하는 현상이에요. 당연한 이유로, 피 비라고도 불리죠.

W Student: 그게⋯ 하늘에서 피 비가 내리는 건가요? 끔찍할 것 같은데요.

M: 아니에요, 피는 아닙니다. 하지만 과거에는 사람들이 이를 피라고 생각했죠. 붉은 비는 수천 년 동안 전 세계의 지역에서 내린 것으로 기록되어 있습니다. 사람들은 이를 보통 나쁜 일이 일어날 것이라는 징조로 생각했어요. 제 말은, 어, 말이 되는 이야기입니다, 그렇지 않나요? 땅으로 붉은 비가 내리는 모습을 본다면 어떤 느낌이 들 것 같나요?

W: 세상이 곧 끝날 것이라고 생각할 것 같아요.

M: 사람들도 정확히 그렇게 생각을 했어요⋯ 그리고 오늘날도 마찬가지죠. 그래서, 어, 붉은 비는 많은 지역에서 내린 것으로 기록되어 있습니다. 하지만 아무도 그 이유는 정확히 모르고 있어요. 분명 붉은 비와 관련이 있는 다수의 경우는 유성우가 있은 직후에 발생했어요. 그래서 천체의 물질과 관련이 있을 수도 있습니다. 다른 경우, 붉은 비가 내리기에 앞서 화산이 분출했는데, 이로써 산성비는 화산재가 원인인 문제일 수도 있습니다. 그 원인을 빗방울 및 대기로 유입된 이끼류와 섞인 먼지 입자에서 찾는 사람들도 있어요. 기본적으로, 우리는 아직 모르고 있습니다.

Exercises with Long Conversations

Exercise 1 1 Ⓑ 2 Ⓐ 3 Ⓓ p.140

Script 05-06

W Student: Hello. My name is Rebecca Nelson. I wonder if you can help me clear up a question.

M Student Housing Office Employee: Yes, Rebecca. What can I do for you?

W: I picked up my mail this morning to find that I had received some sort of housing fine. I keep a very clean dorm room and am generally quiet, so I have no idea what this fine is regarding. Can you tell me what this is about, please?

M: Okay. Please just bear with me one moment while I check my computer. Ah, it appears as though you are being fined for having a halogen lamp in your room. Is this true? Do you have a halogen lamp in your room?

W: Yes, I do, but are you saying I am being fined for having a lamp? Every student in my dormitory has a lamp in their room. How can it be that my lamp is more dangerous than the others? **That doesn't make any sense.**

M: You are not being fined for having just any lamp. You happen to have a halogen lamp, and the school does not allow these lamps because they are hazards. If left on too long, they can reach very high temperatures and may cause a fire if they come into contact with curtains or papers or something of that nature.

W: But it is only a little desk lamp that I use when I am studying late at night. It's tiny, and I make sure to place it as far away from any books or drapes as possible.

M: I am sure you are very responsible and try to be cautious, but I am afraid the school is very firm on this issue. A few years ago, a student disregarded this rule and unfortunately fell asleep with the halogen lamp on. The lamp was sitting very close to a pile of papers and ignited them. Two rooms in that dormitory burned down, and one student was taken to the hospital to be treated for minor burns. Did you not read the rules when you signed the dorm contract?

W: There were so many rules, and I read it so fast . . . I must have missed the clause about the halogen lamps.

M: The only thing I can suggest is that you stop using your halogen lamp immediately and buy a new desk lamp.

W: But what about my fine? Fifty dollars seems like a lot for a fine.

M: I'll make a deal with you, Rebecca. If you go out today and buy a new lamp and bring me the receipt as proof of your purchase, then I will waive your fine. Does that sound fair?

W: Oh, yes! That sounds very fair. I will go out right now and buy a new desk lamp and then come back here with the receipt. Thank you so much for being so understanding.

M: You are very welcome.

해석

W Student: 안녕하세요. 제 이름은 Rebecca Nelson이에요. 한 가지 문제가 있는데 도움을 주실 수 있는지 궁금해서요.

M Student Housing Office Employee: 그래요, Rebecca. 어떻게 도와 드릴까요?

W: 오늘 아침에 우편물을 받았는데, 주거 벌금 같은 것이 부과되었어요. 저는 방 청소도 잘 하고 보통 조용하게 지내는 편이라서 이 벌금이 무엇과 관련된 것인지 모르겠어요. 이것이 무엇에 대한 것인지 알려 주실 수 있나요?

M: 그래요. 컴퓨터로 확인해 볼 테니 잠시만 기다려 주세요. 아, 방에 할로겐 램프를 두었기 때문에 벌금이 부과된 것 같군요. 그런가요? 방에 할로겐 램프가 있어요?

W: 네, 그렇지만 램프 때문에 벌금이 부과되었다는 말씀이신가요? 제 기숙사에 있는 학생들 전부 방에 램프를 두고 있어요. 어떻게 제 램프가 다른 학생들의 램프보다 위험할 수 있나요? 말이 되지 않잖아요.

M: 아무 램프에나 벌금이 부과되는 것은 아니에요. 학생은 우연히도 할로겐 램프를 두게 되었는데, 그러한 램프는 위험하기 때문에 학교에서 허용되지가 않아요. 너무 오래 켜 둘 경우 온도가 크게 높아져서 커튼이나 종이, 혹은 그러한 성분의 물체에 닿으면 화재가 발생할 수도 있죠.

W: 하지만 밤늦게 공부하는 경우에만 사용하는 소형 책상 스탠드일 뿐이에요. 크기도 작은데다가, 저는 최대한 책이나 커튼에서 멀리 떨어진 곳에 놔 둔단 말이에요.

M: 학생은 분명 책임감이 크고 조심성이 많은 것으로 보이지만, 유감스럽게도 이러한 문제에 대한 학교측 입장은 매우 엄격해요. 몇 년 전 한 학생이 이러한 규정을 무시하고 안타깝게도 할로겐 램프를 켜 둔 채 잠이 들었어요. 램프가 종이 더미 가까이에 있어서 불이 났어요. 기숙사 두 개의 방이 불에 탔고, 한 명의 학생이 병원으로 옮겨져 가벼운 화상을 치료받아 했죠. 기숙사 계약서에 서명할 때 규정을 읽어보지 않았나요?

W: 규정이 너무 많은데다가 너무 빨리 읽어서… 할로겐 램프에 관한 조항은 분명 제가 놓친 것 같군요.

M: 제가 제안할 수 있는 건 당장 할로겐 램프의 사용을 중지하고 책상 스탠드를 새로 사야 한다는 것이에요.

W: 하지만 벌금은 어떻게 해야 하죠? 벌금으로 50달러는 너무 많은 것 같아요.

M: 학생과 협상을 할게요, Rebecca. 오늘 나가서 스탠드를 새로 구입하고 구입한 증거로 제게 영수증을 가져다 주면 제가 학생의 벌금을 면제해 줄게요. 괜찮게 들리나요?

W: 오, 그럼요! 정말 괜찮게 들리는군요. 지금 당장 가서 책상 스탠드를 새로 구입한 다음에 영수증을 가지고 다시 이곳으로 돌아올게요. 이해해 주셔서 정말 감사합니다.

M: 천만에요.

Summary Note

A

❶ housing fine
❷ clean
❸ halogen lamp
❹ fire hazards
❺ caused fire
❻ new lamp today

B

The student goes to the housing office and inquires about a fine she has received. The man checks his computer and finds that the student has been fined for keeping a halogen lamp in her dorm room. The student is shocked by the news. She does not understand how having a lamp could result in a fine. She tells the man that she is a very responsible student. The man explains that although the student may be cautious, halogen lamps pose a fire danger because the bulbs heat up to such a high degree. The man suggests that the student buy a new lamp as soon as possible. The student asks if she can keep the lamp if she is very careful where she places it, but the man stands by the school rules. The student then complains that the fine is too high, so the man offers to waive the fine if the student goes out and buys a new lamp immediately and then brings the man the receipt.

Exercise 2 1 Ⓐ 2 Ⓓ 3 Ⓑ p.142

Script 05-07

M Student: Hello, Professor Harris. I am here to inquire about how I can volunteer to become a host for visiting students. My roommate said he did it last semester and had a great time meeting and helping new students.

W Professor: David, I'm so glad you are willing to volunteer for this job. We are always looking for new students to help us, and you seem like a great candidate.

M: That is very kind of you, Professor Harris. But before I commit, can you tell me exactly what the job entails?

W: I would be happy to. Your main responsibility is to lead a group of prospective students around campus, show them the facilities, and answer any questions they might have along the way. You should be courteous and show enthusiasm when the students ask questions about our school.

M: I will show plenty of enthusiasm because I love our school. But would I be showing them not only dorms but also classrooms?

W: Oh, yes. We want visiting students to see as much of the campus as possible. We want the students to see everything from dorms and cafeterias to classrooms and the recreation center. This way, the students can get a feel for the entire operation of our campus.

M: That sounds like something I could do although I am not very good with big crowds. How many students are coming?

W: We have 200 prospective students scheduled to visit this coming week.

M: 200 students! I could never speak in front of that many people. I would be too nervous.

W: That is how many students are coming in total. We break the students down into smaller groups. Could you handle ten or fifteen in a group?

M: Oh, yes. That sounds much better. I thought you were asking me to lead a group of 200. That is about the same number of people who come to watch our dramatic performances.

W: Wonderful. Now, students have another option, which is to sit in on classes that interest them. So say a student comes and says he is interested in chemistry and would like to sit in on a class. Then, you would lead him to the appropriate lecture hall and retrieve him when the lecture is finished. This is optional, however, and not mandatory. You may have a lot of students who wish to sit in on a class in your group or you may have none at all.

M: I think I would like to do this. Is there anything else I need to know? What are the logistics of this particular group of 200 that is arriving?

W: There are two orientations scheduled during the week. One is on Monday afternoon, and the other is on Thursday evening. These orientations are mandatory, so make sure everyone in your group goes to one of them.

M: I will, Professor Harris, and thank you for considering me for this job.

W: You're welcome. I'm sure you'll do great.

해석

M Student: 안녕하세요, Harris 교수님. 자원봉사로 방문 학생을 맞이하는 방법을 여쭤 보려고 왔어요. 제 룸메이트가 지난 학기에 그렇게 했는데, 새로운 학생을 만나고 돕는 일이 정말 좋았다고 하더군요.

W Professor: David, 이번 일에 자원봉사를 하려고 한다니 기쁘네요. 도움을 줄 수 있는 새로운 학생들을 항상 찾고 있는데, 학생은 훌륭한 지원자가 될 것 같아요.

M: 정말 친절하시군요, Harris 교수님. 하지만 결정을 하기 전에 정확히 어떤 일을 하게 되는지 말씀해 주시겠어요?

W: 물론 그러죠. 주로 하게 될 일은 예비 신입생들과 함께 캠퍼스를 돌아다니면서 시설을 소개시켜 주고, 그러한 과정에서 생길 수도 있는 질문에 대답해 주는 것이에요. 학생들이 학교에 대한 질문을 하는 경우에는 정중한 태도로 열정적인 모습을 보여 주어야 하고요.

M: 저는 우리 학교를 좋아하니까 열정은 충분히 보여 줄 거예요. 하지만 기숙사뿐만 아니라 강의실도 보여 주어야 하나요?

W: 오, 그래요. 방문 학생들이 가능한 캠퍼스의 많은 부분을 보았으면 좋겠어요. 기숙사 및 교내 식당부터 강의실과 레크리에이션 센터까지 전부 보았으면 좋겠어요. 그렇게 하면 학생들이 우리 캠퍼스가 전체적으로 어떻게 돌아가는지 알 수 있을 거예요.

M: 제가 많은 사람들을 상대하는 일은 잘 못하지만 저도 할 수 있을 것처럼 들리는군요. 방문할 학생들이 몇 명인가요?

W: 이번 주에 200명의 예비 신입생들이 오기로 예정되어 있어요.

M: 200명이요! 그렇게 많은 사람들 앞에서는 말해 본 적이 없어요. 너무 긴장될 것 같아요.

W: 그 수는 학교에 올 전체 학생 수예요. 우리가 학생들을 소그룹으로 나누죠. 10명이나 15명 정도의 그룹은 상대할 수 있겠죠?

M: 오, 네. 훨씬 나을 것 같군요. 저보고 200명을 데리고 다니라는 말씀인 줄 알았어요. 그 정도면 저희의 연극 공연을 보러 오는 사람들의 수와 거의 비슷하네요.

W: 잘 됐군요. 자, 학생들에게는 또 다른 선택권이 있는데, 관심이 있는 수업에 들어가는 것이죠. 그래서 가령 한 학생이 와서 자신은 화학에 관심이 있고 수업을 들어보고 싶다고 말한다고 가정해 보죠. 그러면 학생은 이 학생을 적절한 강의실로 데리고 가서 강의가 끝난 후 그를 데리고 와야 할 거예요. 하지만 이것은 선택 사항이지 의무 사항은 아니에요. 학생의 그룹에 수업을 듣고자 하는 학생이 많을 수도 있고, 아니면 전혀 없을 수도 있어요.

M: 이 일은 해 보고 싶군요. 제가 더 알아야 할 것이 있나요? 도착할 이번 200명의 그룹에 대한 계획은 무엇인가요?

W: 해당 주에 두 번의 오리엔테이션이 예정되어 있어요. 하나는 월요일 오후에, 그리고 다른 하나는 화요일 저녁에 있죠. 이 오리엔테이션은 의무적인 것이기 때문에 학생 그룹에 소속되어 있는 모두가 반드시 이 중 하나에 참석하도록 해야 해요.

M: 그럴게요, Harris 교수님. 그리고 이번 일에 저를 참여시켜 주셔서 감사합니다.

W: 천만에요. 잘 해낼 것으로 믿어요.

Summary Note

A

❶ volunteering
❷ visiting students
❸ around campus
❹ courteous
❺ enthusiastic
❻ 10-15 students

B

The student wants to volunteer to help host visiting students at his college, so he visits the professor to see how he can do that. The professor tells the student that he would be responsible for leading a small group of students on a tour around campus. The professor also says that the students have the option of sitting in on a class of their choice, but this is not obligatory. The student says he will accept the job, so the professor gives him the final details, which are to have each of his students attend at least one of two mandatory orientations, either on Monday afternoon or on Thursday at night.

Exercise 3 1 Ⓑ 2 Ⓐ 3 Ⓓ p.144

Script 05-08

M Post Office Employee: Yes? How can I help you?

W Student: Hello. My name is Cindy Anderson. I am going to study in Spain for three months next semester, and I am a little worried about my mail situation. I don't want any of my mail to be misplaced while I am gone. **What are my options for how my mail will be handled when I am away?**

M: You have one of two choices. First, you can give us the address you will be living at in Spain, and we can have your mail forwarded there, or you can choose to have your mail held here at the post office.

W: You will hold my mail here indefinitely?

M: No, not indefinitely. We will only hold mail for an individual for three months, but that seems to be the exact amount of time you will be gone. For three months, right?

W: Yes, I suppose that is an option. I guess I really don't know what to do. **What would you decide to do if you were in my position?**

M: I guess that depends on if you have anything of value coming through the mail that you would urgently need within the next three months. If the answer to that question is yes, then I would suggest you have us forward your mail to Spain. If you are only receiving a few items in the mail and they are not very urgent, then I would suggest you just have us hold your mail since it will take a while for your forwarded mail to arrive in Spain. I traveled to Italy when I was in college, and I chose to have my mail held until I returned.

W: I really don't have anything of urgency coming through the mail in the next three months, so I guess I will go ahead and have you hold my mail for me.

M: Okay, that sounds fine. If you could just fill out this form for me, that would be wonderful. Oh! I almost forgot. If you choose to have your mail held here, I must tell you that if you currently receive the school newspaper, I am afraid we cannot hold it as it would take up too much room in our storage area.

W: That is okay. I will just go ahead and cancel my school newspaper subscription right now. I don't read it regularly anyway. I would also like to cancel my subscription to any school event fliers since I won't be here to go to the events anyway.

M: Excellent. That sounds good. You are all set. When you get back from Spain, just pop into the office, and we will have a tub of mail waiting for you.

W: Thank you very much. I appreciate your time.

M: You are very welcome. Have a great trip!

해석

M Post Office Employee: 네? 무엇을 도와 드릴까요?

W Student: 안녕하세요. 제 이름은 Cindy Anderson이에요. 다음 학기에 3개월 동안 스페인에서 공부할 계획인데, 우편물이 좀 걱정되어서요. 제가 없는 동안 우편물을 잃어 버리고 싶지는 않거든요. 제가 없는 경우 제 우편물을 처리할 수 있는 방법으로 어떤 것들이 있나요?

M: 두 가지 중 하나를 선택할 수 있어요. 먼저 스페인에서 지낼 집주소를 저희에게 알려 주시면 그곳으로 우편물을 전달해 드릴 수 있고, 아니면 이곳 우체국에 보관하는 것을 선택하실 수도 있죠.

W: 이곳에서 제 우편물을 무기한으로 보관해 주시나요?

M: 아니요, 무기한은 아니에요. 개인 우편물은 3개월까지만 보관해 드리는데, 학생이 떠나 있는 기간과 정확히 일치하는 것 같군요. 3개월이죠, 그렇죠?

W: 네, 그렇게 할 수도 있겠네요. 사실 어떻게 해야 할지 잘 모르겠어요. 만약 선생님께서 제 입장이라면 어떤 결정을 내리실 건가요?

M: 3개월 이내에 우편으로 학생에게 급하게 필요한 물품이 도착할 것인지에 달린 것 같아요. 이 문제에 '네'라고 답한다면 우편물을 스페인으로 전달하는 쪽을 추천할게요. 우편으로 받을 물품이 얼마 되지 않고 그다지 급한 것이 아니라면, 전달된 우편물이 스페인에 도착하기까지 시간이 좀 걸리기 때문에, 우편물을 보관하는 쪽을 추천할게요. 제가 대학을 다닐 때 이탈리아로 여행을 떠났는데, 저는 돌아올 때까지 제 우편물을 우체국에 보관하는 쪽을 택했어요.

W: 다음 3개월 동안 긴급히 받아야 하는 우편물은 없기 때문에 저도 제 우편물을 우체국에 보관하도록 해야 할 것 같군요.

M: 그래요, 잘 선택했어요. 이 서류만 작성해 주시면 좋을 것 같군요. 오! 깜빡 잊을 뻔 했네요. 이곳에 우편물을 보관하기로 하신 경우, 현재 학교 신문을 받고 계시다면, 신문이 보관 장소에서 자리를 너무 많이 차지하기 때문에 신문은 보관해 드릴 수 없다는 점을 말씀드려야 할 것 같아요.

W: 그건 괜찮아요. 지금 바로 학교 신문의 구독 신청을 취소할게요. 잘 읽지도 않거든요. 학교 행사에도 갈 수 없을 테니 교내 행사들의 안내서도 구독 신청을 취소해야겠어요.

M: 잘 생각했어요. 그게 좋겠군요. 이제 다 되었어요. 스페인에서 돌아오셔서 우체국에 들르시면 우편물들이 학생을 기다리고 있을 거예요.

W: 정말 감사합니다. 시간 내 주셔서 감사해요.

M: 천만에요. 잘 다녀오세요!

Summary Note

A

❶ campus post office
❷ a semester
❸ receiving mail
❹ three months
❺ holding mail
❻ student newspaper subscription

B

The student goes to the school post office because she is leaving the country for three months and is concerned about what will happen to her mail during that time. The student asks the post office employee about her options. The man tells her that she either has the option of having her mail forwarded to Spain or having the post office hold her mail. The only provisions are that if the she chooses to have her mail held, the post office can only hold it for up to three months, and it cannot hold the school newspaper as it would take up too much space. The student tells the man that because she does not have anything urgent coming to her in the mail, she would like to have her mail held. She tells the man that she currently receives the school newspaper but will cancel her subscription since she does not read it regularly.

Exercise 4 1 Ⓐ 2 Ⓑ 3 Ⓒ p.146

Script 05-09

W Professor: Hello, John. I see you made an appointment with me today. What can I help you with?

M Student: Hello, Professor Higgins. Yes, I did make an appointment with you, and the reason is that I am slightly baffled by my final grade in your biology class, especially since I did so well on the last few tests. I felt like I understood all of the concepts this year and cannot understand why you marked me so poorly.

W: Well, let me just go into my computer, John, and check my records. You never know I have been known to make mistakes in my grade book in the past. Let me see . . . Yes, it looks like you had some outstanding scores on the last few tests, the last two in particular, when we were studying microorganisms.

M: Exactly! I really enjoyed learning about amoebas. **Do you think it could be some kind of scoring error?**

W: Possibly, but . . . Oops! Look here. When I view your attendance record for this semester, it shows that you missed more than a third of my classes. This is the reason that your grade is so low.

M: But, Professor Higgins, why does attendance matter? Isn't the important thing that I earned good test scores? It proves that I am learning the material.

W: Yes, John, you are learning the material that can be found in the textbooks I provide, but when you do not attend class, you are still missing out on the lively discussions we have that add to your overall knowledge of the material. For example, during one of the classes in which you were absent, a student brought in an interesting article about microbes that happened to be in the newspaper. We were then able to apply the concepts we learned through the lecture and out of the textbook to a current-events article that dealt with cutting-edge research. What good are all of the things I am teaching if they are never applied to the thoughts and research of today?

M: I guess I never thought that I'd miss too much from the discussions, but it's apparent that I did.

W: It also appears as though quite a few of the classes you missed were classes in which we conducted labs. These are a vital part to my course as they provide hands-on experience. The fact that you missed them would be comparable to the analogy of getting 100% on a written driving exam but never having actually driven an automobile. Would I trust you to drive me around town? I don't think so.

M: I see your point, Professor Higgins. I am sorry I missed so many of your classes, and I now realize why my grade was lower than what I had anticipated.

W: It is okay, John. I just hope that our conversation has made you realize the importance of attending your classes.

해석

W Professor: 안녕하세요, John. 오늘 저와 약속이 있다는 건 알고 있었어요. 어떻게 도와 드릴까요?

M Student: 안녕하세요, Higgins 교수님. 네, 교수님과 약속을 잡은 이유는 교수님의 생물학 수업에서 제 기말 고사 성적이 약간 의외이기 때문인데, 특히 저는 지난 몇 차례의 시험을 정말로 잘 봤거든요. 올해 저는 모든 개념들을 이해하고 있다고 생각해서 교수님께서 왜 그처럼 낮은 점수를 주셨는지 이해가 가지 않아요.

W: 음, John, 컴퓨터로 들어가서 기록을 확인해 볼게요. 결코 몰랐겠지만 과거에도 제가 성적표에 실수를 한 적이 있거든요. 지금 보니… 네, 지난 몇 번의 시험에서, 특히 미생물을 배웠을 때 본 지난 두 번 시험에서, 점수가 굉장히 높았던 것 같군요.

M: 맞아요! 아메바 수업이 정말 재미있었어요. 채점하실 때 실수가 있었던 것 같나요?

W: 그럴 수도 있는데… 이런! 여기를 보세요. 이번 학기 학생의 출석 기록을 보니 제 수업의 3분의 1 이상을 듣지 않았군요. 학생 성적이 그처럼 낮은 이유가 바로 이 때문이에요.

M: 하지만 Higgins 교수님, 출석률이 왜 중요하죠? 시험 성적을 잘 받은 것은 중요하지 않나요? 제가 수업 내용을 잘 이해하고 있다는 점을 입증해 주잖아요.

W: 그래요, John, 학생이 제 수업 교재에서 찾아볼 수 있는 내용들은 잘 이해하고 있지만, 수업에 참여하지 않으면 수업 내용에 대한 전반적인 지식을 넓힐 수 있는 활발한 토론에 참여하지 못하게 되죠. 예를 들어 학생이 빠졌던 한 수업에서는 한 학생이 신문에 실린 미생물에 대한 흥미로운 기사를 가지고 왔어요. 그래서 우리는 강의와 교재에서 배운 개념을 최첨단 연구를 다룬 시사 문제 기사에 적용시킬 수 있었죠. 오늘날의 사고와 연구에 적용시키지 못한다면 제가 가르치는 모든 것들이 무슨 소용이 있겠어요?

M: 토론에서 제가 그처럼 많은 것을 놓치고 있는지는 결코 몰랐는데, 확실히 그랬던 것 같군요.

W: 게다가 학생이 놓친 몇 개의 수업들은 실험이 진행되었던 수업으로 보여요. 실험 수업에서는 직접적인 경험을 할 수 있기 때문에 실험 수업은 제 수업에서 필수적인 부분이죠. 이때 출석하지 않았다는 것은 운전 면허 시험의 필기 시험에서 100점을 받았지만 실제로 운전을 해 본 적은 없는 경우와 마찬가지 일 거예요. 제가 학생을 믿고 학생 차로 시내를 한 바퀴 돌 수 있을까요? 그렇지 않을 거예요.

M: 무슨 말씀이신지 알겠습니다. Higgins 교수님. 수업에 너무 많이 빠져서 죄송하고, 이제 제 예상보다 성적이 낮게 나온 이유를 알겠어요.

W: 괜찮아요, John. 이번 대화를 통해 수업에 참석하는 것이 얼마나 중요한지 학생이 깨달았으면 좋겠어요.

Summary Note

A

❶ biology grade
❷ low score
❸ good
❹ very bad
❺ importance of attendance
❻ important
❼ participate in
❽ hands-on experience

B

The student makes an appointment with his professor because he is confused by his final score in her class. The student points out that he received very good test scores on the last few tests, so he cannot understand why his final grade was so low, especially when he enjoyed learning about so many of the concepts. The professor checks her records to find that the student did receive good test scores but failed to attend a third of her classes. The student does not see how this is a problem. He believes that if his test scores are good, it proves he is learning all of the material. The professor points out that what the student is missing when he does not attend classes are lively discussions, evidence of new and cutting-edge research, and important hands-on experience in labs, which can be applied to the ideas and research of the current time.

Exercises with Long Lectures

Exercise 1 1 Ⓐ 2 Ⓐ 3 Ⓑ, Ⓒ p.148

Script 05-10

M Professor: Okay, everyone. Have you all handed in your homework assignments? Please do so now because I will not accept any late ones as soon as I start my lecture . . . Nobody . . . ? Great. Let's get started then. We have a busy day, and I need to talk about several things with you.

We're going to start by discussing the carbon cycle. Now, uh, you all know what the water cycle is. It's important to life on the planet. And so is the carbon cycle. Let's remember that we humans are carbon-based lifeforms. As such, carbon in all of its forms is of incredible importance to us.

First, let me tell you a bit about carbon. Its atomic number is six, and its symbol on the periodic chart is C. It's one of the most abundant elements on the planet. In its elemental form, it can be graphite, diamond, and fullerene. These are some of its allotropes. Ah, allotropes are structurally different forms of the same element. For instance, diamond is transparent and extremely hard whereas graphite is black and opaque. Yet they are both forms of the element carbon. Carbon combines with other elements to create various carbonates in minerals, and in its gaseous form, it's typically carbon dioxide. Of course, carbon monoxide is another form of carbon as a gas.

Now, uh, the carbon cycle. What is it . . . ? It's the process through which carbon compounds change forms as they move through the Earth's atmosphere, biosphere, geosphere, and hydrosphere. There are a few steps in this process, so please listen carefully as I describe them.

Let's start with carbon dioxide gas, which exists in the atmosphere. Can anyone tell me how it's used?

W Student: Plants, sir. Trees, bushes, flowers, and other plants use carbon dioxide when they undergo photosynthesis.

M: Perfect. Carbon dioxide is an extremely important gas because without it, plants would not be able to undergo photosynthesis. And here's something interesting. Do you know what percentage of the Earth's atmosphere is carbon dioxide? I bet most of you have no idea.

W: Um . . . three percent?

M: **You're off by a tremendous amount.** On the contrary, its 0.04 percent. That's a miniscule amount, yet it's enough to support all of the green plants on the planet. Let me remind you about what happens in photosynthesis. Plants use carbon dioxide, water, and the sun's light to produce glucose, which they use as food, and oxygen, which they emit and which people and animals breathe. That's the first step in the carbon cycle.

So plants absorb carbon during photosynthesis. Then, various plants are consumed by animals, so the carbon then accumulates into their bodies. So now we have carbon both in plants and animals. Over time, the plants and the animals die. As their bodies decompose, some of the carbon in them is released as a gas, so it reenters the atmosphere. Other carbon is not released as a gas but remains in the ground. Over time, it transforms into various fossil fuels, such as gas, coal, and oil. These fuels are then used by humans, which produces carbon dioxide gas that reenters the atmosphere.

W: I heard that carbon gets absorbed in the ocean. Is that a part of the carbon cycle as well?

M: It sure is. The ocean actually takes in a lot of carbon. Various marine animals then convert carbon into calcium carbonate. This is used to create the hard shells of clams, oysters, and other shellfish. When they die, their shells remain. Let me tell you what happens next. I think you'll find it interesting.

해석

M Professor: 좋아요, 여러분. 모두들 과제를 제출하셨나요? 강의를 시작한 후에는 받지 않을 테니 지금 제출하시기 바랍니다… 없나요…? 좋습니다. 그럼 시작해 보죠. 오늘은 바쁜 하루로, 여러분들과 논의할 것들이 몇 가지 있습니다.

탄소 순환에 관한 논의로 시작할게요. 자, 어, 여러분 모두 물의 순환이 무엇인지 아실 것입니다. 지구의 생명체에게 중요한 것이죠. 그리고 탄소 순환도 마찬가지예요. 우리 인간은 탄소를 기반으로 한 생명체입니다. 또한 어떤 형태이든지 탄소는 우리에게 극도로 중요합니다.

먼저 탄소에 대해 잠시 말씀을 드릴게요. 탄소의 원자 번호는 6이며 주기율표 상의 기호는 C입니다. 지구에서 가장 풍부한 원소 중 하나이죠. 원소 상태에서 탄소는 흑연, 다이아몬드, 그리고 풀러린으로 존재할 수 있어요. 이들은 탄소의 동소체들입니다. 아, 동소체란 구조는 서로 다르지만 같은 원소들로 이루어진 것이에요. 예를 들어 다이아몬드는 투명하고 매우 단단한 반면에 흑연은 까맣고 불투명합니다. 하지만 이들 모두 탄소 원소로 이루어진 형태들이에요. 탄소는 다른 원소들과 결합해서 광물질 형태로는 다양한 탄산염을, 가스 형태로는 보통 이산화탄소를 만들어 내죠. 물론, 일산화탄소 역시 탄소로 이루어진 기체입니다.

자, 어, 탄소 순환이요. 이것이 무엇일까요…? 그것은 탄소 화합물이 지구의 대기, 생물권, 그리고 수권에서 이동할 때 그 형태가 바뀌는 과정이에요. 이러한 과정에는 몇 가지 단계가 있기 때문에 제가 드리는 설명을 주의해서 들으시기 바랍니다.

대기에 존재하는 이산화탄소 기체로 시작해 보죠. 어떻게 이용되는지 아는 사람이 있나요?

W Student: 식물입니다, 교수님. 나무, 관목, 꽃, 그리고 기타 식물들이 광합성을 할 때 이산화탄소를 이용하죠.

M: 완벽해요. 이산화탄소는 극도로 중요한 기체인데, 이산화탄소가 없다면 식물들은 광합성을 할 수 없을 거예요. 그리고 흥미로운 점이 있습니다. 지구 대기의 몇 퍼센트가 이산화탄소인지 아시나요? 여러분 대부분이 분명 모르실 것 같군요.

W: 음… 3퍼센트요?

M: 차이가 엄청나게 크군요. 그와 달리 0.04퍼센트입니다. 극소량이지만 지구의 모든 녹색 식물을 부양할 수 있는 충분한 양이죠. 광합성으로 어떤 일이 일어나는지 상기시켜 드리겠습니다. 식물들이 이산화탄소, 물, 그리고 햇빛을 이용해 포도당과 산소를 만들어 내는데, 포도당은 식물이 양분으로 이용하고, 식물에서 방출되는 산소는 인간과 동물들의 호흡에 사용되죠. 이것이 탄소 순환의 첫 번째 단계입니다.

따라서 식물들이 광합성을 하는 동안 탄소를 흡수합니다. 그 후 다양한 식물들이 동물의 먹이가 되면 탄소가 동물의 체내에 축적됩니다. 그러면 이제 식물과 동물 모두에 탄소가 들어 있게 되죠. 시간이 지나면서 식물과 동물이 죽습니다. 이들의 신체가 부패하면 체내의 일부 탄소가 기체로서 방출되어 다시 대기 속으로 들어가게 되죠. 기체로 방출되지 않고 땅에 머물러 있는 탄소도 있어요. 시간이 지나면 이러한 탄소는 가스, 석탄, 그리고 석유와 같은 다양한 화석 연료가 됩니다. 이러한 연료들은 이후 인간에 의해 사용되는데, 이로써 이산화탄소가 배출되고 이는 다시 대기 속으로 들어가게 되죠.

W: 탄소가 바다에 흡수된다는 이야기를 들었어요. 그것도 탄소 순환의 일부인가요?

M: 그럼요. 실제로 바다가 많은 양의 탄소를 흡수합니다. 그러면 다양한 해양 동물들이 탄소를 탄산칼륨으로 변화시키죠. 이는 조개, 굴, 그리고 기타 조개류의 단단한 껍질을 만드는데 사용됩니다. 이들이 죽으면 껍질이 남게 되죠. 그 다음에 어떤 일이 일어나는지 말씀을 드리겠습니다. 여러분도 꽤 흥미롭게 생각하실 것 같군요.

Summary Note

A

❶ carbon cycle
❷ carbon-based lifeforms
❸ other elements
❹ Carbon dioxide
❺ undergo photosynthesis
❻ fossil fuels
❼ atmosphere
❽ Oceans

B

The professor says that he will cover the carbon cycle. Since humans are carbon-based lifeforms, it is of great importance. Carbon has an atomic number of six, and its symbol on the periodic chart is C. It can be found in elemental forms as graphite, diamond, and fullerene, it can be carbonates when it combines with elements, and its gaseous form is often carbon dioxide. The carbon cycle begins when plants take in carbon dioxide when they undergo photosynthesis. Then, plants are eaten by animals, so both plants and animals have carbon. When the plants and animals die, some carbon is released as a gas. Other carbon remains in the ground and becomes fossil fuels. When the fossil fuels are used by humans, the carbon returns to the atmosphere as a gas. The ocean can also absorb lots of carbon, which is used by shellfish to create their hard shells.

Exercise 2 1 Ⓓ 2 Ⓒ 3 Ⓐ p.150

Script 05-11

W Professor: Right now, I would like to leave the planet Earth and talk to you about a weather phenomenon that is known to happen on the planet Mars. I'd like to tell you about something called a Martian dust devil. Now, uh, before I get into this fascinating phenomenon, I think I should talk about dust devils and how they appear on our own planet. Can any of you tell me what a dust devil is? Harold, I wonder if you know the answer.

M Student: I'm not really sure, but I think a dust devil is like a tornado.

W: You're on the right track. However, it's not precisely like a tornado for a couple of reasons. To begin with, a tornado forms a downdraft from a thundercloud while a dust devil forms an updraft when hot air from the surface of the ground rises quickly into a pocket of cooler low-pressure air. In addition, for the most part, dust devils are relatively harmless, but I doubt anyone here would ever call a tornado harmless.

M: Wait a minute. I think I've seen a dust devil before. My family was on a trip in Australia, and I saw this swirling cloud of dust moving over the ground while we were in the Outback. It looked really cool. Was that a dust devil?

W: Yes, from your description, what you saw was a dust devil. In fact, they are quite prevalent in Australia. Now, uh, let me clarify a couple of things regarding dust devils so that none of you are confused. A dust devil forms when very hot air rises quickly and passes through cooler air. This causes the air to rotate, thereby creating a swirling effect. The air then swirls in a column, and the dust devil stays intact as more hot air rushes toward the vortex to replace the moving air. This forms something like a funnel, which is why people sometimes mistake dust devils for tornadoes.

Dust devils are not stationary either. They are capable of movement. The fast spinning or swirling gives dust devils momentum, and that is what causes them to appear as though they are gliding over the ground. Most dust devils are only a few meters in height, but the dust devils that were filmed on Mars were much larger.

M: How did scientists get pictures of dust devils on Mars? I mean, uh, as far as I know, we haven't landed any astronauts on Mars.

W: You're correct about that. The images were taken by various space probes that were sent to the planet. Remember that the United States has been sending probes to Mars since the 1960s. In recent years, rovers and even a flying drone have made it to Mars, where they have made some important discoveries regarding Martian dust devils. What was crucial for astronauts and space engineers to discover was that because dust devils on Mars can be up to fifty times wider and up to ten times higher than dust devils on the Earth, Martian dust devils pose a serious threat to terrestrial technology sent to Mars. However, on one occasion, a Martian dust devil actually helped clean the solar panels of the robot *Spirit Rover*.

M: So the dust devil helped the space mission?

W: It did indeed, and it also gave scientists valuable information about how dust devils on Mars compare to dust devils on the Earth.

해석

W Professor: 이제 지구 행성에 대한 논의는 그만하고 화성 행성에서 발생하는 것으로 알려진 기상 현상에 대해 이야기를 하고자 합니다. 화성의 회오리 바람이라고 불리는 현상에 대해 말씀을 드리려고 해요. 자, 어, 이 매력적인 현상을 설명하기 전에, 회오리 바람에 대해서, 그리고 이들이 우리 행성에서는 어떻게 보이는지에 대해서 말씀을 드려야 할 것 같네요. 여러분 중에 회오리 바람이 무엇인지 말해 볼 사람이 있나요? Harold, 답을 알고 있는지 궁금하군요.

M Student: 확실하지는 않지만 회오리 바람은 토네이도와 같은 것이라고 생각해요.

W: 방향은 잘 잡았군요. 하지만 두 가지 이유에서 토네이도와 똑같지는 않아요. 우선, 토네이도는 뇌운에서 아래쪽으로 하강 기류가 만들어질 때 발생하는 반면, 회오리 바람은 지표면의 뜨거운 공기가 빠르게 상승해 보다 차갑고 저기압 상태인 기류 안으로 들어갈 때 발생합니다. 게다가, 대부분의 경우, 회오리 바람은 비교적 해를 끼치지 않지만, 이곳에 계신 여러분들 중 누구도 토네이도가 무해하다고 말씀하시지는 않을 것 같군요.

M: 잠시만요. 제가 전에 회오리 바람을 본 것 같아요. 저희 가족이 호주를 여행하고 있었는데, 아웃백에 있었을 당시 그러한 소용돌이 형태의 모래 구름이 지면 위로 올라가는 것을 보았어요. 정말로 멋져 보였죠. 그것이 회오리 바람이었을까요?

W: 네, 학생의 설명으로 볼 때 학생이 본 것은 회오리 바람이었어요. 실제로 호주에서는 꽤 일반적인 현상이죠. 자, 어, 여러분 모두 헷갈리지 않도록, 회오리 바람과 관련해서 두 가지 사항을 설명해 드릴게요. 회오리 바람은 뜨거운 바람이 빠르게 상승하면서 보다 차가운 공기를 통과할 때 발생합니다. 이로써 차가운 공기가 회전하게 되고, 그 결과 소용돌이 효과가 만들어지죠. 그런 다음 공기가 기둥 형태로 소용돌이를 치고 보다 뜨거운 공기가 소용돌이를 따라 위로 올라가서 이동 중인 공기를 대체하게 되면 회오리 바람의 형태가 유지됩니다. 이로써 깔때기와 같은 형태가 만들어지는데, 이러한 점 때문에 사람들이 때때로 회오리 바람과 토네이도를 혼동하는 것이에요.

회오리 바람 역시 정지해 있지 않습니다. 이동할 수 있어요. 빠른 회전, 즉 소용돌이로 인해 회오리 바람이 추진력을 얻게 되고, 이로써 이들이 마치 지면 위를 활강하는 것처럼 보이게 됩니다. 대부분의 회오리 바람의 높이는 불과 몇 미터에 불과하지만, 화성에서 촬영된 모래 바람은 훨씬 더 크기가 컸어요.

M: 과학자들이 어떻게 화성의 회오리 바람을 촬영했나요? 제 말은, 어, 제가 알기로는 화성에 우주 비행사들이 착륙한 적이 없었던 것 같아서요.

W: 그 점에 대해서는 학생 말이 맞아요. 이미지들은 그 행성으로 보내진 다양한 우주 탐사선들에 의해 촬영되었어요. 1960년대 이후로 미국은 계속해서 화성에 탐사선을 보내고 있다는 점을 기억하세요. 최근에는 탐사 차량 및 심지어는 드론 비행체들이 화성에 도착해서 화성의 회오리 바람에 관한 몇 가지 중요한 사실들을 밝혀 냈습니다. 우주 비행사와 우주 항공 기술자들이 알아낸 중요한 점은 화성의 회오리 바람이 지구의 회오리 바람보다 최대 50배 더 넓고 10배 더 높기 때문에 화성에 보내진 지상 기술 장비에 심각한 위협이 된다는 것이었어요. 하지만 한 번은 화성의 회오리 바람이 *스피릿 로버*라는 로봇의 태양 전지판을 청소하는 데 실제로 도움을 주기도 했습니다.

M: 그러면 회오리 바람이 우주 탐사에 도움이 되었던 것이죠?

W: 실제로 그랬고, 또한 과학자들에게 화성의 회오리 바람이 지구의 회오리 바람과 어떻게 다른지에 대한 귀중한 정보도 주었습니다.

Summary Note

A

❶ Martian dust devils
❷ tornadoes
❸ cooler air
❹ Australia
❺ cooler air
❻ swirling effect
❼ funnel
❽ space probes

B

Dust devils are formed when very hot air near the ground forms an updraft into cooler, low pressure air. The quickly rising hot air creates a swirling motion that forms into a funnel-shaped column of air capable of moving along the ground due to air speed and friction. Dust devils on the Earth are relatively small and harmless while Martian dust devils, as evidenced by pictures from space probes, can be up to fifty times wider and ten times higher than their earthbound cousins. Some concern arose regarding the safety of terrestrial space equipment on Mars should a dust devil form and destroy the equipment due to its size and power. However, there was an instance when a Martian dust devil actually cleaned the solar panels on a robot.

Exercise 3 1 Ⓒ 2 Ⓒ 3 Ⓓ p.152

Script 05-12

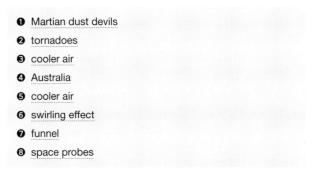

W Professor: Today, class, I am going to be speaking to you about the Industrial Revolution. The term "industrial revolution" refers to the technological, social, economic, and cultural changes that occurred in England in the late eighteenth century. This change eventually spread around the world, creating many big cities based upon the ideals of manufacturing and capitalism. Prior to the Industrial Revolution, the production and harvesting of products was completed through manual labor. The Industrial Revolution replaced this manpower with machine power.

One of the initial, and perhaps most important, developments of the Industrial Revolution was the steam engine. This advance in transportation allowed for the faster delivery of manufactured goods. However, the steam engine wasn't only used for transportation but instead for the construction of machine engines that enabled faster production. For example, before the Industrial Revolution, most tasks were undertaken by either wind or water power or by the sheer strength of man or horse. But in 1698, a man by the name of Thomas Savery constructed the first steam-powered engine in London. His idea was to create a machine that would pump water from mines. Different types of steam engines were created over the following hundred years, culminating with a Cornish blacksmith named Richard Trevithick's work on steam boilers, which eventually led to the production of locomotive steam engines.

The development of the steam engine sparked a host of other changes technologically, socially, and economically within British culture. Steam engine technology led to the development of factories, where products were turned out in the hundreds or even thousands. The first manufacturing change involved the production of textiles in the English city of Manchester. Before the revolution, British textile manufacturing was handled by individual artisans who did spinning and weaving in their own homes. This meant that the process of making a pair of pants or a shirt could take days or even weeks depending on how fast the artisan was at his trade. Imagine having to wait weeks for a new pair of pants, when the only pair of pants you owned was suddenly unwearable. In the mid-eighteenth century, two Englishmen from Birmingham, Lewis Paul and John Wyatt, advanced the process slightly by developing a roller spinning machine and the fly-and-bobbin system of making clothes; however, it wasn't until Richard Arkwright created the cotton mill, which ultimately utilized steam power for its production, that cotton production became a mechanized industry.

The factory industry eventually gave rise to what we now know as the modern city. Manchester, for example, due to its cotton mills, became known as Cottonopolis because there were so many factories producing textiles. However, these early cities were not as clean or well-kept as the ones we are familiar with today. Along with the growth of industry came the proliferation of sometimes harsh or dirty living conditions. Children were forced to work long hours in factories until the Factory Act of 1833 came into effect. It stated that children under nine were not allowed to work and that children over nine were not to work at night or for more than twelve-hour shifts. Trade unions were also born out of the Industrial Revolution, giving workers rights and freedoms that they had not had in the past.

Prior to the Industrial Revolution, working conditions for British workers were not favorable. Men, women, and children worked long hours for little money. The poor conditions of the working class prompted many educated British historians and authors to write Marxist and communist manifestos lamenting the state of the working class. And even those that were not British, such as Friedrich Engels, a German political philosopher, used England as a model for change when he wrote *The Condition of the Working Class in England* in 1844. Within this text, Engels spoke of the Industrial Revolution and how it was to change the whole fabric of society.

해석

W Professor: 여러분, 오늘은 산업 혁명에 대한 이야기를 하려고 해요. "산업 혁명"이라는 용어는 18세기 후반 영국에서 일어났던 기술적, 사회적, 경제적, 그리고 문화적 변화들을 지칭합니다. 이러한 변화는 결국 전 세계로 확대되었고, 이로써 제조업과 자본주의라는 이상에 기반하여 많은 대도시들이 생겨났어요. 산업 혁명 이전에는 제품의 생산과 산출이 육체 노동을 통해 이루어졌습니다. 산업 혁명은 이러한 인력을 기계의 힘으로 대체시켰죠.

산업 혁명에서 최초이자 아마도 가장 중요한 개발품 중 하나는 증기 기관이었어요. 수송 분야에서 이러한 발전이 이루어짐에 따라 제품이 보다 빠르게 운송될 수 있었습니다. 하지만 증기 기관은 수송 목적만이 아니라 기계 엔진의 제작에서도 사용되었는데, 이로써 보다 빠른 생산이 가능해졌어요. 예를 들어 산업 혁명 이전에는 대부분의 일이 풍력이나 수력, 또는 순전히 사람의 힘이나 말의 힘으로 이루어졌어요. 하지만 1698년 토머스 세이버리라는 사람이 런던에서 최초의 증기 기관을 만들었습니다. 그의 아이디어는 광산에서 물을 퍼 올릴 수 있는 기계를 만드는 것이었죠. 이후 100년에 걸쳐 다양한 종류의 증기 기관이 만들어졌고, 콘월 지방의 대장장이였던 리처드 트레비식이 스팀 보일러를 개발하면서 증기 기관은 정점을 맞이했는데, 이로써 마침내 증기 기관차의 엔진이 탄생하게 되었습니다.

증기 기관의 개발로 영국 문화에서 기타 여러 가지의 기술적, 사회적, 그리고 경제적인 변화들이 나타났어요. 증기 기관 기술은 공장의 발전으로 이어졌고, 공장에서는 수백 개의, 심지어는 수천 개의 제품들이 쏟아져 나왔습니다. 제조업에서의 첫 번째 변화는 영국 맨체스터시의 직물 생산과 관련된 것이었어요. 산업 혁명 이전 영국의 직물 제조업은 자신의 집에서 직접 실을 잣고 직물을 짰던 개개 장인들에 의해 이루어졌습니다. 이는 바지 한 벌이나 셔츠 한 벌을 만드는 과정에, 장인이 일을 얼마나 빨리 하는가에 따라, 며칠에서 심지어는 몇 주의 시간이 걸릴 수도 있다는 점을 의미했죠. 가지고 있는 한 벌뿐인 바지를 갑자기 입지 못하게 된 경우, 새 바지를 구하기까지 몇 주를 기다려야 한다고 생각해 보세요. 18세기 중반 버밍험 출신의 두 영국인인 루이스 폴과 존 와이어트가 롤러 방적기와 플라이앤보빈 의류 제작 시스템을 개발함으로써 그러한 과정이 개선되었습니다. 하지만 리처드 오크라이트가 결국 증기 기관을 이용해 면을 생산하는 방적 공장을 지은 후에야 면 생산이 기계화되었죠.

공장 산업으로 인해 드디어 오늘날 우리가 현대적인 도시라고 알고 있는 도시들이 탄생했어요. 예를 들어 맨체스터는 그곳의 방적 공장들로 인해 코트노폴리스라고 알려지게 되었는데, 그 이유는 그곳에 직물을 생산하는 공장이 너무 많았기 때문이었습니다. 하지만 이러한 초창기 도시들은 오늘날 우리가 알고 있는 도시만큼 깨끗하거나 잘 관리되지 못했어요. 산업의 성장과 함께 때로는 불쾌하거나 불결한 생활 환경이 확대되었습니다. 1833년 공장 조례가 시행되기 전까지는 아이들도 장시간에 걸쳐 공장에서 일을 해야 했어요. 이 조례는 9세 미만의 아동은 일을 할 수 없으며, 9세 이상의 아동도 야간 근무를 하거나 12시간 이상의 노동을 해서는 안 된다고 규정을 했죠. 또한 산업 혁명의 산물인 노동 조합이 등장함으로써 과거에는 가지지 못했던 권리와 자유를 노동자들이 갖게 되었습니다.

산업 혁명 이전에는 영국 노동자들의 노동 환경이 좋지 못했어요. 남자, 여자, 그리고 아동들이 푼돈을 받기 위해 장시간 노동을 했죠. 노동 계급의 열악한 상황은 많은 교육을 받은 영국의 역사가 및 작가들로 하여금 노동 계층의 상황을 개탄하는, 마르크스주의 및 공산주의 성향의 성명을 발표하도록 만들었어요. 그리고 영국인이 아닌, 예컨대 독일 정치철학자인 프리드리히 엥겔스 같은 사람조차 1844년 *잉글랜드 노동 계급의 상황*이라는 책을 쓸 때 영국을 변화를 위한 모델로 삼았습니다. 이 책에서 엥겔스는 산업 혁명에 대해, 그리고 산업 혁명으로 전체 사회 구조가 어떻게 바뀔 것인가에 대해 논의했어요.

Summary Note

A

❶ Industrial Revolution
❷ late eighteenth century
❸ manufacturing
❹ machine power
❺ transportation
❻ steam engines
❼ cotton mill
❽ protect people

B

The Industrial Revolution refers to the technological, socioeconomic, and cultural changes that took place in Britain in the late eighteenth century. Prior to this period, goods and services were provided through man or horsepower. The development of the steam engine revolutionized manufacturing forever by allowing machinery to do the jobs of men and at much faster rates. Factories sprang up and grew into what we now know as modern cities as people left their rural homes and flocked to the cities for work. Trade unions sprang up to protect the working class from harsh laws and intolerable conditions. Transportation was also changed forever with the invention of the steam engine locomotive. As a result, people and goods could be transported across the country at a much faster rate. Many British historians and philosophers at the time wrote manifestos concerning the state of the working class in England and how the Industrial Revolution would change their lives forever.

Exercise 4 1 Ⓒ 2 Ⓒ 3 Ⓐ, Ⓑ p.154

Script 05-13

M Professor: Carrying on with our discussion of symbiosis, today, we are going to be talking about one of the forms of symbiosis, mutualism. However, before we begin, let me define symbiosis again. Symbiosis is when two dissimilar organisms interact either in a very intimate living situation or when they merge together and live as one unit. And if the two organisms happen to merge, the larger, or macro, organism is called the host, and the smaller, or micro, organism is called the symbiont. Please remember that yesterday, we talked about parasites and how, when we contract a virus, we are the host, and the virus is the symbiont.

So today we are going to move on with our discussion of symbiosis and talk about the form known as mutualism. Mutual symbiosis, or mutualism, is a relationship between two differing organisms in which both organisms profit from the relationship. A very famous incidence of mutual symbiosis is the relationship between the Egyptian plover bird and the crocodile. One would think that a relationship between these two organisms would be impossible. Surely the crocodile would eat the Egyptian plover if it got too close to its jaws. However, this is not the case. The Egyptian plover depends on certain parasites for food, which, in turn, feed upon crocodiles. Because the parasites are potentially lethal to the crocodile, the crocodile allows the Egyptian plover to search its body for these parasites, even opening its jaws and letting the bird pluck parasites from its mouth. Now, going back to the definition of mutualism, can someone tell me what both of these organisms are gaining from their relationship to one another?

W Student: The crocodile is benefiting because the Egyptian plover is eliminating the harmful parasites from its body, and the Egyptian plover is benefiting because it is getting an easy meal.

M: Yes. Another example is the relationship between the goby fish and shrimp. The shrimp is responsible for digging out a burrow in the sand for both the goby fish and the shrimp to cohabitate. In return, because the shrimp has such poor vision, the goby fish keeps a lookout for predators, and when under threat, the goby fish touches the tail of the shrimp to warn it of the impending danger.

W: Does the relationships between these animals ever change? For example, what if food were scarce for the crocodile and the crocodile decided to start eating the Egyptian plovers?

M: This is an insightful question. The scenario you provide is highly unlikely. However, forms of symbiosis are not always exclusive but are often fluid with each other. For example, it was often thought that the relationship between the oxpecker bird of Africa and certain African mammals, such as the buffalo and the zebra, shared a relationship based on mutualism. The oxpecker would eat the parasites off of the buffalo or zebra and, in turn, the oxpecker would get a meal. However, it was found that sometimes, when the oxpeckers are feeding on the parasites, they are also opening wounds on the animals and drinking their blood. This changes their relationship from one of mutualism to one of parasitism, which is like the example that I provided between a parasite and its host at the beginning of class.

해석

M Professor: 공생에 대한 논의를 계속 이어가고 있는데, 오늘은 공생의 한 가지 형태인 상리 공생에 대해 이야기하려고 합니다. 하지만 시작하기에 앞서 공생의 정의를 다시 한 번 알려 드릴게요. 공생은 서로 다른 두 생물이 매우 친밀한 관계로 상대와 상호 작용을 하거나 이들이 합쳐서 하나의 단위로서 살아가는 경우를 말합니다. 그리고 두 생물이 합쳐지는 경우, 보다 큰 대형 생물을 숙주라고 부르고 보다 작은 소형 생물은 공생자라고 부르죠.

그래서 오늘은 공생 관계에 대한 논의를 이어가면서 상리 공생이라는 형태에 대해 이야기하고자 해요. 상호적인 공생, 즉 상리 공생은 서로 다른 두 생물이 그러한 관계로부터 모두 이익을 얻는 관계입니다. 상리 공생에 대한 매우 유명한 예는 악어새와 악어 간의 관계죠. 이 두 가지 생물 간의 관계가 불가능한 것이라고 생각할 수도 있을 거예요. 분명 악어새가 악어 입에 너무 가까이 있으면 악어가 악어새를 잡아먹을 것 같죠. 하지만 실제로는 그렇지가 않습니다. 악어새는 특정 기생충을 먹이로 삼는데, 기생충은, 이들 또한, 악어에 기생해 살아요. 기생충은 악어에게 잠재적으로 치명적인 존재이기 때문에 악어는 악어새가 자신의 몸에서 기생충들을 찾도록 놔두며, 심지어 턱을 벌려 이 새가 입에서 기생충을 찾아서 먹도록 하죠. 자, 상리 공생의 정의로 돌아가서, 그러한 상호 관계로부터 이러한 두 생물이 어떤 이익을 얻는지 누가 이야기해 볼까요?

W Student: 악어는 자신의 몸에 있는 해로운 기생충을 악어새가 제거해 주니까 이익이고, 악어새는 쉽게 먹이를 구할 수 있으니까 이익인 것이죠.

M: 그래요. 또 다른 예는 망둥어와 새우 간의 관계입니다. 새우는 모래에 망둥어와 새우가 함께 지낼 수 있는 굴을 팝니다. 이에 대한 보답으로, 새우가 시력이 매우 나쁘기 때문에, 망둥어는 포식자를 찾기 위한 경계를 서서 상황이 위험해지면 새우의 꼬리를 건드려 곧 있을 위험을 경고해 줍니다.

W: 이들 동물 사이의 관계가 바뀌기도 하나요? 예를 들어 악어의 먹이가 부족해서 악어가 악어새를 잡아먹기로 결정하면 어떻게 되나요?

M: 날카로운 질문이군요. 학생이 얘기한 시나리오는 발생할 가능성이 매우 낮아요. 하지만 공생 관계가 항상 고정된 것은 아니고 서로에게 유동적인 경우도 종종 있습니다. 예를 들어 아프리카의 소등쪼기새와 물소 혹은 얼룩말 같은 아프리카의 포유 동물 사이의 관계는 상리 공생에 기초한 관계라고 종종 생각됩니다. 소등쪼기새는 물소나 얼룩말의 기생충을 제거해 주고, 그 대가로 먹이를 먹는 것이죠. 하지만 때로는 소등쪼기새가 기생충을 잡아먹을 때 동물들에게 상처를 내서 피도 빨아먹는 모습이 종종 관찰되었어요. 이로써 그들의 관계는 상리 공생에서 기생으로 바뀌게 되며, 이는 제가 수업 초반에 알려 드린 기생충과 숙주 간의 경우에 해당됩니다.

Summary Note

A

❶ symbiosis
❷ dissimilar organisms
❸ symbiont
❹ both partners
❺ crocodile
❻ beneficial

B

Mutualism is defined as a form of symbiosis in which two differing organisms benefit from a close relationship. An example of mutualism is the relationship between the Egyptian plover and the crocodile, in which the Egyptian plover eats the parasites off of the crocodile's body. The Egyptian plover benefits from the relationship by getting an easy meal, and the crocodile benefits from the relationship by having potentially fatal parasites removed from its body. Mutualism can sometimes merge into parasitism, however, if one of the organisms begins harming the other. For example, a different kind of bird, the oxpecker, normally enjoys a relationship of mutualism with certain African land mammals. However, once in a while, the oxpecker will draw blood from the mammals to drink so therefore benefits when the mammal does not.

Integrated Listening & Speaking p.156

A

Script 05-14

M Professor: In our last class, we covered the carbon cycle. Since humans are carbon-based lifeforms, it is of great importance to us, so we really need to know. First, remember that carbon has an atomic number of six, and its symbol on the periodic chart is C. It can be found in elemental forms as graphite, diamond, and fullerene, it can be carbonates when it combines with elements, and its gaseous form is often carbon dioxide. The carbon cycle begins when plants take in carbon dioxide when they undergo photosynthesis. Then, plants are eaten by animals, so both plants and animals have carbon inside them. When the plants and animals die, some of that carbon is released as a gas such as carbon dioxide. Other carbon remains in the ground and eventually becomes fossil fuels. When the fossil fuels are used by humans, the carbon returns to the atmosphere as a gas. The ocean can also absorb lots of carbon, which is used by shellfish to create their hard shells.

1 Humans are carbon-based lifeforms.

2 They are graphite, diamond, and fullerene.

3 The carbon cycle begins when plants take in carbon dioxide when they undergo photosynthesis.

B

Script 05-15

M Professor: Yesterday, we explored the idea of mutualism. Mutualism is a form of symbiosis where two dissimilar organisms benefit from a close relationship or even an invasive relationship. An example of mutualism is the relationship between the Egyptian plover and the crocodile. The Egyptia plover eats parasites that live on the crocodile's body. The Egyptian plover benefits from the relationship by getting an easy meal, and the crocodile benefits from the relationship by having the parasites removed from its body. Mutualism sometimes merges into parasitism if one of the organisms begins harming the other. The oxpecker bird, for example, usually eats bugs and other parasites off the backs of certain African land mammals, but every once in a while, the oxpecker will draw blood from the mammals to drink so therefore benefits when the mammal does not.

1 It is parasitism; the virus is benefiting from the relationship, but you are not.

2 The Egyptian plover gets an easy meal.

3 If the oxpecker starts to draw and drink the buffalo's blood, then the relationship is parasitic.

Mini TOEFL iBT Practice Test p.158

1 Ⓑ	2 Ⓑ, Ⓒ	3 Ⓐ	4 Ⓒ	5 Ⓓ
6 Ⓓ	7 Ⓐ	8 Ⓒ	9 Ⓐ, Ⓑ	
10 Ⓒ	11 Ⓑ			

[1-5]

Script 05-16

M Professor: Good afternoon, Erika. What can I help you with?

W Student: Hi, Professor Phillips. I need some advice because I am having a lot of trouble deciding which graduate school to apply to.

M: Well, the last thing you need is to be stressed by such a process. Let's start off with you telling me what kind of subject you hope to pursue.

W: My bachelor's degree is in education with a minor in psychology. I've enjoyed both and hope I can combine the two subjects by getting a master's degree in psychology either to teach or to be a school counselor.

M: This certainly sounds like a great career choice. Would you like to teach elementary students, high school kids, or college students?

W: I enjoy teaching little children so much and love the way their faces light up when they discover a new concept. I have been student-teaching six and seven-year-old children the last two semesters and have really enjoyed it.

M: Okay, so now you know what to pursue in graduate school. The next consideration is to ask yourself where you would like to live. My philosophy about graduate school is to try to take advantage of a new place. That way, you not only learn at the school of your choosing but also learn by meeting new people, seeing new places, and perhaps experiencing a different culture.

W: Where did you go to graduate school?

M: I did my undergraduate work in the United States, but I decided to travel abroad for graduate school. I settled on a very good program in Britain and got to live in London.

W: London! Wow! I am from a small town, so I cannot imagine the size and pace of a city like London.

M: Well, now's your chance to experience something new. Perhaps a big city experience would be good for you. The best thing is to pick two or three education graduation school programs in different settings. For example, I'd say you should apply to a graduate school located in a rural location, one located in a large city, and one located in a foreign country. This way you spread your options, and if accepted to all three, then you can sit down and think about what new things you want to experience.

W: That sounds like a great idea. Do you have any pamphlets specific to graduate schools that specialize in education?

M: I sure do. Here are half a dozen or so education programs in different parts of the world. Review these, and when you have narrowed your choices to three or four, come back to my office, and I will help you fill out the applications.

W: Thank you so much. Is there anything else I need to do before I come back in?

M: Yes. Try to find three people to write recommendations for you. That is one of the things required to be submitted with each application. I would suggest getting two letters of recommendation from professors and one from an employer.

W: Okay, I can do that. Would you be willing to write one of my letters of recommendation?

M: Of course, Erika. I was hoping you would ask. You have always been one of my best students.

W: Thank you so much. I will see you soon.

해석

M Professor: 좋은 오후군요, Erika. 어떻게 도와 드릴까요?

W Student: 안녕하세요, Phillips 교수님. 제가 어떤 대학원에 지원을 해야 할지 결정을 못 내리고 있어서 조언이 필요해요.

M: 음, 결코 그러한 과정에서 스트레스를 받으면 안 돼요. 먼저 어떤 학문을 공부하려고 하는지 이야기해 보세요.

W: 학사 학위는 교육학으로 받았고 부전공은 심리학이에요. 둘 다 좋아했는데, 심리학 석사 학위를 받아서 이 둘을 결합해 교사나 상담 교사가 되면 좋을 것 같아요.

M: 확실히 진로를 잘 선택한 것 같군요. 초등학생, 중학생, 아니면 대학생을 가르치고 싶나요?

W: 저는 정말로 어린 아이들을 가르치고 싶고, 아이들이 새로운 개념을 알게 되었을 때 얼굴이 환해지는 것을 너무 좋아해요. 지난 두 학기 동안 6세 및 7세 아이들을 상대로 교생 업무를 했는데 정말 재미있었어요.

M: 좋아요, 그러면 이제 대학원에서 무엇을 공부해야 할지는 알게 되었군요. 다음으로 생각해 볼 것은 어디에서 지내고 싶은지에 대해 스스로에게 묻는 것이죠. 대학원에 대한 제 신조는 새로운 곳을 기회로 삼자는 것이에요. 그렇게 하면 학생이 선택한 학교에서 공부를 할 수 있을 뿐만 아니라 새로운 사람들을 만나고, 새로운 장소에 가보고, 그리고 어쩌면 다른 문화를 경험함으로써 배우게 되죠.

W: 교수님은 대학원을 어디에서 나오셨어요?

M: 저는 미국에서 학부를 졸업했지만 대학원은 외국에서 다니기로 결심했어요. 영국에 있던 매우 좋은 프로그램을 선택해서 런던에서 살게 되었죠.

W: 런던이요! 와! 저는 소도시 출신이라 런던 같은 도시의 크기와 속도는 상상이 가지 않아요.

M: 음, 지금이 새로운 것을 경험할 수 있는 기회에요. 아마도 대도시에서의 경험이 학생에게 도움이 될 거예요. 가장 좋은 것은 서로 다른 두세 군데의 교육학 대학원 프로그램을 선택하는 거예요. 예를 들어 시골 지역에 있는 대학원 하나, 대도시에 있는 대학원 하나, 그리고 해외에 있는 대학원 하나에 지원을 하면 좋을 것 같아요. 그러면 선택폭이 넓어질 텐데, 세 군데 모두 합격이 되는 경우, 가만히 앉아서 어떤 새로운 경험을 하고 싶은지에 대해 생각해 보세요.

W: 멋진 아이디어로 들리는군요. 혹시 교육학에 특화된 대학원들만을 소개하는 팜플렛이 있나요?

M: 그럼요. 여기에 전 세계 여러 지역의 교육학 프로그램들이 6개 정도 나와 있어요. 살펴보고 서너 군데로 선택을 좁혀서 제 사무실로 찾아오면 제가 지원서 작성하는 것을 도와 줄게요.

W: 정말 감사합니다. 제가 다시 오기 전에 해야 할 또 다른 일이 있을까요?

M: 네. 학생에게 추천서를 써 줄 세 명의 사람을 찾아 보세요. 이는 지원서와 함께 제출해야 하는 것들 중 하나이죠. 교수님들의 추천서 두 통과 고용인의 추천서 한 통을 받는 것을 추천할게요.

W: 알겠습니다, 그렇게 할게요. 교수님께서 제 추천서 중 한 통을 써 주실 수 있으신가요?

M: 물론이죠, Erika. 내심 기대하고 있었어요. 학생은 항상 최고의 학생 중 한 명이었으니까요.

W: 정말 감사합니다. 곧 다시 뵐게요.

[6-11]

Script 05-17

W Professor: Good morning, class. Today, we are going to continue our life sciences lectures with a discussion on the introduction of new species within the plant world. More specifically, we are going to be looking at the effects of introducing exotic plants, also known as naturalized plants, into an area containing established native plants, also known as endemic plants. Someone start off our discussion by telling us what I mean when I say introduced. How does a plant become introduced?

M Student: Introduced simply means that the plant has been brought into an area that it has not previously been before.

W: Good. Who is bringing it and how?

M: Well, the plant can be brought into an area either deliberately, with the intention of planting it, or accidentally by a human being.

W: Very good. In many cases, introducing a plant species to a new area is a bad thing. For instance, what if a scientist introduced a new plant to an area where it had never previously been before, and the introduced plant killed off an endemic plant? Sadly, this happens from time to time in places around the world. But before we develop this idea, let us think about why people would want to introduce exotic plants into other areas in the first place.

One of these reasons is that when people immigrate to other countries, they often want to be able to take plants they are familiar with to make it feel like home. Another reason is that some people want to introduce a new plant just for aesthetic reasons. For example, perhaps a new park is being built, and the landscape artist wants certain colored flowers. He might try to import certain flowers from another country because they are what he believes are necessary to make the park look good.

Here, uh, let me give you a specific example of something that happened in the past. The Norway maple is a beloved tree in Scandinavia, and when Scandinavians began migrating to Canada, they brought the Norway maple with them. Fortunately, the Norway maple has thrived well in Canada, eventually spreading to all of North America with little harm to other native species; however, sometimes a well-intentioned introduction has led either to the overpopulation of the introduced species or the curbing or even completely killing off of other native species.

M: Can you give us an example of this?

W: Certainly. The purple loosestrife is an herbaceous perennial plant that grows in colonies and produces a lovely reddish-purple flower. The purple loosestrife has been introduced into nonnative habitats because of its beautiful flower; however, what people did not know was that it can easily escape horticultural control because of its rapid and widespread growth, and when it does, the purple loosestrife chokes off all other plant life in the area. When a plant escapes control like this, it is termed invasive.

M: Can another reason for introducing new species also be because certain plants help maintain a particular habitat?

W: Absolutely. The flowering plant known as the garlic mustard is a plant that helps combat erosion control. It is native to Europe, parts of Africa, and Asia but was introduced to North America in the mid-nineteenth century after people found that when garlic mustard was planted, it helped combat soil washouts and wind erosion. In that case, the plant was able to benefit its new environment.

M: What about national parks? Sometimes plants are protected there, right? Are they native plants or introduced plants?

W: Both. National parks are great places to foster the life of both native and nonnative plants as the areas can be tightly controlled and monitored. Oftentimes, the introduction of exotic plants into these areas is for means of protection since there are very specific rules governing land and growth in national parks. Whether an endemic plant or introduced plant, what is important is that all plants be protected in their best possible environment to prevent absolute and irreversible outcomes such as extinction.

해석

W Professor: 안녕하세요, 여러분. 오늘은 식물계 내로 새로운 종이 유입되는 것에 관한 논의로 생명 과학 강의를 계속하도록 하죠. 보다 자세하게는, 귀화 식물이라고도 불리는 외래 식물이 고유 식물이라고도 불리는 기존 토종 식물이 있는 지역에 유입된 경우에 대해 살펴볼 거예요. 제가 말한 유입이 무엇을 의미하는지 누군가 얘기해 봄으로써 논의를 시작해 보죠. 식물은 어떻게 유입이 될까요?

M Student: 유입은 식물이 이전에 존재하지 않았던 지역 안으로 들어오는 것을 말합니다.

W: 좋은 대답이군요. 누가 어떻게 들여올까요?

M: 음, 식물을 심을 의도를 가지고 고의로 들여올 수도 있고, 아니면 인간에 의해 우연히 들어올 수도 있겠죠.

W: 잘 했어요. 많은 경우, 새로운 지역에 식물종이 유입되는 것은 좋지 않은 일이에요. 예를 들어 어떤 과학자가 이전에는 그러한 식물이 없었던 지역에 새로운 식물을 유입시키고, 유입된 식물이 고유 식물들을 죽인다면 어떻게 될까요? 안타깝게도 그런 일이 전 세계 각지에서 때때로 일어납니다. 하지만 이러한 아이디어를 발전시키기에 앞서 사람들이 왜 외래종을 다른 곳에 유입시키고자 하는지 생각해 보죠.

한 가지 이유는 사람들이 다른 나라로 이민을 가는 경우, 종종 고향과 같은 기분을 느끼기 위해서 자신에게 친숙한 식물들을 가져가려고 하기 때문이에요. 또 다른 이유는 미적인 이유로서 몇몇 사람들이 새로운 식물을 유입하고자 하기 때문이죠. 예를 들어 아마도 새로운 공원이 조성되는 중인데, 조경 디자이너가 특정한 색의 꽃을 원할 수도 있을 거예요. 공원을 아름답게 만들기 위해서는 그러한 꽃이 필요하다고 생각해서 해외로부터 특정한 꽃들을 수입하고자 할 수도 있죠.

이제, 어, 과거에 있었던 구체적인 사례를 하나 알려 드릴게요. 노르웨이단풍은 스칸디나비아반도에서 사랑받는 나무인데, 스칸디나비아의 사람들이 캐나다로 이주하기 시작하면서 이들이 노르웨이단풍을 가지고 왔습니다. 다행히도 노르웨이단풍은 캐나다에서 잘 자랐고, 다른 토착종에 해를 거의 끼치지 않으면서 북아메리카 전역으로 퍼졌어요. 하지만 때때로 좋은 의도로 유입되었지만, 유입된 종이 과도하게 증가하는 경우도 있었고, 다른 토착종의 성장을 억제하거나 이들을 멸종시키는 경우도 있었습니다.

M: 그에 대한 예를 하나 들어 주실 수 있나요?

W: 물론이죠. 털부처꽃은 군락을 이루어 자라면서 아름다운 자주색 꽃을 피우는 다년초입니다. 털부처꽃은 그 꽃이 아름다워서 자생지가 아닌 지역으로 유입되었지만, 이것이 빠르게 성장하고 퍼져 나가기 때문에 원예학적인 통제에서 쉽게 벗어날 수 있으며, 그렇게 되는 경우 털부처꽃이 지역 내의 다른 모든 식물들을 고사시킨다는 점은 사람들이 모르고 있었죠. 어떤 식물이 이처럼 통제 불능이 되는 경우, 이 식물에 침습성이 있다고 말을 합니다.

M: 몇몇 식물들이 특정 서식지의 유지에 도움을 준다는 이유로 새로운 종이 유입될 수도 있나요?

W: 물론이죠. 알리아리아라고 알려진 화초는 침식 작용을 예방하는데 도움을 주는 식물입니다. 이 식물은 유럽, 아프리카 일부, 그리고 아시아에서 자라는 토착종이지만, 알리아리아를 심으면 토양 침식 및 풍식을 예방하는데 도움이 된다는 점이 알려진 후, 19세기 중반에 북아메리카에 유입되었어요. 이 경우에는 식물이 새로운 환경에 이로움을 가져다 줄 수 있었습니다.

M: 국립 공원은 어떤가요? 그곳 식물들은 때때로 보호를 받잖아요, 그렇죠? 그런 식물들은 토종 식물인가요, 아니면 유입된 식물인가요?

W: 둘 다 있어요. 국립 공원은 매우 엄격하게 통제되고 관리되기 때문에 토종 식물 및 비토종 식물 모두가 잘 자랄 수 있는 좋은 장소입니다. 국립 공원에는 토양 및 성장과 관련된 매우 구체적인 규정이 존재하기 때문에 종종 보호 수단으로서 외래 식물들을 그곳으로 들여오기도 하죠. 고유 식물이든 유입된 식물이든, 중요한 점은 멸종과 같은 절대적이고 회복 불가능한 결과를 막기 위해 가능한 최적의 환경에서 모든 식물들을 보호해야 한다는 점이에요.

Vocabulary Check-Up

p.163

A

1 Ⓛ	2 Ⓝ	3 Ⓞ	4 Ⓖ	5 Ⓕ
6 Ⓒ	7 Ⓔ	8 Ⓐ	9 Ⓙ	10 Ⓑ
11 Ⓗ	12 Ⓚ	13 Ⓘ	14 Ⓜ	15 Ⓓ

B

1 Ⓒ	2 Ⓑ	3 Ⓔ	4 Ⓐ	5 Ⓓ

UNIT 06 Understanding Organization

Basic Drill p.168

Drill 1 Ⓓ

Script 06-02

M Student: Professor Wallace, are you available for a quick chat?

W Professor: Sure, Edward. What can I do for you?

M: I saw that you're going to be teaching a seminar next semester. Would it be possible for me to sign up for it?

W: Hmm . . . Are you going to be a junior or senior next semester?

M: I'll be a senior. Is that important?

W: Yes, it is. Attendance for seminars is restricted to a low number. It's usually eighteen or twenty. So seniors are given the opportunity to sign up for seminars first.

M: I had no idea. But, um . . . I'm not an English literature major. I'm just getting a minor in it.

W: That's quite all right. You can still receive permission from me to sign up for the class. Would you like that?

M: Definitely. I'm really looking forward to studying nineteenth-century novels.

W: I'm glad that you're so interested in the class. I'll put your name on the list.

해석

M Student: Wallace 교수님, 잠깐 이야기를 나눌 수 있으신가요?

W Professor: 그럼요. Edward. 어떻게 도와 드릴까요?

M: 교수님께서 다음 학기에 세미나 수업을 맡으신다는 점을 알게 되었어요. 제가 그 수업에 등록을 할 수 있을까요?

W: 흠… 다음 학기에 3학년이 되나요, 아니면 4학년이 되나요?

M: 4학년이요. 그것이 중요한가요?

W: 네, 그래요. 세미나 수업의 참석 인원은 소수로 제한되어 있어요. 보통은 18명이나 20명이죠. 그래서 4학년생들에게 먼저 세미나 수업에 등록할 수 있는 기회가 주어져요.

M: 그건 제가 몰랐네요. 하지만, 음… 제 전공이 영문학은 아니에요. 부전공일 뿐이죠.

W: 그건 괜찮아요. 그래도 제게 승인을 받아서 수업에 등록할 수 있어요. 그렇게 하고 싶나요?

M: 그럼요. 19세기 소설에 대해 정말로 공부해 보고 싶어요.

W: 학생이 그처럼 수업에 관심이 많다니 기쁘군요. 수업 명단에 학생 이름을 올려 놓을게요.

Drill 2 Ⓑ

Script 06-03

M Bursar's Office Employee: Good afternoon. How may I be of assistance today?

W Student: Hello. I'd like to get a refund on my classes.

M: Could you be more specific, please?

W: Sure. I was signed up for two classes during the summer session. But I had to drop both of them because I got a full-time job for the summer.

M: I see. May I have your student ID, please? I need to call your name up on the screen.

W: Of course. Here you are . . .

M: Let me see . . . Doris Mercer . . . According to the computer, you should be reimbursed 1,000 dollars.

W: Huh? I thought it should be double that amount. After all, I paid 2,000 dollars for the classes.

M: Yes, but you dropped the classes on July 10. The deadline for dropping classes to get a full refund was July 8. You missed it by two days.

W: Okay. I didn't realize that. I guess I was too slow.

해석

M Bursar's Office Employee: 좋은 오후군요. 어떻게 도와 드릴까요?

W Student: 안녕하세요. 수업에 대한 환불을 받고 싶어서요.

M: 보다 자세히 말씀해 주시겠어요?

W: 그럴게요. 저는 두 개의 여름 학기 수업에 등록했어요. 하지만 여름에 풀타임으로 일을 하게 되어서 둘 다 수강을 철회해야 했죠.

M: 알겠어요. 제가 학생증을 봐도 될까요? 화면에 학생의 이름이 나오도록 해야 해서요.

W: 물론이에요. 여기 있어요…

M: 제가 볼게요… Doris Mercer… 컴퓨터에 의하면 학생은 1,000달러를 돌려 받게 될 거예요.

W: 네? 그 두 배의 금액일 것으로 생각했는데요. 어쨌거나 저는 수업료로 2,000달러를 냈으니까요.

M: 네, 하지만 학생은 7월 10일에 수강 철회를 했어요. 전액 환불이 가능한 수강 철회 마감일은 7월 8일이었고요. 이틀 늦었군요.

W: 알겠어요. 그 점은 제가 몰랐네요. 제 행동이 너무 느렸던 것 같아요.

Drill 3 Ⓑ

Script 06-04

W Professor: One of the most brilliant artists in history was Sandro Botticelli. He was an Italian who lived during the Renaissance. He was born in 1445 and died in 1510. Let me show you a couple of his works of art right now so that you can see his genius. Here is one . . . Here is another . . . And another . . . Impressive, aren't they?

Botticelli lived during the Early Renaissance, and he was a humanist painter. This means he didn't focus so much on religious topics like artists did during the Middle Ages. Botticelli instead focused on more secular topics. He was strongly affected by the introduction of Greek and Roman ideas from ancient times. That's not to say that he didn't paint religious topics. He did. Here is his painting called *The Adoration of the Magi*. Take a close look . . . It's one of my favorites. However, his paintings focusing on ancient mythology are much better known. Here is *The Birth of Venus*. Venus was the goddess of love in Greek mythology. She is depicted sailing to shore on a giant shell. This painting is entitled *Venus and Mars*. Mars was the Greek god of war and the lover of Venus. You've probably seen this one, too. It's called *Primavera*. It shows various figures from mythology. It's one of my personal favorites.

해석

W Professor: 역사상 가장 뛰어났던 화가 중 한 명은 산드로 보티첼리였어요. 그는 이탈리아의 화가였고 르네상스 시대에 살았죠. 1445년에 태어나서 1510년에 사망했습니다. 그의 천재성을 아실 수 있도록 지금 그의 미술 작품들을 두어 점 보여 드릴게요. 여기에 하나가 있고… 여기에 하나가 더 있는데…. 그리고 또 하나가 있습니다… 인상적이죠, 그렇지 않나요?

보티첼리는 초기 르네상스 시대에 살았으며 휴머니즘 화가였어요. 이는 그가 중세 시대의 화가들과 달리 주로 종교적인 주제에만 초점을 맞추지는 않았다는 점을 의미해요. 대신 보티첼리는 보다 세속적인 주제에 초점을 맞추었습니다. 고대의 그리스 및 로마의 사상이 소개됨으로써 많은 영향을 받았죠. 그가 종교적인 주제를 그리지 않았다는 뜻은 아닙니다. 그렸어요. 여기에 *동방박사의 경배*라는 그림이 있습니다. 자세히 보시면… 제가 가장 좋아하는 작품 중 하나죠. 하지만 고대 신화에 초점을 맞춘 그림들이 훨씬 더 잘 알려져 있어요. 여기에 *비너스의 탄생*이 있습니다. 비너스는 그리스 신화의 사랑의 여신이였어요. 거대한 조개 껍질을 타고 해변으로 항해하는 모습이 묘사되어 있죠. 이 그림의 제목은 *비너스와 마르스*입니다. 마르스는 그리스의 전쟁의 신이자 비너스의 연인이었어요. 아마 이 그림도 보셨을 것 같군요. *프리마베라*라는 작품입니다. 신화에 등장하는 다양한 인물들을 보여 주죠. 제가 개인적으로 가장 좋아하는 작품 중 하나예요.

Drill 4 Ⓑ

Script 06-05

M Professor: Most archaeological digs take place on land. Archaeologists dig in the ground to unearth treasures and ruins buried in the past. There's also something called underwater archaeology. This can be done for various reasons. Many times, archaeologists dive on shipwrecks in order to study ships and to recover their contents. In some places, rising water levels have covered entire civilizations, so archaeologists must go down into the water to explore them.

This is one of the most challenging types of archaeology to practice for obvious reasons. Let me tell you some of the difficulties. First, the conditions beneath the surface can be very harsh, especially in ocean and river environments. Currents can make it hard for archaeologists simply to go where they want, and visibility can be low at times. Second, people who practice underwater archaeology require specialized training. They have to know how to scuba dive. Even experienced divers have problems when they are deep in the ocean, and accidents, some of which may kill divers, happen from time to time. Specialized equipment, which can cost huge sums of money, is required. And divers not only have to focus on doing proper dives but then also have to examine artifacts or try to unearth them. Underwater archaeology is really extremely difficult and dangerous, and few people are brave and trained enough to do it.

해석

M Professor: 대부분의 고고학적 발굴은 땅에서 이루어집니다. 고고학자들은 땅을 파서 과거에 묻혀진 보물 및 유적을 발굴하죠. 수중 고고학이라는 것도 존재합니다. 다양한 이유에서 이러한 활동이 이루어질 수 있어요. 많은 경우, 고고학자들은 선박을 연구하고 그 안에 들어 있는 것을 찾아내기 위해 난파선 안으로 잠수를 합니다. 일부 장소에서는, 수위가 상승한 물이 문명 전체를 덮고 있기 때문에, 고고학자들이 물속으로 들어가서 탐험을 해야 하죠.

이것은 명백한 이유로 가장 실시하기가 어려운 고고학적 활동 중 하나입니다. 어려운 점들을 몇 개 말씀드릴게요. 첫째, 수면 아래의 상황은, 특히 바다와 강 환경에서, 매우 혹독할 수 있습니다. 해류로 인해 고고학자들이 원하는 곳으로 가기가 힘들 수도 있고, 때로는 시야가 좁아질 수도 있어요. 둘째, 수중 고고학 활동을 하는 사람들은 전문적인 훈련을 받아야 합니다. 스쿠버다이빙하는 법을 알아야만 하죠. 숙련된 다이버들도 바다 깊은 곳에서는 문제를 겪으며, 다이버를 사망하게 만들 수도 있는 사고들이 때때로 발생하기도 합니다. 막대한 비용이 들 수 있는 전문적인 장비도 필요해요. 그리고 다이버들은 잠수하는 일에 집중해야 할 뿐만 아니라 유물을 조사하거나 이들을 발굴해 내야 하죠. 수중 고고학은 극도로 힘들고 위험하며, 그러한 활동을 할 수 있을 정도로 용감하고 훈련되어 있는 사람은 극소수입니다.

Exercises with Long Conversations

Exercise 1 1 Ⓐ 2 Ⓓ 3 Ⓑ p.172

Script 06-06

W Student: Hello, Professor Cleveland. I received a phone call from the departmental secretary. She told me that you would like to speak with me about something.

M Professor: Ah, Lucinda. Thanks for responding so quickly. I appreciate that.

W: Sure. I don't have any classes today, so I have plenty of free time every Wednesday.

M: That sounds like a pleasant day. So, uh, anyway, the reason I want to speak with you . . .

W: Yes?

M: Well, I'm a bit concerned about your performance in my class.

W: My performance? What do you mean? I've done all of the homework assignments and received good grades for the ones that you handed back. I also got a ninety-six on the midterm exam. I'm not sure how much better I can do.

M: Yes, it's true that the scores on your homework and midterm exam are outstanding. However, you seem to be forgetting one vital thing.

W: What's that?

M: Twenty percent of your class grade is determined by class participation. As you know, for the last twenty or thirty minutes of every class, we have discussion time. During this period, all students are encouraged to chime in with their questions and comments. However, I don't recall you ever saying a single word in any class. Is there a reason for that?

W: Um . . . Actually, there is.

M: What is it?

W: I get really nervous speaking in front of other people. I sometimes develop a stutter, and I start to sweat a lot.

M: I see. Has this problem always existed?

W: I'm afraid so. For as long as I can remember, I haven't been comfortable speaking in public. You know, I probably wouldn't have signed up for this class if I had known about the participation aspect of the grade ahead of time. I just . . . I just can't do it.

M: Have you ever spoken with a specialist? The school provides free consultations with specialists. If you make an appointment with one, you just might get the help you need. Are you interested in that?

W: You bet I am. I would love to be able to contribute to this class and others if I could just overcome my phobia. Do you know who to contact?

M: I'm actually on my way to Westin Hall right now. Why don't I escort you there? I know one of the specialists personally, so I can introduce you to her. If you work with her, you just might be able to make a contribution or two to class before the semester is over.

W: Thanks so much, Professor. I really appreciate your concern. It's nice of you to take a personal interest in my issue instead of just getting mad at me for not speaking in class.

해석

W Student: 안녕하세요, Cleveland 교수님. 학과 사무실 직원으로부터 전화를 받았어요. 교수님께서 저와 이야기를 나누고 싶어하신다고 전해 주더군요.

M Professor: 아, Lucinda. 이렇게 빨리 와 주다니 고마워요. 감사해요.

W: 천만에요. 오늘은 수업이 전혀 없는 날이라서 매주 수요일에는 시간이 많이 남아요.

M: 기분 좋은 날처럼 들리는군요. 그러면, 어, 어쨌든, 제가 학생과 이야기를 하고자 했던 이유는…

W: 네?

M: 음, 제 수업에서의 학생의 성적이 약간 걱정스러워서요.

W: 제 성적이요? 무슨 말씀이시죠? 저는 과제도 다했고 돌려 주신 과제에서 좋은 점수도 받았어요. 또한 중간 고사에서는 96점을 받았고요. 제가 얼마나 더 잘할 수 있는지 모르겠어요.

M: 네, 과제와 중간고사 점수가 뛰어난 것은 사실이에요. 하지만 중요한 한 가지를 잊은 것 같군요.

W: 그것이 무엇인가요?

M: 수업 성적의 20%는 수업 참여로 결정되어요. 알겠지만, 모든 수업에서 마지막 20분내지 30분 동안 토론 시간을 갖고 있죠. 이때 모든 학생들은 질문과 의견을 제시하면서 토론에 참여할 것이 권장되어요. 하지만 제 기억에 학생은 어떤 수업에서도 단 한 마디 말도 하지 않았어요. 그에 대한 이유가 있나요?

W: 어… 사실 있어요.

M: 그게 무엇이죠?

W: 저는 다른 사람들 앞에서 말을 할 때 정말로 긴장이 되어요. 때때로 말을 더듬기도 하고, 땀도 많이 흘리죠.

M: 그렇군요. 그런 문제를 항상 겪어 왔나요?

W: 그랬던 것 같아요. 제 기억으로는, 공개적으로 말하는 것에 불편함을 느껴 왔어요. 아시겠지만, 제가 수업 참여와 관련된 내용을 미리 알았더라면, 아마도 이번 수업에 등록하지 않았을 거예요. 저는 그냥… 저는 그냥 못하겠어요.

M: 전문가와 이야기를 해 본 적이 있나요? 학교에서 무료로 전문 상담 서비스를 제공하고 있어요. 한 분과 약속을 잡으면 필요한 도움을 받을 수 있을 거예요. 관심이 있나요?

W: 물론 있어요. 제가 공포증을 극복할 수 있다면 이 수업과 다른 수업의 토론에도 참여할 수 있을 거예요. 누구에게 연락하면 되는지 아시나요?

M: 사실 저는 지금 Westin 홀에 가려는 중이었어요. 저와 함께 그곳으로 가는 것이 어때요? 개인적으로 전문가 한 분을 알고 있는데, 제가 그분에게 학생을 소개시켜 줄 수 있어요. 그분의 도움을 받으면 학기가 끝나기 전에 수업에서 한두 차례 말을 하게 될 수도 있을 거예요.

W: 감사합니다, 교수님. 걱정해 주셔서 정말 고맙습니다. 수업 시간에 말을 하지 않는다고 화를 내시는 대신, 제 문제에 개인적인 관심을 기울여 주시다니 정말 친절하시군요.

Summary Note

A

❶ student's performance
❷ exam grades
❸ class participation
❹ never speaks
❺ public speaking
❻ specialist

B
The student visits the professor because he wants to speak with her. He states that he is concerned about the student's class performance, and the student is surprised. She states that her homework and exam grades were high, so she feels she is doing well in the class. The professor remarks that class participation is twenty percent of her grade, but she has never said anything during class discussions. The student says she gets nervous when speaking in front of others. The professor asks if she would like to speak with a specialist at the school. The student agrees, so the professor volunteers to introduce her to one of the specialists. The student expresses her thanks that the professor is helping her rather than getting mad at her.

Exercise 2 1 Ⓐ 2 Ⓑ 3 Ⓓ p.174

Script 06-07

M Dean of Students: Greetings. You must be Denise Mellon. It's a pleasure to meet you.

W Student: It's a pleasure to meet you, too, Mr. Peterson.

M: Please have a seat and make yourself comfortable . . . Now, uh, you requested a meeting with me, but you didn't indicate what you'd like to discuss.

W: That's right. Hmm . . . Let me think about how I should begin . . . I'm a foreign student, and things are a lot different here than in my home country.

M: Right. How are you adjusting here? Is everything okay?

W: For the most part, everything is fine. I grew up speaking English, so that's not a problem. However, there are a few aspects of the culture that I find difficult to understand. I'm trying to overcome these issues though, so I think I'm doing well.

M: That's great to hear. So is the reason you want to speak with me a cultural issue?

W: I'm not really sure, but I think it may be. You see, um, it concerns one of my professors. Her name is Professor Lombard, and she's in the Anthropology Department.

M: I've heard her name before, but I've never met her. I believe she just started teaching here this past semester. What is your complaint about her?

W: Well, I find her class very interesting, but there is one thing that she does which bothers me a lot. You see, every once in a while, I raise my hand to ask a question. I know she sees me because I sit in the second row in the middle of the classroom, but she never asks me to speak.

M: Does she call on other students when they raise their hands?

W: Yes, she does. That's what's annoying. Yesterday, I had my hand up, and so did the student next to me. She asked him what he wanted to say, but she completely ignored me. And there's something else.

M: What's that?

W: A couple of times, when she refused to call on me, I waited until there was a pause in the class, and I just asked my question. She ignored it and just continued to lecture.

M: Have you tried talking to her after class?

W: I waited after class once, but she walked right by me. I really don't understand what's going on. So I thought that I should speak with someone here who might be able to give me a hand.

M: Okay. I'm going to chat with her either today or tomorrow. I'll find out her side of the story. Then, I'll arrange for both of you to meet me in my office. How does that sound to you?

W: Perfect. Thank you so much.

M: Why don't you let my secretary know when you have time to meet on Friday? I imagine this meeting will take around thirty minutes.

W: I'll do that right now. Thank you, sir.

해석

M Dean of Students: 안녕하세요. 분명 Denise Mellon이겠군요. 만나서 반가워요.

W Student: 저도 만나서 반갑습니다, Peterson 학생처장님.

M: 편하게 앉으세요… 자, 어, 학생은 저와 면담을 요청했지만, 무엇에 대해 논의하고 싶은 것은지는 밝히지 않았더군요.

W: 맞아요. 흠… 어떻게 시작하면 좋을지… 저는 외국인 학생인데, 이곳은 제 본국과 크게 다르더군요.

M: 그래요. 이곳에 어떻게 적응하고 있나요? 모든 것이 다 괜찮나요?

W: 대부분의 경우 다 괜찮아요. 저는 영어를 사용하면서 자랐기 때문에 영어는 문제가 안되죠. 하지만 제가 이해하기 힘든 몇 가지 문화적인 문제들이 있어요. 하지만 그러한 문제들을 극복하려고 노력 중이기 때문에 잘 지내고 있는 것 같아요.

M: 그런 이야기를 들으니 다행이네요. 그러면 저와 문화적인 문제에 대해 이야기를 하고 싶었기 때문인가요?

W: 확실하지는 않지만, 그런 것일 수도 있다고 생각해요. 그러니까, 음, 제 교수님 중 한 분과 관련된 일이에요. 그분의 성함은 Lombard 교수님으로, 인류학과 교수님이시죠.

M: 전에 이름은 들어 본 적이 있는데, 만나 본 적은 없네요. 지난 학기에 이곳에서 처음 강의를 맡으신 것으로 알고 있어요. 그분에 대해 어떤 불만이 있나요?

W: 음, 저는 그분의 수업이 매우 흥미롭다고 생각하지만, 그분의 한 가지 행동이 저를 정말로 힘들게 만들어요. 그러니까, 저는 가끔씩 손을 들어서 질문을 해요. 제가 강의실에서 두 번째 줄에 앉기 때문에 그분이 저를 본다는 건 알지만, 결코 제가 말을 하도록 시키지 않으세요.

M: 다른 학생들이 손을 드는 경우에는 발언을 허용하시나요?

W: 네, 그래요. 바로 그러한 점이 기분을 상하게 만들어요. 어제는 제가 손을 들고 제 옆 학생도 손을 들었어요. 교수님께서는 그 학생으로 하여금 말하고 싶은

것을 말하라고 하고, 저는 완전히 무시하셨죠. 그리고 또 있어요.

M: 무엇인가요?

W: 두어 번은, 교수님께서 제 발언을 거부하셨을 때, 강의가 잠깐 끊길 때까지 기다렸다가 질문을 했어요. 교수님께서는 그것도 무시하시고 강의를 이어 나가셨죠.

M: 수업이 끝난 후에 교수님과 이야기를 나누어 보았나요?

W: 한 번은 수업이 끝날 때까지 기다렸는데, 저를 그냥 지나쳐 가시더군요. 저는 이게 무슨 일인지 정말로 이해가 가지 않아요. 그래서 제게 도움을 주실 수 있는 이곳 누군가와 이야기를 해야겠다고 생각했죠.

M: 알겠어요. 제가 오늘이나 내일 그분과 이야기를 해 볼게요. 그분의 입장이 무엇인지 알아 볼게요. 그런 다음에 제 사무실에서 두 사람 모두와 약속을 잡도록 할게요. 어떻게 들리나요?

W: 완벽해요. 정말 고맙습니다.

M: 금요일에 만날 수 있는 시간을 제 비서에게 알려 주는 것이 어떨까요? 제 생각에 이번 모임은 약 30분정도 소요될 것 같아요.

W: 지금 바로 그렇게 할게요. 감사합니다, 처장님.

Summary Note

A

❶ professor
❷ cultural issue
❸ ask questions
❹ ignores
❺ arrange meeting
❻ good time to meet

B

The student arranged to meet the dean of students because she has a problem. She thinks it might be something cultural because she is from a foreign land. She says that she has a problem with one of her professors. When the student raises her hand to ask a question in class, the professor ignores her. She calls on other students but ignores the student. The student tries speaking up in class and has waited for the professor after class, but the professor says nothing to her. The man says that he will talk to the professor and then arrange for the two of them to meet in his office on Friday. He tells the student to let his secretary know what time is good for her on Friday.

Exercise 3 1 Ⓓ 2 Ⓑ 3 Ⓐ p.176

Script 06-08

M Student: Professor Sabharwal, I need to talk to you about something.

W Professor: Please come into my office, young man. How might I help you?

M: I'm in your quantum physics class and looked at my grade. I think you must have made some kind of mistake when you calculated it.

W: Are you sure? I never make mistakes with grades!

M: Really?

W: Well, I must admit that from time to time, I do make errors. What makes you think there's a problem with my grade?

M: Well, you gave us a spreadsheet with our updated grades, right? And right now, my score is seventy-two, which should be impossible because on the midterm exam, I got an eighty-five, and on the quiz, I got a ninety. So I think my score should be about eighty-six.

W: Oh, goodness. Let me take a look at your scores . . . Just a minute, please . . . Why don't you sit down? I'll need a minute just to locate the file . . . Aha! I got it . . . What is your student number?

M: It's 2-0-0-6-1-1-8-7.

W: Hmm . . . This is strange . . . very strange . . . I can't find you. You're not on my list. It's as if you don't exist.

M: Well, I'm in your morning class that meets every Tuesday and Thursday at 10:00.

W: Oh, I believe you, and I remember you . . . but I just can't seem to find you . . . Oops! I was looking at the wrong file. Just a minute . . . Aha. I got it. Your midterm exam was an eighty-five, and you got a ninety on your quiz. Does that sound correct?

M: Yes, that's exactly what I told you a minute ago.

W: Well, you're doing very well in my class. And you're right. I did make a mistake. Your score should be an eighty-six right now. That's a good score. It's one of the highest in the class.

M: So you'll change my grade, right?

W: Yes, of course. I'm really sorry I caused you such an inconvenience. Next time, if you have any problems, just call me, okay? You don't have to come all the way down here. You can even talk to me about it during class time. I don't mind. And don't hesitate to ask me any questions in class.

M: Okay. But I didn't have to go out of my way or anything.

W: Well, I'm truly sorry. I did the grades late at night after I had had a long day at work. I hope I didn't make any other mistakes like that. And thank you for bringing this to my attention.

M: It's no problem. Thanks for your help.

W: Okay. I'd better check the other students' grades in case I made more mistakes like that . . . In any event, have a nice weekend.

해석

M Student: Sabharwal 교수님, 교수님께 드릴 말씀이 있어서요.

W Professor: 사무실 안으로 들어오세요. 어떻게 도와 드릴까요?

M: 저는 교수님의 양자 물리학 수업을 듣고 있는데, 제 성적을 보았어요. 제 생각에 교수님께서 채점하실 때 틀림없이 실수를 하신 것 같아요.

W: 정말인가요? 성적에 있어서는 제가 절대로 실수를 하지 않아요!

M: 정말인가요?

W: 음, 가끔 실수를 한다는 점은 인정해야겠군요. 어떤 점 때문에 성적에 문제가 있다고 생각하나요?

M: 음, 교수님께서 저희에게 성적이 갱신된 성적표를 주셨어요, 그렇죠? 그리고 지금 제 점수는 72점인데, 중간고사에서 제가 85점을 받았고 퀴즈에서는 90점을 받았기 때문에 그러한 점수는 불가능한 것이에요. 따라서 저는 제 점수가 86점 정도 되어야 한다고 생각해요.

W: 오, 이런. 학생 점수를 확인해 볼게요… 잠시만요… 앉는 것이 어떨까요? 파일을 찾는데 시간이 필요해서… 아하! 찾았어요… 학번이 어떻게 되나요?

M: 2-0-0-6-1-1-8-7입니다.

W: 흠… 이상하네요… 정말 이상한데… 학생을 찾을 수가 없어요. 제 명단에 없군요. 마치 없는 학생처럼요.

M: 음, 저는 매주 화요일과 목요일 10시에 진행되는 교수님의 오전 수업을 듣고 있어요.

W: 오, 맞아요, 학생이 기억나요… 그런데 찾을 수가 없네요… 이런! 제가 다른 파일을 보고 있었군요. 잠시 기다리시면… 그래요. 찾았어요. 중간고사 성적이 85점이었고 퀴즈에서는 90점을 받았군요. 맞는 것 같나요?

M: 네, 제가 조금 전에 말씀드린 그대로예요.

W: 음, 제 수업에서 성적이 정말 좋군요. 그리고 학생 말이 맞아요. 제가 실수를 했네요. 학생 점수는 이제 86점이 될 거예요. 높은 점수군요. 수업에서 가장 높은 점수 중 하나예요.

M: 그러면 제 성적도 바꿔 주실 거죠, 그렇죠?

W: 네, 물론이에요. 불편을 끼쳐 드려서 정말 죄송해요. 다음 번에 문제가 생기면 전화를 주세요, 알겠죠? 여기까지 찾아올 필요는 없어요. 수업 시간에 제게 이 야기를 해도 좋고요. 저는 개의치 않아요. 그리고 수업 중에 질문이 있으면 주저하지 말고 하세요.

M: 알겠습니다. 일부러 찾아오고 할 필요가 없었군요.

W: 음, 정말 미안해요. 일하느라 긴 하루를 보낸 후에 밤늦게 채점을 했거든요. 그러한 실수가 또 있지는 않았으면 좋겠네요. 그리고 지적해 줘서 고마워요.

M: 천만에요. 도와 주셔서 감사합니다.

W: 좋아요. 그와 같은 실수가 더 있을 수도 있으니 다른 학생들의 성적도 확인해 보는 것이 좋겠네요… 어쨌든 주말 잘 보내세요.

Summary Note

A

❶ his grade
❷ the scores
❸ list
❹ wrong file
❺ wrong
❻ Apologizes

B

The student goes to the professor's office to tell her that he suspects that the professor made a mistake when she calculated the student's quantum physics grade. The student says that according to the professor's spreadsheet, his grade is only a seventy-two, but his midterm score was an eighty-five, and his quiz score was a ninety. Therefore, he feels that his grade should be higher than a seventy-two. The professor tells him that she sometimes makes mistakes calculating grades. She asks for the student's ID number but cannot find the student on the class list. Eventually, the professor realizes that she is looking at the wrong list. Then, she finds the right list and confirms that student's statements are correct. She informs the student that the correct grade is an eighty-six. She apologizes for the mistake and tells the student that she did the grades late at night.

Exercise 4 1 Ⓒ 2 Ⓐ 3 Ⓒ p.178

Script 06-09

M Student: Good afternoon, ma'am. I think my books are almost due, so I'd like to renew them. I don't have to bring them to the library, do I?

W Librarian: Oh, no, of course you don't have to do that. Just let me see your student ID card, and I can call up your record on the screen.

M: You have no idea how much of a relief it is to hear those words come out of your mouth. I've got a ton of books checked out, so lugging them up here wouldn't be fun. Here's my card.

W: Okay, let me take a look . . . Your name is Jason Stevens, right? And you have . . . Wow . . . That's a lot of books you have checked out. Thirty-five in total? You must be some kind of a bookworm.

M: Not really. It's just that I have this upcoming report due in one of my classes, so I'm trying to do as much research as I can. So when are the books due now?

W: They aren't due until November 29. That's four weeks from today, so you should have plenty of time to finish everything by then.

M: Excellent. You've been quite a lot of help . . . Oh, I have a question for you. I've been trying to find this book . . . It's really crucial to my research, but it appears to have been checked out by someone. Do you think you could check to see if it has been returned yet?

W: I don't mind at all. That's exactly what I'm here for. Why don't you give me the title of the book so that I can check on its status?

M: Sure, I can do that. The title of the book is *Exploring New Methods in Historiography*.

W: Hmm, I didn't know that there were any new methods in history. But I guess you're the expert, huh?

M: Yeah, it's not exactly the most fascinating topic in the world, but without it, I don't know what I'll do. I guess I'll have to purchase it from a bookstore, but considering that it costs around fifty dollars, I'd much rather check it out instead. So what's the verdict on the book?

W: I'd have to say that today is your lucky day. It appears that whoever had it checked out just returned it to the library. Here's the call number for the book. Let me write it down for you . . . Now here's something you need to keep in mind. Since it just got returned, it might not be shelved yet. Why don't you head down to the stacks and take a look? If it's not where it should be, come back up here, and I'll find it in the returned books section.

M: Wow. That is some seriously awesome news. Thanks a lot.

W: You don't have to thank me. I'm just doing my job.

해석

M Student: 안녕하세요, 선생님. 책 반납일이 거의 다 된 것 같아서 갱신을 하려고 해요. 도서관으로 가지고 오지 않아도 되죠, 그렇죠?

W Librarian: 오, 그럼요, 물론 그럴 필요가 없죠. 제게 학생증만 보여 주시면 제가 화면에서 학생의 기록을 불러 올게요.

M: 그러한 말씀이 제게 얼마나 다행인 것인지 결코 모르실 거예요. 엄청나게 많은 책을 대출했기 때문에 책들을 여기까지 가지고 오면 장난이 아닐 거예요. 여기 제 학생증이요.

W: 좋아요, 제가 한번 볼게요··· 이름이 Jason Stevens군요, 맞죠? 그리고 학생은··· 와··· 많은 책을 대출했네요. 전부 35권인가요? 분명 책벌레인 것 같군요.

M: 꼭 그렇지는 않아요. 제가 듣는 수업 중 하나의 리포트 마감일이 다가오고 있어서 최대한 조사를 많이 하려고 노력 중이죠. 그러면 이제 책 반납일이 언제가 되나요?

W: 11월 29일까지에요. 오늘부터 4주 후라서 그때까지 모든 작업을 마무리할 시간은 충분할 거예요.

M: 잘 됐네요. 큰 도움을 주셨군요··· 오, 질문이 하나 있어요. 이 책을 찾고 있는 중인데··· 조사에 정말 중요한 책이지만 누군가 이미 대출을 한 것처럼 보여서요. 혹시 반납이 되었는지 확인해 주실 수 있을까요?

W: 그럼요. 그게 제 일이니까요. 제가 도서 상태를 확인할 수 있도록 책 제목을 말씀해 주시겠어요?

M: 물론 그러죠. 책 제목이 *역사 기록학의 새로운 방법 연구*예요.

W: 흠, 역사에 새로운 방법이 있었는지는 제가 모르고 있었네요. 하지만 학생은 전문가겠죠, 그렇죠?

M: 예, 분명 세상에서 가장 매력적인 주제는 아니지만, 그 책이 없으면 제가 어떻게 해야 할지 모르겠어요. 서점에서 책을 사야 할 것 같은데, 50달러 정도의 책 가격을 생각하면 그 대신에 대출을 하는 편이 훨씬 낫죠. 그러면 도서 상태가 어떻게 나오나요?

W: 오늘 운이 좋다고 말씀드려야겠네요. 대출을 했던 사람이 조금 전에 책을 도서관에 반납했어요. 이게 그 책의 도서 청구 번호예요. 적어 드리죠··· 이제 기억하셔야 할 것을 알려 드릴게요. 방금 반납이 되었기 때문에 아직 서가에 진열되어 있지 않을 거예요. 서고로 내려가서 찾아보는 것이 어떨까요? 만약 있어야 할 곳에 없는 경우, 이곳으로 다시 오시면 제가 반납 도서 코너에서 찾아볼게요.

M: 와, 진짜 놀라운 소식이군요. 정말 감사합니다.

W: 고마워할 필요 없어요. 제 일이니까요.

Summary Note

A

❶ library
❷ renew books
❸ bring books with him
❹ research project
❺ buy it
❻ call number

B

The student goes to the library to renew some of his books. He asks the librarian if he needs to bring the books with him, but she tells him that is not necessary. He gives her his ID card, and she calls his name up on the computer. She then renews the student's books for him. The student proceeds to ask a question about a book that he needs to complete his research project. He says that the book is currently checked out, and because it is so expensive, he does not want to purchase it. The librarian checks its availability and notices that the book was returned that day. She gives the man the book's call number and then tells him that if the book is not on the shelves, he should tell her, and she will find the book in the returned books section.

Exercises with Long Lectures

Exercise 1 1 Ⓒ 2 Ⓓ 3 Ⓒ p.180

Script 06-10

M1 Professor: So what is free trade?

M2 Student: Free trade means no tariffs and no quotas between countries that trade goods with one another.

M1: Good answer. But it's not only the free flow of goods. It also means the free flow of services between nations. It's a system that allows people to buy and sell whatever they desire with whomever they desire. Advocates argue that total free trade will result in a net gain in wealth for both trading partners. Some of the characteristics of free trade are . . . Uh, let me list them for you . . . First is the absence of tariffs, which are taxes on imported goods and services. Second is the absence of quotas and other trade barriers. Third . . . is the free flow of labor between two trading partners. Fourth . . . is the free flow of capital between two trading partners. And fifth is the absence of subsidies and regulations on locally produced goods and services that give businesses in the home country an advantage over those in a foreign country. Now having said all this, keep in mind that free trade is a relatively loose term that means different things to different people. For instance, it can be any combination of these characteristics I just mentioned to you, and it's typically never completely 100% free. When you have a free-trade agreement between two countries, there are usually some protective policies in place.

Protectionism, on the other hand, means government restraint on trade between two nations. Protective trade or protective tariffs are a nation's efforts to prevent its own people from trading. Such protective measures include tariffs on imported goods and services, restrictive quotas on imported goods and services, government regulations which discourage imports, anti-dumping laws, and subsidies for local producers.

There are a number of advantages to free trade. Perhaps the most important advantage of free trade is that it lowers the costs of goods and services. This is possible for a number of reasons. For example, production can take place in nations where labor and other operating costs are lower. So companies might manufacture in developing nations, where labor costs are much cheaper. Likewise, it allows cheaper foreign manufactured goods from foreign businesses easily to be imported into a country where manufacturers cannot produce goods as cheaply. An example would be garment manufacturers in China. In addition, jobs can be outsourced to other countries where labor is much cheaper. This explains why a lot of telephone call centers are located in India. So with free trade, consumers can pay lower prices for foreign manufactured goods or foreign services rather than pay higher costs to local high-cost producers. Free trade also attracts investors to developing nations, improving the economies of those nations. It allows corporations easily to operate across borders. It also results in social advantages such as the spread of democratic ideas to developing nations and the reduction of the likelihood of war between developed nations.

Despite its apparent advantages, there are a number of critics of free trade. Many people prefer protectionism. And as I mentioned a moment ago, in the real world, even when we have free trade or a free-trade agreement, there's still some protectionism. Protectionists feel it's better for local consumers to pay higher prices and thereby maintain quality jobs. So protectionism protects businesses, jobs, and wages, but it also means higher prices.

해석

M1 Professor: 그러면 자유 무역이란 무엇일까요?

M2 Student: 자유 무역은 서로 상품을 거래하는 두 나라 사이에 관세와 쿼터가 존재하지 않는 것을 의미합니다.

M1: 잘 대답했어요. 하지만 상품의 자유로운 흐름만은 아니에요. 국가 간의 서비스의 자유로운 흐름도 의미하죠. 이러한 시스템에서는 사람들이 원하는 어떤 사람과도 원하는 어떤 것이든 팔고 살 수 있어요. 지지자들은 완전한 자유 무역으로 무역 당사자들 모두가 부에 있어서 순수익을 거두게 될 것이라고 주장합니다. 자유 무역의 특징 중 일부는… 어, 말씀을 드리면… 첫 번째는 관세가 없다는 점인데, 관세는 수입 상품 및 서비스에 부과되는 세금입니다. 두 번째는 쿼터 및 기타 무역 장벽이 없다는 점이에요. 세 번째는… 두 무역 당사자 간에서 노동이 자유롭게 이동한다는 점입니다. 네 번째는… 두 무역 당사자 간에 자본이 자유롭게 이동한다는 점이죠. 그리고 다섯 번째는 타국 기업보다 자국 기업에게 이점을 주는, 역내에서 생산된 제품 및 서비스에 대한 보조금이나 규제가 없다는 것이에요. 이제 다 말씀을 드렸는데, 자유 무역은 각자에게 서로 다른 의미를 갖는 비교적 불명확한 용어라는 점을 명심하세요. 예를 들어 자유 무역은 제가 조금 전에 말씀드린 특징들 중 일부가 결합된 형태일 수 있으며, 일반적으로 완벽히 100%인 자유 무역은 없습니다. 두 국가 간에 자유 무역 협정이 체결되어 있는 경우, 보통은 몇 가지 보호 무역 정책들이 있기 마련이죠.

반면에 보호 무역주의는 두 국가 간의 무역에 대한 정부 규제를 의미합니다. 보호 무역이나 보호 관세는 무역에 있어서 자국 국민들을 보호하기 위한 국가의 노력이에요. 그러한 보호 무역 조치에는 수입 상품 및 서비스에 부과되는 관세, 수입 상품 및 서비스의 수량 제한, 수입을 어렵게 만드는 정부 규제 및 반덤핑법, 그리고 자국 기업에 제공되는 보조금이 포함되죠.

자유 무역에는 다수의 이점이 존재합니다. 자유 무역의 가장 중요한 이점은 아마도 상품 및 서비스의 가격을 낮춘다는 점일 거예요. 이는 여러 가지 이유에서 가능합니다. 예를 들어 생산은 인건비 및 기타 운영비가 낮은 국가에서 이루어질 수 있어요. 따라서 기업들은 인건비가 훨씬 더 저렴한 개발 도상국에서 생산을 할 수 있죠. 이로써 해외 기업에 의해 해외에서 생산된 보다 저렴한 상품들이, 그처럼 저렴한 비용으로는 생산자가 제품을 생산할 수 없는 국가로 쉽게 수입될 수 있습니다. 한 가지 예가 중국의 의류 생산업체들일 거예요. 또한 인건비가 훨씬 저렴한 다른 국가로 작업을 아웃소싱할 수도 있습니다. 많은 콜센터가 인도에 있는 것이 바로 이러한 이유 때문이죠. 따라서 자유 무역 하에서는 소비자들이 자국의 고비용 생산자에게 높은 비용을 지불하는 대신 해외에서 생산된 상품이나 서비스를 낮은 가격으로 구입할 수가 있습니다. 자유 무역은 또한 투자가들을 개발 도상국으로 끌어들여서 이들의 경제를 발전시켜요. 기업들이 쉽게 국경을 넘어 활동할 수 있게 만들죠. 또한 그 결과로, 예컨대 개발 도상국으로 민주주의 사상이 확산되고 선진국 간의 전쟁 가능성이 감소되는 것과 같은, 사회적인 이점이 나타납니다.

명백한 이점에도 불구하고, 자유 무역을 비판하는 사람들도 많아요. 많은 사람들이 보호 무역주의를 선호합니다. 그리고 제가 조금 전에 언급했던 것처럼, 실제 세계에서는 자유 무역이나 자유 무역 협정이 존재하는 경우조차 어느 정도 보호 무역주의가 존재합니다. 보호 무역주의자들은 자국 소비자들이 더 높은 가격을 지불함으로써 양질의 일자리가 유지되는 것이 더 낫다고 생각해요. 따라서 보호 무역주의는 기업, 일자리, 그리고 임금을 보호해 주지만, 또한 가격 상승을 의미하기도 합니다.

Summary Note

A

❶ free trade
❷ goods and services
❸ wealth
❹ different meanings
❺ trading
❻ tariffs
❼ Cheap
❽ developing nations

B

Free trade is the free flow of goods and services between nations. Some of the characteristics of free trade are the absence of tariffs, quotas, subsidies, and various other regulations that limit the free flow of business. Free trade agreements usually involve some protective policies. Protectionism is government restraint on trade between two nations. It is one nation's efforts to prevent its own people from trading. Such protective measures include tariffs, restrictive quotas, government regulations, anti-dumping laws, and subsidies. One major advantage of free trade is that it keeps prices down, but at the same time, a big disadvantage is that it might cause many domestic businesses to suffer economically, domestic jobs to disappear, and domestic wages to decrease. Foreign businesses, especially in poorer countries, can provide the same goods and services at cheaper prices because of lower labor costs.

Exercise 2 1 Ⓓ 2 Ⓒ 3 Ⓒ p.182

Script 06-11

W Professor: Before we get into details about the art of photography and discuss the mechanics of cameras, I want to give you a brief history of some of the major events in the development of photography so that you'll have a greater appreciation for the art and technology that we have today.

You might have already read in your textbooks that in the fourth and fifth centuries B.C., philosophers in China and Greece described the basic principles of cameras. Now, this might not seem like a big deal because they were still far from inventing a camera, but what is of particular interest here is that they were already familiar with the basic principles of optics. In the 1660s, Isaac Newton discovered that white light was actually composed of different colors. By this time, darkrooms had already existed as a tool to assist in drawings. Then, in 1727, we get our first important chemical discovery. Johann Heinrich Schulze discovered that exposure to light would darken silver nitrate. Finally, in 1814, a Frenchman, Joseph Nicéphore Niépce, became the first person to create a photographic image. However, his discovery wasn't a very practical one because his image needed to be exposed to light for at least eight hours. And more importantly, the image quickly faded. However, after this, the development of photography quickly snowballed, and within a generation, we had what very closely resembled modern-day photography. Niépce died in 1833. But his business partner, Louis Daguerre, continued to experiment.

Finally, in 1837, Daguerre performed possibly the greatest or most important feat in the history of photography when he became the first person successfully to capture an image that did not fade. In other words, this was the first permanent image. He accomplished this by immersing the image in salt. He also developed photographic plates, which significantly reduced the required exposure time to thirty minutes. As a result of this, many artists at that time felt that this would seriously jeopardize their livelihoods, and some predicted that painting would cease to exist.

In 1841, William Henry Talbot developed the first negative-positive process, which made it possible to have multiple copies of the same image. But exposure times still took three to fifteen minutes. Modern-day photography is based on the same principles that he used. Finally, in 1851, Frederick Scott Archer invented the Collodion process, in which images only required a few seconds of light exposure. This was also cheaper and therefore made it possible for most middle-class people to have their portraits done. The first mass-market camera was sold in 1900. It was called the Brownie. In 1913, the first 35mm still camera was developed, and then, in 1927, General Electric invented the first modern flashbulb. Polaroid cameras were first marketed in 1948. In 1973, instant cameras were introduced, and then, in the mid-1980s, we had the arrival of digital cameras.

해석

W Professor: 사진술을 자세히 살펴보고 카메라의 역학을 논의하기 전에, 오늘날의 사진과 그 기술을 보다 잘 평가하실 수 있도록, 사진의 발달에 중요했던 사건들의 역사를 간략히 알려 드리고자 합니다.

여러분은 이미 교재에서 기원전 4세기와 5세기에 중국과 그리스의 철학자들이 사진기의 기본 원리를 설명했다는 내용을 읽었을 거예요. 자, 사진기가 발명되기 한참 전이었기 때문에 이러한 점이 대단한 것으로 보이지 않을 수도 있지만, 여기에서 특히 흥미로운 점은 그들이 광학의 기본 원리를 이미 알고 있었다는 점입니다. 1660년대에 아이작 뉴턴은 흰색의 빛이 실제로는 여러 가지 색깔로 이루어져 있다는 점을 밝혀냈어요. 당시 그림의 보조 도구로서 이미 암실이 존재하고 있었죠. 그러다가 1727년에 화학적으로 중요한 최초의 발견이 이루어졌습니다. 요한 하인리히 슐츠가 질산은이 빛에 노출되면 어두운 색으로 변한다는 점을 알아냈죠. 마침내 1814년에 프랑스인인 조제프 니세포르 니에프스가 최초로 사진 이미지를 만들었습니다. 하지만 이미지를 최소한 8시간 이상 빛에 노출시켜야 했기 때문에 그의 발견은 그다지 실용적이지 못했어요. 그리고 보다 중요한 점은 이미지가 빠르게 희미해졌다는 점이었어요. 하지만 이후 사진술이 급속도로 발전을 했고, 한 세대가 지나기 전에 현대와 매우 유사한 사진술이 등장하게 되었습니다. 니에프스는 1833년에 사망했어요. 하지만 그의 사업 파트너였던 루이 다게르가 계속 실험을 진행했습니다.

마침내 1837년에 다게르가 처음으로 희미해지지 않는 이미지를 만드는데 성공함으로써 역사상 가장 위대한, 혹은 가장 중요한 업적을 이루었는데, 이것이 바로 최초의 영구적인 사진이었어요. 이미지를 소금에 담금으로써 그럴 수 있었습니다. 그는 또한 인화지를 개발했으며, 이는 노출 시간을 30분으로 크게 감소시켰어요. 그 결과 당시의 많은 화가들이 생계에 심각한 위협을 느꼈고, 몇몇 사람들은 그림이 사라지게 될 것이라는 예언을 하기도 했죠.

1841년 윌리엄 헨리 톨봇이 최초로 네거티브-포지티브법을 개발함으로써 같은 이미지를 여러 장 얻을 수 있게 되었습니다. 하지만 노출 시간은 여전히 3분에서 15분 정도였죠. 현대의 사진술도 그가 사용했던 것과 동일한 원리에 기초하고 있습니다. 드디어 1851년에 프레드릭 스코트 아처가 콜로디온 습판법을 발명했는데, 이 방법에서는 이미지를 몇 초만 빛에 노출시키면 되었어요. 이는 또한 가격도 저렴했기 때문에 대부분의 중산층 사람들도 초상 사진을 찍을 수가 있었죠. 최초의 대량 판매용 사진기는 1900년에 판매되었습니다. 브라우니라는 이름의 사진기였죠. 1913년에는 최초의 35mm 스틸 카메라가 만들어졌고, 1927년에는 제너럴 일릭트릭사에서 최초의 현대식 플래쉬 전구가 개발되었어요. 폴라로이드 사진기는 1948년에 최초로 출시되었습니다. 1973년에는 인스턴트 사진기가 소개되었고, 이후 1980년대 중반에는 디지털 카메라가 등장을 했죠.

Summary Note

A

❶ history of camera
❷ Chinese and Greek
❸ all colors
❹ darken
❺ photographic image
❻ didn't fade
❼ negative-positive
❽ mass-marketed

B

The history of photography is a long one. In the fourth and fifth centuries B.C., Greek and Chinese philosophers were already familiar with the basic principles of cameras. In 1727, Johann Heinrich Schulze discovered that exposure to light would darken silver nitrate. Finally, in 1814, a Frenchman, Joseph Nicéphore Niépce, created a photographic image, but it was not very practical because it needed to be exposed to light for at least eight hours and the image quickly faded. In 1833, his business partner, Louis Daguerre, became the first to capture a permanent image. He accomplished this by immersing the image in salt. He also developed photographic plates, which significantly reduced the required exposure time to thirty minutes. In 1841, William Henry Talbot invented a process that only required a few seconds to have multiple copies of the same image. Finally, in 1851, Frederick Scott Archer invented the Collodion process, in which images made it possible of light exposure.

Exercise 3 1 Ⓑ 2 Ⓐ 3 Ⓑ p.184

Script 06-12

W Professor: I'm glad you've all done your reading assignment . . . So now, um, perhaps, someone can remind us what archaeology is about.

M Student: Well, according to what we have read, it's a science which studies ancient cultures and past human activities.

W: And how do we study these ancient activities?

M: The ancients left little or no written records, but archaeologists can learn a lot by examining ancient remains such as buildings, tools, graves, artifacts, and stuff like that. They use these to reconstruct the past.

W: Correct. These remains are our chief source of knowledge of prehistoric and ancient cultures. And archaeologists mainly get their information by digging. In other words, they excavate the ground. Usually, this means digging a big hole. They expose, process, and record the remains of each archaeological site. One kind of archaeology is rescue archaeology, which is sometimes referred to in your readings as salvage archaeology or preventive archaeology. Rescue archaeology is the survey and excavation of areas of archaeological interest that have recently been revealed and are threatened by land development or construction. Usually, development is imminent, so archaeologists must urgently excavate so that they don't impede the developers. In other words, they have to rescue the site before the bulldozers move in. Uh . . . these archaeologists have to operate with tight deadlines. This means they need to record the details of the remains quickly. The actual fieldwork is conducted by an army of mobile professional archaeologists who are skilled in this type of work. Rescue archaeology is more common in cities because that's normally where ancient civilizations were located and where the remains lie. It's also where development usually occurs.

The bulldozer is not the only concern for rescuers. Many sites have suffered a lot of erosion, which adds to the peril of the situation. This is another reason for the urgent need to rescue. The excavation becomes an exercise in damage control as the team tries to limit the amount of damage that has occurred or will inevitably occur. We call this damage control.

M: Is there always such an urgency to excavate? Don't they ever take their time?

W: Oh, of course. What I described were the urgent cases. Often, there is no emergency or deadlines, so they have a lot more time and can examine things more closely. We call this research excavation. During research excavation, archaeologists have a lot more resources to assist in their work. They can work at a relaxed pace, and they can excavate more fully. Time is simply not of the essence. Usually, the people working on such sites are the academics and private societies who have sufficient labor and funding. Right now, as I speak, there are thousands of digs taking place all over the world.

While there aren't any excavations taking place near us, there are others elsewhere. However, surprisingly, despite their size, there are not many excavation sites in Canada and the United States. In fact, right now, Mexico has more digs than anywhere else in the Americas. The countries where extensive ancient civilizations were located tend to have more archaeological sites. In the Americas, Mexico and Peru have the most excavations. But at any given time, you would likely find a lot of digging in places like Iran, Egypt, Greece, and Italy. Ah, a good example would be Pompeii, the ancient Roman city that was destroyed by a volcano in 79 A.D. It was rediscovered in 1748, and ever since that time, a lot of excavations have been going on there even now in the present day.

해석

W Professor: 모두들 읽기 과제를 다 해서 기쁘네요… 그러면 이제, 음, 아마도 누군가가 고고학이 무엇인지 우리에게 상기시켜 줄 수 있을 것 같군요.

M Student: 음, 제가 읽은 바에 따르면, 고고학은 고대 문화와 과거 인류의 활동을 연구하는 학문이에요.

W: 그러면 그러한 고대의 활동은 어떻게 연구하나요?

M: 고대인들은 문서 기록을 거의 혹은 전혀 남기지 않았지만, 고고학자들은 건물, 도구, 무덤, 공예품, 그리고 기타 물건과 같은 고대 유적을 조사함으로써 많은 것을 알아낼 수 있어요.

W: 맞아요. 그러한 유적들은 선사 시대 및 고대 문화에 대해 알려 주는 중요한 자료가 됩니다. 그리고 고고학자들은 주로 땅을 파서 정보를 얻어요. 다시 말해서 발굴을 하는 것이죠. 이는 보통 커다란 구덩이를 파는 것을 의미해요. 고고학자들은 각 고고학 발굴 현장의 유적들을 드러내고, 처리하고, 그리고 기록합니다. 고고학의 한 분야는 구제 발굴인데, 여러분 책에서는 이것이 구제 고고학이나 예방 고고학으로 종종 지칭되기도 할 거예요. 구제 발굴은 최근에 발견되었지만 토지 개발이나 건설로 인해 위협을 받는, 고고학적인 관심을 불러일으키는 지역을 조사하고 발굴하는 것입니다. 일반적으로 개발이 임박한 경우가 많기 때문에 고고학자들은 개발업자들에게 방해가 되지 않도록 신속하게 발굴을 해야 해요. 다시 말해서 불도저가 밀고 들어오기 전에 발굴 현장을 구조해야 하는 것이죠. 어… 이러한 고고학자들은 빠듯한 마감 시간 하에서 작업을 해야 해요. 이는 유적의 세부적인 면들을 빠르게 기록해야 한다는 점을 의미하죠. 실제 현장에서는 이러한 작업에 능숙한 기동력 있는 전문적인 고고학자들에 의해 작업이 이루어집니다. 구제 발굴은 도시에서 보다 흔히 볼 수 있는데, 그 이유는 도시에 주로 고대 문명이 위치해 있었고 그곳에 유적이 남아 있기 때문이죠. 또한 보통 개발이 이루어지는 곳도 도시고요.

구제 발굴의 고고학자들이 걱정하는 것은 불도저만이 아닙니다. 많은 발굴 현장에서 심한 침식이 이루어지며, 이로써 상황이 더욱 악화되죠. 이는 긴급히 구제를 해야 하는 또 다른 이유가 됩니다. 발굴은 일종의 피해 대책 활동이 되는데, 발굴팀이 이미 발생한 혹은 불가피하게 발생할 피해를 최소화하기 위해 노력하기 때문이에요. 이를 피해 대책이라고 부릅니다.

M: 발굴이 항상 그렇게 촉박하게 이루어지나요? 여유가 있는 경우는 없나요?

W: 오, 당연히 있죠. 제가 설명드린 것은 긴급한 경우였어요. 종종 전혀 긴급하지 않거나 마감 시간이 없는 경우도 있는데, 따라서 시간이 훨씬 더 많아지며 보다 자세한 관찰도 가능해집니다. 우리는 이를 학술 발굴이라고 불러요. 학술 발굴을 할 때에는 고고학자들이 작업에 도움이 되는 자원을 더 많이 갖게 됩니다. 여유로운 속도로 작업을 할 수 있고, 발굴 작업도 보다 충실하게 할 수가 있죠. 시간은 중요하지 않습니다. 보통 그러한 발굴 현장에서 작업하는 사람들은 충분한 인력과 자금을 갖추고 있는 학술 단체 및 민간 단체에 소속된 사람들이에요. 제가 말씀드리는 이 순간에도 전 세계 각지에서 수천 개의 발굴 작업이 이루어지고 있죠.

이곳 근처에서 이루어지고 있는 발굴 작업은 없지만 다른 곳에는 있습니다. 하지만 놀라운 점은, 그 크기에도 불구하고, 캐나다와 미국에는 발굴 현장이 많지가 않아요. 실제로 현재 아메리카 대륙에서는 그 어떤 곳보다도 멕시코에 가장 발굴 현장이 많습니다. 광범위한 고대 문명이 존재했던 국가에 고고학적인 유적지가 더 많이 있는 경향이 있어요. 아메리카 대륙에서는 멕시코와 페루에 발굴 현장이 가장 많이 존재합니다. 하지만 어떤 경우이던 이란, 이집트, 그리스, 그리고 이탈리아와 같은 곳에서는 많은 발굴 작업을 찾아보실 수 있을 거예요. 아, 한 가지 좋은 예는 폼페이가 될 텐데, 폼페이는 기원후 79년에 화산 폭발로 파괴된 고대 로마의 도시였어요. 폼페이는 1748년에 다시 발견되었고, 그 이후로 현재까지 많은 발굴 작업들이 그곳에서 이루어져 왔습니다.

Summary Note

A

1. archaeology
2. ancient cultures
3. ancient remains
4. endangered areas
5. cities
6. Mexico

B

Ancient cultures left little or no written history, but archaeologists can learn a lot about these cultures by examining ancient remains such as buildings, tools, graves, and artifacts. These remains are the chief source of knowledge of prehistoric and ancient cultures. Archaeologists get their information by digging or excavating. One kind of archaeology is rescue archaeology, which is the examination of sites threatened by land development. Usually, development is imminent, so archaeologists must urgently excavate before the bulldozers move in. Many sites also suffer a lot of erosion, which adds to the peril of the situation. In such a case, excavation becomes an exercise in damage control. Sometimes excavation can be done at a relaxed pace with no deadlines. This is called research excavation. During this type of excavation, archaeologists have more resources and can excavate more fully. Right now, there are thousands of digs taking place all over the world. The countries where ancient civilizations were located tend to have the most archaeological sites.

Exercise 4 1 Ⓑ 2 Ⓒ 3 Ⓐ p.186

Script 06-13

M Professor: So we've discussed and looked at architecture, sculptures, and a number of paintings. But we haven't discussed ceramics yet. You see, uh, a lot of art students are not interested in this art form because they don't see it as being glamorous. But I think it does deserve some of our attention. So let me ask you a question. What exactly is ceramics?

W Student: Ceramics are objects that are made from clay. It's things like mugs, cups, plates, pots, tiles, and I think bricks, too.

M: Yes. Generally, ceramic arts, which are sometimes referred to as pottery, are pieces made from a combination of inorganic nonmetallic materials and heat. In other words, it's earthenware. And indeed, the most common ingredient is clay, but it's usually mixed with various minerals. Typically, pottery is something you've been using your entire life. I mean it's usually kitchenware and various other kinds of containers. It usually has utilitarian purposes, but sometimes it's designed purely for decorative reasons. Because of its practicality and durability, it's probably the oldest form of art. Many pieces date back several thousand years to the age of prehistoric man. Early man had little time for decorative art but developed pots primarily for practical reasons. Imagine drinking water all these centuries without cups or eating without plates.

W: How do they make it look so refined? What you see in the stores and museums hardly looks like clay.

M: Oh, I'm glad you asked that question. First, much of the kitchenware that you see in stores is mass-produced in factories. But making beautiful, refined-looking pottery is not difficult. Many pots are made in old-fashioned, modest studios just like they were hundreds of years ago. And they're made by hand. Potters might use a potter's wheel, but that's all. The potter starts with a hunk of clay, shapes it with his hands, and then lays it out to dry. Later, the potter heats it up in an oven, which we call a kiln. This hardens the clay. Once it's heated, the shape becomes permanent and can no longer be modified. This is why pottery is so durable. Pots are usually heated at an extremely high temperature, which varies with the purpose. Sometimes the pots are heated twice, but they're always glazed before the final firing, which gives them that refined look and makes them nonporous. In addition, when painters use pots or plates as a canvas and devote a lot of attention and detail to the design, that works wonders.

W: So how high do the pots have to be heated?

M: Well, as I said, that depends on the purpose of the art form. If the temperature is heated to more than 1,200 degrees Celsius, it will essentially turn the clay into manmade stone. We call this stoneware. It's hard enough to resist scratching. A lot of fancy plates are made this way, and with the touch of a skilled painter, they can be made to look very beautiful. There are other types of pottery, such as earthenware and porcelain. Earthenware is heated below 1,200 degrees.

해석

M Professor: 그러면 건축, 조각, 그리고 많은 회화들에 대해 논의하고 살펴보았군요. 하지만 아직 도기에 대해서는 논의하지 않았어요. 아시다시피, 어, 많은 학생들은 매력적인 것으로 보이지 않는다는 이유로 이러한 예술에 관심을 보이지 않습니다. 하지만 저는 충분히 우리의 관심을 끌만한 것이라고 생각해요. 그리니 제가 질문을 하나 하죠. 도기가 정확히 무엇일까요?

W Student: 도기는 점토로 만들어진 물건입니다. 머그잔, 컵, 접시, 항아리같은 것인데, 제 생각에는 타일도 포함될 것 같아요.

M: 맞아요. 일반적으로 도기는, 때때로 도자기라고도 불리는데, 비금속 무기질과 열로 만든 물건입니다. 다시 말해서 흙으로 만든 제품이죠. 그리고 실제로 가장 많은 성분은 점토이지만 보통은 다양한 물질들이 혼합되어 있어요. 전형적으로 도자기는 평생 동안 사용하는 물건입니다. 보통 주방용품 및 다양한 종류의 용기라는 뜻이죠. 통상적으로는 실용적인 기능을 지니지만, 때로는 순전히 장식적인 목적으로 만들어지기도 해요. 실용성과 내구성 때문에, 도기는 아마도 가장 오래된 형태의 예술일 것입니다. 많은 도기들이 수천 년 전 선사 시대 때 만들어졌어요. 초기 인류에게는 장식 예술을 할 만한 시간이 거의 없어서 주로 실용적인 목적으로 도자기 그릇이 만들어졌죠. 수 세기 동안 컵 없이 물을 마시거나 접시 없이 음식을 먹었다고 상상해 보세요.

W: 어떻게 그처럼 세련되게 만드나요? 상점과 박물관에서 볼 수 있는 것들은 전혀 점토 같지 않아서요.

M: 오, 그런 질문을 하다니 기쁘군요. 우선, 상점에서 볼 수 있는 상당수의 주방용품은 공장에서 대량으로 만들어집니다. 하지만 아름답고 멋진 도기를 만드는 것은 어렵지 않아요. 많은 도자기 그릇들이 수백 년 전과 똑같은 옛날 방식의 초라한 작업실에서 만들어집니다. 그리고 손으로 만들어져요. 도공들이 물레를 사용할 수도 있지만, 그것이 다입니다. 도공은 점토 한 덩이로 작업을 시작해서, 손으로 모양을 잡은 다음, 이를 건조시킵니다. 그 후 도공은 이를 가마라고 불리는 화덕에 두고 굽습니다. 열이 가해지면 형태는 영구적인 것이 되고 더 이상 변형이 불가능해지죠. 바로 이러한 점 때문에 도자기의 내구성이 우수한 것입니다. 도자기 그릇은 보통 엄청난 고온으로 구워지며, 온도는 목적에 따라 달라져요. 때로는 도자기에 두벌구이를 하는 경우도 있지만, 마지막으로 굽기 전에는 항상 유약을 바르는데, 유약을 바르면 이들이 세련되게 보이고 구멍도 없어지죠. 또한 화공들이 도자기 그릇이나 접시를 캔버스로 사용해서 많은 주의를 기울여 세부적인 문양을 그리면 환상적인 작품이 탄생하게 됩니다.

W: 그러면 얼마나 높은 온도로 도자기 그릇이 구워져야 하나요?

M: 음, 말씀을 드린 것처럼 도예의 목적에 따라 달라져요. 섭씨 1200도 이상으로 가열하는 경우에는 반드시 점토가 인공석으로 바뀌게 됩니다. 이를 사기 제품이라고 부르죠. 긁어도 상처가 나지 않을 정도로 단단합니다. 많은 멋진 접시들이 이러한 방식으로 만들어지며, 솜씨가 뛰어난 화공의 손길이 더해지면 매우 아름다운 작품이 만들어질 수 있습니다. 토기 제품이나 자기 제품과 같은 다른 형태의 도기들도 존재해요. 토기는 1200도 이하의 온도에서 구워집니다.

Summary Note

A

❶ ceramics
❷ clay
❸ pottery
❹ kitchenware
❺ potter's wheel
❻ firing again

B

Generally, ceramic arts, which are sometimes referred to as pottery, are pieces made from a combination of inorganic nonmetallic materials and heat. The most common ingredient is clay, but it is usually mixed with various minerals. Typically, pottery is something people have used their entire lives: kitchenware. It usually has utilitarian purposes, but sometimes it is designed purely for decorative reasons. It is very durable, and it is the oldest form of art. Many pieces date back to the age of prehistoric man. Much of the kitchenware seen in the stores is mass-produced in factories. However, many pots are made in old-fashioned, modest studios. They are also made by hand. The potter starts with a hunk of clay, shapes it with his hands, and then heats it up in a kiln. This hardens the clay. Pots and other ceramic arts are usually heated at extremely high temperatures, but they are always glazed before the final firing, which gives them a refined look and makes them nonporous. Artists may add a final touch to them as well.

Integrated Listening & Speaking

p.188

A

Script 06-14

M Professor: As I already mentioned, there'll be a number of questions about free trade and protectionism on next week's exam. So keep in mind that free trade is basically the free flow of goods and services between nations. Usually, this means the absence of tariffs, quotas, subsidies, and restrictive regulations which limit the flow of business between two nations. Protectionism is the government restraining trade between two nations. It is basically the opposite of free trade and includes such protective measures as tariffs, quotas, government regulations, anti-dumping laws, and subsidies. One major advantage of free trade is that it keeps prices down, but at the same time, it can hurt domestic businesses and reduce domestic wages. Protectionism protects domestic businesses, domestic jobs, and domestic wages while keeping prices higher.

1 It is the free flow of goods and services between nations.

2 Protectionism

3 Stronger domestic businesses, more domestic jobs, and higher domestic wages.

B

Script 06-15

M Professor: Ceramic arts, or pottery, are items that are made from various natural ingredients like clay or other minerals. Most pottery has a practical use, like for bowls and plates. So how do we make pottery? Well, if doing that by hand, first the potter uses a potter's wheel to mold a piece of clay into the shape he wants. Then, he lets it dry, and after that, he bakes it in an oven called a kiln. When the clay is heated, it hardens, thereby making its shape permanent. After that, the pot is done. Of course, sometimes the potter heats it again, but not before glazing the pot. That is a process which gives pots the nice look that most of them have. It sounds like a difficult process, but it is really not that hard at all.

1 They use it for bowls, plates, and other practical reasons.

2 Shape some clay, let it dry, cook it in a kiln, and let it harden.

3 It is the process that makes pots look nice.

Mini TOEFL iBT Practice Test

p.190

1 Ⓓ 2 Ⓐ 3 Ⓒ 4 Ⓑ 5 Ⓐ

6 Ⓑ 7 Ⓓ 8 Ⓐ 9 Ⓒ 10 Torpor

Hibernators: 1, 3 Deep Hibernators: 2, 4

11 Ⓑ

[1-5]

Script 06-16

M Student: Good afternoon, Professor Rico. How are you doing today? I'm a bit surprised to see you in your office now. I was expecting you to have gone home by now.

W Professor: Ah, how fortunate you just dropped by, Brandon. I was really hoping that I would get to see you today.

M: Really? How come?

W: Do you remember the field trip that we went on to the Sanderson Art Gallery in our class last semester? I seem to recall that you really enjoyed it.

M: Oh, yes. I had a great time there. It was rather nice to see some new paintings that I hadn't had the opportunity to observe before. I go there regularly because it has such a great collection of artwork.

W: I'm very glad to hear that.

M: Yeah?

W: Yes. You see, uh, I'm taking another class to the gallery this weekend, and I'd like for you to accompany us on the trip.

M: But . . . I'm not in your class this semester. Why would you want me to go with you?

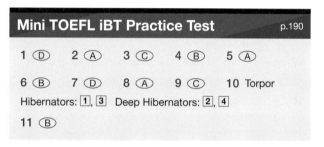

W: The one thing that the gallery doesn't have is any guides. Visitors have to learn about the paintings and the artists by themselves.

M: Yeah, I know. It's kind of unfortunate.

W: Well . . . I'd like you to be something of a guide for the students if you have the time. This class is kind of big. It's got around forty students, and that is too many for me to handle by myself. None of my colleagues has time on the weekend, so I thought I'd ask you. Do you think that you could lead a group of around twenty students?

M: Um . . . I'm really flattered that you're asking me for assistance, but I'm not sure I'm up to the task.

W: Oh, of course you are. The new exhibit features some works by Renaissance masters, and I remember you wrote an outstanding paper about them for me two years ago. I also remember hearing you telling the other students about some of the artists whose works were featured at the gallery last semester.

M: Yeah, I guess you're right.

W: So you can do it?

M: **What time is the bus leaving?** And where should I meet you?

W: We'll be departing at ten in the morning from in front of Granderson Hall. Will that be a problem for you?

M: Not at all. I no longer work part time on weekends, so I'm free all day long on Saturday.

W: That's great to hear. And just so you know, this isn't volunteer work. I'll make sure that you get paid to do it. I'm not sure how much I can give you. I'll have to speak with the head of my department about this matter. I'll be able to let you know how much you're making on the day of the field trip.

M: That's fine. Thanks for letting me know. I wasn't expecting to get paid though, so I really appreciate your generosity.

W: You're doing work and doing a big favor for me, so you should get paid for your effort. It's the least that I can do.

해석

M Student: 안녕하세요, Rico 교수님. 오늘 어떠신가요? 지금 교수님 사무실에서 교수님을 뵙게 되다니 약간 놀랐어요. 지금쯤이면 댁으로 가셨을 것이라고 생각했거든요.

W Professor: 아, 학생이 들리다니 정말 다행이군요, Brandon. 오늘 학생을 만날 수 있기를 정말로 바라고 있었어요.

M: 정말인가요? 왜요?

W: 지난 학기에 우리 수업에서 Sanders 미술관으로 현장 학습을 갔던 것이 기억나나요? 제 기억으로는 학생이 정말로 좋아했던 것 같아요.

M: 오, 네. 그곳에서 즐거운 시간을 보냈죠. 전에 볼 기회가 없었던 새로운 그림들을 보게 되어 상당히 좋았어요. 그곳에 미술 작품들이 꽤 많이 전시되어 있기 때문에 정기적으로 그곳에 가고 있죠.

W: 그런 이야기를 들으니 기쁘네요.

M: 그러신가요?

W: 네. 그러니까, 어, 저는 이번 주말에 다른 수업의 학생들을 데리고 미술관에 가려고 하는데, 학생이 현장 학습에 같이 가 주면 좋겠어요.

M: 하지만… 저는 이번 학기에 교수님 수업을 듣지 않는데요. 왜 저와 함께 가고 싶으신가요?

W: 한 가지 이유는 미술관에 가이드가 없기 때문이죠. 관람객들이 스스로 그림과 화가들에 대해 알아내야 해요.

M: 예, 저도 알아요. 안타까운 일이죠.

W: 음… 시간이 있는 경우, 학생이 학생들을 위한 가이드 같은 역할을 해 주면 좋겠어요. 이번 수업은 대형 강의 수업이에요. 약 40명의 학생들이 수업을 듣고 있는데, 저 혼자 감당하기에는 수가 너무 많아요. 동료 교수님들 중에서 주말이 시간이 되시는 분도 없어서 학생에게 요청을 해 봐야겠다고 생각했죠. 약 20명 정도의 학생들을 이끌 수 있을 것 같나요?

M: 음… 제게 도움을 요청하시니 정말로 기분이 들뜨기는 하지만, 제가 그 일을 해낼 수 있을지 잘 모르겠어요.

W: 오, 물론 할 수 있을 거예요. 새로운 전시에서는 르네상스 시대의 거장들의 작품이 전시되는데, 저는 학생이 2년 전에 그들에 대한 뛰어난 보고서를 썼던 것을 기억해요. 또한 지난 학기 미술관에서 전시된 작품들의 화가들 중 몇 명에 대해 학생이 다른 학생들에게 이야기하는 것을 들은 기억도 있고요.

M: 예, 교수님 말씀이 맞는 것 같군요.

W: 그러면 할 수 있겠죠?

M: 버스가 언제 떠나나요? 그리고 어디에서 교수님과 만나면 될까요?

W: 우리는 Granderson 홀 앞에서 오전 10시에 출발할 거예요. 그러한 점이 학생에게 문제가 될까요?

M: 전혀요. 주말에 더 이상 아르바이트를 하지 않게 되어서 토요일에는 하루 종일 시간이 있어요.

W: 반가운 소리군요. 그리고 알다시피 이번 일은 자원 봉사가 아니에요. 제가 일에 대해서는 학생이 꼭 보수를 받을 수 있도록 할게요. 얼마나 줄 수 있는지는 잘 모르겠어요. 이 문제에 대해서는 학과장님과 이야기를 해야 하거든요. 현장 학습 일에 학생이 얼마나 받게 될 것인지 알려 줄 수 있을 거예요.

M: 좋아요. 알려 주셔서 감사합니다. 하지만 보수를 받게 될 것이라는 점은 예상하지 못했기 때문에 신경 써 주신 부분에 대해서는 정말 감사해요.

W: 일을 해서 제 어려운 부탁을 들어줄 테니 노고에 대한 보상은 받아야죠. 제가 할 수 있는 최소한의 일이에요.

[6-11]

Script 06-17

M Professor: So for these reasons, when you're camping, be sure that you take all of the necessary precautions to avoid bear encounters, or else your trip might have a very unpleasant ending.

W Student: This winter, I'll be going camping. It'll be the first time I've ever tried winter camping. I was wondering, um, since bears usually hibernate during the winter, do we, ah, do we still have to take the same precautions as when we go camping in the summer?

M: Yes, you do. First of all, you don't know when bears are going to start hibernating, and you don't know when they're going to stop hibernating, and most importantly, bears don't hibernate.

W: Really?

M: Yes, really. The stories you were told as a child about bears hibernating are not true. Bears are not true hibernators. Let me repeat that. Bears don't hibernate. True hibernation essentially means total inactivity for several days or weeks. It's a state or a phase that some animals experience when the days become very short, the temperature cools, and food quantities are limited. Furthermore, there are different kinds of hibernators. True hibernation is also referred to as deep hibernation because the animal's body is inactive for a very long period, its body temperature decreases to five degrees or less, its metabolism decreases, and its breathing slows down. True hibernation is a survival mechanism during the long, cold winter season, when food is scarce. Deep hibernation allows the animal to conserve its energy. Its sleep is so deep that it cannot be awakened. This allows animals to skip the cold, stressful winter. Bears, however, are not true hibernators. They can awaken during the winter. Please remember that.

So . . . what are bears? Basically, they are torpor hibernators. This means they are not true hibernators like some smaller animals. Torpor hibernators are inactive only for a short time, perhaps during the coldest hours of the night. They don't sleep for several weeks like true hibernators, and their temperature never drops to five degrees. In fact, bears' temperatures rarely drop below thirty degrees. When an animal is in torpor, it's capable of quick arousal. Some bears will sleep for several weeks, but even if they do, they are capable of waking up very quickly. That's why bears are dangerous all year round.

How do animals know when to hibernate? Well, some hibernators, like reptiles, are capable of predictive dormancy, which means that as the days decrease in length, they can anticipate winter approaching, and then they begin hibernating automatically. Because they can anticipate cold weather, they can avoid the potentially lethal cold season by going into hibernation. Other animals are not capable of this anticipation. They're only capable of consequential dormancy. In other words, they don't hibernate until they've been exposed to cold weather. If the winter is mild or the animal is located in an area where seasonal weather conditions are unpredictable, it might stay active all winter if conditions permit. If it gets too cold, it can start hibernating.

What about deep hibernators? Some deep hibernators are chipmunks, woodchucks, snakes, box turtles, and toads. Torpor hibernators include bears, raccoons, and skunks. **Non-hibernating animals are red foxes, gray squirrels, and wild turkeys, among others.**

해석

M Professor: 따라서 이러한 이유들 때문에 캠핑을 할 때에는 곰을 마주치지 않도록 필요한 모든 예방 조치를 취해야 하며, 그렇지 않을 경우에는 여러분의 여행이 매우 불행한 결말로 끝날 수도 있습니다.

W Student: 저는 이번 겨울에 캠핑을 갈 거예요. 겨울 캠핑은 처음이죠. 궁금한 점이, 음, 곰은 보통 겨울에 동면을 하기 때문에 저희가, 어, 저희가 여름에 캠핑을 갈 때와 똑같은 예방 조치를 해야 하나요?

M: 네, 그래요. 무엇보다, 곰이 언제 동면을 시작할지 모르고, 언제 동면에서 깨어날지 모를 텐데, 가장 중요한 것은 곰은 동면을 하지 않는다는 점이에요.

W: 정말인가요?

M: 네, 정말이죠. 여러분이 어렸을 때 들었던 겨울잠을 자는 곰 이야기는 사실이 아닙니다. 곰은 실제로 동면을 하는 동물이 아니에요. 다시 한 번 얘기해 드리죠. 곰은 동면을 하지 않습니다. 진정한 동면은 기본적으로 며칠 또는 몇 주 동안 완전히 활동을 하지 않는 것을 의미해요. 이는 낮이 매우 짧아지고, 기온이 내려가며, 그리고 먹이가 줄어들 때 일부 동물들이 겪는 상태나 단계입니다. 게다가 다양한 형태의 동면을 하는 동물들이 존재해요. 진정한 동면은 깊은 동면으로도 불리는데, 그 이유는 동물의 신체가 매우 오랫동안 활동을 하지 않으며, 체온이 5도 이하로 떨어지고, 대사량이 줄어들며, 그리고 호흡이 느려지기 때문이죠. 진정한 동면은 먹이가 부족한 길고 추운 겨울을 보낼 수 있는 생존 메커니즘입니다. 깊은 동면을 통해 동물들은 에너지를 보존할 수 있어요. 매우 깊은 잠을 자기 때문에 깨어날 수가 없습니다. 이 때문에 동물들이 춥고 힘든 겨울을 날 수 있는 것이죠. 하지만 곰은 진정한 동면을 하는 동물이 아니에요. 겨울에 깨어날 수도 있습니다. 이 점을 기억해 주세요.

그러면… 곰은 무엇일까요? 기본적으로 휴면을 하는 동물이에요. 몸집이 보다 작은 동물들처럼 진정한 동면을 하지는 않는다는 뜻입니다. 휴면을 하는 동물들은 짧은 시간 동안만, 아마도 가장 추운 야간 시간대에만 활동을 하지 않아요. 진정한 동면을 하는 동물들처럼 몇 주 동안 잠을 자는 것은 아니며, 체온도 결코 5도까지 떨어지지 않죠. 실제로 곰의 체온은 30도 이하로 떨어지는 경우가 거의 없습니다. 동물이 휴면 상태에 들어가면 빨리 일어날 수 있어요. 일부 곰들은 몇 주 동안 잠을 자겠지만, 그러한 경우조차 매우 빨리 잠에서 깨어날 수 있습니다. 바로 이러한 이유 때문에 곰은 1년 내내 위험한 동물인 것이죠.

동물들이 언제 동면에 들어가야 하는지를 어떻게 알까요? 음, 동면을 하는 일부 동물들은, 예컨대 파충류는 예측에 의해 동면을 하는데, 이는 낮 길이가 짧아지면 이들이 겨울이 온다는 것을 알고 자동적으로 동면에 들어간다는 의미입니다. 추운 겨울을 예상할 수 있기 때문에 동면에 들어감으로써 치명적일 수도 있는 추운 시기를 피하는 것이죠. 이러한 예상을 하지 못하는 동물들도 있습니다. 이들은 상황에 따른 동면만을 할 수 있어요. 다시 말해서, 추운 날씨를 접한 후에야 동면을 하게 되는 것이죠. 만약 겨울 날씨가 따뜻하거나 계절 날씨를 예측할 수 없는 지역에 동물이 있는 경우, 이 동물은 상황이 허락하는 한 겨울 내내 활동을 할 수도 있어요. 날씨가 너무 추워지는 경우에는 동면에 들어갈 수 있죠.

깊은 동면을 하는 동물들은 어떨까요? 깊은 동면을 하는 동물로는 얼룩다람쥐, 우드척, 뱀, 상자거북, 두꺼비 등이 있습니다. 휴면을 하는 동물에는 곰, 너구리, 그리고 스컹크가 포함되고요. 동면을 하지 않는 동물로는 붉은여우, 회색다람쥐, 그리고 야생 칠면조 등이 있습니다.

Vocabulary Check-Up

p.195

A

1 (E)	2 (A)	3 (F)	4 (H)	5 (C)
6 (K)	7 (D)	8 (J)	9 (B)	10 (I)
11 (L)	12 (G)	13 (O)	14 (N)	15 (M)

B

1 (B)	2 (E)	3 (C)	4 (D)	5 (A)

UNIT
07 Connecting Content

Basic Drill p.198

Drill 1 Ⓐ

Script 07-02

W Student: Good afternoon. I have something on my mind, Professor Daniels, so I'd like to speak with you, please.

M Professor: Can you make it fast? I've got a seminar to teach in five minutes.

W: Sure. This won't take long.

M: Great. What's up?

W: I've been thinking of doing a double major, but I'm not sure which subject to choose. My major is art history, but I have enough time to get a second major.

M: What are you considering?

W: I'm thinking about either doing history or chemistry. What do you think?

M: Well, both of them are good choices. You'll have to do a lot of work in chemistry because of the labs. You won't be quite so busy in history. But history might be the better choice.

W: Why is that?

M: You'll be able to understand the historical conditions in which many artists worked. As you know, artists are influenced by their times, so I would go with history if I were you.

해석

W Student: 안녕하세요. 고민이 하나 있는데요, Daniels 교수님, 교수님과 이야기를 나누고 싶습니다.

M Professor: 빨리 할 수 있나요? 5분 후에 세미나 수업에 가야 하거든요.

W: 그럼요. 오래 걸리지 않을 거예요.

M: 잘 되었네요. 무슨 일인가요?

W: 저는 복수 전공을 생각 중인데, 어떤 학과를 선택해야 할지 잘 모르겠어요. 제 전공은 미술사로, 두 번째 전공을 공부할 수 있는 시간은 충분하죠.

M: 무엇을 고려하고 있었나요?

W: 역사학이나 화학 중 하나를 생각 중이에요. 어떻게 생각하시나요?

M: 음, 둘 다 좋은 선택이군요. 화학에서는 실험 때문에 해야 할 일이 많을 거예요. 역사학의 경우 그다지 바쁘지는 않을 것이고요. 그런데 역사학이 더 좋은 선택일 것 같아요.

W: 왜 그런가요?

M: 많은 화가들이 작업을 했던 역사적인 배경을 이해할 수 있을 테니까요. 알겠지만, 화가들은 시대의 영향을 받기 때문에 제가 학생이라면 역사학을 선택할 것 같아요.

Drill 2 Ⓓ

Script 07-03

W Museum Curator: I'm very sorry, young man, but we're about to close for the day.

M Student: Really? That's too bad. I was hoping to see the new exhibit of Chinese pottery.

W: It's very impressive. Are you planning to view it because of a class you're taking?

M: Yes, that's right. My professor suggested that everyone in class look at it. Professor Westin spoke very highly of it in class.

W: Ah, so Candice sent you.

M: Candice?

W: That's Professor Westin's first name. We attended college together a long time ago.

M: Ah, I see. Well, I guess that I'll come back tomorrow.

W: That's quite all right. Since you're here for her class, I can let you stay for around twenty minutes. Will that be enough time?

M: More than plenty. Thank you so much, ma'am.

해석

W Museum Curator: 정말 죄송하지만, 곧 문을 닫을 거예요.

M Student: 정말인가요? 난감하군요. 저는 중국 도자기에 관한 새로운 전시회를 보고 싶었거든요.

W: 정말 인상적이죠. 듣고 있는 수업 때문에 관람할 생각인가요?

M: 네, 맞아요. 교수님께서 수업을 듣는 모든 학생들에게 관람을 추천하셨어요. Westin 교수님께서 수업 시간에 전시회를 매우 높게 평가하셨죠.

W: 아, 그러면 Candice가 학생을 보낸 것이군요.

M: Candice요?

W: Westin 교수님의 이름이에요. 우리는 오래전에 같이 대학을 다녔죠.

M: 아, 그러셨군요. 음, 제가 내일 다시 와야 할 것 같네요.

W: 괜찮아요. 학생이 이곳에서 그분의 수업을 듣고 있으니 20분 정도 머물러 있을 수 있도록 해 드리죠. 그 정도 시간이면 충분할까요?

M: 충분해요. 정말 고맙습니다, 선생님.

Drill 3 Reptiles: 2 Amphibians: 1, 3, 4

Script 07-04

W Professor: We all know that reptiles and amphibians are different kinds of animals. Nevertheless, people often get them confused with each other. Just remember that for the most part, lizards, turtles, snakes, alligators, and crocodiles are reptiles. As for amphibians, they include toads, frogs, salamanders, and newts.

Of course, uh, both reptiles and amphibians are vertebrates, meaning that they have backbones. However, their skin is different. Amphibians have moist skin whereas the skin of reptiles is dry and scaly. Reptiles' skin helps protect them in various ways. As for amphibians, their skin is permeable both to air and water as they sometimes breathe through their skin. Amphibians also live parts of their lives in water and part on land. While some reptiles live in the water, many never venture into it. For instance, crocodiles, alligators, and some species of snakes spend plenty of time in the water. Ah, yes, turtles as well. However, various reptiles and snakes don't go into the water at all.

Something else you often see is that highly toxic amphibians are brightly colored. This warns other animals to stay away from them. This is particularly the case for certain species of frogs. Oh, I nearly forgot. Because of amphibians' special skin, they need unique living conditions. If they get too much sun, their skin cells will get damaged. And if the wind blows too much, their skin can dry out, which dehydrates them.

해석

W Professor: 우리 모두는 파충류와 양서류가 다른 동물들이라는 것을 알고 있어요. 그럼에도 불구하고, 사람들이 이들을 혼동하는 경우가 많습니다. 대부분의 경우, 도마뱀, 거북, 뱀, 앨리게이터, 크로커다일은 파충류입니다. 양서류에 대해 말씀을 드리면, 여기에는 두꺼비, 개구리, 도롱뇽, 그리고 영원이 포함되죠.

물론, 어, 파충류와 양서류 모두 척추 동물인데, 이는 그들이 등뼈를 가지고 있다는 점을 의미해요. 하지만 이들의 피부는 서로 다릅니다. 양서류는 촉촉한 피부를 가지고 있는 반면에 파충류의 피부는 건조하고 비늘을 가지고 있죠. 파충류의 피부는 다양한 방법으로 이들을 보호해 줍니다. 양서류에 대해 말씀을 드리면, 이들은 때때로 피부로 호흡을 하기 때문에 공기와 물 모두 이들의 피부를 통과할 수 있어요. 양서류는 또한 삶의 일부는 물속에서, 그리고 일부는 육지에서 보냅니다. 물속에 사는 파충류도 있기는 하지만 다수의 파충류는 결코 물에 들어가지 않아요. 예를 들어 앨리게이터, 크로커다일, 그리고 일부 뱀들은 대부분의 시간을 물속에서 보냅니다. 아, 그래요, 거북도 마찬가지고요. 하지만 다양한 파충류 및 뱀들은 전혀 물에 들어가지 않습니다.

여러분이 종종 볼 수 있는 또 다른 점은 강력한 독성을 지닌 양서류들이 매우 밝은 색을 띤다는 것이에요. 이는 다른 동물들에게 자신으로부터 멀리 떨어지라는 경고를 해 주죠. 이러한 점은 특히 특정 종의 개구리들에게 해당됩니다. 오, 깜빡 잊을 뻔 했네요. 특별한 피부 덕분에 양서류들은 독특한 생활 환경을 필요로 해요. 햇빛에 너무 많이 노출되는 경우 이들의 피부 세포는 손상될 것입니다. 그리고 바람이 너무 많이 부는 경우에는 피부가 말라 버릴 수 있는데, 이는 탈수를 일으키죠.

Drill 4 Sir Francis Drake: [2], [3] Horatio Nelson: [1], [4]

Script 07-05

M Professor: An island nation, Great Britain has always depended upon its navy for protection. As such, it has produced countless highly capable seamen. Two of the greatest were Sir Francis Drake and Horatio Nelson. Interestingly, the two men accomplished their goals in different ways.

Drake lived in the 1500s, which was when Great Britain was beginning to send ships across the Atlantic Ocean to the Americas. He was a privateer, which is basically another word for pirate. He had a grudge against the Spanish, so he mostly attacked Spanish ships. He plundered their cargo and sank the ships, becoming a rich man in the process. In 1588, the Spanish sent an enormous fleet—now called the Spanish Armada—to invade Britain. The queen made Drake an admiral, and he led the British defense. Thanks to Drake's use of fireships and a powerful storm, Drake managed to defeat the Spanish Armada.

Horatio Nelson lived from 1758 to 1805. He served in the British Navy, where he fought both the French and the Spanish during the Napoleonic Wars. He fought in numerous battles, and he lost an eye and his right arm in two of them. In 1798, he won the Battle of the Nile against the French. In 1805, he led the British fleet at the Battle of Trafalgar. Prior to battle, he made the famous quote "England expects that every man will do his duty." Nelson was killed by a sniper, but Britain won the battle.

해석

M Professor: 섬나라인 영국은 항상 해군에 의존해 자국을 보호했습니다. 그래서 매우 유능한 선원들을 수없이 배출했죠. 가장 뛰어난 선원 중 두 명은 프랜시스 드레이크 경과 호레이쇼 넬슨이었습니다. 흥미롭게도, 이 두 사람은 서로 다른 방식으로 자신의 목표를 달성했습니다.

드레이크는 영국이 대서양을 건너 아메리카 대륙으로 선박을 보내기 시작한 1500년대에 살았습니다. 그는 사략선의 선장이었는데, 이는 기본적으로 그가 다름아닌 해적이었다는 뜻이에요. 그는 스페인에 대한 원한을 가지고 있었기 때문에 주로 스페인 선박들을 공격했습니다. 화물을 약탈하고 배를 침몰시키는 과정에서 그는 부자가 되었습니다. 1588년 스페인은 영국을 침략하기 위해, 현재 스페인 무적 함대라고 불리는, 대규모 함대를 보냈어요. 여왕은 드레이크를 해군 제독으로 임명했고, 그가 영국의 방어를 이끌게 되었습니다. 드레이크가 화공선과 강력한 폭풍을 이용한 덕분에 드레이크는 스페인의 무적 함대를 물리칠 수 있었습니다.

호레이쇼 넬슨은 1758년에서 1805년까지 살았어요. 그는 영국 해군에서 복무했으며, 나폴레옹 전쟁 당시 프랑스 및 스페인 모두와 맞서 싸웠습니다. 그는 수많은 전투에 참여했는데, 그중 두 차례 전투에서 한쪽 눈과 오른쪽 팔을 잃었습니다. 1798년에는 프랑스를 상대로 나일 전투에서 승리했습니다. 1805년에는 트라팔가 전투에서 영국 함대를 이끌었죠. 그는 전투에 앞서 "영국은 모든 사람이 자신의 의무를 다하기 바란다."라는 유명한 명언을 남겼습니다. 넬슨은 저격수에 의해 살해되었지만 영국은 전투에서 승리했습니다.

Exercises with Long Conversations

Exercise 1 1 Ⓑ 2 Ⓑ 3 Ⓐ p.202

Script 07-06

M Student: Hello, Professor Cronkite. I was just wondering if I could speak to you for a few minutes.

W Professor: Certainly, Patrick.

M: I had a little trouble understanding your lecture today when you were discussing mountaineering and the dangers of high-altitude sickness. Could you go over what causes it again if it's not too much trouble?

W: Of course, Patrick. Let me start at the beginning so there is no confusion. First of all, high-altitude sickness refers to an illness that can occur when people travel above a certain number of feet, such as, uh, if they are driving a car up a steep mountain, mountain climbing, or flying in an airplane. Was that part of the lecture clear?

M: Oh, yes. I only started getting confused when you began discussing the chemistry behind it and what happens inside the body.

W: What causes high-altitude sickness is the lack of oxygen in the atmosphere the higher you ascend. The concentration of oxygen in the air people are used to is around twenty-one percent. As you ascend, the concentration of oxygen in the air doesn't change, but what does change is that the number of oxygen molecules per breath is reduced. For example, if you were to climb a mountain that peaked at 12,000 feet, you would be inhaling forty percent fewer oxygen molecules per breath at the top than at the bottom.

M: So a person feels ill because he cannot get as much oxygen into his bloodstream as he is used to. But how does a person know he has high-altitude sickness? What symptoms does he display?

W: Well, if you've ever flown in an airplane, you know one or two people on board always feel lightheaded or nauseous. However, others may not show any symptoms since they are acclimatized to the conditions.

M: Sorry, but what does acclimatized mean?

W: Acclimatized means you've allowed yourself to become used to the conditions little by little. There are some simple things each person can do to become acclimatized to altitude. The main cause of high-altitude sickness is that you ascend too quickly, so your body has no time to adjust, but here are some things you can do to help you acclimatize. Try to start your ascent under 10,000 feet and ascend slowly. If you are flying, try not to do anything too strenuous the following day. Always try to stay well hydrated.

M: What does hydration have to do with preventing high altitude sickness?

W: Oftentimes, the process of acclimatization is accompanied by fluid loss, so staying properly hydrated will help replenish your body.

M: Thank you very much for your time, Professor Cronkite. I think I understand high altitude sickness much better now.

W: You're very welcome, Patrick. **And thank you for being brave enough to come by and ask for my help.** So many students are too embarrassed to admit they need help, but that is what we are here for . . . to make sure you understand the concepts and to help you realize your full potential.

해석

M Student: 안녕하세요, Cronkite 교수님. 교수님과 잠시 이야기를 나눌 수 있는지 궁금해서요.

W Professor: 물론 가능하죠, Patrick.

M: 오늘 강의에서 등산과 고산병의 위험에 대한 부분이 잘 이해가 가지 않았어요. 번거롭지 않으시면 고산병이 왜 일어나는지 설명해 주실 수 있나요?

W: 그럼요, Patrick. 헷갈리지 않도록 처음부터 시작해 보죠. 우선 고산병은, 예컨대 어 자동차를 타고 가파른 산에 가거나, 등산을 하거나, 혹은 비행기를 타는 경우처럼, 일정 피트 이상의 고도로 올라갈 때 발생할 수 있는 병을 가리켜요. 강의에서 그 부분은 이해를 했나요?

M: 오, 네. 고산병의 화학적인 원리와 체내에서 일어나는 현상을 말씀하실 때 헷갈리기 시작했어요.

W: 고산병이 일어나는 이유는 고도가 높아질수록 대기 중의 산소가 부족해지기 때문이에요. 사람들에게 익숙한 대기 중 산소 농도는 약 21%이죠. 더 높은 곳으로 올라가면 대기 중 산소 농도는 변하지 않지만, 변하는 것은 호흡을 할 때마다 산소 분자의 수가 감소한다는 점이에요. 예를 들어 12,000피트 높이의 산을 오르는 경우, 산 정상에서는 산 아래쪽에 있을 때보다 40% 적은 산소 분자를 들이마시게 될 거예요.

M: 그러면 익숙했던 양의 산소가 혈액 속으로 들어가지 않기 때문에 증상을 느끼는 것이군요. 하지만 고산병에 걸렸다는 것은 어떻게 알게 되나요? 어떤 증상이 나타나죠?

W: 음, 비행기를 타본 적이 있다면 항상 탑승객 중 한두 명은 어지러움이나 메스꺼움을 느낀다는 점을 알 거예요. 하지만 다른 사람들은 그런 환경에 적응했기 때문에 아무런 증상을 나타내지 않을 수 있죠.

M: 죄송하지만, 적응한다는 것이 어떤 뜻인가요?

W: 적응한다는 것은 상황에 조금씩 익숙해진다는 것을 의미해요. 고도에 적응하기 위해 개인이 할 수 있는 간단한 일들이 있어요. 고산병의 주요 원인은 너무 빨리 올라가서 신체가 적응할 시간을 갖지 못하기 때문인데, 적응을 위해 할 수 있는 것들을 몇 개 알려 드리죠. 10,000피트 이하의 장소에서 등산을 시작해서 천천히 산을 오르세요. 비행기를 타고 있는 경우라면 그 다음 날에 너무 격렬한 활동은 하지 않도록 하세요. 항상 수분을 충분히 섭취하시고요.

M: 수분 섭취가 고산병 예방과 어떤 관련이 있나요?

W: 종종 적응 과정에서 수분이 손실되기 때문에 충분한 수분을 섭취하면 신체에 수분이 보충되죠.

M: 시간 내 주셔서 정말 감사합니다, Cronkite 교수님. 이제 고산병을 훨씬 잘

이해할 수 있게 된 것 같아요.

W: 천만에요, Patrick. 그리고 용기를 내서 이렇게 찾아와 도움을 요청하다니 저도 고마워요. 몇몇 학생들은 너무 쑥스러워서 도움이 필요하다는 걸 인정하지 않지만 저희가 여기에 있는 건… 학생들에게 개념을 이해시키고 자신의 능력을 완전히 발휘할 수 있도록 돕기 위한 것이니까요.

Summary Note

A

❶ explain more
❷ high-altitude sickness
❸ going high up
❹ oxygen
❺ nausea
❻ Hydration

B

The student asks the professor to help him understand a concept from an earlier lecture. The lecture was about high-altitude sickness. The professor starts by defining high-altitude sickness as an illness that occurs when people ascend into the atmosphere too quickly. People tend to feel ill because they are not breathing as many oxygen molecules as they normally do. If a person were on a plane that was flying at 12,000 feet, he would be taking in forty percent fewer oxygen molecules with each breath. This depletion of oxygen intake can cause the person to feel dizzy or nauseous. The professor then tells the student about some of the ways to acclimatize in high altitudes. The person could start to ascend from no more than 10,000 feet and ascend slowly. The professor also points out the benefits of drinking plenty of fluids and of refraining from strenuous activity for the first twenty-four hours after flying.

Exercise 2 1 Ⓓ 2 Ⓐ 3 Ⓐ p.204

Script 07-07

M Student Housing Office Employee: Hello. How may I be of assistance?

W Student: Hi. My name is Sally Morgan, and I am a senior on campus. I'm here because I would like to extend my stay in my dorm room for one more semester.

M: And why is it that you need to extend your stay?

W: Well, you see, I am getting my major in education, and I thought I would be finished with all of my classes by this winter, but my professor reminded me that I need to remain in the area for one more semester to do student-teaching. Student-teaching is the main part of my degree.

M: Okay, can you tell me what dormitory you currently live in?

W: Carter Hall.

M: Okay, let me check my computer here to see what it says about the Carter Hall . . . Oh, I'm sorry, but it looks like we have allocated all of the rooms in your dorm to some incoming foreign students next semester. I am afraid you will have to make other arrangements.

W: But why can't I stay? I am a paying student, and this is my fourth year. I have to remain in the area. If I don't do my student-teaching here, then I won't get my degree.

M: I understand that, but you must remember that you signed an agreement last semester stating that you would not need your dorm room after the term. Do you remember that agreement? We have given that room to a foreign student.

W: But can't you just tell the student that you made a mistake? She could live off campus or in another dorm. Surely, I should have first choice since I have been here longer.

M: All of the other dorm rooms are accounted for, and to have the student try to fend for herself off campus would be very irresponsible on the part of this university. Imagine if you were only just learning Chinese and decided to study abroad in China for one semester. Do you think you could take it upon yourself to find your own housing if your student housing fell through? How would that make you feel?

W: I suppose I would feel very alone and scared. Oh . . . I see your point.

M: I am sorry you cannot live in your dorm room next term, but think about it this way. Those dorm rooms are due for an upgrade. You see how old they are and how desperately they need repair work done. I am sure you can find a really nice place off campus, perhaps with your friends, where your room is much nicer than the one you are in right now.

W: Yeah, I guess so. My friend did say that she needed another roommate for next semester. Sorry I was so upset. I apologize.

M: That's no problem. Thank you very much for understanding the situation.

해석

M Student Housing Office Employee: 안녕하세요. 무엇을 도와 드릴까요?

W Student: 안녕하세요. 제 이름은 Sally Morgan이고, 이 학교 4학년생이죠. 기숙사에서 한 학기 더 지내고 싶어서 왔어요.

M: 왜 더 지내고 싶은 건가요?

W: 음, 그러니까, 제 전공이 교육학인데, 이번 겨울이면 모든 수업이 다 끝날 것으로 생각했지만, 제가 교생 실습을 하려면 한 학기 더 이곳에 머물어야 한다는 점을 교수님께서 상기시켜 주셨어요. 교생 실습은 제 학위에서 중요한 부분이죠.

M: 그렇군요, 현재 어느 기숙사에서 지내는지 말씀해 주시겠어요?

W: Carter 홀이요.

M: 좋아요, 여기 제 컴퓨터로 Carter 홀에 관한 사항을 확인해 볼게요··· 오, 유감이지만 다음 학기에 그곳 기숙사에 있는 모든 방들은 곧 오게 될 유학생들에게 배정된 것 같군요. 안타깝지만 학생은 다른 곳을 찾아봐야 할 것 같아요.

W: 왜 제가 지낼 수 없는 거죠? 저는 학비도 지불하고 있고 올해 4학년이에요. 여기에서 지내야만 해요. 이곳에서 교생 실습을 하지 못한다면 학위도 받지 못하게 될 거예요.

M: 저도 이해하지만, 학생은 지난 학기에 학기가 끝나면 기숙사 방이 필요 없다는 계약에 서명했던 점을 기억해야 해요. 그 계약이 기억나나요? 그 방은 유학생에게 배정되었어요.

W: 하지만 그 유학생에게 실수가 있었다고 말해 주실 수는 없나요? 학교 밖이나 다른 기숙사에서 지낼 수도 있을 거예요. 제가 여기에 더 오래 있었으니 분명 제가 1순위가 되어야 해요.

M: 다른 기숙사 방들도 모두 배정이 되었고, 유학생을 학교 밖에서 혼자 살게끔 하는 것은 학교 측에서 봤을 때 매우 무책임한 일이 될 거예요. 학생이 중국어를 배우고 있는데 한 학기 동안 중국에서 유학하기로 결심했다고 가정해 봐요. 학생이 머물 곳이 없어진 경우 스스로 지낼 곳을 찾을 수 있다고 생각하나요? 그러면 어떤 기분이 들 것 같나요?

W: 정말 외롭고 두려울 것 같아요. 오··· 무슨 말인지 알겠어요.

M: 학생이 다음 학기에 기숙사 방에서 지낼 수 없게 되어 저도 유감이지만 이렇게 생각해 보세요. 그 기숙사는 리모델링이 예정되어 있어요. 알겠지만 너무 낡아서 보수 작업이 절대적으로 필요하죠. 분명 학생은 학교 밖에서, 아마도 친구랑 같이, 지금 지내는 방보다 훨씬 더 좋은 방이 있는 정말로 좋은 숙소를 찾을 수 있을 거예요.

W: 예, 그럴 수도 있겠네요. 제 친구가 다음 학기에 다른 룸메이트가 필요하다고 얘기했어요. 너무 흥분해서 죄송해요. 사과할게요.

M: 천만에요. 상황을 이해해 줘서 정말 고마워요.

Summary Note

A

❶ housing office
❷ stay in dormitory
❸ foreign student
❹ upset
❺ foreign student
❻ understands

B

The student stops by the student housing office to let the man know that she needs to remain in her dorm room for an extra semester because she forgot she had to complete her student-teaching. The man checks the computer and finds that her room has already been allocated to a foreign student for next semester, so the student must find new housing arrangements. This angers the student since she feels she should be able to remain in her room since she is a senior. The man kindly informs her that the reason the university puts foreign students in dorm rooms is to help them get comfortable in a new country and on a new campus. The man suggests that she find an off-campus house with one of her friends. The student understands the man's point of view and mentions a friend she knows that needs a roommate.

Exercise 3 1 Ⓒ 2 Ⓓ 3 Ⓑ p.206

Script 07-08

W Student: Excuse me?

M Music Hall Employee: Yes? Can I help you?

W: I certainly hope so. My name is Cherie, and I booked a room in Lincoln Hall to practice the piano. However, when I went in the room just now, I heard a large group of men working on the building. They are making so much noise pounding and sawing that I can hardly hear myself play.

M: Oh, yes. I am so sorry for the inconvenience, Cherie, but I am afraid we are in the middle of renovating the hall, and we need to get this construction done before the big concert. I know it seems very inconvenient for you, but now was the best time for the construction crew to come in.

W: But I am also preparing for the concert, and it's only six weeks away. I have decided to play a challenging Bach piece, and I need all the practice I can get. Can't the construction workers come in after hours or early in the morning?

M: Well, perhaps the construction workers coming in during the early morning or evening would be convenient for you, but I doubt it would be very convenient for all of the students trying to sleep in the dorms next door. No one wants to hear the sound of a hammer or saw at midnight. I do not want to sound rude, but you are not the only person who is involved with the concert. There are many students who seem to be making other arrangements while the men finish the work.

W: Yes, but I don't want to hear the sound of a hammer or a saw when I am practicing. And of course, it may be easier for other students to practice. A flutist can take his flute wherever he wants to practice, but a piano is not very mobile.

M: Again, I understand that this is an inconvenience, but the construction workers will only be here for one week, so we decided that if the workers need to be here for a week, we would at least book them early enough before the concert so that everyone would be guaranteed good, silent practice times five weeks prior to the performance.

W: But what am I supposed to do? I need a full six weeks of practice to get this Bach piece polished.

M: How about making a compromise? There is a piano in the basement of the theater building that is utilized during stage musicals that is not being used at the moment. I could give you written permission to get into the building for one week so that you can practice your piece in silence while these construction workers are finishing up. Does that sound fair?

W: Oh, yes, that sounds wonderful. I am sorry for being so pushy about this, but it is the final performance of my senior year, and I want it to go perfectly. Thank you very much.

M: You are welcome.

해석

W Student: 실례해도 될까요?

M Music Hall Employee: 네? 제가 도와 드릴까요?

W: 꼭 도와 주셨으면 좋겠어요. 제 이름은 Cherie로, 피아노 연습을 하기 위해 Lincoln 홀의 연습실을 예약했어요. 하지만 조금 전에 연습실에 갔다가 건물에서 여러 사람들이 공사를 하는 소리를 들었어요. 두드리고 톱질하는 소리가 너무 커서 제 연주를 거의 들을 수가 없어요.

M: 오, 그렇군요. 불편을 끼쳐 드려서 정말 죄송하지만, Cherie, 안타깝게도 그 홀을 리모델링하는 중인데, 대형 콘서트가 있기 전에 이번 공사를 끝내야 해요. 매우 불편한 일로 생각될 수 있다는 점은 저도 알지만, 공사 인부들이 들어올 수 있는 가장 좋은 때가 바로 지금이죠.

W: 하지만 저 역시 연주회를 준비하는 중인데, 연주회는 6주밖에 남지 않았어요. 어려운 바흐의 곡을 연주하기로 했기 때문에 연습을 최대한 많이 해야 하죠. 공사 인부들이 몇 시간 후에, 아니면 아침 일찍 올 수는 없나요?

M: 음, 공사 인부들이 이른 아침이나 저녁에 오는 경우 학생은 편할지 모르지만 바로 옆 기숙사에서 잠을 자려는 학생들은 매우 큰 불편을 느끼게 될 것 같군요. 한밤중에 망치나 톱 소리를 듣고 싶어하는 사람은 없으니까요. 기분 나쁜 말을 하고 싶지는 않지만, 연주회가 있는 사람은 학생만이 아니에요. 인부들이 작업을 마치기까지 다른 방법을 찾고 있는 학생들이 많아요.

W: 그래요, 하지만 저는 연습을 할 때 망치나 톱 소리를 듣고 싶지 않아요. 그리고 물론 다른 학생들은 연습하기가 더 쉬울 수도 있어요. 플루트 연주자는 원하는 어디에서나 플루트를 집을 수가 있지만, 피아노는 옮기기가 쉽지 않아요.

M: 다시 말씀을 드리면, 이번 일로 불편하신 점은 이해하지만 공사 인부들이 일주일 동안만 이곳에 있을 것이기 때문에, 일주일 동안 인부들이 이곳에 있어야 하는 경우, 공연 5주 전에는 모두가 쾌적하고 조용한 연습 시간을 보장받을 수 있도록 공연 전 충분히 일찍 예약을 받기로 결정했어요.

W: 하지만 저는 어떻게 해야 하죠? 이번 바흐 곡을 제대로 연습하려면 6주 내내 연습을 해야 해요.

M: 타협을 하는 것이 어떨까요? 극장 건물 지하에 뮤지컬 공연 때 사용되는 피아노가 한 대 있는데, 현재 이 피아노를 사용하는 사람이 없어요. 공사 인부들이 공사를 마무리하는 동안 학생이 조용하게 곡을 연습할 수 있도록 일주일간 그 건물에 들어갈 수 있는 허가증을 발급해 줄게요. 괜찮게 들리나요?

W: 오, 네, 좋을 것 같아요. 너무 쏘아붙인 것 같아 죄송하지만, 이번이 4학년 마지막 연주회라서 완벽하게 연주하고 싶거든요. 정말 감사합니다.

Summary Note

A

❶ Construction
❷ piano playing
❸ practice for concert
❹ one week

B

The student visits Lincoln Hall and complains to the employee on duty that she cannot hear herself practicing the piano because there are construction workers in the building making too much noise. The man apologizes but tells her that the upgrades on Lincoln Hall are necessary before the big concert and that the construction workers are only booked for one week. The student says that she requires a full six weeks of practice on her Bach piece and simply cannot have that much noise. The man offers her a compromise. He will give her written permission to use the piano in the theater building for one week while the construction workers finish their job. The student agrees to this compromise and thanks the man.

Exercise 4 1 Ⓐ 2 Ⓑ 3 Ⓐ p.208

Script 07-09

M Student: Excuse me, but can I ask you a question?

W Student Services Center Employee: Yes, what can I do for you?

M: My name is Charlie Myers. I applied to go on the ecology field trip to Inglewood Forest next week, but for some reason, my application was denied and returned to me in the mail. I can't seem to figure out why it would be denied as I should have preferential admission for this trip since I am in the class. I was just wondering if you knew why I was denied.

W: Ah, yes, Charlie Myers. When I look into your file, it says here that you applied to go on the same field trip last term but did not go. Is this information correct?

M: Yes, that is correct. I signed up to go on the field trip last term but came down with a bad case of the flu. I was too sick to make the trip that day. It took me one week to get over my illness, and that excluded any possibility of me going to Inglewood.

W: Did you call the office to let anyone know you were sick, or did you cancel your application? Did you let your professor know so that he could delete your entry for the trip?

M: No, I'm afraid I didn't. I asked a friend to cancel my application for me, but he forgot. I was also going to call myself, but I lost my voice due to my illness.

W: That is too bad. I am so sorry you came down with the flu, but I'm afraid that due to the popularity of this field trip, the science office has a policy that you must call and cancel your application if you cannot attend. The waiting list is always long for this trip, and had you called, we could have filled your spot with someone else. I'm afraid that because you did not call, you've now forfeited your chance to attend the field trip. It is the office policy.

M: But this field trip is a crucial part of my major. If I don't go on it, I won't graduate.

W: I'm sorry, Charlie, but you should have read the application more closely. The only consolation I can offer is that there are always a couple of students, like yourself, that cannot make the trip for whatever reason. On the morning of the field trip, wait at the bus stop, and if a student does not show up, you can fill that vacancy. I would suggest that you get up early, however, as the vacancies are filled on a first-come, first-served basis, so you will want to make sure you are first in line.

M: Okay, if this is the only way, then I will do it. And I will definitely be the first one there.

W: That sounds like a good idea, Charlie. Sorry I cannot do anything else for you.

해석

M Student: 실례지만 질문을 하나 해도 될까요?

W Student Services Center Employee: 네, 무엇을 도와 드릴까요?

M: 제 이름은 Charlie Myers예요. 저는 다음 주 잉글우드의 숲 생태학 현장 학습을 신청했는데, 어떤 이유로 신청서가 거부를 당해서 우편으로 돌아왔어요. 저는 해당 수업을 듣고 있기 때문에 이번 현장 학습 참여에 우선권이 있는 것으로 알고 있어서 왜 거부가 되었는지 모르겠어요. 제가 거절당한 이유를 알 수 있을지 궁금했어요.

W: 아, 예, Charlie Myers요. 학생 파일을 보니까 학생이 지난 학기에 동일한 현장 학습을 신청하고서 가지 않았다고 나와 있네요. 이 내용이 맞나요?

M: 네, 맞아요. 지난 학기에 현장 학습을 신청했지만 심한 독감에 걸렸어요. 그날 너무 몸이 아파서 현장 학습을 가지 못했죠. 몸이 회복되기까지 일주일이 걸렸고, 그렇기 때문에 제가 잉글우드에 갈 수가 없었어요.

W: 사무실에 전화를 해서 누구에게라도 학생이 아프다는 사실을 알리거나 신청을 취소했나요? 학생이 현장 학습에서 빠질 수 있도록 교수님께 연락을 드렸나요?

M: 아니요, 그렇게는 안 했던 것 같아요. 친구한테 신청을 취소해 달라고 부탁했는데, 그 친구가 잊어 버렸어요. 제가 직접 취소를 하려고도 했지만, 아파서 목소리가 나오질 않았죠.

W: 정말 안 되었군요. 독감에 걸렸다는 말을 들으니 유감이지만, 이 현장 학습은 인기가 많기 때문에 과학부에서는 참석이 불가능한 경우에는 반드시 전화로 신청을 취소해야 한다는 규정을 두고 있죠. 항상 현장 학습의 대기자 명단이 길기 때문에 만약 학생이 전화를 했더라면 학생 대신 다른 누군가가 참석을 할 수 있었을 거예요. 학생이 전화를 하지 않아서 지금 현장 학습에 참가할 기회를 박탈당한 것이고요. 그것이 사무실 방침이에요.

M: 하지만 이 현장 학습은 제 전공에서 매우 중요한 부분이에요. 만약 가지 못한다면 졸업을 못하게 될 거예요.

W: 유감이지만, Charlie, 신청서를 보다 자세히 읽어 보았어야 해요. 제가 할 수 있는 유일한 위로는 어떠한 이유로 학생과 같이 현장 학습에 가지 못하는 학생이 항상 한두 명은 있다는 점이죠. 현장 학습일 아침에 버스 정류장에서 기다리면, 어떤 학생이 나타나지 않는 경우, 학생이 그 자리에 들어갈 수 있을 거예요. 하지만 빈 자리는 선착순으로 채워지기 때문에 맨 앞에 서 있는 것을 원하게 될 테니 학생에게 일찍 일어나는 것을 추천할게요.

M: 좋아요, 그것이 유일한 방법이라면 그렇게 할게요. 그리고 반드시 맨 앞에 서도록 할게요.

W: 좋은 생각이에요, Charlie. 달리 해 줄 수 있는 일이 없어서 유감이군요.

Summary Note

A

❶ go on field trip
❷ denied
❸ skipped last time
❹ popular
❺ graduate
❻ show up

B

The student goes to the science office because he does not understand why his application to attend the Inglewood Forest field trip has been denied. The woman informs him that the reason he was denied was that he submitted an application for the same field trip last term but did not show up on that day. The student explains that he did not attend the trip because he had the flu. The clerk tells him that because he did not bother to call in and inform the science office, he forfeited his chance to go on the trip. The student tells the woman that he needs to attend the field trip in order to graduate and that there must be a way he can go. The woman says that she is sorry, but the only way he has a chance at going is to wait at the bus stop on the day of the trip and hope to fill a vacancy left by another student.

Exercises with Long Lectures

Exercise 1 1 Cause: [4] Effect: [1], [2], [3] 2 (B) 3 (B) p.210

Script 07-10

M Professor: Stress is something which we all suffer from at various times in our lives. Let me start by giving you a quick definition of stress so that I can be sure everyone understands precisely what I'm talking about. Stress is basically a state of worry or tension in the mind caused by some kind of unpleasant or difficult situation. Is that clear to everyone . . . ? Excellent.

Now, what causes stress? Well, there are many things in our lives that can cause people to suffer from stress. It often depends upon the person. By that, I mean that something which causes stress for me may not bother some of you in the least bit. On the other hand, something that some of you may get stressed out about could be seen by me as nothing at all to worry about. However, there are certain factors which tend to create stress in a large number of people.

For the most part, stress is caused by work, school, and personal issues. Let's look at them one by one. At work, which is something most of you don't have to worry about now, an unpleasant or overly demanding boss can create stress. So can a heavy workload, an impending deadline, and coworkers. At school . . . anyone?

W Student: Your test next week is causing me stress.

M: Not too much, I hope. I know she's just joking around, but Stephanie is right, class. Tests, homework, and other assignments can cause stress. So can class presentations, especially for those who don't like public speaking. In personal lives, trouble with a significant other can be a major cause of stress. So can divorce and the death of a family member or friend. Money problems often cause stress, too. People who are about to get married frequently get stressed out, and so do individuals who are unemployed or who are looking for employment. An illness, uh, particularly a chronic one, can stress people out. I'm sure all of you can think of many others. I just told you the most common ones.

What about the effects of stress? Well, there are many of them. People who suffer from short-term stress may find themselves with headaches and upset stomachs. They may be overly tired and have difficulty both falling asleep and concentrating. After all, they are basically thinking about what is stressing them out, so they simply can't focus on other things, even, uh, even sleeping. Stressed-out people are typically very irritable. Think about it. When you're suffering from stress, you tend to get mad at people easily and are bothered by small things that you might not even normally notice.

At times, when stress doesn't go away but persists for a long time, people may suffer more severe symptoms. One major problem is depression. People with depression should seek a specialist to help them because this can lead to numerous issues. Some people suffer weight problems. Some may gain lots of weight while others may lose lots of weight due to long-term stress. Some people get skin problems, including acne and eczema while others may suffer from heartburn and even ulcers. In serious cases, stressed-out people can suffer various heart problems. These include heart attacks, which can kill people.

As you can see, stress is something that needs to be managed properly lest people become ill and even die from it. Fortunately, there are quite a few things that we can do to mitigate stress in our lives. I'm going to tell you all about them, but why don't we take a break right now? We've been going for quite a while, and some of you are looking tired. Let's take five minutes off.

해석

M Professor: 스트레스는 인생의 다양한 시기에서 우리 모두가 겪게 되는 것입니다. 제가 말씀드리는 것을 모두가 정확히 이해할 수 있도록, 스트레스에 대한 정의를 짧게 알려 드리면서 시작해 보죠. 스트레스는 기본적으로 불쾌하거나 힘든 상황에 의해 야기되는 정신적인 불안 및 긴장 상태입니다. 모두들 이해하셨나요…? 좋습니다.

자, 무엇이 스트레스를 일으킬까요? 음, 우리의 삶에서 스트레스를 일으킬 수 있는 것들은 많습니다. 종종 그 사람에 달려 있죠. 이 말은, 제게 스트레스를 일으키는 것이 여러분 중 일부에게는 전혀 문제가 되지 않을 수도 있다는 뜻입니다. 반면에 여러분 중 일부가 스트레스를 받는 일이 제게는 전혀 걱정할 필요가 없는 것으로 비춰질 수도 있죠. 하지만 대다수의 사람들에게 스트레스를 일으키는 특정한 요인들이 존재합니다.

대부분의 경우 스트레스는 업무, 학업, 그리고 개인적인 문제들로 발생해요. 하나씩 살펴보죠. 직장에서, 여러분 대다수는 아직 이에 대해 걱정할 필요는 없지만, 불쾌하거나 과도한 요구를 하는 상사가 스트레스를 유발할 수 있습니다. 과중한 업무, 촉박한 마감 시간, 그리고 동료도 마찬가지죠. 학교에서는… 말해 볼 사람이 있을까요?

W Student: 교수님의 다음 주 시험이 제게 스트레스를 주고 있어요.

M: 너무 많이 주지는 않았으면 좋겠군요. 학생이 농담을 하고 있다는 것은 저도 알지만 Stephanie의 말이 맞습니다, 여러분. 시험, 숙제, 그리고 기타 과제들이 스트레스를 일으킬 수 있어요. 수업 발표도, 특히 사람들 앞에서 말하는 것을 좋아하지 않는 학생들에게는, 마찬가지고요. 사생활에 있어서는, 중요한 주변 사람과의 갈등이 스트레스의 주요 원인이 될 수 있어요. 이혼이나 가족 혹은 친구의 죽음도 마찬가지죠. 돈 문제 역시 종종 스트레스를 일으킵니다. 곧 결혼하려는 사람들은 종종 스트레스를 받으며, 실직자 혹은 취업 준비생들도 마찬가지입니다. 질병은, 어, 특히 만성적인 질병 또한 스트레스를 일으킬 수 있어요. 여러분 모두가 기타 많은 것들도 생각해낼 수 있으리라 확신합니다. 저는 가장 일반적인 것들만 말씀을 드렸어요.

스트레스의 영향은 어떨까요? 음, 많은 영향들을 끼칩니다. 단기적인 스트레스를 겪는 사람들은 두통 및 복통을 느낄 수 있어요. 지나치게 피곤함을 느낄 수도 있고, 잠드는 것과 집중하는 것 모두에 어려움을 겪을 수도 있습니다. 어쨌거나 기본적으로 스트레스를 주는 일에 대해 생각을 하고 있기 때문에 다른 일에는, 심지어, 어, 수면에도 집중할 수가 없습니다. 스트레스를 받는 사람들은 전형적으로 매우 초조해합니다. 생각해 보세요. 여러분이 스트레스를 겪고 있을 때 여러분들은 다른 사람에게 쉽게 화를 내는 경향이 있으며 평소라면 눈치채지 못했을 사소한 일에도 기분이 상하게 되죠.

때때로 스트레스가 사라지지 않고 오랫동안 남아 있는 경우, 사람들은 보다 심각한 증상을 겪을 수 있습니다. 그러한 문제 중 하나가 우울증이에요. 우울증에 걸린 사람들은 그로 인한 여러 가지 문제들이 발생할 수 있기 때문에 전문가를 찾아 도움을 받아야 해요. 체중과 관련된 문제를 겪는 사람들도 있습니다. 장기간의 스트레스로 체중이 크게 증가하는 사람도 있고, 체중이 크게 감소하는 사람도 있을 수 있죠. 여드름 및 습진을 포함하여 피부와 관련된 문제를 겪는 사람들도 있으며, 속쓰림 및 심지어 궤양을 겪는 사람들도 있을 수 있습니다. 심각한 경우, 스트레스가 쌓인 사람들은 다양한 심장 질환을 겪을 수도 있어요. 여기에는 심장마비도 포함되는데, 이로 인해 사람이 사망할 수도 있습니다.

보시다시피, 사람들이 병에 걸리지 않고 심지어 그로 인해 사망하지 않기 위해서는 스트레스가 적절하게 관리되어야 합니다. 다행히 삶에서 스트레스를 경감시키기 위해 우리가 할 수 있는 일들이 몇 가지 있어요. 그에 대한 모든 것을 여러분들께 말씀드릴 텐데, 잠시 휴식 시간을 갖는 것이 어떨까요? 꽤 오랜 시간 수업을 했기 때문에 여러분 중 몇 분은 피곤해 보이는군요. 5분간 쉬도록 하겠습니다.

Summary Note

A

❶ stress
❷ be caused
❸ work
❹ demanding bosses
❺ tests
❻ divorce
❼ headaches
❽ heart attacks

B

The professor defines stress as a state of worry or tension in the mind caused by something unpleasant or difficult. He then notes that many things can cause stress and that what causes stress for some people may not cause stress for others. He then states that there are some things that tend to cause stress in most people. Among them are work, school, and personal issues. A demanding boss, a heavy workload, and an impending deadline can cause stress at work. Tests, homework, and assignments can cause stress at school. Divorce, death, money problems, and illnesses can cause stress in private lives. The effects of stress include headaches, upset stomachs, a lack of sleep, and being irritable. Long-term stress can lead to bigger problems, including weight gain or loss, skin problems, and even heart attacks.

Exercise 2 1 Toothed Whale: [3], [4] Baleen Whale: [1], [2] 2 Ⓒ 3 Ⓑ p.212

Script 07-11

W Professor: This afternoon, we are going to talk about one of the largest mammals on the Earth, which just so happens to live in the ocean. I'm talking, of course, about the whale. And during today's class, we are going to focus not only on the different types of whales and their body structures, but we will also discuss whale migration and intelligence. Can anyone here name a type of whale and then tell us about one of its distinct features?

M Student: There is the humpback whale, and it is called that because it has a hump on its back.

W: Good. The distinguishing feature of the humpback whale is pretty self-evident in its name, isn't it? Another type of whale is the blue whale, which happens to be the largest living animal in the world. Blue whales can grow up to thirty meters in length, and some have exceeded 177 metric tons in weight. We have named two whales that also share something in common, something that is used to divide all whales into two different groups. I'm talking about baleen. Baleen is the sieve-like structure in a whale's mouth that filters the water from the plankton that it eats. It is made of out of keratin. Non-baleen whales, such as the sperm whale, are known as toothed whales because they have teeth, so they feed on larger creatures such as fish or squid. Two other types of toothed whales are the bottlenose whale and the killer whale. And blue whales and humpback whales are two types of whales that have baleen.

Now, uh, what about feeding? Whales sometimes have to swim very far to get to their feeding grounds. Whale migration is a complex and time-consuming event in the lives of whales. Each type of whale varies slightly, but the two main reasons for migration are mating and feeding. Now, does anyone have an idea as to why a whale must migrate for these activities and why it does not just stay in one region?

M: Aren't some of the waters they live in too cold to give birth in?

W: That is part of the reason, yes. Typically, whales travel to warmer water to give birth and colder water to feed. Whales are known to travel for thousands of kilometers to complete these activities. One type of whale, the southern right whale, lives along the southern coast of Africa during its mating season and then swims all the way to water near Antarctica in the summer so that it can feed.

M: But that doesn't seem to make any sense. A whale must expend so much energy to get to its food source. Wouldn't it be safer and smarter for the whale just to try to find food where it is?

W: One would think so, but once the whale gets to where it is going, it is able to gorge itself on plentiful food, thus gaining more energy than it ever would if it were to stay in one type of water year round. And let us not forget that whales are very intelligent mammals. First of all, they have larger brains than every mammal, including human beings. Whales are highly social animals, able to communicate with one another through complex sounds, and if need be, they form groups and swim together as a means of protecting one another. Evidence of this can be noted when whales are under threat by whaling ships. The whales either find new migration routes, or they swim in a tight formation to try to protect one another.

해석

W Professor: 오늘 오후에는 지구에서 가장 큰 포유 동물 중 하나로서 바다에서 사는 동물에 대해 이야기하려고 합니다. 물론 고래를 말씀드리는 것이에요. 그리고 오늘 수업에서는 고래의 다양한 종류 및 이들의 신체 구조뿐만 아니라 고래의 이동과 지능에 대해서도 논의를 할 것입니다. 한 종류의 고래의 이름을 말하고 그 고래의 한 가지 특징에 대해 이야기해 볼 사람이 있나요?

M Student: 혹등고래가 있는데, 등에 혹이 있어서 그렇게 불립니다.

W: 잘 대답했어요. 혹등고래의 특징은 그 이름에 잘 드러나 있어요, 그렇죠? 또 다른 종류의 고래로는 흰긴수염고래가 있는데, 이 고래가 현재 세상에서 가장 큰 동물입니다. 흰긴수염고래는 최대 30미터의 길이로 자랄 수 있으며, 일부 고래의 무게는 177톤이 넘기도 하죠. 또한 모든 고래를 각기 다른 두 그룹으로 나눌 때 사용되는 특성을 공유하는 두 고래에 대한 명칭이 존재합니다. 바로 고래수염을 말씀드리는 거예요. 고래수염은 고래의 입에 있는 체와 같은 부분으로, 고래가 먹는 플랑크톤에서 물을 빼냅니다. 각질로 이루어져 있죠. 향유고래처럼 고래수염이 없는 고래들은 이빨을 가지고 있기 때문에 이빨고래라고 불리며, 따라서 물고기나 오징어 같은 보다 큰 동물들을 먹습니다. 기타 이빨고래의 두 가지 종류로는 범고래와 범고래가 있어요. 그리고 흰긴수염고래와 혹등고래는 고래수염을 가지고 있는 고래의 유형에 속하죠.

자, 어, 먹이는 어떨까요? 고래들은 때때로 매우 멀리까지 헤엄을 쳐서 먹이가 있는 곳으로 가야 해요. 고래의 삶에 있어서 이동은 복잡하고 시간이 많이 걸리는 일이죠. 고래의 종류에 따라 약간씩 다르지만, 이동을 하는 두 가지 주된 이유는 짝짓기와 섭식 때문입니다. 자, 고래가 그러한 일을 위해 왜 이동을 해야 하는지, 그리고 왜 한곳에 머물러 있지 않는지 아는 사람이 있나요?

M: 고래가 사는 수역의 물이 너무 차가워서 새끼를 낳을 수가 없기 때문이 아닌가요?

W: 네, 그것도 부분적인 이유가 됩니다. 일반적으로 고래는 새끼를 낳기 위해 보다 따뜻한 수역으로 이동을 하고 먹이를 먹기 위해 보다 차가운 수역으로 이동을 해요. 그렇게 하기 위해 수천 킬로미터를 이동하는 것으로 알려져 있죠. 고래의 한 종류인 남방긴수염고래의 경우 짝짓기 기간에는 아프리카 남해안 쪽에서 지내다가 여름이 되면 먹이를 먹기 위해 남극 근처의 수역으로 이동을 합니다.

M: 하지만 그건 말이 안 되잖아요. 먹이가 있는 곳까지 가기 위해서 고래는 틀림없이 엄청난 에너지를 소비해야만 할 거예요. 자기가 사는 곳에서 먹이를 구하는 것이 고래에게 더 안전하고 현명한 일이 아닐까요?

W: 그렇게 생각할 수도 있지만, 고래가 일단 목적지에 도달하면 엄청난 양의 먹이를 먹을 수 있기 때문에, 일년 내내 한 수역에서 머무르는 경우보다 이때 더 많은 에너지를 얻을 수가 있죠. 그리고 고래가 매우 똑똑한 포유 동물이라는 점을 잊지 않기로 하죠. 무엇보다 고래는 인간을 포함해 어떤 포유 동물보다도 커다란 뇌를 가지고 있어요. 고래는 매우 사회성이 높은 동물로 복잡한 소리를 통해 서로 의사소통을 할 수 있으며, 필요한 경우, 서로를 보호하기 위한 수단으로서 떼를 지어 함께 헤엄을 칩니다. 이에 대한 예는 고래가 포경선의 위협을 받는 경우에 찾아볼 수 있어요. 고래는 새로운 이동 경로를 찾거나, 혹은 서로를 보호하기 위해 촘촘한 대형을 이루어 헤엄을 칩니다.

Summary Note

A

❶ whales
❷ plankton
❸ Killer whale
❹ mating
❺ brains
❻ complex sounds

B

The mammals known as whales can be divided into two main groups: those with baleen and those with teeth. Baleen is a sieve-like structure made of keratin that filters out plankton for baleen whales to eat. Two types of baleen whales are the blue whale and the humpback whale. Toothed whales, such as the sperm whale and the killer whale, prey on larger animals such as fish or squid. Whales also migrate. They migrate to warmer waters to breed and give birth, and then they migrate into colder waters to feed. One would think that the energy spent for these mass migrations would not be worth it; however, once whales are in their feeding waters, they are able to gorge to their hearts' content. Whales are very intelligent and often work together in groups to try to avoid danger.

Exercise 3 1 Mount Rushmore: [2], [4] The Statue of Liberty: [1], [3] 2 Ⓒ 3 Ⓐ p.214

Script 07-12

M Professor: This morning, I am going to be giving a lecture on the differences in the origins of two American landmarks, Mount Rushmore and the Statue of Liberty. To start off, let me talk about Mount Rushmore. Mount Rushmore is a national memorial located in South Dakota. The monument represents the first one hundred and fifty years of the American presidency and is comprised of sixty-foot-tall sculptures of four American presidents: George Washington, Thomas Jefferson, Theodore Roosevelt, and Abraham Lincoln.

One interesting fact about Mount Rushmore is that it was originally known to the Lakota tribe of Native Americans as Six Grandfathers. At that time, the most notable point of the Black Hills was Harney Peak, the highest mountain in the range. It wasn't long, however, before American settlers eventually moved through and into the area, at that time giving Harney Peak a succession of names: Cougar Mountain, Sugarloaf Mountain, Slaughterhouse Mountain, and Keystone Cliffs. In 1885, the peak was renamed Mount Rushmore after a New York lawyer who was representing a mining company in the Black Hills area.

Looking to increase tourism into the Black Hills area, in 1923, historian Doane Robinson conceived of the idea of chiseling the visages of different United States presidents into the granite hillsides. The following year, Robinson was able to persuade sculptor Gutzon Borglum to complete the task. It took Borglum and a group of 400 other workers over fourteen years, from October 4, 1927, to October 31, 1941, to complete the sculptures on Mount Rushmore. Mount Rushmore became part of the National Park Service in 1933 with the total cost of the project nearly reaching one billion dollars. Remarkably, no workers died during the project despite some very precarious working situations.

The second monument I'd like to discuss is the Statue of Liberty. This monument, also known as Liberty

Enlightening the World, is a statue of a woman dressed in a robe and wearing a crown while holding a stone tablet in her left hand and a flaming torch in her right hand, and it was given to the United States by the Parisian-based Franco-American Union in 1885. The statue was given to the United States by the French as a gesture of friendship and goodwill between the two nations.

The Statue of Liberty stands on Liberty Island in New York Harbor as a welcome to all visitors and immigrants and returning Americans. If anyone has ever seen this monument, it is a welcome sight to behold. The statue is made of pure copper, with the exception of the torch flame, which has a coating of gold leaf. Etched on the tablet that the woman is holding is the text July IV MDCCLXXVI, which was the date of the United States's Declaration of Independence, July 4, 1776.

The Statue of Liberty was constructed by two Frenchmen, sculptor Frederic Auguste Bartholdi and architect Alexandre Gustave Eiffel, who was also the designer of the Eiffel Tower. In July of 1884, the Statue of Liberty was completed in France and broken down into three hundred and fifty pieces and crated so that it could be stacked onto the French frigate *Isere* and shipped to the United States. It arrived in New York Harbor on June 17, 1885. Reassembly took four months to complete, but finally, on October 28, 1886, the Statue of Liberty was dedicated by President Grover Cleveland. For the first sixteen years that it stood in New York Harbor, the Statue of Liberty served as a lighthouse. Now, the Statue of Liberty is one of the most recognizable American icons, and millions of tourists visit the monument each year.

해석

M Professor: 오늘 아침에는 미국의 두 랜드마크라고 할 수 있는 러시모어산과 자유의 여신상의 기원의 차이에 대해 강의를 하고자 합니다. 우선 러시모어산에 대한 이야기를 해 보죠. 러시모아산은 사우스다코타에 있는 국립 기념지입니다. 이 기념지는 미국의 첫 150년 동안의 대통령들을 나타내며, 조지 워싱턴, 토머스 제퍼슨, 시어도어 루스벨트, 그리고 아브라함 링컨 네 대통령을 묘사한 18미터 높이의 조각상들로 이루어져 있죠.

러시모어산에 관한 한 가지 흥미로운 점은 원래 이곳이 라코타 미 원주민들에게 6인의 조상으로 알려진 곳이었다는 점입니다. 당시 블랙힐스에서 가장 유명한 곳은 산맥에서 가장 높은 산인 하니피크였어요. 하지만 얼마 지나지 않아 미국 식민지 주민들이 결국 이주를 해서 이 지역으로 유입되었고, 이때 하니피크에 쿠거산, 슈거로프산, 슬로터하우스산, 그리고 키스톤클리프와 같은 일련의 이름들이 붙여졌습니다. 1885년에 하니피크는 블랙힐스 지역의 광산 회사의 대표였던 한 뉴욕 변호사의 이름을 따서 다시 러시모어라는 이름을 얻게 되었죠.

1923년, 블랙힐스를 찾는 관광객 수를 늘리기 위해, 역사가였던 돈 로빈슨이 화강암 산허리에 여러 미국 대통령의 얼굴을 조각해야 한다는 아이디어를 떠올렸습니다. 이듬해 로빈슨은 조각가 거촌 보글럼을 설득해서 그 일을 하도록 했죠. 보글럼과 기타 400명의 인부가 1927년 10월 4일부터 1941년 10월 31일까지 14년에 걸쳐 러시모어산에 조각 작품을 완성시켰습니다. 러시모어산은 1933년 미 국립 공원 관리청 시스템의 일부가 되었고, 총 공사 비용은 10억 달러에 육박했어요. 놀라운 점은 작업 환경이 상당히 위험했음에도 불구하고 공사 기간 중 사망한 인부가 없었다는 점이었습니다.

논의하려는 두 번째 기념비는 자유의 여신상이에요. 세계를 밝히는 자유라고도 알려져 있는 이 기념물은 가운과 왕관을 착용하고 왼손에는 석판을, 오른손에는 횃불을 들고 있는 여성을 나타낸 조각상으로, 1885년 파리에 본부를 둔 프랑스-미국 협회가 미국에 기증한 것입니다. 이 조각상은 프랑스인들이 양국 간의 우의와 친선의 표시로 미국에 기증한 것이었죠.

자유의 여신상은 모든 방문객과 이민자, 그리고 귀국하는 미국인들을 환영하기 위해 뉴욕항의 리버티아일랜드에 세워져 있습니다. 이 기념물을 본 적이 있는 사람이라면 알겠지만 반가운 모습이 아닐 수 없습니다. 이 조각상은 순동으로 만들어져 있고, 예외적으로 횃불에만 금박이 입혀져 있어요. 여인이 들고 있는 석판에는 July IV MDCCLXXVI이라는 글이 새겨져 있는데, 이는 미국의 독립 기념일인 1776년 7월 4일을 의미합니다.

자유의 여신상은 두 명의 프랑스인, 조각가 프레데리크 오귀스트 바르톨디와, 에펠탑의 설계자이기도 한 건축가 알렉상드르 귀스타브 에펠에 의해 제작되었어요. 자유의 여신상은 1884년 7월에 프랑스에서 완성되어 350개의 조각으로 분해된 뒤 상자에 넣어져 프랑스의 프리깃함인 *이제르*에 의해 미국으로 운반되었죠. 뉴욕항에는 1885년 7월 17일에 도착을 했습니다. 다시 조립을 하기까지 4개월이 걸렸지만, 마침내 1886년 10월 28일에 그로버 클리블랜드 대통령의 주재로 자유의 여신상에 대한 제막식이 열렸습니다. 뉴욕항에 세워진 후 처음 16년 동안은 자유의 여신상이 등대로 사용되었어요. 현재 자유의 여신상은 미국을 나타내는 가장 유명한 상징 중 하나로, 매년 수백 만 명의 관광객들이 이 기념물을 찾고 있습니다.

Summary Note

A

❶ Mount Rushmore
❷ Sculptures
❸ tourism
❹ Statue of Liberty
❺ crown
❻ France
❼ symbols
❽ Very recognizable

B

Two famous monuments in the United States are Mount Rushmore and the Statue of Liberty. Mount Rushmore is located in South Dakota and is a large sculpture of four United States presidents etched into the granite hillside of the tallest peak in the Black Hills. The four presidents represented are George Washington, Thomas Jefferson, Theodore Roosevelt, and Abraham Lincoln. The monument was conceived by Doane Robinson, who was trying to think of a way to bring more tourists to the Black Hills region. A sculptor by the name of Gutzon Borglum and four hundred workers completed Mount Rushmore in 1941. The Statue of Liberty is a monument of a woman wearing a robe and crown while holding a stone tablet and a flaming torch. She was given to the Americans by the French in 1884 as a gesture of friendship and goodwill. One of its designers was Alexandre Gustave Eiffel, the same man who designed the

Eiffel Tower in Paris, France. The Statue of Liberty is made of pure copper and stands on an island in the middle of New York Harbor.

Exercise 4 1 Ⓒ 2 Ⓑ 3 Ⓑ p.216

Script 07-13

W Professor: Good morning, class. Today, for our history lecture, we are going to be discussing the rise of tyranny that occurred in ancient Greece around the seventh century B.C. A good way for us to begin is for someone to give us the definition of tyranny. Anyone?

M Student: Doesn't tyranny refer to the unjust exercising of power by one ruler?

W: Yes, good. This is the definition that we use nowadays. Harsh, isn't it? However, the origins of this type of power were not quite this brutal. This form of government began in ancient Greece, when aristocrats found that they could gain power over others first by securing the support of poor people either by giving them land or money or even freeing them from slavery or prison. Eventually, the aristocrat was able to acquire absolute power because the people he had previously bribed for their support were now beholden to him.

M: But that is such an unfair form of gaining power. How did the poor people allow that?

W: Well, it was unfair, but people did not have the same rights as we do now, and let's try to approach it from the point of view of a poor ancient Greek in the seventh century B.C. Greece fell into what has come to be called the archaic period. New political structures were only just beginning to be formed following the previous period, which didn't have much structure. The rise of democracy was in its infancy, and the population was booming, from hundreds of thousands of people to millions. Originally, Greek cities were monarchies in which a rich land owner had control over the subjects that worked his land and became their king; however, these monarchies were soon overthrown by groups of populist aristocrats from outlying rural areas because these particular groups of populists, also known as tyrants, were promising the poor money or freedom.

M: Populists? What is a populist? I thought we were talking about tyrants?

W: A tyrant is a type of populist leader. A populist is a person who believes in standing up for the little guy or poor man. A populist wants equal representation between the elite and the underclass. That is why the populists became so popular with the poor . . . They were speaking on the poor person's behalf. If you were poor or perhaps a slave, what would look more appealing to you . . . to be offered money or freedom if you supported the populist or to stay and work on a piece of land for little or no money?

M: I guess I understand why a poor person would support the populist initially, but doesn't the word tyrant conjure up negative connotations?

W: Nowadays, yes. When we refer to a tyrant, we are referring to a leader who has ridden roughshod over his people while making empty promises along the way and ruling with an iron fist of absolute power. Initially, tyrants were trying to buoy the poor people against the elite. However, as it happens in many situations, those who had lofty and moral aspirations in the beginning were gradually corrupted by power. Eventually, the ancient Greek tyrants, like the Greek monarchs before them, abused their positions over the people, and the term tyrant gained the definition that we use today.

해석

W Professor: 안녕하세요, 여러분. 오늘 역사 수업에서는 기원전 7세기경 고대 그리스에서 시작되었던 참주 정치에 대해 논의하려고 해요. 누군가 참주 정치에 대한 정의를 말함으로써 강의를 시작하면 좋을 것 같군요. 누구 없나요?

M Student: 참주 정치는 한 명의 통치자에 의해 권력이 부당하게 행사되는 것을 뜻하지 않나요?

W: 네, 좋은 대답이군요. 그것이 오늘날 우리가 사용하는 정의이죠. 무자비하지 않나요? 하지만 이러한 권력의 기원은 그처럼 잔인한 것이 아니었어요. 이러한 형태의 통치는 고대 그리스에서 시작되었는데, 귀족들은 가난한 사람들에게 토지나 돈을 주거나 노예 또는 수감자 신분에서 이들을 해방시킴으로써 가난한 사람들의 지지를 확보하여 다른 사람들을 지배하는 권력을 얻을 수 있다는 점을 처음으로 깨닫게 되었죠. 마침내 귀족은, 지지를 얻기 위해 뇌물을 바쳤던 사람들이 자신에게 신세를 지게 되자, 절대적인 권력을 얻을 수 있었습니다.

M: 하지만 그건 매우 부당한 방식의 권력 획득이잖아요. 어떻게 가난한 사람들이 허용을 했나요?

W: 음, 부당하기는 했지만 사람들이 현재 우리가 가진 것과 같은 권리를 가지고 있지는 않았기 때문에, 기원전 7세기의 가난한 고대 그리스인의 관점에서 접근을 하도록 하죠. 그리스는 고대 시대라는 시기에 속해 있었어요. 정치 기구가 별로 존재하지 않았던 시기가 지나가고 새로운 정치 기구들이 막 형성되기 시작했죠. 민주주의가 싹트기 시작했고, 인구는 수십 만 명에서 수백 만 명으로 불어나고 있었습니다. 원래 그리스 도시에서는 부유한 지주가 자신의 토지를 경작하는 백성들을 지배하고 그들의 왕이 되는 군주제가 실시되고 있었어요. 하지만 이러한 군주들은 곧 외진 농촌 지역 출신의 포퓰리스트 귀족들에게 자리를 빼앗겼는데, 그 이유는 참주라고도 알려진 이러한 특정 그룹의 포퓰리스트들이 가난한 사람들에게 돈이나 자유를 약속해 주었기 때문이었죠.

M: 포퓰리스트요? 포퓰리스트가 무엇인가요? 우리가 참주에 대해 이야기를 하고 있다고 생각했어요.

W: 참주는 포퓰리스트 지도자의 한 유형이에요. 포퓰리스트는 평범하거나 가난한 사람의 편에 서야 한다고 생각하는 사람이고요. 포퓰리스트는 엘리트와 최하층 계급을 동등하게 대변하고자 합니다. 바로 이러한 점 때문에 포퓰리스트들이 가난한 사람들에게 큰 인기를 얻었는데… 이들은 가난한 사람들의 편에 서서 말을 하고 있었습니다. 만약 여러분이 가난하거나 아마 노예인 경우라면 무엇이 더 매력적으로… 포퓰리스트를 지지해서 돈이나 자유를 얻게 되는 것과, 아니면 거의 또는 전혀 돈을 받지 못한 채 한 뼘의 땅에서 일하는 것 중 무엇이 더 매력적

으로 보일 것 같나요?

M: 가난한 사람이 처음에 왜 포퓰리스트를 지지했는지 이해할 수 있을 것 같은데, 참주라는 말은 왜 부정적인 의미를 갖게 되었나요?

W: 현재에는 그렇습니다. 참주라고 말하는 경우, 백성을 함부로 대하고 헛된 공약만을 일삼으며 무자비하게 절대 권력을 휘두르는 지도자를 가리키죠. 처음에는 참주들이 엘리트 계층에 대항하여 가난한 사람들의 사기를 진작시키기 위해 노력했어요. 하지만 많은 경우에 그러하듯이, 처음에는 고귀하고 도덕적인 열망을 가졌던 사람들이 점차 권력에 의해 타락하기 시작했습니다. 마침내 고대 그리스의 참주들은, 이전의 그리스 군주들과 마찬가지로, 국민 위를 군림하며 자신의 지위를 남용하게 되었고, 참주라는 용어는 오늘날 우리가 사용하는 의미를 갖게 되었죠.

Summary Note

A

❶ tyranny
❷ helping poor
❸ archaic period
❹ monarchies
❺ overthrew
❻ populists
❼ poor people
❽ equal representation

B

The term tyranny is defined as the unjust exercising of power by one absolute ruler over a group of people. Although the current term has negative connotations, the first tyrants were not harsh rulers but were in fact a group of aristocrats known as populists who wished to represent the poor people who were being undervalued and mistreated by the elite. Some of these populists gained control and became known as tyrants because their method of amassing support from the poor or slaves was to bribe them with money or promises of freedom.

Integrated Listening & Speaking p.218

A

Script 07-14

M Professor: Last week, we took a look at two different national monuments in the United States: Mount Rushmore in South Dakota and the Statue of Liberty in New York Harbor. The monument at Mount Rushmore is a giant sculpture of four United States presidents that is etched into the highest peak in the Black Hills Mountain Range. George Washington, Thomas Jefferson, Theodore Roosevelt, and Abraham Lincoln are the featured presidents, and the monument represents the first one hundred and fifty years of the American presidency. The monument was first conceived as a way to lure tourists to the Black Hills. The monument was sculpted by a man named Gortzon Borglum and four hundred workers. It was completed in 1941. The Statue of Liberty is a monument of a woman wearing a robe and crown and holding a stone tablet and a flaming torch. It sits on a small island in New York Harbor. The Statue of Liberty was given as a gift of friendship to the Americans by the French in 1884. The designer of the Statue of Liberty was Alexandre Gustave Eiffel, the man also responsible for designing the Eiffel Tower.

1 South Dakota

2 The first one hundred and fifty years of the American presidency

3 A stone tablet and a flaming torch

B

Script 07-15

W Professor: During the last class period, I gave a lecture on the rise of tyranny in ancient Greece. We started the lecture by identifying today's definition of tyranny as the unjust exercising of power by one absolute ruler. The origin of tyranny, however, was not quite so harsh. The rise of tyranny came about in ancient Greece, when a certain group of aristocrats, known as populists, were unhappy with the way poor people were treated under monarchies. A populist is simply a person who advocates not just for the elite but also for the poor. He wants representation for all people. The tyrants gained the support of the poor and slaves by promising them money, freedom, or both. Initially, the tyrants ruled by the ethics they first believed in, but eventually, the power they gained led to corruption and the bribery of poor people without fulfilling the early promises became commonplace.

1 The tyrants promised money, property, or freedom.

2 Eventually, power corrupted the tyrants, and they no longer made good on the promises they made to the lower class.

3 It originated in ancient Greece.

Mini TOEFL iBT Practice Test p.220

1 Ⓒ 2 Ⓐ 3 Ⓑ 4 Ⓓ 5 Ⓐ, Ⓒ
6 Ⓑ 7 Ⓐ 8 Ⓐ 9 Ⓑ 10 Ⓑ
11 Ⓒ

[1-5]

Script 07-16

W Student: That was a very interesting lecture today, Professor Wilcox. I learned a great deal about excavations in ancient Egypt. I had no idea about some of things you taught us.

M Professor: I'm glad you found it interesting, Celine. I thought the two questions you asked in class were rather insightful. Not many students ever think about what you asked about.

W: Thank you, sir.

M: So . . . is there something I can do for you?

W: Actually, yes, there is. Do you mind if I sit down?

M: Not at all. Please go ahead.

W: Thank you . . . So . . . I've been doing some thinking about my future, and I believe I would like to major in archaeology.

M: That's wonderful. It's a really fascinating subject. But . . . are you sure? Archaeology is a rewarding subject to study, but it can sometimes be hard for people to get jobs. I mean, uh, you'll be limiting yourself in some ways if you major in it.

W: I think I'll be all right. I'm strongly considering going to graduate school in the future. And I've already started teaching myself Egyptian hieroglyphics because I want to learn more about ancient Egypt.

M: Well, that's very ambitious of you.

W: So I was wondering . . . if I declare as an archaeology major, I'm going to need an academic advisor. Would you be interested in being my advisor?

M: Of course. The honor would be all mine. Just so you know, you have to fill out a form declaring your major. Then, you need to get your current academic advisor to sign it, and I'll have to sign it, too. You can pick up the form at the Registrar's office.

W: Yes, one of my friends told me about it. I didn't want to get the form until you said yes. I plan on going there this afternoon and getting the form. My current advisor won't be at school until Thursday, so I'll talk to him then and return here once he signs the paper.

M: That sounds perfect. Oh, wait a minute. Before you go, there's something I want to tell you.

W: Yes?

M: Did you know that a professor at a local college is going to be going on a dig in Egypt this summer? He invited me to go along, and I accepted his offer. We're putting together a team of students who will go with us. We'll be doing an excavation out in the desert near Luxor for around a month. Are you interested in going?

W: What do I need to do?

M: Well, mostly, you just need to express interest in going. But you should be aware that this is an unpaid position. In fact, you'll be responsible for paying your way to Egypt and also paying for your expenses while you're there. On trips like this, students normally spend around four or five thousand dollars. That includes airfare.

W: Hmm . . . I'll have to talk to my parents about that since that's a lot of money, but I believe they'll be inclined to let me go.

M: That's wonderful news. Why don't you let me know by the end of the month because I need to turn in the list of which students are going to Professor Dumas?

W: I'll have an answer for you by the time that I return on Thursday.

해석

W Student: 오늘 강의는 매우 흥미로웠어요, Wilcox 교수님. 고대 이집트에 관한 발굴 작업에 대해 많은 것을 배웠죠. 저희에게 알려 주신 것들 중 일부는 제가 몰랐던 것이었어요.

M Professor: 흥미롭게 생각했다니 기쁘군요, Celine. 수업 중에 학생이 했던 두 가지 질문은 매우 예리한 것이라고 생각했어요. 학생이 질문한 것에 대해 생각해 본 학생은 많지 않을 거예요.

W: 감사합니다, 교수님.

M: 그러면… 제가 도울 일이라도 있나요?

W: 실은, 네, 그래요. 제가 앉아도 될까요?

M: 그럼요. 앉으세요.

W: 감사합니다… 그러니까… 저는 제 미래에 대해 생각 중인데, 제가 고고학을 전공하면 좋을 것 같아서요.

M: 잘 되었군요. 정말로 멋진 학문이죠. 하지만… 정말인가요? 고고학이 연구하기에는 보람 있는 학문이지만, 취직에 있어서는 때때로 어려움을 줄 수가 있어요. 제 말은, 어, 고고학을 전공하면 일정 부문 제약이 생기게 될 거예요.

W: 저는 괜찮을 것 같아요. 추후 대학원에 진학하는 것을 적극적으로 고려 중이거든요. 그리고 고대 이집트에 대해 더 많이 배우고 싶어서 이미 이집트의 상형문자를 독학하기 시작했어요.

M: 음, 의욕이 대단하군요.

W: 그래서 궁금한 점이… 제가 고고학을 전공으로 삼으면 지도 교수님이 필요할 거예요. 제 지도 교수님이 되어 주실 생각이 있으신가요?

M: 물론이죠. 제가 영광이에요. 알다시피, 학생은 전공 신청서를 작성해야 해요. 그런 다음에는 현재의 지도 교수님께 서명을 받아야 하고, 저 또한 서명을 해야 할 거예요. 신청서는 학적과에서 받을 수 있어요.

W: 네, 제 친구 중 한 명이 그에 대해 이야기를 해 주었어요. 교수님께서 승낙을 하시기 전에는 신청서를 받고 싶지 않았거든요. 오늘 오후에 그곳으로 가서 신청서를 받을 생각이에요. 현재 제 지도 교수님은 목요일 이후에 학교로 돌아오시기 때문에 그분께는 그때 말씀을 드려서 서류에 서명을 받고 이곳으로 다시 돌아올 거예요.

M: 완벽하게 들리는군요. 오, 잠깐만요. 학생이 가기 전에 제가 하고 싶은 말이 있어요.

W: 네?

M: 인근 대학의 한 교수님께서 이번 여름 이집트에서 발굴 작업을 할 것이라는 점을 알고 있나요? 같이 가자는 초청을 하셔서 제가 그분 제의를 수락했죠. 우리는 함께 갈 학생들을 모집하고 있는 중이에요. 약 한 달 동안 룩소르 인근 사막에서 발굴 작업을 하게 될 것이고요. 가는데 관심이 있나요?

W: 제가 어떻게 하면 되죠?

M: 음, 주로, 가고 싶다는 의향을 밝히기만 하면 돼요. 하지만 이번 일은 보수가 따르지 않는 일이라는 점을 알아야 할 거예요. 실제로 이집트까지 가는 경비는 학생이 부담하게 될 것이고, 또한 그곳에 있는 동안의 경비도 부담해야 할 거예요. 이러한 여행에서 학생들은 보통 4천 혹은 5천 달러를 쓰게 되죠. 항공료를 포함해서요.

W: 흠… 금액이 크기 때문에 그에 대해서는 부모님과 이야기를 해야 하지만, 제가 가는 것을 허락하실 것 같기는 해요.

M: 정말 좋은 소식이군요. 가게 될 학생들의 리스트를 Dumas 교수님께 제출해야 하니 제게 이달 말까지 알려 줄래요?

W: 목요일에 다시 이곳으로 올 때 답을 드릴게요.

[6-11]

Script 07-17

M Professor: Today, we are going to be learning about John Dewey, an American educational reformer who was also a psychologist and philosopher. Has anyone here heard of John Dewey?

W Student: I think I have. Wasn't he one of the men who supported the idea of progressive education?

M: Yes, very good. We will get to that in today's lecture. But let's start with a little background. John Dewey was born during the late nineteenth century in the state of Vermont. He received his bachelor's degree from the University of Vermont and then went on to get his PhD from the Krieger School of Arts and Sciences at Johns Hopkins University in Baltimore, Maryland. Starting in 1904, John Dewey taught philosophy at Columbia University. It was during these years that Dewey began forming his ideas about psychology and education. In his book *Democracy and Education*, John Dewey formulized his educational philosophy. Dewey believed that the development of the human mind was a communal process and that a person only became truly meaningful when that individual fully engaged within his or her society. John Dewey strongly believed that children should not be taught by rote, nor should they learn simply by having a teacher regurgitate facts. Dewey believed in the process we know as learning by doing. Can someone tell me what this means?

W: Well, let's say you were teaching us a concept in chemistry. Learning by rote would mean that you would stand in front of us and perhaps read us something or write something about the concept on the board. John Dewey's way of teaching us the concept would be to have us actually do something in the laboratory, right?

M: That is a very good way of putting it. Yes, John Dewey believed in more of a hands-on approach to learning and also in having the students be involved with the society they lived in, so the idea of field trips or talking to professionals outside of school would be something that he would also support.

Dewey was continuously formulating his ideas in the early part of the twentieth century, and initially, his idea of progressive education was popular and widely accepted. During the 1950s, however, during the Cold War years, there was a slight reaction against progressive education, as many Americans felt that students in other parts of the world, namely the Soviet Union, were accelerating faster in the classroom than Americans. In the post-Cold War period, Dewey's ideas reemerged, and they have thrived in classrooms ever since.

W: Can you elaborate on the concept of progressive education? What does that mean?

M: Of course. Educational progressivism is the idea that because humans are social animals, we learn better if we are involved in real-life activities with other people. John Dewey had a five-step approach to learning. First, become aware of the problem. Second, define the problem. Third, propose a hypothesis or set of propositions to solve the problem. Fourth, evaluate the consequences of the problem from one's past experience, and fifth, test the most likely solution.

W: Wait a minute. **That's kind of like the step-by-step process that is used by scientists conducting laboratory experiments.**

M: That's right. It is. Today, this model of evaluating a problem is the one that is the most widely used in classrooms.

W: So if you could summarize John Dewey's philosophy on education, what would it be?

M: The main concept behind John Dewey's educational philosophy is that the most important part of learning is the broadening of the intellect and the strengthening of critical thinking and problem-solving skills as opposed simply to memorizing facts from a book. For instance, if John Dewey were alive today, he might put it to us this way . . . Would you learn more about swimming if you were to read about some man's exploits of swimming in a book, or would you learn more about swimming if you actually got into the water yourself?

해석

M Professor: 오늘은 심리학자이면서 철학자이기도 했던 미국의 교육 개혁가 존 듀이에 대해 공부해 보려고 합니다. 여기에 존 듀이에 대해 들어본 사람이 있나요?

W Student: 제가 들어본 것 같아요. 진보적인 교육이라는 아이디어를 주장했던 사람 중 한 명 아니었나요?

M: 네, 훌륭한 대답이군요. 오늘 강의에서 그 점에 대해 살펴볼 거예요. 하지만 먼저 약간의 배경 지식부터 알아보도록 하죠. 존 듀이는 19세기 말 버몬트주에서 태어났습니다. 버몬트 대학에서 학사 학위를 받은 뒤 메릴랜드의 볼티모어에 있는 존 홉킨스 대학의 크리거 문리 대학으로 가서 박사 학위를 받았죠. 1904년부터 존 듀이는 콜롬비아 대학에서 철학을 가르쳤습니다. 바로 이 시기에 존 듀이가 심리학 및 교육에 대한 아이디어를 생각해 내기 시작했어요. 자신의 책 *민주주의와 교육*에서 존 듀이는 본인의 교육 철학을 구체화시켰습니다. 듀이는 인간 지성의 발달이 공동의 과정이며, 개인은 자신이 속한 사회 속에서 완전한 관계를 맺고 있을 때 진정한 의미를 지니게 된다고 믿었어요. 존 듀이는 아이들을 주입식 암기법으로 가르쳐서는 안 되며, 교사가 사실을 그대로 반복해서 말하는 방식으로도 아이들을 가르쳐서는 안 된다는 확고한 믿음을 가지고 있었습니다. 듀이는 우리가 경험에 의한 학습이라고 알고 있는 과정을 믿었어요. 이것이 무엇을 의미하는지 누가 말해볼까요?

W: 음, 교수님께서 화학의 한 개념을 저희에게 가르쳐 주신다고 가정해 볼게요. 주입식 암기법의 경우 아마도 교수님께서는 저희 앞에서 그러한 개념에 관한 내용을 읽어 주시거나 칠판에 써 주실 거예요. 존 듀이의 교수법으로 그러한 개념을 가르치는 경우에는 우리가 실험실에서 실제로 무언가를 하게 될 것이고요, 맞나요?

M: 예를 잘 들었군요. 그래요, 존 듀이는 실제로 해 보는 학습을 선호했고 또한 학생들이 자신이 살고 있는 사회에 관여하는 것을 선호했기 때문에, 현장 학습이나 학교 밖에서 전문가와 나누는 대화도 지지했을 거예요.

듀이는 20세기 초반에 끊임없이 자신의 아이디어를 구체화시켰는데, 초기에는 진보적인 교육에 대한 그의 아이디어가 인기를 얻고 폭넓은 지지를 받았습니다. 하지만 냉전 기간이었던 1950년대에는 많은 미국인들이 다른 세상에 있는 학생들, 즉 소련에 있는 학생들이 미국인보다 더 빨리 진전을 보인다고 느끼면서, 진보적인 교육에 대해 약간의 반발이 일어났어요. 냉전이 끝난 후에는 듀이의 아이디어가 다시 부각되어서 그 이후에는 교실에서 널리 적용되었죠.

W: 진보적인 교육의 개념을 설명해 주실 수 있나요? 그것이 어떤 의미인가요?

M: 물론이에요. 진보주의 교육은 인간이 사회적인 동물이기 때문에 우리가 다른 사람과 함께 현실의 활동에 참여할 때 보다 잘 배우게 된다는 아이디어예요. 존 듀이는 학습에 대한 5단계 접근법을 주장했어요. 첫 번째는 문제 인식입니다. 두 번째는 문제 규정이고요. 세 번째는 문제 해결을 위한 가설 또는 명제 설정입니다. 네 번째는 과거의 경험으로부터 문제의 결과를 예측하는 것이고, 다섯 번째는 가장 가능성이 높은 해결책을 시험해 보는 것이죠.

W: 잠시만요. 과학자들이 실험실에서 실험을 할 때 사용하는 단계별 과정과 비슷하군요.

M: 맞아요. 실제로 그렇습니다. 오늘날 이러한 문제 평가 모델은 교실에서도 가장 널리 사용되는 모델이죠.

W: 그러면 교육에 대한 존 듀이의 철학을 요약한다면 어떻게 말할 수 있을까요?

M: 존 듀이의 교육 철학에 깔려 있는 주된 개념은 학습에서 가장 중요한 부분이 지식을 넓히고 비판적인 사고 및 문제 해결 능력을 강화하는 것이라는 점인데, 이는 단순히 책에 있는 사실들을 외우는 것과 반대되는 것이죠. 예를 들어 존 듀이가 오늘날 살아 있다면 우리에게 이런 식으로 물었을 텐데… 책에서 수영을 잘 하는 사람에 대한 이야기를 읽을 때 수영을 더 잘 배우게 될까요, 아니면 실제로 여러분이 물에 들어갈 때 수영을 더 잘 배우게 될까요?

Vocabulary Check-Up p.225

A

1 Ⓗ	2 Ⓚ	3 Ⓙ	4 Ⓐ	5 Ⓒ
6 Ⓘ	7 Ⓞ	8 Ⓝ	9 Ⓜ	10 Ⓕ
11 Ⓖ	12 Ⓛ	13 Ⓓ	14 Ⓔ	15 Ⓑ

B

1 Ⓑ	2 Ⓐ	3 Ⓓ	4 Ⓔ	5 Ⓒ

UNIT 08 Making Inferences

Basic Drill p.228

Drill 1 Ⓑ

Script 08-02

M Professor: Janet, I need you to rewrite part of the paper you submitted on Tuesday.

W Student: Rewrite it? What did I do wrong?

M: You failed to include a conclusion in your paper.

W: Really? I distinctly remember writing one.

M: Apparently, you remember incorrectly. You had an excellent introduction, and the body of your paper was quite good, but then it just ended. There was no paragraph summing up the paper.

W: Hmm . . . Would you mind if I looked at the paper for a minute, please?

M: Not at all . . . Here you are.

W: Oh . . . Oh, no. I see what happened. I must not have printed the last page of the paper. I can go back to my dorm, print it, and bring it to you. Is that all right?

M: Sure. That's fine. These things happen from time to time.

W: Thanks so much, sir. I'll be back in around thirty or forty minutes.

해석

M Professor: Janet, 화요일에 제출한 보고서의 일부를 다시 써야 할 것 같더군요.

W Student: 다시 쓴다고요? 제가 무엇을 잘못했나요?

M: 보고서에 결론을 포함시키지 않았어요.

W: 정말인가요? 분명 썼다고 기억하고 있는데요.

M: 보아하니 잘못 기억하고 있는 것 같군요. 서론도 훌륭하고 보고서의 본론도

상당히 좋았지만, 바로 끝나 버렸어요. 보고서를 요약하는 단락이 없었죠.

W: 흠… 제가 보고서를 잠시 살펴봐도 될까요?

M: 그럼요… 여기 있어요.

W: 오… 오, 맙소사. 무슨 일이 있었는지 알겠어요. 제가 보고서의 마지막 페이지를 출력하지 않은 것이 확실해요. 기숙사로 돌아가서 출력을 한 후에 가져다 드릴게요. 그렇게 하면 될까요?

M: 그래요. 좋아요. 그런 일들이 때때로 일어나는 법이죠.

W: 정말 고맙습니다, 교수님. 30분이나 40분 후에 돌아올게요.

Drill 2 Ⓓ

Script 08-03

M Student: Hello. My name is Brad Welker. I have an appointment with you for 3:30.

W Financial Aid Office Employee: It's a pleasure to meet you, Mr. Welker. Please come in and have a seat.

M: Thank you very much. I appreciate it.

W: So . . . what kind of financial aid are you looking for?

M: Well, as you know, tuition at the school is going up next semester. It's already high, and it's hard for my family to support me. I have three younger sisters, so my parents are trying to raise them as well.

W: I see. About how much more financial aid are you looking for?

M: Around two thousand dollars would be great. I brought along all of my family's financial information so that you can look at it. My grades are good, too. I have a 3.74 GPA.

W: That's a very impressive GPA. You must study very hard.

M: I do my best. I want to be successful so that I can pay my parents back all the money they've spent on me.

W: I like your attitude. Let me look at all of the information you've provided. I'm pretty sure that we will be able to help you out at the number you mentioned. I'll call you back in a couple of days.

M: That sounds perfect. Thank you very much.

해석

M Student: 안녕하세요. 제 이름은 Brad Welker예요. 선생님과 3시 30분에 약속이 되어 있죠.

W Financial Aid Office Employee: 만나서 반가워요, Welker 씨. 들어와서 앉으세요.

M: 정말 고맙습니다. 감사해요.

W: 그러면… 어떤 종류의 학자금 지원이 필요하신가요?

M: 음, 아시다시피, 학교 등록금이 다음 학기에 인상될 예정이에요. 이미 높은 편이어서 제 가족이 저를 지원하기가 힘들어요. 여동생도 3명이 있는데, 부모님들께서 동생들도 지원해 주고 계시죠.

W: 그렇군요. 학자금 지원이 어느 정도 더 필요하신가요?

M: 2천 달러 정도면 될 것 같아요. 선생님께서 보실 수 있도록 저희 가족의 금융 관련 정보들을 모두 가지고 왔어요. 또한 제 학점은 좋은 편이에요. GPA가 3.74이죠.

W: GPA가 매우 높군요. 분명 열심히 공부하고 계신 것 같아요.

M: 최선을 다하고 있어요. 부모님께서 저를 위해 쓰신 돈을 모두 갚기 위해 성공하고 싶거든요.

W: 자세가 마음에 드네요. 가지고 오신 정보를 모두 볼게요. 분명 학생이 언급한 금액으로 학생을 도와 드릴 수 있을 거예요. 이틀 후에 전화를 드릴게요.

M: 좋아요. 정말 감사합니다.

Drill 3 Ⓒ

Script 08-04

W Professor: Good morning, everyone. My name is Professor Powell. This semester, I'll be teaching you all about meteorology. I hope we can all learn a lot in this class.

Now, uh, meteorologists have a number of tools that we use to measure the weather. I'd like you to pay close attention as I explain them to you. I'm going to talk about them in every class, so you must know their functions. Please take a look up here at the screen as I'll show you some pictures of the devices we use in our endeavors.

The first is something I'm sure you're familiar with: the thermometer. This simple device measures the temperature. That is, it tells us how hot or cold the conditions are in a place. Next is this device, which is a barometer. It measures air pressure, which is quite useful for telling when it's going to rain or snow or if a powerful storm is coming. An anemometer is a device that measures the speed of the wind. You can see it here . . . And a weather vane, which I'm sure everyone has seen on the tops of barns, tells us the direction that the wind is blowing. Here's one you may not know . . . It's a hygrometer. This device measures the amount of humidity in the air. And a rain gauge tells us how much precipitation has fallen. Those are all fairly simple devices. Let me show you some more complicated ones now.

해석

W Professor: 모두들 안녕하세요. 저는 Powell 교수입니다. 이번 학기에 여러분들께 기상학을 가르쳐 드릴 예정이에요. 이번 수업에서 모두들 많이 배우시기 바랍니다.

자, 어, 기상학자들은 날씨를 측정할 때 사용되는 다수의 도구들을 가지고 있어요. 제가 설명해 드릴 때 주의를 기울여 주시면 좋겠군요. 수업을 할 때마다 이에 대한 이야기할 것이므로 이들의 기능을 반드시 알고 계셔야 합니다. 실제로 사용되는 기구들의 사진을 몇 장 보여 드릴 테니 여기 화면을 봐 주세요.

첫 번째는 여러분들도 분명 알고 계시는 것으로, 바로 온도계입니다. 이 간단한 기구는 온도를 측정하죠. 다시 말해서 어떤 장소의 날씨가 얼마나 더운지, 혹은 추운지 알려 줍니다. 다음은 이 기구인데, 기압계입니다. 이는 기압을 측정하며, 언제 비나 눈이 내릴지, 혹은 강력한 폭풍이 다가오고 있는지 알려 주는 매우 유용한 기구예요. 풍속계는 바람의 속도를 측정하는 기구입니다. 여기에서 보실 수 있고… 그리고 풍향계는, 여러분 모두 헛간의 꼭대기에서 보신 적이 있을 것으로 생각되는데, 바람이 부는 방향을 알려 줍니다. 여러분이 모르실 수도 있는 것도 하나 있어요… 바로 습도계입니다. 이 기구는 공기 중의 습기의 양을 측정하죠. 그리고 우량계는 비가 얼마나 많이 내렸는지 알려 줍니다. 이들 모두가 상당히 간단한 기구들입니다. 이제 보다 복잡한 것들을 보여 드릴게요.

Drill 4 Ⓒ

Script 08-05

M Professor: Some of the oldest art other than cave paintings comes from Egypt. I'm referring, of course, to the Egyptian art which can be seen in the ruins of old buildings as well as inside ancient tombs. Some of the oldest art ever found in Egypt dates back around 5,000 years ago.

There are a few characteristics about ancient Egyptian art that I'm sure most of you have seen but may not have really paid much attention to. Take a look at this picture here . . . and this one . . . and this one . . . You all saw that the paintings were somewhat similar, right? Now . . . how were they similar? First, each character in the pictures was painted in profile. That means you can only see one side. The pose each character was making was identical, too, wasn't it? And you only saw one eye. Finally, each picture was two dimensional. The Egyptians never learned how to give the appearance of three dimensions in their paintings. Or, uh, if they did learn it, they didn't practice it.

Interestingly, this style of art did not change for thousands of years. Think about all of the different styles of art that have taken place in the Western world. Hmm . . . Wait. Just think about the different styles there were in the 1900s. There were Cubism . . . Dadaism . . . Impressionism, Art Deco, Pop Art, and numerous others. But for thousands of years, Egyptian art simply remained the same.

해석

M Professor: 동굴 벽화를 제외하고 가장 오래된 미술 작품 중 몇몇은 이집트에서 만들어진 것들입니다. 당연하게도, 오래된 건물 유적뿐만 아니라 고대 무덤의 내부에서 찾아볼 수 있는 이집트 미술을 말씀드리는 것이에요. 이집트에서 발견된 가장 오래된 미술 작품 중 일부는 약 5,000년 전에 만들어진 것입니다.

고대 이집트 미술에는 여러분 대다수가 분명 본 적이 있지만 실제로는 별 관심을 기울이지 못했을 만한 몇 가지 특징들이 있습니다. 여기 이 사진을 봐 주세요… 그리고 이것도… 그리고 이것도요… 여러분 모두 그림들이 다소 비슷하게 보인다는 점을 아셨을 거예요, 그렇죠? 자… 어떻게 비슷했을까요? 먼저, 그림에 각 인물들의 옆모습이 그려졌습니다. 한 쪽 면만 볼 수 있다는 뜻이에요. 각각의 인물들이 취하고 있는 자세 역시 동일하죠, 그렇지 않나요? 그리고 눈은 한 개만 보였습니다. 마지막으로, 각 그림들은 2차원으로 그려졌어요. 이집트 사람들은 그림에서 3차원 효과를 나타내는 법을 결코 알지 못했습니다. 혹은, 어, 알았다면, 실행하지 않은 것이었죠.

흥미롭게도 이러한 미술 스타일은 수천 년 동안 바뀌지 않았습니다. 서구에서 나타났던 다양한 미술 스타일에 대해 생각해 보세요. 흠… 잠시만요. 1900년대에 존재했던 다양한 스타일에 대해서만 생각해 보세요. 입체주의… 다다이즘… 인상주의, 아르데코, 팝아트, 그리고 기타 수많은 것들이 있었습니다. 하지만 수천 년 동안 이집트 미술은 똑같았어요.

Exercises with Long Conversations

Exercise 1 1 Ⓑ 2 Ⓓ 3 Ⓑ, Ⓒ p.232

Script 08-06

W Bookstore Employee: Hello. That's a huge stack of books you've got. But, uh, isn't it a bit late in the semester to be buying books? I mean, um, we're already halfway done with the term.

M Student: Oh, no. I'm here to sell these books. I just don't need them anymore.

W: I see. Well, I can handle that for you. But you might want to know a couple of things before we start.

M: What's that?

W: We often don't buy back books, and students are usually pretty unhappy about the amount of money we offer them when we do buy books.

M: Thanks for the warning. Out of curiosity, why don't you buy back any books?

W: The primary reason is that the publishing company that makes the book is creating a new edition. When that happens, professors use the new edition, so the old one isn't desired anymore.

M: What's the other reason?

W: The other reason is that we simply have too many books in inventory. So we don't need to buy any more of those books back.

M: Well, I hope that isn't the case for the books I have. Would you mind taking a look at them for me, please?

W: Okay . . . You're in luck. We can buy this one back. And we'll even give you fifty percent of the cover price for it. That almost never happens.

M: Fifty percent of the cover price is good?

W: Totally. In most cases, we might just offer one or two dollars for a book.

M: Seriously? Most of these books cost between forty and sixty dollars. But you'll only offer a dollar for it?

W: Yeah, I know. I'm a student here, too, and I really

dislike that. But I just have to go by what the computer tells me.

M: What do most students wind up doing?

W: A lot of them refuse to sell their books for such a low amount. And some take their books to a nearby used bookshop and try to get more money there.

M: Huh. It looks like you've scanned all of the books. Can you tell me what the deal with them is now?

W: I have. We can't take the books back in this pile. But we will offer you money for these books. We can give you a total of sixty dollars, which, if you ask me, is a really good amount.

M: I'll take it. Thanks for all of your help. It has been rather educational talking to you about this. Maybe if the employees here talked like this to other students, they would understand why they aren't getting too much back for the books that they spent a lot of money on.

해석

W Bookstore Employee: 안녕하세요. 가지고 있는 책이 엄청나게 많군요. 하지만, 어, 책을 사기에는 학기가 이미 좀 지나지 않았나요? 제 말은, 음, 벌써 학기 중반이잖아요.

M Student: 오, 아니에요. 저는 이 책을 팔려고 온 거예요. 더 이상 필요하지가 않아서요.

W: 그렇군요. 음, 제가 처리해 드릴게요. 하지만 그 전에 두어 가지 아시면 좋을 것들이 있어요.

M: 무엇인가요?

W: 저희가 종종 책을 구입하지 않는 경우도 있고, 저희가 책을 구입하는 경우에도 저희가 제시하는 금액에 학생들이 상당한 불만을 갖는 경우도 많아요.

M: 미리 알려 주셔서 고마워요. 궁금해서 그런데, 왜 책을 다시 구입하지 않나요?

W: 가장 큰 이유는 해당 도서를 출판한 출판사가 개정판을 만들고 있기 때문이에요. 그렇게 되면 교수님들께서 개정판을 사용하시기 때문에 더 이상 구판을 찾는 사람이 없게 되죠.

M: 또 다른 이유는요?

W: 또 다른 이유는 재고 도서가 너무 많이 남아 있기 때문이에요. 그러면 해당 도서들을 추가로 다시 구입할 필요가 없죠.

M: 음, 제가 가진 책들에는 해당되지 않는 내용이면 좋겠군요. 한번 봐 주시겠어요?

W: 그럴게요… 운이 좋군요. 이 책은 저희가 다시 구입할 수 있어요. 그리고 정가의 50%를 드릴 거예요. 이런 경우는 거의 없어요.

M: 정가의 50%가 좋은 편인가요?

W: 그럼요. 대부분의 경우, 권당 1달러나 2달러만 제시할 수도 있어요.

M: 정말인가요? 이 책들의 가격은 대부분 40달러에서 60달러 사이에요. 하지만 그에 대해 1달러만 제시를 한다고요?

W: 네, 저도 알아요. 저도 이곳 학생인데, 정말로 마음에 들지 않는 부분이죠. 하지만 저는 컴퓨터가 알려 주는 것을 따라야만 해요.

M: 대부분의 학생들이 결국 어떻게 하나요?

W: 많은 학생들이 그처럼 낮은 가격으로 책을 파는 것을 받아들이지 않아요. 그리고 일부는 책을 근처 중고 서점으로 가져가서 더 많은 돈을 받으려고 하죠.

M: 흠. 책들을 다 스캔하신 것 같군요. 이제 그 책들의 조건이 어떤지 말씀해 주시겠어요?

W: 다 했어요. 이 더미에 있는 책들은 다시 받을 수가 없어요. 그리고 이 책들에 대해서는 금액을 제시할게요. 총 60달러를 드릴 수 있는데, 만약 제게 묻는다면 정말로 좋은 가격이에요.

M: 받아들이죠. 도와 줘서 고마워요. 그에 대한 이야기를 나누어서 상당히 많은 것을 알게 되었어요. 아마 이곳 직원들이 다른 학생들에게 그러한 이야기를 해 준다면, 그들도 많은 돈을 쓴 책에 대해 그다지 많이 돌려받지 못하는 이유를 이해할 것 같아요.

Summary Note

A

❶ bookstore
❷ textbooks
❸ not buy
❹ old editions
❺ inventory
❻ sixty dollars

B

The student visits the bookstore with a huge stack of books. They are textbooks that he does not need anymore, so he wants to sell them. The woman says that the bookstore sometimes does not buy back books, and when it does buy them, the prices are not high. The student asks why the bookstore does not buy books at times. The student responds that if a publishing company is making a new edition, the bookstore will not buy the old edition. In addition, if it has too many of a certain textbook in stock, it will not buy more of them. The woman checks one book and says the bookstore will give the student half price for that. She thinks it is a good offer. Then, she scans all of the books and offers him sixty dollars for some. She cannot buy the others. The student agrees to her offer.

Exercise 2 1 Ⓒ 2 Ⓓ 3 Ⓒ p.234

Script 08-07

M Student: Marcia, are you busy right now? I would like to talk to you about something that's kind of important.

W Residential Assistant: I'm not too occupied right now, Enrique. What's on your mind?

M: I saw a flyer on the front door of the dorm. It's about a quiet period which is going to happen during the midterm exam period. Um . . . I've never heard of anything like that. Could you tell me what this quiet period is, please?

W: You've never heard of it? But we have it all the time.

M: **I'm a freshman.** Remember?

W: Oh, I had totally forgotten about that. My apologies.

M: No worries.

W: So the quiet period is something that takes place here twice each semester. It happens for midterm exams and final exams. It starts two days before the beginning of each period and ends as soon as the last exam is over.

M: I understood that much from the flyer. But what happens during this time? That's what I'm curious about.

W: It's pretty simple. You have to be quiet so that you don't disturb any students who are trying to study for their exams. That means no yelling, shouting, or singing. You can't listen to loud music or play musical instruments like guitars.

M: Oh, my roommate isn't going to be happy about that.

W: Right. I forgot that he's a musician. I'll have to have a chat with him personally to make sure he doesn't do that.

M: So we need to be quiet all day and night long? That's actually going to be pretty stressful for some people.

W: There's a one-hour period that starts at seven PM and ends at eight when students are allowed to make as much noise as they want.

M: That probably gets a bit crazy. I can't wait to hear that.

W: Yes, there's lots of yelling, shouting, and music during that time. Now, uh, you really need to be quiet, or you can get fined. The fines start at a hundred dollars, and if you get multiple fines, you'll get in trouble with the dean of students. You're a pretty quiet guy, so I don't think that you'll have any problems. However, there are a few students on your floor who are not going to enjoy this time.

M: Yeah. I think Eddie and Lewis will have trouble during this time.

W: Those are precisely the people that I was thinking about. Anyway, it's just for a few days, and it lets people emphasize their schoolwork. So overall, I'd say it's a good thing. I know that I find it beneficial to my studies when I don't have to ask the students next to me to turn the TV down or to stop playing their music so loudly. It's also nice to get uninterrupted sleep without waking up to loud music at three in the morning.

해석

M Student: Marcia, 지금 바쁜가요? 중요한 일에 대해 이야기를 나누고 싶어요.

W Residential Assistant: 그렇게 바쁜 편은 아니에요, Enrique. 무슨 일인가요?

M: 기숙사 정문에 붙여 있는 안내문을 보았어요. 중간 고사 기간에 진행될 정숙 기간에 관한 것이죠. 음… 제가 전에 그런 것을 들어본 적이 없어서요. 정숙 기간이 무엇인지 알려 주실 수 있나요?

W: 전에 들어본 적이 없다고요? 하지만 항상 정숙 기간을 두는데요.

M: 저는 신입생이에요. 기억하시죠?

W: 오, 제가 완전히 잊고 있었군요. 미안해요.

M: 괜찮아요.

W: 이곳에서는 학기마다 두 번씩 정숙 기간을 두고 있어요. 중간고사와 기말고사 때 실시되죠. 각 시험이 시작되기 이틀 전에 시작해서 마지막 시험이 끝나자마자 종료되고요.

M: 그에 대해서는 안내문을 봐서 알고 있었어요. 하지만 이 기간에 어떤 일이 일어나죠? 그것이 바로 제가 궁금한 점이에요.

W: 꽤 간단해요. 시험 공부를 하고 있는 학생들에게 방해가 되지 않도록 조용히 지내야 하죠. 소리를 지르거나, 고함을 치거나, 또는 노래를 해서는 안 된다는 뜻이에요. 시끄러운 음악을 들어서도 안 되고, 기타와 같은 악기를 연주해서도 안 되죠.

M: 오, 제 룸메이트가 실망할 것 같군요.

W: 맞아요. 그가 연주를 한다는 점은 제가 잊고 있었네요. 그와 개인적으로 이야기를 나누어서 연주를 하지 못하도록 해야겠네요.

M: 그러면 밤낮으로 계속 조용히 해야 하는 건가요? 몇몇 사람들은 실제로 상당한 스트레스를 받게 되겠군요.

W: 저녁 7시에 시작해서 8시까지 한 시간 동안 학생들이 원하는 만큼 소리를 낼 수 있는 시간이 주어져요.

M: 아마도 그땐 정신이 없을 것 같군요. 빨리 들어보고 싶네요.

W: 네, 이때 시끄러운 고함 소리와 음악을 많이 들을 수 있죠. 자, 어, 정말로 조용히 해야 하는데, 그렇지 않으면 벌금을 물게 될 수도 있어요. 벌금은 10달러부터 시작하고, 여러 차례 벌금이 부과되면 학생처장님과의 관계가 곤란해질 거예요. 학생은 상당히 조용한 편이기 때문에 학생에게 문제가 생길 것으로는 생각하지 않아요. 하지만 이러한 기간을 좋아하지 않는 학생들이 학생의 층에 몇 명 있어요.

M: 그래요. Eddie와 Lewis가 그러한 기간에 문제를 겪을 것 같아요.

W: 제가 생각하고 있던 사람이 바로 그들이에요. 어쨌든, 단 며칠만 진행되며, 이때 사람들이 학업에 집중할 수 있어요. 그러니 전체적으로 좋은 일이라고 말하고 싶군요. 옆 학생들에게 TV 볼륨을 낮추라거나 음악을 그렇게 크게 틀지 말라고 부탁할 필요가 없어서 제 공부에도 도움이 된다는 걸 알고 있죠. 또한 새벽 3시에 시끄러운 음악을 듣고 깰 필요없이 숙면을 취할 수 있다는 점도 좋아요.

Summary Note

A

❶ flyer
❷ midterm exam
❸ quiet
❹ disturb
❺ dean of students
❻ quiet

B

The student asks the residential assistant about a flyer he saw. It provided information about a quiet period that is going to happen during the midterm exam period. Because he is a freshman, he does not know about it. The woman says that it starts two days before midterm exams and finishes when the last exam ends. All students must be quiet to avoid disturbing other students. There should be no yelling, shouting, singing, listening to music, or playing musical instruments. The woman will talk to the student's roommate since he is a musician. From seven to eight PM every day, students can make as much noise as they want. Students who make noise during the quiet period will get fined and may have to talk to the dean of students. The woman says that the student should be fine since he is quiet, but other students may have difficulty during this time.

Exercise 3 1 Ⓒ 2 Ⓓ 3 Ⓑ p.236

Script 08-08

W Professor: I'd say that the classes you've chosen to take next semester all look good, George. You've got two classes in your major, a class in a related field, a language class, and an elective. Overall, you've made some wonderful choices, and I think you'll do well in those classes next spring.

M Student: Thanks for saying that, Professor Chamberlain. I thought about which classes to take very hard, and I'm really looking forward to taking them when the new semester begins. I've heard great things about all of the professors I'll be taking, so I know that I'll learn a lot in those classes.

W: Great. Now, uh, before you leave, I would like to chat with you about something.

M: Sure. What's that?

W: When the spring semester finishes, you'll be done with your sophomore year. So you'll be a junior next fall.

M: Right.

W: Have you given any thought to spending a semester or two abroad? Junior year is when most students do that.

M: Hmm . . . I can't say that I have thought much about it.

W: Is there a reason why? I mean, uh, I don't want to pry into your family finances, but is money stopping you from going?

M: Oh, not at all. My family is comfortable enough that my parents could afford to let me study abroad. I guess I just never really considered doing it. Should I?

W: Well, your major is international relations. In my opinion, it would be a great idea for you to spend at least one semester abroad. That would enable you to live in a foreign country and learn about international relations firsthand.

M: That makes sense. I'm open to doing it, but I have no idea where I should go.

W: What foreign languages are you comfortable in?

M: I'm pretty good at both German and Italian. I took a semester of Chinese, but I wasn't particularly talented at it. And I can speak a few words of French.

W: So . . . it would be best if you went to a European country. I would suggest going to Germany or Italy since you know those languages. By the time you return, you'll likely be fluent in one of them.

M: Oh, wow. That would be really cool and would help me get a job after graduation.

W: Precisely. So what do you think?

M: I'll strongly consider it. Can I talk to you about this again after I chat with my parents?

W: It would be my pleasure. I hope that they are in favor of it because I really believe that going abroad would not only improve your skills but would also be helpful to you with regard to your personal development.

해석

W Professor: 다음 학기에 수강하려고 선택한 수업들이 모두 좋아 보인다고 말하고 싶어요, Gorge. 전공 과목이 두 개, 관련 과목 수업이 한 개, 언어 수업 한 개, 그리고 선택 과목이 하나군요. 전제적으로 선택을 잘 했기 때문에 내년 봄에 이들 수업에서 좋은 성적을 거둘 것 같아요.

M Student: 그렇게 말씀해 주시다니 감사합니다, Chamberlain 교수님. 어떤 수업을 들을지 많이 고민했는데, 새로운 학기가 시작되면 빨리 그 수업들을 들어 보고 싶어요. 제가 듣게 될 수업의 모든 교수님들에 대해서도 좋은 이야기를 들었기 때문에 수업에서 많은 것을 배우게 될 것 같아요.

W: 잘 되었군요. 자, 어, 학생이 가기 전에 학생과 나누고 싶은 이야기가 있어요.

M: 좋아요. 어떤 것인가요?

W: 봄 학기가 끝나면 학생의 2학년이 끝나게 될 거예요. 그러면 다음 가을에는 3학년이 되겠죠.

M: 맞습니다.

W: 한두 학기 정도 해외에서 공부하는 것을 생각해 본 적이 있나요? 대부분의 학생들이 3학년 때 유학을 가죠.

M: 흠… 그에 대해서는 많은 생각을 해 보지 못했던 것 같아요.

W: 이유가 있나요? 제 말은, 어, 학생 가족의 경제적인 상황은 캐묻고 싶지 않지만, 돈 때문에 가지 못하는 건가요?

M: 오, 전혀 그렇지 않아요. 집안 형편이 괜찮은 편이어서 부모님들께서 제 유학 비용을 감당하실 수 있을 거예요. 실제로 그에 대해서는 한 번도 고려해 본 적이 없는 것 같아요. 그래야 할까요?

W: 음, 학생의 전공이 국제 관계학이잖아요. 제 생각으로는 최소한 한 학기 정도 해외에서 보내는 것이 좋을 것 같아요. 그러면 해외에서 생활하면서 국제 관계를 직접적으로 배우게 될 거예요.

M: 일리가 있는 말이군요. 의향은 있는데, 어디로 가야 할지는 모르겠어요.

W: 능숙하게 하는 외국어가 있나요?

M: 독일어와 이탈리아어 모두 꽤 잘하는 편이죠. 한 학기 동안 중국어 수업도 들었지만 특별하게 잘하지는 못해요. 그리고 프랑스어도 몇 마디 할 줄 알고요.

W: 그러면… 유럽에 있는 국가로 가는 것이 최선일 것 같군요. 학생이 해당 언어를 알고 있으니 독일이나 이탈리아에 가는 것을 추천하고 싶어요. 돌아올 때쯤이면 그중 하나는 유창하게 하고 있겠네요.

M: 오, 우아. 그러면 정말 좋을 것 같은데, 졸업 후 구직 활동을 할 때에도 도움이 될 것 같아요.

W: 맞아요. 그러면 어떻게 생각하나요?

M: 적극적으로 고려해 볼게요. 부모님께 말씀을 드린 후에 다시 교수님과 이야기를 나눌 수 있을까요?

W: 기꺼이 그럴게요. 저는 해외 유학이 학생의 실력을 향상시켜 줄 뿐만 아니라 학생의 자기 계발에도 도움이 될 것이라고 생각하기 때문에 그분들께서 찬성하셨으면 좋겠어요.

Summary Note

A

❶ next semester
❷ looking forward to
❸ junior year
❹ international relations
❺ German
❻ become fluent

B

The professor compliments the student on his choice of classes to take next semester. The student says that he is looking forward to taking all of the classes. The professor then asks the student if he has considered studying abroad during his junior year. The student says he has not thought about it. The professor thinks that since the student is an international relations major, he should go abroad. She asks what languages he knows, and he says that he is pretty good at German and Italian. She recommends that he go to Germany or Italy since he will become fluent in either German or Italian when he is there. The student says that he needs to talk to his parents but that he will come back later to talk to the professor.

Exercise 4 1 Ⓑ 2 Ⓑ 3 Ⓓ p.238

Script 08-09

W Student: Professor Collins, I'd like a word with you about my recent exam. I'm really curious about why I got such a poor grade on it.

M Professor: Of course, Brenda. I was also extremely surprised by your performance on it. You did quite well on the first test we took, and your contributions in class discussions have been excellent as well. I couldn't believe your score was so low, so I actually graded your test again to make sure that I hadn't made any mistakes on it. But, uh, no. There was nothing wrong with my grading.

W: I see. Well, I've never gotten a D on a test until this one, so I was quite upset. Do you think we can go over the test now? I brought it with me.

M: Sure. May I see it, please?

W: Of course. Here you are . . .

M: So, uh, the first part of the test was simply multiple choice. You missed nine of those questions.

W: Yeah, I'm not sure how I managed to do that. I mean, uh, I studied really hard for the test, and I knew all of the information.

M: Let's look carefully. The answer to number one is C, but you wrote D. The answer to number two is D, but you wrote B.

W: Wait a minute. Is the answer to number three B?

M: Yes, it is. Why do you ask?

W: Oh, my. I see what I did. I answered the questions correctly, but I put each answer with the wrong number. Do you see that?

M: Hmm . . . Oh, yeah. I see what you did. You put the right answer for number two in the space for number 1. And you kept doing that for all of the other answers. That's why you only got one correct.

W: I can't believe it. Now, uh, what about the other answers? Did I do the same thing?

M: Let me see . . . No, it doesn't appear so. It looks like the chief reason you lost points is that you got a lot of dates wrong.

W: I did? Let me see . . . Oh, yeah. You're right. I don't know what I was thinking here. And here . . . And here, too. I don't know what happened, but I just totally messed up this test.

M: These things happen, Brenda. We all make mistakes. The best thing that you can do is learn from your mistakes and try not to repeat them. We still have three more exams and a paper this semester, so you've got plenty of time to improve your grade. You might even pull off an A if you do well on everything.

W: I'll do my best. Thanks so much for explaining things. I feel much better already.

M: Good luck. I'm expecting great things from you the rest of this semester.

해석

W Student: Collins 교수님, 최근 시험에 관해서 교수님과 이야기를 나누고 싶어요. 제가 시험에서 왜 그처럼 낮은 점수를 받았는지 정말로 궁금해서요.

M Professor: 그래요, Brenda. 저 또한 학생의 점수를 보고 크게 놀랐어요. 학생은 우리가 봤던 첫 번째 시험에서 성적이 꽤 좋았고, 수업 토론 참여도 역시 매우 우수했으니까요. 학생의 점수가 그처럼 낮은 것을 저도 믿을 수가 없어서 채점할 때 실수가 있었는지 확인하기 위해 실제로 학생의 시험지를 한 번 더 채점하기까지 했죠. 하지만, 어, 없었어요. 제 채점에는 잘못된 것이 없었죠.

W: 그렇군요. 음, 저는 그 전까지 한 번도 시험에서 D를 받아본 적이 없기 때문에 상당히 당황스러웠어요. 지금 시험지를 같이 검토해 주실 수 있을까요? 제가 가지고 왔어요.

M: 그럼요. 제가 봐도 될까요?

W: 물론이죠. 여기 있습니다…

M: 그러면, 어, 시험지의 첫 번째 파트는 객관식이었어요. 그중 9개를 틀렸군요.

W: 네, 제가 어떻게 틀렸는지 잘 모르겠어요. 제 말은, 어, 저는 정말로 열심히 시험 공부를 해서 내용은 모두 알고 있었거든요.

M: 자세히 살펴보죠. 1번 문제의 답은 C이지만, 학생은 D라고 적었어요. 두 번째 문제의 답은 D인데, 학생은 B라고 적었고요.

W: 잠시만요. 3번 문제의 답이 B인가요?

M: 네, 그래요. 왜 묻는 것이죠?

W: 오, 이런. 제가 어떻게 했는지 알겠어요. 답은 맞췄는데, 모든 답의 문제 번호를 잘못 적었어요. 보이시나요?

M: 흠… 오, 그래요. 학생이 어떻게 했는지 알겠어요. 1번 문제의 자리에 2번 문제의 정답을 적었네요. 그리고 나머지 답들도 모두 그런 식으로 적었고요. 바로 이 때문에 한 문제만 맞췄던 것이군요.

W: 믿기지가 않네요. 자, 어, 다른 답들은 어떤가요? 제가 똑같이 했나요?

M: 봅시다… 아니에요, 그런 것 같지는 않군요. 학생이 점수를 잃은 주된 이유는 학생이 다수의 날짜들을 잘못 썼기 때문이에요.

W: 제가요? 저도 볼게요… 오, 그래요. 교수님 말씀이 맞아요. 여기에서 제가 어떤 생각을 하고 있었는지 모르겠어요. 그리고 여기에도… 그리고 여기도 마찬가지고요. 무슨 일이 있었는지는 모르겠지만, 이번 시험은 완전히 망쳤어요.

M: 때때로 일어날 수 있는 일이에요, Brenda. 우리 모두 실수를 하죠. 학생이 할 수 있는 최선의 행동은 본인의 실수로부터 배우고 그런 일이 반복되지 않도록 노력하는 것이죠. 이번 학기에 아직 세 번의 시험과 한 번의 보고서가 남아 있으니 성적을 향상시킬 수 있는 시간은 많아요. 모든 것에서 좋은 성적을 받으면 A도 받을 있을 거예요.

W: 최선을 다할게요. 설명해 주셔서 정말 감사합니다. 기분이 훨씬 나아졌어요.

M: 행운을 빌어요. 이번 학기 나머지 기간 동안 많은 기대를 하고 있을게요.

Summary Note

A

❶ low grade
❷ D
❸ wrong blanks
❹ dates
❺ mistakes
❻ paper

B

The student wants to talk about the low grade she got on an exam. The professor says that he was surprised the grade was so low, so he checked it again. The student wants to see the test because she is upset about getting a D. She checks the multiple-choice part and realizes that she had the correct answers but put them in the wrong blanks. Then, on the other part of the test, she got a lot of dates wrong. She says that she just messed up on the test. The professor tells her to learn from her mistakes and to do well on the three remaining exams and paper. He thinks she can get an A in the class if she does well.

Exercises with Long Lectures

Exercise 1 1 Ⓐ 2 Ⓐ 3 Ⓑ, Ⓓ p.240

Script 08-10

M Professor: Another form of indigenous art is Inuit art, which has flourished in recent years both in quantity and commercial demand. The Inuit are the northern people who live in the Arctic areas of Canada, Alaska, Russia, and Greenland. We used to call them Eskimos, but today, that term is regarded by many Inuit as derogatory. The Inuit seem to be associated with Canada more than with any other country, possibly because the Canadian government has incorporated and promoted Inuit culture as a part of Canada's cultural identity. If you have ever been a tourist in Canada and you've visited a souvenir shop there, you'll know exactly what I'm talking about because the shop is almost surely overflowing with Inuit art, which may include sculptures, paintings, and prints. As for architecture, you're all familiar with the igloo.

But I want to focus more specifically on Inuit sculptures, which have become very commercialized in the last few decades. Prior to the 1950s, the carvings were small enough to hold inside your fist. When a Canadian government official visiting the Artic in the 1940s was approached by an Inuit carrying a piece inside his fist, the official mistakenly believed the Inuit individual was going to start a fistfight. The official was so impressed with the miniature carving that he bought all of the sculptures in the community. This began the commercialization of Inuit carvings. Today, many of the carvings are very small because the Inuit were historically a nomadic people who traveled lightly. Since the 1950s, many carvings have become bigger because the Inuit have settled into permanent settlements and because many buyers prefer larger sculptures. Today, we have miniatures and larger sculptures. In addition, since the 1980s, the carvings have become more polished and realistic, again because of market demands in Canada and internationally, where they are now considered fine art.

The subjects of these carvings are usually animals and humans. Some pieces are very realistic looking while others have less detail and are cruder or more primitive in appearance. The animals are bears, seals, whales, walruses, and sometimes birds. Some of the carvings are now highly polished while others are unpolished or dull. The themes may be humorous, such as a waving walrus and a dancing bear. Others are more serious, such as hunting scenes. The characteristics of these carvings vary from region to region and with the specific artist. A unique characteristic of Inuit carvings is that they are never made of wood. The reason is that there are no trees in the Arctic. So the artists use whatever raw materials are available from the land and the sea. Animal bone, ivory, and, most commonly, stone are the primary materials. Soapstone is very soft, but most parts of the

Arctic don't have soapstone. So many Arctic artists use serpentine, which is not as soft. It's available in a range of colors from green to black. Other stones used includes marble, quartz, and dolomite. Finished sculptures are sometimes imbedded with metallic minerals. In recent years, soapstone has been imported from other countries, resulting in the perception of the sculptures being less authentic. Nevertheless, many successful Inuit artists use the imported stone.

We're running out of time, so we'll continue our discussion of Inuit carvings and also look at Inuit art prints and Inuit baskets in our next class.

해석

M Professor: 또 다른 형태의 원주민 예술은 이누이트 예술로, 이는 최근에 양적인 면과 상업적인 수요에 있어서 큰 성과를 보이고 있습니다. 이누이트족은 북쪽에 사는 사람들로, 캐나다의 북극 지방, 알래스카, 러시아, 그리고 그린란드에서 살고 있어요. 이들은 한때 에스키모족이라고 불리기도 했지만, 오늘날 그러한 용어는 많은 이누이트족 사람들에게 경멸적인 것으로 여겨지고 있죠. 이누이트족은 다른 어떤 나라보다 캐나다와 밀접한 관계를 맺고 있는 것처럼 보이는데, 그 이유는 아마도 캐나다 정부가 이누이트족의 문화를 캐나다의 문화적인 정체성의 일부로 통합시키고 발전시켰기 때문일 것입니다. 캐나다에서 관광을 하면서 그곳 기념품 매장을 방문한 적이 있다면 제가 드리는 말씀을 정확히 이해하실 수 있을 텐데, 그곳 매장은 조각, 회화, 그리고 인쇄물이 포함된 이누이트 예술품들로 분명 넘쳐나고 있을 것입니다. 건축에 대해 말씀을 드리면, 여러분 모두 이글루를 잘 아실 것 같군요.

하지만 저는 지난 수십 년 동안 크게 상업화된 이누이트 조각에 대해 보다 초점을 맞추고자 해요. 1950년대 이전에는 조각품들이 손 안에 들어갈 정도로 작았습니다. 1940년대에 북극을 방문했던 한 캐나다 정부 관리는 손에 무언가를 쥐고 있는 이누이트족 사람이 다가오자 이 이누이트족 사람이 주먹다짐을 시작할 것으로 오해하기도 했죠. 그 관리는 조그마한 조각품에 크게 감명을 받아서 마을에 있는 조각품들을 모두 구입했어요. 이로써 이누이트 조각품이 상업화되기 시작했죠. 오늘날 많은 조각품의 크기가 매우 작은 이유는 이누이트족 사람들이 역사적으로 가볍게 이동을 했던 유목민이었기 때문입니다. 1950년대 이후 이누이트족이 영구적인 정착지에서 생활하기 시작하고 다수의 구매자들이 보다 큰 조각품을 선호하자 많은 조각품들의 크기가 커졌습니다. 또한 1980년대 이후에는 조각품을 순수 예술 작품으로 간주하는 캐나다 및 국제 시장에서의 수요 때문에 이러한 조각품들이 보다 세련되고 사실적인 형태를 띠게 되었어요.

이러한 조각품의 대상은 보통 동물과 인간입니다. 매우 사실적으로 보이는 작품들도 있고, 디테일이 떨어지고 형태가 보다 조잡하거나 원시적인 작품들도 있죠. 동물로는 곰, 물개, 고래, 바다코끼리, 그리고 때로는 새가 있습니다. 현재 매우 세련된 조각품들도 있지만, 세련되지 못하거나 단조로운 것들도 있습니다. 테마는 손을 흔드는 바다코끼리 및 춤추는 곰과 같이 재미있는 것일 수도 있어요. 사냥 장면처럼 보다 진지한 것들도 있죠. 이러한 조각품의 특징은 지역에 따라, 그리고 특정 조각가에 따라 다양합니다.

이누이트 조각의 독특한 특징은 결코 나무로 만들어지지 않는다는 점이에요. 그 이유는 북극에 나무가 없기 때문이죠. 그래서 조각가들은 육지 및 바다에서 얻을 수 있는 재료라면 무엇이든 다 이용합니다. 동물의 뼈, 상아, 그리고, 가장 흔하게는, 돌이 주재료가 되죠. 동석은 매우 무르지만, 북극의 대부분 지역에는 동석이 존재하지 않습니다. 그래서 북극의 여러 조각가들은 무르지 않은 사문석을 사용해요. 녹색에서 검정색까지 다양한 색의 사문석을 구할 수가 있습니다. 그 밖의 돌로는 대리석, 석영, 그리고 백운석을 들 수 있습니다. 완성된 조각품에 때때로 금속성 광물을 넣기도 해요. 최근에는 동석을 외국에서 수입하는데, 그 결과 조각품의 정통성이 떨어지는 것으로 인식되고 있습니다. 그럼에도 불구하고 성공한 많은 조각가들이 수입한 돌을 사용하고 있죠.

시간이 다 되었으니 다음 시간에 계속해서 이누이트 조각에 대해 이야기를 하고, 또한 이누이트 인쇄품과 이누이트 바구니 제품들도 살펴보도록 하겠습니다.

Summary Note

A

❶ Inuit art
❷ Arctic areas
❸ Canada
❹ sculptures
❺ realistic
❻ wood

B

The Inuit are northern people who live in the Arctic areas of Canada, Alaska, Russia, and Greenland. Inuit art includes sculptures, paintings, and prints. Prior to the 1950s, Inuit carvings were small enough to hold in one's fist. Today, the carvings have become bigger because the Inuit have settled into permanent settlements and are trying to satisfy market demand. So there are now miniatures and larger sculptures. In addition, since the 1980s, Inuit carvings have become more polished and realistic. The subjects of these carvings are usually animals and humans. The animals are bears, seals, whales, walruses, and sometimes birds. Some themes are humorous while others are more serious. A unique characteristic of Inuit carvings is that they are never made of wood. The artists use whatever raw materials are available from the land and sea. The most common substance is a stone called serpentine. It's available in a range of colors from green to black. Other stones used include marble, quartz, and dolomite.

Exercise 2 1 Ⓑ 2 Ⓐ 3 Ⓒ p.242

Script 08-11

M Professor: You should realize that not all weather phenomena are perfectly understood by meteorologists. That's one reason why we can't always make accurate forecasts. You will read a number of explanations in your textbook as to what causes El Nino and La Nina, but, in reality, nobody knows for certain what causes these phenomena.

W Student: Sorry, uh, I get El Nino and La Nina confused. Which one occurs in the Northern Hemisphere, and which one is in the Southern Hemisphere?

M: They both originate in the Southern Hemisphere, and both take place in the Pacific Ocean. And they both cause major temperature changes in the surface waters of the Pacific Ocean and eventually trigger unusual weather phenomena worldwide.

W: So what's the difference between the two?

M: Okay, perhaps, this might help. El Nino brings warm water to the west coast of South America, and La Nina brings cold water to the west coast of South America. El Nino occurs every five to eight years whereas La Nina occurs about half as frequently. El Nino causes changes to the currents of the ocean by bringing uncharacteristically warm water to the coast of South America, particularly in the northern areas of South America. Warm water spreads from the Western Pacific, moves eastward, and eventually reaches the coast of South America. By the time the warm water reaches the coastal waters of Peru, it rises and replaces the cool nutrient-rich seawater at the surface. Because the warmer water has no nutrients, it drastically reduces the amount of plant life and fish in the area.

El Nino's impact can be felt worldwide as it causes unusual weather in many different areas. For instance, it can cause droughts from Indonesia to Mexico and Central America. Its impact on the United States is less obvious, but it can cause or at least contribute toexcessive rainfall in the states around the Gulf of Mexico and in California. In 1982 and 1983, much of California suffered record amounts of rainfall and consequent floods and mudslides. Some of the mudslides obliterated communities in a flash, killing many people. It also brings rain to deserts in South America, which normally don't receive rain in non-El Nino years. This causes floods, a subsequent swarm of mosquitoes, and then disease. Flooding occurs in Bolivia, Peru, Ecuador, Cuba, and the American states on the Gulf coast.

W: Does El Nino have any positive impacts?

M: Good question. It's my understanding that El Nino can snuff out hurricanes with its warm winds at 40,000 feet above sea level. Ah, La Nina, because of its cool water, can dramatically change upper-level air currents, contributing to storm development. La Nina can also affect winter weather in the United States. As an example, it can cause Florida, which is already dry, to become warmer and drier in winter, which may increase the number of forest fires. In winter, it tends to accentuate regular weather patterns, causing colder areas to become colder and warm areas to become warmer.

해석

M Professor: 기상학자들도 모든 기상 현상을 완벽하게 이해하지는 못한다는 점을 아셔야 해요. 그렇기 때문에 정확한 일기 예보가 항상 가능한 것은 아닙니다. 여러분 교재에서 엘니뇨와 라니냐의 원인에 대한 여러 가지 설명을 읽을 수는 있겠지만, 실제로 이러한 현상이 왜 일어나는지를 정확히 아는 사람은 없습니다.

W Student: 죄송하지만, 어, 저는 엘니뇨와 라니냐가 헷갈려요. 어떤 것이 북반구에서 일어나는 것이고, 어떤 것이 남반구에서 일어나는 것인가요?

M: 둘 다 남반구에서 발생해서 둘 다 태평양에서 진행이 되죠. 그리고 둘 다 태평양의 표층수 온도에 커다란 변화를 일으켜서, 결국 전 세계적으로 비정상적인 기후 현상이 나타나게 됩니다.

W: 그러면 이 둘의 차이점이 무엇인가요?

M: 좋아요, 아마도 이렇게 말하면 도움이 될 것 같군요. 엘니뇨는 따뜻한 물을 남아메리카 서해안에 가져다 주고, 라니냐는 찬 물을 남아메리카 서해안에 가져다 줍니다. 엘니뇨는 5년에서 8년 간격으로 발생하는 반면에 라니냐 발생 빈도는 그것의 절반 정도예요. 엘니뇨는 평소와 다르게 따뜻한 물을 남아메리카 해안, 특히 남아메리카의 북쪽 지역에 가져다 줌으로써 해류에 변화를 일으킵니다. 따뜻한 물은 서태평양에서 시작되어, 동쪽으로 이동한 후, 마침내 남아메리카 해안에 도달하게 되죠. 따뜻한 물이 페루의 해안가에 도착할 무렵이면 따뜻한 물이 불어나서 수면에 있던 양분이 풍부한 차가운 물이 밀려납니다. 따뜻한 물에는 양분이 없기 때문에 이로 인해 해당 지역의 식물과 어류의 양이 급격하게 줄어들게 되죠.

엘니뇨는 많은 지역에서 비정상적인 날씨를 유발하기 때문에 그 효과는 전 세계에서 느낄 수가 있어요. 예를 들어 인도네시아에서 멕시코 및 중앙아메리카에 이르기까지 가뭄이 일어날 수 있습니다. 미국에 미치는 영향은 적은 편이지만, 엘리뇨는 멕시코만 주변에 있는 주들과 캘리포니아에 발생하는 폭우의 전적인, 혹은 최소한 부분적인 원인일 수 있습니다. 1982년과 1983년에 캘리포니아의 상당 지역에서 기록적인 양의 비가 내림으로써 홍수와 이류가 발생했습니다. 몇몇 이류는 눈 깜짝할 사이에 마을을 집어삼켰고, 이로써 많은 사람들이 목숨을 잃었습니다. 또한 엘니뇨가 발생하지 않는 해에는 보통 비가 내리지 않는 남아메리카에 비를 내리게 만들 수도 있습니다. 그렇게 되면 홍수가 발생해서, 그 결과 모기떼가 창궐하고, 그런 다음에는 질병이 발생하죠. 볼리비아, 페루, 에콰도르, 쿠바, 그리고 멕시코만의 미국의 주에서는 홍수가 발생합니다.

W: 엘니뇨에 긍정적인 효과도 있나요?

M: 좋은 질문이에요. 제가 알기로는 엘리뇨에 수반되는 해수면 위 40,000피트 상공의 따뜻한 바람 때문에 허리케인이 소멸할 수 있습니다. 아, 라니냐는 차가운 물 때문에 상층 기류에 극적인 변화를 일으킬 수 있는데, 이로써 폭풍이 발생할 수 있어요. 또한 라니냐는 미국의 겨울 날씨에도 영향을 미칠 수 있습니다. 한 가지 예로서, 이미 건조한 플로리다가 그로 인해 겨울에 더 따뜻해지고 건조해질 수 있는데, 이로써 산불의 발생 횟수가 증가하게 되죠. 겨울에는 정상적인 날씨 패턴을 두드러지게 만드는 경향이 있어서, 그 결과 추운 지역은 더 추워지고 따뜻한 지역은 더 따뜻해집니다.

Summary Note

A

❶ meteorology
❷ warm water
❸ fish and plant life
❹ cold water
❺ half
❻ positive and negative

B

El Nino and La Nina are weather phenomena that both originate in the Southern Hemisphere and occur in the Pacific Ocean. Both cause major temperature changes in the surface waters of the Pacific Ocean and eventually trigger unusual weather phenomena worldwide. El Nino brings warm water to the west coast of South America, and La Nina brings cold water to the west coast of South America. The warm water El Nino brings to the coastal waters of Peru rises, replaces the cool nutrient-rich water at the surface, and drastically reduces the amount of plant life and fish in the area. El Nino causes unusual weather in many different areas, including droughts and severe rainstorms. La Nina contributes to hurricane development and in winter accentuates the climate in certain areas. For example, in winter, it may cause Florida to be warmer and drier than usual.

Exercise 3 1 Ⓐ 2 Ⓓ 3 Ⓒ p.244

Script 08-12

W Professor: I think that's about enough for today. It's a nice day, so I'd like to finish up a bit early. However, before I let you all go, I need to give you your next writing assignment.

M Student: Excellent! What's the next assignment?

W: Your assignment is to write a memoir. Now, uh, I suppose that I need to explain to you what a memoir is and then give you some suggestions as to how you can write it. It's essentially a story about one part of your life.

M: Wait! What's the difference between a memoir and a biography?

W: A biography is an account of another person's life rather than your own. Please don't write a biography. I want you to write only about your own life. And don't write an autobiography either. That's different, too. It would take too long. An autobiography is a detailed story of your life, usually from childhood to old age. It's a chronological personal history that requires a lot of research and interviews. You're just writing a memoir. That doesn't require any research.

For your information, memoirs are a type of autobiography. An autobiography typically requires a lot of detailed research to reconstruct a detailed chronological story of your whole life. Memoirs, on the other hand, have a narrower focus. You merely write what you recall. So you don't have to look anything up. You don't have to go to the library. You don't have to use the Internet. You can literally go outside, sit down, and start writing. But remember that you should not write about your whole life. Just write about part of it. Let me repeat. You are not writing an autobiography.

Ah, as I said, a memoir is restricted in scope, and it can be short. You focus on part of your life which you feel was important or significant to you. And don't be afraid to describe your feelings because a memoir is usually an intimate account that gets into the writer's head and describes his or her emotions as they relate to certain periods and events in his or her life.

M: Aren't memoirs just for famous people?

W: Historically, they were usually written by world leaders, politicians, government officials, and military leaders to explain their thinking during critical moments in their public lives. Leon Trotsky, Albert Speer, Mahatma Gandhi, and Richard Nixon all wrote memoirs. Some memoirs are eyewitness reports by private citizens who participated in significant historical events. Among these are American slaves and survivors of wars . . . All you need to do is tell a story based on what you can recall about an important time in your life. And keep in mind that memoirs are usually written in narrative form. So you can include a lot of the usual elements of storytelling . . . plot, characterization, imagery, conflict, flashback, foreshadowing, symbolism, irony, and anything else you think will make it an interesting read. While writing a memoir, a writer usually contemplates the meanings of events in retrospect. So it can be a very therapeutic experience, especially for those who focus on stories of survival and hardship. Perhaps you'll feel the same.

Oh! And to answer your question, you don't have to be a famous person to write a memoir. Until twenty years ago, they were written mostly by famous people, but that seems to be changing. Look at Frank McCourt. He was an ordinary person, yet he wrote *Angela's Ashes*.

Okay. Does everyone understand your assignment, which, by the way, is due next Wednesday? Do you have any questions about it?

해석

W Professor: 오늘은 그 정도면 충분한 것 같네요. 날씨가 좋기 때문에 약간 일찍 수업을 끝내고자 합니다. 하지만 모두들 나가시기 전에 다음 글쓰기 과제를 내 드려야 할 것 같군요.

M Student: 좋습니다! 다음 과제는 무엇인가요?

W: 과제는 회고록을 쓰는 것이에요. 자, 어, 회고록이 무엇인지 설명한 다음에 회고록을 쓰는 방법에 관한 몇 가지 제안을 해야 할 것 같네요. 기본적으로 회고록은 여러분 인생의 한 부분에 관한 이야기입니다.

M: 잠깐만요! 회고록과 전기의 차이점이 무엇인가요?

W: 전기는 본인이 아니라 타인의 인생에 관한 글이에요. 전기를 쓰지는 마세요. 저는 여러분들이 여러분 자신의 인생에 대해서만 글을 쓰기를 바랍니다. 그리고 자서전을 쓰지도 마세요. 이 또한 다른 것이죠. 시간이 너무 오래 걸릴 거예요. 자서전은 여러분의 인생, 보통 유년 시절부터 노년에 이르기까지의 인생에 대해 상세히 쓴 글이에요. 이는 시간 순서에 따라 쓴 개인의 역사로서, 많은 조사와 인터뷰가 요구되죠. 여러분은 그저 회고록을 쓰는 거예요. 아무런 조사도 필요하지 않죠.

참고로 회고록은 일종의 자서전입니다. 자서전에서는 보통 인생 전체에 대한 상세한 이야기를 시간 순서대로 재구성하기 위해 많은 세부 조사가 요구되어요. 반면에 회고록은 보다 좁은 부분에 초점을 맞춥니다. 단순히 기억나는 것을 쓰는 것이죠. 그래서 아무것도 찾아볼 필요가 없어요. 도서관에 갈 필요도 없죠. 인터넷을 이용할 필요도 없고요. 말 그대로 나가서, 앉아서, 글쓰기를 시작하면 됩니다. 하지만 인생 전체에 대한 글을 써서는 안 된다는 점을 기억하세요. 그중 일부에 대해서만 쓰세요. 한 번 더 말씀을 드리죠. 자서전을 쓰는 것이 아닙니다.

아, 말씀을 드렸던 것처럼 회고록은 범위가 제한되어 있기 때문에 길이가 짧을 수 있어요. 여러분이 느끼기에 인생에서 자신에게 중요하거나 의미가 있다고 생각되는 부분에 초점을 맞추세요. 그리고 회고록은 보통 작가의 머릿속에 들어가서 인생의 특정 시기 및 사건과 관련된 본인의 감정을 나타낸 사적인 이야기이기 때문에, 여러분의 감정을 드러내는 것을 두려워하지 마세요.

M: 회고록은 유명인들만을 위한 것이 아닌가요?

W: 역사적으로 세계의 지도자, 정치가, 정부 관리, 그리고 군 지도자들이 공직 생활 중 중요한 순간에 자신의 생각을 나타내기 위해 쓰는 경우가 많았죠. 레온 트로츠키, 알베르트 슈피에르, 마하트마 간디, 그리고 리처드 닉슨 모두 회고록을 썼어요. 일부 회고록은 역사적으로 중요한 사건에 참가했던 일반 시민의 목격담이기도 합니다. 미국 노예와 전쟁에서 살아남은 사람들이 여기에 해당되죠… 여러분이 해야 할 것은 여러분 인생에서 중요한 시기에 대해 기억나는 것을 기반으로 이야기를 하는 것이에요. 그리고 회고록은 보통 서술적인 형태로 쓰여진다는 점을 명심하세요. 따라서 스토리텔링의 일반적인 요소들을 다수 포함시킬 수 있는데… 플롯, 인물 묘사, 심상, 갈등, 회상, 전조, 상징, 아이러니, 그리고 그 밖에 글을 흥미롭게 만들 수 있다고 생각되는 모든 것들이 포함될 수 있죠. 회고록을 쓰는 동안 작가는 보통 사건들이 갖는 의미에 대해 회고하게 됩니다. 따라서 이러한 경험은, 특히 생존과 고난의 이야기에 초점을 두는 사람들에게, 큰 치료 효과를 나타낼 수 있어요, 아마 여러분도 같은 느낌을 받게 될 것입니다.

오! 학생의 질문에 답을 하자면 회고록을 쓰는 사람이 유명한 사람일 필요는 없어요. 20년 전까지는 주로 유명한 사람들이 회고록을 썼지만, 이러한 점은 바뀌고 있는 것처럼 보입니다. 프랭크 맥코트를 보세요. 그는 평범한 사람이었지만 *안젤라의 재*를 썼어요.

좋습니다. 그건 그렇고, 과제의 기한은 다음 주 수요일인데, 모두들 과제를 이해하셨나요? 그에 관한 질문이 있나요?

Summary Note

A

❶ write memoir
❷ biography
❸ writer's own life
❹ autobiography
❺ important people
❻ narrative

B

A biography is an account of another person's life rather than one's own. An autobiography is a detailed story of one's own life, usually from childhood to old age. It is a chronological, detailed, personal history that requires a lot of research and interviews. A memoir, however, is a type of autobiography which focuses on only a part of someone's life. The writer merely needs to recall some events that occurred in his or her life. No research is required. It is usually shorter than an autobiography. It focuses on events that are significant to the writer. If the person is a public figure, then that person writes his or her recollections and emotions regarding some of the important public events of his or her life. Historically, they were written by world leaders, politicians, military leaders, and other famous people, but that is changing nowadays.

Exercise 4 1 Ⓓ 2 Ⓐ 3 Ⓑ p.246

Script 08-13

W Professor: To understand earthquakes, you first need to understand the content and workings of the lithosphere and the asthenosphere. So, I'll begin by describing the lithosphere.

The lithosphere is the Earth's exterior. It's the crust. It includes all of the continents, the rocks, and the ocean floor. It also includes the upper part of the asthenosphere, or mantle, located just below the crust. On the continents, the crust is about eighty kilometers deep, but below the ocean, it's only about five kilometers thick.

The lithosphere is very much like a giant puzzle. In fact, if you were to buy one of those puzzle globes . . . I mean those puzzles that are shaped like a globe, it would give you a pretty good idea of what the lithosphere is like. The exterior of the Earth, therefore, is like a puzzle broken up into giant plates that fit around the Earth as though it were a jigsaw puzzle. We call these giant pieces tectonic plates. The continents rest on these plates, and the plates move about two inches every year. Their movement is a sliding motion as they glide along the upper part of the asthenosphere, which is not as solid as the surface.

The asthenosphere consists of a semi-plastic molten rock material, which is like silly putty. It is more fluid, and it moves as it responds to the churning motions of the extremely hot interior of the Earth below. These movements inside the asthenosphere cause the tectonic plates to move as they glide or float on the moving asthenosphere. The plates, by the way, are made of rock, but these plates are lighter than the denser, fluid layer beneath. This allows them to flow on top of the denser material.

Over millions of years, the movement of the plates has given the surface the look that it has today. The movement of tectonic plates is called plate tectonics, and as we'll learn later, it plays a major role in earthquakes and other Earth-shaping events. An example of how the movement shapes the surface is when two plates collide head-on with one another, followed by an upward movement of the edge of the plates. This lifting of the crust is how mountain ranges form. The Rocky Mountains formed as a result of two plates crashing head on, and then their edges moving upward and lifted the crust. The resulting uplift created the Rockies.

There are seven major plates and about twelve minor ones. The plates have also been given names, usually according to their geographic location. For example, there are the Pacific plate, the North American plate, the African plate, the Australian plate, and the Philippine plate. Because the plates only move a few inches a year, it takes millions of years for the continents to move. But at one time, the continents and the oceans were in different locations, and about 250 million years ago, the continents were mostly connected with one another.

Remember that the interior of the Earth is extremely hot. It is this heat that generates movement above. However, the core is expected, someday, millions of years from now, to cool off. When that happens, the movement of the asthenosphere will stop, causing the tectonic plates to stop moving and thereby stabilizing the surface. In other words, the continents will stop moving. This has already happened on the moon, on Mars, and on other planets and satellites.

해석

W Professor: 지진을 이해하기 위해서는 먼저 암석권과 암류권의 구성 및 활동에 대해 알아야 해요. 그러면 암석권에 대한 설명으로 시작해 보겠습니다.

암석권은 지구의 외부입니다. 바로 지각이죠. 여기에는 모든 대륙, 암석, 그리고 해저가 포함됩니다. 또한 지각 바로 아래에 있는 암류권의 상부, 즉 맨틀도 포함되고요. 대륙에서는 약 80킬로미터 아래까지 지각이지만, 해양의 경우에는 지각의 두께가 약 5킬로미터밖에 되지 않습니다.

암석권은 마치 거대한 퍼즐과 같아요. 실제로 여러분이 그 퍼즐 지구본… 지구본처럼 생긴 퍼즐을 말씀드리는 것인데, 그 퍼즐을 보면 암석권이 무엇인지 쉽게 알 수 있을 거예요. 따라서 지구의 외부는 마치 직소 퍼즐처럼 지구에 꼭 들어맞는 거대한 판으로 나뉘어진 퍼즐과 같습니다. 우리는 이 거대한 조각들을 지각판이라고 불러요. 대륙은 이들 판 위에 놓여 있으며, 판들은 매년 약 2인치씩 이동합니다. 이러한 움직임은 활강 형태를 띠는데, 그 이유는 판이 지표면만큼 단단하지 않은 암류권의 상부를 따라 미끄러지기 때문이죠.

암류권은 고무 장난감과도 같은 반소성 용융 암석 물질로 이루어져 있어요. 보다 액체에 가깝고, 극도로 뜨거운 지구 내부의 교반 운동에 반응해서 움직입니다. 암류권 내에서 이루어지는 이러한 움직임 때문에 지각판이 이동하게 되며, 지각판은 움직이는 암류권 위에서 미끄러지듯 이동하거나 떠다니게 되죠. 그건 그렇고, 판은 암석으로 이루어져 있지만, 이러한 판들은 아래쪽에 있는 보다 밀도가 높은 액체층보다 더 가볍습니다. 그래서 밀도가 더 높은 물질의 맨 윗부분에서 흘러갈 수 있는 것이죠.

수백 만년에 걸쳐 판들이 이동함에 따라 오늘날의 지표면 형태가 만들어졌습니다. 지각판의 움직임은 판구조론이라고 불리며, 나중에 배우겠지만, 지진 및 지형을 형성시키는 기타 현상들에 있어서 중요한 역할을 하죠. 그러한 움직임이 지표면 형태에 영향을 미치는 과정에 대한 한 가지 예를 들면, 두 개의 판이 서로 정면 충돌을 하는 경우 판들의 가장 자리가 위로 올라가게 됩니다. 이렇게 지각이 융기하면 산맥이 형성되는 것이죠. 로키산맥은 두 개의 판이 정면 충돌한 결과로 만들어진 것으로, 이후 이곳의 가장자리가 위로 올라가면서 지각이 융기하게 되었습니다. 이러한 결과로서 생긴 융기로 인해 로키산맥이 만들어진 것이에요.

7개의 커다란 판과 약 12개의 작은 판이 존재합니다. 또한 이 판들은, 보통 지리적인 위치에 따라, 이름을 가지고 있어요. 예를 들면 태평양판, 북아메리카판, 아프리카판, 호주판, 그리고 필리핀판이 있습니다. 판들은 1년에 단 몇 인치만 이동하기 때문에 대륙이 이동하려면 수백 만 년이 걸립니다. 하지만 한때는 대륙과 해양의 위치가 현재와 달랐고, 약 2억 5천만 년 전에는 대륙들이 대체로 서로 연결되어 있었죠.

지구의 내부는 극도로 뜨겁다는 점을 기억하세요. 그 위에서 움직임이 나타나는 것은 바로 이러한 열 때문입니다. 하지만 핵은 지금으로부터 수백만 년 후 언젠가 식게 될 것으로 생각되고 있어요. 그렇게 되면 암류권의 움직임이 중단될 것이고, 이로 인해 지각판들의 움직임도 멈춤으로써, 그 결과 지표면이 안정될 것입니다. 다시 말해서 대륙의 움직임이 중단되는 것이죠. 이러한 일은 이미 달, 화성, 그리고 기타 행성 및 위성에서 일어났습니다.

Summary Note

A

❶ lithosphere
❷ the crust
❸ ocean floor
❹ molten rock material
❺ tectonic plates
❻ earthquakes

B

The lithosphere is the Earth's exterior. It is the crust, which includes the continents, the rocks, and the ocean floor. It also includes the upper part of the asthenosphere, which is located just below the crust. On the continents, the crust is about eighty kilometers deep, but below the ocean, it is about five kilometers thick. The exterior of the Earth is like many pieces broken into giant plates that fit together like a jigsaw puzzle. These pieces are called tectonic plates. The continents rest on these plates. They slide along the upper part of the asthenosphere, which consists of a semi-plastic molten rock material. It is more fluid and moves as it responds to the churning motions of the extremely hot interior of the Earth below. These movements in the asthenosphere cause the tectonic plates to move as they glide or float on the moving asthenosphere. There are seven major plates and twelve minor plates. Because the plates only move a few inches a year, it takes millions of years for the continents to move. But at one time, the continents were mostly connected.

Integrated Listening & Speaking p.248

A

Script 08-14

M Professor: Today, we're going to continue talking about Inuit baskets and paintings. Last week, if you'll recall, I told you that the Inuit are the northern people who live in the Arctic areas of Canada, Alaska, Russia, and Greenland. I mentioned to you the different kinds of Inuit art, but we spoke mostly about Inuit carvings. Prior to the 1950s, Inuit carvings were small enough to hold inside your fist. Today, some are much bigger to satisfy market demand and because the Inuit are no longer nomadic. In addition, since the 1980s, Inuit carvings have become more polished and realistic looking. The subjects of these carvings are usually animals and humans. The animals are bears, seals, whales, walruses, and sometimes birds. Some of the sculptures are humorous, such as the dancing bear. Others are more serious. Because of a lack of trees in the Arctic, Inuit carvings are never made of wood. The artists use whatever raw materials are available. The most common substance is a stone called serpentine that is available in a range of colors from green to black. Other stone used includes marble, quartz, and dolomite. Soapstone is also imported from other countries.

1 They are small enough to fit in the palm of a hand.

2 They live in the Arctic areas of Canada, Alaska, Russia, and Greenland.

3 They are made of stones like serpentine, marble, quartz, dolomite, and soapstone.

B

Script 08-15

W Professor: There are a few more things I'd like to review with you before we have our . . . ah, written examination, next week . . . One of the things you'll need to do during the exam is distinguish autobiographies from memoirs. Remember that an autobiography is a detailed story of your own life, usually from childhood to old age. It's a chronological, detailed, personal history that requires a lot of research and interviews. It takes a lot of work. A memoir is a type of autobiography which focuses on only a part your life. The writer merely needs to recall some events that have occurred in his or her life. It doesn't require any research. The writer doesn't have to go to the library or use the Internet. It's usually shorter than an autobiography and focuses on events that are significant to the writer. A public figure would probably write recollections and emotions regarding some of the important public events of his or her life. Historically, memoirs were written by world leaders, politicians, military leaders, and other famous people, but that's changing now.

1 Autobiographies describe one's entire life while memoirs only focus on part of a person's life.

2 There's no research required to write a memoir.

3 Historically, they were written by world leaders, military leaders, politicians, and other famous people.

Mini TOEFL iBT Practice Test

p.250

1 Ⓓ 2 Ⓓ 3 Ⓒ 4 Ⓐ 5 Ⓒ
6 Ⓒ 7 Ⓓ 8 Ⓒ 9 Ⓑ 10 Ⓑ, Ⓓ
11 Ⓑ

[1-5]

Script 08-16

W Gym Employee: Hello. You look a little lost. Is there anything that I can help you with?

M Student: I just transferred from another college this semester, and I was wondering about the school's gym. Can anyone use it?

W: That depends on your enrollment status. Let me see your ID card, and I can tell you exactly what kind of usage you're allowed.

M: Oh, sure . . . Here you are . . .

W: Okay, according to your ID card, you are a full-time student, so that means you can use just about every single one of our facilities for free. Let me tell you what that means . . . You can use both of the basketball courts . . . when there isn't a game or practice going on, of course. You can use the squash and racquetball courts as well. They are located on the second floor. You can also use the swimming pool on the third floor.

M: Wow, that sounds pretty cool. At my last school, we had to pay extra money to use the facilities. It's really nice not to have to do that here.

W: I'm glad you're happy about our arrangements. If you don't have any more questions . . .

M: Wait a minute. How about using the locker rooms? Do we get our own lockers or what?

W: **Only members of the school's athletic teams get permanent lockers.** But don't worry about your stuff. You can get a temporary locker anytime. All you have to do is talk to the attendant outside the locker room . . . That's me, by the way . . . And I'll give you a key you can use for a locker to store your clothes and valuables in. Once you're finished, give the key back to me. And no, it doesn't cost a thing.

M: That's great. Some of my stuff at my last school got stolen when I was working out before. Somebody just came in and took my wallet and a few CDs right from my bag. That was unbelievable.

W: I'm sorry to hear that. So . . . do you have any more questions?

M: Er, yes, I do. I'm a little curious about the weight room. Can anyone use it, or do we need a membership?

W: That's a good question. We have two weight rooms.

The big one is Collier Gym. That's open to the entire school. It has pretty much everything that you could possibly need to work out. And it won't cost a single dime. The smaller one is Peterson Gym. It's located up on the fifth floor. It's much more specialized and has some really cool equipment. But it's only open to members of the athletic teams and paying members. If you want to become a member of that gym, it will cost you 200 dollars a semester. Are you interested in that?

M: Oh, no, I don't think so. Not at that price. I just like to get in a light workout every now and then. I'm not that serious about it.

W: Yeah, most people are satisfied with Collier Gym. It's really nice. That's where I work out most of the time.

M: Great. Well, you've been a real fountain of knowledge. Thanks so much for all of your help. I'll see you around.

W: See you later.

해석

W Gym Employee: 안녕하세요. 문제가 있으신 것처럼 보이는군요. 제가 도울 일이라도 있을까요?

M Student: 저는 이번 학기에 다른 대학에서 편입을 했는데, 이 학교의 체육관이 궁금했어요. 누구라도 사용이 가능한가요?

W: 등록 상태에 따라 달라요. 학생증을 보여 주시면 제가 어떻게 사용하실 수 있는지 정확히 알려 드릴게요.

M: 오, 그러죠… 여기 있어요.

W: 좋아요, 학생증을 보니 풀타임 학생이기 때문에, 이러한 경우 저희의 모든 시설을 무료로 사용하실 수 있어요. 무슨 말인지 설명해 드리면… 두 개의 농구 코트 모두 사용하실 수 있는데… 물론 경기나 연습이 없는 경우에요. 스쿼시와 라켓볼 코트도 사용하실 수 있어요. 2층에 있죠. 또한 3층에 있는 수영장도 사용하실 수 있고요.

M: 와, 정말 잘 되었군요. 이전 학교에서는 추가 요금을 내야만 시설을 이용할 수 있었거든요. 여기에서는 그럴 필요가 없어서 정말 좋네요.

W: 저희 방식이 마음에 드신다니 저도 기뻐요. 질문이 더 없으시면…

M: 잠깐만요. 사물함 이용은 어떤가요? 개인 사물함 같은 것이 있나요?

W: 교내 운동부에 속한 학생들에게만 개인 사물함이 있어요. 하지만 짐에 대해서는 걱정하지 마세요. 언제든지 일반 사물함을 이용하실 수 있으니까요. 라커룸 밖에 있는 직원에게 말씀만 하시면 되는데… 그건 그렇고, 그게 바로 저예요… 옷과 귀중품을 보관할 수 있는 사물함을 이용하실 때 필요한 열쇠를 드릴게요. 끝나면 열쇠를 제게 반납해 주세요. 그리고 이것도 무료로, 비용이 들지 않죠.

M: 잘 됐군요. 이전 학교에서 운동을 하다가 물건을 도난당한 적이 있었거든요. 누군가 들어와서는 제 가방에서 지갑과 몇 장의 CD를 가지고 갔죠. 믿을 수가 없더군요.

W: 그런 이야기를 들으니 유감이네요. 그러면… 질문이 더 있나요?

M: 어, 네, 있어요. 헬스장에 대해서도 좀 궁금해요. 누구라도 사용이 가능한가요, 아니면 회원으로 가입을 해야 하나요?

W: 좋은 질문이군요. 두 개의 헬스장이 있어요. 큰 곳이 Collier 짐이죠. 그곳은 전체 학생들에게 개방되어요. 아마 운동하는데 필요한 것은 거의 모두 갖추어져 있을 거예요. 그리고 요금도 따로 없고요. 보다 작은 곳은 Peterson 짐이에요. 4층에 있죠. 훨씬 전문적이고 정말 좋은 설비들이 갖추어져 있어요. 하지만 그곳은 운동부 소속 학생 및 유료 회원들에게만 개방이 되어요. 만약 그 헬스장의 회원이 되고 싶으면 학기당 200달러를 내야 하죠. 관심이 있으신가요?

M: 오, 아니요, 그렇지 않아요. 그 가격에는 아니에요. 저는 가끔씩 가볍게 운동하는 것을 좋아해요. 운동에 그렇게 빠져 있는 사람은 아니죠.

W: 그래요, 대부분의 사람들은 Collier 짐에 만족해해요. 정말 좋거든요. 제가 주로 운동을 하는 곳도 그곳이죠.

M: 좋아요. 음, 정말 많은 것을 알고 계시는군요. 도와 주셔서 정말 감사합니다. 다음에 또 뵐게요.

W: 다음에 봬요.

[6-11]

Script 08-17

W Professor: I think that we can move on to another animal before we take a short break. We need to cover a lot today, so let's get busy. Now, uh, I need to discuss spiders with you. There are at least 34,000 species of spiders known to scientists. That makes spiders the seventh most diverse species in the world. Scientists believe that many species of spiders have not been discovered yet, especially in the tropics. So you can expect that number to grow over time. In fact, some arachnologists believe that we've only discovered about twenty percent of the total existing number of spider species . . . Here is a question. Are spiders predators?

M Student: Yes! That's why they have webs. They catch prey with their webs and then eat it.

W: Okay, good. In fact, spiders are the world's most diverse species of predators. And their webs are made of silk. The silk is a thin but very strong protein strand. Can anyone tell me where it comes from?

M: Um . . . from their hands?

W: Hmm . . . I think you've been watching a bit too many superhero movies. Spiders don't have hands or anything that resembles hands. Instead, they have eight legs. And the silk . . . Well, the silk actually comes from spinnerets. These can be found at the end of the abdomen. They're more like fingers, not hands or limbs.

Now, uh, let me give you some more information about spider silk. All spiders produce it. However, not all species of spiders spin webs. Additionally, spider silk has a number of functions. It is not just used for trapping and killing insects. Spiders can use it to climb, to wrap prey, to build egg sacs, to rear their young, to make shelter, and to temporarily hold sperm. As you can see, it has a multitude of purposes.

M: Can spiders hunt without silk?

W: Most species can hunt without silk, but some cannot. Most species inject venom, which they use to kill prey or for self-defense. So most types of spiders are able to kill without spinning webs. If they don't have a web, they simply wait for prey to come near them, and then they pounce on it.

M: Can they kill people with their venom?

W: Hmm . . . Only 200 species can harm humans with their bites. Most of the injuries that people sustain from spider bites are minor in nature. Occasionally, a wound from a minor bite might become infected, which could be a concern. But usually, spiders are not a serious threat to humans unless their venom is very toxic. Toxicity of venom varies from spider to spider. Few species possess enough toxicity to endanger humans. Usually, the humans most susceptible to spider venom are children and the infirm. By far the most dangerous species to mankind are widow spiders. **The black widow spider, which I'm sure you have all heard of, is one of them.** The female will bite if its web is tampered with or if it feels threatened. They have killed more humans than any other spider.

M: How do spiders reproduce?

W: Okay. For sexual reproduction, male spiders transfer sperm to females by using a special appendage near the mouth called a pedipalps. In fact, this is how we distinguish male spiders from females. Female pedipalps look like short legs while male pedipalps look like boxing gloves. The female will lay a batch of eggs. Then, she will wrap them in silken egg sacs. Spiderlings eventually hatch within the sac and then leave to begin feeding. Spiders have to molt their external skeleton before they can grow larger. Molt means shed. Most species of spider tend to live about one or two years. And most species of spider molt about five or six times as they grow. Once they become adults, they stop growing and no longer molt.

해석

W Professor: 잠깐 휴식을 취하기에 앞서 또 다른 동물에 대한 이야기로 넘어갈 수 있을 것 같군요. 오늘은 많은 내용을 다루어야 하기 때문에 서두르기로 하죠. 자, 어, 거미에 대해 논의할게요. 과학자들에게 알려진 거미는 최소한 34,000종이 넘습니다. 이로써 거미는 세상에서 7번째로 다양한 종이 됩니다. 과학자들은 많은 종의 거미들이, 특히 열대 지역에서, 아직 발견되지 못했다고 믿고 있어요. 따라서 시간이 지나면 그 수가 늘어날 것으로 생각해도 될 것 같군요. 실제로 일부 거미학자들은 전체 거미 종 중의 약 20% 정도만 발견되었다고 생각하는데… 질문을 하나 할게요. 거미는 포식 동물일까요?

M Student: 네! 그래서 거미집이 있는 것이죠. 거미집으로 먹이를 붙잡은 후에 먹이를 잡아 먹으니까요.

W: 그래요, 잘 대답했군요. 실제로 거미는 포식 동물 중 세상에서 가장 다양한 종입니다. 그리고 거미집은 거미줄로 만들어져요. 거미줄은 얇지만 매우 튼튼한 단백질 실입니다. 거미줄이 어디에서 나오는지 아는 사람이 있나요?

M: 음… 손에서요?

W: 흠… 수퍼 히어로 영화를 너무 많이 보는 것 같군요. 거미는 손이나 손과 비슷한 것도 가지고 있지 않아요. 대신 8개의 다리를 가지고 있죠. 그리고 거미줄은… 음, 거미줄은 사실 방적 돌기에서 나옵니다. 이는 배의 끝 부분에서 찾아볼 수 있어요. 손이나 팔다리보다는 손가락과 더 비슷하죠.

자, 어, 거미줄에 관한 내용을 더 알려 드릴게요. 모든 거미들이 거미줄을 생산해 냅니다. 하지만 모든 거미종이 거미집을 만드는 것은 아니에요. 게다가, 거미줄은 다양한 용도를 지니고 있습니다. 곤충을 붙잡고 죽이는 용도로만 쓰이는 것이 아니에요. 거미들은 거미줄을 이용해서 기어오르고, 먹이를 감싸고, 알주머니를 만들고, 새끼를 기르고, 집을 짓고, 그리고 일시적으로 정자를 품습니다. 보시다시피 다양한 용도로 활용이 되죠.

M: 거미들이 거미줄 없이도 사냥을 할 수 있나요?

W: 대부분의 종은 거미줄이 없이도 사냥을 할 수 있지만 그렇지 않은 종들도 있어요. 대부분의 종은 먹이를 죽이거나 자기 방어를 할 때 사용하는 독을 주입합니다. 그래서 대부분의 거미들은 거미집을 만들지 않고도 먹이를 사냥할 수 있어요. 거미집이 없는 경우에는 먹이가 다가오기를 기다리다가 다가오면 먹이에게 달려들죠.

M: 독으로 사람을 죽일 수도 있나요?

W: 흠… 단 200종만 사람을 물어서 해를 끼칠 수 있어요. 사람들이 거미에게 물려서 입는 대부분의 상처는 사실 경미한 것이에요. 때때로 가볍게 물린 상처가 감염이 되어 문제가 될 수는 있을 거예요. 하지만 일반적으로 거미의 독이 매우 강하지 않은 한 인간에게 심각한 위협이 되는 경우는 없어요. 거미의 독성은 거미에 따라 다릅니다. 사람을 위험에 빠뜨릴 만큼 강한 독성을 지닌 종은 거의 없어요. 일반적으로 거미의 독에 가장 피해를 입기 쉬운 사람들은 아이와 노약자들입니다. 인류에게 가장 위험한 종은 과부거미에요. 흑색과부거미가, 여러분 모두 들어보셨을 것 같은데, 그중 하나이죠. 암컷은 자신의 거미집이 방해를 받거나 자신이 위협을 느끼는 경우 물게 됩니다. 이들이 다른 어떤 거미보다 많은 사람들의 목숨을 앗아갔어요.

M: 거미는 어떻게 번식하나요?

W: 좋아요. 번식의 경우, 수컷 거미가 촉수라고 불리는 입 주변의 특별한 부속기관을 이용해 암컷에게 정액을 보냅니다. 실제로 이 촉수를 가지고 수컷과 암컷 거미를 구별해요. 암컷의 촉수는 짧은 다리처럼 생긴 반면에 수컷의 촉수는 권투 글러브처럼 생겼습니다. 암컷이 알을 낳습니다. 그러면 암컷은 거미줄로 만든 알주머니로 알을 감쌉니다. 알주머니 안에 있던 새끼 거미들이 마침내 부화를 하면 밖으로 나와서 먹이를 먹기 시작해요. 거미들은 외골격을 탈피한 후에야 더 크게 자랄 수 있습니다. 탈피는 껍질을 벗는다는 의미에요. 대부분의 거미종은 1년이나 2년 정도 사는 경향이 있습니다. 그리고 대부분의 거미 종들은 자라면서 다섯 번이나 여섯 번 정도 탈피를 하죠. 다 자라면 성장이 멈추고 더 이상 탈피를 하지 않게 됩니다.

Vocabulary Check-Up

p.255

A 1 Ⓐ 2 Ⓕ 3 Ⓒ 4 Ⓘ 5 Ⓚ 6 Ⓖ 7 Ⓞ 8 Ⓗ 9 Ⓔ 10 Ⓙ 11 Ⓓ 12 Ⓝ 13 Ⓑ 14 Ⓛ 15 Ⓜ

B 1 Ⓓ 2 Ⓑ 3 Ⓔ 4 Ⓒ 5 Ⓐ

Actual Test

Actual Test 01

p.258

PART 1

1 Ⓒ　2 Ⓐ　3 Ⓑ, Ⓓ　4 Ⓐ　5 Ⓑ
6 Ⓑ　7 Fact: [2], [3]　Not a Fact: [1], [4]　8 Ⓐ
9 Ⓓ　10 Ⓓ　11 Ⓑ

PART 2

1 Ⓓ　2 Ⓒ　3 Ⓑ, Ⓓ　4 Ⓓ　5 Ⓐ
6 Ⓑ　7 Ⓒ　8 Ⓒ　9 Ⓒ　10 Ⓓ
11 Ⓐ
12 Ⓒ　13 Ⓑ　14 Ⓑ　15 Ⓐ　16 Ⓓ
17 Ⓑ

PART 1

[1-5]

Script 09-03

M Student: Excuse me. You're the lab assistant for Professor Bascomb's biology 154 class, aren't you?

W Laboratory Assistant: That's correct. Did you forget something in the lab? That would make you the third person of the day who has done that. What did you forget? Your book?

M: Um . . . No, I didn't forget anything. I'm not here for that.

W: That's a relief. What do you need?

M: I need to get into the laboratory to conduct an experiment. Professor Bascomb said you have the key to it, so could you either unlock the lab for me or let me borrow the key, please?

W: I'm really sorry, but the lab is supposed to stay locked today. I can't open it for you.

M: But . . . Professor Bascomb told me that you could unlock it for me. I missed last week's class because I was ill, so I need to make up the lab as soon as possible.

W: I'm afraid there's not anything I can do for you.

M: Well, he wrote this note for me. Maybe this will help change your mind.

W: Let me see it, please . . . Hmm . . . It reads, "Melanie, please open the lab for Trace. He doesn't need to be supervised. It should take him about one hour. Professor Bascomb." Okay, I guess the professor knows what he's talking about. I've got the key right here. Let's go to the lab.

M: Thanks a lot. I really appreciate your assistance.

W: Okay, uh, there are a couple of things that you need to know.

M: Yes?

W: First, the door automatically locks as soon as it shuts, so if you leave, and the door closes, you'll be locked out. And I have a seminar to attend in ten minutes. It's going to last for three hours, so you won't be getting back in until it's over.

M: I'm not planning on leaving the lab until I'm done.

W: Great. I hope that happens. In addition, there are some rules. Put everything back where you got it when you're finished. You also need to clean up any messes that you make.

M: Of course. I do that every time I do an experiment. You won't even be able to tell that I was there once I leave.

W: I sure hope you're right. Finally, uh, don't take anything from the lab. A lot of the chemicals are expensive, and they're also dangerous. If you take something, we'll know about it. And the results won't be pleasant. Oh, and if you break anything, you're responsible for replacing it.

M: I understand. Thanks for letting me know the rules. What if I have a problem with my experiment?

W: You'd better call someone in the class because as I just mentioned, I'll be unavailable for three hours. I hope you have a friend in class.

M: I do. I'll be sure to contact her if something goes wrong. Thanks for your help.

W: You're welcome. Okay, uh, here we are. Let me open the door and turn on the lights for you . . . There you go . . . Good luck with the experiment and please remember everything that I told you. I'll be back after my seminar just in case you're still here. Oh, don't let anyone else in the lab no matter who knocks on the door.

M: Got it.

해석

M Student: 실례합니다. Bascomb 교수님의 생물학 154 수업의 실험실 조교님이시죠, 그렇지 않나요?

W Laboratory Assistant: 맞아요. 실험실에서 놓고 온 것이라도 있나요? 그렇다면 오늘 세 번째로 물건을 놓고 온 사람이 되겠군요. 무엇을 놓고 왔나요? 책인가요?

M: 음… 아니에요, 놓고 온 것은 없어요. 그 때문에 온 것이 아니에요.

W: 다행이군요. 무엇이 필요한가요?

M: 저는 실험실에 들어가서 실험을 해야 해요. Bascomb 교수님께서 조교님이 실험실 열쇠를 가지고 있다고 말씀하셨는데, 저를 위해 실험실 문을 열어 주시거나 혹은 열쇠를 제게 빌려 주실 수 있나요?

W: 정말 미안하지만 실험실은 오늘 계속 잠겨 있기로 되어 있어요. 학생에게 문을 열어 줄 수는 없어요.

M: 하지만··· Bascomb 교수님께서 조교님이 문을 열어 주실 수 있다고 말씀을 하셨거든요. 저는 아파서 지난 주 수업을 듣지 못했기 때문에 가능한 빨리 보충 실험을 해야 해요.

W: 유감이지만 제가 도울 수 있는 일은 없는 것 같군요.

M: 음, 교수님께서 제게 이 메모를 써 주셨어요. 이걸 보시면 아마도 생각이 바뀌실 거예요.

W: 한번 볼게요··· 흠··· "Melanie, Trace에게 실험실 문을 열어 주세요. 감독을 할 필요는 없어요. 한 시간 정도 걸릴 거예요. Bascomb 교수,"라고 써 있군요. 좋아요, 교수님께서 무슨 말씀을 하시는지 알 것 같아요. 여기에 키가 있어요. 실험실로 가죠.

M: 정말 고맙습니다. 도와 주셔서 정말 감사해요.

W: 좋아요, 어, 학생이 알아야 두 가지가 있어요.

M: 네?

W: 먼저, 문이 닫히면 저절로 문이 잠기기 때문에 밖으로 나갈 때 문이 닫히면 다시 들어가지 못하게 될 거예요. 그리고 저는 10분 후에 세미나 수업에 가야 해요. 3시간 동안 진행될 예정이라서 수업이 끝나기 전까지는 학생이 다시 안으로 들어갈 수 없을 거예요.

M: 실험이 끝나기 전에는 실험실을 떠날 생각이 없어요.

W: 잘 되었군요. 그랬으면 좋겠어요. 또한 몇 가지 규정들이 있어요. 실험이 끝나면 모든 것을 제자리에 다시 갖다 놓으세요. 또한 학생 때문에 어질러진 것들은 정리해야 해요.

M: 물론이에요. 실험을 할 때마다 그렇게 하고 있죠. 제가 그곳을 떠나면 제가 그곳에 있었다는 것 조차 알아차리지 못하실 거예요.

W: 학생 말이 맞기를 바랄게요. 마지막으로, 어, 실험실에서 어떤 것도 가져가지 마세요. 많은 화학 물질들이 비싼 것들이고, 또한 위험한 것이기도 하죠. 무언가를 가져간다면 우리가 알게 될 거예요. 그리고 그 결과는 좋지 않을 것이고요. 오, 무언가를 망가뜨리는 경우에는 교체할 책임이 학생에게 있어요.

M: 이해해요. 규정을 알려 주셔서 고맙습니다. 실험에서 문제가 생기면 어떻게 해야 하나요?

W: 조금 전에 말씀을 드린 대로 저는 3시간 동안 자리를 비울 것이기 때문에 수업을 듣는 누군가에게 전화를 하는 편이 나을 것 같군요. 같이 수업을 듣는 친구가 있기를 바라요.

M: 있어요. 무언가 문제가 생기면 반드시 친구에게 연락하도록 할게요. 도와 주셔서 고마워요.

W: 천만에요. 좋아요, 어, 여기 있어요. 문을 열어드리고 불을 켜 드리죠··· 됐어요··· 좋아요, 실험에 행운이 있기를 바라고, 제가 말씀드린 것을 모두 기억해 주세요. 수업이 끝나면 학생이 아직 여기에 있는 경우를 대비해서 제가 다시 올 거예요. 오, 누가 노크를 하더라도 실험실 안으로 들어오게 해서는 안 돼요.

M: 알겠습니다.

[6-11]

Script 09-04

W Professor: All right, everybody. Let's all settle down in our seats and be quiet. We have a great amount of material to cover today, so I would like to get started immediately. Okay. Thank you. Right now, I'm going to give you an overview on the topic of attachment theory, which covers the way that we establish bonds with our caregivers when we're babies and how that continues into our adolescent and adult lives. This theory is especially important when exploring psychology since it affects each and every one of us at the core level of our personalities. Now, the basis of attachment theory hinges on what psychologists call an affectional bond. This is a type of attachment behavior which one person has for another individual. This bond is most typically held between a mother and her child. In this type of bond, the mother and the child are partners, and they tend to remain within close proximity to each other.

Just so you know, the term was developed decades ago by psychologist John Bowlby, who published an important paper entitled "The Nature of the Child's Tie to His Mother" in 1958. According to Bowlby, there are five main criteria that must be present in order for an affectional bond to be established and a sixth for it to become a lasting bond.

The first of the main criteria is that an affectional bond is persistent rather than transitory. This means that it lasts. It doesn't come and go like less meaningful relationships. The second criterion is that an affectional bond involves one particular person. The person cannot be exchanged or replaced with anybody else. The third is that the affectional bond involves a relationship that is emotionally significant. And, uh . . . the fourth criterion is that the individual who has established the bond wants to remain physically close or within proximity of the person with whom he or she is bonded. The fifth and last of the main criteria is that the individual will become saddened or distressed if he or she is ever involuntarily separated from the person with whom the bonding has occurred. Does this remind any of you of being a kid with your mom? I'm sure that it does for many—if not most—of you.

Okay . . . moving along . . . after the five main criteria, it's important to tack on this extra sixth one, which is a characteristic of a true attachment bond. This is that the person who has formed the bond will always seek security and comfort in the relationship.

Now, um, another important paper that was published in 1958 was written by Harry Harlow. It was entitled "The Nature of Love." This seminal work was based on a series of groundbreaking experiments with infant rhesus monkeys. These experiments showed that the baby monkeys preferred an emotional attachment with the object of their affectional bond rather than with life-sustaining food. In short, the experiment worked like this: The baby monkeys were separated from their mothers at birth. Then, they were introduced to two surrogate mothers. The first mother was made of cold metal wire mesh. The second mother was the same mesh frame, but it was covered in soft cloth and foam. The cold metal mother also contained a bottle with milk, and the soft mother had nothing. What Harlow found was that the young monkeys would quickly drink the milk from the cold metal mother and then promptly seek contact with the soft mother, with whom they had already formed affectional bonds.

This study showed that babies ultimately desire their mother's warmth rather than their physical survival needs. But even the soft doll did not totally satisfy the baby monkey's needs. Later on, the baby monkeys that were raised apart from their natural mothers proved to be maladjusted to social situations with the other monkeys. They . . . uh . . . acted abnormally when they were placed in these situations. In most cases, they were either very fearful of the other monkeys they encountered or responded with unprovoked aggression.

In addition, the female monkeys that were raised in isolation often abused and neglected their own infants when they too became mothers. These experiments were very important, especially since long-running and deep-seeded tests such as these could never be ethically performed on human beings. And as researchers have found in so many cases, these rhesus monkeys serve as excellent analogues to human beings, especially in the infant stages.

So, uh . . . now that we've discussed Bowlby's and Harlow's scientific contributions to establishing the field of attachment theory, let's move on to a new topic. Right now, I think that we need to cover the positive and negative aspects of affectional bonding.

해석

W Professor: 좋아요, 여러분. 모두들 자리에 앉아서 조용히 해 주세요. 오늘 다룰 내용이 상당히 많기 때문에 바로 시작하고자 합니다. 좋아요. 고마워요. 이제 애착 이론이라는 주제를 살펴보려고 하는데, 애착 이론은 아기들이 보호자와 유대감을 형성하는 과정과 그러한 유대감이 사춘기 및 성인기로 어떻게 이어지는지를 다룹니다. 애착은 인격이 형성되는 핵심적인 시기에 우리 모두에게 영향을 미치기 때문에, 특히 심리학 연구에서 그러한 이론이 중요합니다. 자, 애착 이론의 기초는 심리학자들이 정서적 유대감이라고 부르는 것에 기반해 있어요. 이는 한 사람이 또 다른 개인을 위해 나타내는 일종의 애착 행동입니다. 이러한 유대감은 엄마와 아기 사이에서 형성되는 것이 가장 일반적이죠. 이러한 형태의 유대감에서는 엄마와 아기가 파트너 관계를 이루며, 서로가 가까이 있고자 하는 경향을 나타냅니다.

아시다시피 이러한 용어는 수십년 전 심리학자인 존 보울비에 의해 만들어졌는데, 그는 1958년 *아이와 어머니가 형성하는 유대의 본질*이라는 제목의 중요한 논문을 발표한 사람이었어요. 보울비에 따르면 정서적 유대감이 형성되기 위해서는 다섯 가지의 주요한 조건이 만족되어야 하며, 이러한 유대감이 지속되기 위해서는 여섯 번째의 조건이 충족되어야 하죠.

첫 번째 조건은 정서적 유대감이 일시적인 것이 아니라 지속적인 것이어야 한다는 것이에요. 이는 계속되어야 한다는 의미입니다. 보다 의미가 없는 관계처럼 왔다가 가는 것이 아닙니다. 두 번째 조건은 정서적 유대감이 특정한 한 사람과 관련되어야 한다는 것이에요. 그 사람은 바뀔 수도 없고, 혹은 다른 사람으로 대체될 수도 없죠. 세 번째 조건은 정서적 유대감이 감정적으로 중요한 관계와 관련되어 있어야 한다는 점입니다. 그리고, 어… 네 번째 조건은 유대감을 형성한 사람이 유대감을 느끼는 인물과 물리적으로 가까운 곳에, 혹은 그 주변에 있으려고 해야 한다는 것이죠. 다섯 번째이자 마지막 척도는 개인이 유대감을 느끼는 인물과 비자발적으로 떨어지게 되는 경우 슬픔이나 괴로움을 느껴야 한다는 점이에요. 어렸을 때 엄마와 함께 있던 기억이 떠오르시나요? 여러분 중, 대부분은 아니더라도, 많은 분들께서 기억하실 것으로 확신합니다.

좋아요… 계속해서… 다섯 가지 척도 외에도 진정한 유대감의 특징을 이루는 여섯 번째 조건을 추가하는 것이 중요합니다. 이는 유대감을 형성한 사람이 그러한 관계 속에서 항상 안전함과 편안함을 느껴야 한다는 것이에요.

자, 음, 1958년에 발표된 또 다른 중요한 논문은 해리 할로우가 작성한 것이었어요. *사랑의 본질*이라는 제목이었죠. 매우 독창적인 이 논문은 새끼 붉은털원숭이를 대상으로 한 획기적인 실험들에 기초해 있었습니다. 이러한 실험에서 새끼 원숭이들은 생존에 필요한 먹이보다 정서적 유대감을 느끼는 대상에 감정적으로 더 애착을 느끼는 것으로 밝혀졌어요. 요약하자면 실험은 다음과 같이 이루어졌어요. 새끼 원숭이들은 태어났을 때 어미로부터 격리되었어요. 그런 다음 이들에게 두 가지 대리모를 주었습니다. 첫 번째 대리모는 차가운 금속 철망으로 만들어진 것이었어요. 두 번째 대리모는 동일한 철망으로 만들어졌지만 부드러운 천과 스폰지로 덮여 있었죠. 또한 차가운 금속으로 된 대리모에게는 우유병이 있었고, 부드러운 대리모에게는 아무것도 없었어요. 할로우는 새끼 원숭이들이 차가운 철사 대리모보루터 우유를 먹은 다음 재빨리 부드러운 대리모 쪽으로 이동하는 것을 관찰했는데, 새끼 원숭이들은 부드러운 대리모들과 이미 정서적 유대감을 형성하고 있었어요.

이러한 연구 결과 새끼들은 신체적인 생존의 욕구보다 결국 어미의 온기를 더 원한다는 점이 밝혀졌습니다. 하지만 심지어 부드러운 인형도 새끼 원숭이의 욕구를 완전히 충족시키지는 못했어요. 이후 진짜 어미와 격리되어 길러진 새끼 원숭이들은 다른 원숭이들과 지내는 사회적 환경에 잘 적응하지 못한다는 점이 입증되었죠. 이들은… 어… 그러한 상황에 놓이면 비정상적인 행동을 했어요. 대부분의 경우, 다른 원숭이들을 만나면 크게 겁을 먹거나 정당한 이유 없이 공격성을 나타냈죠.

또한 격리되어 길러진 암컷 원숭이들은 자신이 어미가 되었을 때 종종 새끼들을 학대하거나 방치했습니다. 이러한 실험은, 특히 이처럼 장기간에 걸쳐 지속적으로 진행되는 실험은 윤리적인 측면에서 결코 인간에게 행할 수 없기 때문에, 매우 중요했어요. 그리고 그렇게 많은 실험에서 연구자들이 알아낸 것처럼, 이 붉은털원숭이들은 특히 유아기 때의 인간에 대한 훌륭한 비교 대상이 되고 있죠.

그러면, 어… 애착 이론의 확립에 있어서 보울비와 할로우의 업적을 살펴보았으니 새로운 주제로 넘어가도록 할게요. 이제 정서적 유대감의 긍정적인 측면과 부정적인 측면에 대해 다루어야 할 것 같군요.

PART 2

[1-5]

Script 09-06

M Professor: Good morning, Lisa. Thank you for being on time for your appointment. I'm glad to see that at least one of my students is punctual.

W Student: Good morning, sir. Ah, I'm a morning person, so having a meeting at eight thirty isn't a problem for me. I guess it might be an issue for other people though.

M: Yes, I suppose you're right. Anyway, let's get started. I've got to meet with several students this morning, so I don't have time to spend on idle chitchat.

W: No problem, sir. I've got to do an experiment in my chemistry class at nine, and it's in Heflin Hall on the other side of campus, so I don't have too much time as well.

M: Okay. Now, we need to talk about the story that you submitted to me for your creative writing assignment.

W: Sure.

M: This is something I like to do with all students on their first assignment. Some students can get a bit upset about having their work criticized in class, so I like to do it in the privacy of my own office the first time.

W: Of course. How did you like my story?

M: Hmm . . . I really enjoyed it. I thought it was a nice creative work. You also have a way with words, and you manage to put sentences together well.

W: Thank you, sir. I did my best.

M: And it shows. Oh, you also have good grammar. That's something you should be proud of. Over the years, I've seen many students that simply have poor grammar and make too many mistakes ever to become good writers.

W: I see.

M: Now, I enjoyed a lot of your story, but it has some shortcomings. Before I tell you my opinion, I'd like to ask you a question . . . What would you say your weaknesses as a writer are?

W: Hmm . . . That's a good question. First, I really have trouble writing dialogue. I sometimes know how my characters should react, but I just can't get the right words into the story. You might have noticed that.

M: Go on.

W: I guess the genre that I tried writing in isn't really that good for a ten-page story.

M: Yes, that's a good point. You wrote a mystery, and while it was quite clever and well written, it really needed to be at least double in length. Still, for a very short story, it was a nice mystery.

W: Thank you.

M: You're also correct about the dialogue. I marked a few things on your paper regarding it. I also suggested some ways to improve the dialogue in the story.

W: That's great, sir. I appreciate the assistance.

M: That's what I'm here for. Now, uh, I want to give you your second assignment, and then you can head off to your class. For this paper, I want you to write ten pages of a fantasy story. Now, more than fifty percent of the story must be dialogue. I don't want you to focus on exposition too much. Tell me the story through dialogue. If you focus on writing conversations, you should improve. Can you do that?

W: I sure can. Thanks a lot, Professor Marigold. I'll do my best on this project.

해석

M Professor: 안녕하세요, Lisa. 약속 시간에 늦지 않게 와 줘서 고마워요. 학생들 중 최소한 한 명은 약속 시간을 잘 지켜 주다니 기쁘네요.

W Student: 안녕하세요, 교수님. 아, 저는 아침형 인간이라서 8시 30분 약속이 전혀 문제가 되지 않아요. 하지만 다른 사람에게는 문제가 될 수도 있을 같네요.

M: 네, 학생 말이 맞는 것 같군요. 어쨌든, 시작해 보죠. 오늘 아침에 몇 명의 학생들과 약속이 되어 있어서 한가한 얘기를 할 시간은 없어요.

W: 괜찮습니다, 교수님. 저도 9시에 화학 실험 수업이 있는데, 캠퍼스 반대편에 있는 Heflin 홀 수업이라서 저도 시간이 그다지 많지는 않거든요.

M: 좋아요. 자, 창작물 쓰기 과제로 학생이 제출한 이야기에 대해 이야기해 보죠.

W: 좋습니다.

M: 이는 첫 번째 과제와 관련해서 제가 모든 학생들과 하고자 하는 일이에요. 수업 시간에 자신의 글이 평가되는 것을 약간 언짢게 생각하는 학생들이 있을 수 있기 때문에, 처음에는 제 사무실에서 비공개적으로 그렇게 하려고 하죠.

W: 그러시군요. 제 이야기가 어떠셨나요?

M: 흠… 정말 재미있었어요. 훌륭한 창작물이라고 생각했죠. 또한 단어들도 잘 선택해서 문장으로 표현했고요.

W: 감사합니다, 교수님. 최선을 다했거든요.

M: 그렇게 보여요. 오, 학생은 또한 문법 실력도 우수해요. 그에 대해서는 자부심을 가져도 될 것 같아요. 여러 해 동안 저는 문법 실력이 부족하고 너무나 많은 실수를 해서 글을 잘 쓰지 못하는 학생들을 많이 보아 왔거든요.

W: 그러셨군요.

M: 자, 학생의 이야기가 무척 마음에 들지만, 단점도 있었어요. 제 생각을 말하기에 앞서 학생에게 질문을 하나 하면… 작가로서 학생의 단점이 무엇이라고 얘기하고 싶나요?

W: 흠… 좋은 질문이군요. 먼저 저는 대화를 쓰는 것이 정말 힘들어요. 때때로 제 등장 인물들이 어떻게 반응해야 하는지는 알고 있는데, 하지만 적절한 단어들을 이야기에 집어 넣을 수가 없어요. 그 점을 알아차리신 것 같은데요.

M: 계속해 보세요.

W: 제가 쓰려고 했던 장르가 10페이지 분량의 소설로서는 그다지 좋지 않은 것 같아요.

M: 네, 좋은 지적이군요. 학생은 추리 소설을 썼고 그 소설은 상당히 기발하고 잘 쓰여졌지만, 분량이 최소한 그 두 배가 되어야 했어요. 하지만 매우 짧은 소설로서는 멋진 추리 소설이었어요.

W: 감사합니다.

M: 대화에 관한 학생의 이야기도 맞아요. 그와 관련해서 학생 보고서에 몇 군데 표시를 해 두었죠. 또한 이야기의 대화를 개선시킬 수 있는 몇 가지 방법들도 제안했고요.

W: 감사합니다, 교수님. 도와 주셔서 고마워요.

M: 그것에 제 일인 걸요. 자, 어, 학생에게 두 번째 과제를 내 주고 싶은데, 그런 다음에는 수업에 가도 좋아요. 이번 글에서는 학생이 10페이지 분량의 판타지 소설을 쓰면 좋겠어요. 자, 이야기의 50퍼센트 이상이 대화여야 해요. 설명에 너무 많이 집중하지 않았으면 좋겠고요. 대화로 이야기를 전달해 주세요. 대화를 쓰는 일에 집중한다면 학생 실력이 더 나아질 거예요. 그럴 수 있죠?

W: 물론이죠. 정말 감사합니다, Marigold 교수님. 최선을 다 해서 이번 프로젝트를 하도록 할게요.

[6-11]

Script 09-07

M Professor: Okay, uh, if you are all ready to begin class, I'd like to continue our discussion from last week on pollution. I would like to focus in particular on water pollution for the duration of this class. We can begin by defining water pollution as a large set of negative effects upon water bodies such as lakes, rivers, oceans, and groundwater that is caused by human activities.

W Student: Um, are you saying that all water pollution is caused by man? I'm not sure that I would agree with you regarding that statement.

M: Hmm . . . I understand what you are alluding to, but this is something important that you all need to know. Although natural phenomena such as, um, volcanoes, storms, and earthquakes are capable of causing major changes in water quality and the ecological status of water, the damage that they cause is not considered pollution. You see, uh, nature has a way of taking care of problems that are caused by natural processes, but it's much more difficult for Mother Nature to take care of manmade problems. So let's just stick with manmade water pollution for this class.

Now, uh, water pollution has many causes and characteristics. Let's begin with, ah, organic waste that is introduced into the water system by humans. This waste can take on many forms. It includes sewage and farm waste, which put high oxygen demands on the receiving water reservoirs, such as rivers. This leads to oxygen depletion or . . . a loss of oxygen within the river system itself, which has the potential severely to impact the entire ecosystem. For instance, without oxygen, fish are unable to survive, so they will all die. When they float to the top of the water and begin decomposing, that presents an entire new set of problems.

W: What about industry? I thought that factories and other manufacturers are the worst polluters of all?

M: You bet they are. Industries discharge a variety of pollutants in their wastewater. Among them are heavy metals, organic toxins, oils, nutrients, and solids. Discharges can also have thermal effects, especially those from power stations, and these too reduce the available oxygen within the system.

W: So we have industry and, um, organic waste that is put into the water system by people. Are there any other causes of water pollution?

M: Sure. Silt-bearing runoff or dirt from many activities, including construction sites, forestry, and farms, can stop the penetration of sunlight through water. This prevents water plants from utilizing photosynthesis and causes the, ah, blanketing of lake or riverbeds, which, in turn, damages the ecology. And if that isn't enough, pollutants in the water include a wide spectrum of chemicals, pathogens, and physical chemistry or sensory changes. Many of the chemical substances are toxic or even carcinogenic. Pathogens can obviously produce . . . um, waterborne diseases in either human or animal hosts. In short, various water systems all around the world are in pretty big trouble on account of a wide variety of pollutants. You see, uh, water pollution has now become a serious global problem. It has been suggested that it is the leading worldwide cause of death and disease and that it accounts for the deaths of more than, uh, get this . . . 14,000 people daily.

W: Really? I had no idea that it was that bad. I mean, uh, that's an enormous number of deaths. It's rather scary.

M: It is. Let me put it this way. Most water pollutants are eventually carried by rivers into the Earth's oceans. In some areas of the world, the influence can be traced, um, hundreds of miles from the mouth of a river by studies that utilize hydrology transport models. Advanced computer models have been used in many locations worldwide to examine the effects of pollutants in aquatic systems. For example, filter feeding species such as crayfish have also been used to study the effects of pollution, um, in the New York Bight, an area in the Atlantic Ocean that is centered around New York City. In this study, the highest toxin loads were not directly at the mouth of the Hudson River but were instead sixty miles south since several days are required for incorporation into planktonic tissue. Farther south were areas of oxygen depletion caused by chemicals using up oxygen and by algae blooms caused by excess nutrients from algal cell death and decomposition.

W: So what you're saying is that the loss of oxygen in the water system has negative effects on all living water creatures?

M: **You've got it.** It's a vicious cycle. Fish and shellfish kills were reported because toxins climb the food chain after small fish consume copepods like crayfish, then large fish eat smaller fish, and, well, you get the point. Each step up the food chain concentrates certain toxins such as heavy metals and pesticides by approximately a factor of, um, ten. All right, who has questions?

해석

M Professor: 좋아요, 어, 수업을 시작할 준비가 다 되었으면 오염에 관한 지난 주 논의를 계속 이어가고자 합니다. 이번 수업에서는 수질 오염에 대해 특히 초점을 맞추고자 해요. 수질 오염을 인간의 활동으로 인해 호수, 강, 바다, 그리고 지하수와 같은 수역에 미치는 부정적인 영향이라고 정의함으로써 시작해 보죠.

W Student: 음, 모든 수질 오염이 인간에 의해 일어난다는 말씀이신가요? 그러한 주장에 동의할 수 있을지 잘 모르겠어요.

M: 흠… 어떤 말을 하려고 하는지는 알겠는데, 여러분 모두가 아셔야 하는 중요한 점이 있습니다. 자연 현상들, 예컨대, 음, 화산, 폭풍, 그리고 지진이 수질 및 물

의 생태에 커다란 변화를 일으킬 수 있다고 해도 그로 인한 피해를 오염으로 간주하지는 않죠. 아시다시피, 어, 자연은 자연적인 과정으로 생긴 문제들을 해결하는 능력을 가지고 있지만, 자연이 인간에 의한 문제를 해결하는 것은 훨씬 더 어려운 일입니다. 따라서 이번 수업에서는 인간이 초래한 수질 오염에 대해서만 살펴보도록 할게요.

자, 어, 수질 오염의 원인과 특징은 많습니다. 우선, 어, 인간에 의해 물에 유입되는 유기 폐기물로 시작해 볼게요. 이러한 폐기물은 다양한 형태를 취할 수 있습니다. 여기에는 하수와 농장 폐수가 포함되는데, 이들은 강물과 같이 물이 모이는 곳에서 산소 요구량을 증가시킵니다. 이로써 산소가 고갈되거나… 강 자체에서 산소가 손실되어 전체 생태계에 잠재적으로 심각한 영향을 미치게 되죠. 예를 들어 산소가 없어지면 물고기가 생존할 수 없기 때문에 이들 모두 죽게 될 것입니다. 물고기들이 수면 위를 떠다니면서 부패하기 시작하면 완전히 새로운 문제들이 나타나게 되고요.

W: 기업은 어떤가요? 공장 및 기타 제조 시설에서 가장 많은 오염 물질이 배출된다고 생각했어요.

M: 물론 그렇습니다. 기업은 폐수를 통해 다양한 오염 물질들을 방류합니다. 여기에는 중금속, 독성 유기 물질, 석유, 영양분, 그리고 고형 물질들이 포함되죠. 또한 그러한 방류로 인해, 특히 발전소에서 열효과가 발생할 수 있으며, 이로써 수계 내의 유효 산소가 지나치게 감소하게 됩니다.

W: 그러면 기업과, 음, 인간에 의해 수계로 유입되는 유기 폐기물이 원인이군요. 수질 오염의 또 다른 원인이 있나요?

M: 물론이죠. 공사 현장, 숲, 그리고 농장 등에서 이루어지는 다수의 활동에서 비롯된 토사를 포함하고 있는 유거수나 흙 때문에 햇빛이 물속을 통과하지 못할 수 있어요. 이로 인해 수중 식물들이 광합성을 하지 못하게 되면, 어, 호수나 강의 바닥에 블랭킷팅 현상이 일어나는데, 이는 또 다시 생태계를 파괴시키죠. 그리고 그걸로 충분하지 않다면, 물속 오염 물질에는 다양한 화학 물질, 병균, 그리고 물리 화학적인 또는 감각적인 변화를 일으키는 물질들이 포함되어 있습니다. 다수의 화학 물질들이 독성을 띄고 있으며, 심지어 발암 물질들도 존재해요. 병균은 명백하게도… 음, 인간이나 동물 숙주에게 수인성 질병을 일으킬 수 있습니다. 간단히 말해서 전 세계에 있는 다양한 수계들이 많은 오염 물질 때문에 커다란 문제를 겪고 있어요. 아시다시피, 어, 수질 오염은 현재 전 세계적으로 심각한 문제가 되고 있죠. 수질 오염이 전 세계적인 죽음과 질병의 주요한 원인이 되고 있다는 주장과 이로 인해 어… 매일 14,000명 이상의 사람들이 목숨을 잃고 있다는 주장이 제기 되고 있습니다.

W: 정말인가요? 그 정도로 심각한지 모르고 있었어요. 제 말은, 어, 사망자 수가 너무 많다는 뜻이에요. 정말 끔찍하군요.

M: 끔찍하죠. 이렇게 설명을 드릴게요. 대부분의 수질 오염 물질은 결국 강에서 바다로 흘러 들어갑니다. 전 세계의 일부 지역에서 그러한 영향은 수문학 이동 모델을 이용한 연구를 통해, 음, 강 하구로부터 수백 마일 떨어진 곳까지 추적할 수 있어요. 오염 물질이 수상 시스템에 미치는 영향을 조사하기 위해 보다 발달한 컴퓨터 모델이 전 세계 여러 지역에서 사용되고 있습니다. 예를 들어 대서양에 속한 지역으로 뉴욕시 중심에 위치한 뉴욕만에서는 오염 물질의 영향을 연구하기 위해 가재와 같은 여과섭식종이 이용되고 있습니다. 이 연구에서 가장 많은 독성 물질이 검출된 곳은 허드슨강 하구가 아니라 그곳에서 남쪽으로 60마일 떨어진 곳으로 나타났는데, 그 이유는 혼합물이 플랑크톤 조직으로 들어가기까지 수일이 소요되기 때문입니다. 더 남쪽 지역에서는 산소를 소모시키는 화학 물질과 해조류의 죽음 및 부패로 인한 영양분의 과다 증가로 발생한 적조 현상 때문에 산소가 고갈되었어요.

W: 그러니까 교수님 말씀은 수계의 산소 손실이 모든 수중 생물에게 부정적인 영향을 미친다는 것이죠?

M: 맞아요. 악순환인 거죠. 작은 물고기들이 가재와 같은 요각류를 잡아먹고, 큰 물고기들이 작은 물고기를 잡아먹고, 음, 계속 그런 식으로 독성 물질이 먹이 사슬을 타고 올라가기 때문에 어패류들의 폐사가 보고되었어요. 한 단계씩 먹이 사슬을 올라갈 때마다 중금속 및 살충제에서 나오는 특정 독성 물질의 농도가 대략, 음, 10배씩 증가하게 됩니다. 좋아요, 질문이 있나요?

[12-17]

Script 09-08

M Professor: Okay, everybody. For this morning's lecture, um, I have some pretty technical stuff to discuss, so I will try to give this information to you as simply as possible. While I don't usually allow this, you are all free to record this lecture if you want. That way, you can review everything I say so that you are familiar with the information for your test this Thursday . . . Okay, uh, ready or not, here we go. You have probably all seen or read news stories about fascinating ancient artifacts. For example, at an archaeological dig, a wooden tool is unearthed, and the archaeologist finds out that it is around 5,000 years old. A child mummy is found high in the Andes, and the archaeologist says that the child lived more than 2,000 years ago. With this in mind, you may be asking yourself this question: How do scientists know how old an object or human remains which they unearth are? Well, let me go through a process which will help all of you understand how it is possible for archaeologists to date old objects.

The fact of the matter is that all plants and animals on the planet are made principally of carbon. How is this possible? Well, carbon goes through many living things because it is an enormous part of the cycle of life. Let me start at the beginning of this cycle. During the period of a plant's life, the plant takes in carbon dioxide through the process of photosynthesis, which is how it makes energy and grows. Animals eat plants, and some eat other animals in the food chain. Carbon follows this pathway through the food chain on the Earth so that all living things are using carbon, which is building their bodies until they die. Does everyone follow me so far . . . ? Wonderful.

Moving on then . . . A tiny part of the carbon on the Earth is called carbon-14. It's also known as radiocarbon. It is called radiocarbon because it is radioactive. This means that, ah, its atomic structure is not stable and also that there is an uneasy relationship between the particles in the nucleus of the atom itself. Eventually, a particle is emitted from a carbon-14 atom, and the carbon-14 subsequently disappears. Most of the carbon on the Earth exists in a slightly different atomic form although it is, chemically speaking, identical to all carbon. How are we doing up to this point . . . ? So far, so good? All right.

Now that we know carbon atoms follow many living things through the food chain, I can now explain how carbon-14 dating works. In the 1940s, scientists succeeded in finding out how long it takes for radiocarbon to disappear or decay from a sample of carbon taken from a dead plant or animal. A scientist named Willard Libby first measured the half-life of radiocarbon. Now, um, here's an important definition, so write this down. The half-life refers to the amount of time it takes for half of the radiocarbon in a sample of bone or shell or any carbon sample to disappear.

Well, Libby found that it took 5,568 years for half of the radiocarbon to decay. After twice that amount of time, which is about 11,000 years, another half of that remaining amount will have disappeared. After another 5,568 years, again another half will have disappeared. You can work out so that after about 50,000 years of time, all the radiocarbon will have vanished. Libby figured out that radiocarbon dating is not able to date anything older than 70,000 years old.

Since carbon is very common on the Earth, um, there are a lot of different types of material which can be dated by scientists. For example, Libby tested the new radiocarbon method on carbon samples from prehistoric Egypt whose ages were known. A sample of, um, acacia wood from the tomb of the pharaoh Zoser was dated, for example. Zoser lived during the Third Dynasty in Egypt. Libby figured that since the half-life of carbon-14 was 5,568 years, then he should obtain a radiocarbon amount of about fifty percent of that found in living wood because Zoser's death took place about 5,000 years ago. The results he obtained indicated this was the case. Many other radiocarbon tests were conducted on samples of wood whose ages were also known. Again, the results were as expected. In 1949, Libby and his team published their results.

So as you can see, radiocarbon dating is a . . . very important field of science. The carbon-14 method has been and continues to be applied and used in many different fields, including hydrology, atmospheric science, oceanography, geology, paleo-climatology, archaeology, and biomedicine. Whew! Okay, do you have any questions for me before I continue?

해석

M Professor: 좋아요, 여러분. 오늘 아침 강의에서는, 음, 상당히 전문적인 내용을 다룰 것이기 때문에, 최대한 간단하게 그에 대해 설명해 드리도록 하겠습니다. 보통은 허용을 하지 않지만, 원하시는 경우 여러분 모두 자유롭게 이번 강의를 녹음하셔도 좋습니다. 그렇게 하시면 제가 말한 내용을 다시 들으시고 이번 목요일에 있는 시험을 잘 준비하실 수 있을 테니까요… 좋아요, 어, 준비가 됐든 안 됐든 시작해 보죠. 아마도 여러분 모두가 놀라운 고대 유물에 관한 뉴스를 보거나 읽은 적이 있으실 것입니다. 예를 들어 고고학 유적지에서 목재 도구가 발굴되었는데, 고고학자는 그것이 약 5,000년 전의 것이라는 점을 밝혀냅니다. 한 아이의 미이라가 안데스산맥의 고지대에서 발견되었는데, 고고학자는 그 아이가 2000년도 더 전에 살았던 아이라고 주장합니다. 이러한 점을 염두에 두고서 여러분 스스로에게 다음과 같이 물어볼 수 있을 거예요. 발굴된 물건이나 사람의 유해가 얼마나 오래전의 것인지 과학자들이 어떻게 알 수 있을까요? 음, 고고학자들이 오래된 물건의 연대를 어떻게 측정하는지 여러분 모두가 이해하실 수 있도록 그 과정을 살펴보도록 하겠습니다.

사실 지구상의 모든 동식물은 기본적으로 탄소로 이루어져 있습니다. 어떻게 이런 일이 가능할까요? 음, 탄소는 많은 생물을 거쳐 가는데, 그 이유는 탄소가 생애 주기의 커다란 부분을 차지하기 때문입니다. 이러한 주기의 처음부터 시작해 보죠. 식물의 생애에 있어서 식물은, 에너지를 얻고 성장하는 과정인, 광합성 작용을 통해 이산화탄소를 흡수합니다. 동물은 식물을 먹고, 일부 동물은 먹이 사슬에 있는 다른 동물을 잡아먹습니다. 지구에서는 먹이 사슬을 통해 탄소가 그러한 경로로 이동하기 때문에 모든 생물은 탄소를 이용하고 있으며, 생물이 죽을 때까지 탄소가 이들의 신체를 구성하게 됩니다. 여기까지 이해가 되시나요…? 좋습니다.

그럼 더 나아가서… 지구상에 존재하는 탄소 중 극히 적은 일부는 탄소-14라는 것입니다. 이는 또한 방사성 탄소라고도 알려져 있죠. 방사성을 띠기 때문에 방사성 탄소라고 불립니다. 이는, 어, 원자 구조가 안정적이지 않으며 또한 원자의 핵에 있는 입자들의 관계가 불안정하다는 것을 의미합니다. 결국 탄소-14에서 하나의 입자가 방출되면 그 결과 탄소-14는 사라지게 되죠. 지구상 대부분의 탄소는, 화학적으로 말하면 모두 동일한 탄소이지만, 원자 형태에 있어서는 약간씩 서로 다른 상태로 존재합니다. 여기까지는 어떤가요…? 지금까지는 괜찮죠? 좋습니다.

탄소 원자가 먹이 사슬을 통해 여러 생물을 거쳐 간다는 점은 알았으니 이제 방사성 탄소 연대 측정법의 원리를 설명해 드릴 수 있겠군요. 1940년대에 과학자들은 죽은 동식물에서 얻은 탄소 샘플에서 방사성 탄소가 사라지거나 붕괴되는데 걸리는 시간을 알아내는데 성공했어요. 윌러드 리비라는 과학자가 최초로 방사성 탄소의 반감기를 측정했습니다. 자, 음, 중요한 정의를 알려 드릴 테니 적으시기 바랍니다. 반감기란 뼈, 껍질, 또는 모든 탄소 샘플 속에 들어 있는 방사성 탄소의 절반이 사라지기까지 걸리는 시간을 가리킵니다.

음, 리비는 방사성 탄소의 절반이 붕괴되는데 5,568년이 걸린다는 것을 알아냈어요. 그 두 배의 시간인 약 11,000년이 지나면 남아 있는 양의 반이 또 다시 사라질 것이고요. 그 후 또 다시 5,568년이 지나면 그 절반이 다시 사라질 것입니다. 그래서 약 50,000년이 지나면 모든 방사성 탄소가 사라질 것으로 생각해 볼 수 있어요. 리비는 70,000년 이전의 것에 대해서는 방사성 탄소 연대 측정법으로 연대를 측정할 수 없다는 점을 알아냈습니다.

지구에서 탄소는 매우 흔하기 때문에, 음, 다양한 물질들을 대상으로 과학자들이 연대를 측정할 수 있습니다. 예를 들어 리비는 연대가 알려져 있는 선사 시대 이집트에서 나온 탄소 샘플에 대해 새 방사성 탄소법을 실험해 보았어요. 한 가지 예로, 음, 파라오 조세르의 무덤에서 나온 아카시아 나무 샘플에 대한 연대를 측정했습니다. 조세르는 이집트의 세 번째 왕조 때의 인물이었죠. 탄소-14의 반감기가 5,568년이고 조세르가 약 5,000년에 사망했기 때문에 살아 있는 나무에서 발견된 방사성 탄소의 양은 약 50퍼센트여야 했습니다. 그가 얻은 결과는 이와 같았어요. 또한 이미 시대를 알고 있는 나무 샘플들을 대상으로도 많은 방사성 탄소 측정법이 실시되었습니다. 또 다시, 예상 그대로의 결과들이 나타났죠. 1949년에 리비와 그의 연구팀은 연구 결과를 발표했습니다.

이제 아시다시피 방사성 탄소 연대 측정법은… 과학에서 매우 중요한 분야예요. 방사성 탄소 연대 측정법은 수문학, 대기 과학, 해양학, 지질학, 고기후학, 고고학, 그리고 생물 의학 등을 포함하여 여러 분야에서 적용되고 사용되어 왔습니다. 휴! 좋아요, 제가 계속하기 전에 혹시 질문이 있는 사람이 있나요?

Actual Test 02

p.274

PART 1

1 Ⓒ 2 Ⓒ 3 Ⓒ 4 Ⓐ 5 Ⓐ
6 Ⓑ 7 Ⓑ 8 Ⓑ 9 Ⓐ
10 Ⓑ, Ⓒ 11 Ⓑ

PART 2

1 Ⓓ 2 Ⓐ 3 Ⓐ, Ⓒ 4 Ⓒ 5 Ⓓ
6 Ⓓ 7 Ⓒ 8 Ⓐ 9 Fact: 1, 3
Not a Fact: 2, 4 10 Ⓓ 11 Ⓑ
12 Ⓐ 13 Ⓒ 14 Ⓓ 15 Ⓐ, Ⓓ
16 Ⓐ 17 Ⓐ

PART 1

[1-5]

Script 09-11

M Student: Hello. My name is Cedric Nelson. I was told that I should come up here and speak with you.

W Campus Dining Employee: It's a pleasure to meet you, Cedric. Who sent you here?

M: Mr. Carrington down in the café on the first floor of this building.

W: All right. So what do you want to talk about with me?

M: Well, I heard that there is a job opening at the café, so I went there to talk to the manager. I guess that's Mr. Carrington. He told me that he doesn't make the hiring decisions. However, he said that if he likes someone and thinks that person would be a good worker, he tells that individual to speak with you. So, uh, here I am.

W: Okay. It looks like you got an endorsement from Mr. Carrington. That's a good start. I need to ask you a few questions before I can hire you though.

M: Sure.

W: First, do you have any experience working at a café or anywhere in the food service industry?

M: Yes, I do. I worked at a coffee shop during summer vacation for two years when I was a high school student a few years ago.

W: What kinds of duties did you have?

M: Just about everything. I made coffee for customers. I took orders at times and accepted payment for purchases. I even helped make some of the baked goods when the store got really busy. So I learned how to make different kinds of cakes, cookies, bagels, donuts, muffins, and other stuff like that.

W: It sounds like you have a good bit of experience. That's nice.

M: Yes. I really enjoyed working at the coffee shop, so I thought I would apply to work at one here. I love talking to customers and just being in that kind of an environment.

W: Hmm . . . I'm willing to give you a chance here. We have quite a few shifts available. About how many hours would you like to work?

M: As many as possible. I'd definitely like ten hours at least. I'd do more if you have more.

W: Take a look at this schedule. The blocks that are in blue are ones that have not been filled. Do any of them fit your class schedule?

M: Hmm . . . Oh, this is unfortunate. It looks like the only shift that you have which I can do is on Thursday night from seven to eleven.

W: Do you want to take it?

M: Yes, please.

W: Great. Now, uh, I do the hiring for all of the businesses in this building. And a couple of other food establishments are looking for workers. Since you have experience making pastries, why don't you check out this schedule for the bakery located in the basement? It has quite a few more openings, so I think that some of them will fit your schedule.

M: Okay. Let me see . . . Wow . . . I can do the shifts on Monday afternoon . . . on Wednesday morning . . . and on Friday evening. Um, that isn't too many hours, is it?

W: **It's not a problem for me.** If you think that you can handle it, I can give you all three of those shifts plus the other one at the café. What do you think?

해석

M Student: 안녕하세요. 제 이름은 Cedric Nelson이에요. 제가 여기에 와서 선생님과 이야기를 해야 한다는 말을 들었어요.

W Campus Dining Employee: 만나서 반가워요, Cedric. 누가 보냈나요?

M: 이 건물 1층에 있는 카페의 Carrington 씨요.

W: 그렇군요. 그러면 저와 어떤 이야기를 나누고 싶으신가요?

M: 음, 저는 카페에 빈 자리가 있다는 말을 듣고 그곳에 가서 매니저와 이야기를 나누려고 했어요. 그 분이 Carrington 씨라고 생각을 했죠. 그분은 자신에게 채용에 관한 결정권이 없다고 하시더군요. 하지만 누군가가 마음에 들고 그 사람이 일을 잘할 것 같다고 생각하는 경우, 그러한 사람에게 선생님과 이야기를 해 보라고 말한다고 말씀하셨어요. 그래서, 어, 제가 여기에 온 것이고요.

W: 그렇군요. Carrington 씨가 학생을 보증해 준 것처럼 들리는군요. 시작이 좋네요. 하지만 학생을 고용하기에 앞서 제가 몇 가지 질문을 할게요.

M: 좋아요.

W: 첫째, 카페나 혹은 음식물과 관련된 업소에서 일을 해 본 경험이 있나요?

M: 네, 있어요. 몇 년 전 제가 고등학생이었을 때 2년 동안 여름 방학을 이용해 커피숍에서 일을 했어요.

W: 어떠한 일을 담당했나요?

M: 모든 일이요. 손님들에게 커피를 만들어 줬어요. 때때로 주문도 받고 계산도 해 드렸죠. 매장이 정말로 바쁜 경우에는 제과 업무를 돕기도 했어요. 그래서 다양한 종류의 케이크, 쿠키, 베이글, 도넛, 머핀, 그리고 그러한 기타 제품들을 만

드는 법도 알게 되었죠.

W: 상당한 경력을 가지고 있는 것처럼 들리는군요. 좋아요.

M: 네. 커피숍에서 일하는 것이 정말 즐거웠기 때문에 이곳에서도 그러한 곳에 지원을 해야겠다고 생각했죠. 손님들과 이야기하는 것도 좋아하고, 그러한 환경에 있는 것 자체도 좋아해요.

W: 흠… 기꺼이 기회를 드리고 싶네요. 근무 가능한 시간대는 꽤 있어요. 몇 시간 동안 일을 하고 싶나요?

M: 가능한 많이요. 적어도 10시간 이상 일했으면 정말 좋겠어요. 더 많은 시간을 원하시면 그럴 수도 있고요.

W: 이 시간표를 봐 주세요. 파란색으로 칠해진 것들이 비어 있는 시간대예요. 학생의 시간표에 맞는 것들이 있나요?

M: 흠… 오, 운이 없네요. 제가 일할 수 있는 유일한 시간대는 목요일 저녁 7시에서 11시까지 뿐인 것 같아요.

W: 그때 하시고 싶나요?

M: 네, 그래요.

W: 좋아요. 자, 어, 저는 이 건물 내 모든 업체들의 고용 업무를 담당하고 있어요. 그리고 두 곳의 식당에서도 직원을 구하고 있는 중이죠. 학생이 제과 업무 경험이 있으니 지하에 있는 빵집의 이 시간표를 확인해 보는 것이 어떨까요? 비어 있는 자리가 꽤 있기 때문에 그중 몇 개는 학생의 시간표에 맞을 것 같아요.

M: 좋아요. 제가 한번 볼게요… 와… 월요일 오후에 근무를 할 수 있고… 수요일 오전에도… 그리고 금요일 저녁에도 가능해요. 음, 너무 많이 일하는 건 아니겠죠, 그렇죠?

W: 제게는 아무런 문제가 안 되죠. 학생이 할 수 있다고 생각하면 그 세 개의 시간대뿐만 아니라 카페에서의 한 개의 시간대를 더 배정해 드릴 수 있어요. 어떻게 생각하나요?

[6-11]

Script 09-12

W Professor: Today, class, we are going to focus on the history of American theater. So if you're all ready, I'll begin. I strongly encourage you all to take good notes for two reasons. First, the material that I cover today will be on your midterm exam in a few weeks. Second, I'm going to refer back to a lot of the names that I mention today in later classes, so I will expect you to be familiar with all of them. Does everyone understand . . . ? All right, uh, taken from a historical context, the birth of professional theater in America is usually thought to have begun with the Lewis Hallan troupe, which arrived in Williamsburg, Virginia in 1752.

M Student: **It really started that far back?**

W: It sure did. How do you think the early settlers entertained themselves? Now, uh, not everybody approved of theater back then. There was active opposition to this form of entertainment all throughout the eighteenth century. For example, in the puritanical climate of the time, especially in the northern colonies, the theater was considered a "highway to hell." Laws forbidding the performing of plays were passed in Massachusetts in 1750 and in Rhode Island in 1761, and performances were banned in most of the American colonies during the American Revolutionary War at the urging of the Continental Congress.

However, by the early nineteenth century, theater became more common in the United States, and many celebrity actors from Europe visited the United States and went on tour, giving performances wherever they went. The Walnut Theater is the oldest, um, continuously operating theater in the country. It's located in Philadelphia, Pennsylvania and was built in 1809.

M: Do you mean that Philadelphia was the only city in the entire United States with a theater at that time?

W: Oh, no. Not at all. However, most cities only had a single theater. Productions were much more rudimentary then, and sometimes plays would be staged in barns or in dining rooms when no theater was available. Provincial theaters frequently lacked heat and even minimal props and scenery. They were really kind of basic. Anyway, as the westward expansion of the country progressed, some entrepreneurs staged, um, floating theaters on boats which would travel from town to town. Eventually, towns grew to such sizes that they could afford long runs of a production, and in 1841, a single play was shown in New York City for an unprecedented three weeks.

M: What kinds of plays did they perform in the 1800s?

W: Well, ah, Shakespeare was the most commonly performed playwright, yet various other European playwrights had their plays performed at times. American plays of the period were mostly melodramas, often weaving in local themes or characters such as the heroic but ill-fated Indian. The most enduring melodrama of this period was, um, you guessed it, *Uncle Tom's Cabin*.

M: Other than the kinds of plays you already mentioned, did they do anything else?

W: Sure. One popular form of theater during this time was the minstrel show. It was arguably the first uniquely American style of performance. These shows featured white actors dressed in blackface and playing up racial stereotypes. Ah, another type of performance was the burlesque show. Burlesque became a popular form of entertainment in the middle of the nineteenth century. Originally a form of farce in which females in male roles mocked the politics and culture of the day, burlesque was condemned by opinion makers for its sexuality and outspokenness. The form was hounded off the legitimate stage and found itself relegated to saloons and barrooms.

M: Well, how did the modern theater come about in the United States?

W: By the 1880s, theaters on Broadway in New York City and along 42nd Street took on a flavor of their own, giving rise to new stage forms such as the Broadway musical. These were strongly influenced by the feelings of immigrants with great hopes and ambition who were coming to the country, and many of these immigrants went into the theater. New York became the organizing center for theater throughout the United States.

M: So is it safe to say that Broadway was the most influential part of what we call modern American theater?

W: Well, you are partly correct, but there are other important factors that have influenced the modern theater in the United States. For example, vaudeville was common in the late nineteenth and early twentieth centuries and is notable for heavily influencing early film, radio, and television productions. This was born from an earlier American practice of having singers and novelty acts perform between acts in a standard play. Hmm . . . I'd say that about covers my overview of the history of theater. Now, I'd like to backtrack and go into more detail.

해석

W Professor: 오늘은 미국의 극의 역사에 대해 초점을 맞추도록 하겠습니다. 다들 준비가 되었으면 시작해 볼게요. 두 가지 이유에서 필기를 잘 하실 것을 강력히 추천해 드립니다. 첫째, 제가 오늘 다룰 내용은 몇 주 후 중간고사의 시험 범위에 들어가는 것이에요. 둘째, 오늘 언급되는 여러 가지 명칭들은 이후 수업에서 제가 다시 말하게 될 것이므로 여러분 모두가 잘 알고 계셨으면 좋겠습니다. 모두 이해하셨나요…? 좋아요. 어, 역사적인 맥락에서 볼 때 미국에서의 전문적인 극은 1752년 버지니아의 윌리엄스버그에 도착한 루이스 할란 극단에서 시작되었다고 보통 생각됩니다.

M: 정말로 그처럼 오래 전에 시작되었나요?

W: 물론이죠. 초기의 식민지 정착민들에게 어떤 오락거리가 있었을 것 같나요? 자, 어, 당시 모든 사람이 극을 반겼던 것은 아니었어요. 18세기를 통틀어 이러한 형태의 오락거리를 적극적으로 반대하는 사람들이 있었죠. 예를 들어 당시 청교도적인 분위기에서, 특히 북부의 식민지에서는 극장이 "지옥으로 가는 고속도로"라로 간주되었습니다. 공연을 금지시키는 법안이 1750년에 매사추세츠에서, 그리고 1761년에 로드아일랜드에서 통과되었고, 미국 독립 전쟁 당시에는 대륙 회의의 권고에 따라 대부분의 미 식민지에서 공연이 금지되었습니다.

하지만 19세기 초반 미국에서 공연은 보다 보편적인 것이 되었고, 유럽에서 온 많은 유명 배우들이 미국을 찾아 순회 공연을 함으로써 이들이 방문하는 곳마다 공연이 이루어졌어요. 월넛 시어터가 미국에서 가장 오래된 극장인데, 음, 이곳에서 지속적으로 공연이 이루어졌습니다. 이곳은 펜시베니아의 필라델피아에 위치해 있으며 1809년에 설립되었어요.

M: 당시 미국 전체에서 극장이 있던 도시가 필라델피아뿐이었다는 말씀이신가요?

W: 오, 아니에요. 전혀 그렇지 않아요. 하지만 대부분의 도시에는 극장이 하나밖에 없었어요. 당시 제작 수준은 훨씬 더 원시적인 수준이었고, 극장이 없는 경우에는 때때로 헛간이나 식당에서 공연이 이루어지기도 했어요. 지방 극장의 경우, 종종 난방이 되지 않았고, 심지어는 최소한의 소품이나 무대 장치가 없는 경우도 흔했어요. 정말로 원시적인 수준이었죠. 어쨌든, 미국의 서부가 개척되면서 몇몇 사업가들이, 음, 이 마을에서 저 마을로 이동이 가능한 수상 극장에 공연을 올렸어요. 마침내 장기 공연이 가능할 정도로 도시들이 크게 성장하게 되었고, 1841년에는 하나의 연극이 뉴욕시에서 3주 동안 상연되었는데, 이는 전례가 없던 일이었죠.

M: 1800년대에는 어떤 극이 공연되었나요?

W: 음, 어, 셰익스피어의 희곡이 가장 흔히 무대에 올려졌지만, 기타 다양한 유럽 작가의 희곡들도 때때로 무대에 올려졌어요. 당시 미국의 극들은 대부분 신파극으로, 영웅적이지만 불행했던 인디언과 같은, 지역적인 주제나 인물들을 나타냈습니다. 당시 가장 오래 공연된 멜로드라마는, 음, 여러분도 짐작하겠지만, *톰 아저씨의 오두막*이었어요.

M: 이미 언급하신 종류의 극 외에 다른 것들도 있었나요?

W: 물론이죠. 이 시기에 인기를 끌었던 한 가지 극의 형태는 민스트럴쇼였어요. 분명 최초의 미국식 공연이라고 할 수 있는 것이죠. 이 쇼에서는 흑인 분장을 한 백인 배우들이 나와서 인종적인 고정 관념을 강조했습니다. 아, 또 다른 공연 형태로 벌레스크쇼가 있었어요. 벌레스크는 19세기 중반에 인기를 끈 공연이었죠. 원래는 남장을 한 여자가 당시의 정치와 문화를 조롱했던 소극 형태였는데, 성적 묘사와 노골적인 측면 때문에 벌레스크는 오피니언 리더들의 비난을 받았습니다. 이러한 형태는 합법적인 무대에서 쫓겨나 바와 술집으로 옮겨 가게 되었어요.

M: 미국에서 현대적인 극은 어떻게 나타나게 되었나요?

W: 1880년대 뉴욕시의 브로드웨이와 42번가에 극장들이 자리를 잡음으로써 브로드웨이 뮤지컬이라는 새로운 형태의 공연이 등장하게 되었습니다. 이는 커다란 희망과 포부를 가지고 뉴욕에 온 이민자들의 감정에 큰 영향을 받았으며, 그러한 많은 이민자들이 극장으로 유입되었어요. 뉴욕은 미국 전역에서 극장의 중심지가 되었습니다.

M: 브로드웨이가 현대 미국 극에서 가장 큰 영향력을 행사했다고 말할 수 있다는 뜻인가요?

W: 음, 틀린 말은 아니지만, 미국의 현대 극에 영향을 미친 또 다른 중요한 요소들도 있습니다. 예를 들어 보드빌은 19세기 말과 20세기 초반에 일반적이었으며, 초창기의 영화, 라디오, 그리고 텔레비전 방송 제작에 상당한 영향을 끼친 것으로 잘 알려져 있어요. 이는 일반적인 극의 막 사이에 가수와 새로운 배우가 공연을 하는 초창기 미국의 전통에서 비롯된 것이었죠. 흠… 이 정도면 극의 역사에 대한 개괄적인 설명은 다 드린 것 같군요. 자, 다시 돌아가서 보다 상세하게 살펴보도록 하죠.

PART 2

[1-5]

Script 09-14

W Student: Hello, Professor Adams. May I speak with you for a moment?

M Professor: Sure, Mary. Please come into my office and have a seat. How can I be of assistance to you today?

W: Well, I'm here to talk to you about our group project in your intro class . . .

M: Okay, yes . . . You're talking about the group projects that are due next week . . . How is your group faring?

W: Well, uh, not so well. That's what I was hoping to discuss with you. We met last night and failed to make any progress. We just kind of sat around, and nobody said much of anything.

M: So the first thing I want to know is who did your group elect as the leader? I'm assuming it was you since you're the one who is here representing them now.

W: No, we kind of avoided selecting a leader. It was like nobody wanted to step up and take any responsibility.

M: Aha, I see. Nobody wanted to assume the leadership role; therefore, no productive decisions were made.

W: That's right. We couldn't decide on what topic to choose for our research project or even how we should go about choosing a subject.

M: Well, Mary, I think the correct decision is sitting there right in front of me. It's you. You should elect yourself leader of this quiet little group and start making decisions in order to get something accomplished.

W: Yes, but being the leader takes so much effort. With my other studies, I just don't know if I have the time and energy to invest in this.

M: Do you want a good grade?

W: Of course.

M: Well, since you're willing to invest the time and effort into coming to see me here and you really want a good grade, I think it's in your best interests to assume leadership of this group and to start making some strong decisions.

W: Uh . . . Okay . . . Tell me more.

M: Well, the benefits are trifold. First of all, you'll steer your group toward success. This will give you the respect and admiration of your fellow students. Secondly, by asserting yourself, there will be some long-term benefits in the boost in confidence and the increase in ability you'll receive.

W: Sure . . . I'll feel stronger, sharper . . . more capable.

M: That's right. You've got it. By stepping up into the leader's role, you'll play a role that is required in any human endeavor. And thirdly, you'll impress me . . . your teacher . . . which means that you'll get a better grade than the other students in your group since they were too meek to do anything for themselves.

W: Okay. I think you've talked me into it. I'm going to call another group meeting and nominate myself as group leader.

M: Well done. But don't assume all of the burden yourself. As soon as you're the leader, you need to allocate the responsibilities. Make one of the group members in charge of researching the various topics and another member in charge of assembling information. Before you know it, your group will be working toward its goal like a well-oiled machine!

W: Oh, thanks so much for your valuable guidance.

M: No problem. That's what I'm here for.

해석

W Student: 안녕하세요, Adams 교수님. 잠깐 이야기를 나눌 수 있으신가요?

M Professor: 물론이죠, Mary. 사무실로 들어와서 앉으세요. 어떻게 도와 드릴까요?

W: 음, 저는 교수님의 개론 수업의 조별 과제에 대해 말씀을 드리려고 왔는데…

M: 그래요, 네… 다음 주가 마감인 조별 과제를 얘기하는 것이군요… 학생 조는 어떻게 되고 있나요?

W: 음, 어, 그다지 잘 되고 있지 않아요. 그래서 논의를 하고 싶었던 것이고요. 저희는 어제 밤에 모였는데 아무런 진전이 없었어요. 그냥 둘러 앉아 있었고, 아무도 말을 많이 하지 않았어요.

M: 그렇다면 우선 알고 싶은 것이, 누구를 조장으로 뽑았나요? 지금 여기에서 그들을 대표하고 있는 것이 학생이니 학생이라고 생각이 드는군요.

W: 아니에요, 저희는 조장을 선정하지 않았어요. 앞에 나서서 책임을 지려는 사람이 아무도 없는 것 같았어요.

M: 아, 알겠어요. 어느 누구도 조장 역할을 맡으려고 하지 않았기 때문에 생산적인 결정이 내려지지 못했다는 것이군요.

W: 맞아요. 연구 과제로 어떤 주제를 선택할지, 혹은 심지어 어떻게 주제를 선택해야 할지도 정할 수가 없었어요.

M: 음, Mary, 올바른 결정은 바로 제 앞에 있다고 생각해요. 바로 학생이죠. 학생이 조용하고 크지 않은 조의 조장을 자처해서 무언가를 이루기 위해 결정을 내려보는 것이 어떨까요?

W: 하지만 조장이 되면 너무 많은 수고가 필요하죠. 다른 공부도 해야 하는데 이 일에 투자할 만한 시간과 에너지가 제가 있는지 잘 모르겠어요.

M: 좋은 성적을 받기를 바라나요?

W: 물론이죠.

M: 음, 학생이 기꺼이 시간과 노력을 투자해서 여기까지 저를 보러 오고 정말로 좋은 성적을 얻고 싶어하기 때문에, 제 생각에는 학생이 이번 조의 조장을 맡아서 확실한 결정을 내리는 것이 최선일 것 같아요.

W: 어… 그렇군요… 말씀을 더 해 주세요.

M: 음, 세 가지 이점이 있어요. 우선 학생의 조를 성공적으로 이끌 수 있어요. 그렇게 하면 급우들로부터 인정과 존경을 받게 될 거예요. 둘째, 자신의 주장을 폄으로써 장기적으로 자신감을 기를 수 있고 능력이 향상될 거예요.

W: 그렇겠군요… 더 강하고, 더 날카롭고… 더 능력 있게 느껴지겠죠.

M: 맞아요. 바로 그거예요. 지도자의 역할을 맡음으로써 인간의 모든 활동에서 요구되는 역할을 해 보게 될 거예요. 그리고 세 번째로 학생은 제게… 학생을 가르치는 사람에게 좋은 인상을 남길 텐데… 그러면 너무 미온적으로 아무것도 하지 않으려는 다른 조원들보다 좋은 점수를 받게 될 거예요.

W: 좋아요. 교수님 말씀에 마음이 동하네요. 조원들을 소집해서 제가 조장 후보로 제 자신을 추천할게요.

M: 장하군요. 하지만 모든 짐을 혼자 떠맡지는 마세요. 조장이 되자마자 업무를 할당하세요. 조원 중 한 명에게는 다양한 주제를 조사하도록 하고 다른 조원에게는 정보 수집 업무를 맡기세요. 학생도 모르는 사이에 기름이 잘 쳐진 기계처럼 학생의 조가 목표를 향해 움직이고 있을 거예요.

W: 오, 소중한 조언에 정말로 감사를 드려요.

M: 천만에요. 그것이 제가 해야 할 일이죠.

[6-11]

Script 09-15

W Professor: Okay, class. Before we end today's class, I'd like to tell you all about one of my favorite animals. I'm referring to the badger, which is a little-known but fascinating animal. I'm going to discuss its natural habitats, its feeding habits, its families, and, most interestingly, its coloration. So to get started, what can you tell me about badgers' habits and habitats?

M Student: They are nocturnal creatures that hunt at

night, usually by digging. They are also carnivores and feed on several species of insects and small mammals. They live in marshlands across North America as well as in the United Kingdom. They're great tunnel diggers, and they hibernate through the winter.

W: Very good, uh, except, contrary to popular belief, it has been proven that badgers do not actually hibernate. But they do have certain adaptations which allow them to survive on less food during the hard winter months, which are when their regular diet of earthworms and grubs is in shorter supply. Essentially, uh, they have adapted to be able to survive the lean winter months in the places where they live.

Badgers live in underground tunnel networks that are called setts. Just so you know, sett is spelled S-E-T-T. Note that there are two T's at the end of the word, please. Setts are usually found on sloping ground where there is some cover. Badgers dig their setts with their incredibly strong front claws. There's a picture of them on page ninety-five in your books. If you brought your textbook to class, why don't you take a look at that picture right now? I think you'll find it very impressive . . . Now, um, badgers live in their setts in groups of about fifteen and are led by a dominant male and female. Their setts usually have either one or two main entrances in addition to several lesser-used entryways.

I just mentioned male and female badgers. Just so you know, male badgers are referred to as boars whereas female badgers are called sows. As for the males, they are extremely tough. They are also highly territorial and are known to patrol their setts constantly, especially during the mating season. Let me tell you a bit about badger mating right now.

M: Uh, I'm not totally sure about this, but isn't their mating method a little different than that of most animals? I seem to recall reading that somewhere, but I could be confusing them with a different animal.

W: You're not mistaken. You're absolutely right. Badgers reproduce through delayed implantation. They can mate at any time of year, but the embryo does not implant into the womb and start growing until winter. This means that all cubs are born around the same time of year, which is between January and March. Litter sizes range from one to five cubs, but most females average about three.

When the babies are born, they're blind and pink with silky white fur. They suckle for about eight weeks, and once they have sufficient fat reserves, they begin to achieve independence from their mother. This, however, doesn't usually fully occur until their fifteenth week of life.

Okay. Let me tell you about the badger's coloration. It has black and white stripes on both its head and its face. Does anyone want to guess why the badger has those stripes . . . ? No . . . ? Okay, I'll tell you why since nobody wants to guess. It's not the randomness of nature in case you're curious. The markings are a kind of adaptation, but they are not intended to disguise badgers from predators. Instead, they are a warning to other animals that might be considering messing with a badger. Those sharp black and white stripes are one of nature's ways of saying, "Stay back! Don't bother me!" Keep in mind that you can see similar color markings on other animals that also utilize them as a warning. These animals include certain species of snakes, skunks, and even some insects.

M: Aha, so those markings are like a danger sign.

W: That's exactly what they are. They basically indicate that the badger is dangerous and that other animals need to leave it alone. However, you should be aware that not all badgers are fortunate enough to have this built-in defense system. It all depends on the amount of melanin pigmentation that is found in the badger's skin and fur. That is the genetic chemical which decides whether the badger has the warning stripes on its head or if it's an albino or black or even ginger colored.

All right. I think that will be enough for today. Please don't forget to study your notes because we're going to have a short quiz at the beginning of class next Monday. And yes, the badger will be on it. Good luck. See you next week.

해석

W Professor: 좋아요, 여러분. 오늘 수업을 끝내기에 앞서 제가 가장 좋아하는 동물 중 하나에 대해 이야기를 하고자 합니다. 잘 알려져 있지는 않지만 매우 흥미로운 동물인 오소리를 말씀드리는 거예요. 이들의 자연 서식지, 식습관, 가족, 그리고 가장 흥미로운 점인 색깔에 대해 논의할 것입니다. 먼저, 오소리의 습성과 서식지에 대해 말해 볼 사람이 있나요?

M Student: 오소리는 야간에, 주로 땅을 파서 사냥을 하는 야행성 동물입니다. 또한 육식 동물로서 몇 가지 종류의 곤충과 작은 포유 동물들을 잡아먹죠. 북아메리카와 영국의 습지에서 서식을 하고요. 굴을 매우 잘 파는 동물이고, 겨울에는 동면을 합니다.

W: 훌륭한 대답이긴 한데, 어, 일반적인 생각과는 달리 오소리는 사실 동면을 하지 않는 것으로 밝혀져 있습니다. 적응을 했기 때문에 오소리의 주요 먹이인 지렁이와 구더기가 부족해지는 추운 겨울에도 먹이를 적게 먹고 생존할 수 있어요. 기본적으로, 어, 자신들이 살고 있는 장소에서 먹이가 부족한 겨울을 날 수 있도록 적응해 온 것이죠.

오소리들은 오소리굴이라고 불리는 땅굴에서 생활해요. 아시다시피 철자는 S-E-T-T입니다. 단어의 마지막에 T가 두 개 있다는 점에 주의하시고요. 오소리굴은 보통 덮개가 있는 경사진 땅에서 찾아볼 수 있어요. 오소리는 엄청나게 튼튼한 앞쪽 발톱을 이용해 오소리굴을 팝니다. 여러분 교재의 95페이지에 그에 대한 사진이 있어요. 수업에 교재를 가져 오셨으면 지금 사진을 한번 보시는 것이 어떨까요? 매우 인상적인 것으로 생각되실 거예요… 자, 음, 오소리는 약 15마리의 무리를 이루어 오소리굴에서 살며 대장 역할을 하는 수컷과 암컷이 무리를 이끕니다. 오소리굴의 주요 출입구는 한 개 혹은 두 개이며, 잘 사용되지 않는 입구들이 몇 개 더 있죠.

조금 전에 제가 수컷과 암컷 오소리를 언급했습니다. 아시다시피, 수컷 오소리는 보를 가리키고 암컷 오소리는 소우라고 불리죠. 암컷에 대해 말하자면, 이들은 상당히 거칩니다. 또한 텃세가 매우 심해서, 특히 짝짓기 기간에는, 오소리 굴 주변을 항상 경계하는 것으로 알려져 있어요. 이제 오소리의 짝짓기에 대해 약간 설명을 드리도록 하겠습니다.

M: 어, 확실하지는 않지만, 이들의 짝짓기 방법이 다른 대부분의 동물들과 약간 다르지 않나요? 어디에선가 읽은 것 같은데요, 제가 다른 동물과 헷갈리는 것일 수도 있어요.

W: 잘못 알고 있는 것이 아니에요. 학생 말이 맞습니다. 오소리는 착상 지연으로 번식을 해요. 연중 어느 때라도 짝짓기를 할 수 있지만, 태아가 자궁에 착상을 하지 않고 겨울까지 자랍니다. 이는 모든 새끼들이 연중 같은 시기에, 즉 1월과 3월 사이에 태어난다는 점을 의미해요. 한 번에 태어나는 새끼는 한 마리에서 다섯 마리 사이이지만, 대부분의 암컷들은 평균적으로 3마리 정도를 낳습니다.

갓 태어난 새끼들은 눈이 보이지 않으며 분홍색을 띠고 하얀색 비단과 같은 털을 지니고 있어요. 이들은 약 8주 동안 젖을 먹으며, 지방이 충분히 축적되면 어미로부터 독립하기 시작합니다. 하지만 생후 15주가 지난 후에야 완전한 독립이 가능합니다.

좋아요. 이제 오소리의 색깔에 대해 말씀을 드리죠. 오소리의 머리와 얼굴에는 검고 흰 줄무늬가 있습니다. 오소리가 왜 그러한 줄무늬를 가지고 있는지 추측해 볼 사람이 있나요…? 없나요…? 좋아요, 아무도 추측해 보려고 하지 않기 때문에 제가 이유를 말씀드리죠. 궁금해 하시는 경우를 위해 말씀을 드리면 아무 의미 없이 그런 것은 아니에요. 무늬는 일종의 적응이라 할 수 있지만, 포식자로부터 오소리를 위장시키려는 목적은 아닙니다. 대신 오소리를 건드리려는 다른 동물들에게 경고를 해 주죠. 날카로운 검정색과 하얀색 줄무늬는 "물러서! 방해하지마!"라고 말해 주는 자연적인 방법 중 하나입니다. 다른 동물들도 경고의 수단으로서 이와 비슷한 색의 무늬를 이용한다는 점을 명심하세요. 이러한 동물에는 뱀, 스컹크, 그리고 심지어 일부 곤충종들도 포함됩니다.

M: 아, 그러면 그러한 무늬가 위험 표시와 같은 것이군요.

W: 정확해요. 기본적으로 오소리는 위험한 존재라는 점과 다른 동물들은 오소리를 그대로 놔두어야 한다는 점을 알려 주죠. 하지만 모든 오소리들이 이러한 선천적인 방어 시스템을 가지고 있을 정도로 운이 좋은 것은 아니라는 점을 기억해 주세요. 오소리의 피부와 털에서 찾아볼 수 있는 멜라닌 색소의 양에 따라 결정되는 것이죠. 이는 오소리의 머리에 경고성 줄무늬가 나타날 것인지, 혹은 오소리가 희거나 검은색을 띨 것인지, 심지어는 적갈색을 띨 것인지를 결정해 주는 유전적인 화학 물질입니다.

좋아요. 오늘은 이만하면 충분한 것 같군요. 다음 주 월요일에 수업을 시작하면서 짧은 퀴즈를 볼 예정이니 필기한 것을 잊지 마시고 공부해 오세요. 그리고, 그래요, 오소리에 대한 내용이 나올 것입니다. 행운을 빌게요. 다음 주에 뵙죠.

[12-17]

Script 09-16

M Professor: Now, let me talk a little more in depth about the lens. The crystalline lens is a transparent biconvex structure in the eye that, along with the corneae, helps refract light to focus on the retina. Its function is thus similar to a manmade optical lens. Are you following me . . . ?

So, uh . . . during the fetal stage, the development of the lens is aided by the hyaloid artery. In adults, the lens depends entirely upon the aqueous and vitreous humors for nourishment. Some of the most important characteristics of the lens are that it is nonrenewable and transparent and has no blood vessels and no organelles.

In humans, the refractive power of the lens in its natural environment is approximately fifteen diopters, which is roughly one-fourth of the eye's total power. The lens is . . . uh . . . made of transparent proteins called crystallins. The average concentration of lens proteins is about twice that of other intracellular proteins, and they are thought to play a structural role in the lens. It is about five millimeters thick and has a diameter of about nine millimeters for an adult human. However, please be aware that these figures can vary. The proteins are arranged in approximately 20,000 thin concentric layers with a refractive index varying from approximately 1.406 in the central layers down to 1.386 in the less dense cortex of the lens. This index gradient enhances the optical power of the lens. The lens is included in the capsular bag, maintained by the zonules of Zinn.

It is composed of fibers that come from hormone-producing cells. In fact, the cytoplasm of these cells makes up the transparent substance of the lens. The crystalline lens is composed of four layers from the surface to the center. They are the capsule, the subcapsular epithelium, the cortex, and the nucleus.

The lens capsule is a clear membrane-like structure that is quite elastic, a quality that keeps it under constant tension. As a result, the lens naturally tends toward a rounder or more globular configuration, a shape it must assume for the eye to focus at a near distance. Slender but very strong suspensor ligaments, also known as zonules, which attach at one end to the lens capsule and at the other end to the ciliary processes of the circular ciliary body around the inside of the eye, hold the lens in place.

When the eye is viewing an object at a far distance so that parallel rays of light are entering the eye, the ciliary muscle within the ciliary body relaxes. The ciliary processes pull on the zonules, which, in turn, pull on the lens capsule around its equator. This causes the entire lens to flatten or to become less convex, enabling the lens to attempt to focus light from the faraway object. Conversely, when the ciliary muscle works or contracts, tension is released on the suspensor ligaments and subsequently on the lens capsule, causing both lens surfaces to become more convex and the eye to be able to focus on near objects.

Okay, so the lens is flexible, and its curvature is controlled by ciliary muscles through the zonules. By changing the curvature of the lens, one can focus the eye on objects at different distances from it. This process is called accommodation. You need to pay close attention here because it is extremely important to understand how the lens ages. The lens continually grows throughout life, laying new cells over the old cells, which results in a stiffer lens. The lens gradually loses its accommodation ability as an individual ages.

The loss of an individual's ability to focus is termed presbyopia. It's really important that you become very familiar with the principals of the accommodative process since much of your future work in the field of optics will consist of helping your patients adapt to changes in their own accommodative process over time . . . Okay?

Normally, the accommodative process of the crystalline lens is smooth and effortless. When one changes one's focus from far to near, the ciliary muscle quickly contracts, causing the crystalline lens to accommodate the person by becoming thicker and the object at a near distance to become clear. Then, when looking back again at a far distance, the ciliary muscle immediately relaxes, causing the crystalline lens to revert to a thin shape and one's far-distance vision to become clear again.

Now, I know I just hit you with a mouthful. But I hope you've got it covered in your notes because your final exam is coming up next week. Don't be afraid to come to my office in case you want to ask any questions. Or feel free to drop me an email.

해석

M Professor: 자, 수정체에 대해 보다 상세한 이야기를 하도록 하죠. 수정체는 눈에 있는 투명한 양면 볼록 렌즈 형태의 조직으로, 각막과 함께 빛을 굴절시켜서 망막에 상이 맺히도록 만듭니다. 수정체의 기능은 인간이 만든 광학 렌즈와 비슷해요. 무슨 말인지 아시겠죠…?

그러면, 어… 태아 단계에서 수정체는 유리질 동맥의 도움을 받아 발달하게 됩니다. 성인의 경우 수정체는 전적으로 수양액과 유리액에 의존해서 양분을 얻죠. 수정체의 가장 중요한 특징으로는 재생이 불가능하고 투명하다는 점과, 혈관과 세포 기관이 존재하지 않는다는 점을 들 수 있어요.

인간의 경우 자연적인 환경에서 수정체의 굴절력은 약 15디옵터 정도로, 이는 눈의 전체 굴절력의 4분의 1정도에 해당됩니다. 수정체는… 어… 크리스탈린이라는 투명한 단백질로 이루어져 있어요. 수정체 단백질의 평균적인 농도는 기타 세포간 단백질의 농도의 두 배 정도이며, 이들은 수정체에서 구조적인 역할을 하는 것으로 생각됩니다. 성인의 경우 수정체의 두께는 약 5mm이며 지름은 약 9mm입니다. 하지만 이 수치는 달라질 수 있다는 점에 주의하세요. 단백질은 약 2만 개의 중심이 같은 얇은 층으로 배치되어 있으며, 굴절률은 중심층의 경우 약 1.406에서부터 수정체의 밀도가 낮은 피질 부분의 경우 1.386에 이르기까지 다양합니다. 이처럼 굴절률이 분포되어 있기 때문에 수정체의 광출력이 향상됩니다. 수정체는 모양체소대에 의해 유지되는 수정체낭 안에 들어 있어요.

수정체는 호르몬을 분비하는 세포에서 나오는 섬유질로 이루어져 있습니다. 실제로 이러한 세포의 세포질이 수정체의 투명 물질을 구성하고 있죠. 수정체는 표면에서부터 중심부까지 네 개의 층으로 이루어져 있습니다. 낭, 낭하 상피, 피질, 그리고 핵이에요.

수정체낭은 투명한 막처럼 생긴 조직으로 상당한 탄성을 지니며, 이러한 탄성 덕분에 항상 장력이 존재하게 됩니다. 그 결과 수정체는 자연적으로 둥글어지고 보다 구형을 띠는 경향이 있는데, 근거리에서 초점을 맞출 때 이런 모양을 취하게 되죠. 모양체소대라고도 알려진 가늘지만 매우 튼튼한 현수인대는, 한쪽 끝은 수정낭에 다른 쪽 끝은 눈의 안쪽 주변에 원형 섬모체의 섬모체돌기에 연결되어 있으며, 수정체를 고정시켜 줍니다.

눈이 멀리 있는 물체를 보는 경우, 평행한 광선이 눈으로 들어갈 수 있도록 섬모체 내의 섬모체근이 이완됩니다. 섬모체돌기는 모양체소대를 잡아당기고, 이로 인해 또 다시, 적도 주변의 수정체낭이 당겨지게 됩니다. 이로서 수정체 전체가 납작해지거나 덜 볼록하게 되어 수정체가 멀리 있는 물체에서 온 빛을 모을 수 있게 되죠. 섬모체근이 수축하면 현수인대에 가해지는 장력이 약해지고 수정체낭에 가해지는 장력 역시 약해져 수정체의 양면이 보다 볼록해지는데, 이로써 눈이 가까운 물체에 초점을 맞출 수 있게 됩니다.

좋아요, 그러면 수정체는 유연하며, 곡률은 모양체소대를 통해 섬모체근에 의해 조절됩니다. 수정체의 곡률을 변화시킴으로써 눈이 서로 다른 거리에 있는 물체에 초점을 맞출 수가 있어요. 이러한 과정을 조절이라고 부릅니다. 여기에서 주의를 잘 기울이셔야 하는데, 조절은 수정체의 노화 과정을 이해하는데 매우 중요하기 때문이에요. 수정체는 평생 동안 계속해서 자라며, 기존 세포 위에 새로운 세포가 놓임으로써 수정체는 점점 뻣뻣하게 됩니다. 나이가 들수록 수정체는 조절 능력을 서서히 잃게 되죠.

초점 조절 능력이 상실된 눈을 노안이라고 부릅니다. 추후 광학 분야에서 여러분이 하게 될 일 중 상당 부분이 환자들로 하여금 시간에 따른 조절 과정의 변화에 적응하도록 돕는 것이기 때문에 조절 과정의 원리를 잘 이해하는 것이 대단히 중요합니다… 알겠죠?

보통 수정체의 조절 과정은 순조로우며 아무런 노력이 요구되지 않습니다. 먼 곳에서 가까운 곳으로 초점이 옮겨지는 경우 섬모체근이 빠르게 수축하는데, 그 결과 조절이 이루어져 수정체가 더 두꺼워지면 가까이 있는 물체가 선명하게 보이게 됩니다. 그 후 다시 멀리 있는 물체를 보면 섬모체근이 즉시 이완됨으로써 수정체가 얇아지고 먼 곳에 있는 물체가 선명하게 보이게 되죠.

자, 머리가 멍해지셨을 것으로 압니다. 하지만 기말고사가 다음 주에 있으니 필기를 잘 하셨기를 바라요. 질문이 있는 경우에는 주저하지 마시고 제 사무실로 찾아와 주세요. 혹은 이메일을 보내셔도 좋습니다.

MEMO

How to
Master Skills for the

TOEFL® iBT

LISTENING

Advanced

Second Edition